CW01262558

HISTORY OF
THE SECOND WORLD WAR
UNITED KINGDOM MILITARY SERIES

Edited by Sir James Butler

The authors of the Military Histories have been given full access to official documents. They and the editor are alone responsible for the statements made and the views expressed.

Marshal of the Royal Air Force Lord Portal, K.G., G.C.B., O.M., D.S.O., M.C., Air Officer Commanding-in-Chief, Bomber Command, April to October 1940. Chief of the Air Staff from October 1940.

THE STRATEGIC AIR OFFENSIVE AGAINST GERMANY 1939–1945

BY
SIR CHARLES WEBSTER,
K.C.M.G., F.B.A., D.LITT

AND

NOBLE FRANKLAND,
D.F.C., M.A., D.PHIL

VOLUME I
PREPARATION
Parts 1, 2 and 3

This edition of
The Strategic Air Offensive Against Germany: Volume One
first published in 2006
by The Naval & Military Press Ltd

Published by
The Naval & Military Press Ltd
Unit 10 Ridgewood Industrial Park,
Uckfield, East Sussex,
TN22 5QE England
Tel: +44 (0) 1825 749494
Fax: +44 (0) 1825 765701
www.naval-military-press.com

The Strategic Air Offensive Against Germany 1939–1945:
Volume One first published in 1961.
© Crown copyright. Reprinted with the permission of
the Controller of HMSO and Queen's Printer for Scotland.

In reprinting in facsimile from the original, any imperfections are inevitably reproduced and the quality may fall short of modern type and cartographic standards.

Printed and bound by CPI Antony Rowe, Eastbourne

PREFACE

THE history of the Strategic Air Offensive against Germany presents a number of formidable problems of scope and method.

The offensive was, from 1943 onwards, joined by the United States Army Air Forces and the two offensives became more and more merged together as the campaign proceeded. In the later stages of this work, therefore, constant reference is made to the Eighth and Fifteenth Air Forces, but it does not pretend to give a comprehensive account or appraisal of their operations. These can be followed in the United States official history, *The Army Air Forces in World War II*, published in advance of our own work, which has also been of much service to us in other ways.

But, in addition, strategic bombing is a relatively new form of warfare and its conduct and achievements have been highly controversial subjects before, during and after the war. We have, therefore, thought it necessary to use methods of presentation somewhat different from those adopted in the other volumes of this official series.

In the first place the conception of strategic bombing and the terms used to describe it have not been analysed, defined and standardised to the same degree as those of naval and land warfare. In a short preliminary chapter, therefore, we have discussed the theory of strategic bombing and explained the meanings which we attach to the terms most commonly used.

Secondly, both the theory and practice of the strategic air offensive were greatly influenced by doctrines formed in the years between the wars on the basis of the experience of the First World War. We have, therefore, devoted a long chapter to the design and structure of the force and the strategic and tactical plans devised in the years before 1939.

Thirdly, we have found it necessary to keep separate the three main aspects of the offensive—namely, its strategy, its operations and what we have termed its appreciations and results. These aspects are closely related, but each requires both description and analysis. If they are treated together chronologically, the narrative tends to become too involved. We have, therefore, though dividing the main portion of the book into four chronological divisions termed Parts, again divided each Part into three chapters dealing respectively with strategy, operations and appreciations and results. This plan inevitably leads to some repetition, but we consider its disadvantages outweighed by the opportunity thus afforded for greater clarity in description and analysis. We hope also that the introduction to each

Part and the overall survey of the final chapter will show the connections between the various aspects and the conclusions which, in our opinion, can be drawn from the whole.

Fourthly, because of the controversial and complicated nature of the subject, fuller documentation is necessary than has usually been employed in the official histories. We have thought it advisable, therefore, to show in the footnotes not only where we are relying on specific evidence but also the nature of it. Precise reference to the official files which contain it is not allowed by current regulations and would serve no useful purpose, since they are not yet open to public inspection.

Fifthly, it seemed necessary to provide more appendices than is usual, and these have been placed in a separate volume. This is composed of annexes on some technical matters about which some readers may wish to have more information than can be conveniently given in the narrative and important memoranda, correspondence and statistics on which in part our conclusions are based. Any omissions in these latter are, as is usual, indicated by a dotted line, except that we have omitted without notification references to the files of some of the documents alluded to in the text for the reason given in the immediately preceding paragraph.

Sixthly, even though the book is longer than was originally designed, there are contributory aspects of the subject which we have not been able to treat as fully, perhaps, as their importance merits, such as training, production, scientific research and the organisation of the Air Ministry. These affect other aspects of aerial warfare as well as the strategic offensive, and a comprehensive account of them was beyond the scope of this book.

Finally, it should be remarked that this work is the product of a joint effort extending over a period of ten years. In some cases the chapters are founded on two separate drafts, one by each of us; in other cases they are the result of joint examination of a draft by one of us. In every case each of us has satisfied himself, so far as is possible, of the accuracy of the facts and the validity of the arguments and we are jointly responsible for the whole. We gratefully acknowledge the assistance which Mrs. Oakley has given us since 1955 in marshalling the material, checking the facts, preparing the material for the maps and providing a link between our activities. She is also responsible for the index.

The book is mainly based on the documentary evidence in the archives of the Cabinet Office, the Air Ministry and Bomber Command to all of which we have had full access. We have also had the advantage of being able to consult the official despatch of Sir Arthur Harris with its many appendices. In addition, we have examined the German documents in London, especially the three series of Speer papers and the interrogations of Speer, his associates and other leading Germans. Only a small portion of the archives of the Ministry of Economic Warfare relevant to our purpose appears to have survived.

Considerable assistance has been derived from the unpublished preliminary narratives of the Air Historical Branch. Among these, that of Professor R. B. Wernham on the pre-war evolution of Bomber Command has been especially useful. For the points at which our subject is connected with maritime warfare we have found invaluable the meticulously compiled narrative on the share of the Royal Air Force in it by Captain D. V. Peyton-Ward, R.N. Since this aspect is included in the volumes of *The War at Sea* by Captain Roskill, R.N., we have not dealt with its operations in our own survey. Similarly we have had to deal with some aspects of the air operations of the land offensive and have discussed its problems with Major L. F. Ellis, the author of the forthcoming volumes on this subject in the official series. We have also gained much from other published volumes of the official history and the advice of colleagues who are engaged in their preparation. For the statistics of casualties in Bomber Command we are greatly indebted to officials of the Manning Statistics Department of the Directorate of Manning in the Air Ministry who made a special investigation at our request.

Except in a few cases, which are indicated, we have relied on documentary evidence and not upon oral testimony as to what actually happened. But we have been greatly aided in our work by the generous help of many persons who were engaged in the offensive, including several of the highest-ranking British and United States officers who planned and directed it, as well as many scientists and others who played an important part in it. Some of them have read the whole or parts of the book in manuscript. As a result, we have in many cases been able to prosecute our research with a fuller understanding of the problems involved and in some we have had our attention directed to aspects of the subject to which we might otherwise have paid less attention. None of those so advising us are in any way responsible for the statements and arguments used in this book and for that reason we have not included a list of their names. But we tender to all our most grateful thanks for their freely given and invaluable assistance.

We are indebted to the Institute for Advanced Studies at Princeton and to the Rockefeller Foundation for grants which enabled both of us to extend our studies and consultations to the United States. At Princeton the late Professor Edward M. Earle placed his great experience at our disposal. We also both visited the United States Air University at Maxwell Air Force Base, and Dr. Frankland was permitted access to the Army Air Force archives in the Research Studies Institute there as well as at the Federal Record Center at

Alexandria. We received great help and kindness from Dr. Albert Simpson and members of his staff at the Research Studies Institute and we wish particularly to express our indebtedness to Mr. Martin R. Goldman.

Throughout our studies we have been fortunate in being able to rely upon the indispensable assistance of the Air Ministry, Air Historical Branch in tracing documents and in many other ways. We record our most grateful thanks to the former Head of the Branch, Mr. J. C. Nerney, and to his successor, Mr. L. A. Jackets, who has also for many years been in charge of the Branch's German archives. From the latter and his staff we have obtained much statistical information and translations of many German documents.

We are indebted to our general editor, Professor Sir James Butler, and to the members of his advisory panel for advice and criticism.

The late Mr. Acheson of the Cabinet Secretariat was often most helpful, and two members of the office, Mr. F. J. Trigger and Mr. C. E. Jones, have throughout assisted us in many ways in the production of the book. Nor must we omit to pay a tribute to the skill and consideration of H.M. Stationery Office.

The maps were prepared by Colonel Penney and Mr. Kelleway with the same care and accomplished expertise which they have shown in all the official histories. The photographs are derived from the remarkable collection in the Imperial War Museum.

August, 1960.   C. K. W.
                                                             N. F.

CONTENTS

VOLUME I: PREPARATION

AUTHORS' PREFACE . . . . . . Page v

PART I
THE NATURE OF AND PREPARATION FOR A STRATEGIC AIR OFFENSIVE

INTRODUCTION 3

CHAPTER I: THE NATURE OF A STRATEGIC AIR OFFENSIVE 5
    (a) General considerations 6
    (b) Strategic factors 12
    (c) Operational factors 17
    (d) Factors in appreciations and results . 23

CHAPTER II: THE PREPARATION FOR A STRATEGIC AIR OFFENSIVE, 1914–1939 . 33
  1. The origin in the war of 1914–1918 . . . 34
  2. Laying the foundations, 1919–1933 . . . 52
  3. The reconstruction of the bombing force, 1934–1939   65
    (a) New types and strengths . . . 65
    (b) Organisation and infrastructure . . 81
  4. Strategic principles and plans, 1934–1939 . . 86
  5. Training and tactics, 1934–1939 107

PART II
THE OPENING OF THE OFFENSIVE AND THE TRANSITION TO AREA BOMBING
September 1939–November 1941

INTRODUCTION 129

CHAPTER III: THE OPENING OF THE OFFENSIVE: THE MAKING OF BOMBING STRATEGY. September 1939–November 1941 . . 133
  1. The lull before the storm, September 1939–April 1940 134

CONTENTS

Page

2. The opening of the strategic offensive and the Battles of France and Britain, May–September 1940   144
3. The oil plan and the Battle of the Atlantic, October 1940–March 1941 155
4. The decline of selective attack and the coming of area bombing, March–November 1941 . . 167

CHAPTER IV: THE OPENING OF THE OFFENSIVE: BOMBER COMMAND IN OPERATION. September 1939–November 1941 189

1. Trial and error: The conversion of Bomber Command into a night force, September 1939–April 1940   190
2. Night precision bombing, May 1940–March 1941 . 213
3. The tactical foundations of area bombing, March–November 1941 233

CHAPTER V: THE OPENING OF THE OFFENSIVE: APPRECIATIONS AND RESULTS. September 1939–November 1941 259

1. The machinery for target selection and appraisal of results 260
2. The nature of the German war economy and the British estimate of it 271
3. The nature of the target systems . . . 284
4. The estimated and actual results, 1940–1941 . . 299

PART III

THE MOUNTING OFFENSIVE AND THE IMPACT OF EXPERIENCE

November 1941–December 1942

INTRODUCTION 309

CHAPTER VI: THE MOUNTING OFFENSIVE: THE CRISIS OF STRATEGIC BOMBING. November 1941–December 1942 315

Note on Bomber Command radar aids introduced between March 1942 and January 1943 316

1. The consequences of failure: Bombing policy assailed, November 1941–March 1942 . . . 318
2. An improving prospect. General and selective policies, April–September 1942 337

Page

 3. The American intervention and the strategic problems of a daylight policy, September–November 1942 353
 4. The role of strategic bombing and the outlook for 1943, October–December 1942 364

CHAPTER VII: THE MOUNTING OFFENSIVE: ADVANCES IN THE FIELD OF OPERATIONS. November 1941–December 1942 381
 1. The introduction of *Gee* and the development of night bombing tactics, November 1941–May 1942 382
 2. The Thousand Bomber Raids, May–June 1942 . 402
 3. The creation of the Pathfinder Force and the further development of bombing tactics, July–December 1942 418
 4. Daylight bombing in 1942 437

CHAPTER VIII: THE MOUNTING OFFENSIVE: APPRECIATIONS AND RESULTS. November 1941–January 1943 457
 1. The economic appraisal of area and precision bombing 458
 2. The estimated and actual results 473

PRINCIPAL STAFF AND COMMAND APPOINTMENTS 1918–1942 493

ABBREVIATIONS 497

CODE NAMES 500

INDEX 501

MAPS

		Page
1. General Map of Europe	. . . . .	*facing* 135
2. Bomber Command, 15th May 1940	. . .	*facing* 215
3. Focke-Wulf factory at Bremen, 12th March 1941	. .	246
4. Bomber Command, 5th March 1942	. . .	*facing* 387
5. Augsburg Operation, 17th April 1942	. . . .	442
6. Le Creusot Operation, 17th October 1942	. . .	445

PHOTOGRAPHS

Marshal of the Royal Air Force Lord Portal . . *Frontispiece*

1. Air Chief Marshal Sir Edgar Ludlow-Hewitt
2. Air Chief Marshal Sir Richard Peirse . . . } *between pages* 154 *and* 155
3. Lord Thurso (The Rt. Hon. Sir Archibald Sinclair)
4. Air Marshal Sir Robert Saundby . . .
5. A Blenheim . . . .
6. Wellingtons . . . .
7. A Whitley . . . .
8. Hampdens . . . . } *between pages* 194 *and* 195
9. Emden. Bomber Command's first 4,000 lb. bombs .
10. A Wellington after returning from an attack on Bremen . . . .
11. The Renault Works after the attack on the night of 3rd March 1942 . . . . . .
12. Lübeck after the attack on the night of 28th March 1942 . . . .
13. Rostock after attacks in April 1942 . . . } *between pages* 410 *and* 411
14. Cologne five days after the Thousand Bomber Raid on the night of 30th May 1942 . . .
15. Marshalling yards at Cologne before and after the Thousand Raid . . . . . .
16. Mainz after attacks in August 1942 . . .
17. Duisburg after attack on the night of 20th December 1942 . . . .
18. The Philips Radio Works at Eindhoven after the daylight attack of 6th December 1942 . . } *between pages* 442 *and* 443
19. M.A.N. Works, Augsburg, after the daylight attack of 17th April 1942 . . . . .
20. Air Vice-Marshal D. C. T. Bennett . . .

PART I

The Nature of and Preparation for a Strategic Air Offensive

INTRODUCTION

THE British strategic air offensive against Germany began in May 1940 and ended in April 1945. Owing to the complete collapse of Nazi Germany and no less to the extraordinary revolution in strategy, which has occurred since as a result of the harnessing of nuclear energy, the end which came in April 1945 may be regarded by military historians as a real end. But the beginning which occurred in May 1940 was not, in the same sense, a real beginning. What happened then and in the five years which followed was, in large measure, determined or at least, to a great extent, influenced, by the development of theory and practice which had taken place in the previous twenty-six years, that is since the beginning of the First World War. An historical appraisal of the strategic air offensive of the Second World War must, therefore, not only take account of the events and decisions of 1940–1945, but also make a preliminary survey of those which occurred in 1914–1940.

It also seems necessary to discuss at the outset the general principles and definitions of a strategic air offensive. Despite its earlier origins, the kind of warfare which Bomber Command embarked upon in May 1940, was substantially new and naturally it created its own peculiar vocabulary which was also new and sometimes obscure. Terms such as *air superiority*, *target system*, *selective* or *area* bombing, *tactical* or *strategic* operations and *auxiliary* or *independent* offensive are often used without definition. Moreover, even when they are defined, they tend to be defined differently by different authorities.[1]

These and other no less important terms used in the succeeding narrative have been given some definition in Chapter I of this introductory part. The definitions have been accompanied by a discussion of some of the fundamental aspects of the nature of a strategic air offensive which is designed to make clearer the meaning of the definitions themselves. This discussion, after some initial general observations, has been arranged under the headings of the three principal factors in the strategic air offensive, namely, its strategy, its operations and its appreciations and results. This division into three corresponds with the division into three chapters which has been made in each of the succeeding Parts of these volumes.

---

[1] The monumental *United States Air Force Dictionary* published by the Air University Press in 1956 under the editorship of Dr. Woodford Heflin, is an invaluable work of reference. But apart from the fact that it is naturally in American, it cannot be regarded as a determining reference work by students of the published British literature or the unpublished secret archives on air warfare. It is interesting to note that the Concise Oxford Dictionary (Third Edition 1934, Revised Appendix 1944) does not include the abbreviation C.A.S. though that of C.I.G.S. is included.

INTRODUCTION

The second chapter of this Part consists of the historical introduction to the history of the war years. In the opening section it is shown how the creation of a separate air service, of which the Royal Air Force was the first in the world, was due primarily to the wish of the British Government to pursue a strategic air offensive against Germany during the First World War. In the following sections it is shown how the whole development of the Royal Air Force in the years between the wars was influenced by this dominating idea. The strategic and tactical doctrine which was developed by the Air Staff for a bombing offensive is surveyed, the effect which the rise of Hitler and the rearmament of Germany had upon these doctrines is examined, and the plans, strategic, operational, productive and training, which made Bomber Command what it was in 1939, are briefly described.

In many respects the story is a melancholy one. It is the story not only of what was done, but also of what was done inadequately, and of what was not done at all. When war came Bomber Command could make little impression upon Germany and the first great victory of the Royal Air Force, which had been born of the desire to attack, came, not from the offensive, but from a glorious defence in the Battle of Britain. Nevertheless, Bomber Command, initially so weak and ineffective, was eventually to grow into a weapon which, with the United States Strategic Air Forces in Europe, was of decisive importance in the ultimate and total defeat of Nazi Germany. The initial failure and scarcely less the ultimate success were, in large measure, determined by the decisions of the pre-war years.

CHAPTER I

THE NATURE OF A STRATEGIC AIR OFFENSIVE

(a) General considerations
(b) Strategic factors
(c) Operational factors
(d) Factors in appreciations and results

'Tactics and strategy are two activities mutually permeating each other in time and space, at the same time essentially different activities, the inner laws and mutual relations of which cannot be intelligible at all to the mind until a clear conception of the nature of each activity is established.'

CLAUSEWITZ: *On War*

(a) GENERAL CONSIDERATIONS

THE strategic air offensive is a means of direct attack on the enemy state with the object of depriving it of the means or the will to continue the war. It may, in itself, be the instrument of victory or it may be the means by which victory can be won by other forces. It differs from all previous kinds of armed attack in that it alone can be brought to bear immediately, directly and destructively against the heartland of the enemy. Its sphere of activity is, therefore, not only above, but also beyond that of armies or navies. Nevertheless, it was from the mere extension of military and naval warfare into the third dimension that the revolutionary conception of strategic bombing initially sprang.

The use of the air as a medium of warfare came, indeed, before the first man-made flight in a powered aeroplane on 17th December 1903. Even as long ago as the Revolutionary and Napoleonic Wars the art of ballooning had been put to a military application. Before the Battle of Fleurus in 1794, for example, General Jourdan learnt something of the Austrian dispositions through men who had surveyed their lines from the air. But by the time of the Franco-Prussian War in 1870–71, when balloons, drifting freely on the wind, were used by the beleaguered garrison in Paris for the conveyance of despatches and when, more remarkably, Gambetta left the city by balloon to organise further resistance from the south of France, such relatively helpless instruments of war were already scientifically obsolescent. In 1852, Giffard had made the first powered flight in an elongated balloon whose propeller was driven by a steam engine. Later, in 1883, the Tissandier brothers made headway against the wind in another elongated balloon powered this time by an electric motor and, in 1900, Count Zeppelin ascended from Lake Constance in an airship of some four hundred and twenty feet in length which was driven by two Daimler internal combustion engines, each of sixteen horsepower. Even so, it is a wholly remarkable fact that within fourteen years of Count Zeppelin's achievement, German Zeppelins were carrying out bombing attacks upon Britain and that within eleven years of the first flight of the Wright Brothers, German, French and British military aeroplanes were making the first essays in bombing operations.

The first and certainly one of the most important factors in the strategic air offensive of 1939–1945 was the astonishing speed with which that kind of warfare had been evolved. It was as though, in naval terms, the development from the stage of the primitive viking ship to that of the Super Dreadnought, or, in military terms, from that of the chariot to the tank, had been compressed into the lifetime of a young man. But it was even more than that for the use of the air as a means of waging war created not merely a new degree but also a new kind of war potential.

The harnessing of air power offered to the makers of war a wide range of possibilities. As far as bombing was concerned, aircraft might be used as an extension of existing military and naval methods of warfare. In much the same way as the air had already been used as an extension of the means of reconnaissance on the surface, so also, it could be used as an extension of military artillery. Similarly it might be not only the eyes but also the guns of a fleet. In these senses, the nature, though not necessarily the location, of the targets would be the same as those which had always been sought by artillery and by naval guns. The object of the operations would be to assist armies and navies in the achievement of their historic aims. For that reason, it is convenient to describe such uses of air power as 'auxiliary'.

However, in the pursuit of these auxiliary aims, air power might be brought to bear against two quite distinctively different types of target. Dumps of ammunition or other military and naval supplies, concentrations of troops, lines of immediate communication and ships at sea might be bombed. But because the range of aircraft was greater than that of guns and because aircraft could fly indifferently over sea and land and over plain and mountain range, the sources of these military and naval manifestations could also be bombed. The factories in which the dumps of ammunition were to be manufactured and the shipyards in which the warships were to be built might be attacked. The difference between these kinds of target—the difference between attacking the manifestations of enemy armed strength in the immediate vicinity of actual fighting and attacking the sources of it—may conveniently, though not always entirely precisely, be distinguished by the use of the terms 'tactical' and 'strategic'.

But the possibilities of bombing were by no means exhausted by the consideration of the strategic and tactical ways in which it might be used as an extension of existing military and naval conceptions of war. There was the possibility that bombing might be harnessed, not merely to a new degree, but also to a new kind of warfare. Nor was it simply a question of air power developing its own battle in which the aeroplane would grapple with the aeroplane and in which guns on the ground or at sea would have to be pointed upwards as well as outwards. It was possible that bombing might be used in the pursuit of objects which were beyond, not only the range, but also the strategy of armies and navies. Thus, air power was likely to produce a strategy of its own and a series of bombing operations which were not auxiliary in the sense of being directly related to military and naval operations. Such bombing operations may conveniently be described by the term 'independent'.

In the tactical sense, independent bombing operations might be used as a contribution to the air battle. They might be directed against enemy aircraft parked upon their bases or they might be directed towards the destruction of the bases themselves. In the strategic sense, they might be directed against the factories producing aircraft, their engines and their components or against the plants manufacturing or processing the fuel to drive those aircraft.

All the possible roles of bombing, auxiliary or independent and tactical or strategic, which have so far been discussed, are, it will have been noticed, directly related to the course of battles at sea, on the land and in the air. Their intention, in the case of auxiliary operations, could only be to assist the army and the navy in prevailing against the opposing armies and navies, with the object of gaining positions of strength from which their ulterior aims might be achieved. These ulterior aims would be concerned with the imposition of peace terms upon the enemy. The army might seek to do this by occupying enemy territory or, perhaps, by demonstrating to the enemy by other means the futility of further resistance. Alternatively, the army might seek to do it by occupying and holding naval bases and thus assisting the navy to achieve the aim. In the first case, from the military point of view, the strategy would be independent, and in the second, it would be auxiliary.

Similarly, the navy might seek to achieve the aim by blockade which, through starvation, either literal or industrial, might bring the enemy to terms. Alternatively, the navy might seek the aim by transporting, supporting and reinforcing the army. From the naval point of view, the first strategy would be independent and the second auxiliary.

But the air force too was presented with the same kind of alternatives. In addition to being used in its auxiliary functions and in addition to being used independently as an element in the air battle, bombing might also be used as a means of an independent strategy —as a means of producing the enemy surrender. If bombing could be brought to bear strategically upon the sources of enemy naval, military and air force production, it could also be brought to bear upon other sources of production. It might be used not merely to dislocate the enemy's production of armaments required for impending battles, but to dislocate the enemy country itself and render it incapable or unwilling to continue the struggle.

This might be done by physical or by moral means. It might be done by the destruction of the keys to industrial activity such as might be found in the production of electricity, gas, or oil. It might be done by the general attrition of industrial activity on a much broader scale. It might be done by striking at communications or at the workers themselves in their homes. It might be done by the destruction of the centres of government and administration and in all these cases the result might be achieved either through the destruction itself or through the sense of destruction and the consequent fear, terror or panic which might be induced. In this sense the weapon of strategic bombing was analogous to that of naval blockade, but there were two important differences. Sea power, though it might affect the heartland of the enemy, could only be exerted against his perimeters. Air power could strike at the centres directly. Secondly, naval blockade could achieve its aim only by the dislocation of enemy sea communications. Air power could achieve its aim by this and a large variety of other means.

Before proceeding to examine the implications of these possibilities, it is, however, necessary to make some further observations about the independent and auxiliary functions of armed force where the distinctions are less clear in practice than in theory. In practice, the alternatives between the auxiliary and independent employment of armies and navies tended to be alternatives of emphasis rather than of absolute difference. Moreover, the choice tended to be, not between one alternative and the other, but between various blends of the two. Thus, for example, in the Napoleonic War, British sea power was used both to enforce a continental blockade and to transport British troops to various seats of war. In addition, it has to be realised that the independent operations of one service are seldom and, if successful, never irrelevant to the other services. Quite obviously, an independent naval blockade is likely to improve the prospects of an army offensive against the injured enemy, and this might be so both for direct and indirect reasons. Directly, the blockade might lead to a shortage of military equipment in the enemy camp or a decline in the fighting spirit of his troops. Indirectly, it might result in a redeployment of the enemy troops and, perhaps, their launching on a campaign which would not otherwise have been undertaken. So also was the prospect for the independent strategic air offensive. Clearly, an air offensive which could destroy all the major sources of enemy industrial production would afford great, though not necessarily immediate, advantages in the conduct of naval and military operations against the same enemy. Even an independent strategic air offensive which largely failed to achieve its objects might produce beneficial and even decisive results for an accompanying naval and military offensive. The enemy, for example, might be compelled to devote and, perhaps, to divert manpower and material resources to combating the air attack and these efforts, even if successful, might deny him the means of maintaining an adequate defence against military or naval attack.

Thus, the admission that the development of air power produced the possibility of an independent air strategy was not necessarily an admission that strategic air power could operate effectively independently and in a vacuum—it was not necessarily an admission that strategic air power alone could win a war—it was not a claim that naval and military operations were irrelevant and out of date. Some of the prophets of air power and later some of its exponents did, it is true, believe that this was the case. General Smuts hinted at the possibility as early as 1917 and there were moments during the Second World War when Sir Arthur Harris seemed to have adopted the idea. Perhaps it even entered into Sir Winston Churchill's calculations when, in 1940, British naval and military arms were, so to speak, in reverse and when Britain was without allies outside the Commonwealth and Empire.

Such ideas, nevertheless, were aberrations inspired by excessive optimism or excessive depression. In essence they were a reaction against the horrible conditions of trench warfare and no less against the hopeless odds of the campaign which ended at Dunkirk. They were also an expression of the natural excitement which accompanied the conquest of the air—a development not, after all, less significant than the discovery of gunpowder. But, as aberrations, they were the exception which proved the rule. The theory of victory through air power alone never gained currency in the high strategic counsels of the Chiefs of Staff during the period of the Second World War. It was not merely that such ideas were unacceptable to the Chief of Naval Staff and to the Chief of the Imperial General Staff. They were also foreign to the thinking of the Chief of the Air Staff.

This is not, however, to suggest that the development of the theory of strategic air power was not a controversial matter. From the time when the first experiments were made in it during the First World War until the great Bomber Command attack on Dresden and the discharge of the first atomic bombs by the United States Army Air Forces thirty years later, the whole development and direction of strategic bombing was a highly and a continuously controversial matter. And the controversy ranged over the whole field of the offensive which embraced questions of strategic desirability, operational possibility, economic, industrial and moral vulnerability, and legal and moral responsibility.

These were all closely related questions. For example, a strategy which was desirable could not be a proposition of war unless it was operationally possible and morally acceptable. Or again, a course of action which was operationally possible could not be strategically desirable unless it bore upon some aspect of the enemy activity which was regarded as vital.

Such considerations, perhaps, will indicate the principal elements in the conduct of the strategic air offensive. The first may be regarded as the strategy of the offensive, that is to say, the determination of the aim and the relating of that aim to the grand strategy of the war. The second is the operation of the offensive, that is to say, its actual execution. The third, which may be described as the appreciation and the result is, as far as the appreciation is concerned, a problem of the intelligence services and, as far as the result is concerned, a judgment upon the whole. In all these factors, and especially in the third, it is important to distinguish between the supposed and the actual. An appreciation may be the basis of a strategic decision or of an operational development. An appreciation, at the strategic level, may, for example, suggest that the enemy is weak in the production of some particular commodity and that may lead to an attack on that kind of production. In fact, however, the appreciation is liable to error. The enemy may not actually be weak in that respect at all, and for that reason the attack may be fruitless. An appreciation of the results is equally liable to error and may produce the same bad consequences. For example, an appreciation may indicate that a particular operation against a group of factories has been highly successful and on that evidence further attacks may be cancelled. The attack, all the same, may actually have miscarried and an opportunity of doing real damage might be lost. Nor even after the war is over are the results of the strategy and operations employed necessarily crystal clear. The result is always due to a number of different causes acting at the same time, and the exact contribution of each is not always apparent. If this is true of naval and land warfare it is still more true of a strategic bombing offensive where results may be produced in many indirect and unexpected ways.

The question of operational possibility is also liable to the same kind of hiatus between the supposed and the actual. A plan may, for example, be found strategically acceptable on the grounds that a certain series of operations is held on the basis of previous experience or of theoretical calculation to be possible. Those operations, all the same, may prove, in the event, to be impossible.

Thus, the conduct of a strategic air offensive is clearly a hazardous and an uncertain business. In this respect it resembles the other expressions of armed strength but its hazards are greater and its uncertainties more uncertain because the art of air warfare is a new one and because the targets it seeks are often not only geographically remote but also, both in their structure and in their significance, of almost incredible complexity. In the strategic air offensive the 'other side of the hill' tends to be farther away than in any other kind of warfare, except, perhaps, that of naval blockade.

Finally, it has to be kept in mind that there are various criteria by which the success or failure of a strategic air offensive may be judged. A great operational success such as the complete destruction of the appointed target may not produce a corresponding strategic success. The target may prove to be dispensable from the point of view of the enemy, it may be quickly repaired or it may have an alternative or a substitute elsewhere. On the other hand, a series of operations which fail to achieve the designed strategic result are often liable to achieve some other result which may be no less important, and this may be done either directly or indirectly. Something else may be destroyed, or the enemy may be compelled to initiate some unforeseen counter-measure which weakens him in another and, perhaps, equally unforeseen manner.

With these general considerations in mind, it is now possible to proceed to a somewhat more detailed examination of the three elements which have to be considered in the history of the strategic air offensive, namely, the strategy, the operations and the appreciations and results.

(b) STRATEGIC FACTORS

The selection of the aim is generally regarded as the first principle of war. In its most general sense and at the level of grand strategy, it concerns such questions as whether the enemy is to be reduced to the point at which he will accept terms of surrender or whether the object is merely to reduce his bargaining position in a negotiated settlement which may not be of vital importance to either side. This latter object is, however, outside the scope of this chapter and this book. We are dealing here with the great conflicts between states on which their whole future may rest.

At the level of the direction of the air offensive itself the selection of the aim concerns the question of the point or the area which is to be attacked on a particular occasion. Between these levels, there is the question of what the general course of the offensive should be and how it should be adjusted to other means of attack in the pursuit of the grand strategy of the war. At this level, the selection of the aim may conveniently be described as the 'strategy' of the offensive.

All bombing, of course, is operationally offensive, just as all shooting is operationally offensive, but in the strategic sense, whether it is offensive or defensive, is determined not simply by the action but by the aim. Positive aims, such as forcing the enemy to give ground either by attacking his defending forces or by destroying the sources from which they derive their power, are strategically offensive. Negative aims, such as resisting his attacking forces or destroying their means of attack, are strategically defensive. The choice is clearly an important one. Major wars cannot be won by defence alone but they can be lost by untimely attack or by the neglect of the defence.

Another, and an equally important factor is whether the offensive should be primarily independent or primarily auxiliary. This tends to be a delicate question because each of the fighting services is anxious to make the greatest and the most apparent contribution to victory. From the point of view of the strategic air offensive there is an apparent danger in auxiliary employment. Apart from the fact that in the Royal Air Force there was always the memory of the time when the Army and the Navy had attempted to reabsorb the new service, there was also what seemed to most air strategists, to be the danger of being drawn predominately into tactical bombing. The Air Staff always had a conviction that the true role of an air force was strategic bombing, whether of an independent or auxiliary character. The military and naval general staffs, on the other hand, tended to believe more strongly in tactical bombing. To them, the destruction of a warship at sea or in port, or the cutting of a railway or destruction of a bridge in a vital battle area generally seemed to be preferable to and more useful than the destruction, for example, of a naval construction yard or a tank factory. The decision between the alternatives of independent and auxiliary bombing, therefore, tended to become associated and sometimes even confused with the decision between the alternatives of strategic and tactical bombing.

The issue clearly involved to a greater extent than any other the establishment of the relationship between the three services, not only as regards their respective employments, but also as regards their respective budgets, production priorities, manpower allocations, and so on. This was a problem for the Chiefs of Staff to advise the Cabinet about, but that is not to say that they could always give clear advice. The various points of view, which sometimes amounted almost to a dispute, were always a major factor in the strategy of the offensive and, in the nature of things, they were always likely to be so.

Within narrower limits, the problem of the selection of the strategic aim is equally baffling. It has to be decided whether the offensive should be concentrated by selective bombing against a group of related targets all of which are associated with the same activity, that is to say a 'target system', or dispersed over a wider range of activities in a general bombing offensive. These were complicated alternatives which are sometimes confused with another choice, namely, that between precision and area bombing. In fact, however, a selective offensive, for example, could be pursued either by area or precision attack. The choice between area and precision attack is primarily governed by operational factors; the choice between a selective and a general bombing offensive is a question of strategy.

The point may be illustrated by considering, for example, the theory of an attack upon the aircraft industry. Within this target system several potential objectives can be discerned. Among them are the groups of factories engaged in airframe and aero-engine production, the plants making ball-bearings and other components such as tyres, instruments, and so on. There are the communications upon which the bringing together of all these components depends. In addition, there are the sources of power—gas, electricity, coal and oil—upon which the factories depend, and there are also the workers who operate the machines in the factories. This, of course, would be a selective attack in the sense that one industry, namely, the aircraft industry, would be the object, but it might be undertaken by more or by less selective operations. The less selective application would be the destruction of as much and as many of these systems as possible. The most selective application would be the concentration upon one of the activities. But in either case, precision or area bombing or both could be used as the instrument. The selective aim of disrupting aircraft production might be achieved by area attacks upon towns associated with that production or by precision attacks upon factories actually engaged upon it.

It will, however, be apparent that, apart from operational factors, the choice between area and precision bombing as the instrument was liable to be influenced by the nature of the targets. If, for example, in the case which has just been mentioned, the targets which were chosen consisted of small objects in open country, then precision bombing would be more desirable than area bombing, for in the latter case most of the bombs would, through the intention of the bomb aimers, fall in open country. If, on the other hand, the decision had been to concentrate upon the factory workers by the destruction of their homes, then clearly area bombing would be more appropriate, if only for the reason that it would scarcely be practicable to aim individually at a whole series of houses.

This last consideration introduces another factor, the moral factor, which is of great importance in the strategy of the offensive. There were various attempts to draw up internationally agreeable rules of air warfare, notably at The Hague in 1922–1923, but none of these came to fruition and the so-called Hague Rules were never ratified by any of the powers. Nevertheless, nations and individuals continued to have various views of what, in terms of strategic bombing, was morally permissible and what was not.

Part of the argument centred upon the difference between 'military' and 'civilian' targets and developed somewhat along the lines of the conventions which had been attached to military and naval warfare. There was a school of thought which demanded that bombing should be restricted to 'military targets' which could be destroyed without undue risk to 'civilian' life or property. This argument turned upon what was meant by the term 'military target'. Clearly, a tank on the battlefield was a military target, but was a tank on the assembly line in a factory a civilian target? Clearly a soldier in the front line was a military target, but was a worker engaged in the manufacture of his rifle a civilian target? There was also the question of what constituted an 'undue risk' to civilian life and property. A battleship at sea, it might be assumed, would be manned only by naval personnel and a badly aimed bomb would be unlikely to fall anywhere other than in the water. But the same battleship in port might have civilian workers on board and a badly aimed bomb might destroy anything from a warehouse to a church.

Obviously a strict interpretation of these obscure questions meant the absolute prohibition of all strategic bombing and the confinement of all operations to the actual area of land fighting or to warships at sea. It meant, indeed, the kind of restriction which was, in fact, applied to Bomber Command at the outset of the Second World War. On the other hand, once it had been agreed that this restriction was too narrow—once it had been decided to extend the definition of 'military targets'—then the limit was very difficult to see. In modern war between major powers there is, after all, practically nothing worth attacking which does not have some bearing upon the national war effort. Even the national churches pray for national victory. They exhort troops to fight for it and workers to work for it.

Thus, the moral argument about strategic bombing, once that kind of warfare had been accepted at all, tended to degenerate into the drawing of distinctions between necessary and unnecessary destruction. But at this point it merged with and became indistinguishable from the strategic argument, for clearly it was against every strategic precept to waste bombs, bombers and bomber crews upon attacks which were not held to be necessary. There were naturally strategic differences of opinion as to what was necessary and what was unnecessary, and these strategic differences often arose between those who were regarded as strategists and those who were regarded as moralists. But there was never any difference of opinion about the obvious fact that what was regarded as unnecessary should not be done.

Nevertheless, even amongst those who accepted the wider definition of military targets in such a way as to embrace the enemy war economy, there were still certain moral arguments which could be, or, at any rate, were, advanced. There was, for example, a school of thought which maintained that, though it was morally permissible to attack specific industrial targets such as factories, oil plants and railway centres even at an incidental risk to surrounding life and property, it was immoral to attack that surrounding life and property. In other words, the implication was that targets in or near towns could be attacked but that towns themselves could not. Operationally this, as was to be shown by a comparison between United States Army Air Force attacks upon factories and Bomber Command attacks upon towns, was often a distinction which disappeared in practice. It was, indeed, an argument which was generally put forward without operational factors in mind or even in sight. It did, nevertheless, define the principal moral issue of the strategic air offensive in the Second World War.

From what has been said about the strategic and moral opportunities of the strategic air offensive it will be seen that the alternatives are apparently of immense variety. A further reason for that fact is the also apparently enormous flexibility and versatility of air power. We have already discussed the possibilities of auxiliary tactical operations such as attacks upon troops in action and communications in the battle area, or warships at sea. We have discussed auxiliary strategic operations such as attacks upon the production of naval and military weapons and vehicles and we have discussed independent strategic operations such as attacks upon the sources of war production, of administration or morale. No other form of armed force could embrace such a variety of objects, yet, in theory at least, a bomber force could not only undertake all these tasks and others as well, but it could within hours be diverted from one to another. Armies are confined to the land and to certain channels of advance. A change of objective means a regrouping of forces which may occupy weeks or even months. Navies are confined to the sea and are intrinsically limited to certain objectives. Air forces are confined neither to land nor to sea, and a change in objective may be achieved by a wireless message travelling at the speed of light and carried out at not much less than the speed of sound. The same bomber force operating from the same bases may attack a naval construction yard in northern Germany on one night and a railway viaduct in southern France on the next, and the same force may carry out bombing, reconnaissance, leaflet and infiltration warfare either alternatively or simultaneously.

This apparently great flexibility and versatility of the bomber as an instrument of war is one of the reasons for which it is so difficult to concentrate an air offensive sufficiently and for long enough; for, even amongst experts, there are always differences of opinion as to where the decisive point lies. It is also one of the reasons for which the air offensive is so liable to the advice of armchair strategists. It is hard for the amateur to see that where the crow can fly the bomber cannot always fly. Yet, as we shall see when we come to the consideration of the operational factors in the strategic air offensive, there are many restricting obstacles which give the bomber less flexibility and less versatility than is often supposed.

There are also strategic obstacles which tend to have the same effect. In addition to the moral restraints which may be imposed there is also the question of the enemy's capacity for retaliation. It is seldom certain that the enemy's retaliation will be in kind, but the supposition is often that this will be the case. The side which feels itself to be inferior in strategic air power or to be more vulnerable to strategic air attack may well hesitate to initiate strategic bombing, or, even if it does not, it may impose restrictions upon the nature and the scope of its offensive. In the propaganda of war it may also attribute the reasons for such hesitations or restrictions to the promptings of moral restraint, but moral restraint and the fear of retaliation are distinct and different things.

The bombing offensive is also restricted by the amount and the nature of the productive effort which is devoted to it, and the whole question of this productive effort is obviously one of the cardinal factors in the strategy of the offensive. Moreover, the strategic decision as to what kind and size of bomber force is required has to be taken many years before the operations of that force can be carried out. Changes in circumstances and errors in expectation are always liable to render the force inappropriate or irrelevant to the tasks for which it was designed, and these factors, in turn, therefore, also tend to exert a restricting effect upon the strategic options of the offensive.

Finally, and in the case of coalition warfare, there is, for the strategic air offensive as for other forms of warfare, the necessity for allies to co-ordinate their plans, for obviously two offensives which have some complementary connection are more than twice as likely to be effective as two offensives which have no connection beyond being directed against the same enemy.

(c) OPERATIONAL FACTORS

The opportunities as also the limitations of the strategic ideas depend ultimately upon operational capacities. 'We have to make war,' Lord Kitchener observed, 'as we must and not as we would like to.'[1] The determining factor between the theoretical intention and the practical possibility is the operational element.

The operational requirements of a strategic bombing force are easy to express and difficult to attain. First, the force must have the ability to reach the designated targets, which is a question of range,

---

[1] Field-Marshal Sir William Robertson: *Soldiers and Statesmen, 1914–1918*, Vol. I, (1926), p. 92.

penetration and navigation. Secondly, it must be able to strike effectively at those targets, which is a question of bombs adequate both in quality and in quantity and of the accuracy with which they can be aimed. Thirdly, the force must be able to return to base without suffering more than the bearable casualty rate.

The first two of these three basic requirements are self-explanatory. The third is not. The bearable casualty rate is a variable and a relative factor which is influenced by the rate of destruction which can be achieved. The greater the rate of destruction, the greater is the casualty rate which can be sustained on each operation, for the fewer will be the number of operations which are required. If the offensive is one of gradual attrition, the bomber force is liable to decay from individually quite low casualties which extend over a long period. The bearable casualty rate depends upon the morale of the surviving crews, the extent to which the crews and aircraft lost can be replaced and the extent to which the dilution of experience by inexperience can be overcome. The factors in the bearable casualty rate range, therefore, from the psychological aspect of the fighting spirit of the crews to the material one of aircraft production.

The natural hazards which impede the fulfilment of these operational requirements are meteorological, geographical and, in the case of night bombing, the problem of seeing in the dark. The weather may make flying impossible or highly dangerous, and unless it is corectly forecast it may do so after the force has taken off. A sudden change of wind, formation of cloud, rising of fog or even change in temperature may ruin an operation and, perhaps, produce a disaster. Less variable but sometimes equally formidable is the geographical factor. Mountain ranges are liable to cause accidents, and some kinds of terrain such as densely built up areas or featureless plains produce peculiar navigational problems. Measures to overcome the difficulties of night vision are, as will presently be noticed, liable to produce man-made hazards of their own.

The man-made hazards consist of the enemy defences—the fighters, anti-aircraft guns, searchlights and other counter-measures such as radio-jamming, bogus radio or visual navigational or bomb aiming signals, dummy targets, and so on. They also include the exploitation by the enemy of the devices, such as flares or radio emissions, upon which the bombers may depend.

The resources with which to meet these hazards, man-made and natural, lie in the efficiency and determination of the crews, the design of their aircraft, its equipment and armament and the provision of adequate protection against the enemy counter-measures. Again, the first two of these resources are self-explanatory, but the third is not. The adequacy of the protection provided obviously depends upon the nature of the task being attempted and upon the nature and the intensity of the enemy defences. It may vary, in fact, from the fitting of a small piece of armour plating behind the pilot's head to the provision of a fleet of long-range fighters as large as the bomber force itself. It may include the introduction of scientific measures, such as radio-jamming or simulated activities, or of tactical devices, such as feint attacks, diversionary routing or night bombing. But these devices themselves are often liable to produce new operational limitations.

Thus, the principal operational elements in the strategic air offensive are: first, the calibre of the crews, which is a question of selection, training, experience, leadership and fighting spirit; secondly, the performance of the aircraft and of the equipment and bases upon which they depend; thirdly, the weather; fourthly, the tactical methods adopted and, fifthly, the nature of the enemy opposition.

These elements in combination and especially at the outset of a war naturally tend to exert a seriously diminishing effect upon the apparently great strategic flexibility and versatility of the bomber, and it will be seen in due course that this diminishing effect was inadequately appreciated before the war and in its early years. The intricacies of long-range bomber operations tended to be underestimated and the destructive power of bombs tended to be overestimated. The invulnerability of targets and the effectiveness of defences tended also to be underestimated. The shock of war showed that many of the operational alternatives which had appeared to exist, did not really exist at all. This was a significant operational limitation of greater importance than that imposed by the also inadequate size of the force. The fact that its application to Bomber Command was not unique and that the failure to anticipate it was at least to some extent unavoidable did not diminish its importance.

Nor was this a limitation which could be quickly overcome. It took some two years to train a bomber pilot or navigator to the operational standards of 1943, about six to introduce a new type of bomber aircraft and nearly three to develop and produce an effective radar aid to navigation.

On the other hand, measures to overcome initial operational limitations of this kind have an inherent tendency to increase the specialisation and the complexity of the bomber force. More complicated and more powerful aircraft require more complicated base installations and services. Mobility tends, therefore, to be reduced. The heavy bomber of 1919 could be flown off from practically any flat surface. That of 1942 required concrete runways. The introduction of more complicated tactics and more complicated operational procedures calls for more highly specialised training, and in the haste of war there is seldom time to train a crew for more than its immediate purpose. Thus, as a crew qualifies itself for one kind of operation it tends to disqualify itself for another. A pilot, for example, who has been trained in the difficult art of daylight formation flying can scarcely, in wartime, be equally well trained in the also difficult art of night landing in poor visibility. The same principle applies to the equipment of the aircraft. One, for example, which is heavily coated with armour plating cannot carry the maximum bomb load, and an aircraft equipped with *H2S* for detecting built up areas cannot also be simultaneously equipped with A.S.V. for spotting ships at sea. Thus, tactical decisions such as those between day or night bombing or strategic decisions such as those between auxiliary, tactical or independent strategic operations tend to be binding for long periods. Even advances in operational technique may in these respects tend to produce the effect of operational limitations.

Moreover, the need to improve operational techniques is not the only one which leads to specialisation and, therefore, to a degree of rigidity. The problem of discovering what the operational limitations are is itself a formidable one, which apart from the requirement of operational research, demands the development of much complicated equipment, such as photographic devices for recording the positions of bomb bursts or the readings of instruments. In addition, parts of the force have to be specially trained and equipped for purposes such as photographic and radar reconnaissance.

All these kinds of difficulty were, in the period of the Second World War, primarily due to two principal factors. The first was the relatively low destructive power of the bombs in use and the second was the relatively high efficiency of the defences developed by the enemy. Both these factors, as has already been mentioned, bore upon the crucial question of the bearable casualty rate, which was always the principal operational limitation in the strategic air offensive. On the extent to which these obstacles could be overcome largely depended the degree of air superiority achieved.

Air superiority is a term which has been in constant but generally vague and often conflicting use almost since the first military employment of aircraft. To some, it means simply the possession of a larger air force, or one that can lift a greater weight of bombs, than that of the enemy. To others, it means the ability to drive the enemy air force on to the defensive and so to deprive it of the means of sustaining a counter-offensive. To yet others, it is purely a question of air communications and means only the ability to fly at will over enemy territory and at least to a great extent to prevent the enemy from doing the same thing. But, though these definitions undoubtedly indicate aspects of air superiority, the sense in which the term is used in these volumes means something wider and more complicated.

Air superiority can be measured by the extent to which it is possible for one side and impossible for the other to carry out constant and effective naval, military and air operations in spite of opposition from the enemy air force. It is thus more than a question of the relative size or bomblift of the opposing air forces. The *Luftwaffe* in 1940 was larger and had a greater bomblift than the Royal Air Force in 1940 yet, as was shown in the Battle of Britain, it could not carry out its operations without constant and effective opposition from the Royal Air Force. It is similarly more than merely a question of driving the enemy air force on to the defensive for, again in 1940, the *Luftwaffe* had driven the Royal Air Force on to the defensive and, in turn, by the autumn of 1943, had itself been driven on to the defensive. Yet, in 1940, the *Luftwaffe*, and, in 1943, Bomber Command and the United States Eighth Air Force, were not able to carry out their operations without constant and effective opposition from the enemy air force. Finally, it is more than simply a question of air communications. Throughout the war both sides were able at will to send their air forces over the territory of each other, at any rate at night.

This last consideration, however, indicates the heart of the matter. Air superiority is not simply a question of being able to use an air force. It is a question of being able to use it effectively. From the point of view of bombers, for example, it is not simply a question of getting through. It is a question of getting through and doing effective damage. Thus, to put the matter the other way round, the extent to which a defending air force is able to deny air superiority to the attacking one is to be measured by the extent of the handicap which is imposed. This clearly applies to all kinds of air operations, whether for the purpose of strategic bombing, reconnaissance or support to naval and military operations.

Now this handicap may be imposed by a number of different means or by a combination of them. It may be done by the method of direct defence, that is by the infliction of a casualty rate upon the attacking air force which, for reasons of morale, production of aircraft and replacement of crews, is higher than can be sustained for the necessary duration of the campaign. It may be done by a less direct method of defence, that is by harassing, though not necessarily destroying, the attacking air force to such an extent that it is unable to make its operations effective. It may also be done by counter-offensive means, that is by a counter-attack which diverts the air force originally attacking and compels it to devote its energies to defence.

It will, therefore, be obvious that air superiority can hardly be an absolute state of affairs. If there is a defending air force at all it will by some or all of these means be able to inflict some handicap upon the attacking one. What counts, of course, is the extent of the handicap. It is also true that the defending air force may be able to impose a greater handicap in some areas, situations or times than in others. What counts is the decisive area, situation or time. Thus, local air superiority, air superiority for limited purposes or air superiority for temporary periods has to be distinguished from air superiority in the full sense.

It will also be clear that it is impossible to establish a theoretical standard of what is needed to impose an adequate handicap upon an attacking air force. That, to a considerable extent, will be conditioned by the strategy, operational method and technical development of the attacking force. It will also depend upon the morale of the crews, their commanders and indeed of the nation which supports them. If, for example, in the case of a strategic air offensive, the attacking bombers are of particularly high performance and carry weapons of a particularly destructive nature, it will then be more difficult for the defending air force to impose a sufficiently severe handicap upon them. Clearly a bomber force which can bring its campaign to a successful conclusion in a shorter period of time can afford a higher casualty rate than one which needs a longer period of time for the same achievement. Thus, depending upon these factors of strategy, operational ability and efficiency of weapons, a bomber force, though suffering a casualty rate of fifty per cent or more, may be in possession of air superiority, while one suffering a casualty rate of five per cent or less, may not.

But the ability to deny the enemy air superiority is not, of course, the same thing as asserting air superiority over him. It is no more than a step in that direction. The assertion of air superiority depends upon the extent to which the enemy air force can be prevented from imposing a significant handicap. It can, as has been indicated, be measured by the extent to which, by neutralisation or destruction, the enemy air force can be prevented from interfering with one's own naval, military and air operations. As far as bombing operations are concerned, this may be done by enabling the bombers to defend themselves effectively in air combat, or to evade interception by their tactical methods. It may also be done by other measures of attack upon the enemy air force such as the bombing of his bases and sources of production, the provision of a long-range fighter force to engage him in the air, or by the over-running of his forward installations by military action. Or, of course, it may be created by a combination of some or all of these factors.

Air superiority, however, can never be absolute. It is no more than a means to an end which is invariably impeded by other agencies such as anti-aircraft fire, the weather and geographical facts. Nevertheless, the history of the strategic air offensive, no less than that of the principal military and naval campaigns of the Second World War, does indicate that air superiority was not only an indispensable but also the most important means to the ends which were sought. Most of the operational factors in the strategic air offensive were directly or indirectly related to the question of air superiority, as also, incidentally, were many of the operational factors in land and sea campaigns.

(d) FACTORS IN APPRECIATIONS AND RESULTS

The decision as to which targets should be attacked depended, in addition to operational factors, on an appreciation of their economic, military and moral importance. It also depended upon an appreciation of the results of previous attacks. Both these appreciations, as in all operations of war, depended for their validity upon accurate intelligence, but it was intelligence of a somewhat different character from that used in other kinds of warfare. How far they were soundly based could indeed only be ascertained with any certainty by investigation of the enemy records when the war was over.

Obviously the choice of targets would depend on the operational efficiency of the bombing forces at any particular moment of time. It was no use choosing a target when the means to destroy it did not exist. The choice of a target system, therefore, depended on a combination of operational and economic factors. It must not be so widespread, so remote or so difficult to find that it could not be attacked with success; it must also be one liable to be seriously damaged by high-explosive bombs or incendiaries and one where destruction or serious injury would impair the ability of the enemy to continue the war. Only the Air Force itself could be the judge of the first group of these factors, but the second was a matter for technicians and economic experts to pronounce upon. In a field so new and controversial it was inevitable that in both cases no very certain forecast could be made. Nevertheless, the two groups of factors were closely associated; for the importance of the effect produced depended to a large extent on the rapidity with which it could be achieved.

It was, however, possible to discover certain general principles as to the nature of target systems and to apply them to the various alternatives that had to be considered. Some of these principles were known before the war began; others were evolved in the course of the war itself. But whatever principle was adopted, clearly everything depended on the amount and reliability of the information available about the target system to be attacked. Before the probable result of a successful attack on a target system could be estimated it was necessary to know its function in the supply of weapons or in the national economy, the statistics of its production, rate of consumption and stocks, and many other things. The accurate appreciation of a target system depended, therefore, first and last upon the accuracy of the information concerning such matters. But even if this were extensive and reasonably correct, there could still be no certainty as to what the result would be. Even those engaged in the industry itself with full knowledge of all the facts often disagreed as to what the effect of an attack upon it would be. Still, unless some such assessment were made there could be no more than a vague guess at the result, and in order to obtain and clarify the information and enable it to be used for its purpose large and elaborate intelligence systems were set up.

This machinery was evolved from that which had for some time been developing in modern warfare. Since all operations of war depend in large part on a correct appreciation of the strength and disposition of the enemy forces, machinery for providing and classifying such information had long been in existence. It had also been found more and more necessary to obtain as much information as possible concerning the existing and potential production of the enemy, for on this would depend in large part the numbers and efficiency of their armed forces. General staffs had paid great attention to this problem and set up special departments of their intelligence to deal with it.

In the First World War new machinery outside the service departments had to be devised to deal with the intelligence required for the economic blockade which was one of the main means of pressure on the enemy. It had had great success, and by long practice much had been learnt about the best methods of estimating the enemy's resources both actual and potential. In this country, as in others, however, the armed services continued to have their own economic intelligence sections. They naturally considered themselves more expert than the civilians on many questions concerning the supply of weapons. They were not always ready to accept civilian advice as to the proper objectives of economic pressure.

Similar machinery was obviously required to obtain the information necessary to assess the various target systems for a strategic air offensive, and it was in fact developed from that which had been used in the First World War. But much more detailed and varied information was now required. It was not sufficient to know such general questions as the amount produced and consumed and existing stocks, though this was still very important. It was also necessary to know the exact situation of each factory, including those built during the war, and, if possible, the contribution of each factory to the total production. This information could to a large extent be obtained by the same methods as had long been employed in economic intelligence. All industrial countries necessarily publish in peace time voluminous information about their economy. Nor can they avoid providing much information in war time, however much they desire to keep such matters secret. In order that the economy may function efficiently it is necessary to issue numbers of orders and directives on all kinds of subjects. Civilian consumption of many articles has to be rationed. Labour has to be regulated and directed and the orders for this purpose throw light on the industries served by it. This public information, which for its own purposes had to be accurate, was the main foundation of the economic intelligence.

The information about the pre-war situation could be supplemented by the knowledge of business men and technicians resident in this country, many of whom had had close contact with their counterparts in other countries. In some cases the contact had been so close as to amount to a partnership, and in many others there were opportunities for knowing in detail the structure of an industry. This information when war came could be placed at the disposal of those engaged in the task of assessment. Indeed, these were often such people themselves, business men, engineers and experts of all kinds, who had had close contacts with industry in other countries and, especially in this case, with German industry.

There were other important sources, such as reports of friendly neutrals who were in a position to obtain information from the enemy country or intercepts of cables and letters which might give more recent and more accurate accounts of new developments than it was possible to obtain elsewhere. Much information could be derived from a scientific study of the press, including the technical press, which often revealed important facts without intending to do so. Another source was the interrogation of prisoners of war, perhaps in each single case seemingly of small value, but, when large numbers were available, capable of throwing much light on some problems. Spies in enemy countries could rarely supply much economic information with sufficient accuracy and rapidity to compete with other sources, though they might suggest a new line of enquiry and, where there were subversive elements in the population, provide facts of real importance. Refugees and other exiles could sometimes supply secret information otherwise quite unavailable, and check with an informed mind knowledge obtained from other sources. In addition there was a new source of information supplied by the Royal Air Force itself, that of photographic reconnaissance, which was in many ways more important than all the others, as will be abundantly seen in the course of this narrative.

To accumulate and classify such information and make it readily available for use obviously needed a large staff of experts under skilled direction. In Britain the process of making such an organisation had begun long before the war began. In Germany, though the general staff had an elaborate economic intelligence organisation, it had not been much elaborated for this particular purpose, because

Germany did not plan to use her air force in a scientifically directed strategic bombing offensive. Nor did such an organisation exist in the Soviet Union or in the United States before the war began, while that in France had not been much developed and in any case was rendered useless by German occupation before the strategic offensive began. In this kind of warfare, therefore, it can be said that Britain had an advantage over others in this respect. That was a natural result of the fact that economic pressure by blockade and a strategic bombing offensive had for a long time been considered as the main weapons which Britain would employ if war came.

The purpose of such an organisation was to determine the priority among the possible target systems and within the target systems what targets should be attacked. By what criteria should the advice of the economic experts be guided? It was of course possible to have the view that no such advice was necessary. There could be a general attack on industrial areas without attempting to concentrate on any special target system. The general devastation so brought about would, it was sometimes suggested, produce the necessary effect on the enemy in two main ways. First, by depriving the workers of their homes and amenities, such as electricity, water and gas, it would prevent them from carrying on their work and so make production difficult or even impossible. Secondly, it was thought that because of the threat of death and mutilation and the deprivation of the amenities of life the will of the people to continue the war would be so much weakened that they might force their government to sue for peace. There would also be other results. Some factories, even though not specifically aimed at, would inevitably be destroyed in the towns attacked and the general level of production thus substantially reduced. The production of weapons would be also reduced by the necessity of repairing and replacing the damaged housing and amenities, while it might also be diverted to the production of the essential consumer goods needed by the population which had been destroyed in the general offensive.

But there were also many reasons against making such a general attack. As has already been explained, both its legality and its morality had been challenged. But in addition there were other more concrete reasons. It was claimed by those who opposed it that the war could be won more quickly and with a greater economy of force by an attack on some target system which would more immediately reduce the enemy's fighting capacity. A well planned attack might destroy in a short time all the production of an essential weapon or deprive the enemy of some indispensable raw material or component of weapon production. The first thing to determine, therefore, was to what extent the product attacked was essential to the war effort. Would the fighting capacity of the enemy be seriously reduced if he were deprived of it? Once an affirmative answer had been given to this question many other considerations had to be taken into account. How soon, for example, would the destruction of the chosen target system affect the supply of weapons or the means of using them? This would depend on the amount of time necessary to turn the commodity into finished weapons and on the stocks of it in existence. An attack on the factories making the weapons would produce a more rapid result than one on the plants making the steel which they used. If the stocks were large in relation to the existing rates of production and consumption, no immediate effect might be forthcoming and opportunity would be given for repair, dispersal and substitution.

The vulnerability of the targets had also to be considered.[1] Were they of such a character as to be easily destroyed by the high-explosive bombs or incendiaries in use? On this question there was when war broke out very little accurate intelligence. Some targets might be self-destructive because made of or containing much inflammable material. Some would be much more stoutly built than others and thus more resistant to attack. Hardly anything was in fact known of the effect of blast on different kinds of structures. Engineers and construction experts had given little thought to such problems and but few experiments had been made. Nevertheless, the question was of fundamental importance and affected both the choice of a target system and the choice of the means by which it should be attacked. When Britain was herself subjected to a bombing attack the experience was to provide valuable information on this important problem.

It had also to be recognised that the enemy would use every means in his power to avert the destruction of his weapons or other indispensable commodities. The defences of the plants in the threatened target system would be rapidly increased. It might also be possible for him to disperse the industry into a larger number of factories, possibly in more remote localities, without incurring a crippling loss of production. Every effort would also be made to repair the plants as quickly as possible. Their recuperability would vary and might well determine whether it would be worth while to attack them. In some there might be indispensable machinery which it was known could only be replaced after a long interval if it were seriously damaged. In others the machinery might be of a kind which the machine tool industry could easily duplicate. The destruction of the structure of the factories would not be sufficient if the machinery in

---

[1] 'Vulnerable' means open to damaging attack. The word is sometimes applied to a target system implying that it is so situated that a sufficient proportion of its production can be attacked. It is also used, as here, of a target or part of a target implying that it can be seriously injured or destroyed by high explosives or incendiaries.

them remained intact, for it could be moved elsewhere to other existing or easily constructed buildings. Damaged buildings might be made usable by temporary roofing or other repairs. On all these matters the experts on the industries themselves and those on industrial construction found it difficult to give decisive opinions. There was also the possibility of the supplies urgently needed being provided by neutrals so far as the enemy had access to them.

It was clear, therefore, that an attack on a target system of any large size might take a long time to produce effective results, and in the interval means might be found to reconstruct the industry or obtain a supply from other sources. There was thus a strong inducement to seek for a target system containing only a few targets the destruction of which would have an immediate effect on the enemy's power of resistance. These were the target systems which were to be called 'bottlenecks' or, in Sir Arthur Harris's phrase, 'panacea targets'. The necessary qualifications were that the industry was of major importance to the production or use of armaments, that a substantial proportion of the total output was concentrated in a few plants, that there was no appreciable spare production capacity standing idle in the occupied countries or elsewhere, that only limited possibilities existed for economy in its use, that the machinery used could not be quickly repaired or replaced and that the industry could not be dispersed without great loss of production for a considerable period of time. Clearly some of these criteria were difficult to determine. But, in view of the difficulty of destroying a large target system, there was great inducement to discover one which might be destroyed with much less effort and yet produce an equally important effect on the supply of armaments.

Finally there was one target system, communications or transport,[1] damage to which would affect not only the production of armaments but the whole economy of the enemy and the distribution of his armed forces. If movement on railways and waterways could be stopped or seriously reduced, factories would be unable to obtain their raw materials or despatch their finished products. In an economy so complex as that of Germany the effect would be devastating if it could be produced. But such a target system was difficult to attack effectively. Railways in a modern industrial state are highly organised and serviced. Repair of damage or defects is part of the normal functions of the system and facilities for it exist throughout its length. There are also in most cases a number of alternative routes between different areas. So large a target system would need an immense force to attack it with success and repair might well keep pace with any damage inflicted on it.

---

[1] We have followed the usage of the documents though the two terms are not really the equivalents of each other.

Here also, however, 'bottlenecks' might be discovered. There might be important canals, aqueducts, viaducts, tunnels or junctions the destruction of which would disrupt the communications of a large area. Or again, it might be possible by an attack on a limited number of targets to seal off an important producing area from communication with the rest of the country. This was also a target system which had attracted the attention of army staffs, for a successful attack upon it might paralyse the movement of the enemy's armies from one part of the country to another. More thought had, indeed, been given to it in the pre-war period than to any other target system. There was, however, no general agreement as to the best methods of inflicting damage upon it, though this was one of the few target systems whose vulnerability had been tested by experiment before the war broke out.

Thus, whatever was chosen as the objective of the attack, clearly account had to be taken of a number of different factors some of which could not be exactly calculated. In addition, no one could be sure that the prescribed operations could be carried out with the necessary efficiency. The result was, therefore, always problematical and that made it all the more necessary to discover as quickly as possible what that result was. A process of trial and error was always necessary, but how was error to be assessed and decisions made as to whether it was remediable unless the result was accurately known? This problem was to be one of the main difficulties of a strategic bombing offensive and it was never completely solved, though in the end sufficiently so to enable an effective attack to be made. The usual sources of information concerning the enemy were not sufficiently precise and for the most part received too slowly for an accurate appraisal to be based on them. For this purpose the targets had to be reconnoitred from the air and a judgment made as to what had been accomplished from the reports thus received. The bombing crews themselves could, of course, describe what they had seen during the attack, but were they likely to give an accurate account of what they had done in the excitement of battle when most of the time also the target would be obscured by smoke? Even the crew of a reconnaissance aircraft would find it difficult to see what had been done when the target was clear. This fact had long been recognised and the camera used to provide a more exact and permanent record which could be intensively studied. It had been used extensively in the First World War for tactical reconnaissance with invaluable results. But despite this fact, provision for photographic reconnaissance before the Second World War was quite inadequate and many of the inherent difficulties of the problem had not been recognised, let alone solved. It was found that special aircraft and special apparatus were necessary if the photographs taken inevitably from a great height, were to provide the necessary information. The interpretation of such photographs also needed a new technique which at the outbreak of the war was still in process of development.

In the course of the war this problem was to a large extent solved, so far as it could be solved in the normal weather conditions of Western Europe. But it took much time to solve it. And the failure to do so in the earlier stages of the war exerted a profound influence on the course of the strategic bombing offensive, while to the success of the offensive in the later stages photographic reconnaissance made an all-important contribution.

After the end of a war it is possible to compare the intelligence appreciations with the real facts so far as these can be ascertained from the records of the warring countries and the evidence of those who took part in the war. On such investigations have depended in large part the judgments which historians have made on the strategy and tactics of commanders. 'This may be called', wrote Clausewitz, '*judgment according to the result.* Such a judgment appears at first sight inadmissible and yet it is not . . . What can be more natural than to say that in the years 1805, 1807, 1809 Buonaparte judged his opponents correctly, and that in 1812 he erred on that point? On the former occasions, therefore, he was right, in the latter wrong, and in both cases we judge by the *result.*'[1] At the same time, historians have often fallen into the error of expecting commanders and their staffs to know facts which the historian himself has found out but which could not be known or inferred from the information available while the war was in progress. It is also true that in some cases the result may not be exactly known, even after the most extensive investigations.

It is now possible to compare the intelligence appreciations made during the war with the actual results of the strategic bombing offensive as shown by the post-war investigations. These have been more extensive and detailed than is usual, though necessarily made rather hastily and without access to an important area of Germany. It has, however, been possible to obtain a fairly comprehensive survey of German production during the war and the extent to which it was reduced by the strategic bombing offensive. The statistics concerning production, consumptions and stocks have been compiled and analysed and in most cases are trustworthy up to the end of 1944. The result of an attack on a particular town can be measured in some cases with fair accuracy and compared with the estimates made at the time. The effect of high-explosive bombs and incendiaries on different kinds of structures has also been studied on

---

[1] General Carl von Clausewitz: *On War*, (1949), Vol. I, pp. 149–151.

FACTORS IN APPRECIATIONS AND RESULTS

the spot with the help of the statistics of individual firms and factories. The various means by which factories and machines were protected and rapidly repaired have also been investigated. Thus the physical effects of the offensive have been extensively surveyed and in many cases can be accurately measured. The subject is, however, a complicated one, for many different factors were exerting an influence at the same time and it is not always possible to determine the extent of the contribution of each to the final result. This is especially true of the last stage of the war when the armies were close to or inside the German frontier and statistics became less reliable or non-existent because of the chaos produced in Germany at that time.

It is still more difficult to determine the effect of the offensive on more intangible matters such as morale, while there are indirect results on the strategy and tactics of the enemy which must always remain less susceptible of precise measurement. But the contribution of the strategic bombing offensive to the defeat of Germany can only be fairly judged if all these factors be taken into account.

Finally, it should be remembered that the strategic bombing offensive was a combined effort of the British and United States air forces. The co-operation was always close and continuous. Intelligence services were largely fused together and a common strategy was worked out at the highest level. There was, however, a greater difference between the aircraft, training and tactics of the two bombing forces than existed between any components of the land and sea forces of the two countries and the United States Army Air Forces did not begin active operations against Germany until January 1943. During the greater part of the war the one operated almost entirely at night and the other by day. This fact complicated the problem of concentration on one particular target system. It also complicates the problem of assessing the results produced by different methods of attack. But they were produced by a joint offensive and neither air force could have produced them by itself. 'We must never forget', wrote General Arnold in his final despatch, 'that the air war over Europe was a case of the closest joint effort with the RAF, from beginning to end. At times the AAF and the RAF employed different tactics and their secondary objectives differed, but at all times it was done with complete understanding of each other's capabilities and limitations. A case in point is the coordinated efforts of RAF night bombing and AAF daylight bombing of Nazi industry; each complemented the other.'[1] This fact should be constantly kept in mind throughout all the discussions which follow.

---

[1] *Third Report of the Commanding General of the Army Air Forces to the Secretary of War.* 12th Nov. 1945, p. 29.

CHAPTER II

THE PREPARATION FOR A STRATEGIC AIR OFFENSIVE

1. The origin in the war of 1914–1918
2. Laying the foundations, 1919–1933
3. The reconstruction of the bombing force, 1934–1939
    (a) New types and strengths
    (b) Organisation and infrastructure
4. Strategic principles and plans, 1934–1939
5. Tactics and training, 1934–1939

'To make an Air Force worthy of the name, we must create an Air Force spirit, or rather foster this spirit which undoubtedly existed in a high degree during the war, by every means in our power.'
    SIR HUGH TRENCHARD, 25th November 1919

'The task of translating a Cabinet directive into terms which are readily understandable by the captain of a bomber aircraft is not an easy one and requires time and care of Command, Group and Station Headquarters.'
    Air Staff Memorandum, 1939

1. The origin in the war of 1914–1918[1]

IN the war of 1914–1918 strategic bombing was begun by the Germans. During 1915–1916 they sent their Zeppelins mainly to the North of England and the Midlands, though one or two managed to reach London, always a prime objective. These raids were ostensibly aimed at military objectives, but the Zeppelin commanders often did not know where they were and their bombs were dropped largely at random. They did on occasion more by luck than management cause some damage and a number of civilian casualties. They also caused some slight diminution of production by the effect of the blackouts and nervous tension on the population.

For some time no effective defence could be set up against them and it was mainly the weather that protected England. But gradually the fighters learnt to go up at night without causing more damage to themselves than the enemy. The number of anti-aircraft guns was also gradually increased. In 1916 several Zeppelins were destroyed and for a time the raids almost ceased. So far aeroplanes had only been used for this purpose by Germany in a few sporadic attacks on British coastal towns which had caused little damage.

During this period the only British attempt to do anything of the kind was by naval aircraft first stationed at Dunkirk and subsequently in 1916 at Luxeuil which attacked targets specially obnoxious to the Navy. The Naval wing had considerable success at first in bombing Zeppelin sheds and naval harbours on the Belgian coast. It was less successful in attacks of longer range on German towns and factories concerned with the production of submarines. It was broken up in the spring of 1917 in order to support the hard-pressed squadrons of the Royal Flying Corps. Throughout its strategic operations it received little encouragement from the headquarters of the British Expeditionary Force in France, and in May 1917 the Admiralty abandoned them.

But in the spring of 1917 the Germans began a more serious strategic offensive. They established bomber bases in Belgium and from them Gothas began to attack the south and south-east coast, one aircraft reaching London itself. On 25th May a squadron of Gothas flying very high attacked Shorncliffe Camp and Folkestone, killing ninety-five and injuring 195 people. No less than seventy-four British aircraft went up to attack them, but they only succeeded in destroying one enemy bomber.

---

[1] This section is based on the methodical and exhaustive survey made by Mr. H. A. Jones in the official history of the war of 1914–1918, *The War in the Air* (six volumes and a volume of appendices), supplemented by references to that war in the papers of the Air Ministry, especially in the early formative period.

This raid revealed the inadequacy of the defending forces. No organisation existed to co-ordinate them. The aircraft used were of all kinds and some of the pilots were still engaged in training. Most of them failed to find the enemy, and, if they did, often could not reach sufficient height to intercept the bombers. No warnings had been given to the towns attacked.

There had been many demands for better protection against the Zeppelins from towns in the North and Midlands. There was now, after such heavy casualties, an immediate public outcry that something should be done. Lord French, the Commander-in-Chief Home Forces, explained to the War Cabinet that he had an inadequate number of fighters and anti-aircraft guns and that the warning system was practically useless. Before this report could be considered another raid was directed against London itself. On 13th June 1917 twenty-one Gothas crossed the south-east coast, and, after small towns in Kent and Essex had been bombed, fourteen went on in a diamond formation to London which they reached at 11.35 a.m. and there dropped high-explosive bombs. 162 people were killed and 432 injured by this raid, nearly all in London itself. Ninety-two British aircraft of one sort or another went up to attack the enemy but all the Gothas returned safely to their aerodromes. On 7th July 1917 a second daylight raid on London caused the death of sixty-five people and injured 245, of whom ten were killed and fifty-five injured by the increased air barrage. Only one Gotha was destroyed by the ninety-five British aircraft which attempted to intercept the raiders.

These raids and the subsequent aircraft and Zeppelin attacks of the autumn did much to determine the future of the British Air Service. To them was largely due the reorganisation of the Royal Flying Corps and the Royal Naval Air Service into an independent arm, the Royal Air Force. From them also sprang much of the strategic theory of the Royal Air Force when its independence had been achieved. In these questions, as in others of major importance in later years, civilian leaders played a leading role.

By the autumn of 1917 the British air services had already become an all-important factor in the fighting in France and other theatres of war. When the war began they had been behind both Germany and France in the number and quality of their aircraft and aircraft engines. But in a comparatively short time the Royal Flying Corps, as part of the army, had made good these deficiencies. Under its great Commander, Major-General Trenchard, who succeeded Sir David Henderson in 1915, its aircraft now provided indispensable reconnaissance of the enemy forces, added immensely to the effectiveness of the British artillery and carried out tactical bombing of the forward bases, dumps, billets, transport and lines of communication of the German armies both by day and by night. In order to pursue these tasks efficiently its fighter squadrons had to obtain air superiority in the airspace above no-man's land and the front areas of the contending armies. In this struggle there had been fluctuations, but in the main, in conjunction with their French allies, the British air force had been able to obtain the upper hand. It had done this by pursuing a vigorous offensive which had forced the enemy on to the defence. When the French air force had for a time taken a defensive rather than an offensive attitude the consequences had been such as to confirm the confidence of the British Command in their own tactics.[1] The Royal Naval Air Service had had less to do and one result had been that it had devoted part of its forces to strategic bombing, as has already been noted. It had also at the beginning of the war been entrusted with the defence of Britain against aerial attack, a duty, which, as the attack increased, it shared with the Royal Flying Corps and the anti-aircraft artillery.

During all this time the two air services remained quite separate and the only link between them was at first an Air Committee and later an Air Board, on which both were represented, as well as the Department of Aircraft Production of the Ministry of Munitions. But these were never more than centres for the exchange of views and the settlement of the demands of the two services, who jealously guarded their control over their own air forces and employed them to carry out the objectives of the military and naval staffs.

The German raids of May, June and July 1917 set in motion forces which transformed this situation. The first step was to increase the defences of London and for this purpose towards the end of June two fighter squadrons were taken from the British Expeditionary Force and stationed on both sides of the Straits of Dover at Calais and Canterbury. This step had only been reluctantly agreed to by Sir Douglas Haig and Major-General Trenchard, the Commander-in-Chief of the Royal Flying Corps, on whom Sir Douglas Haig relied completely for advice on aerial warfare. The aeroplane, Major-General Trenchard had constantly asserted, was a weapon of offence, not defence. The best way to defend London, the Cabinet were told, was to reconquer Belgium as soon as possible, a task which Sir Douglas Haig hoped to accomplish in 1917. Meanwhile, the best defence was to wage a counter-offensive on the German hangars and aerodromes behind the German front. In any case the two squadrons could not be spared beyond 5th July, when they would be needed to assist the British land offensive. Accordingly on 5th and 6th July, having done nothing in the meantime, they were withdrawn and on 7th July the second raid on London, described above, took place.

---

[1] H. A. Jones: *The War in the Air*, Vol. II, App. IX, Future Policy in the Air (September 1916).

It was now recognised that a serious situation had arisen. If such attacks should continue and increase in force, as seemed probable, the life of the capital would be threatened and the conduct of the war rendered difficult. The adequate defence of the base is the first charge on all armed forces. It was, therefore, not surprising that though the Chief of the Imperial General Staff, General Robertson, apologised to Sir Douglas Haig for agreeing to it, the demand was made for the return of one squadron of fighters from France. But clearly this was not enough in such an emergency. The War Cabinet appointed, therefore, a Committee of two, the Prime Minister and General Smuts, to review the situation and make further recommendations. Mr. Lloyd George, much preoccupied with other questions, wisely left the problem in the hands of General Smuts and it was he, advised by military experts and officials, who made the proposals which transformed the position of the air services.

His first proposal concerned the establishment of a better organised defence. Major-General E. B. Ashmore was appointed Commander-in-Chief for the defence of London and he was given control of the observers, anti-aircraft guns, balloon barrage and fighter squadrons. His command extended over a wide area and soon became reasonably effective. Two daylight raids in August were turned back with some loss to the enemy, and, because of the increased resistance and the fact that the German General Staff had never placed any very serious hopes on the bombing offensive, this form of attack now practically ceased and the Germans henceforward only raided London by night.[1]

But in addition General Smuts adopted the doctrine already established in the Royal Flying Corps by Major-General Trenchard that a counter-offensive was the best form of defence. For this purpose he proposed, in a second memorandum, not only that the strength of the air services should be doubled, but that a large strategic bombing force should be created. Since the formation and direction of such a force would lie entirely outside the experience of existing military and naval staffs, it necessitated the institution of an independent Air Service in which the present military and naval air forces should be combined and which should be provided with a separate administration and a general staff of its own to control the strategy of the air. The creation of such an independent arm had long been the desire of some of those who led the Royal Flying Corps, but it had always failed to materialise because of the difficulty of establishing an entirely new service in the midst of a world-wide war. There was still naturally much opposition from the other two services. Sir Douglas Haig, who was not consulted until the decision

---

[1] There is a detailed description and analysis of the raids on London in the book published by Major-General E. B. Ashmore in 1929, *Air Defence*.

was announced, sent back an acid commentary on the scheme and insisted on the necessity of keeping up the air forces under his own command to the necessary strength. Major-General Trenchard had the same outlook at this time and was in full agreement with his Commander-in-Chief. The Admiralty was even less enthusiastic. Nevertheless, the decision to create an independent Air Force was taken with surprising speed, though the detailed negotiations took some time and were not completed without much controversy.

But, though the daylight raids ceased, other strategic bombing attacks continued. New Zeppelins had been constructed which had a ceiling beyond that of the British fighters and only a providential gale in the upper atmosphere and a disastrous explosion in the Zeppelin sheds saved England from repeated attacks. Meanwhile the Gothas had begun to bomb by night, being able when the moon was full, or nearly so, easily to find their way to London. Some of these aircraft were specially constructed 'Giants' (*Riesenflugzeuge*) which had four engines and were able to carry a much heavier bomb load.[1] For a time it seemed as if these attacks would be even harder to deal with than those made by day. Many casualties were caused and large numbers of the people of London took refuge by night in the tubes and other shelters.

Thus the necessary impetus was given to make the change. The Cabinet accepted the Smuts report, a Bill was passed through Parliament in November, a committee set up to plan the necessary reorganisation and on 1st April 1918 the Royal Air Force came into existence. Its separate identity was, therefore, closely bound up with the plan of a strategic bombing offensive and this very fact tended to make such an offensive the centre of the strategic thinking of the new independent service. As this had provided the main argument for the creation of a separate service, so it was also the main reason for the continued existence of a separate service when, as will be seen, that was again threatened.

Despite the protests of Sir Douglas Haig, Major-General Trenchard was brought back from France in January 1918 to be the first Chief of the Air Staff. The latter had, however, at once a serious difference of opinion with Lord Rothermere, whom Mr. Lloyd George had appointed as first Secretary of State for Air. Major-General Trenchard did not at that time wish to establish the independent force at the expense of the tactical air forces in France. Major-General Sykes, one of the pioneers of the service, was appointed in his place; but Lord Rothermere's health was uncertain and other

---

[1] The night raiders were also gradually mastered and in the last raid of 19th May 1918 out of a force of thirty-three aircraft, three were destroyed by night fighters, three by anti-aircraft fire, three crashed and one was lost through engine failure. Ashmore: *Air Defence*, pp. 85 ff.

high officers, including Sir David Henderson, who had done so much to bring the independent air service into existence, were critical of the new Minister. Lord Rothermere therefore soon resigned and was succeeded by Sir William Weir, the Director of Aircraft Production in the Ministry of Munitions. Major-General Trenchard was then appointed to the command of the independent bombing force already set up in France which it had been planned to increase to formidable strength in the course of the year.[1]

The British Government could decide that an independent air service should come into existence, but there were still great difficulties in the way before an effective 'independent' strategic bombing force could be created. By the time these difficulties were overcome, the war had only a few months to run and the new arm, still only a small force, was never in a position to demonstrate what strategic bombing could accomplish. In the first place it never reached anything like the numbers at first contemplated. It was originally suggested that it should have one hundred squadrons, one third of the expanded air force. But these estimates were ruthlessly reduced in face of the lack of suitable engines, the demands of the tactical air force and the unexpected prospect of an early end to the war. In the end Major-General Trenchard never disposed of more than nine squadrons of the Royal Air Force and several of these were quite unsuitable for their purpose. The aircraft of the one squadron of fighters allotted to him were so poor in quality that they could not do anything to protect the day bombers during their sorties.[2]

In addition to the lack of sufficient aircraft there was great difficulty in establishing the 'independence' of the new force. The nucleus of such a force had been created at Ochey near Nancy in October 1917, while Major-General Trenchard was still Commander-in-Chief of the Royal Flying Corps in France, in the 41st Wing consisting of one day and two night bombing squadrons. It had been set up in conjunction with the French to fulfil the wish of the British Government and people that a reply should be made to the repeated bombing of Britain by the enemy. It was under the control of G.H.Q. and was regarded as of small consequence in the general strategic scheme. Neither Sir Douglas Haig nor his new Commander-in-Chief of the Royal Air Force in France, Sir John Salmond, believed that strategic bombing could accomplish very much in the immediate struggle. At any rate, they were more concerned to provide the maximum number of fighters and bombers

---

[1] Lord Beaverbrook: *Men and Power, 1917–1918*, (1956), pp. 219–238.
Robert Blake: *The Private Papers of Douglas Haig, 1914–1919*, (1952), p. 280.

[2] On 8th August 1918 the Independent Force consisted of five bombing squadrons (three day and two night), and on 11th November 1918 of nine bombing squadrons (four day and five night) and one fighter squadron. *The War in the Air*, Appendices vol., pp. 122, 128.

for co-operation with the armies which were to an ever-increasing degree depending on air support for success in the field. Between 17th October 1917 and 5th June 1918, when the Independent Force proper came into existence, fifty-seven raids were made by the British element of the strategic air force.

Meanwhile the German offensive in March 1918 resulted in the appointment of Marshal Foch to direct the strategy of all the allied forces in France. It was only natural that he should object strongly to the establishment of an 'independent' bomber force over which he had not final control. The main strategic object of the allies, he said, was to defeat the German armies, and for this purpose he must be able to use, if necessary, all the air power in France. It took some time before a compromise could be worked out by which, while Marshal Foch was given overriding authority, Major-General Trenchard was made Commander-in-Chief under him of an 'independent' strategic force, which, it was hoped, would become interallied by the inclusion of French, Italian and American squadrons. By the time all this was settled the Germans were being rapidly driven out of France and one of the main purposes of the strategic air force, to break the deadlock on the Western front, was seen to be no longer necessary.

Had the war continued until 1919, a much greater effort would have been made and a considerable part of the force engaged would have been based in Britain instead of France. One of the motives behind this plan was the desire to be outside the control of the Allied Command in France. Indeed, at the height of the controversy narrated above it had been proposed to remove the whole force to Norfolk and only use aerodromes in France as refuelling bases.[1] As will be seen, this same difficulty was to exercise an influence on the strategy of the Royal Air Force when the next contest with Germany drew near. This attack from Britain was to be carried out at night by long-range bombers which were partly suggested by the 'Giants' which the Germans had used in attacks on London. They were to be constructed by Handley-Page with four engines, a crew of six and a range which would have enabled them to reach Berlin with a heavy bomb load. Two hundred and twenty-five of these aircraft had been ordered, but by the end of the war only three had been delivered and none made a sortie over enemy territory. Thus, this ambitious project had no result, though it showed the possibilities of a strategic air force, if it were given adequate instruments for its purpose. But no successor to these aircraft was planned until 1932, and no four-engined bomber until 1936.

In these circumstances the independent strategic force could not

---

[1] There was also a plan to base some of the long-range bombers in Czechoslovakia when that country should have been freed.

accomplish much and its influence on the struggle in France was almost imperceptible. Within its range were the Saar iron mines and the chemical industries of Mannheim and Freiburg. Some of its raids penetrated 100 to 120 miles beyond the allied lines. Some small material loss was caused both by actual destruction and by the effect on the workers; a number of civilians were killed and a certain diversion of effort was caused by forcing the Germans to assign aircraft to defence and to provide a barrage of anti-aircraft guns and balloon protection. A considerable amount of the effort of the Independent Force was spent on attacking the enemy's aerodromes. It also assisted on occasion, at the request of Marshal Foch, in tactical bombing of railways. But the total weight of bombs dropped on Germany was too small to have more than a nuisance value. The daylight raids were generally only one squadron strong, about twelve aircraft flying in formation. An increasing proportion was made at night in single sorties. The total losses were not large, 3·9 per cent of the number despatched, but in addition a number of aircraft were destroyed on the ground by German bombing. All this was a very small thing compared to the immense effort that was being put into the air forces co-operating with the armies. The Independent Air Force was no more than an aspiration. Its significance was in the future, not in the struggle of 1918.[1]

Thus, on the Western Front, there was a limited experience upon which to base plans for the future. There was also the experience of the German strategic air offensive against England and, in addition, a fuller experience of tactical bombing both in France and in other theatres of war which had occupied far more of the attention of the Air Force. Many attempts had been made, for example, to cut railway communications and thus deprive armies of their supplies both in France and in the Middle East. The defeat of the Turkish armies in Palestine had been produced by obtaining mastery of the air, and its effects much increased by the use of fighter bombers at a critical moment. Bombing also helped to demoralise the Bulgarian Army in its retreat from the Salonica front. In these cases the opposition was feeble or non-existent and that fact, perhaps, helped to bring about an exaggerated view of the accuracy with which bombs could be dropped in warfare.

Still, this was all the experience available and it was on it that the

---

[1] Of the 543 tons dropped by the Independent Force 220 were dropped on German aerodromes. Seventy-six per cent of the areoplanes sent out dropped bombs somewhere in Germany, fifty-five per cent of these on the primary or alternative targets given to them and the rest with no very specific object. Engine trouble or the weather caused fourteen per cent to turn back without dropping their bombs on Germany. *The War in the Air*, Vol. VI, pp. 158, 163 fn. In Appendix XIII of the Appendices volume a detailed list of all the British raids of the 41st Wing and Independent Air Force is given. The latter made 239 raids in all, including attacks on the same day or night on different places

strategic thinking of the Air Staff had in future years to be based. It is necessary, therefore, to sum up their attitude towards it. Naturally there was not always full agreement as to the facts or to the interpretation of them.[1] But Sir Hugh Trenchard, Commander of the Independent Air Force, was Chief of the Air Staff from 1919 to 1929, and his estimate of what had been done was of decisive influence on the future of the Royal Air Force.

In the first place there was the doctrine that an air force is far more effective in offence than defence. It had first been evolved as a result of the fighting over the fronts of the armies in the trench warfare which had existed since 1915. Its truth had been clearly demonstrated, as has been noted, when the enemy was forced to fight over his own territory in an endeavour to prevent tactical bombing and reconnaissance. What this amounted to was that, if one side could obtain air superiority in the front areas over the other, then its air force could be employed for those other uses which injured the enemy, while the latter was prevented from making similar use of his own aircraft. Neither freedom of action on one side nor prohibition on the other was total, except in rare and local cases. Nor did it apply to night bombing since the means of detection of hostile aircraft were yet primitive. There were, indeed, two periods when the Germans obtained the ascendancy. In the autumn of 1915 the new Fokker aircraft and in the spring of 1917 the *Richthofen* offensive won for the enemy temporary air superiority. But in each case it was regained by the British and French air forces and for the greater part of the war in the West the allied aircraft were able in daytime to survey the enemy ground forces and bomb his back areas to a greater extent than the enemy could use such means against the *entente* powers. The initiative lay with the latter; they controlled the air space over the fronts to a much greater degree than the Germans. And it should be noted that this superiority was not achieved by close escort of the reconnaissance and bombing aircraft. It was obtained by sending out large forces which attacked the enemy wherever they could find them and drive them off. Under the shelter of such protection, supplemented at times by close escort, the reconnaissance and bombing aircraft could perform their duties, not without some molestation, but on the whole in such security that they could reach their objectives and accomplish their purposes. Meanwhile the land armies of the side that had air superiority could move with greater freedom and had greater opportunities for surprise attack.

This lesson from the battlefields was not, however, applied to strategic bombing. Neither the British nor the Germans used fighters

---

[1] *The War in the Air* took nearly eighteen years to produce, and the final volume which contained an account of the Independent Bombing Force did not appear until 1937.

to clear the air for the use of their long-range bombers. But as regards tactical bombing the doctrine had been laid down as early as autumn 1915, and it was confirmed by subsequent experience.[1] It is stated quite definitely in a remarkable memorandum of the General Staff of the British Expeditionary Force in March 1917. 'To seek out and destroy the enemy's forces', it said, 'must be the guiding principle of our tactics just as it is on land and sea.' It also insisted that bombers needed protection: 'A bomb raid in the air may be compared to a convoy on the ground, and similar measures are required for its protection, namely, an escort designed to act offensively and keep the enemy at a distance, and, in addition, an escort keeping with the raid for the local protection of bombing machines, should the enemy succeed in getting to close quarters.'[2] This does not quite lay down the thesis that a general air superiority must be obtained, but it goes far in that direction by advocating a separate fighter force for offence against the opposing fighters. Sir Douglas Haig himself, while sceptical of the effects of strategic bombing, had, in a memorandum which no doubt reflected the views of Sir Hugh Trenchard, insisted on the importance to the armies in the field of gaining and maintaining 'supremacy in the air'.[3] But the general doctrine that the first necessity for all air operations was the defeat of the enemy air forces had been laid down in 1917 in a great state paper by the Minister of Munitions, Mr. Winston Churchill. 'But the indispensable preliminary to all results in the air,' his memorandum stated, 'as in every other sphere of war, is to defeat the armed forces of the enemy.'[4] The Minister of Munitions had long been a student of the strategy of war and was familiar with the doctrines of Clausewitz and Mahan.

It is not surprising, therefore, that when the first scheme for a large strategic air force was put forth by Sir Douglas Haig in November 1917, the necessity of obtaining air superiority for it had been at first accepted. It was then suggested that it should include twenty squadrons of long-range fighters, almost as many as the number of daylight bombing squadrons. But when it became clear that nothing like such numbers could be obtained, Major-General Trenchard said that he would dispense with fighters. He took this course not only because fighters were urgently needed for the tactical air forces when the struggle in France was at its height, but also because he did not know exactly what type of fighter would be necessary.[5] Thus he sent out his bombing force in the daytime without fighter protection and made no effort to command the air by that means beyond the front areas. In these front areas some protection

---

[1] *The War in the Air*, Vol. II, pp. 164–168. [2] do. Vol. III, App. XI, p. 408.
[3] do. Appendices vol., p. 16. [4] do. p. 21.
[5] do. Vol. VI, pp. 170–172.

was afforded by the tactical air forces, but beyond them the bombers were left to defend themselves.[1] The squadrons generally flew in formation so that the bombers could protect one another from the attacking fighters, and the losses were on the whole surprisingly small. The art of fighter defence against a long-range bombing force was imperfectly developed. The warning system was rudimentary and the means of directing a compact force quickly against the attackers had not yet been worked out. There had, it is true, been considerable success against the German raiders in August and September 1917. But that attack had been on a small scale, had not been persevered with and, as is noted below, had been met with immensely superior forces. It is, perhaps, not surprising that the result of this limited experience was to suggest that the bombers could always get through, and that it was not necessary to provide fighter protection in the air space through which they would have to operate. Moreover, the strategic bombers were themselves armed, and, though they had not shot down many enemy aircraft, this fact made the task of the opposing fighters more difficult and initiated the doctrine that the bombers could defend themselves. In any case, it was held, no deductions as to fighter support of long-range strategic bombing could be made from the experience of short-range operations over the battle fronts. There the enemy could be easily found by fighters whose bases were only twenty miles distant and needed no more fuel than the enemy aircraft. But the contest would be an unequal one if the escorting fighter had to traverse a long distance. It would have no fuel for manœuvre, would soon have to leave the bombers to their fate and would itself be in grave danger on its homeward journey ill supplied with fuel. All this was the more easily believed since not much thought had yet been given to the problem of designing a long-range fighter which could hold its own with the short-range interceptor.

These views had also seemed to be confirmed by the defence of Britain against the German attacks. It had cost in men and materials an immense amount more than the attack had cost the Germans. Sixteen squadrons of fighters had been employed continuously as a defence against the Zeppelins. The attacks of the Gotha squadrons, never more than forty aircraft strong in all, had, it was often recalled in later years, caused a force of 440 to be assembled against them and even then the defence was for some time ineffective.[2]

---

[1] As Major-General J. M. Salmond pointed out in his report of October 1918, the D.H.9s, the least serviceable of the bombing squadrons, had practically to restrict their raids to areas where protection could be given by the tactical patrols over the front areas. *The War in the Air*, Vol. VI, pp. 142–143 fn.

[2] According to Major-General Ashmore his force at the maximum was 159 day and 123 night fighters. The total of 440 is presumably made up by the odds and ends that sometimes joined in the defence. There were in addition in April 1918, 266 guns and

The High Command had protested against this diversion of strength but the Government had been forced into this defensive attitude, so it was said, by the pressure of public opinion. The fact that two squadrons of fighters had had to be withdrawn from France at a critical moment was never forgotten.

This incident aroused the fear that the demand for protection at home would prevent the best use of air power. There had, of course, during the Zeppelin and aeroplane attacks been strongly expressed demands for more protection. But the situation had been accepted and there had been little panic and not much unreasonable agitation. 'In our own case', wrote Mr. Churchill in October 1917, 'we have seen the combative spirit of the people roused, and not quelled, by the German air raids.' The preponderant feeling was a desire to strike back. 'There was at this time', wrote Major-General Ashmore, 'a tremendous public outcry for reprisals on German towns.'[1] Nevertheless, the view prevailed that public opinion might prevent the air force from being used in the manner best calculated to defeat the enemy.

Moreover, right up to the Second World War the fear persisted in both civil and military circles that the British people would become so panic-stricken under bombing that special measures would be necessary to maintain order. A report of the Air Raids Precautions Committee in 1930 proposed to create three battalions of troops for action in air raids and the Chairman stated that if this were not done 'he had little doubt that such a state of panic would be produced as might bring about a collapse, certainly of the community in London, if not of the whole country'. In 1937 the Minister for the Co-ordination of Defence suggested to the Cabinet that 'certain territorial units might, therefore, be earmarked for duties in connection with the maintenance of order and of essential services in this country in time of war'. The Cabinet agreed that 'some part of both the Regular Army and the Territorial Army may be used for internal security', though no battalions were to be especially allotted to that task.[2]

This judgment was partly due to the heavy casualties produced by the daylight raids on London in the First World War. On the basis of such figures calculations were later made that staggering

---

353 searchlights as well as the considerable personnel of the balloon barrage. *Air Defence*, p. 79. The Germans, it was later said, employed a mixed force of 240 bombers and fighters in the defence of the Rhineland against the Independent Air Force of 122 aircraft. C.A.S. Memo., 12th June 1934.

[1] *The War in the Air*, Appendices, p. 19. Ashmore: *Air Defence*, p. 63.

[2] Cf. an Air Staff Minute, 24th March 1930: 'N.B. We have got a folio full of appeals from mayors and M.P's for all sorts of odd places in the Midlands screaming for direct protection against half a dozen old Zeppelins; and a crashed flying officer was hauled out of an ambulance in Norwich and mobbed as a result of—I think—*two* raids in which about a dozen little bombs were scattered about.' Min. by Slessor. C.I.D. Mtg., 29th Sept. 1930. Report by Inskip, 15th Dec. 1937. Cabinet Mtg., 22nd Dec. 1937.

civilian casualties would be incurred in the first weeks of an air war, which would virtually make London uninhabitable. Little attempt was made to compare these casualties with those produced by the British bombing of German towns which would have suggested a different result. Nor was the unprepared state of the defences and of the Air Raid Precaution measures taken sufficiently into account. This exaggeration of the number of casualties which strategic bombing was likely to produce was a major factor in all strategic thinking before the Second World War and exercised a profound influence on the minds of the services, the political chiefs, and, being translated into even more sensational language by journalists and publicists, on public opinion at large.

This judgment was also a main cause of Major-General Trenchard's constantly repeated dictum to the effect that in strategic bombing the moral effect was greater than the material effect. This might seem to mean that casualties and damage to public amenities and personal property would produce such an effect on civilians as to change the whole course of a war. In its most extreme form this doctrine claimed that the next war could be won by bombing alone by destroying the enemy's will to resist. Armies would thus be no more than police forces to occupy a country already conquered from the air. During the 1914–1918 war Major-General Trenchard had always insisted that strategic bombing was directed against military objectives and not at the civilian population. He had protested, for example, when it was suggested that the British air raids on Germany after the bombing of London should be termed 'reprisals'. But it was always recognised that in such a process heavy civilian casualties were inevitable. As Major-General Trenchard pointed out in his survey of 1st January 1919, he was only prevented from destroying completely one industrial centre after another in Germany because he lacked the means to do so. Such a task, he thought, would in any case take four or five years. But meanwhile, by spreading the raids over as many towns as possible, he could produce great moral effect. 'At present,' he wrote, 'the moral effect of bombing stands undoubtedly to the material effect in a proportion of 20 to 1.'[1] Major-General Sykes, then Chief of the Air Staff, had written on 27th June 1918 in a memorandum for the Cabinet:

> 'The aim of such attacks would be to sow alarm broadcast, set up nervous tension, check output, and generally tend to bring military, financial, and industrial interests into opposition ... The wholesale bombing of densely populated industrial centres would go far to destroy the morale of the operatives.'[2]

---

[1] Despatch of Trenchard, 1st Jan. 1919. *The War in the Air*, Vol. VI, p. 136.
[2] C.A.S. Memo., 27th June 1918.

There were always some who challenged the view that the effect on civilian morale would be decisive. Mr. Churchill, for example, in the memorandum already quoted, refused to believe 'that any terrorisation of the civil population which could be achieved by air attack would compel the Government of a great nation to surrender.' The Germans were as courageous as the British. 'Nothing that we have learned of the capacity of the German population to endure suffering justifies us in assuming that they could be cowed into submission by such methods.' He thought that the armies would decide the issue of the war, but that the air force could make its best contribution to this end by precise bombing of the bases and communications of the enemy and that it might be possible, as some experts believed, by use of more scientific instruments and better tactics, to attack them with an accuracy 'similar to that which has been attained at sea under extraordinarily difficult circumstances,' if only, as has been noted, the enemy air forces were first defeated.[1]

Some precision bombing had, indeed, been attempted by the Independent Force during the war and occasional successes were obtained by the primitive methods then available. But there could have been no illusions as to the difficulty of hitting a precise object, a fact which was recognised even in tactical bombing. Still, the idea that the best results could be obtained from precision bombing was already conceived if only the means could be found for carrying it out.

Much of the strategic bombing on both sides had been done at night when a precision attack would be more difficult, if not impossible. But the German aircraft had had little difficulty in finding London on fine nights. And it was often asserted, especially by the Naval Wing, that bombers could find their way better by night than day, provided that there was a moon or that the night was a clear one. Moreover, because they were less liable to interception, they did not require the same weight of defensive armament and could, therefore, carry a greater weight of bombs. For these reasons it seemed to some that the bomber forces could be used with the greatest effect at night.[2] It was at any rate, in view of later experience, surprising that the night bombers had apparently found their target areas as well as they had. The distances covered were, of course, small, the aircraft flew at a fairly low height and they only attempted a night attack when the weather was good. The Royal Naval Air Service had been the most successful in night flying and it was thought that exact navigation could be produced by the same methods as were used at sea. But though the effect of the clouds and ground haze of Western Europe had been fully revealed, few instruments had been devised to assist navigation under such conditions.

---

[1] *The War in the Air*, Appendices vol., pp. 19, 21.
[2] do. Vol. VI, pp. 167 ff.

It can be said, indeed, that the magnitude of the problem of navigating an aircraft at night or in cloudy weather to a target area over such a distance as separated Britain from Germany had not been appreciated when the war came to an end. It was sometimes claimed that not only the target area but the target itself could be found on moonlight nights as well as in daytime, since at night the bombers could fly at a lower height, being harder to hit by anti-aircraft fire. No doubt sometimes definite targets were hit, but there was little precise knowledge on this subject and the reports of the crews were accepted without later photographic confirmation. Flares had been used on occasions but no very searching tests had been made. Still it was realised that precision bombing by night would be difficult—and, indeed, by day as well.[1]

Similarly, there was insufficient experience of defence by fighters against night bombers. Special night fighters working in conjunction with the searchlights had had success against the Zeppelins, but these were vulnerable targets. Bombing attacks had generally been carried out by single aircraft flying with considerable intervals of time between them. Such aircraft, flying alone, were hard to find, though successes had sometimes been gained against them by night fighters. Many factors in night flying were thus still a matter of debate, and it was inevitable that there should remain much difference of opinion on the advantages of night and day bombing when the new air force came to be planned.

Since fighters were as yet considered to be an imperfect defence against bombers, whether by night or by day, both sides tried to reduce the enemy forces by attacks on aerodromes whence the bombers came. The Royal Naval Air Service had attacked the Zeppelin sheds and compelled the removal of the Zeppelins to a safer area. Such a course had been suggested as a means to prevent the daylight raids on Britain in 1917. The Germans delivered some attacks on British aerodromes and aircraft depots with considerable success, though the main damage was done in the depots. Major-General Trenchard replied in the same manner, both to reduce this form of attack and also to reduce the fighter attack on his bombers which he had no other means of combating. No less than 220 of the 543 tons dropped by the Independent Force were aimed at enemy aerodromes. The results were not known at the time and were, indeed, never assessed exactly in later days, but they also had some considerable success, though, as no depot was hit, less than that of the German air force. The impression of the importance of such attacks

---

[1] In 1924 a careful examination of the records of the war 1914–1918 was made because of the controversy between the advocates of night and day bombing: 'An examination of the records of the I.A.F. [Independent Air Force] shows that the number of night attacks which failed to reach their objective was proportionately far in excess of the number of unsuccessful day attacks.' Plans Note, 16th April 1924.

remained, though, as will be seen, it was later removed to a considerable extent by experiments in such bombing in peace time. At the same time such use was held to be in a sense 'defensive' and to produce a reduction in offence, the real objective of the force.[1]

Such a reduction was all the more to be regretted because the total weight of bombs dropped on Germany was so small and, since only a small bomb load could be carried, the bombs themselves were of small size, generally 112 or 230 lb. Most of the British aircraft used could carry no more than four of the larger ones, and even the largest aircraft not more than a total of about 1,750 lb.[2] Some bombs of a larger size had been used by the Germans in their 'Giants'. But little was known of the comparative effects of such bombs and the subject seems to have attracted little attention, a fact that would be surprising if there had not been a similar neglect in the period between the wars. Nor was much yet known of the ballistics of bombs on which the right method of aiming depended. Incendiaries had been used, but the comparative failure of those dropped by the Germans on London had caused their value to be discounted and there was little conception of the possibilities of this type of weapon.[3]

There was, therefore, a tendency to exaggerate the indirect effects of bombing. The suspension of work in Britain during air-raid warnings and the absenteeism after raids, caused, it was often said later, more loss than the actual damage inflicted by the bombs themselves. Major-General Trenchard tried to produce similar effects in Germany by spreading his attacks over a wide area rather than by concentrating on a specific objective. In tactical bombing the importance of 'saturating' the defence by a concentrated attack had already been realised. But as yet the value of concentration in strategic bombing for a similar purpose had not been perceived.

Finally, there were two large and general impressions made by the war of 1914–1918 not only on the professional soldiers, sailors and airmen but also on British public opinion, which exercised great influence on all the strategic thinking in the period between the wars. The heavy casualties produced by the prolonged static warfare had shocked the world and especially the British people, who had never had a previous experience of continental fighting on such a large scale. It was constantly asserted that Britain must never again take

---

[1] *The War in the Air*, Vol. VI, pp. 158–164. This summary, written under the impression of later doctrine in the Air Force, is rather critical of the use of bombers for this purpose, suggesting that they would have been better employed in bombing towns.

[2] The new Handley Page four-engine bomber would have been able to carry 7,500 lb. a long way if not, perhaps, as far as Berlin. Their bomb-load range had not been fully tested.

[3] The Germans had designed towards the end of the war a new 2-lb. incendiary bomb with which they had the intention of devastating Paris, but they thought it unwise to use it in defeat.

part in such warfare. Not until the Second World War was close at hand was the decision taken to send an army to the Continent. How then could a future war be won? The naval blockade which had played so great a part in the Napoleonic and the First World Wars could only produce an effect after a long period of time, and it was generally thought that the aggressor in the next war, if it came, would aim at attaining a quick decision. An insular power like Britain, with an army recruited by voluntary service and largely occupied with the defence of the Empire, could only make a rapid counter-attack by means of a strategic air force. Its influence in a future struggle would depend on its ability to strike back immediately with greater force than its opponent could employ.

On the other hand, because of its small area and the concentration of its inhabitants in large towns, nearly one quarter of the whole in greater London, Britain was specially vulnerable to attack from the air. It seemed, as a result of the war, to many soldiers and sailors as well as to civilians, that her interests would be best served if strategic bombing was abolished altogether. And this attitude was reinforced by doubts as to its morality. In 1918 the suggestion had been made by the King of Spain, perhaps at the instance of the German Government, that some restraint should be placed on bombing. Statements in the Bavarian Chamber had seemed to indicate that the German Government would be prepared to make an agreement that open towns should not be bombed. This offer was due to the effect on the Rhineland of the limited strategic bombing that had already taken place and the fact that the German General Staff had never placed much faith in a strategic bombing offensive as an aid to winning the war. But such an agreement would have allowed tactical bombing to continue and this would have meant that only French and Belgian towns would be bombed. The claim that tactical bombing was legitimate, however many casualties it caused to civilians, while strategic bombing was not, was to be made in later years. At any rate the hint, for it was nothing more, was regarded by the British Government as a sign that the Germans thought that they would suffer more damage by strategic bombing than they could inflict and it was consequently rejected. The rejection was accompanied by a declaration that, except on one or two occasions as reprisals, British bombing had been directed against military objectives and would continue to be so. Everything possible, it was added, would be done to reduce civilian casualties.[1] But it was not indicated how this last object was to be accomplished even in daylight bombing. The Air Staff had, of course, few illusions on this subject. Strategic bombing was bound to cause civilian casualties.

---

[1] *The War in the Air*, Vol. VI, pp. 101–103.

This was, indeed, as has been seen, one of the means of producing that moral effect which was considered by some to be so much more important than the physical damage inflicted on the enemy. In any case, was not this method of warfare more humane than one which produced starvation or at least malnutrition in the civilian population by blockade and condemned the youth of all countries to mass slaughter on the battlefields?

But this view of the Air Staff was not, after the war, accepted by the Admiralty or the General Staff and still less by public opinion. Determined efforts were to be made to find some means by which bombing from the air could be banished from civilised warfare. The obstacles in the way of placing such restraint on the use of a new weapon of war were much too great to be overcome. They depended ultimately on an advance in international organisation which was never attained. But the fact that strategic bombing was considered in many circles as an illegitimate method of warfare was bound to exercise an influence on planning the use of the strategic bombing force.

2. Laying the foundations, 1919–1933[1]

At the close of the war of 1914–1918 the Royal Air Force was the most powerful air force in the world. Moreover, it alone had designed and organised a strategic bombing force independent of the control of the other services. But in a short time this great instrument of war had, as Air Marshal Sir Hugh Trenchard wrote, 'withered away like Jonah's gourd'. Much of this process was inevitable. In all countries, and in none more than Britain, there was a loathing of war and the hope that means would be found to prevent its recurrence. In such a climate of opinion it was impossible to obtain adequate support for a new service, hastily, if brilliantly, improvised during the war and lacking nearly all the permanent installations which the older services possessed.

At the end of the war Air Marshal Sir Hugh Trenchard was made Chief of the Air Staff. He recognised at once that he must plan for a small force, which, in addition to its duties overseas, would be mainly concerned with training and research, so that the foundations could be laid for a more efficient and modern air force in the future. The great state paper, in which he sketched the outline of the peace-time organisation, laid down all the necessary requirements for this purpose. Everything, of course, depended on its retaining its separate identity. The necessary air forces had to be provided for the Navy and the Army, both at home and overseas, and it was even recognised that these forces might become detached from the Royal Air Force. But 'the main portion of it would consist of an Independent Force together with Service personnel required in carrying out Aeronautical Research'. The Royal Air Force must train its own officers, airmen and artificers and thus preserve the 'Air Force spirit'. The force must, indeed, be highly trained and the paper enumerated the essentials, navigation ('practically a new science'), wireless, photography and engineering. Research was of supreme importance and the existing establishments at Biggin Hill, Martlesham Heath and Grain must be retained and developed. Since everything during the war had been done in temporary buildings, much capital expenditure would be required.[2]

Had the Air Ministry been given the means to carry out this programme, it could have developed in a short time an efficient and progressive force, able to cope with the new and formidable

---

[1] In this and the following three sections much help has been obtained from Vol. I of the Narrative, *The R.A.F. in the Bombing Offensive against Germany. Prewar evolution of Bomber Command 1917–1939*, prepared by Professor R. B. Wernham, under the direction of the Air Historical Branch, Air Ministry.

[2] C.A.S. Memo., 25th Nov. 1919. Cmd. 467.

problems of air warfare. The scheme, submitted by Mr. Churchill, then Secretary of State for Air as well as for War, and prepared under his direction, was, indeed, approved in principle by the Cabinet. But the amount which it was proposed to allot to carry it out was but £15 million a year, a sum quite inadequate for the purpose. This meant that many indispensable parts of the plan had to be postponed for an indefinite period.

There also was at the outset an even greater danger than crippling finance; for the independent position of the Air Force was again threatened. Neither the Navy nor the Army looked with favour on a new competitor for the limited sums available for the armed services. The former claimed control not only of all seaborne aircraft, but also of all land-based aircraft used for any purpose over the sea or in defence of naval establishments. The latter not only asserted that 'coordination between the air and the surface is more fundamental than that between the land and the sea', but suggested that great economies would be effected if the air force were incorporated so far as possible in the army and common services set up—even perhaps in the training of officers.[1] The battle for an independent air force had to be fought all over again, and naturally special emphasis was again laid on the strategic bombing force, which, as has been seen, was the main reason for bringing an independent air force into existence. Not until 1923 as a result of the findings of the Salisbury Committee was the issue finally settled and the Royal Air Force enabled to look forward to an established future. At the same time, by the creation of the Chiefs of Staff Committee, the Chief of the Air Staff was placed on an equal footing with his colleagues of the Navy and Army.[2]

Until this struggle was decided no very definite planning could take place. The new role of the air force in overseas territories was realised during this period and its success in maintaining order by air power in the Middle East with a minimum of personnel and expense contributed to the maintenance of its position as an independent service. But meanwhile the force at home had dwindled to a mere handful. The situation was viewed by the Government and Parliament with equanimity, since the German air force had been abolished and no other threat from the air had appeared.

---

[1] One of the reasons put forward by the army was that the active life of a pilot was so short, an average of five years, so that there would be no room in the higher ranks of the air force for their employment, while the army could easily absorb them. Memo. by Worthington-Evans (Sec. of State for War, Feb. 1921–Oct. 1922, Postmaster-General, 1923–1924), 3rd July 1923. The Chief of the Air Staff who denied that the active period would be so short, pointed out the number of short-service officers and looked forward to higher ranks retaining their flying ability. 'It is not improbable that Air Vice-Marshals should themselves go into the air and lead in the next war.' Address by Trenchard at War Office Staff Exercise, 9th–13th April 1923. One or two of them did on occasion.

[2] Cmd. 1938, July 1923.

It was the growing friction with France, which had retained a much larger air force, that enabled the Chief of the Air Staff in 1923 to begin to plan in more detail. The Cabinet approved and submitted to Parliament a recommendation of a Sub-committee of the Committee of Imperial Defence that there should be a 'Home Defence Air Force of sufficient strength to protect us against air attack by the strongest air force within striking distance of this country'. Part of it was to be composed of permanent and regular squadrons, part of auxiliary volunteer squadrons and cadre reserve squadrons. The total was to be equal to the French 'independent' force of about 600 aircraft or fifty-two squadrons in the first stage of development.[1]

On this basis the Air Staff began to plan a home defence force, interpreting defence in its own way. The problem received in the summer of 1923 close examination at a number of meetings presided over by the Chief of the Air Staff himself. From these discussions came decisions which determined not only the composition of the future Bomber Command, but also to a considerable extent its strategy and tactics, and some account must, therefore, be given of them. These decisions were partly due to the desire to safeguard the independence of the Air Force, partly to the enforced economy of the time and partly to the experience of the war of 1914–1918, as interpreted at that period. The discussions were dominated by the personality of the Chief of the Air Staff, the main creator of the Air Force, who had an experience and authority which no one else could rival.[2]

It was he who decided before the discussions began that fighters should consist only of short-range interceptors for home defence and that there should be no long-range fighters to protect the bombing squadrons. His object was to obtain as many bombing squadrons as possible and thus increase the offensive power of the Air Force. This decision, of fundamental importance to the whole development of the Air Force, could not therefore be challenged, though some of those present insisted that unescorted day bombers would be likely to suffer heavy casualties.

The discussions were dominated by the view that the right method of using an Air Force was to attack, and that only an offensive force could win the next war. Fighter defence must also, therefore, be kept to the smallest possible number. It was, in the view of the Chief of the Air Staff, in a sense only a concession to the weak-

---

[1] Shortly afterwards the French 'independent' air force ceased to exist as such and was subordinated to the army even more than before.
[2] The minutes of the meetings which were held at intervals between 10th July and 8th August 1923 were kept together in a separate file with a few other documents. For the minutes of 19th July 1923 see App. 1.

ness of the civilians, who would demand protection and cause the Cabinet and even the Secretary of State for Air to do so likewise. These demands, he insisted, must be resisted as far as possible. This view met with some criticism. It was pointed out that fighters might prevent more damage being done to Britain than an equivalent number of bombers could inflict on France. But Sir Hugh Trenchard insisted that everything must be done to ensure that the heaviest possible bomb load could be dropped on the enemy country so that the morale of its inhabitants could be destroyed. When it was pointed out that the morale of the bombing force might deteriorate, if it had heavy losses, he answered that 'this would have a greater effect on the morale of the French pilots than it would on ours.' Casualties affected the French more than they did the British. That consideration must be taken into account, but the most vital point was to hit the French nation and cause them to cry out before the British did. 'The question had been asked at Camberley "Why is it that your policy of attack from the air is so different from the policy of the Army, whose policy it is to attack the enemy's army, while yours is to attack the civil population." The answer was that we were able to do this while the Army were not, and so go straight to the source of supply and stop it. Instead of attacking a machine with 10 bombs we would go straight to the source of supply of the bombs and demolish it, and the same with the source of production of the machines. It was a quicker process than allowing the output to go on. The Army policy was to defeat the enemy Army—ours to defeat the enemy nation'.[1]

It will be at once noted that there was a confusion of thought here between two methods of defeating the enemy, one by destroying his will to resist, the other by depriving him of the means of resistance. It could, of course, be said that the two objects could be prosecuted together since an attack on the sources of production would, inevitably, cause heavy civilian casualties and the destruction of housing and public amenities. But a great deal might depend on which of the two was the primary objective—the type of aircraft needed, the training of the crews, the choice between day and night bombing.

It was at any rate assumed that the bomber force would be able to penetrate to its targets and destroy them. The new force must, therefore, consist mainly of bombers with fighters kept to the lowest possible level and reserved for home defence only.

It had then to be determined how many squadrons should be regarded as night bombers and how many as day bombers. On this point there was considerable difference of opinion and it was never finally settled. With the strategic objective so defined and with the

---

[1] For the whole discussion see App. 1.

technical knowledge then available, it was, indeed, an insoluble problem. Those who dreaded the casualties which might be inflicted by day on the bombers tended to prefer action mainly by night; those who thought that day bombers would find the target more easily and bomb it more accurately by day were prepared to take that risk. There was general agreement that in order to obtain the maximum effect, bombing both by day and by night would be necessary.[1]

This led naturally to a discussion as to whether it was necessary to have different types of machines for day and night. The Chief of the Air Staff insisted that the same machines should be used both for day and night fighters, and it was generally agreed that fighter pilots should be trained for both purposes. There was more difference of opinion as to whether night and day bombing could be done with the same kind of aircraft. It was recognised that day bombers would have to fight their way to their targets and might, therefore, need more speed as well as more armament and, perhaps, armour. But this end might be secured by modifications of the same aircraft. Perhaps, it was suggested, a few squadrons of special high-performance aircraft should be solely directed to day bombing and a few others with a specially heavy bomb load to night bombing. The rest, it was hoped, might serve for both purposes according to circumstances. This was all the more necessary since the hours of daylight and darkness varied so much in the course of the year.

There was, indeed, not only then but up to and even during the war, a strong body of opinion against specialisation in aircraft. Too many different types, it was thought, not only meant that smaller numbers of aircraft would be produced; they also reduced the flexibility of the air force and prevented it from being concentrated as a whole against the most important objective, a fundamental principle of strategy. It was at this time pointed out that after all there was no great difference between fighters and bombers and that the light bombers, so much used in the war, were as swift and manœuvreable as the interceptors. Light bombers were also more easily transferred overseas than heavier aircraft, unless these were so big as to be able to fly there. There was thus a tendency, in spite of the emphasis on the size of the bomb load, to develop aircraft of this kind.[2]

---

[1] A note by the Plans Division of 16th April 1924 stated: 'There is no doubt that failure to reach the objective from this cause [failure in determination to find it] is less likely to occur with the day bombing squadrons, flying as they will be in large formations. The night-bomber, on the other hand, as far as can be foreseen at present, must always fly alone, which, added to the difficulties of navigation and identification of targets, will undoubtedly lead to great weights of bombs being dropped on comparatively unimportant objectives.' A prophetic warning of the years 1939–1941!

[2] The aim was constantly to have an aircraft that could be used both for day and night, but it was thought in 1929 that the night bombers would not be able to be used by day. In 1932 it was suggested by Air Defence of Great Britain Command that the introduction of the automatic pilot made an interchange easier, while the two-seater

LAYING THE FOUNDATIONS, 1919–1933

The guiding decision was that the ratio of bombers to fighters in the new force was to be two to one, thirty-five bomber squadrons and seventeen fighter squadrons. The proportion of night to day was laid down in 1925 as twenty day to fifteen night. These figures were, however, only rough guides. Some of the squadrons would be auxiliary or reserve cadre, and thus probably of less value than the regular ones. And in any case the new force would only gradually come into existence. It was intended at the outset that the fifty-two squadrons should be attained by 1928, but this aim was soon abandoned and it remained doubtful what the final composition of the force would be.

For the slow increase there were two main reasons. There was in the first place no immediate enemy in sight. The tension with France was soon replaced by the co-operation that resulted in the Treaties of Locarno, and Sir Austen Chamberlain's dictum that war with France was inconceivable was generally accepted. If Italy and Japan were developing their air forces to a greater degree than Britain, they were not within striking distance of her shores. Moreover, the provision for the armed services was based on the assumption, first laid down by the Cabinet in 1919, that no major war was to be expected for ten years. All sense of urgency was thus lost. No one was more vigorous in economy than Mr. Churchill, who was Chancellor of the Exchequer from 1924 to 1929, and in 1928 he reaffirmed the Ten Year Rule in an even more drastic form. So fortified, it endured for five years longer. True, it could be reconsidered at any time, but up to that time it meant that the essentials of a rapid expansion were absent. The aircraft firms had so few orders that they were largely establishments for design and development and there was no experience of planning large-scale production. What money was available had to be spread thinly amongst them just to keep them in existence. Their number was limited for the Air Staff did not think that more could be supported by the funds at their disposal. No doubt in the circumstances the creation of this circle of 'family firms', as they were termed, was a wise one, but it made too small a base when the period of rapid expansion came. The Air Force itself also lacked the necessary means of research and development to keep at the highest possible level the quality of its aircraft and other equipment.[1]

---

fighter could be used as a day bomber. 'In such an organisation, the A.O.C.-in-C. would have the flexibility which he requires . . . Under the present organisation we are inclined to strangle ourselves with specialist types.' Letter Salmond (A.O.C.-in-C., A.D.G.B.) to Air Min., 9th April 1932. In 1931 the May Committee, which otherwise could find no possible economies in the Air Estimates, suggested that money could be saved if the number of types was reduced, there then being according to the report forty-six types of aircraft and thirty-six types of engines.

[1] For the Ten Year Rule see App. 3. Mr. Churchill's account is in *The Second World War*, Vol. 1 (1948), p. 40. It is true of course that Germany could have been prevented

In 1929 the great world-wide depression began and Mr. Churchill's successors were even less anxious than he had been to spend money on armaments. But a further cause for the neglect of the Air Force throughout this period was the serious attempt made under the League of Nations to reduce and limit armaments by international agreement. A commission began in 1925 to draw up a convention for that purpose. In the discussions the British Government had consistently urged drastic limitation of air armaments and the abolition of bombing from the air, if agreement could be obtained on practical proposals for that object. In 1931 it was decided to summon the Conference, though agreement had by no means been reached as to what was practicable or desirable. But there could be no doubt that there was a strong current of opinion in favour of limitation and reduction of armaments, all the more so in Britain because Germany had been promised that the limitations imposed on her by the Treaty of Versailles would be followed by the acceptance of reduction and limitation by the victorious powers, though not, as German propaganda continually insisted, to the same level as that of Germany.

In the discussions at the Conference which met in February 1932, when it was found difficult to get agreement as to quantity of arms, the idea of 'qualitative' disarmament obtained much support. By this was meant the abolition of those weapons 'whose character is the most specifically offensive or those most efficacious against national defence, or most threatening to civilians.' And this idea was naturally especially applied to bombing aircraft, the offensive weapon *par excellence*. There can be no doubt but that this development would have been welcomed by the British Government and the British people if it could have been made effective. Such abolition was, indeed, more than once proposed by the British Government and a resolution to that effect was agreed to by the British delegation at Geneva, although it would have struck at the heart of the doctrine of the counter-offensive on which British air strategy was based. The Air Staff were, however, always of the opinion that its inherent difficulties would cause the plan to fail and that, even if it were accepted, it would not be maintained in the stress of modern war. They incurred a certain odium by a reservation of the use of bombers for police purposes against barbarous disturbers of the peace in outlying regions, but this was certainly in no way the cause of the failure

---

by force from rearming any time up to 1934. But, if that were not done, British difficulties in the period 1934–1939 were enhanced by the lack of preparation in the previous period. When Mr. Churchill took a Conservative deputation to urge more ample rearming on the Cabinet in 1936, the Prime Minister began his reply with a reference to the Ten Year Rule, which he implied had become more stringent in 1928. The position of the aircraft firms is described by M. M. Postan: *Aircraft Production: (Quantity)* (unpublished monograph).

of the negotiations and would have been abandoned if it had remained as the only obstacle after agreement had been reached on more fundamental points.

But the major obstacles were never overcome. One of these was the necessity, as it was supposed, to control or even internationalise civil aviation, if bombing aircraft were abolished, since civil aircraft could be used for bombing with, it was said, only small modifications. There were, indeed, proposals for the creation of an international air force, but this implied the creation of a world government to give it orders and no power was prepared to accept such a solution. Prohibition of bombing the civil population was useless if any bombing was to be allowed. The suggestion that bombing should be prohibited on the European continent was also obviously impracticable if France and Italy were to retain bombing squadrons in Africa. The only possible line of approach would have been limitation by numbers and possibly also by weight of aircraft on the lines by which naval limitation had already been put into force in the Washington and London Conferences. There were more formidable technical difficulties than in the case of surface ships; but these might have been overcome, if there had been such a sense of common danger as to make nations accept wholeheartedly a community of interest in one another's defence.[1]

But there was on the contrary a desire amongst the foremost advocates of drastic limitation to limit their own commitments to a minimum. The plan was finally made impossible by the German claim for equality and her withdrawal from the Conference when equality was refused, at any rate as an immediate concession. The Conference dragged on in 1933, but by the end of that year the situation in Germany had caused all plans for the reduction of armaments to become unreal, though many people refused to believe it.

But for some time there had been great hopes of success in the most responsible circles, and in Britain public opinion compelled the Government to do everything to show that it was in earnest in trying to secure an agreement, as indeed it was. In 1931 a proposal had been made at Geneva that there should be no increase of armaments while the Conference lasted. This was a reasonable proposal and was accepted by all, but it bore specially hard on the Royal Air Force, whose fifty-two squadron scheme had reached no more than twenty-six regular and eleven auxiliary and cadre squadrons at that date. Nor was the lack of quantity compensated by an advance in quality.

---

[1] The public declarations and proposals of the British Government are well summarised in R. A. Chaput: *Disarmament in British Foreign Policy*, (1935), Ch. V. The view of the Air Staff is given in a Cabinet paper of 9th May 1932 which names many of the points given above. Examples of the modification of civil aircraft for war purposes are the Heinkel 111, used extensively in the Battle of Britain, and the Focke-Wulf Condor which inflicted losses on our shipping during the Battle of the Atlantic.

In the early thirties the bulk of the Air Force was still made up of aircraft types dating from the war of 1914–1918. The standard of its equipment was falling below that of foreign countries such as Italy and the United States.[1] The aircraft were still for the most part biplanes made of wood and their speed and bombload such that some of the problems of the future were necessarily hidden. Nor in such a climate of opinion was the necessary amount of research and planning given to the creation of new types. The Air Ministry had devoted too little thought to such questions. When in 1934 they were faced with the problem of making an air force which could compete with that of Germany, even the preliminary steps had hardly been taken. Between 1931 and 1933 the services were preoccupied with the threat in the Far East from Japan and this attitude continued for more than a year after Hitler had come into power and the rearmament of Germany had made great progress. Moreover, a proposal had been made at Geneva by Britain that the maximum weight of an aeroplane should not be more than three tons. During this period, therefore, no design for a really heavy bomber could be seriously considered.

In these circumstances, it is not surprising that in spite of much devoted service from its higher officers as well as from the active personnel, including those in the auxiliary squadrons, little progress was made in solving the technical and intricate problems of strategic bombing. Such experience as the Air Force had in Iraq, Somaliland and the North-Western Frontier was no clue as to the tactics to be employed in Europe, and, because there was no opposition in the air, tended to produce misleading ideas as to the ease with which targets could be found and hit.[2]

The basic flying training was always of the highest standard. Based on the principles discovered in the First World War when the Gosport Training School had been an outstanding success, the Central Flying School never relaxed its standards. But there was always insufficient provision for more advanced training. The aircraft in the Training Schools were also often obsolescent and much basic training as well as the whole of the training on multiple-engined aircraft had to be done in the operational squadrons themselves. Exercises beyond squadron strength were rare. Navigation was neglected and no director of navigation existed in the air staff. Navigation was as yet, of course, in the hands of the pilot and it was because he had many other things to learn that navigation training was made as short as possible. The problems of long flights over un-

---

[1] M. M. Postan: *British War Production*, (1952), p. 5.

[2] 'We were informed by the Chief of the Air Staff that accuracy of aim has improved so much that on the North-West Frontier of India aircraft are able to bomb a house of a particular sheikh.' Report of a Cttee. on Coast Defence, 9th May 1932.

familiar territory were not realised. Much flying was done in the vicinity of aerodromes where landmarks were familiar. But little attention was paid to navigation by night, though a large, if indeterminate, portion of the bomber force was to be used at night. There was considerable experiment to test whether aircraft could hit battleships and cruisers, a question to which the sensational achievements and even more sensational advocacy of Brigadier General Mitchell in the United States had given great prominence. Much less attention was paid to the problem of how precise objectives on land were to be hit, whether by day or by night. It was thought that the day bombers could avoid crippling casualties by speed and evasion. But less thought was given to protecting them by armour, nor were their petrol tanks self-sealing. Their guns remained the same as those used in the First World War. Their stock of bombs largely consisted of those left over from 1918 and hardly anything was done to find out what effects they could produce or whether improvements could be made in their destructive power.[1] The provision of cameras was inadequate and their necessity not fully understood.[2]

One notable advance was, however, made in developing a meteorological service after the Air Ministry had taken over the Meteorological Office in 1920. It was recognised that the weather was a vital factor in determining strategy and tactics and the foundations of this indispensable service were well and truly laid. But the application of the knowledge thus acquired had yet to come.

This lack of progress was mainly due to the small size of the bombing force and the paucity of the resources for training, experiment and research. But it is also true that those in authority were less aware of the problems to be solved than might, perhaps, have been expected. They had, however, another great difficulty, the provision of the necessary space for exercise and experiment in a small country like Britain. Even though the force was still so small there were many obstacles in the way of obtaining suitable aerodromes and suitable areas where live bombing could be carried out under realistic conditions.

The aerodromes of the bombing force were planned with great care. It was at once realised that the fighter defence must be placed in an arc defending London from the south with its aerodromes situated far back from the coast so as to give as much time as possible for the fighters to get into the air when the enemy had been detected.[3]

---

[1] As late as July 1932 it was ruled by the D.C.A.S. that no bomb heavier than 500 lb. would be needed. Min. Burnett to Dowding (A.M.S.R.), 28th July 1932. Some heavier bombs were in existence, but these were intended mainly for the destruction of battleships.

[2] See below, pp. 121-123.

[3] Basil Collier: *History of the Second World War. The Defence of the United Kingdom*, (1957), pp. 15-16.

The anti-aircraft defence was similarly placed. After much discussion it was finally decided that the bombing squadrons should be located behind this screen, in spite of the inconvenience that might be caused by the necessity of passing through it in order to attack. If stationed before it on the coast, the aerodromes would be too vulnerable.

The final result was to set up an Air Defence of Great Britain under a Commander-in-Chief with a fighter force and three bomber area commands subordinate to him, though only one of these latter was fully in operation by 1933. The exact relation of the Commander-in-Chief to the Air Staff was still not entirely settled. The main lines of strategy were, of course, to be decided by the Air Staff under the political direction of the Cabinet. But the Air Staff exercised considerable control not only over the training but also the tactics of the Air Defence of Great Britain. This development was partly due to the long tenure of Sir Hugh Trenchard as Chief of the Air Staff, an office in which he had to exercise supervision over nearly every aspect of the Air Force. There was an Air Council on the lines of the Army Council with Air Marshals in charge of Personnel and of Research and Development. But the problems to be solved were so new, the technical advances so rapid, the difficulties of creating an entirely new service so formidable, that the authority and experience of the Chief of the Air Staff were constantly appealed to on questions which in the other two services would have been decided in other ways. The fact that Sir Hugh Trenchard remained ten years in that post showed how indispensable he seemed to be in the creation of the Royal Air Force.[1]

Nevertheless, whatever the setbacks imposed by excessive economy in the design and training of the bombing force, the Chief of the Air Staff had maintained intact the strategic objective for which it existed, the overthrow of the enemy by a bombing offensive without which neither the Navy nor the Army could achieve victory in a continental war. This was, indeed, the *raison d'être* of an independent Air Force and its main claim to a substantial proportion of the slender funds devoted to armaments.

Two examples will illustrate the doctrine which was consistently upheld during these years. In October 1925 a Committee of civil servants and representatives of the Admiralty, War Office and the Air Ministry made a report on Air Raid Precautions. They naturally turned to the Air Staff for an appreciation of the possible effects of an attack by France, then the only possible enemy. The Air Staff made a calculation of the number of bombs which the French Air Force

---

[1] Air Chief Marshal Trenchard, who became the first Marshal of the Royal Air Force in 1927, recognised that this was not a precedent to be followed and recommended that his successors should not have more than four or five years of office: Min. Trenchard to Hoare (S. of S. for Air), 13th Nov. 1928.

could deliver on London, and, basing their conclusions on the German attack in the war of 1914–1918, estimated the casualties as 1,700 killed and 3,300 wounded in the first twenty-four hours, 1,275 killed and 2,475 wounded in the second twenty-four hours and 850 killed and 1,650 wounded every subsequent twenty-four hours. 'It is well known', the Air Staff memorandum stated, 'that the moral effect of Air Attack is out of all proportion greater than the material results achieved. While, therefore, serious material damage may be expected from bomb attack, the most probable cause of chaos in the community will be the *moral* collapse of the personnel employed in the working of the vital public services, such as transport, lighting, water and food distribution.' Nor was there any defence possible even if the means of defence were much increased. 'Sir Hugh Trenchard', reported the Committee, 'was so emphatically of the opinion that an increase of the defence forces beyond a certain proportion would not secure greater immunity from attack, that we felt we had no alternative but to continue our investigations with a view to mitigating, so far as possible, the evils attendant upon aerial bombardment.' This view was criticised by the General Staff, who pointed out that only half the German aeroplanes dispatched in daylight reached London and that, once the air defences of London were made reasonably efficient, twenty-two per cent of the attacking planes were destroyed. They also thought the estimate of casualties by the Air Staff was an exaggeration and they deprecated alarming the public. The Air Staff in reply reiterated their warning, 'which, so far from exaggerating the menace, errs perhaps to a slight extent in understating the gravity of the situation.'[1] From this report came ultimately the measures of Air Raid Precautions, which were undoubtedly of great value, but it is one reason why the anti-aircraft defences were in such a weak state in 1938.

The view that offence is all-important and defence completely ineffective was consistently maintained throughout these years. Sir Hugh Trenchard restated his conception of the role of the Air Force during his last year of office in an uncompromising paper, which he submitted to the Chiefs of Staff Sub-Committee. It was not to attack the enemy's armed forces but to penetrate his air defences and 'attack direct the centres of production, transportation and communication from which the enemy war effort is maintained. . . .' In this way '[the stronger side] will throw the enemy on to the defensive and it will be in this manner that air superiority will be obtained, and not by direct destruction of air forces.' The objectives aimed at would be military objectives, if the adjective were properly construed. There would inevitably be civilian casualties incidental

---

[1] Report by Cttee. on Air Raid Precautions, 8th July 1925. General Staff Memo., 14th Oct. 1925. Air Staff Memo., 24th Oct. 1925.

to the operation. 'Moral effect is created by the bombing in such circumstances but it is the inevitable result of a lawful operation of war.' The result would be far greater than anything produced in the last war and might, as Marshal Foch himself had suggested, ' "impress the public opinion to a point of disarming the Government and thus becoming decisive." ' Thus, though the Chief of the Air Staff disclaimed, as always, the idea that the war could be won by air power alone, some of his arguments went far in that direction and they were based, as in the 1923 discussions, on the destruction not only of the means of resistance but of the will to resist of the civilian population.[1]

For both practical and moral reasons these arguments were not accepted by his two colleagues, who answered them in reasoned memoranda.[2] There was, they said, no evidence that the results anticipated by the Chief of the Air Staff would ensue and the unrestricted bombing, which he in effect advocated, was, in addition to the moral aspect, more likely to be dangerous to Britain than to any other country. Also, if the enemy defence forces could be ignored, what was the purpose of the Air Defence of Great Britain? No one could foresee, Sir George Milne asserted, how far defence against aeroplanes would develop in the years to come. 'Indeed,' he went on, 'it is difficult to see how in the end the issue will not be determined by the superiority of one air force over another just as fighting on the ground is determined by the superiority of one army over another.'

There the matter rested. But the doctrine of the Air Force still remained that the bomber would always get through and be able to inflict such destruction on the enemy as would, with the help of the other services, undermine his resistance; whether this result was to be obtained by the destruction of his sources of supply and communications or by the effect produced on the civilian population was still left in doubt in the language used to describe the strategic objectives of the bombing force.

---

[1] Memo. by Trenchard, 2nd May 1928, App. 2 (i).
[2] Memo. by Milne, 16th May 1928. Memo. by Madden (First Sea Lord), 21st May 1928. For both documents see App. 2 (ii) and (iii).

3. The reconstruction of the bombing force, 1934–1939

(a) NEW TYPES AND STRENGTHS

Because of the mounting danger from Hitler's Germany the lean years of 1923–1933 were followed by five years of rapid expansion. Yet even so Bomber Command entered the war with a force inadequate for its tasks and exercised little direct effect on the course of the struggle during its first two years. This result was primarily due to the impossibility of repairing its deficiencies in the time available except by such an effort as the British people were not prepared to undertake until the danger had become acute. No doubt they could have been induced to do much more if a clear call had come from the Government. But this was not forthcoming until war was close at hand and British policy meanwhile wavered between appeasement and panic preparation, a course which encouraged enemies and discouraged friends. France was in an even worse state, while Italy was added to Japan as a potential enemy, if war with Germany came.

Moreover, it was some time before the Air Ministry knew exactly what kind of a bombing force it desired to make. Thus, it was forced to adopt methods of expansion which were not best calculated to produce an efficient and balanced Air Force. Yet, if the immediate efficiency of the bombing force suffered, it was in this period that the defence of Britain was so reorganised that Hitler could not prevail against it in 1940 and the foundations were laid of the attacking force which ultimately contributed so much to his final overthrow.

The problem was made much more difficult by the rapid advance in the design and construction of aircraft which had just begun to take place. Metal monoplanes were displacing the wooden biplanes with which the Air Force was almost exclusively equipped at the beginning of 1934. New devices such as the automatic pilot, the retractable undercarriage, and the variable pitch propeller were coming into existence and aero engines were undergoing a rapid development. As was to be proved, the designers of the 'family firms' and the expert staff of the Air Ministry were as capable as any in the world of producing these new types of aircraft. But time was needed. It was necessary in the first place to have a clear conception of what type of bombing aircraft was to be produced and the use to which it would be put. The relative advantages of speed, range, armour, bombload and rapidity and ease of production had to be weighed. It was two years before these preliminary decisions could be made.

The discussions as to German 'equality' went on during 1934 and were followed in 1935 by a proposal for an Air Pact between the principal European powers, which was to contain some provision against bombing. The Italian conquest of Abyssinia and the failure of the boycott organised under the League of Nations to prevent it, put an end to this plan which never had much chance of success. Meanwhile, Germany was rearming and no one was prepared to prevent her by force. In 1934, therefore, the British Government re-examined the situation and as a result determined to rearm also, while still declaring its readiness to accept any fair and practicable scheme of general reduction and limitation, if one could be found. The Air Estimates of March 1934 added no more than a paltry two squadrons, but Mr. Baldwin then made a notable declaration in the House of Commons that 'in air strength and in air power this country shall no longer be in a position inferior to any country within striking distance of our shores'. On 28th November, when larger increases were planned, he repeated the promise specifically as regards Germany. These statements did no more than reaffirm the undertaking made in 1923 which all succeeding Governments had failed to implement. But this claim to 'parity', as it was called, exercised a great influence on the method of expansion. For a considerable time the Cabinet were preoccupied with the desire to show somehow or other that the promise would be fulfilled.[1]

The purpose of 'parity' was to create a deterrent to German aggression by a threat of immediate reprisals by a force equal to her own. But parity, a word inherited from the discussions with the United States on control of naval armaments, was extremely difficult to define. Clearly it depended on the character of the aircraft, built or building, as much as on their numbers. Light bombers with neither the range nor the bombload sufficient to allow much damage to be inflicted on Germany could not rank with heavier bombers of longer range. The exact character of the German air force was not yet fully known, but it seemed to be designed mainly for co-operation with the Army. No one knew exactly what role such a force could play in an attack on Britain. 'Parity' came to be defined first as the number of aircraft, then as the number of bombers, then as the number of long-range bombers and finally as the weight of bombs that could be dropped on Germany and Britain by the opposing air forces. Even then everything would depend not only on the first line of operational aircraft but on the reserves of aircraft and men behind

---

[1] Parliamentary Debates. Commons. Vol. 286, Col. 2078, 8th March 1934. Vol. 295, Cols. 882–883, 28th Nov. 1934. Mr. Churchill's first attacks contributed to this mood but he later always emphasised the superiority of the German war potential both publicly and in the memoranda which he sent for the consideration of the C.I.D. The Labour opposition which decried the notion of parity in 1934 were in 1938 taunting the Government for not having obtained it.

it. Neither the Germans nor the British declared their reserves. There was thus a temptation, to which all succumbed, to make the first line, present and planned, seem as strong as possible at the expense of the reserves. This went so far that it was at last admitted in Government discussions, though not, of course, publicly, that the official figures of 'first line' aircraft contained what was really a second line which would have to be 'rolled up', if war came before 1941, in order to replace the aircraft and crews which it was expected would be lost in the first weeks of the war.

In 1934 new Cabinet committees made a serious examination of the situation caused by German rearmament on top of the threat from Japan and soon came to the conclusion that Germany was potentially the greater danger, if not immediately so.[1] All the three services had been neglected and large sums of money would be needed to make them capable of defending Britain and the Empire and to carry out British obligations under the Locarno treaties. The Ministers were, however, more impressed by the danger from the air than by any other threat, and when the Chancellor of the Exchequer refused to find the necessary funds for all the services, they were ready to give priority to the Air Force in order to counter it. These discussions resulted in Scheme A of July 1934 which would in five years have increased the Metropolitan Air Force from fifty to eighty-four squadrons, but would not have provided it for another three years with the necessary reserves. Some of this increase was for the Fleet Air Arm, and the General Reconnaissance and Army Co-operation squadrons. Moreover, the increased need for defence was such that the Bomber Force was only to reach forty-one squadrons while the Fighter Force was to be expanded to twenty-eight squadrons.[2] This increase in the proportion of the force devoted to defence was not welcomed by the Air Ministry, but it had to be admitted that the German threat to the East and North of Britain necessitated the formation of new fighter squadrons.[3]

A still greater weakness was the fact that twenty-two of the forty-one squadrons were to be light bombers of no great use in an attack on Germany. The reason for this decision was partly financial, for light bombers cost less and so more squadrons could be formed.

---

[1] The Defence Requirements Sub-Committee of the C.I.D. was set up in 1933 and its report was referred to the Ministerial Committee on Disarmament. This latter committee was renamed 'Ministerial Committee on Defence Requirements' and reconstituted in July 1938 as a Sub-Committee of the C.I.D. on Defence Policy and Requirements.

[2] In the interim report of the Ministerial Committee of which Mr. Baldwin himself was Chairman it was stated that the Chancellor of the Exchequer did not make a firm commitment that the necessary extra money (£20 million spread over five years) would be forthcoming.

[3] Two of the squadrons were to be torpedo-bombers. See App. 7, where the details of the various schemes of these years are shown in a schedule.

But it was also due to the fact that no satisfactory medium or heavy bomber had yet been put into production. The Cabinet disliked this, but there was nothing else to be done if expansion was to proceed and a 'deterrent' to be created. This situation was the result of past history and could not be immediately remedied. The allowance for reserves was also far below what was considered necessary. They were only to be brought up to the proper figure between 1939 and 1942. There were, however, compensating advantages. The new bombers would enable more pilots to be trained operationally for the better machines which might one day be available, and smaller reserves meant that less obsolescent aircraft would be ordered. Meanwhile, the best crews were to be allotted to the medium and heavy bombers and bases for the light bombers were to be sought for on the Continent.

The Air Ministry, however, did not for some time appreciate the situation in Germany and underrated the rapidity with which a totalitarian state could bring an effective air force into being, if it had such a potential capacity as Germany possessed. Nevertheless, great efforts were now made to design and produce a modern bomber force. New committees were set up in the Air Ministry to lay down the specifications of new bombers which would be able to attack Germany from bases in England, and the organisation of the Air Ministry was overhauled for this purpose. The Operational Requirements branch which in 1934 was only a small section under the Director of Operations and Intelligence was gradually transformed until in 1938 it was put in the charge of a new Assistant Chief of the Air Staff and in 1939 its head was made a full Director. Changes were also made in the machinery controlling production and Sir Wilfrid Freeman, who had been made Air Member for Research and Development on 1st April 1936, was appointed Air Member for Development and Production on 1st August 1938. He, more than any other man, was responsible for the decisions to build such aircraft as eventually enabled Bomber Command to become an effective arm of war.[1]

But all this took time, and, perhaps, a longer time because the Air Ministry had failed to realise quickly enough the formidable nature of the challenge which they had to meet. In November 1934 Mr. Baldwin had spoken to the House in such terms as seemed to make it certain that Britain would easily be able to maintain a first-line strength superior to that of Germany for at least two years. He spoke

---

[1] M. M. Postan: *British War Production*, pp. 20–21. Unpublished monograph, *Aircraft Production Quality*, pp. 61–68. In 1938 Mr. Ernest Lemon was made by Sir Wilfrid Freeman Director General of Production and the importance of the position was marked by making him a member of the Air Council. He took general charge of the programme, created some six directorates and reorganised the whole department which was able to hive off as the Ministry of Aircraft Production in May 1940.

thus on the advice of the Air Staff who, however, had wisely qualified their estimate with the provision that there should be no increase in the German rate of production. Mr. Baldwin accordingly inserted in his statement the words 'if she [Germany] continues to execute her air programme without acceleration'. These words, however, seem to have made as little impression on the speaker himself as they did on the House at the time.[1]

Yet such a qualification was an obvious one for no one could be sure as to the extent of the German preparations. In June 1934 the Air Staff believed that she aimed at producing 480 first-line aircraft by the autumn of 1935 and then to have two further stages of expansion each of 480 aircraft so that by 1942 she would possess 1,440 first-line machines of which, perhaps, 1,230 would be bombers. It was, however, always recognised that such figures did not take into account the full potential capacity of Germany of which she had given such proof in the First World War. Thus, for example, in discussing in the Chiefs of Staff Committee the German danger in June 1934 the Chief of the Air Staff, Sir Edward Ellington, told his colleagues that Germany could in six months' time maintain a force of 800 aircraft with the necessary reserves, and he concluded that she 'could, if she wished, build up rapidly in peace time to a force of 2,000 aircraft, and that the preparations which she is now beginning to make may within, say, five years enable her to *maintain such a force at practically its full strength in war*'.[2] But this paper, which his colleagues thought unduly alarmist, was not sent on to Ministers, nor did the Air Staff use such arguments in asking for approval of their own scheme. They did not believe that Germany could build up rapidly a force at all equal in efficiency to that of Britain. This was the tone of the discussion with Ministers and the qualification had been inserted as a safeguard against too exact a statement rather than as a serious warning of a likely contingency.

But in March 1935 Hitler told Sir John Simon and Mr. Eden, who had gone to Berlin to discuss the possibility of a limitation of air armaments, that Germany already possessed first-line parity with Britain's metropolitan force and intended soon to have a first line equal to that of the French metropolitan and African air force, a number variously estimated at between 1,500 and 2,000 aircraft. This statement was inaccurate as regards the immediate present, though true enough as to the future. It created something like a panic in the Cabinet. It was reinforced by reports from Berlin that Germany's first-line air force was already at least thirty per cent stronger than that stationed in Britain. The Air Ministry, however, still maintained

---

[1] Parliamentary Debates. Commons. Vol. 295, Col. 882.
[2] Memo. by Ellington, 12th June 1934.

that whatever the number of aircraft which Germany possessed she was still far behind Britain in organisation and training. 'We are at present,' wrote Lord Londonderry, the Secretary of State for Air, 'and for the next three years, at least, far ahead of the German Air Force in efficiency. The position as to reserves, however, is less satisfactory and there is reason to believe that the organisation of the aircraft industry for war purposes in Germany is already in advance of that in this country.' He urged, therefore, that the position should be re-examined with a view to increasing our air armament. The Air Staff were still reluctant to expand the force prematurely to meet this new threat and proposed a gradual increase which would produce something like 1,500 first-line aircraft by 1940. But the Government, though at first they denied in Parliament that Germany had reached parity with Britain, were very conscious of the weakness of their position and, on 22nd May 1935, Mr. Baldwin made his notable confession in the House of Commons that his Government had been completely mistaken as to the rate of German rearmament in the air. Meanwhile, the Cabinet had appointed an Air Parity Committee to go into the situation of which Sir Philip Cunliffe-Lister was Chairman, and, on 7th June 1935, he became Secretary of State for Air in place of the Marquess of Londonderry, who had been the mouthpiece of the Air Ministry's scepticism. The Air Ministry was thus represented in the House of Commons by its Secretary of State, but not for long, for in November 1935 Sir Philip Cunliffe-Lister entered the House of Lords as Lord Swinton. Lord Weir, who had had great experience in the First World War, was also at this time brought in to assist the Air Ministry with the problems of construction.[1]

As a result of these discussions two new schemes were made in 1935 which increased the number of bombing squadrons and reduced the period during which the increase was to be made. The first of these (Scheme C) proposed sixty-eight bomber squadrons of 816 aircraft to be produced by 1937, the second (Scheme F), by increasing the initial establishment, was to produce 990 bombing aircraft for the same number of squadrons by 1939. But Scheme F also made

---

[1] Letter Simon to MacDonald, 19th April 1935, memo. by Londonderry, 15th April 1935. Defence Requirements Cttee. Mtg., 30th April 1935. Parliamentary Debates. Commons. Vol. 302, Col. 367, 22nd May 1935. The Air Staff's attitude is defended in Denis Richards: *Royal Air Force 1939–1945*, Vol. I, (1953), pp. 11–14, where it is proved that Hitler lied or was confused. It has been subsequently stated that the German General Staff prepared a false statement for this purpose (Ernst Heinkel: *He 1000* (1956), p. 213, where, however, the year is wrongly given as 1936). But when on 29th April 1935 Mr. Winston Churchill sent a memorandum to the Government which endeavoured to show that Germany already had superiority both in number and quality of aircraft the comment of Wing Commander C. E. H. Medhurst of the Directorate of Operations and Intelligence, was 'My general comment is that Mr. Churchill's statements are substantially correct, looked at from a broad aspect, but incorrect in relatively unimportant detail.' Memo. by Churchill, 29th April 1935. Min. Medhurst to Ellington, 3rd May 1935.

RECONSTRUCTION OF THE FORCE, 1934–1939

provision for adequate reserves and, in addition, for heavier bombers. With the addition of the fighters and other first-line aircraft the total home force planned for Scheme C would be 1,512 in 1937 and for Scheme F 1,736 in 1939. Smaller additions were made to the fighter squadrons. Neither of these schemes really provided for parity with the German forces likely to be in existence at the time they could be completed, but they could be announced as such and, therefore, as able to produce a suitable deterrent.[1]

One feature of Scheme F was the substitution of as many new medium bombers as possible for light bombers, orders being given for the Blenheims which had not then been fully tested. The other types available were inferior in range and bombload to those of the German air force. Thus, by now the Heyford, the Hart, and the Hind, and even the Wellesley and Harrow bombers were all out of date. The new types first planned in 1932, the Whitley, the Hampden and the Wellington, were not yet ready for mass production. This was, indeed, one reason why the Air Ministry had deprecated a too-rapid expansion of the force.

Scheme C had been approved by the Cabinet on 21st May 1935 and Scheme F on 25th February 1936.[2] The latter remained for nearly two years as the blueprint of expansion, while, at Lord Swinton's insistence, efforts were made to increase the potential supply of aircraft by at last going outside the circle of 'family firms' and inducing others, and especially the motor firms, to set up 'shadow factories' which could come into production if war broke out. This plan had the added advantage that it might avoid the necessity of providing large reserves of obsolescent aircraft though Scheme F still retained, on paper at least, the objective of 225 per cent reserves (seventy-five per cent immediate in the squadrons and 150 per cent war reserve) which had been laid down as necessary to sustain an offensive if war came.

Fortunately the new fighters, the eight-gun Hurricane and Spitfire, were equal, if not superior, to anything that Germany possessed. At the same time the prospect of faster and better-armed fighters made it necessary to reconsider the armament of the bombers. This meant greater weight, particularly as, if an adequate field of fire was to be obtained, the guns must be put in turrets, and an extra gunner would have to be carried. Moreover, the necessity of building aircraft with a longer range had been underlined in the Abyssinian

---

[1] Memo. by Swinton, 10th Feb. 1936. For the details of the aircraft proposed see Vol. IV, Sect. II, App. 7. There was no agreement as to what the German air force front-line strength would be in 1939, but it was hardly likely to be as low as 1,736 if it were 1,512 in 1937. Nor could the strength of the German reserves be adequately gauged.

[2] Cabinet Mtgs., 21st May 1935, 25th Feb. 1936. Schemes D and E had been made but never presented as the necessity for larger reserves and heavier bombers became apparent.

crisis when the British bases in Egypt had to be placed dangerously near the frontier if attack were to be possible on the Italian bases in Libya. All this seemed to show that there was no future for the light bomber and that even a medium bomber would hardly be large enough to contain all the necessary equipment, the crew and a paying bombload.[1]

Thus, in 1936 the Air Ministry began to think more and more in terms of heavy bombers and bombers that became heavier as the necessary qualities of range, bombload, armament and crew became apparent. The new types of heavy bombers, the Wellington, the Whitley and the Hampden were now nearing production stage but the Air Ministry were still not satisfied. Two new types, one a twin-engine and one a four-engine bomber, were now evolved, and by the end of 1936 their specifications had been drawn up. These were the prototypes of the heavy bombers which were the real striking force of Britain after 1942. There was, it is true, a quite different type of aeroplane produced as early as 1934 by the De Havilland firm. This was the Comet, which had been built to compete in the Melbourne air race. It was made of wood and was so fast that it was claimed that no fighter would be able to catch it if it was adapted to the role of a light bomber. From this aircraft came in 1940 the Mosquito, the most versatile and efficient of the whole war, which was to play a role as fighter, bomber and reconnaissance aircraft of immense importance. But at this moment, and for many years to come, its full possibilities were not foreseen by the Air Ministry.

Meanwhile, further information was obtained of the expansion of the German aircraft industry and it became clear that Scheme F was not sufficient to attain 'parity' with the probable German first line of 1939. The political situation was also growing continually worse. The occupation of the Rhineland, the undisguised interference of Germany and Italy in the Spanish Civil War, the establishment of the 'Axis' bond between them, the growing truculence of Japan, now associated with them in the Anti-Comintern Pact, showed to most the urgency of the situation. Yet even with the immediate use of the new 'shadow' factories the number of aircraft proposed in F was not likely to be reached. The inevitable teething troubles held up new types. There was a shortage of skilled workers. Indeed, it also now became apparent that there would not be a sufficient number of pilots, observers and gunners to man the new aircraft if they could be produced.

---

[1] A Memorandum of the Deputy Director of Plans, Group Captain A. T. Harris, had already on 16th January 1935 stated that the light bomber was outmoded and advocated a policy of seeking maximum range and bomb capacity so that even the medium bomber would disappear. 'The term [fighter bomber]', he wrote, 'came into use solely to pacify the demand for a fighter in certain stations overseas, when we ourselves did not wish to provide fighters but preferred bombers.'

Thus, in new Schemes G and H made to supplement Scheme F the Air Ministry began to reduce the reserves so as to give Bomber Command, established in 1936, a show of front-line parity with Germany. By this means and by increasing the number of aircraft per squadron they were able to suggest the possibility of constructing a force of nearly 2,500 front-line aircraft 'at the earliest practicable date' after April 1939, of which 1,659 would be bombers, while fighters were only slightly increased to 476. They were all the more ready to do this since the reserves planned for Scheme F would consist of aircraft which according to their new train of thought would rapidly become obsolescent. The fewer of these in reserve, the sooner they could be replaced by the new types already under construction. It was, however, still necessary to place orders for such aircraft as the Battle, which it was now recognised were not really capable of being usefully employed in a war against Germany. In these aircraft, indeed, many good crews were to be sent into an unequal fight in 1939–40. However, the Cabinet did not approve the suggested scheme partly owing to assurances from General Milch that the increase in the German air force would not be as great as had been anticipated. They agreed, however, that further expansion might become necessary and authorised the provision of new aerodromes and an increase of skilled men.[1]

In October 1937 General Milch visited Britain as part of the policy of appeasement, which the majority of the Cabinet still thought was the best way of dealing with the difficult situation into which Britain had now fallen. He gave assurances as to the limits of German expansion. But events had already justified the Air Ministry's distrust of such assurances and in December it was learnt, on his own confession, that Milch had lied or erred and that Germany's number of 'front-line' aircraft would be greater than had been imagined.[2] It was not, however, any German assurances that caused the rejection of the new Scheme J which was submitted to the Cabinet in October 1937.

For meanwhile both the economic situation and the strategic situation needed re-examination. The Chancellor of the Exchequer was perturbed at the mounting cost of rearmament and wished to know where it was leading. The worsening of the political situation had

---

[1] It was recognised that Germany would have a larger first-line strength, but this scheme would give Britain 'parity' in bombers and a fighter force of a strength required to meet the probable scale of attack. Such aircraft as were contained in the German Army Co-operation Force or the British Fleet Arm need not enter into the comparison. Memo. by Swinton, 14th Jan. 1937. The Cabinet made its decision on 24th February 1937. Cabinet Mtg.

[2] Report by Vachell (Air Attaché, Berlin), 3rd Dec. 1937. The increase was in the initial establishment of the squadrons, which would have soon become evident in any case.

caused Belgium to seek refuge in a new neutrality and this fact underlined the strategic importance of the Low Countries in the conflict. If Germany occupied them her air force would be in a position to make a far heavier attack on Britain. If France and Britain could defend them they might have a similar advantage against Germany. Yet military plans had hardly yet envisaged the construction of an expeditionary force to assist France in their defence. Meanwhile the Navy was clearly not strong enough to cope with threats from Germany, Italy and Japan simultaneously. It was not only a question of expanding the Air Force, but of reconsidering the whole question of defence and the relative shares of the three services in it. Sir Thomas Inskip had been appointed Minister for the Co-ordination of Defence, a newly created post, specifically to assist the Cabinet to make decisions on this kind of vital question and a new Cabinet sub-committee, Defence Plans (Policy), had been set up in April 1937 to review the whole situation.

Accordingly, at the beginning of July 1937 the services were called upon to make a comprehensive review of their needs in order to ascertain not only the cost of their programmes, but what the cost would be in the future when the existing programmes were completed.[1] Meanwhile, the Army and the Navy had been putting forward through a Sub-Committee of the Committee of Imperial Defence proposals for greatly increased estimates and they included these in the overall review. The Air Ministry only found out in October that the other two services were thus using this opportunity to make new and much larger claims on the funds to be allotted for defence. Until then they had confined themselves mainly to a review of the situation as it had been left by Schemes F and H. They now realised that it was necessary to make a detailed plan for future development before allotments were made to the other services which might make any further air force expansion impossible.[2] Thus, in some haste, they proceeded to draw up a new and detailed Scheme J. From the discussions on this scheme came two great decisions which affected profoundly the whole future of the Air Force.

In the first place the Air Ministry finally decided that it must seek to have the bomber force rearmed as soon as possible with the new heavy bombers. For they still remained faithful to the main strategic principle that only an offensive force capable of throwing on Germany a greater weight of bombs than Germany could throw on Britain would enable the war to be won. It was true that new radar aids to air defence were coming into existence. These the scientists

---

[1] Cabinet Mtg., 30th June 1937.

[2] Extract of Mins. Newall to Swinton, 4th Oct. 1937, and Swinton to Newall, 6th Oct. 1937.

under the lead of Sir Henry Tizard, Mr. R. A. Watson Watt, Mr. H. E. Wimperis and Mr. A. P. Rowe, in the closest co-operation with Fighter Command, were to develop with surprising rapidity into an instrument which transformed the possibilities of defence against bombers.[1] But this fact by no means, in the view of the Air Staff, altered the basic principle that only an offensive of superior weight could secure the victory. To be driven back to relying on defence, they thought, would be to lose the war.

It seemed now to be established that the most economical method of dropping the heaviest bombload on Germany was to construct a force composed almost entirely of the new heavy bombers—if, indeed, an even larger and heavier one were not designed. Germany had no such aircraft, but the United States' development of the Boeing had some effect on the thinking of the Air Ministry. The decision was not an easy one. There were many difficulties to be overcome. Such a force would be difficult to accommodate on the aerodromes and hangars already existing or planned. It was thought that the former would be unable to bear the weight of the new machines. At one time it was considered that the use of catapults might be necessary to get the heavy load off the ground. In any case the take-off and landing of such heavy aircraft seemed to raise formidable problems. The question of how many engines would be necessary was also difficult to decide. Four would not only mean expansion of engine production but a larger maintenance force. Sir Wilfrid Freeman himself was for a time in favour of retaining smaller two-engined aircraft. But fortunately specifications were drawn up in 1936 for both a four-engined heavy bomber and a two-engined 'heavy medium' bomber, which gradually developed into a heavy bomber also. From these came the four-engined Stirlings, the Halifaxes and Lancasters and the twin-engined Manchesters.

The new scheme, therefore, though it contained a comprehensive review of all the requirements of the Air Force, still laid the main emphasis on the bombers. Considerable increase was suggested for overseas forces and fighters were given a modest increase of fifty-six aircraft. But Bomber Command was to be increased to ninety squadrons (1,442 aircraft). Full reserves of 225 per cent were to be made for both bombers and fighters.

But most important of all, Bomber Command's aircraft were to become progressively larger so that at first the Whitleys, Hampdens and Wellingtons would become a major part of the force, while gradually they would be replaced by the new types until by 1943 the whole force would be so rearmed. This decision which had been under discussion for the last two years was now definitely made as

---

[1] Basil Collier: *The Defence of the United Kingdom*, pp. 36–40.

the only real answer to the great increases which the Air Ministry now expected to be made in the German air force and it was firmly held to in spite of great pressure to alter it both from Ministers and later from the aircraft industry itself. There would, of course, be a great increase in expense over Scheme F in construction and maintenance,[1] and it was doubtful also whether the manufacturing capacity of Britain could produce the aircraft or the necessary personnel could be found to man them. But these difficulties could be overcome, at any rate in part, if the necessary priorities were given to the Air Force which, so it was claimed, alone could provide the necessary deterrent against war or the means by which victory could be won, if war came.[2]

But the attitude of Sir Thomas Inskip to this proposal brought about another decision of the greatest importance. For Sir Thomas Inskip refused to put forward this programme and demanded that the sum allotted in Scheme F should not be increased by more than £110 million. Part of the saving was to be obtained by making no increase in the overseas force, the rest by drastic reduction in the proposed strength of Bomber Command. In communicating this view to the Secretary of State for Air he challenged the strategic doctrine on which the Air Force had based its estimates. German bombers, he claimed, could be better destroyed over Britain by a fighter force than by bombing her aerodromes and factories. If her attack could be repelled, or at least considerably reduced, time would be gained for Britain to use her traditional methods of war. 'The point I want to put to you, therefore,' he wrote, 'is as to whether you can devise a revised programme based on the conception that at the outset of a war our first task is to repulse a knock-out blow within the first few weeks, trusting thereafter to defeat the enemy by a process of exhaustion, resulting from our command at sea, in the later stages.' He suggested, therefore, that it would be better to develop the medium and light bombers (which might be operated from continental bases) than to concentrate on constructing a heavy bomber force, that a large cut should be made in the bomber reserves, with some compensating increase in the provision of factory space and machine tools, and that all idea of parity should be abandoned. It was in any case, he wrote, impossible to achieve it not merely in first-line aircraft but also in reserves and war potential. Britain, he insisted, did not need the same kind of air force as Germany. The fighter force should, therefore, be made as strong as possible and given full reserves, while the bombers, though capable of retaliation and, therefore, a deterrent, should be reduced in numbers and, perhaps,

---

[1] It was estimated that in 1937–1942 Scheme J would cost £650,000,000 as against the £467,500,000 envisaged under Scheme F.

[2] Air Staff Memo., 8th and 12th Oct. 1937. Memo. by Swinton, 27th Oct. 1937.

also in size. He even added that some medium bombers could be transformed into fighters, in order to throw the balance at once in that direction.[1]

The Air Staff reacted violently to this appreciation. It challenged the doctrine on which all their policy was based. To lay the emphasis on defence and even to transform bombers into fighters would be to accept defeat at the outset. The victory could only be won by attack, and, whether the war was short or long, the Air Force would have to play a main role in such attack. They could not deny that Sir Thomas Inskip could not dispose of sufficient resources to carry out their scheme under the conditions then obtaining. But the Cabinet must be told that his scheme definitely accepted a position of air inferiority to Germany. On one point, however, they insisted. It was necessary to plan a heavy bomber force in the manner that they had suggested even if it took longer to build and man.[2]

Despite a strong protest from the Foreign Office, the Cabinet on 22nd December 1937 accepted Sir Thomas Inskip's point of view. The increase was reduced to £100 million and it was left to the Air Ministry and Sir Thomas Inskip to decide how it was to be spent. The Cabinet were also anxious to replace bombers by fighters because fighters were cheaper and easier to construct.[3] The Air Ministry, therefore, in the new Scheme K, which they made with Sir Thomas Inskip's help, retained the fighter numbers with full reserves. They also retained as an objective nearly the same first-line strength in bombers but cut down drastically the number of squadrons and made a big cut in the reserves. The replacement by heavy bombers was also to proceed at a slower pace. Nevertheless, the plan for rearming of the force at some time in the future with the new heavy bombers was retained.

The Cabinet were, however, not yet ready to provide as much money as Scheme K necessitated, and when the scheme was further examined the Air Staff were dismayed at the result. Elaborate calculations had recently been made as to the probable rate of wastage of bombers and fighters in the event of an all-out war with Germany, if, as was considered quite likely, the *Luftwaffe* decided to begin the war by an attempt to knock out Britain. On the basis of these estimates, the Chief of the Air Staff told his colleagues, they would be left with only nine weeks' reserves, a small training establishment and a war potential which, though considerable, would not be in full production for many months after the outbreak of the war. 'It appeared

---

[1] Memo. by Inskip, 9th Dec. 1937, App. 5.
[2] Air Staff Note on Aide Memoire by Inskip, 11th Dec. 1937.
[3] Two arguments carried great weight: (1) the necessity of financial and economic stability as an essential element of defence, (2) reserves involved waste if no war ensued while war potential was an asset to the country.

probable,' he said, 'that there would be a period when the Air Force would come to a standstill owing to lack of reserves and the potential would consequently be useless (since the war would have been lost) if it were not destroyed.'[1] It was agreed, therefore, that it would be wise to reduce the provision for war potential and provide more reserves of heavy bombers. In order to do this with the funds available further economies were also suggested in training establishments and permanent buildings.[2]

That such expedients should have been necessary only twenty-two months before war broke out shows how far the Government yet was from the realisation of what was necessary to be done to preserve the safety of the country. Parliament and public were, it is true, now thoroughly alarmed. There was an increasing stream of criticism on the failure of the Government to achieve parity with Germany. Attacks had long been made on the policy of reserving production for the 'family' firms and at this time new efforts were made to increase those engaged in production. Some of the 'shadow' factories were already at work and components and parts were farmed out to smaller firms. If the men could not be brought to the job, the jobs must be taken to the men. At long last also a system of double shifts was authorised in some factories. In May 1938, partly as a result of the criticisms, Lord Swinton gave up his post of Secretary of State for Air which was taken by a member of the Lower House, Sir Kingsley Wood. Lord Weir also resigned. Though conscription was still delayed, the resources of the country were now being more fully employed, perhaps as rapidly as could be done in peace-time conditions. It is also true that the *Luftwaffe* was incapable of dealing Britain from German bases any such knock-out blow as the Air Staff feared.[3] The German Government had, indeed, no plans for any such an action, however much it might boast and intimidate. It is to be noted also that the Air Staff, though not the Commander-in-Chief, Fighter Command, placed less confidence than the civilian Ministers on the capacity of the fighter to stop the German attack, if it came. The emphasis on defence was imposed on the Air Staff from outside. Nevertheless, an examination of the tactical position in March 1938 led to the conclusion that the prospects of defence had improved.[4]

The Cabinet's decision meant, indeed, two things. First, that the

---

[1] Notes of C.A.S. Mtg., 18th Jan. 1938.
[2] Note by Air Min., 21st Jan. 1938.
[3] The view of the Air Staff was summed up by the C.A.S. as follows: 'No one can say with absolute certainty that a nation can be knocked out from the air, because no one has yet attempted it. There can be no doubt, however, that Germany and Italy believe it possible as there can be no other explanation for their piling up armaments to a level which they could not hope to maintain in a long war. When, as I firmly believe, the issue is that of the survival of British civilisation we cannot afford to take so great a chance for the sake of £60 or £100 millions.' Min. Newall to Swinton, 8th April 1938.
[4] See below, Section 4, pp. 101–103.

attempt to obtain 'parity' with Germany whether in numbers or striking power had been postponed to an indefinite future, and, secondly, that priority must now be given to defence. But it did not mean that the Air Staff had abandoned their strategic doctrine, though for the time being it had to be subordinated to the necessity of home defence. Moreover, most important of all from their point of view, they had retained the objective of an all-heavy-bomber force, which might one day make it possible to put their theories into practice.

The situation was in any case a fluid one. Before the last proposals could be passed through the Cabinet the rape of Austria occurred and the Cabinet were ready, in spite of the protest of the Chancellor of the Exchequer, to allow the Air Force to be further expanded and to order aircraft up to the capacity of the available production of the next two years which it was thought would be 12,000 aircraft. The Cabinet now cancelled their decision that the course of normal trade should not be impeded by defence requirements.[1] But as far as bombers were concerned all that could be hoped for in the new Scheme L was to accelerate the programme by a year. It was, however, possible to make better progress with fighters and their planned first-line numbers were increased to 608, while it was definitely laid down that priority was to be given to fighter production.[2] By this time also the Air Staff had begun to realise that a counter-offensive by Bomber Command could at present do little to check the German attack on Britain and that that task must be almost entirely left to Fighter Command and the ground defences.

This was the situation when the Munich crisis of September 1938 showed how unprepared for a contest Bomber Command now was, not only in numbers but in capacity, organisation and maintenance. Forty-two squadrons were mobilised, but only ten of these were Whitley and Harrow squadrons, at that time ranked as heavy bombers. The rest were medium or light bombers. There was hardly ten per cent reserve of aircraft, and of the planned 2,500 reserve pilots only 200 were ready for immediate operations. Many of the aircraft available lacked essential equipment, such as turrets. The only way to obtain a sufficiency of spare parts was to break up squadrons. Many of the squadrons had only had their new aircraft for a short period. It was calculated that, if peace-time standards were applied, not fifty per cent of the force was fit to fight. The administrative machinery was also shown to be inadequate. In the circumstances, it was natural that the Commander-in-Chief, Sir Edgar Ludlow-Hewitt, welcomed the suggestion that bombing

---

[1] Cabinet Mtg., 22nd March 1938.
[2] For the details of Scheme L, see App. 7.

should be confined to strictly military objectives in the hope that Germany would follow the same course.[1]

The dread that Germany would endeavour to strike a knock-out blow was, however, widespread among the Government and the public and the gross exaggeration of the threat was one of the factors in the decision to allow Czechoslovakia to fall under the control of Hitler. It was British weakness in the air, insufficient in defence and lacking the ability to make a counter-offensive, which had the greatest effect on contemporary thinking.[2] All the same, there was, as has been seen, no German plan to deliver the feared knock-out blow, and the experience of the war shows that they were quite incapable of performing any such operation at that time.

The revelation to the Government of British weakness during the Munich crisis spurred them to new efforts. More money was available for the Air Force as well as for the Army and Navy. The Air Staff had to review all their arrangements. They were now allowed to order as many aircraft as could be produced, but the rearming of Bomber Command could not be quickly accomplished. An expanding Army and Navy meant that greater provision was necessary for the Army Co-operation Squadrons and the Fleet Air Arm. Moreover, though only a handful of the new fighters had been ready in September, they could be built more easily and more quickly than the new bombers. And they needed only a pilot, while the bombers needed a crew. The new Scheme M therefore not only increased Fighter Command by twelve squadrons to 800 aircraft, but also its reserves, and gave it a first claim on the pilots available as well as on production. It would, however, take more than eighteen months to rearm it with Spitfires and Hurricanes, and meanwhile the immediate shortage was to be met by converting some Blenheim squadrons into fighters while seven others designed for Army co-operation were to be made ready to be converted if required.

This was a step which less than a year ago the Air Staff had characterised as the acceptance of defeat. It caused some misgiving and it was thought necessary to circulate a memorandum explaining that the counter-offensive had not been replaced by a defensive strategy.[3] It was realised, however, that in any event the first line of Bomber Command must be drastically reduced. The Chief of the Air Staff had already issued an order that only such squadrons were to be mobilised as could be provided with six weeks' reserve of aircraft and personnel, and this policy was openly avowed in the new scheme. A

---

[1] 'The position a month ago had been positively tragic. We had then had no real reserve, whether fighters or bombers,' Sir Kingsley Wood told the Committee on Defence Programmes and Acceleration, 28th Oct. 1938.

[2] See, for example, Mr. Churchill's statement quoted below, pp. 184–185.

[3] Air Council letter and Note, 26th Nov. 1938. See pp. 102–103.

RECONSTRUCTION OF THE FORCE, 1934–1939

large number of the new aircraft were to be trainers. But the policy of gradual rearmament by heavy bombers was to persist. Some qualifications were made as a result of the fears of the Chancellor of the Exchequer, but in the main the proposals of the Air Ministry were approved. The advocates of appeasement did, indeed, protest that this policy involved a threat to Germany and that Ministers should at any rate talk about fighters in public instead of bombers. But the Cabinet decided in favour of the heavy-bomber policy so that there might eventually come into being a striking force equal or even superior to that of Germany. In order to keep the factories in full employment until they could be retooled for the latest types, orders for the earlier ones would still have to be given. But by 1942 it was hoped that Bomber Command would be eighty squadrons strong and composed almost entirely of the new bombers. Nor was the Air Ministry discouraged from trying to find even bigger bombers in the future.[1]

But all these plans needed time and time was not to be given, as indeed after March 1939 even the Prime Minister at last realised. Still twenty-four of the fifty-five squadrons were equipped with newer aircraft before war broke out in September 1939. Bomber Command had then only thirty-three operational squadrons, but sixteen were light or medium (ten Battle and six Blenheim) and seventeen heavy (six each of Wellingtons and Hampdens and five of Whitleys).[2] But even so more than half the force could not attack Germany at all except from bases on the Continent, while of the others only the Wellington had possibilities of much improvement, the Whitley being too slow and the Hampden unsuitable in many ways. Since it was estimated that the Germans possessed 1,500 long-range bombers, it was clear that the policy that would best suit Bomber Command was to delay all-out bombing as long as possible until the new and more effective bombers appeared and crews could be trained to operate them.

(b) ORGANISATION AND INFRASTRUCTURE

During the period of expansion a great change was made in the organisation of the Air Force which had considerable effect on strategy and tactics. In 1923 the Metropolitan Air Force consisting

---

[1] Memo. by Wood, 25th Oct. 1938. Cabinet Mtg., 7th Nov. 1938. The proposals were first discussed at a number of meetings of the Defence Programmes and Acceleration Committee of the Cabinet and a report was made by them on 3rd November 1938. The objections of the Chancellor of the Exchequer were left to be settled by subsequent discussion. This resulted in a number of reservations about the re-examination of expenditure in future years. The opposition to the construction of heavy bombers also suggested that the attack plan might provoke Germany to construct a 'super-Halifax' in reply, while the view was put forward in favour of smaller types not only because they would cost less but 'that it would be more difficult to grass the whole covey of small birds than to bring down one large bird.'

[2] See the Order of Battle, 1939, App. 38.

of both fighters and bombers had been placed under one Commander-in-Chief of the Air Defence of Great Britain, who was responsible directly to the Air Council. As only one fighter group was planned, while there were to be three bombing areas, it was intended that he should devote most of his attention to the offensive rather than to home defence, and, since there was no immediate enemy in sight, this attitude could be easily adopted.

But the appearance of Germany as a potential enemy and the proposed rapid expansion of the Air Force transformed this situation. The fighter screen, hitherto giving protection only against an enemy from the South, had now to guard from the East and from the North as well. It had to be reorganised into three groups. At the same time the increase of bombers meant that at least six groups would be necessary. This would be too much for one headquarters to control without the interposition of some intermediate commands. Two methods were possible. Commanders subordinate to the Air Officer Commanding-in-Chief, Air Defence of Great Britain, could be appointed over the bombers and fighters, leaving to the supreme commander the direction and co-ordination of the whole, or separate commands could be set up for bombers and fighters, each placed directly under the Air Council.

For some time the decision hung in the balance. Without a Commander-in-Chief of the two forces a heavy burden of operational co-ordination would be placed on the Chief of the Air Staff. Both the Chiefs of Air Staff concerned, Sir Edward Ellington and Sir Cyril Newall, were in favour of creating such a Commander-in-Chief. But Sir John Steel for the bombers and Sir Hugh Dowding for the fighters opposed the scheme as unwise, because it detracted from the authority of the Chief of the Air Staff, and as unnecessary, because sufficient co-ordination between the two Commands could be effected by the usual liaison channels. There was also the problem of co-ordinating fighter defence with that of anti-aircraft guns and searchlights.

The situation was complicated by the proposal that supreme home commanders should also be appointed for the Army and the Navy, so that the three could together co-ordinate all the home defences. But this idea did not suit the organisation of the Admiralty. The final reason for eliminating the supreme Air Commander appears to have been, however, the fear that he might be too preoccupied with the problems of defence to give the necessary impetus and leadership to the striking force. It was, therefore, decided that separate Bomber and Fighter Commands should be set up and that each should have an Air Officer Commanding-in-Chief directly responsible to the Air Council.[1]

---

[1] R.A.F. Narratives, *Air Defence of Great Britain*, Vol. I, *Growth of Fighter Command July 1936–June 1940*, pp. 30–34. *The R.A.F. in the Bombing Offensive against Germany*, Vol. I,

RECONSTRUCTION OF THE FORCE, 1934–1939

This decision, which came into effect in July 1936, was one of great importance. It made still wider the gulf between attack and defence. The experience of one Command was not so easily transferred to the other. Combined operations were made more difficult. Joint tactical planning was neglected. In the circumstances of the time the decision was no doubt necessary. Fighter Command had to be concentrated on the task of defending Britain against enemy bombers and fighters. It may well be that, had this not been done, the progress that was made between 1937 and 1940 in developing the new system of defence would not have taken place and the Battle of Britain would have been lost.

But an overall commander such as existed in the overseas commands and was later to exist in the United States Eighth Air Force would have been able to effect a closer co-ordination between bombers and fighters. As it was, the division between Bomber and Fighter Commands tended towards the separate employment of each force. It was for the Chief of the Air Staff to remedy any such defects. But he had many other duties to perform and especially the task of formulating with the other Chiefs of Staff and their opposite numbers in the United States the global strategy of the war. A Commander-in-Chief interposed between him and the operational commander of Bomber and Fighter Commands might have helped to solve some of the problems of the strategic offensive.

Other Commands were also necessarily created as the Air Force grew larger. Coastal Command came into existence for that part of the home Air Force which was to co-operate with the Navy. The Admiralty, which obtained in 1937 absolute control of the Fleet Air Arm, had long wished also for fuller control of the Coastal Command aircraft. Their operations, though not their administration, were also in 1937 brought into closer relation to it. Coastal Command was thus trained entirely for another purpose and was not able to play as great a part in the strategic offensive as had at one time been contemplated.[1]

One other new change urgently needed was the creation of Training Command which took over those groups which were responsible for flying training, and, all too tardily, a Maintenance Command was eventually set up followed by a Reserve Command for the Royal

---

Prewar Evolution of Bomber Command 1917–1939, pp. 110A–110E. See also Basil Collier: *The Defence of the United Kingdom*, pp. 34–35.

[1] R.A.F. Narrative Vol. I, *The Pre-War Evolution of Coastal Command 1919–1939*. At the end of 1936 the A.O.C.-in-C. of the Coastal Defence squadrons, Air Marshal Sir Philip Joubert, thought that the main role of this force would still be to support the bombing offensive, but the Air Ministry did not accept this view and decided that it must be specially trained for co-operation with the Navy. On 1st December 1937 after much discussion with the Admiralty they agreed that its primary role was 'trade protection, reconnaissance and co-operation with the Royal Navy', and later gave assurance that shore-based aircraft allocated to such duties would only be detached in time of war for other purposes after approval of the Chiefs of Staff or, if necessary, by the War Cabinet. They did this in order to retain their administrative and operative control and with a genuine desire to remove the fears of the Admiralty. See on the transfer Captain S. W. Roskill, R.N., *History of the Second World War. The War at Sea*, Vol. I, (1954), Chap. III.

Air Force Volunteer Reserve. In 1940 Training and Reserve were combined with two other Commands, Flying Training and Technical Training, while an Army Co-operation Command came into existtence as the Army grew in size. Transport Command was not instituted until 1943. All this was, of course, essential to maintain the organisation and efficiency of the large numbers of aircraft and men that had to be dealt with.

The expansion raised a host of problems in addition to those of supply of aircraft, personnel and organisation. All kinds of things had to be provided, either entirely new or in much greater quantity than before. Much of the equipment had to be completely redesigned. High octane petrol was needed for the new aircraft, new and bigger bombs for the new heavies, new flares for night flying, new and better guns for both fighters and bombers, new equipment for the bombers such as power-operated turrets and the automatic pilot, provision for aids against the hazards of the weather and cameras to map targets and discover the effects of the bombing. Only a few of these problems were solved with any great success; others were neglected or found to be intractable. But one of the most formidable was, perhaps, the re-orientation of the bases of the Air Force to meet the threat that now came from over the North Sea and the large number of additional aerodromes and accommodation that had to be provided for the new squadrons.

Thus, many new sites had to be acquired, and in spite of the imminence of war there was often great difficulty in overcoming local opposition. Moreover, hangars built for the old aircraft were not large enough for the new ones. The Air Staff could not get everything arranged as it would have liked. The medium bombers could not be placed nearest to Germany in East Anglia, where the hangars had been designed for the larger heavy bombers. They had to occupy the central aerodromes. It was realised that the Blenheims would need refuelling grounds nearer the coast, and the Battles in France, if they were to be used in strategic bombing. Some of the aerodromes were on land that became waterlogged in heavy rain. There were as yet only a few concrete runways which the new heavies would need. But, by and large, the difficult task was accomplished and an infrastructure capable of receiving the new Air Force was constructed. There were nearly three times as many aerodromes in 1939 as in 1934. The weakest part of the structure was in storage and maintenance. A year before war broke out there was not a single repair depot in the United Kingdom, though steps were then taken to construct a number. Nor had the Air Force acquired the necessary space for training and bombing practice and experiment.[1]

---

[1] The vulnerability of the aerodromes also caused much anxiety and the construction of underground hangars was seriously considered.

The new organisation was also linked together with an efficient system of rapid communication. This was above all necessary for Fighter Command, where minutes might make all the difference. But it was also indispensable to Bomber Command if its squadrons, scattered over half of England, were to be effectively controlled by its Commander. When war broke out the new headquarters, about five miles from High Wycombe, with its underground operations room was not yet ready, but Bomber Command was able to move there in early 1940, and thereafter its Commander-in-Chief had rapid and secret means of communication with his Group Commanders and they with one another and their squadrons on the airfields. Much had also been done to give the Commander-in-Chief as accurate meteorological information as possible on which all his decisions would largely depend. These decisions must also depend on the strategic plans which the Air Staff had made during this time of feverish activity and how far the tactics and training of the crews made it possible for these plans to be carried out, subjects which are discussed in the two following sections.

4. Strategic principles and plans, 1934–1939

The threat from Germany and the reconstruction of the bomber force necessarily caused a re-examination of the strategic theories which during the period of stagnation had been accepted almost without question. Sir Hugh Trenchard had not only insisted on the maintenance of the offensive at all costs and the reduction of the defensive force to the lowest possible number, but also had implied that the war could be won by producing such moral effect on the civilian population of the enemy that its government would have to sue for peace. This was never stated quite explicitly and the advantage of destroying military installations and factories was recognised, but the essence of the theory was that it was easier to overcome the will to resist among the workers than to destroy the means to resist. Moral effect, it had continually been said, was as to material effect as twenty to one. Thus, the war could be won without the use of large armies. The Navy also, it was suggested, was now so vulnerable to air attack that it could not protect the country as it once had done. All must depend on the striking power of the Air Force.

As soon as Germany began to rearm, these principles, hitherto largely theoretical and based on little experience of warfare, had to be considered in relation to an actual potential enemy. Had Britain been able to maintain a large preponderance of force in the air, they might have remained intact. But on the contrary, the German air force in two years became stronger than that of Britain and in numbers at least it increased its lead with every year that passed. Plans were, indeed, made to equal and even surpass it in striking power. But these could not possibly mature before 1941 and might well, as indeed happened, not produce much effect before 1942.

The other services had never, of course, accepted these theories. But until 1934 they had been preoccupied with other areas, the possible attack by Russia on India and, after 1931, the aggressive spirit shown by Japan in the Far East. The strategy as regards Europe had never been discussed as a matter of immediate decision, though from time to time, as has been seen, the services had stated their conflicting views in the Committee of Imperial Defence or its Chiefs of Staff Sub-Committee.

But in 1934 the issue became a live one, since all three services were demanding large sums of money to repair the neglect of previous years. For a period the Air Staff maintained its position. The Army, for example, continued to be starved and no preparation was made to send an adequate expeditionary force to the Continent. The threat in the air made a deeper impression on Ministers and public opinion than any other danger. Until 1938 the doctrine that a counter-offensive was the only reply to the German threat held the field. But already the position of the Air Staff had been modified and it had been more fully recognised that the combination of all three services was necessary to secure the best strategic position. The Army was responsible for manning the anti-aircraft artillery which, it was gradually perceived, was an essential factor in the struggle in the air. Still more important was the fact that the weight of air attack on either side depended to a large extent on the control of the Low Countries, which would involve all three services in the struggle.

There were also other air forces in Europe. But that of France grew so obsolescent and inefficient that it tended to be left out of account. The alliance with France and her role in preventing the Germans from acquiring bases nearer Britain and providing bases for the medium and light bombers of the Royal Air Force was, however, regarded as fundamental, though no formal staff discussions with France took place until the war was close at hand. Still less account was taken of the air forces of Poland and Czechoslovakia. The Italian air force had to be reckoned with as a threat to France and Egypt after 1935, and it made notable progress in the speed and range of its aircraft, some of which were considered to be the best of their kind. But always the discussion came back to the problem of how the German threat in the air could be met by a counter-attack.

The strategic problem was brought to the fore in 1934 by the Chancellor of the Exchequer, Mr. Neville Chamberlain, who set a limit on the funds which were to be devoted to rearmament in the next five years, the period then assumed as that in which Germany could accomplish her own rearmament. These funds were obviously insufficient to meet all needs, and in order to establish the necessary priorities the strategic situation had to be examined. The Joint Planning Committee of the three Staffs had been established in 1927 for the purpose of discussing such strategic problems and reporting on them to the Chiefs of Staff for their approval and submission to the Committee of Imperial Defence.

In the preliminary discussions amongst the Chiefs of Staff, the Chief of the Air Staff, Sir Edward Ellington, now painted a grim picture of the damage that Germany could do to Britain by an air attack, so grim indeed that the Chief of the Imperial General Staff, General Sir Archibald Montgomery-Massingberd, refused to accept it. Sir Edward Ellington himself did, indeed, admit that much depended on where the German aircraft were based. If Germany were able to occupy Belgium her attack would be overwhelming and most difficult to counter. If the Low Countries remained neutral and France was the ally of Britain, Germany would not be able to do so much harm, while, if the Low Countries were allied with Britain, the advantage would be very much on the other side and Germany would be driven on to the defensive. Germany could, however, by directing her main air attack on British ports, probably make it impossible or difficult to send a British expeditionary force to the Continent, at any rate by the usual Channel route.

The Chief of the Air Staff also agreed that much more attention must be paid in Britain to air raid precautions and to educating the working population of the country so that it might be better able to endure the attack. No reliance could be based on defence by fighters against any raid on objectives less than fifty to a hundred miles from the coast, since sufficient warning would not be given for them to get into position to intercept the bombers. It had always been recognised that standing patrols could not be maintained, since six squadrons would have to be provided to keep one in the air. Thus, London and many of the industrial towns and ports would be at the mercy of the enemy, who might well try to deliver a 'knock-out blow' against Britain at the opening of hostilities. The only reply to this attempt was a counter-offensive, as the Air Staff had so often reiterated, and since the British aircraft had so little range, it was necessary to possess bases in France for this purpose. In such a case the German attack would also be levelled at France as well as at Britain and the weight of bombs dropped on Britain would be reduced.[1]

The General Staff did not agree with this appreciation. 'Air warfare by itself would not end a war.' Nor according to their information was Germany planning such an attack. Her air force was designed for co-operation with the Army and the main attack in the West would be by land, and, it was added, unless repulsed, it might give Germany bases enabling her to bomb Britain with much greater effect. There was also considerable scepticism in the other two services as to the effectiveness of bombing and the papers were not sent forward for the consideration of Ministers.[2] But both the Cabinet and the country as a whole saw in the air attack the greatest threat to Britain, while there was still great dread of becoming involved in a continental war like that of 1914–1918. Accordingly, as has been seen, the Air Force was given a considerable share of the entirely inadequate funds allocated to defence, while, in spite of the necessity to defend the Low Countries, the Army received a much smaller proportion of the meagre increase.

Throughout the discussions of 1935–1936 the Air Staff still insisted on the priority of the bombing force, and after the initial increase in

---

[1] Memo. by Ellington, 12th June and 11th July 1934.
[2] C.O.S. Mtgs., 4th May and 27th June 1934. There was also the possibility of France deciding to crush Germany by a preventive war before the forces of the latter became too strong. In such a case the Chiefs of Staff were of the opinion that Britain would not support France. The war they had to envisage was a defensive war to repel aggression.

1934 only a small expansion of the fighters was proposed. Ministers accepted this doctrine as it seemed to provide the 'deterrent' to a German attack. The Air Ministry went on, therefore, as has been seen, to plan the force of heavy bombers which would be able to bomb Germany from British bases. Hitherto the plan for this counter-offensive had only been stated in the most general terms. But now the actual process had to be carefully studied and the position of all three services in the defence of Britain to be more exactly defined.

This was the task of the Joint Planning Committee which began its study in 1934, but did not complete it until two years had passed. It made, however, an interim report to the Chiefs of Staff on 1st August 1935 which stressed the danger that Germany might begin the war by attempting a 'knock-out blow' at Britain, probably after occupying Belgium, but possibly directly from German bases. This would not be ostensibly aimed at civilian morale, but attacks on 'military' establishments would have the same effect. The results, judging from the experience of the 1914–1918 war, would be catastrophic. London might be made untenable and the feeding of the population impossible by attacks on the ports. Other reports confirmed this pessimistic view and the idea of the 'knock-out blow' was thus in everyone's mind by the end of 1936.[1]

Neither the Army nor the Navy accepted these estimates. The former especially continued to insist that the main German attack would be by land. But the Air Force had a strong position since it was only in the air that an offensive against Germany could be immediately mounted. It was on the Air Force, therefore, that they must rely to counter the German offensive in the early stages of the war.

The discussions came to a head in the autumn of 1936 when the Joint Planners submitted their report to the Chiefs of Staff. This, after prolonged consideration by the Chiefs of Staff themselves, resulted in the formulation of a general plan, which was submitted to the Committee of Imperial Defence and Cabinet and approved by them in May 1937. It was a compromise between the strategic views of the different services, but it gave a prominent position to the bombing force, though utilising it in a more defensive way than had been envisaged in the nineteen-twenties. In an appendix to the report of the Joint Planners there was an alarming account of the possible effects of German air raids on Britain. 150,000 casualties, it was estimated, might occur in the first week of the war. The Chiefs of Staff did not endorse this part of the report or send it forward, but they accepted the view that the war might begin with a German attempt

---

[1] J.P.C. Report, 1st Aug. 1935. This appreciation of the probable effects of German bombing was confirmed by a C.I.D. Sub-Committee set up to estimate the possible German scale of attack. Report of the Cttee., 17th March 1936. The discussion of the defence of the ports and home trade led to similar conclusions.

to deliver a 'knock-out blow' against Britain. This attack could be sustained for a fortnight at least with great intensity and the first duty of the Royal Air Force was to counter it. Since Germany possessed no target as vulnerable as London and there was no other German area or industry on which an attack would produce an immediate effect, the bombing force must direct its first attacks on the bases, centres of concentration and maintenance depots of the *Luftwaffe*. These were considered targets difficult to find and to attack and they were likely to be strongly defended, but this seemed to be the best method by which the German attack could be reduced to something that could be endured. Meanwhile, the Army must stay at home and the Air Force would assist the Navy to repel any attack by sea, whether by surface ships or submarines.

On the other hand, the first German attack might be on land against France and Belgium. In this case it was assumed that Britain would, by whatever route was possible, send a small expeditionary force to the Continent. The bombing force must then be used to attack the communications of the German army and thus assist the land forces to repel their attack.

But, whether the German attack was begun in the air or on the land, this would only be the first phase of the war. During this phase, it was admitted, the role of the Royal Air Force would be defensive. But this phase would be followed by a second one of stabilisation during which each side would try to build up its resources. Then the bombing force might play a decisive role by an attack on German industry, which, like the blockade, but much more quickly, would reduce the German war potential and enable the Western Alliance to obtain such a superiority of force as to allow it to assume the offensive. There was no suggestion that Germany could be defeated solely by action in the air. The use of a land army with mechanised forces would be essential. But the bombing forces would play a great part in the softening up process that would precede the final victory. Except for the exaggerated estimate of air casualties which was generally accepted at that time, this second appreciation was a remarkably accurate forecast of the course of the war and the means by which victory could be attained.[1]

The Chiefs of Staff also made at this time another decision of the

---

[1] J.P.C. Appreciation, 26th Oct. 1936. Extracts are given in Appendix 4. Its members were Captain T. S. V. Phillips, R.N., Colonel R. Forbes Adam and Group Captain A. T. Harris. In a covering note it was pointed out that as Germany was less vulnerable than Britain it was necessary for the British bombing force to be stronger than that of Germany. C.O.S. Report, 15th Feb. 1937. Sir Arthur Harris in *Bomber Offensive*, (1947), pp. 25–26, claims the same foresight for a later appreciation of the Joint Planning Committee in 1938, but he seems to have given the wrong date. These arguments were, indeed, often repeated, but this is the first document that has been found in which they were explicitly set down. It was this document also that led the Chiefs of Staff to order definite plans to be made to carry out the strategy laid down in it.

greatest importance. Now that the general lines of strategy had been laid down they must be translated as soon as possible into plans based on the best information available and worked out in such detail that they could be instantly put into operation if war came. There were to be a number of alternative plans, since no one could foresee exactly what would happen and moreover the plans of Britain's allies would have to be taken into account. For the Air Force, therefore, they drew up ten different categories of plans for which detailed operational instructions were needed. These fell into three divisions, first the role of the Air Force in assisting the Navy, secondly its co-operation with the Army, and finally its own independent action in a bombing offensive. Those affecting the Navy were largely the concern of Coastal Command, but Bomber Command had also a part to play, and this had to be considered in conjunction with the Naval Staff. Similarly there were special Army Co-operation Units for tactical work with the Army which would be under their control, but, as has been seen, in certain circumstances, the Army also desired to use Bomber Command to stop the German offensive, and plans for this purpose had naturally to be worked out with the General Staff. The rest, which comprised the counter-attack on the *Luftwaffe* and the offensive against German industry, were for Bomber Command alone.[1]

It was now, therefore, the duty of the Air Staff to prepare, in conjunction with Bomber Command, the detailed plans called for and the process certainly brought them down to earth. It was one thing to lay down general theories of strategy; it was another to draw up detailed instructions which squadron commanders could carry out. The task was all the more difficult since the exact composition of the Royal Air Force when the moment for action came could not be foreseen. It was soon revealed also that there was no clear idea as to what was operationally possible, what targets could be reached, how far they could be hit, what would happen to them if they were hit or what were likely to be the casualties incurred. The process of examining these problems was a painful one. At the end of it it was revealed that at any rate in 1939–1940 Bomber Command was unlikely to be able to make any great contribution to the defence of Britain or the counter-attack on Germany.

The process was, however, also a very salutary one. For the first time it caused the strategy and tactics of the bombing offensive to be considered with due regard to the actual conditions under which warfare would be carried on. Though it failed to discover the tactics or the methods of training the crews to carry out its strategic objectives, the main lines of its offensive strategy survived until the means

---

[1] C.O.S. Report, 15th Feb. 1937.

were at last found to make them effective. The realisation of its inability to counter the German attack by a bombing offensive caused the Air Staff to accept more easily the policy, already forced on it by the Ministers, if for inadequate reasons, of priority to fighter defence.

There was already prepared in the Air Ministry what was known as the 'Western Plan', a scheme for the mobilisation of all forces when the war came and the distribution of the squadrons to the various aerodromes. This had to be constantly under review by a mobilisation committee, for its components were continually changing. It included provision for sending to France a force of ten medium bomber squadrons, to be followed later by a further ten, designated as the Advanced Air Striking Force. It had also been recognised that refuelling bases might be required there for other squadrons. Plans for the transport and servicing of such squadrons had been made with the Army. It was also possible that bases might be obtained in Belgium as a result of a German attack upon her.[1] Obviously the provision of such bases would affect the extent of the penetration into Germany. Yet it was only after much delay that a provisional list of them could be drawn up and the whole situation remained somewhat conjectural, since the Cabinet had refused to allow staff conversations with the French on the subject and Belgium remained entrenched in her policy of neutrality.

After he began to examine the war plans, the Commander-in-Chief of Bomber Command was also not satisfied that his aircraft were placed in the best position to suit their several performances. He did not obtain all that he sought, but a compromise was arranged by which the medium bombers occupied the Midland aerodromes with the possibility of using refuelling bases in Kent or France, and the rest of the force was distributed more in accordance with his proposals.[2]

Much progress had also been made in procuring the intelligence on which the plans must be based. That concerning the armed forces of the enemy and their stations was the business of the military, naval and air staffs. But, if the German war potential was to be attacked, it was obviously necessary to know of what it consisted and to divide it into suitable targets. The machinery now in use for this purpose had been set up as long ago as 1929, but it had been overhauled in 1936 as the result of a comprehensive report by the Deputy Chiefs of Staff. The Industrial Intelligence Committee, composed of representatives of the Board of Trade and other civilian departments, which had set

---

[1] Min. Portal (D. of O.) to Slessor, 30th Aug. 1937. 'C.A.S.', wrote the Director of Organisation, 'considers it will probably be impossible actually to send any squadrons in the first month or so when the contest for superiority in the air will be in an acute stage.'

[2] Letter Ludlow-Hewitt to Air Min., 4th Feb. 1938. See the order of battle at the outset of the war, Appendix 38.

up an Industrial Intelligence Centre with a small full-time staff, was now given an Air Targets Sub-Committee. Attention was concentrated on Germany and a great deal of valuable material was acquired and analysed so that a fairly comprehensive, if still very inadequate, account could be given of German industry and what were most likely to be the most profitable targets in it.[1]

To some, the main function of the Industrial Intelligence Centre was to prepare the information and machinery for an economic blockade such as had been so powerful a weapon against Germany in the First World War. But its Director, Major D. F. Morton, had from the first regarded it as an instrument of economic warfare in the widest sense. Its economic intelligence, therefore, was also to provide the information for the strategic air offensive and any other operation designed to destroy the economic potential of Germany. As soon as war began it was to become a part of the Ministry of Economic Warfare with all that that name implied. For administrative purposes it was placed under the Department of Overseas Trade. There soon, however, developed a certain difference of opinion as to the role of the Industrial Intelligence Centre. It was not satisfied with providing intelligence but began also to attempt to determine priorities amongst the targets, a task which the Air Staff considered its own, especially as regards the effect likely to be produced on the armed services of Germany.[2] This claim on the part of civilians to determine the targets of Bomber Command persisted throughout the war. But at any rate a comprehensive machine had been set up to provide the material without which such plans could not be made.

What the Air Staff had to do, therefore, was to take into account the character of Bomber Command on mobilisation at some date in the future, its stations, whether in Britain or France (or possibly Belgium), and, in the light of the intelligence with which it was provided, draw up a list of strategic targets for Bomber Command to attack. Since there were so many alternatives, it had also to provide an order of priority, at any rate for attention, if not one that would be used when war came. It would then be for Bomber Command to devise the tactical plans to carry out the strategic objectives and formulate them in a series of operational orders. The tactical appreciation might well determine what targets were likely to be the most remunerative and thus give Bomber Command the final word as to which should be attacked. As will be seen, the Air Staff did not accept

---

[1] D.C.O.S. Report, 1st Jan. 1936. Its Chairman was Sir Maurice Hankey. Industrial Intelligence in Foreign Countries Cttee. Report, 22nd July 1936. The Air Targets Sub-Committee was composed of the Comptroller-General of the Department of Overseas Trade, Sir Edward Crowe, the Deputy Directors of Intelligence of the Admiralty, War Office and Air Ministry or their representatives and the Head of the Industrial Intelligence Centre.
[2] Letter Buss to Morton, 1st. Oct. 1937.

this view and this conflict in authority was to continue throughout the war. The Deputy Director of Plans, Group Captain J. C. Slessor, was the central pivot of all this planning, co-ordinating the information provided by the Intelligence Departments, both those inside and those outside the Air Ministry, tabulating the targets, getting them arranged in some order of priority and keeping in close touch with Bomber Command as regards the tactical appreciations.

The process of the tabulation of the plans took a considerable time. On some of the projects the information was decidedly meagre. It was even more difficult to establish an order of priority. But this was eventually done at a meeting at the Air Ministry on 1st October 1937, which discussed a draft drawn up in the Plans Division. Thus, a list of thirteen plans, called W.A. (Western Air) plans, each with its own number, was sent down to Bomber Command with instructions to concentrate at the outset on three of them which were placed in Group No. 1. Two other plans in this group concerned Coastal Command, while the eight following were not yet regarded as of much immediate importance. This list was subsequently somewhat altered both in numbering and content, but the three plans now given priority occupied the main attention of all concerned until the Munich crisis and it was in considering them that the limitations of Bomber Command were first revealed. They were:

(1) W.A.1. The attack on the German Air Striking Force and its maintenance organisation, to which was later added the German aircraft industry, originally listed under W.A.6.
(2) W.A.4. The attack on German military rail, canal and road communications (a) during the period of the concentration of the armies, (b) to delay a German invasion of the Low Countries and France.
(3) W.A.5. The attack on the German War Industry including the supply of oil with priority to that in the Ruhr, Rhineland and Saar.[1]

In order to carry out the tactical appreciation Bomber Command was given a small increase of staff; a Group Captain (F. P. Don) with three or four assistants. It was little enough to deal with the formidable problems presented to them. It took some time also before Group Captain Don could obtain the necessary information about the kind of aircraft which would be available in 1939 or what forces it was thought that the enemy could use against them. There was also the

---

[1] Several revisions were made which increased the list to fourteen. The last made before the war was dated 1st September 1939. See App. 6. There is no logic in the order except that the main attack on the enemy's armed forces of air, sea and land comes first. The first list of thirteen plans was sent to Bomber Command on 13th December 1937 together with three dossiers of information for W.A.1, W.A.4, W.A.5. Letter and enclosures Peirse (D.O.I.) to Ludlow-Hewitt.

pertinent question of what types of bombs would be available. Answers to these questions were not immediately forthcoming and it is not surprising to find that the date for the completion of the plans was changed from 1st August 1938 to 1st January 1939. Even then only the three main plans could be surveyed. It was, indeed, a tremendous task to survey the methods by which W.A.1, W.A.4 and W.A.5 could be carried out and come to some conclusion about them. The result in the circumstances was bound to be superficial. Nevertheless, the survey brought to light the hard realities of the problem for the first time and revolutionised the thinking not only of Bomber Command but of the Air Staff itself.

The attack on the German air force (W.A.1) had been specially mentioned by the Joint Planners as the best method of reducing the German bombing attack on Britain. As such it might claim to have priority over all the others. But from the first the Air Staff had been pessimistic about obtaining any results from it commensurate with the casualties which must occur in the attempt. It had been ascertained that the Germans were preparing a large number of emergency aerodromes for use when war broke out and the location of these was not known, would be hard to discover and often changed. It appeared likely that there would be no central reserve of aircraft but that it would be distributed over the aerodromes. Aircraft factories were 'large, distinctive and vulnerable targets' but, unless the Germans lost a hundred per cent of their force in a month in their attack on Britain and at least fifty per cent damage could be done to the factories in the first week, the effect on the *Luftwaffe* would be too long delayed to affect the immediate situation. Similar conclusions were reached about engine factories, oil fuel and components such as ball-bearings.[1]

The tactical examination by Bomber Command not only confirmed this view but showed how incapable Bomber Command was of inflicting any such blow from British bases without incurring prohibitive casualties. Sir Edgar Ludlow-Hewitt had already reported that calculations had been made of the probable casualties and that they showed that if a determined attack were made on Germany his medium bomber force would be eliminated in three and a half weeks and the so-called heavy bombers in seven and a half.[2] A later letter of Sir Edgar Ludlow-Hewitt to the Air Ministry, written at a time when his Command might be called into action at any minute, gave an extremely pessimistic appreciation. If Holland and Belgium were neutral, the Blenheims could only just reach a few targets in North-West Germany. The Battles would be ineffective and suffer heavy

---

[1] Air Staff Intelligence Summary, 5th Oct. 1937.
[2] Letter Ludlow-Hewitt to Air Min., 19th March 1938.

casualties. They should, therefore, only be used in the last resort. It would be difficult for such aircraft as could reach the targets to hit them from a high level and the experiments on Salisbury Plain had shown that small damage was inflicted on aircraft well dispersed. But in more general observations, Sir Edgar Ludlow-Hewitt repeated again his doubts as to whether his force could penetrate any distance into Germany without more protection. He even suggested that the Air Ministry should reverse its long-standing doctrine and construct long-range fighters for that purpose:

'Experience both in China and in Spain seems clearly to indicate', he wrote, 'that with the aircraft in use in these two theatres of war at present, Fighter Escorts are considered absolutely essential for the protection of Bomber Aircraft. So far as I am aware this policy runs counter to the views long held by the Air Staff and I must admit that I have myself in the past wondered what the German two-seater Fighter Escorts were supposed to do when they arrive in this country. They should, I assumed, be comfortably outclassed by our single-seater aircraft of the Hurricane and Spitfire class.' But he felt that some such protection was essential and, if fighter escorts could not be sent the long distance from Britain they could at least use bases in France for that purpose as was done in the 1914–1918 war. He advocated, therefore, basing the main part of the force in France, developing long-range fighters for their protection and arming them much more heavily than had hitherto been done. From Britain itself, it was thus clear, nothing could be done about W.A.1, and since it was estimated that at least a month would elapse before the force could be adequately based in France nothing could be done in this way to counter the knock-out blow if the Germans essayed it. Indeed, Sir Edgar Ludlow-Hewitt himself said that Britain must rely on the North Sea and the strongest possible fighter and anti-aircraft defence.[1]

Germany might, however, decide to make its attack by land as the French and the British General Staffs expected. Then the role of the Air Force would be to assist the Army to repel it (W.A.4). There would, of course, be army co-operation squadrons under the direction of the military commander, but, in addition, Bomber Command, from bases in Britain or France, could be used to attack the concentration and communications of the German armies on the Western front. Here it was obviously possible to reach the targets, at any rate from French bases. But the Air Staff had never shown much favour towards a plan which might ultimately bring a large part of Bomber Command under the direction of the Army Commander-in-Chief. The appreciation sent with W.A.4 to Bomber Command more or less

---

[1] Letter Ludlow-Hewitt to Air Min., 30th Aug. 1938. He also pointed out that the range of the Blenheims which had been assumed as 792 miles had been found in practice to be only 700 miles. Letter Ludlow-Hewitt to Air Min., 19th Sept. 1938.

intimated that they did not expect a favourable report. The War Office itself admitted that not much effect would be produced except by a heavy and continuous attack which would absorb much of the force. There was also a difference between the Air Staff and the General Staff as to the method best calculated to disrupt the German communications. The latter wished the targets to be bridges, viaducts and railway lines where they ran through defiles, while the Air Staff thought that greater effect would be obtained by attacks on railway stations, locomotive sheds and junctions. The experience of the Chinese and Spanish wars pointed to this view as well as their own experiments. But either would absorb practically the whole force, would result in heavy casualties and would be doubtful in result. In view of the dense network of railways in western Germany and the Low Countries it was not likely to cause any appreciable delay.[1]

It was thus becoming clear that Bomber Command could not do much to counter German attack either in the air or on the land. There remained W.A.5, the direct offensive on German industry in the Ruhr, which might be pursued in less haste than the other two. From the outset this plan was regarded by the Air Ministry as the most profitable target system for Bomber Command. The Air Targets Sub-Committee had been able to prepare a survey, which seemed to contain a number of highly vulnerable targets. Amongst these it might even be possible to discover those which, in spite of the failure of the Joint Planning Committee to do so in 1936, would tend (though probably not immediately) to cause a reduction of the German air offensive as well as 'have an adverse effect on the German war effort and German economic life generally'.[2]

The appreciation by Bomber Command was even more optimistic. The 1939 force would, of course, not be able to wipe out the industry of the Ruhr. But if it concentrated attack on the nineteen power plants and twenty-six coking plants enumerated in the intelligence report sent to them, they could be put out of action in a fortnight by 3,000 sorties with a loss of 176 aircraft, and Germany's war-making power reduced almost to a standstill.[3] The Air Ministry, indeed, thought the report too optimistic and that the power plants would not be so easy to hit or the coking plants so easy to destroy. It was also pointed out that there was much German manufacturing capacity outside the Ruhr which would need attention. But there was another way of fatally crippling the Ruhr. The Air Targets Sub-Committee was confident that the same amount of damage could be done in

---

[1] Air Staff Note on W.A.4, 30th Nov. 1937.
[2] Letter Peirse to Ludlow-Hewitt, 13th Dec. 1937.
[3] Letter and Appreciation Bomber Cmd. to Air Min., 28th July and May 1938, with pencilled marginal notes.

3,000 sorties or less by destroying the Möhne and Sorpe dams, which would disrupt the industry of the Ruhr and cause great destruction. If this was to be attempted bigger and better bombs would be needed as Bomber Command pointed out. But the plan continued to be pressed by the Targets Sub-Committee. In addition, it was suggested that the locks and aqueducts of the canal system which connected the Ruhr with northern Germany were most vulnerable and contained key points which, if they were destroyed, would throw the whole system out of gear. Coupled with attacks on the principal railway workshops and repair depots this would paralyse the Ruhr for months and the whole German industrial system which depended on it would come to a standstill. It was, of course, doubtful if the 1939 force, even if mainly based in France, could accomplish all this, but it was thought that such aims would be within the power of Bomber Command when it possessed more heavy bombers. At any rate the two plans were kept in the list as W.A.5(a) and W.A.5(b) and were considered practical operations of war.[1]

It is easy to mock at these estimates in the light of the experience of the war. But it was not so much the strategic objectives that were at fault as the failure to appreciate the operational difficulties. In choosing electric power as a primary target amongst those given to it to study in W.A.5 Bomber Command had, according to investigations in Germany after the war, selected a highly vulnerable part of the German industrial machine. The Germans, indeed, were amazed that more attention was not paid to it in the later stages of the war.[2] And though the destruction of the dams could not have caused the amount of damage which the Air Targets Intelligence Sub-Committee thought would ensue, it was possible to destroy the Möhne though not the Sorpe dam in the great raid of May 1943. The paralysis of rail and canal communications was at a later date to be a most effective method of overcoming German resistance. There was an obvious discrepancy between the attitude towards W.A.5 and that adopted towards W.A.4. But it was hardly thought by the Air Staff that such great feats could be accomplished until bombers were obtained which by their speed and armament would be able to penetrate to the Ruhr in daylight and so be able to carry out precision bombing. Meanwhile, therefore, the force must be conserved for the future rather than risk its immediate destruction. Otherwise, when the heavy bombers appeared, there would be no crews ready to use them.

---

[1] Air (Targets) Intelligence Memo., 8th Sept. 1938. This was a third revision of W.A.5.
[2] *United States Strategic Bombing Survey: The Effects of Strategic Bombing on the German War Economy*, (No. 3), p. 126. It may be doubted, however, whether Bomber Command was ever sufficiently accurate in its bombing to destroy so many targets of such small dimensions though experience showed that considerable damage could be done by relatively small attacks.

STRATEGIC PRINCIPLES AND PLANS

There was another reason for which it was doubtful whether such a plan as W.A.5 could be put into operation. In view of the British air inferiority it is not surprising to find that the possibility of restricting bombing to purely military objectives now received fresh and sympathetic consideration. Such restriction had indeed always been part of official policy if the means could be found to make it effective. On 21st June 1938 the Prime Minister announced in the House of Commons that Britain would only bomb purely military objectives and even so would take due care to avoid civilian casualties. There was, of course, no very strict definition of what was a purely military objective. Did it for example include factories manufacturing arms, ammunition or distinctive military supplies? This problem was referred to the Joint Planners, but before they could report a decision had become imperative because of the Munich crisis. Both the Air Officer Commanding-in-Chief, Bomber Command and the Air Ministry were of opinion that restrictions on bombing would be an advantage and official orders were sent to the former to confine his attacks to the W.A.1 and W.A.4 plans which were obviously aimed at military objectives. Even then he was to do nothing that might be construed as an attack on civilians and so give the enemy an excuse to do likewise.[1]

Since Sir William Malkin, the legal adviser of the Foreign Office, was absent at Bad Godesberg with the Prime Minister, these instructions could not be elaborated and officially approved at this time. But the policy of restriction was confirmed by the report of the Joint Planners issued on 24th October 1938. The difficulty of defining military objectives was admitted, but it seemed that the greater the restriction, the better it would be for Britain, and in any case it appeared that 'it would be to our disadvantage to retain the right to attack factories engaged in the manufacture of military supplies, if this involved the right of an enemy to attack London, our supply system and seaborne trade.'[2]

These conclusions were not uninfluenced by the experience of the Munich crisis of 1938, when both the Air Staff and Sir Edgar Ludlow-Hewitt were anxious to do as little as possible. They realised that Bomber Command was in no condition to engage in an all-out battle with Germany. They still held exaggerated fears of what the *Luftwaffe* could do to Britain from German bases. The German forces were already concentrated against Czechoslovakia and the Air Staff shared the Commander-in-Chief's view that there was little to be gained except casualties by attacking the few German aerodromes

---

[1] Parliamentary Debates. Commons. Vol. 337, Cols. 937–938, 21st June 1938. Letter Air Council to Ludlow-Hewitt, 15th Sept. 1938. Letter Newall to Ludlow-Hewitt, 19th Sept. 1938.
[2] J.P.C. Report, 24th Oct. 1938.

S.A.O.—I—H

that could be reached. It was agreed that, if the Germans did start an all-out attack, the Ruhr would be the best target for Bomber Command. But even then Sir Edgar Ludlow-Hewitt was told that there was a shortage of reserves and that he must conserve his force as long as possible.[1]

The Commander-in-Chief had no need of such warning. Half his force was in no condition to fight. He did not think it possible to operate efficiently from refuelling bases in France. A heavy attack could only be made on the Ruhr if it was possible to fly over the Low Countries and he doubted whether Britain would gain if both sides could do so. If the Germans attacked London in force he would retaliate by an attack on the Ruhr. But if they did not do so, he suggested that the Blenheims should be turned into defensive fighters and the Battles sent to France to act in co-operation with the French army. The best use for the night bombers would be to drop propaganda pamphlets over Germany, a course that he thought might produce a most useful effect.[2]

After this it was natural that any review of the position after Munich should be a pessimistic one. For example, at a conference at the Air Ministry at the end of November to discuss a questionnaire on bombing produced by the Plans Directorate, Sir Edgar Ludlow-Hewitt then said that he was not prepared to embark immediately on operations that went any large distance into Germany. 'Such a course,' he said, 'might end in a major disaster.'

These pessimistic conclusions were not entirely accepted by the Air Staff. But the discussions showed that, like the Commander-in-Chief, many thought that the possible degree of penetration into Germany in daytime was only a small one, amounting to a range of 200 miles for about forty per cent of the whole force. Even the new Stirlings, when they came, were expected by the Commander-in-Chief not to be able to do much more. At any rate, different degrees of penetration would have to be laid down for the different kinds of aircraft. At the same time it was thought that, when all types of bombers were capable of both day and night operations, seventy-five per cent of the sorties would be by day. Night attacks, it was agreed, would not be able to achieve appreciable results against precision targets. The Senior Air Staff Officer of Bomber Command, Air Commodore

---

[1] Letter Air Council to Ludlow-Hewitt, 15th Sept. 1938. Letter Newall to Ludlow-Hewitt, 19th Sept. 1938.
[2] Letters Ludlow-Hewitt to Air Min., 19th and 25th Sept. 1938. A note made at this period stated that 'the Air Staff regard propaganda as a weapon.' Britain could not reply to German bombs merely by paper, but if the Germans caused civilian casualties by an attack on a military objective warning notices might be sent before retaliation which might cause great panic and seriously disorganise the industrial life of the Ruhr. It was, however, too much to hope that the scale of attack on Britain would be reduced by this means. Air Staff Note, 25th Sept. 1938.

N. H. Bottomley, however, thought that methods could be found to make such attacks effective and agreed to arrange exercises to discover them.[1]

It is surely remarkable that it was less than a year before the war broke out that the Air Staff should have realised the limited possibilities of Bomber Command. They now knew that its Commander-in-Chief did not think that it was capable of carrying out the operations on which the Air Ministry had based its strategy for the last four years. The conclusion was not indeed entirely accepted even then. Sir Cyril Newall, the Chief of the Air Staff, immediately told Sir Edgar Ludlow-Hewitt that it might be necessary to attack vital targets, and, when the Commander-in-Chief reiterated his policy of conservation and limited experiment, Sir Cyril Newall did not entirely accept this view. Bomber Command, he pointed out, would lose the advantage of surprise and its pilots were likely to deteriorate rather than increase in efficiency. A situation might occur, he wrote, when the attack might have to be pressed home at whatever cost. But no one wanted such a situation to occur, and nothing, therefore, must be done to provoke it.[2]

There was some consolation in the fact that during the year 1938 the prospect of countering the German attack by Fighter Command had much improved. Early in that year this question had also been raised in definite form by the Deputy Director of Plans in one of his searching questionnaires as to what the prospects were when the new Hurricanes and Spitfires came into service. He himself was inclined to maintain the old theory that the bomber would still be supreme because of its increase in speed. But the answers of the Commander-in-Chief of Fighter Command, Sir Hugh Dowding, showed great confidence in a contrary view which was accepted by the Assistant Chief of the Air Staff. 'I do not agree', the latter wrote, 'that the value of the fighter in home defence is, if anything, declining. I think that within the last few months, what with the advent of the 8-gun fighter, R.D.F., and the Biggin Hill Interception scheme, the pendulum has swung the other way and that at the moment—or at any rate as soon as all our Fighter Squadrons are equipped with Hurricanes and Spitfires—the fighter is on top of the contemporary enemy bombers. How

---

[1] Min. Slessor to Douglas, 4th Nov. 1938. Mins. of Air Min. Mtg., 30th Nov. 1938. See also below, p. 190. The D.D. Plans wished a special permanent committee to be formed to review the possibility of strategic bombing at which both Bomber Command and Fighter Command should be represented. The A.C.A.S. refused, however, on the grounds that machinery already existed and only agreed to one *ad hoc* meeting. The Air Tactics and Fighter Operations sections of the Air Ministry were represented by junior officers but not Fighter Command. This is an example of the effect of the separation of the two Commands. The question of whether fighters could assist Bomber Command to solve its problems was ignored.

[2] Letters Newall to Ludlow-Hewitt, 19th Jan. and 1st Feb. 1939. Letter Ludlow-Hewitt to Newall, 21st Jan. 1939.

long this will be the case it is of course difficult to say, but that is my view at the moment.'[1]

This view was confirmed, as Air Vice-Marshal Douglas anticipated, by consideration of the new tactics instituted by the Fighting Committee and its satellite the Air Defence Development Establishment and it must have been reinforced by the views which had been put forward by Bomber Command. As has been seen, the Air Staff now adopted without further question the policy of giving priority in construction and personnel to Fighter Command.

But the Air Staff could not accept this situation as anything but a temporary one. It had to be admitted that their own bombers could not at present always get through and were certainly unable by a counter-offensive to protect Britain from German attack. The policy of defence must, therefore, be given priority for the time being. But the Air Staff still had hopes for the future when Bomber Command would be rearmed with heavier aircraft. It was essential that the Air Force should not lose faith in the offensive for only by the offensive could the war be won. The Air Staff and the Commander-in-Chief were perturbed lest the new policy should undermine the morale of Bomber Command. It could hardly be concealed, for it was evident in the estimates laid before Parliament and the speeches that were made there and elsewhere. To counteract the impression that might be produced, an official circular was drawn up and was given a wide circulation. It was meant to explain the policy announced in Parliament and to refute 'the erroneous deductions that a change of policy is thereby implied in the direction of a defensive strategy at the expense of our capacity for counter-offensive action. It is therefore thought desirable to reaffirm the Air Staff policy and to make it clear that no such change is implied by the measures recently announced or is in any way contemplated.' There was no question of setting up a new ratio of fighters to bombers. The size of the fighter force was determined by the size of the area to be defended and the probable scale of attack. But there must also be a bomber force at least comparable in power with that of the potential enemy. It was essential to any system of defence, a powerful deterrent in peace and the most effective means of exerting pressure in war. It was not enough to avoid losing a war. It had to be won and that could not be done simply by a policy of defence.

The circular went on to admit, however, that the doctrine of the Air Staff had undergone a certain change. 'There has been a tendency in the past to over-state the case that "the bomber will *always* get through", and perhaps also to lay too much stress on the claim that the counter offensive is the *only* effective means of defence in

---

[1] Min. Slessor to Douglas, 11th March 1938. Min. Douglas to Slessor, 23rd March 1938 enclosing answers to questionnaire.

the air. It must be remembered that developments in recent years have undoubtedly added to the actual strength of the defensive in the air.'[1]

This, perhaps, hardly reflected sufficiently the views of the Commander-in-Chief, Bomber Command. But, of course, the Air Staff did not allow that he had the last word. Throughout all these discussions there had been apparent the problem of the division of responsibility between the Air Staff and the Commander-in-Chief of Bomber Command. The Deputy Director of Plans had come to believe that the Air Staff had to take some part in the operational planning.[2] But others thought that, while the selection of the targets was the province of the Air Staff, the Commander-in-Chief was alone responsible for choosing the methods by which they were to be attacked. Sir Edgar Ludlow-Hewitt himself had already made it clear that in his view the final word as to the practicability of any plan lay with himself. 'The line of demarcation of responsibility in war', he had told Air Vice-Marshal Peirse, 'would remain as in peace, namely that the responsibility for the formation and definition of new plans would remain with the Air Ministry. The responsibility for the implementation of plans and for their modification in accordance with the tactical situation would rest with Bomber Command. It is, in my opinion, far more efficient to draw the line there, between planning and implementation, than where it lies now, namely between Intelligence and Planning.'[3]

But Sir Cyril Newall did not agree with this view entirely in the discussion which took place after the Munich crisis. In theory Sir Edgar Ludlow-Hewitt's view of the line of demarcation was accepted. But it was not a clear line and great difficulties were to arise in the course of the war in deciding as to where exactly it was to be drawn.

For the moment, however, the policy of conservation held the field both in the Air Ministry and at Bomber Command Headquarters and was naturally reflected in the papers of the Chiefs of Staff. In a comprehensive review made after Munich the reference to a bombing offensive was couched in very different terms to those of previous papers and more stress was laid on fighter and anti-aircraft defence.[4]

The Air Staff and Bomber Command, however, continued to elaborate the W.A. plans and especially those connected with W.A.5. Meanwhile, a new and promising variation was coming into prominence in the German oil stocks and oil refineries and synthetic plants. Many of these targets were in western Germany and several were in the Ruhr. These were thought to be extremely vulnerable by reason

---
[1] Air Staff Note, 26th Nov. 1938.
[2] Memo. by Slessor, 4th Oct. 1938.
[3] Letter Ludlow-Hewitt to Peirse, 22nd Sept. 1938.
[4] C.O.S. Appreciation, 20th Feb. 1939.

of their contents, though some of the targets were small and would be difficult to hit. Still, here was a promising plan, which might well bring to a standstill the armed forces of Germany.[1]

But neither the oil plan nor any of the W.A.5 plans could be undertaken while the bombing restrictions already announced by the Prime Minister were in force. When the German absorption of Czechoslovakia in March 1939 made even the Prime Minister realise that the policy of appeasement could no longer be maintained and serious staff conversations with the French at last began, it was difficult to find an adequate role for Bomber Command. It was now agreed that a British Expeditionary Force should be sent to the Continent and the excessive estimate of what the *Luftwaffe* could do was shown in the decision to send it through the Western ports. But the French were even less anxious to begin unrestricted bombing than the British. Their own aircraft had little power of penetration and they dreaded the German reply. Since French aerodromes would have to be used for any very heavy attack on Germany, this added to the improbability that it would take place.

Some French air commanders did not altogether accept this position, but the French General Staff, which had the final word, was convinced that the best use for Bomber Command was for it to attempt to delay the expected onslaught of the German army by bombing its points of concentration and communications. There was, however, great difference of opinion between the French and British staffs as to the best methods to accomplish this purpose. The British Air Staff, as the discussion on W.A.4 had revealed, were sceptical as to whether anything very much could be achieved by any method. But there was no alternative and at a very early date 'the two Staffs recognised that the object of all the available bombers would be to contribute to the success of the battle on land.'[2]

Discussion then ensued as to how this should be done and agreement was never reached. The French wished German columns on the march to be bombed and their aerodromes attacked, if, as they thought probable, the *Luftwaffe* devoted its main energies to the French army's back areas. These were not thought by the British to be very profitable targets. Nor did the British Air Staff consider it possible to cut the railway communications as the French insisted could be done. The French were in effect told that they must not expect much result from the assistance of the British bombers. All that had been decided was that an all-out bombing offensive should

---

[1] Another target that was given attention was that of the German forests and crops which, it was suggested, could be set on fire in dry weather by incendiary pellets. It had a place in the *Manual of Air Tactics* (1937) as a means of punishment, having been used for that purpose in outlying areas against primitive peoples.

[2] Mins. of Anglo-French Staff Conversations, 29th March 1939.

be avoided by both countries and that something should be done if possible to attack the lines of communication and bases of the German army and air force.

Nor was any further plan made as a result of the guarantees given to Poland. A survey of the situation led to the conclusion that if Germany began by an attack in the East, as the British General Staff thought probable, nothing could be done to assist Poland. The French, indeed, talked of probing attacks on the Siegfried Line, but it was clear that they did not intend to do very much. Nor could the small British army do much to assist them. The only other means of helping Poland was by a strategic bombing offensive. But neither Britain and still less France, whose bases would be indispensable, had any intention of making one. It is true that the Committee of Imperial Defence was most reluctant to come to such a conclusion and the matter was referred back to the Joint Planners for report. These latter did not recommend any definite decision, but their report stressed the arguments that Britain was more vulnerable than Germany and in any case declarations had been made which ruled out strategic bombing, except such as would not cause civilian casualties, and it was clear what the conclusion was meant to be.[1]

Was there then nothing that Bomber Command could do when the imminent war broke out without giving Germany an excuse to bomb the cities and ports of Britain? Two plans were now given much consideration which preserved the necessary legality. The first (W.A.7 and W.A.12) was an attack on the German fleet either at sea or in harbour either to destroy it or drive it out to sea so that the British fleet could engage it. Long discussions took place on this project with the Admiralty but neither side felt very confident that much could be done. There were also plans for attacking the Kiel Canal (W.A.9) or sowing mines in it, a course which Sir William Malkin thought would be perfectly legal. But this plan also was thought to be very difficult to execute.

Indeed, the only plan which was prosecuted with much enthusiasm in those final months was the one which Sir Edgar Ludlow-Hewitt had suggested during the Munich crisis, the dropping of propaganda leaflets from aircraft at night. The Foreign Office and the new propaganda machinery were set the task of drawing up suitable leaflets. The Air Force itself showed great activity in devising suitable means

---

[1] C.O.S. Memo., 3rd June 1939. C.I.D. Mtg., 22nd June 1939. J.P.C. Draft Report 7th July 1939. On 14th August the British representatives at the Anglo-French Staff Conversations in a review of possible courses of action in effect advocated restricting attacks to purely military objectives and concluded: 'Whatever course we adopt, we should take all possible steps to make clear not only to neutral countries, but also to the German people, that our air action is directed only against those objectives whose destruction is calculated to shorten the course of the war, and that we have no intention of attacking the civil population as such.'

of releasing them over Germany and were concerned as to the character of the propaganda that was thus to be distributed. This was at any rate a task which was operationally possible, while all the other plans were doubtful of execution. This situation was, as has been seen, due partly to the aircraft and equipment which were then available to Bomber Command, but it was also due to the failure to base strategy on operational possibilities, so far as they could be discovered by exercises, and to train crews accordingly. This question must be discussed in the next section.

5. Training and tactics, 1934–1939

How had it come about that Bomber Command felt itself in 1939 unable to carry out the strategic offensive which had for so many years been the basis on which its position had been built up? In part this weakness was due to the fact that it had not yet been equipped with sufficient numbers of aircraft of the necessary range and bombload. But, in addition, it had begun to realise that its crews were not adequately trained to perform such a task. Until two years before the war the operational and technical problems of the strategic offensive had been neglected, and even later no real attempt was made to solve them by more realistic operational exercises. It may of course be said that no solution could have been found until war itself provided the necessary experience. But, however that may be, the result was that even as late as 1939 the Air Staff had little realisation of the tactical problems raised by the strategic plans which had been adopted.

This situation was due to a number of causes. One certainly was the haste with which the Air Force had to be expanded after years of stagnation. The Air Ministry was during 1934–1939 preoccupied with the designing and procurement of aircraft and with obtaining the crews to man them. It had little time left to examine its basic objectives and to consider how the crews were to be trained to achieve them. Training aircraft and the numerous articles of equipment needed by the aircraft and the crews had not been given the necessary priority in production. The realisation that an efficient air force could not be built up if it was too rapidly expanded was one of the main reasons why the Air Ministry had seemed to be reluctant to seize the opportunity afforded to it in 1934–1935. But it had been carried along by the strength of the desire of the Government to achieve 'parity' and provide a 'deterrent' as soon as possible to German aggression. For this reason Bomber Command became to a certain extent a 'shop window' force. It would have been stronger in 1939 if it could have grown more gradually and directed more attention to training and to solving operational problems as they revealed themselves, rather than by seeming to have a large 'first line', much of which, when the test came, turned out not to be a 'first line' at all.

In these years Fighter Command had also greatly expanded. But in this case two indispensable things had been done. The Air Ministry had at an early date planned and put into production two aircraft which were fully capable of executing their objectives. Moreover, the main tactical problem, that of obtaining sufficient warning of the approach of enemy aircraft, had been firmly faced and with the assistance of the scientists had been solved, or nearly so, before war broke out. Two Committees, one a sub-committee of the Committee of Imperial Defence, and one a technical Committee of Scientists presided over by Sir Henry Tizard, the Scientific Adviser of the Air Ministry, had given the necessary impetus and guidance. The latter committee had had the assistance of an operational unit of Fighter Command, while Sir Hugh Dowding had forwarded the project in every possible way.

Admittedly, the problems of the strategic offensive were more complicated. For a bomber a crew had to be trained and not only a pilot as in a fighter and this problem was only fully revealed when the larger bombers came into service. Since long journeys over enemy territory were involved, it was harder to discover in peace time what were the obstacles which had to be overcome. The small size of Britain made it difficult to create conditions in any way equivalent to those of war. And, as will be seen, Bomber Command was not given even the limited amount of training ground necessary to discover the best methods by which a bomb could be dropped on a target. The statement attributed to Colonel Lindbergh, that Britain was too small to possess an air force which could match that of Germany, had some truth in it so far as training was concerned.

This last problem was only solved by utilising the resources of the Commonwealth in one of the greatest co-operative efforts that ever occurred in it. Indeed, before the war ended the Commonwealth was producing almost as many bomber crews as Britain herself, and the majority of British bomber pilots, navigators, bomb aimers and wireless operators were receiving their initial training in territories overseas. During the war this relief enabled the Air Ministry to devote its facilities in Britain to more advanced crew training, but such opportunities were not available during the period of preparation.

In 1934 there were only four Flying Training Schools, including Cranwell where the cadets were trained, and one in Egypt at Abu Sueir. In addition, there was the Central Flying School at Wittering to train instructors and provide a kind of research centre on methods of teaching pilots.[1] The aircraft used for training were largely obsolescent. The 1934 Scheme A meant that a thousand more pilots would be required in addition to the three hundred turned out annually by the existing organisation. As Scheme A was replaced by larger and larger schemes, so the demand for pilots grew and with it came

---

[1] Use has been made of *Flying Training*, Vol. I, *Policy and Planning* issued by the Historical Branch of the Air Ministry in 1952 and R.A.F. Narrative, *Aircrew Training 1934–1942*, prepared under the same direction. Only some of the salient points which especially affect Bomber Command can be discussed here.

the necessity for training a crew behind the pilot. No sooner had a scheme of training been drawn up than it had to be superseded by another.

The first important change made to meet this new situation was to get the civilian flying schools, which had hitherto been used only for reserve officers, to undertake also elementary flying training for new recruits and thus to enable the flying training schools to take the pupil to a more advanced stage. This was the first step taken by Air Commodore Tedder, who was Director of Training in 1934–1936.[1] His object was to produce pilots so trained that they would be able to engage immediately in formation flying when they joined their squadrons. Unfortunately the Royal Air Force expanded too rapidly for the training establishments to catch up with the duties imposed on them. It was only with great difficulty that a sufficient number of pilots were obtained trained in the elements of their art.

First of all there was the necessity of obtaining a sufficient number of recruits under the voluntary system maintained for all services until 1939, not only for the peace-time force but to create the necessary reserves. All Royal Air Force aircrews were always volunteers for that service, but the urgency of the need was not recognised until conscription came. One method used was to increase the number of short-service pilots. Another was to increase the facilities for part-time training of civilians. The model of the Territorial force had been followed in the Royal Air Force by creating county associations with the Lords-Lieutenant at their head, through which at week-ends and on holidays civilians could obtain instruction in flying and so create a reserve of pilots. But this organisation did not expand with the need. There were not sufficient aircraft and the aerodromes were often inconveniently situated for those living in large populous centres. A new kind of voluntary flying school was, therefore, formed with its centre in one of the great cities and its aerodromes in close proximity. This scheme was successful in attracting a large number of enthusiastic recruits, but it took a long time to give basic training to part-time airmen and there were never enough aircraft and instructors.

As the various schemes set an ever higher number of pilots to be reached, the organisation expanded in the effort to produce them. The number of Town Centres grew until there were thirty-eight of them in existence. More and more Flying Training Schools were

---

[1] Proposed officially in October 1934, it was approved early in 1935. The scheme had long before been put before the Air Ministry, but rejected on the ground that such training would not satisfy service requirements. It was also again suggested by Air Marshal Sir John Higgins, Chairman of Armstrong Whitworth Ltd., and A. V. Roe Ltd., and connected with the civilian company, Air Service Training, to Air Marshal Bowhill (A.M.P.) in July 1934, but the definite proposal was made for other reasons by the Director of Training. Letter and Memo. Higgins to Bowhill, 17th July 1934. Min. Tedder to Bowhill, 31st Oct. 1934.

created to give more advanced training. But the course in these still remained only six months in duration instead of the nine months which was really necessary. The consequence was that the objective laid down by Air Commodore Tedder in 1934 was far from being achieved. At the same time a wider basis was given to the training establishment which it was hoped would facilitate the necessary expansion of the system when war came.

The great increase of pilots in the Air Force itself and in the reserve group necessitated a change in organisation. Training Command was overloaded. At the beginning of 1939, therefore, a Reserve Command was created to control the civilian training schools. There was much dissatisfaction with the method of administering navigation and armament training, both of which lacked centralised control and a centre for experiment and research, but little was done about these problems. The need of a further stage where more advanced instruction could be given was fully realised, but when war broke out the crews were still receiving their advanced training in non-operational squadrons of the first line so that fifty per cent of it was being used for that purpose.

These problems could not be dealt with adequately until the radical change brought about by the new scheme of training overseas. The Air Ministry were at an early stage aware of this, and by 1939 the basis had already been laid for the Commonwealth scheme which was to make possible the rapid expansion of the Air Force during the war itself. The delay in putting this scheme into operation was in no way the fault of the Air Ministry or, indeed, of anyone else in Britain. It arose from the political situation in Canada which had been even further removed from reality than that in Britain itself. Australia and New Zealand had for several years been eager for co-operation and done all that lay in their power to get a Commonwealth scheme into operation. But Canada held the key to the problem, and until war was close at hand she could not be persuaded to provide the necessary facilities.[1]

During this period the increase in the size and the range of the bomber aircraft necessitated the training of a crew. Hitherto a pilot and an observer, who was often a 'tradesman' with ground duties, had been considered sufficient. But as time went on three or four or five or even six different individuals, each of whom needed highly specialised training, were required to man a bomber and the problem became much more complicated.

Next to the skill necessary to fly an aircraft, the ability to navigate

---

[1] Mr. MacKenzie King took refuge in silence when the idea of setting up training schools in Canada was first broached. In 1938 he refused to agree to it, with the result that the question was raised in the Canadian Parliament. The actual agreement was not signed until September after war had broken out. For its effect, see Annex III.

TRAINING AND TACTICS

to the required position in space was a prerequisite of all success. In 1934 this was the task of the pilot, and it was many years before it was finally decided that it needed a full-time specialist to perform it. In these years all the thinking of the Air Ministry revolved round the pilot and for a long time the belief persisted that the pilot of even a heavy bomber would be able to navigate it. It was not realised that long-range navigation, and particularly so at night, required special training and facilities in the aircraft which could not be available to the pilot.[1]

Gradually, however, it became apparent that the pilot could not perform all the tasks expected of him. Some thought that the best method would be to add a second pilot, trained in both flying and navigation like the first. The first pilot could then act as navigator while generally supervising the flying of the aircraft, leaving gunnery and wireless to a third person. By this method also the morale of the crews would be strengthened and the less efficient pilots could obtain experience under the instruction of the captain of the aircraft. In 1937, therefore, it was laid down that medium and heavy bombers should have a second pilot, thus necessitating a considerable increase in the numbers to be trained. New courses were instituted for that purpose at Notting Hill Gate and Hamble. These aircraft continued to be supplied with two pilots until late in 1941, when the position of the navigator was at last fully recognised.

But some machines, such as the Hampdens, had no place for a second pilot. It was, therefore, decided that in these navigation should be entrusted to an observer. He had thus to be trained to perform that duty, but, because of the lack of facilities, at first only a short course was provided for him, while the pilot was still given the longer course. It was only gradually realised that the ability required necessitated such an education as often to make commissioned rank as desirable for the navigator as for the pilot. Eventually in 1938 it was recognised that navigation must in war be in the hands of an observer mainly devoted to that subject. The observer was still to be trained in bomb aiming and gunnery so that he might replace one of the gunners if necessary. But the training facilities were then reorganised to give the observer the longer course in navigation and his position in the crew was at last recognised. Only in 1939 was it finally decided that this system was to apply to peace as well as to war conditions.[2]

This was an obvious and sensible decision too long delayed.

---

[1] A course had to be plotted on a chart which could only be done while sitting constantly at a table with a good light.

[2] 'We have created an Air Force of long range and high offensive potential. If we are to use this potential in war and give full scope to its training in peace, a highly skilled full time air observer is just as much an essential as is any other member of the crew, not excluding the pilot.' Air Commodore Sholto Douglas (D.S.D.) November

Accurate navigation was a full-time job. It needed, indeed, as long a course of intensive training as that given to a pilot to teach him to fly an aircraft. It is not surprising that for a long time there was not a sufficient supply of trained navigators. The facilities for training them were quite inadequate. And a great deal of flying was done in the vicinity of the aerodromes or by a hit-and-miss method known in the service as 'by guess and by God'.

Meanwhile, it was essential to ascertain how to make navigation more accurate and to provide equipment which would enable a navigator of average skill to find a way to the target. To navigate at a great height when visibility was not good, and still more to navigate at night, a course had to be set for an aircraft as for a ship. For this it was essential to know accurately the direction and speed of the wind. This could be predicted but with doubtful accuracy. It was, therefore, necessary for the navigator to be able to measure the wind affecting his course and so to check his dead reckoning. It was hoped that he could establish his position by observation of the stars at night, while by day or night he could be assisted by wireless fixes from ground stations.

It was in the large-scale exercises that the weakness of Bomber Command in this respect were first most clearly revealed. But evidence continued to accumulate of the deficiency of the aircrews. Anxiety about this fact was increased because faulty navigation often caused serious accidents. Sir Edgar Ludlow-Hewitt was always specially concerned about this point and constantly pressed on the Air Ministry the need for better training in the Flying Schools and better equipment for the stations and the aircraft to meet the danger. But these deficiencies could not be easily corrected, and when the aircraft had to fly through cloud or at night they were still in 1939 unable to find their way with any certainty.[1] On 17th May 1939, the Air Officer Commanding 3 Group reported that Dead Reckoning navigation by day when above cloud could be expected to bring an aircraft only to within about fifty miles of its target.[2]

1937. Narrative, *Aircrew Training*. In the *Luftwaffe*, until soon after the outbreak of the war, the navigation officer, while, however, also trained as a pilot, was captain of the crew and took the decisions as to what should be done. In Bomber Command the pilot always remained captain, but in actual fact many of his most important decisions were necessarily made on the advice of the navigator until the target itself was found. There was much difference of opinion in 1937 as to the exact role of the first pilot or whether navigation should be left mainly to the second pilot.

[1] The Commander-in-Chief, Fighter Command, was consulted as to the best methods to prevent accidents. In reply he said that the problems of the two Commands were not commensurate. Whereas in twenty-four months Bomber Command had 478 forced landings due to pilots losing their way, in twelve months Fighter Command had only thirty-three cases. He attributed the difference to the fact that Fighter Command aircraft were lighter and that most of its stations were equipped with short wave D/F wireless. Letter Dowding to Ludlow-Hewitt, 23rd April 1938. Bomber Command flights were also much longer in distance and time.

[2] Report Thomson (A.O.C. 3 Group) to Bomber Cmd., 17th May 1939.

Meanwhile, in the last two years before war broke out much attention was given to astro-navigation which, it was hoped, could be so improved in accuracy and ease that all navigators would be able to use it. In order that the object might be achieved it was necessary to have better sextants, better calculating tables and modifications in many of the existing types of aircraft to secure a better view of the heavens. All these matters were taken in hand with great energy, but it was not possible to get quick results. Only one firm in Britain was available to make the sextants and the supply was for a long period very limited. There were also other difficulties connected with the supply of equipment and its use which was always a somewhat complicated task.

The training of crews in night flying was, indeed, obviously a difficult problem and it was never really faced in the pre-war period. In the first place it was impossible to obtain conditions such as would occur in war when no lights would be allowed to show from the ground. There were devices to simulate blind flying such as hoods over the aircraft so that the pilot and the navigator must rely on their instruments. But these were in short supply and some of the squadrons were not yet well enough trained to be able to use them when they were available. They could, of course, fly in the darkness over the sea, but little could be done by this method because the aircraft in the Flying Training Schools were not supplied with life-saving apparatus. Civil aircraft were now able to fly with remarkable consistency in most kinds of weather. They had the assistance of a directional wireless beam and their landing grounds were well lighted. It was, of course, quite a different thing to provide the same facilities for the whole of Bomber Command and they were often lacking. Consequently Group Commanders hardly dared to send up their crews on flights of any length at night or if the weather was not set fair. While all squadrons were required to do some night flying, only a small proportion of it was done in the dark, though it was generally recognised that in war time it would probably often have to be done.[1]

It was realised in the Air Ministry and Bomber Command that further aids to navigation were necessary. The need for the scientific

---

[1] After experiments in 1936 plans were made to equip a dozen stations with wireless beacons to assist landing at night or in bad weather, but nothing was done about it for a long period. As late as 1939 no aircraft of the Flying Training Schools was equipped with wireless; it was, therefore, essential that they should keep in sight of the ground in cross-country flights, and instrument flying could only be done in such visibility that the pilot could keep the visual beacon of his aerodrome in sight; otherwise there was a serious accident risk. The figures of day and night flying hours in Bomber Command were:

	Day	Night
1936	41,644	2,990
1937	129,794	8,773
1938	148,458	14,615

Bomber Cmd. Annual Training Report for 1938.

study of this and other problems was recognised, and at the beginning of 1937 a Committee for the Scientific Survey of Air Offence was set up under the Chairmanship of Sir Henry Tizard, which was meant to do for Bomber Command what its equivalent Committee for the Scientific Survey of Air Defence was doing for Fighter Command.[1]

Many different questions were considered by this Committee, but at the outset the Chairman drew attention to the problem of navigation and at its fourth meeting suggested 'that the possibilities of radio guidance of the aircraft from the ground had not been fully explored'. The subject was raised again from time to time and at the fifteenth meeting in July 1939 it was suggested that 'much was to be gained by using R.D.F. both for bringing the bomber into the vicinity of the enemy and for controlling the release and detonation of the bomb.' But Mr. Watson Watt, who was present, thought that it was difficult to proceed more quickly with research into such questions without holding up other vital work.[2]

In later years these ideas were to be worked out with results that were all-important to the future of Bomber Command. But at this time they could not be followed up with any energy. This was, as has been seen, largely due to the fact that the scientists concerned were occupied with other problems. But there was also a complete lack of direct connection between the Committee and Bomber Command such as had been established between its equivalent and Fighter Command. When their difficulties were filtered through the Air Ministry they tended to become less clear and less urgent.[3] The problems of the navigator were not fully realised by those who alone had the technical skill to solve them. No operational unit was set up for scientific experiment as it was in Fighter Command, and, as will be seen, this was urgently needed in order that these and other technical problems might be understood even if not immediately solved. The necessary co-operation between the scientists and the operational squadrons was thus lacking. The field was not fully explored.

---

[1] Its other members were Professor Melvill Jones, Dr. Pye, Mr. A. P. Rowe and Dr. H. E. Wimperis, the Director of Scientific Research. Mr. Rowe ceased to be a member because of pressure of other work and Dr. Wimperis went to Australia and did not rejoin the Committee on his return. Professors Fowler and Blackett joined the Committee in 1939 just before war broke out. A number of different officers came from the Air Ministry. They were, however, not members of it so that the Air Ministry might not be committed by its recommendations. Wing-Commander Saundby was nominated by the D.C.A.S. for this purpose and Air Vice-Marshal Cave-Browne-Cave also attended.

[2] Mins. of Cttee. for the Scientific Survey of Air Offence, 4th Mtg., 4th May 1937, 15th Mtg., 6th July 1939.

[3] The Chairman was fully conscious of this fact. 'From my point of view', he wrote, 'the Defence Committee works quite well. We know what is going on and we have some effect, at least I hope we do. I cannot say the same for the Offence Committee . . . But the fact is that no one seems very anxious to get our advice on these subjects, or to follow it, if offered. We have had no meeting for a long while and there seems to be no anxiety on the part of Air Ministry that we should meet.' Letter Tizard to Freeman, 8th Nov. 1938.

From 1937 onwards Sir Edgar Ludlow-Hewitt had pointed out the weakness of Bomber Command in navigation. He made a similar protest about the training in armaments, for it was generally recognised that bombers would be attacked not only by anti-aircraft fire but in daylight at least by enemy fighters. In 1934 there were three Armament Training Camps to teach gunnery and bomb aiming and an Air Armament School at Eastchurch which was meant to provide a central authority for questions of armament and armament training. The guns were those which had done good service in the First World War and they were still operated in the same way, either as free guns or mounted on a ring so as to have a wide field of fire. Since the First World War, however, the range of fighter fire had greatly increased and new weapons for the bombers were, therefore, needed. Some consideration was given to the possibility of equipping them with cannon, but in 1937 the ·303 Browning machine-gun was adopted, partly on the ground of its more rapid rate of fire. It was to remain in service throughout the war, with the result that the bombers were almost invariably outranged and outweighted in fire power by the enemy fighters which were gradually armed with cannon.[1]

Much thought was given to the method of handling the guns and giving them a clear field of fire. Here the Royal Air Force made a notable advance. For it was early realised that turrets would be necessary for the new aircraft with their higher speed and the field of sight much restricted by equipment. By 1939 power-operated turrets were being used so that Bomber Command was better provided in this respect than any other air force. The first Fortresses, for example, that were sent to the Royal Air Force from the United States in 1941 lacked this equipment.

But the technique and training necessary to make full use of the new equipment was not so advanced. No central gunnery school was established to explore its possibilities or to lay down a standard set of instructions for the gunners.[2] Their training still depended mainly on visits of the squadrons to the Armament Training Camps. In these there was a great lack of both capable instructors and the necessary equipment. Not sufficient fighter aircraft were available and not sufficient attempt was made to get Fighter and Bomber Commands to co-operate in exercises on which the future of both might depend.

---

[1] The Flying Fortresses used by 2 Group had 0·5 calibre guns and in 1944–1945 Bomber Command finally succeeded in getting turrets for the use of similar guns placed in some of the aircraft of 1 Group. *Harris Despatch.*

[2] Air Vice-Marshal H. M. Cave-Browne-Cave was appointed at the beginning of 1937 to enquire into the armaments requirements of the Royal Air Force. He proposed that an experimental establishment should be set up for this purpose at Orford Ness. The subject was also raised from time to time in the Committee for the Scientific Survey of Air Offence, but little came from these discussions. Mins. of the Cttee., 3rd Mtg., 15th Feb. 1937.

Only in the occasional large-scale exercises were they really pitted against one another.

For a long time the gunners were still part-time airmen with other duties on the ground. It was only gradually realised that this duty was also a whole-time job and observers were enlisted for that purpose and a special school was set up to train them. As the observers gave up gunnery for navigation it was seen that special schools for air gunners were necessary and that they must be whole-time members of the aircrew. But they were still mainly trained by short visits to the armament camps and the results were not satisfactory.

Nevertheless, many of the Western Air Plans were based on the assumption that Bomber Command would, even in daylight, be able to hold its own against the German fighter defences, and operational exercises were laid down for that purpose. How illusory this hope was, was soon to be proved in the war, but even before the war Sir Edgar Ludlow-Hewitt placed little reliance upon it. Thus, in July 1939 he wrote:

> 'As things are at present, the gunners have no real confidence in their ability to use this equipment efficiently in war, and Captains and crews have, I fear, little confidence in the ability of the gunners to defend them against destruction by enemy aircraft. Under these conditions it is unreasonable to expect these crews to press forward to their objectives in the face of heavy attack by enemy fighters.'[1]

Nor was the lack of offensive fire-power in the bombers compensated by any increase of defensive capacity such as could come by using armour. The Air Staff had been against the use of armour as it reduced the weight of the bombload. 'The idea of armouring aircraft for use in the R.A.F. has been definitely abandoned' it was recorded in February 1935.[2] When in November 1936, Air Chief Marshal Sir Hugh Dowding suggested that experiments should be made to find out how far the pilot of a bomber could be protected by armour plating, the Air Staff did not show much interest.[3]

In all these discussions there was no question of providing fighter escort for the bombers. The Commander-in-Chief had, as has been seen, raised the point in his letter of August 1938.[4] But no attention was paid to it by the Air Ministry. Their view was still as it had been in 1923, that effective long-range fighter protection was impossible. The resources to build them were not available, but even if they had

---

[1] Letter Ludlow-Hewitt to Air Min., 17th July 1939.

[2] Note by Plans Division, 28th Feb. 1935.

[3] Letter Dowding to Ellington, 2nd Nov. 1936. Sir Hugh Dowding explained, when his proposal was not very well received, that he was interested in it from the point of view of Fighter Command. If the German bombers were well armoured his tactics might be affected. Note on interview with Dowding, 23rd Feb. 1937.

[4] See above, p. 96.

been obtained, it was not thought they would be effective. If they left the bombers to engage in an unequal battle with the short-range fighters their charges would be as unprotected as if they had not come with them. The possibility of gaining freedom for the bombers by establishing air superiority over enemy territory by this means does not seem to have been contemplated by the Air Staff at this time. Since, therefore, gunnery was ineffective and little armour had been provided, speed and evasion remained as the main means of protection against enemy fighters.

The training so far considered was for the purpose of getting the aircraft safely to the target area. Then came the problem of finding the target and hitting it when it was found. In January 1934, a Bombing Committee was set up in the Air Ministry under the Deputy Chief of the Air Staff, and there was continuous discussion as to the methods by which high- and low-level and dive-bombing should be carried out. Bomb aiming received detailed treatment in the Manual of Air Tactics, drawn up for the use of the Commands. Exercises were prescribed and there were competitions between the squadrons for accurate bombing. As the speed and size of the aircraft changed and the range and accuracy of the anti-aircraft guns increased, the problem became more complicated and the experience of the First World War less reliable. What was clearly needed was a centre for experiment and research. The suggestion that one should be set up had been made in the Bombing Committee at an early stage, but little effort was made to obtain one until 1938.[1]

Thus, the Bombing Committee had to rely on the trials at the Armament Training Camps and theoretical reasoning. But the trials provided no tests for the identification of a target. They were often made at levels which would be impossible in war time against defended targets. They took place in daylight and in good weather. There were hardly any tests as to what could be done at night or in cloudy weather. Under these conditions some squadrons were able in practice to produce a high degree of accuracy. But in the large-scale exercises which approached more closely to war conditions, their deficiencies were exposed. When remedies were proposed and the relative merits of different forms of bombing were discussed, it was realised that there were not sufficient data on which to found reliable conclusions. There was great difference of opinion as to the methods by which a precise target could be hit either by day or by night.[2]

---

[1] The suggestion was made at the 2nd, 3rd, and 10th meetings of the Bombing Committee. Mins. of the Cttee., 30th May 1934, 8th Nov. 1934, 18th May 1936.

[2] At the first meeting of the Sub-Committee on Bombing Policy set up in 1938, Sir Edgar Ludlow-Hewitt said 'that the results recorded at Training Camps bore no relation to bombing under war conditions, and he considered that a definite effort should be made to try to get data as to the war probabilities of bombing.' Mins. of the Cttee., 22nd March 1938.

Nevertheless, the Manual of Air Tactics contained minute instructions on the various kinds of bombing, special attention being given to high-level bombing in daylight.[1] Most of this was necessarily based on theoretical reasoning since there had been so little practical experiment. The considered view of the Air Staff on these questions was summed up in a memorandum issued early in 1938 for the consideration of a special committee on the subject. They divided the targets into two types, (1) the 'precise' target, e.g. a power station, 'this', it was said, 'is our hardest task', (2) the 'target group', 'of considerable area in which are concentrated many targets of equal or nearly equal importance on which accurate bombing is not necessary to achieve valuable hits', e.g. parts of cities, industrial towns, distribution centres or storage areas. This was later to be called 'area bombing'.

Three forms of attack were specified:

(1) *High Level*, and the ideal was to hit a small target by this method. But it was thought 'extremely unlikely that development will ever enable us to do this'. It was asked, however, whether the situation could not be improved by some form of pattern bombing, by reducing speed over the target, by providing better bomb-sights or by using a specially trained crew to mark the target. Night bombing would, it was thought, not be of much use against precise targets and time might be saved if no attempt was made to train crews for that purpose.

(2) *Low Level*, where the average error would be much smaller. But the difficulties were formidable, e.g. the balloon barrage and the need for engines which could give as good a performance at low as at high levels. Yet sometimes visibility would be such that only at a low level would anything be seen at all.

(3) *High and Low Dive Bombing*. Diving from a high level was thought probably impossible in modern aircraft, but some form of shallow dive bombing might be employed.[2]

These questions were stated for the consideration of a Sub-Committee on bombing policy which the Bombing Committee had set up at the beginning of 1938. In addition to a number of members of the Air Staff, it was attended by Sir Edgar Ludlow-Hewitt, his senior officers, and Air Commodore Garrod who commanded No. 25 Armament Group. The discussion revealed great uncertainty on

---

[1] There was a new edition in 1937, with subsequent amendments until war came. It was supplemented by more detailed and technical information for use in the Armament Training Camps and by special Command Instructions issued from time to time.

[2] Air Staff Note, 8th March 1938. Sir Edgar Ludlow-Hewitt suggested that there was a fourth division 'harassing bombing', which would do much damage to the enemy by causing air raid alarms to be given and factories to be closed. Mins. of the Bombing Policy Sub-Cttee., 22nd March 1938. The Air Staff refused to accept this as a logical division and the D.C.A.S. wrote that if it were put in the Manual it would mean 'indiscriminate', but even in 1940–1941 a good deal was done and in later stages of the war harassing raids by Mosquitoes were an important form of attack. Min. Peirse (D.C.A.S.) to Stevenson (D.D. Ops.), 8th June 1938.

nearly all fundamental questions.[1] There was, however, no disagreement with the opinion expressed by Sir Edgar Ludlow-Hewitt, that, whatever the results likely to be attained, all pilots should be trained in precision bombing from high level. Low bombing, he said, might well be found to be impossible. 'Furthermore high level bombing had a definite educational value, e.g. accuracy in flying, accuracy in wind finding, observation, etc.' But Sir Edgar Ludlow-Hewitt also agreed 'that the bombing results likely to be obtained in war by the high level bombing method were such as to rule out this method as a quick and economical way of destroying the precise target.' The suggestion that a few specially trained squadrons should be used for this purpose was not well received. The creation of a *corps d'élite*, even if practicable, would, it was thought, affect the morale of the rest of the force.

Low-level bombing was much more likely to enable a precise target to be hit, if it could be carried out. But apart from the formidable obstacle of the balloon barrage, the effect of anti-aircraft fire could not be exactly gauged. Low-level attack at night was discussed and it was generally agreed that it was possible on moonlight nights, though the target might be difficult to locate. As for dive bombing, it was thought that modifications might be made in modern aircraft to enable it to be done, e.g. by the provision of air brakes. Shallow dive bombing had not been tested. It had been on the programme for some time but there had been no aircraft available for it. 'This lack of aircraft', said one member of the Committee, 'was the root of the trouble.'[2]

However that might be, it was clear that training bore little relation to what it was thought conditions would be in war time. Moreover, on most of the points raised definite opinions could not be given because of lack of information. What was needed was a Bombing Development Unit, which, as has been seen, had long ago been suggested by the Bombing Committee. At an early stage of the discussion the sub-committee decided to recommend that the urgent need of one should be reported to the Air Ministry.

The Air Ministry, however, did not respond quickly, and it needed an official letter from Sir Edgar Ludlow-Hewitt himself to move them.[3] A large and growing number of problems, he wrote, had now

---

[1] It was agreed that a deliberate slowing up over the target was not possible because of the increase of casualties if this were done. The D.C.A.S. in a subsequent minute refused to accept this judgment. It might be necessary to slow down, he wrote, in order to destroy a ship or a bridge and the risk must then be taken. But the C.A.S. wrote 'I do not consider it practical politics to *expect* a pilot to slow up in order to increase bombing accuracy. There may well be opportunities when it can be done but we cannot rely on them being available.' Mins. Peirse to Stevenson, 8th June 1938, Newall to Douglas (A.C.A.S.), 26th June 1938.

[2] Mins. of 1st Mtg. of the Bombing Policy Sub-Cttee., 22nd March 1938.

[3] But see *The Central Blue* (1956) by Marshal of the Royal Air Force Sir John Slessor, pp. 169–170, for some other relevant considerations.

to be referred to one service squadron or another. Some of them were of major importance and concerned the proper use of new equipment or the testing of tactical doctrines. But the work had often to be done by inexperienced crews because those more experienced were employed in training new crews. The result was that the solution of the problem was often long delayed or not produced at all. Amongst the subjects which needed investigation, he wrote, were the suitability of aircraft for various operational roles, the investigation of bombing tactics and bombing accuracy, the development of new methods of bombing, the investigation and development of ancillary equipment, armaments, signals, navigation and night flying, and intensive flying trials and endurance tests to determine operational range. He asked for an allotment of six modern bombers with the necessary crews and suggested that the new establishment unit might be located at Boscombe Down. 'I am convinced', he concluded, 'that the many tactical and technical problems of bomber operations which now confront us would be more expeditiously, more searchingly and more accurately solved if some such establishment were formed at an early date.'[1]

This application, which was strongly supported by the Director of Armament Development, Group Captain G. B. A. Baker, and reiterated by Sir Edgar Ludlow-Hewitt on 14th July 1938, was then agreed to by the Air Ministry, where it was pointed out that the Germans had several such units while, it was believed, that a similar centre existed in Russia.[2] But more time elapsed while the functions of the proposed unit were discussed, though the Air Ministry were now alive to the importance of the question. No range could, however, be obtained in Britain for this vital purpose. An area of twenty-five square miles was all that was required, but objections by civilian authorities were raised to all the proposals that were made, though the danger of war was now acute. Suggestions were made for putting it in the Middle East, but this would have removed it from the necessary contacts with the Air Ministry, Bomber Command and scientific advisers. Not until war had actually broken out could these difficulties be overcome. An establishment was set up in 1940 but it was not a success, for war itself was then providing the bomber crews with instructions to which they were more likely to attend.[3] Meanwhile, in-

---

[1] Letters Ludlow-Hewitt to Air Min., 30th June and 14th July 1938. Mins. of Bombing Cttee., 4th Oct. 1938.

[2] Min. Baker to Douglas, 8th July 1938. In 1937 the *Lehrdivision*, a Technical Development Unit, was set up at Greifswald in which there were special experimental units for each new operational aircraft. It eventually comprised eight *Gruppen* of about thirty aircraft each. It developed into a kind of air research centre to study aerial tactics while also acting as an advanced operational training centre. It seems, however, to have devoted most of its time to exercises for co-operation with the ground forces. Air Ministry monograph, *Rise and Fall of the German Air Force*, (unpublished).

[3] The full story is told in an Air Ministry file entitled Bomber Development Establishment—Formation of.

vestigation into methods of bombing and equipment was proceeding in the squadrons and in a number of diverse schools, committees and research establishments.[1]

Amongst others the Committee for the Scientific Survey of Air Offence devoted considerable attention to the question of exactly how the bomb should be dropped on the target. The question of the improvement of the bomb-sight was much discussed and partly as a result it was improved and simplified and experiments in more complicated instruments discarded. It was generally agreed that here, as in navigation, the equipment must not be too complicated for use by a bomb-aimer of average skill and intelligence. Several of their suggestions bore fruit in later years when it was seen that the whole success of the strategic offensive depended on solving such problems.

Another question of primary importance was that of obtaining such a description of the target that the squadrons would be able to identify it and to discover their success or failure in hitting and destroying it. For this purpose the camera was an indispensable weapon of warfare. The value of air reconnaissance for such purposes and the provision of the necessary aircraft, instruments and organisation had only begun to be realised by the Air Ministry when war broke out. The importance of photographic reconnaissance had been demonstrated in the war of 1914–1918 and it had been used in the construction of target maps for the Independent Air Force. But it had been mainly employed on behalf of the army, and though the Air Force took the photographs, they were interpreted and used for guidance by army officers. This system endured until 1938, though for some years Bomber Command and a few forward-looking officers had realised what ought to be done.[2]

The Air Force meanwhile had made great progress in the art of aerial photography, whose centre was the School of Photography at Farnborough. Such tasks as the survey of the Nile valley and archaeological sites in Britain and the Middle East had added interest to the subject. It was, however, not until the Italian crisis of 1935–1936 and

---

[1] The other bodies mentioned were (1) the Aeroplane experimental establishment, (2) the Royal Aircraft Establishment, (3) the Royal Arsenal, Woolwich, (4) the Air Fighting Development Unit, (5) the Committee for the Scientific Survey of Air Offence, (6) the School of Navigation, (7) the Admiralty, (8) the Chemical Warfare Establishment, (9) the War Office (for anti-aircraft), (10) the Marine Aircraft experimental establishment, (11) the Home Office (for A.R.P.). At the 13th meeting of the Committee for the Scientific Survey of Air Offence, 5th May 1939, it is recorded that 'the Chairman (Sir H. Tizard) said that he had been impressed for some time with the small scale on which research and development work on air armament matters was done in the Air Ministry as compared with the other Services. After some general discussion it was agreed that it would be useful if the Chairman would represent to the Chief of the Air Staff and the Air Member for Development and Production the need for providing facilities for armament research and development on a far larger scale than at present.' Mins. of the Cttee.

[2] This account is mainly based upon the Royal Air Force Narrative, *Photographic Reconnaissance by the Royal Air Force*, Vol. I, prepared under the auspices of the Air Historical Branch of the Air Ministry.

the mounting threat from Germany appeared that attempts were made to obtain secret intelligence of enemy harbours, bases and production centres by this means. Then, in response to urgent Admiralty requests, flying boats had photographed the whole length of the Italian North African coast and the island of Pantellaria. The French also had begun to take secret photographs of the German defences in the west and two British officers provided with a special Lockheed aircraft began to take part in this work. In the last months before the war it was extended to a photographic survey of North-West Germany.

Meanwhile, for several years Bomber Command had been pressing for the means to make photographic reconnaissance effective for its own purposes. Their representations date back to 1936 and the urgency was increased when the planning of the attack on Germany began in 1937–1938. The essentials were clearly seen. Photography had a vital role to play in three respects: (1) to enable the targets to be recognised, (2) to assess the damage done to them, (3) to find out by photographs taken at the moment of bombing which crews had successfully found their targets. The fact that this last task might often have to be done at night had hardly yet been faced. But Sir Edgar Ludlow-Hewitt had pressed the needs of Bomber Command with the same directness and assiduity as he had shown in other questions. He also asked for the appointment to the stations of intelligence officers trained in photographic interpretation to brief the crews before attack and to assess the result after it had taken place. He demanded insistently the provision of special reconnaissance machines.

The Air Ministry responded gradually to these appeals. Conferences were held and machinery set up to deal with the question. In it was a special section to interpret the photographs and a small one was also set up at Bomber Command and some of the intelligence officers were trained at Farnborough. The special reconnaissance machines were, however, not provided. They had not been designed and there was the usual dislike of specialisation. What should be done was shown just before the war by Flying Officer Longbottom, who saw clearly what would be needed when war came—a small high-speed stratoflying aircraft of long range stripped of all but the essentials, which the German fighters would find it impossible to intercept. A Spitfire without its guns and provided with extra tanks would, he suggested, serve the purpose.

Sir Edgar Ludlow-Hewitt, who put forward similar ideas, suggested that an aircraft might be produced which could be used both for photography and for harassing the enemy by light bombing attacks. But meanwhile he had to rely on the Blenheims of 2 Group, which were far too slow and vulnerable for the task. Little was done to provide the cameras for the bombers themselves to record the place in which the bombs were dropped. More than two years passed before the supply was adequate. Their absence was to have a most serious effect on the conduct of operations. At the same time the foundation was laid for the successful organisation which was to play so vital a part in some of the great decisions of the strategic bombing offensive.

The problem of illuminating the target at night had long been under consideration. From 1932 onwards squadrons had been allowed to drop flares over the sea, but only if there was an offshore wind which rarely happened. Trials over the sea were also no real guide to the effectiveness of the flares in lighting up targets on land. Nor were the flares themselves considered to be satisfactory and the best types could only rarely be tried out because they cost too much. Not much was discovered, therefore, about the best method of using them, but interest in the subject was stimulated by a report that the Germans were employing flares successfully in the war in Spain. The question was discussed at the fourteenth meeting of the Bombing Committee on 5th April 1937, when the Chairman, Air Vice-Marshal Peirse, the Deputy Chief of the Air Staff, remarked 'that the subject of night bombing was now, for the first time, before this Committee for detailed discussion'.[1] It was said that there was no squadron in Britain sufficiently skilled to carry out the experiments and that they had better take place in the Middle East, but the Committee refused to accept this conclusion. Group Captain A. T. Harris, the Deputy Director of Plans, said that his own experience made him certain that precision bombing at night was only possible if the target was marked, and suggested that it was necessary to procure a long-burning incendiary for this purpose.

As a result of this discussion further trials were ordered and some took place, but flares such as would be used in war could not be dropped, since their containers were large enough to inflict damage. There were also some experiments with parachute flares. But the final report in 1938 stated: 'It is doubtful whether final conclusions can be drawn with regard to the value of the flares as an aid to locating a target by night under war conditions, as it has been necessary to limit their release to the neighbourhood of an aerodrome or bombing range and in both cases the targets to be located were situated in familiar and lighted areas.'[2]

Exercises under these limitations were continued while a number of experiments were made in the Middle East, where Air Commodore A. T. Harris now had a command, under conditions which approximated to those of war. His conclusion was that targets of small dimensions could not be sufficiently illuminated to be recognised from a high level, while a flare attack from a low level was very dangerous

---
[1] Mins. of Bombing Cttee., 5th April 1937.
[2] Report Ludlow-Hewitt to Air Min., 14th April 1938.

for the pilot, who might well fly into the ground. Some of the essentials of this problem had, therefore, been clearly seen long before war broke out. What was needed was the aid of the scientists to produce better flares and a suitable area and trained squadrons to try them out. But this could not be obtained in Britain for the same reasons as prevented the formation of the Bombing Development Unit. The lack of suitable flares and the lack of experiment as to how they could best illuminate a target at night was to be one of the causes of the weakness of the night attack when it had to be adopted by Bomber Command at an early stage of the war.[1]

Finally, there was the important question of what would be the effect of the bomb on the target. Clearly different targets might require different kinds of bombs, whose ballistics and fusing might also make all the difference to the effect produced. Of all the targets the most thought was given to the attack on naval vessels. This was a subject of controversy between the Navy and the Air Force throughout all these years, and no agreement was ever reached as to the probable result in actual warfare, though a series of trials took place to determine the prospects of hitting a ship. Experiments had also been made to test the vulnerability of two other targets. Bombs were dropped on an aerodrome on Salisbury Plain round which aircraft and vehicles were dispersed. The damage was almost negligible and this experiment, as has been seen, exercised a considerable influence on the strategic thinking of the Air Staff. It showed, as the Commander-in-Chief, Bomber Command, pointed out, how valuable a realistic trial could be. Some considerable tests were also made of the effect of bombing the permanent way of railways both in the open and in cuttings and on embankments. They were, however, inconclusive and further experiments could not be carried out before the war began.[2]

Thus, though the Manual of Air Tactics contained minute directions as to the type of bomb and fusing required for a large number of different targets, these were mainly based on theory rather than

---

[1] The information on the subject is found in a file termed 'Trials of parachute flares for night bombing', though other aspects of illumination are also included. A memorandum of H.Q. Palestine and Transjordan, 1st February 1939, gives, as Air Commodore Harris states in a note, his own views on the subject. A minute of the D.D.Org. to the D.D.S.D., 28th February 1938, states 'I think you will find it impossible to obtain a suitable test ground over land in the British Isles'. The use of Salisbury Plain was, however, allowed under severe restrictions in March 1939, but not much could be done before war broke out. Memo. by H.Q. P. and T.J., Note Harris to Willcock (D.S.D.), Min. Leather (D.D.Org.), to Glenny (D.D.S.D.).

[2] Narrative *The R.A.F. in the Bombing Offensive against Germany*, Vol. I, pp. 34–44. In 1936 a small committee was set up in the Home Office at the instance of Sir Maurice Hankey to plan experiments to test the effectiveness of incendiary bombs against oil-storage tanks. The only occasion on which fused bombs were dropped on an industrial target was in April 1939 when a small number of aircraft attacked a derelict power station at Gretna Green. Lecture by Dewdney, Jan. 1948, p. 1. Some experiments were also made with the incendiary bombs which revealed their defects. For Mr. Dewdney see note on p. 473.

practice. There were those who were anxious to design larger bombs for the new heavy bombers and to experiment with different kinds of containers and explosives. The Ordnance Department of course made such trials, but practice tended to lag behind and new bombs had not come into existence to match the new bombers. When it is remembered how much effort was expended to get an aircraft over a target to drop a bomb on it, it seems surprising that more was not done to make the bomb as effective as possible for its purpose.

Thus, when war came in 1939 Bomber Command was not trained or equipped either to penetrate into enemy territory by day or to find its target areas, let alone its targets, by night. There were, of course, some crews which had reached higher standards of navigation, bomb aiming and gunnery. But the character of their aircraft and guns meant that it was impossible for them, however skilful and brave they might be, to face the enemy over his own territory in daytime. The Air Staff and the Commander-in-Chief already surmised that this was true for the majority of the squadrons of Bomber Command. For this reason they wished everything to be done to restrict the scope of bombing for as long as possible, and for nearly a year owing to Hitler's concentration on Poland and delays in the planned attack in the west this period of restricted warfare was granted to them. They hoped, however, that the Wellingtons and, perhaps, some other squadrons would be able to attack such objectives as naval units or coastal batteries in daylight without incurring crippling losses and that when they appeared, the more powerful four-engine bombers would be able to make further penetration into Germany in daylight. These expectations proved to be in vain, and during all the period of preparation there had hardly been any training for night attack. The Air Ministry had been unable to overcome the difficulties of providing the necessary equipment and instruction for that purpose. Since 1918 their strategy had been based on the conception that the next war could not be won without strategic bombing, but when it broke out Bomber Command was incapable of inflicting anything but insignificant damage on the enemy.

This seems a strange result after twenty years of devoted work. It has been easy to catalogue the deficiencies. But it must be pointed out that in no other country had the problem of strategic bombing been solved or even formulated. In Germany the *Luftwaffe* was by now devoted almost entirely to co-operation with the army and all its strategy and tactics were based on that conception. Though it possessed twin-engined aircraft, such as the Heinkel 111, the Dornier 17 and the Junkers 88, which were capable of reaching Britain from German bases, no strategic offensive had been planned.[1] The Italian

---

[1] Only a small number of Junkers 88s was ready by 1939. Some training had been given in 1939 for attacks on British harbours and shipping.

air force was even less capable of strategic bombing and the Soviet air force was at the end of the war still without the means of making such an attack. The French air force had at one time accepted the necessity of strategic bombing, but when war broke out it had neither the aircraft nor the crews capable of performing it. The United States bombing forces had been designed mainly to protect the American continent from naval attack. They were provided with a better bombsight than any other air force and trained for precision bombing in good weather. But they were no more capable than Bomber Command of penetrating into a strongly defended enemy country in daylight. Their machines in 1939 were no more able to protect themselves than the best British bombers and even lacked the turrets which the British possessed, while no long-range fighters were available to defend them.

It is in war itself that men learn how to fight—if time is given to them in which to learn. During the course of the war the United States, German and British air forces tackled the problem of strategic bombing by different methods which were evolved out of the aircraft available, the nature of the defences against them and the geographical conditions under which they had to fight. The United States was able for two years to observe the fighting of others. It obtained information which caused it to make modifications in its aircraft and their tactics which much increased their defensive power. But it did not discover its prime necessity, a long-range fighter, until it had received crippling losses in its war against Germany. Its acquisition of the Mustang, which did much to save the situation, was almost due to accident.

Germany was given a magnificent opportunity to overcome Britain when she conquered Western Europe and was provided with bases whence her bombers could fly deep into Britain with fighter protection. But she failed entirely to discover the tactics to overcome an air force which, in numbers, was markedly inferior to her own. The German air force, like the British, was forced to resort to night bombing and though its task was far easier in 1940–1941 than that of Bomber Command in 1939–1944 it was unable to accomplish it.

Bomber Command was gradually provided by the prescience of the Air Ministry in 1936 with aircraft that could carry a larger load of bombs than those of any other country. It took more than two years to discover how to drop these bombs on a target area as large as a big city. It took even longer to find out how to hit a precise target. Yet as the narrative will show, all these things were learnt, though at heavy cost. The Royal Air Force was always imbued with the spirit of the offensive, and before the war came to an end Bomber Command was able to carry out the strategic ideas inspired by it.

PART II

The Opening of the Offensive and the Transition to Area Bombing September 1939–November 1941

INTRODUCTION

DURING the first two years of the war Bomber Command was small, ill equipped and ineffective. Its front line in November 1941 consisted mainly, as it had done in September 1939, of Wellingtons, Whitleys and Hampdens, and the daily average of aircraft actually available for operations, though it had increased from just over two hundred in September 1939 to over five hundred in November 1941, was still no more than a fraction of the force thought to be necessary for an effective offensive. Moreover, if the rate of expansion was disappointingly slow, the rate of re-equipment was even slower. The average of 531 long-range bombers available for operations in November 1941 included only eighteen Stirlings, seventeen Halifaxes and thirty-one Manchesters. In many ways also, these new aircraft, and especially the Manchesters, were unsatisfactory.[1]

The small size and, by the end of 1941, the comparative obsolescence of Bomber Command was, however, by no means its only or even its most important limitation. The bombs which it dropped were in many cases inefficient weapons and the places at which they fell were often far removed from the designated targets and, indeed, from any targets. There was in Bomber Command during this period no effective means of accurate long-range navigation and none was provided until March 1942. Nevertheless, from the point of view of the strategy and the tactics of the much more effective offensive which followed, these were the two most important years of the war. In them, on the basis of trial and error, the foundations were laid, and to a great extent they were permanent foundations, upon which the whole structure of the mounting offensive was subsequently built.

At the outset, as will have been seen in the previous chapter, there existed a series of strategic plans for Bomber Command. They included schemes for the disruption of power supplies, oil production, transport and for a localised assault upon key industries in the key area of the Ruhr. There had also been much, if not invariably clear, discussion of the relative merits of bombing designed to achieve pyschological or morale effects and bombing designed to achieve physical effects. But those who had adopted these plans did not know how or whether they could be carried out. They did not know whether Bomber Command would be able to break through the German air defences in daylight or whether it would be forced to seek the cover of darkness. They did not know what targets could be found and hit. They had little knowledge of what physical effects

---

[1] From these reckonings Battles and Blenheims have been excluded because, owing to their performances, neither could be regarded as a strategic bomber.

would be produced if the various targets were hit and they had no idea of how civilian populations, and notably the German population, would react to bombing. There had, after all, never been a strategic air offensive before.

If, however, the Air Staff was largely, and to some extent even unnecessarily, in the dark about the course which the strategic air offensive would take, they were abundantly clear about two things. The first was that strategic bombing, that is the attack upon the sources of the enemy war economy, would be a fundamental and ultimately decisive element in the war, and that its potential should not be frittered away in secondary and auxiliary operations of a tactical nature. The second was that Germany possessed a greater strategic striking power than Britain and that Bomber Command should, therefore, be conserved and, as far as the front line was concerned, even contracted in the interests of consolidation, expansion, re-equipment and training. This consideration made acceptance of a period of limited air warfare a simple proposition and it reinforced the reluctance of the British Government to incur the moral odium of being the first to initiate a strategic air offensive.

The conditions of limited warfare were, however, sufficiently violent to reveal one fundamental operational fact. This was that Bomber Command could not carry out a strategic offensive in daylight. Between September 1939 and the launching of the offensive in May 1940, the force, therefore, turned to night action. The first and the most important lesson of the campaign had been learnt from what was no more than a dress rehearsal of it on a very small scale. Thereafter the strategy of the offensive had to be modified to accord with the operational possibilities of night bombing but these possibilities were only painfully and slowly measured and for too long a policy of day attack was applied to a campaign of night bombing. By November 1941, however, the process was almost complete and bombing policy had progressed through a series of less and less precise aims to that of general area attack on whole towns.

This development is traced in the first of the chapters which follows, but, as will also be shown there, the change in bombing policy was not due solely to the recognition of operational facts, though these alone did make it inevitable. It was also due to a positive eagerness, shared by prominent members of the War Cabinet, that the Germans should get as good as they were giving. In this, the initiative was taken by the civilian and not the service leaders. It will also be shown how the bombing policy of the Air Staff was constantly diverted from its intended course by the overwhelming defensive needs of the period which included the Battle of France, the Battle of Britain and the beginning of the Battle of the Atlantic. Bombing policy was, therefore, not simply a smooth progression

INTRODUCTION

from selective precision attack to general area bombing. On the contrary, it consisted of a series of sudden shifts of aim and of emphasis in only some of which was the logic of the operational facts evident.

These operational facts, or rather the stages by which they were discovered, are analysed in chapter four. Their effect upon the making of bombing policy and, notably, the compelling influence which they had upon the adoption of area bombing, will already have become apparent. There are, however, two other important reasons for examining the operations of Bomber Command even, and, indeed, especially in this primitive stage of their development. The first is that by revealing the limitations of the force, they also indicated the steps which had to be taken in order to increase its efficiency. Notably, they showed the need for the production of many more and much better bombers and above all they showed the necessity for radar and other aids to night navigation and for target marking as a guide to night bombing. Thus, the operational limitations of Bomber Command did not, when they were discovered, only curb the bombing policy of the force, but they also stimulated the production effort and the tactical and technical developments which in turn made more ambitious bombing policies possible later.

The second reason for examining these operations is the tendency which has grown up since the war to believe that the Bomber Command offensive really began in March 1942 or even in March 1943. This, from the point of view of the effects produced on Germany may be substantially true, but from the point of view of the efforts made and the risks run by the crews, it is not. Upon the conduct of these early crews depended the tradition of Bomber Command which by March 1942 had become well established.

This period of trial and error in the operations of Bomber Command was also one of testing old and discovering new methods by which its objectives could best be decided. In the fifth chapter an account will be given of the machinery by which the strategic objectives were determined, the nature of the industrial economy on which the attack was levied and the British estimate of it, the appreciations of the various target systems which were chosen for attack, and the estimated and actual results of the offensive. Many departments of the Government were involved as well as the armed services before the final decisions were taken at the highest level.

The results achieved were, as has been indicated, highly disappointing. But throughout this period there was always in the minds of those planning for the future the hope that Bomber Command would become a much more effective instrument of war when it obtained the new and heavier aircraft which were just coming into operation at the end of this period. Moreover, hope was never abandoned that methods might be found not only to deliver a much greater weight of bombs on Germany but also to enable them to be directed towards more precise objectives. Much of the economic argument was irrelevant under the conditions then existing, but these studies were to bear fruit at a later period when attacks on particular industries could be made with much greater hopes of success.

It was a considerable time before the real limitation of the damage done to Germany was discovered. Only towards the end of this period was an approximation of the real truth admitted by those directing the attack. But during this period great advances were made in the assessment of damage done, though the actual results, as revealed later, were still much less than was yet realised.

These first two years, in which the force was successively led by three Commanders-in-Chief, were years of great endeavour and at the end practically the only reward lay in the lessons which had been learnt. It may well be thought that many of those lessons could have been learnt and acted upon more quickly and therefore more cheaply. Nevertheless, at this time and for years afterwards Bomber Command was the only force which could and did attack Germany directly. To that extent it prevented the initiative from passing entirely into the hands of Hitler.

CHAPTER III

THE OPENING OF THE OFFENSIVE: THE MAKING OF BOMBING STRATEGY

September 1939–November 1941

1. The lull before the storm: September 1939–April 1940
2. The opening of the strategic offensive and the Battles of France and Britain. May–September 1940
3. The oil plan and the Battle of the Atlantic. October 1940–March 1941
4. The decline of selective attack and the coming of area bombing. March–November 1941

> 'It is in bombing, on a scale undreamt of in the last war, that we find the new weapon on which we must principally depend for the destruction of German economic life and morale.'
>
> THE CHIEFS OF STAFF, 31st July 1941

> 'One has to do the best one can, but he is an unwise man who thinks there is any *certain* method of winning this war, or indeed any other war between equals in strength. The only plan is to persevere.'
>
> WINSTON CHURCHILL, 7th October 1941

1. The lull before the storm
September 1939–April 1940

THE atmosphere in Britain at the beginning of the war was charged with hopes and fears of what might be achieved by bombing. Many of these hopes had found expression in the Western Air Plans. Some of the fears had been allayed by the development of the eight-gun fighter and the radar early warning device. Nevertheless, Germany had established a formidable superiority in air strength, and, so long as this lasted, fears were certain to remain as much in the minds of those who now had to take the initial war decisions as in those of the many who populated the crowded towns and cities of Britain. If, as had so often been predicted, the Second World War was to open with mass bombing of cities, ports and industries, there was reason to fear that German superior strength might be turned to immediate account. If, on the other hand, the great onslaught could be delayed for a time, then Britain would have less to fear and more to hope. Time would allow her to increase the strength and efficiency of her defensive Fighter Command. Time would allow her to start the great expansion of her offensive Bomber Command.

This expansion of Bomber Command would in the first instance mean a contraction of first-line strength. Instructors and aircraft would have to be found to train the recruits and work up the reserves. Most of these could only be found in the operational squadrons. A high rate of casualties in the remaining squadrons before the flow of recruits and new aircraft became a flood would not only endanger the existence of the Bomber Command in being, but might well compromise the future of the force. Bomber Command in 1939 was above all an investment for the future. The need to conserve and expand Bomber Command was, at the outset, second only to the need to avert defeat.

For this reason President Roosevelt's appeal to the belligerents to refrain from unrestricted air warfare was welcome and acceptable to the British Government.[1] When, therefore, the *Wehrmacht* turned east to crush Poland, the British were content to carry into effect a policy of restricted bombing, which, with the French, they had planned for this event. This meant that, while the *Luftwaffe* attacked only military targets, Bomber Command would confine its activity to attacks on

---

[1] The Roosevelt appeal was despatched at 10.30 British Summer Time on 1st September 1939. British acceptance was signified the same day. An Anglo-French declaration of approval was made on 2nd September 1939. A German declaration welcoming the Roosevelt appeal was transmitted through the Swedish Minister on 18th September 1939. See J. R. M. Butler: *Grand Strategy*, Vol. II, (1957), App. 1 (a), pp. 567–568.

Map 1

HOLLAND
GERMANY
Target
Münster
Dortmund-Ems Canal
Rhine
Hamm
Huls
Kamen
Soest
Rheinberg
Bottrop
Castrop Rauxel
Hamborn
Gelsenkirchen
Oberhausen
Dortmund
Homberg
Essen
Ruhr
Schwerte
Duisburg
Mülheim
Huls
Krefeld
Maas
Wuppertal
München Gladbach
Düsseldorf
Remscheid
The RUHR
Miles 0 10 20 30 40 50
SWEDEN
BALTIC SEA
Range Circles are measured from Lincoln
International boundaries shown as they were at the outbreak of war
EAST PRUSSIA
Danzig
Marienburg
Warnemünde
Rostock
Wismar
Poelitz
GERMANY
BERLIN
Mittelland C.
Spree
Magdeburg
Froese
Elbe
Oder
Vistula
WARSAW
U.S.S.R.
Posen
POLAND
Ruhland
Leuna
Leipzig
Zeitz
Böhlen
Dresden
Jena
Chemnitz
Schkopau
Bruex
Upper Silesia
PRAGUE
Bayreuth
Pegnitz
Weiden
Nuremberg
CZECHOSLOVAKIA
Regensburg
Danube
VIENNA
Munich
AUSTRIA
BUDAPEST
HUNGARY
RUMANIA
Ploesti
BUCHAREST
BELGRADE
Po
Danube
YUGOSLAVIA
ADRIATIC SEA
BULGARIA
SOFIA

the German Fleet and the spreading of propaganda leaflets over Germany.[1] The difficulty of defining a military land target, as well as the difficulty of hitting no more than the target, was so great that this seemed the most that it was wise to undertake.

This policy of restricted bombing was, however, a matter of expediency as much as of morality, for the performance of the *Luftwaffe* in Poland, where bombing was often indiscriminate, was soon taken by some highly placed officers to free Britain from the moral obligation assumed by the acceptance of the Roosevelt appeal. There remained, however, the evident wisdom of conserving Bomber Command, of averting for as long as possible German air attack on Britain, and of creating a favourable impression upon neutral opinion.[2] Thus, the opportunity of attacking Germany while she was engaged on another front was sacrificed. It was an opportunity which had not escaped the attention of the British Air Staff. Writing on 7th September 1939, the Director of Plans, Air Commodore Slessor, said, 'Although our numerical inferiority in the air is a most important factor, it should not be allowed to obscure other potent considerations. We are now at war with a nation which possesses an imposing façade of armed might, but which, behind that façade, is politically rotten, weak in financial and economic resources, and already heavily engaged on another front. The lessons of history prove that victory does not always go to the big battalions. At present we have the initiative. If we seize it now we may gain important results; if we lose it by waiting we shall probably lose far more than we gain.' Though, as Air Commodore Slessor said, 'Indiscriminate attack on civilian populations as such will never form part of our policy', he felt that it would be legitimate to attack the Ruhr power stations and oil plants.[3]

It was Air Commodore Slessor's duty to examine this question from every side, and his memorandum should not be taken as an indication that he or the Air Staff were at this time definitely opposed to the policy of restricted bombing. The memorandum merely recognised that certain military advantages might be lost by further delay. It was in no sense a denial of the dangers and disadvantages inherent in an early precipitation of full-scale air warfare. As Air Commodore Slessor presently said, 'One must think very hard before beginning the air war against industry'.[4]

The real importance of these suggestions is the conviction which they reveal that Bomber Command, even the Bomber Command of 1939, could inflict a heavy blow upon Germany and that Germany herself was a brittle structure. Nevertheless, whether German armed

---
[1] C.O.S. Memo., 31st Aug. 1939. War Cab. Mtg., 3rd Sept. 1939.
[2] C.O.S. Memo., 11th Sept. 1939, Air Min. to No. 1 Mission, France, 16th Oct. 1939.
[3] D. of Plans Memo., 7th Sept. 1939.
[4] Letter Slessor to Bottomley (S.A.S.O. Bomber Cmd.), 21st Oct. 1939.

strength was a façade or not, that strength would inevitably be turned sooner or later against the Western Powers. The immediate problem which confronted the allies was how to guard against this blow, but, as far as air policy was concerned, severe differences of opinion between France and Britain existed. These differences between the continental and the island powers had already been indicated at the Anglo-French Staff conversations in the last year of peace. Now on the threshold of action they were accentuated.

On 23rd October 1939 Air Vice-Marshal Evill went by air to France to discuss these matters with General Gamelin, the Supreme Commander, and General Vuillemin, who spoke for the French air force. He took with him a paper, prepared by the British Chiefs of Staff and approved by the War Cabinet, which he laid before the French Generals the same evening.[1] This paper was mainly concerned with the action to be taken by Bomber Command after the lull had become the storm. It did not propose any change of policy while the lull continued. '. . . for the present,' it said, 'the initiative is with Germany; our action must be conditioned by her action. It also follows that, so far as enemy action permits, we should conserve and develop our resources until the gap in numerical strength is narrowed. In particular, we should not fritter away our striking force on unprofitable objectives in deference to public clamour for retaliation or public criticism at inaction.'

'On the other hand,' the paper continued, 'we must not shrink from using all that we have got if enemy action against either France or ourselves looks like being decisive. In that event, our striking force must be employed at all costs in the manner that holds out the best hope of obtaining decisive results against Germany.' These were bold words. In effect they meant that when German operations looked like 'being decisive' Bomber Command would be launched on a full-scale daylight assault against the Ruhr, which was believed to contain about sixty per cent of all Germany's vital industry and a population 'which might be expected to crack under intensive air attack'.

Thus, the British view was that when the German attack on the West began to threaten danger the time would have arrived, not merely to take defensive measures, but to launch an attack on the industrial nerve centre of the enemy, which would not only hinder his further advance but which might even ultimately lead to his destruction and defeat.[2]

---

[1] War Cab. Memo., 21st Oct. 1939.

[2] At almost the same time Hitler issued an instruction to the heads of the armed forces in which he stressed the great importance of obtaining bases in the Low Countries from which to prosecute a strategic air offensive against Britain. 'The ruthless employment

All the same, there were difficulties about the Ruhr attack. Though the targets were carefully selected vital points, there would inevitably be heavy casualties among civilians, 'including women and children'. This action would, therefore, the British paper observed, have to be justified by some previous German behaviour of a similar kind, such as the unrestricted bombing of France or Britain, or the infliction of numerous civilian casualties during an invasion of Belgium. Air Commodore Slessor feared that this last proviso, on which he said the Cabinet had 'weakened', would mean delay and possibly the loss of the psychological moment for the attack.[1]

The French Generals, thinking in terms of purely military strategy and imbued with a defensive outlook upon the war, did not show any enthusiasm for the British proposal. They regarded the heavy bomber as merely a weapon of army co-operation. Ill equipped in the air themselves, they were fearful of attracting German air attack on France, and General Vuillemin regarded French industry as very much more vulnerable to bombing than German industry. General Gamelin was not hopeful that the Ruhr attack would cause any significant psychological effect upon the German population. Neither he nor General Vuillemin thought the attack would have any adverse effect upon the German advance through Belgium. General Gamelin thought the less bombing that took place the better would be the prospects of a French victory in the spring of 1940. Such bombing as did take place should, he advised, be directed against German columns of troops, military communications and aerodromes.[2] These, of course, were precisely the targets which the British had in mind when they said that the striking force should not be frittered away 'on unprofitable objectives'.

The French reaction caused consternation in London, where it seemed that Bomber Command might be prevented from taking effective action while the Germans occupied the Low Countries. Once they had done this the *Luftwaffe* would be very favourably placed to launch an attack on England. German fighter escorts would be able to reach London and a sufficient degree of air superiority might be established to make the invasion of England a feasible operation of war. At the same time a German occupation of the Low Countries would cover the Ruhr and might deny to Bomber Command the great prize upon which its eyes were fixed.[3]

Nevertheless, even if French objections to the Ruhr plan could be

---

of the *Luftwaffe* against the heart of the British will-to-resist can and will,' he said, 'follow at the given moment.' Memo. Hitler to Brauchitsch, Raeder, Goering, Keitel, 9th Oct. 1939.

[1] Letter Slessor to Bottomley, 21st Oct. 1939.

[2] Notes of Mtg. at Gamelin's H.Q., 24th Oct. 1939. Letter Gamelin to Evill, 25th Oct. 1939.

[3] Air Staff commentary on Gamelin-Evill talks, 28th Oct. 1939.

overcome, the operation would remain a formidable enterprise. A concerted strategic air attack on a first-class power was something which had never yet been undertaken. No one could say what would be the consequences either for the industries which sustained the attack or for the crews who delivered it. As an experiment, which it was bound to be, the Ruhr plan suffered from grave disadvantages, for it involved committing the whole, or practically the whole, first-line strength of Bomber Command to a surprise attack in daylight over a very highly defended area. The Ruhr attack would involve the Royal Air Force in a gamble for the highest stakes, for it was evident that the very existence of Bomber Command as well as all the hopes for the future which it represented were at issue. Such an action would require the strongest conviction that it was going to succeed, or else a most desperate situation which no alternative action could effectively relieve.

For a long time the Commander-in-Chief, Bomber Command, Sir Edgar Ludlow-Hewitt, though in many respects aware of the limited power of his force, had nourished the hope that the plan would nevertheless succeed, provided his bombers could fly across the Low Countries. Soon after the outbreak of war, however, the Commander-in-Chief began to reach different conclusions and thereafter the more he thought about the plan, the less he liked it. Writing to the Commander-in-Chief, Fighter Command, Sir Hugh Dowding, on 12th October 1939, he said that he could not measure the effectiveness of the Ruhr defences, nor could he predict what the Bomber Command casualties would be if an initial attack was made by a hundred bombers. ' . . . we cannot afford', he said, 'to contemplate losing a large part of it [Bomber Command] in one operation, however successful.'[1] Sir Hugh Dowding warned him that if he made the attack at low level, as was contemplated, his bombers might run into a balloon barrage, and though Sir Hugh Dowding optimistically added, 'Of course, if the German balloons are no better than ours, it would not much matter if you did,'[2] this was evidently cold comfort to Bomber Command, who were soon canvassing the probability that the attack would have to be made at high level.[3] Then, in December, Sir Edgar Ludlow-Hewitt was warned that his Blenheim squadrons might not be available for the Ruhr attack as they might have to be used in support of the French army.[4] Finally, and also in December, these sombre forecasts were confirmed by experience when small formations of Wellingtons, operating in daylight over the North Sea, were engaged by the enemy and very

---

[1] Letter Ludlow-Hewitt to Dowding, 12th Oct. 1939.
[2] Letter Dowding to Ludlow-Hewitt, 14th Oct. 1939.
[3] Memo. Bomber Cmd. to Group Commanders, 12th Dec. 1939.
[4] Letter Slessor to Ludlow-Hewitt, 4th Dec. 1939.

severely mauled. In two actions on 14th and 18th December no less than half the attacking force was destroyed on each occasion.

This confirmation of his worst fears caused Sir Edgar Ludlow-Hewitt to disavow the Ruhr plan. On 28th January 1940 he sent a new appreciation of the prospects to the Air Ministry.[1] This raised considerable doubts about achieving the necessary degree of destruction with the small force of about 170 or 180 day bombers which could take part. If the attack was made from high level the bombing accuracy would not be adequate, and if from low level the bombers might run into a smoke screen and balloon barrage. Casualties might amount to fifty per cent of the force attacking. Such losses, apart from the serious psychological effect, would reduce the efficiency of the force by eighty per cent for months to come. The loss of half of the crews from Bomber Command's Wellingtons and Hampdens would deny the force half its potential leaders of the future who might fly Stirlings and Manchesters. In his covering letter to the Air Ministry, the Commander-in-Chief concluded, 'In view therefore of the risks involved and the doubt which must exist as to the possibility of achieving success, I suggest the urgent necessity to reconsider the whole question and in particular to study the possibility of devising some other means of employing the bomber striking force to the best effect without committing the whole force to such grave risks of heavy loss as is involved in the plan under consideration.'

The Air Staff now realised that the only remaining justification for the Ruhr plan was a desperate situation which could be relieved by no other action. At a conference convened on 22nd February 1940, the Chief of the Air Staff, Sir Cyril Newall, ruled that the Ruhr plan should only be put into operation if a German invasion of the Low Countries had produced a critical situation. For other circumstances he thought it would be wise to consider alternative plans. The most obvious alternative which sprang to mind was the oil plan, which had been highly thought of before the war and which was now strongly supported by the nature of the intelligence, which the Air Ministry was receiving from various sources.[2] The conference agreed that Bomber Command should now make preparations to carry out the oil plan and should be ready to revert to the Ruhr plan only in grave emergency.[3]

The Bomber Command appreciation on the Ruhr plan had, however, set in motion an even more important revolution than a mere change of strategic aim from the Ruhr power plants to the German oil industry. It had begun the conversion of Bomber Command from

---

[1] Letter Ludlow-Hewitt to Air Min., 28th Jan. 1940, Bomber Cmd. Appreciation of Ruhr Plan, 27th Jan. 1940.
[2] See below, pp. 288 ff.
[3] Notes of C.A.S. Conf., 22nd Feb. 1940.

a predominantly day to a predominantly night force. There was for a time no clear ruling on this all important issue, but, at Bomber Command at any rate, the logic of events was recognised. On 8th March 1940 Sir Edgar Ludlow-Hewitt asked his Group Captain, Training, 'whether *night precision* bombing training is being sufficiently carried out, & whether the urgent importance of maximum training in this subject is everywhere appreciated.'[1] A few days later the Senior Air Staff Officer, Air Commodore N. H. Bottomley, wrote, 'in view of the changing tactical conditions which are likely to lead us more and more to night operations I think we need to stress the importance of maximum training in night bombing.'[2] The Bomber Command appreciation on the Ruhr plan had not failed to observe that the leaflet-carrying bombers which had been flying by night over Germany had been almost immune from enemy attack. This coming change from day to night, proceeding as it did from 'tactical conditions', was ultimately to have the most far-reaching consequences upon the whole strategy of the air war.

It was as well that these warning notes had been sounded, for the period of the lull was drawing to a close and the storm was blowing up. On the night of 16th March 1940 German aircraft made a bombing attack on the Scapa Flow area. As far as damage was concerned, this attack was of insignificant importance, but it was the opening shot in a bombing campaign which was presently to engulf nearly all Europe. The Royal Air Force immediately planned a retaliatory action, and on the night of 19th March fifty bombers were ordered to attack the seaplane base at Hörnum on the island of Sylt. This attack was the first ever delivered by Bomber Command against a land target. Hörnum was isolated from inhabited areas and was deliberately chosen as a target whose destruction would not endanger the lives of German civilians. Despite the claims of forty-one crews to have identified and bombed the target, photographic reconnaissance revealed no apparent damage and as a pointer to the possibility of night precision bombing the attack was not encouraging.[3]

This was not, however, the first warning which had been given about the probable limitations of night bombing, for ever since the first nights of the war, Whitleys of 4 Group had been flying through the darkness over Germany carrying leaflets and making, or trying to make, observations. The Group Commander, Air Commodore A. Coningham, had become aware of some of the difficulties and he had seen to it that they were reported to Bomber Command Head-

---

[1] Min. Ludlow-Hewitt to G/C Training, 8th March 1940.
[2] Min. Bottomley to Ludlow-Hewitt, 16th March 1940.
[3] Bomber Cmd. Report, 10th April 1940.

quarters and, in turn, Sir Edgar Ludlow-Hewitt had been passing on the information to the Air Staff.[1]

If the German defences were to make large-scale day attacks by unescorted formations of heavy bombers impossible, and if the night, which would protect the bombers from those defences, was also going to protect their precision targets from identification, then either sweeping changes in bombing policy or great technical and scientific advances would have to be made. In the event, neither was imminent. The policy of precision bombing still held the field, but the means to achieve it did not exist. Such was the state of affairs when, on 3rd April 1940, Air Marshal C. F. A. Portal succeeded Sir Edgar Ludlow-Hewitt as the third Commander-in-Chief, Bomber Command. Within less than a week, on 9th April, Germany invaded Denmark and Norway, and Bomber Command was drawn into the campaign which followed.[2]

The German invasion of the West had begun, and even if the air war was still restricted to purely military, naval and air targets of a tactical nature, it was becoming increasingly likely that its extension to the strategic sphere was imminent. Since their disillusionment about the proposed daylight attack on the Ruhr, the Air Staff had become convinced that the most profitable strategic target remaining to Bomber Command was the German oil industry. Intelligence estimates suggested that German oil stocks had been seriously reduced, and that if they could be further reduced, even by quite a small amount, Germany would find herself in a critical position. When the new Commander-in-Chief, Bomber Command, Air Marshal Portal, was asked on 28th April 1940 whether it would be possible to hit oil targets at night, he told the Vice-Chief of the Air Staff, Air Marshal R. E. C. Peirse, that if the plants proved to be as self-destructive as was reported, Bomber Command could do 'immense damage' with its existing force.[3]

Nevertheless, however attractive the prospects of a strategic attack on oil might be, and however successfully executed it might be, it was, relatively speaking, a long-term policy. Even if it could be shown that it would cause the defeat of Germany in a matter of months, it was not impossible that Germany might meanwhile win the war in a matter of weeks. An oil campaign would give no immediate or direct assistance to the security of the Low Countries, and it was unlikely that the French would welcome it, particularly

---

[1] Letters and Reports between Coningham and Ludlow-Hewitt. Letter Ludlow-Hewitt to Air Min., 6th March 1940.

[2] On 11th April 1940 six Wellingtons and two Blenheims of Bomber Command, operating under the control of Coastal Command, attacked the aerodrome at Stavanger in Norway. This was the first Royal Air Force bombing attack against a mainland target in the Second World War.

[3] Note of Air Min. Conf., 28th April 1940.

if at the time their armies were under hard and immediate pressure. Obviously the prospects of carrying out an oil offensive would be very much better if at the time the Germans were not threatening the allies with a decisive defeat. Yet the War Cabinet were more or less, and the French most certainly, opposed to the initiation of strategic bombing before German operations did look like becoming decisive. Thus, the Air Staff was placed in an awkward dilemma when the problem of writing a directive for Bomber Command had to be faced. In these circumstances it is, perhaps, not surprising that the directive which was sent out on 13th April 1940 was in parts somewhat confused.

There were, the Commander-in-Chief was told, two hypotheses. The first was that unrestricted air warfare might start without the Germans first invading the Low Countries, and the second was that it would start only after such an invasion. In the first case Bomber Command was to undertake night attacks against identifiable oil plants, identifiable electricity plants, coking plants and gas works, and any other 'self-illuminating objectives vulnerable to air attack', in that order of priority. In the second case it was intended 'to initiate attacks on vital objectives in Germany, directed in the first instance against targets in the Ruhr area in order to cause the maximum dislocation on the lines of communication of a German advance through the Low Countries'. The targets were to be troop concentrations, marshalling yards and oil plants in the Ruhr. These operations also were 'to be confined mainly to night action. . . .' This plan, for the second hypothesis, was numbered W.A.4(c), which suggested that it was mainly a communications plan, as indeed was stated. All the same, the directive said that 'The principal weight of attack should be directed against the oil-plants; the attack of marshalling-yards being confined to harassing action.' Neither plan was to be operated without the executive order of the Air Ministry.[1]

If, however, there were doubts as to the circumstances represented by the two hypotheses, in which Bomber Command would go into action, there were also doubts about what it would be able to do when it got into action. The plan adopted for the first hypothesis consisted of a combination of targets selected from W.A.6, the oil plan, W.A.5(a), the Ruhr plan, (the electricity and coking plants and the gas works) and W.A.8, the night harassing plan (the other self-illuminating objectives). Such a selection was of course a direct contravention of the principle of concentration so often enunciated by members of the Air Staff, but it was also a concession to realism. No one knew what targets Bomber Command could hit. It was a question of finding out by trial and error, and the Air Staff could

---

[1] Dir. Slessor to Portal, 13th April 1940, App. 8 (i).

THE LULL BEFORE THE STORM

do no more than indicate to the Commander-in-Chief the order in which he ought to make the experiments, and the circumstances which might vary that order. Nevertheless, it was significant that the plans for both hypotheses had two common factors. In both circumstances the attacks were to be mainly by night, and in both circumstances the attack on oil figured prominently in the instructions.

Meanwhile, the French High Command continued to oppose the British plans for strategic bombing. On 15th April 1940, General Gamelin told Sir Arthur Barratt, Commander-in-Chief, British Air Forces in France, that he was opposed to the attack on marshalling yards and oil plants or industry generally because the Germans would reply with a far more destructive attack. Sir Arthur Barratt told the General that he was living in a 'fools' paradise' if he believed that the Germans would refrain from bombing industry for a moment longer than suited them.[1] This fear of the German air force was not, however, peculiar to the French Generals. At an Air Ministry Conference held on 28th April the Vice-Chief of the Air Staff, Air Marshal Peirse, said that the German bomber effort would be four times as heavy as anything which Bomber Command could put forth. He thought it would be foolish to provoke such an attack needlessly unless Bomber Command could promise decisive results. Though Air Marshal Portal was inclined to favour the initiation of the offensive, he obviously could not promise decisive results. Thus, Air Marshal Peirse, supported by the Deputy Chief of the Air Staff, Air Vice-Marshal W. S. Douglas, was able to state the Air Staff view as being that no offensive operations should be undertaken before Germany invaded the Low Countries, or presumably, though he did not say it, took some other action which looked like being decisive.[2] In any case, by that time even the French had agreed at Government level that, if the Germans invaded the Low Countries, Bomber Command should attack marshalling yards and oil plants in the Ruhr under plan W.A.4(c).[3] Thus, it was left to Germany to strike the first blow. By the time the Royal Air Force bombing offensive against Germany began Britain was already engulfed in a life-and-death defensive struggle in which France was defeated, and in which the British Commonwealth was left alone to face the victorious enemy.

---

[1] Report on Gamelin-Barratt discussions, 15th April 1940.
[2] Note of Air Min. Conf., 28th April 1940.
[3] Supreme War Council Mtg., 23rd April 1940.

2. The opening of the strategic offensive and the Battles of France and Britain May–September 1940

At dawn on 10th May 1940 the German army, preceded and supported by the *Luftwaffe*, swarmed across the Low Countries towards France. Now, indeed, German operations looked like becoming decisive. The new British coalition Government formed by Mr. Churchill on 11th May was immediately confronted with the urgent demand that now at last Bomber Command, whose aircraft were already engaged in support of the land battle, should begin the strategic offensive against Germany. Four more days passed while the War Cabinet hesitated, and every day brought a still more critical situation. Any hopes that the Germans might apply a code of morals in the West different from that which Poland had experienced in the East were quickly shattered by the mass bombing of Rotterdam. This attack caused far less damage and death than was at the time reported, but it was obvious that the gloves were off. Within four days the Germans had broken through the French lines at Sedan and on 15th May all Dutch armed resistance, except for a remnant at Zeeland, collapsed. On the same day the War Cabinet authorised Bomber Command to attack East of the Rhine, and that night ninety-nine bombers were despatched to attack oil and railway targets in the Ruhr.[1]

Thus began the Bomber Command strategic air offensive against Germany. For many years it was the sole means at Britain's disposal for attacking the heart of the enemy, and, more than any other form of armed attack upon the enemy, it never ceased until almost exactly five years later Germany, with many of her cities in ruins, her communications cut, her oil supplies drained dry and her industry reduced to chaos, capitulated to the invading armies of the Grand Alliance. It was probably the most continuous and gruelling operation of war ever carried out.

Through all the vicissitudes of the tremendous events now breaking upon Europe the British Air Staff never lost their faith in the strategic bomber as a war-winning weapon. Yet the course of the offensive was repeatedly marred by conflicting demands and for years by the urgent clamour of defence. Never was this more apparent than at the outset when, before Bomber Command had become the master of any skill, it was forced to become the jack-of-all-trades.

---

[1] War Cab. Mtg., 15th May 1940. Bomber Cmd. Operations Record Book, 15–16th May 1940.

OPENING OF THE STRATEGIC OFFENSIVE

The *Wehrmacht*, fresh from its victories in Poland and Scandinavia, swept into France like an avalanche, and this time there was no miracle of the Marne. The British Expeditionary Force was driven into the sea at Dunkirk, Paris fell, and on 17th June 1940 France capitulated. During this time there had been little which Bomber Command could do to avert the calamity, and what it had tried to do had made serious inroads into the effort which it could put forth against German oil plants. As the Deputy Chief of the Air Staff, Air Vice-Marshal Douglas, rather conservatively told Air Marshal Portal on 4th June 1940, 'the strenuous and gallant efforts of your squadrons against objectives in collaboration with the land battle since the 10th May have not always had results commensurate with the effort exerted.'[1] On the other hand, most encouraging reports were being received from Germany about the effects of the first Bomber Command strategic attacks. Even those which came from what were regarded as reliable sources, suggested that big moral effects were being achieved and that the bombing was the first 'serious shock' to the German public.[2]

It was the constant wish of the Air Staff that as far as possible Bomber Command should be left free to concentrate against these strategic targets. They did everything possible to persuade the French that this would serve the allied cause best. In particular, the Air Staff wished to proceed with the oil campaign, for at the beginning of June they had reason to believe that if German oil reserves could be reduced during the next three months by from 300,000 to 500,000 tons, then in August it would be Germany's turn to confront an 'extremely critical' situation. At the same time, some of the difficulties of identifying oil plants at night were already appreciated, and on 4th June 1940 Air Marshal Portal was told that on nights when oil targets could not be found efforts should be made 'to bring about continuous interruption and dislocation of German war industry, particularly in those areas within range where the aircraft industry is concentrated, namely, the Hamburg, Bremen, Ruhr and Frankfurt areas'. Oil targets were to be the first selection, and aircraft factories the alternative. If neither could be seen, then 'any self-illuminating target or targets which are otherwise identifiable' were to be attacked. In case this instruction should be interpreted too logically, Air Marshal Portal was warned that 'In no circumstances should night bombing be allowed to degenerate into mere indiscriminate action, which is contrary to the policy of His Majesty's Government'. Nevertheless, these plans for strategic attack were subject to a most important qualification. The French Government and High

---

[1] Letter Douglas to Portal, 4th June 1940.
[2] Bomber Cmd. Intelligence Reports. There was, of course, little truth in these reports. See below, pp. 299 ff.

Command had appealed 'in the strongest terms for the greatest possible degree of British air support in the coming battle,' and it was 'the policy of H.M. Government' while that battle was joined, and especially after it had been found imprudent to send further fighter squadrons to France, that Bomber Command should 'give priority to operations in support of the French land forces'. The Air Staff thought that 'attack on rail movement and the dislocation of supply by the bombing of selected points in the enemy's railway system, such as marshalling yards' was probably the most effective contribution which could be made by the heavy bombers.[1]

Thus, during the Battle of France, bombing policy became a compound of the offensive against oil and the defensive against military communications, with the mounting threat of the German air force already beginning to claim attention.[2]

The fall of France confronted Britain with a case which was worse than the famous 'worst case' which had so often been the subject of discussion at the meetings of the Chiefs of Staff before the war. Germany now occupied not only the Low Countries but also the Channel and Biscay ports. The former might become the jumping-off area for the invasion of England, while the latter provided bases for German submarines from which to develop attacks upon Britain's life-line across the Atlantic. The entry of Italy into the war threatened Britain's communications through the Mediterranean and her security in Egypt and the Middle East. The position in the Far East also was already dangerous and precarious. If Hitler assumed that Britain would now rapidly come to terms his error of judgment was, perhaps, understandable.

Britain, however, as the Prime Minister presently indicated, had no intention of coming to terms with Germany. Already on 25th May, anticipating the fall of France, the Chiefs of Staff had prepared a review of the situation which would confront Britain 'in a certain eventuality'. They considered that Germany might be defeated by a combination of economic pressure, the bombing of economic and psychological objectives and the creation of widespread revolt in the occupied territories. In particular, the Chiefs of Staff concluded that the bombing of oil targets would be an important contribution to the defeat of Germany.[3]

Subsequent events have shown that this review was based upon optimistic assumptions and, in fact, presented a picture of Germany's war potential and Britain's ability to damage it which was far

---

[1] Dir. Douglas to Portal, 4th June 1940, App. 8 (iii).

[2] Min. Peirse to Newall, 19th May 1940. Dir. Douglas to Portal, 30th May 1940, App. 8 (ii).

[3] C.O.S. Memo., 25th May 1940. See J. R. M. Butler: *Grand Strategy*, Vol. II, pp. 212–215. The economic basis of this appraisal by the Chiefs of Staff was a report by a representative of the Ministry of Economic Warfare. See below, pp. 281–282.

removed from the reality. All the same, the review indicated a course of action which was ultimately to be an important factor in the defeat of Germany.

In British eyes, then, though the fall of France had indefinitely postponed the opportunity of engaging the German army in the field on the Continent, the prospects of developing an ultimately decisive strategic attack against Germany by blockade and bombing did not seem to be reduced. Indeed, in some respects, they seemed to be increased. It seemed unlikely that Germany and Italy would be able to balance their oil budget, and it was concluded that oil was 'a very weak link in the economy of the European system under German hegemony.'

However promising the ultimate outcome of strategic attack, and particularly an attack on oil, might seem, the immediate outcome of the war depended on other and more pressing factors. Unless the *Luftwaffe* could now establish air superiority over Britain, then the German plan for the invasion of England would not become a feasible operation of war. This was obvious to most of those in authority on both sides of the Channel. In Britain, though not in Germany, the struggle which was now imminent had long received the most constant attention and many preparations had been made. Much had been left undone and many problems had been left unsolved, but what was most important had been done, and the problems which were most pressing had been solved. Under the guns of Fighter Command the *Luftwaffe* sustained a severe defeat and Germany lost a decisive battle of the war. The margin of victory was, however, precariously narrow, and though no satisfactory plan for the employment of heavy bombers in the defence of England against air attack had ever been evolved, Bomber Command was inevitably drawn into the Battle of Britain as it had previously been drawn into the Battle of France. Already on 20th June 1940, before the battle had begun, Air Marshal Portal was told in an Air Staff directive that 'in the present situation, it has been decided that the primary offensive of the Air Striking Force must be directed towards those objectives which will have the most immediate effect on reducing the scale of air attack on this country.' Accordingly, Bomber Command was to attack aluminium plants, airframe assembly factories and air stores parks in western Germany.[1] Even so, there were members of the Air Staff who suspected that this was neither a hopeful nor a realistic policy. In the case of the airframe plants, for example, there was reason to believe that even the destruction of all of them would have only a temporary effect upon the immediate operations of the *Luftwaffe*. The destruction of a smaller proportion would, the Air

---

[1] Dir. Douglas to Portal, 20th June 1940, App. 8 (iv).

Staff recognised, be unlikely to have any important effect.[1] But the Air Staff directive of 20th June allotted six assembly plants as targets for Bomber Command.

Whatever doubts Air Vice-Marshal Douglas may have had about this part of the directive when he signed it, the fact that he did so may, perhaps, be explained by the urgent desire that Bomber Command should play some part, however unpromising, in the struggle against the *Luftwaffe*. It was also, perhaps, these doubts about the effectiveness of the attacks which led the Air Staff once again to deny the principle of concentration and to direct that, in addition to these attacks upon the aircraft industry, Bomber Command should also undertake operations against communications and oil targets, that it should continue sea mining and that it should prepare to set alight German crops and forests with a special incendiary pellet which was expected to be ready early in July. The medium bombers of 2 Group were to harass aerodromes in north-western France and the Low Countries.

But the Germans still hesitated before launching a full-scale attack on Britain in the expectation that she might capitulate. Meanwhile, variations in bombing policy were inevitable, if only because the majority of the targets given in the directive of 20th June could only be attacked in moonlight. Also a military invasion of England might be attempted at any time. Accordingly, on 4th July 1940, Air Marshal Portal was told that his first priority must now be the bombing of German ports and shipping. Attacks were to be made on Kiel, where the *Scharnhorst* and the *Deutschland* were reported to be lying, the docks at Hamburg, where the *Bismarck* might be hit, the docks at Bremen, Rotterdam and any other Dutch ports where concentrations of barges could be found, and the naval bases at Wilhelmshaven and Brunsbüttel. The sea-mining effort was to be increased to the equivalent of at least three squadrons. Attacks against the aircraft industry and oil targets were to continue, and though the directive suggested that communications targets should be dropped, the request from Bomber Command that a limited effort should continue against them was agreed to the next day. The medium bombers were now to concentrate primarily against invasion barges.[2] Almost immediately after this directive, designed principally as a countermeasure to invasion, had gone out, Germany began, not the military invasion, but the preliminary air battle, and the Air Staff once more reviewed their plans for the coming moon phase.

At the Air Ministry the conclusion had now been reached that 'attacks on industrial objectives have hitherto been too dispersed

---

[1] Air Min. Memo., 31st May 1940.
[2] Dir. Douglas to Portal, 4th July 1940, App. 8 (v). Air Min. to Bomber Cmd., 5th July 1940.

and that, in consequence, few objectives have sustained sufficient damage to put them out of action for any length of time.' On 13th July 1940 Sir Charles Portal was, therefore, 'requested to direct a greater weight of attack on fewer targets with a view to complete destruction rather than harassing effect.' To this end Bomber Command was now directed to concentrate against three target systems, the aircraft industry, oil and communications. At first priority five aircraft assembly factories and five depots were to be destroyed. It was estimated that approximately one hundred and forty 500-lb. bombs should be aimed at each factory to achieve the desired destruction. At second priority five oil plants were to be attacked. It was not thought that the oil attacks would have any immediate effect upon the performance of the *Luftwaffe*, but it was believed that 'the effect when felt will be permanent. Moreover, as your operations have shown,' the Commander-in-Chief was told, 'oil targets are very vulnerable and do not call for as great an expenditure of effort as factories.' There were thus only fifteen targets which were called 'primary'. In addition, however, there were also to be limited attacks against communications, including 'a determined effort' against an aqueduct north of Münster. Sea mining was to continue and 2 Group was to concentrate on the invasion barges.[1]

It became evident from the number and form of the directives which had been issued since May 1940 that the Air Staff in Whitehall intended to exercise the closest supervision over the operations carried out by Bomber Command. The general idea, as will have been seen, was that the Air Staff should determine the policy to be adopted and that the Commander-in-Chief should decide upon the means to carry out that policy. This, however, was a division of responsibility which had always been difficult to define in theory and, as it now began to appear, even more difficult to apply in practice. After reading the directive of 13th July, Sir Charles Portal felt that the Air Staff were not making due allowance for the fact that to a large extent the means must determine the end. On 16th July 1940 he told the Air Staff that he did not feel 'entitled to comment at any length upon the policy underlying this directive.' Nevertheless, he could not refrain from asking what could be the use of attacking five aircraft assembly plants when it had already been calculated that the destruction of nine would be unlikely to have any appreciable effect upon the scale of the *Luftwaffe's* attack. What was more serious and also more directly within his province was that Sir Charles Portal did not believe that his Command was operationally capable of carrying out the policy which had been urged upon him. Of the ten primary aircraft industry targets, he said, 'only three can be found

---

[1] Dir. Douglas to Portal, 13th July 1940, App. 8 (vi).

with any certainty in moonlight by average crews. Expert crews may be expected to find the remainder on clear nights with a full moon, and average crews will sometimes find them after a good deal of time has been spent in searching. Moreover,' he continued, 'most of these targets are so far East as to give very little time for finding and attacking them and then returning beyond the German fighter zone before daybreak.' Sir Charles Portal, therefore, expected to see a high proportion of the effort devoted to these targets wasted.[1]

Another serious disadvantage in the selection of these targets which occurred to Sir Charles Portal was that 'since almost all the primary first priority targets are isolated and in sparsely inhabited districts, the very high percentage of bombs which inevitably miss the actual target will hit nothing else of importance and do no damage, and the minimum amount of dislocation and disturbance will be caused by the operations as a whole.' This was a most important observation, and ultimately when carried to its logical conclusion was to have a decisive effect upon the making of bombing policy. It was, perhaps, one of the reasons explaining why Sir Charles Portal now once again urged that 'moderate and constant attacks' against railway targets should be continued.

In addition, however, to these objections to the particular policy of attacking the German aircraft industry, Sir Charles Portal also drew attention to the difficulties of carrying out a policy of concentration against any particular group of targets. For tactical reasons, he observed, 'a considerable degree of dispersal' is 'unavoidable.' Sometimes it would be known that the weather and visibility would be better in one area than in another and at others that visibility would be 'patchy in all areas.' In both these conditions, Sir Charles Portal said, 'alternative targets are necessary, if bombs are not to be wasted, and these alternatives are geographical in the former of the two conditions mentioned and local in the latter.' Sir Charles Portal did not think that this dispersal was necessarily a bad thing, for he believed, as Lord Trenchard had believed in 1918, that it 'largely increases the moral effect of our operations by the alarm and disturbance created over the wider area.' Here was another highly important consideration which in time was to exert its influence upon policy-making.[2]

At the Air Ministry some concern and surprise was felt at the criticisms of the directive made by Sir Charles Portal. The Air Staff felt that 'moral effect, although an extremely important subsidiary result of air bombardment, cannot in itself be decisive. There must

---

[1] The targets were: Rotenburg, Göttingen, Eschwege, Diepholz and Paderborn (Aircraft Depots); Bremen, Wenzendorf, Wismar, Kassel and Gotha (Airframe Assembly Plants).
[2] Letter Portal to Air Min., 16th July 1940.

OPENING OF THE STRATEGIC OFFENSIVE 151

be material destruction as a primary object. If there is to be effective and economical material destruction, there must be a strategical object as well as a tactical objective for our bombing.' The Air Staff agreed that tactical factors had to be considered, but, they said, these 'should not influence strategical factors to the point where moral effect is taken as the primary, instead of the subsidiary, object.' Strategically, the Air Staff still believed that power targets, which had been the basis of the original Ruhr plan, were the most desirable, but they recognised that tactically they were too small. They, therefore, held to the view that when their many defensive commitments could be reduced, a full-scale offensive against oil should begin.[1]

This was as far as the Air Staff were prepared at present to allow 'tactical considerations' to influence 'strategical factors', and it seemed to be far enough, for Sir Charles Portal did believe that oil targets could be hit and, indeed, that they could be 'seriously damaged by a relatively light scale of attack.'[2] Nevertheless, while the Battle of Britain lasted, the difficulty about the targets in the German aircraft industry persisted. The Air Staff understood 'that almost any reasonably large objective could be located and identified in bright moonlight. Factories on aerodromes would not, it was thought, be less easy to find than selected industrial targets in built-up areas.' However this may have been, Sir Charles Portal observed that the factories in question were not on aerodromes, but in woods.[3]

In view of the Air Staff attitude there were no startling innovations in the revised directive issued on 24th July 1940. The main object of Bomber Command's operations remained the reduction of the *Luftwaffe's* scale of effort. The ten offending targets, to which two more were added, remained on the list, and aluminium plants were once more restored to the schedule. The passage about oil was strengthened. 'Recent reports and information', the directive said, 'have confirmed that oil is the weakest link in Germany's war economy, and I am to say that the destruction of Germany's oil resources remains the basis of the main offensive strategy directed towards the reduction and dislocation of German war potential.' A longer list of alternative targets to meet Sir Charles Portal's wishes was also being prepared and was sent to him a few days later.[4]

All the same, and in spite of anything which Bomber Command could do, the full strength of the *Luftwaffe* was turned against Britain in August and September 1940. It was left to Fighter Command to bear the main brunt of the battle which was then joined, and it is

---

[1] Agenda for Air Staff Conf. sent to Portal 21st July 1940.
[2] Letter Portal to Air Min., 16th July 1940.
[3] Agenda for Air Staff Conf. pencil annotations by Portal.
[4] Dir. Douglas to Portal, 24th July 1940. Dir. Slessor to Portal 30th July 1940. For both directives, see App. 8 (vii) and (viii).

still, as it was at the time in the Prime Minister's famous words, to Fighter Command that the glory of victory must be ascribed. On 15th August, two days after the proclamation of 'Eagle Day', German air attacks by day extended from Newcastle to Weymouth, with aerodromes as the principal targets. In these attacks, which proved to be the heaviest of the battle, the Germans lost seventy-six aircraft. On the night of 24th August the first bombs fell on central London, and on the same night attacks were also made on Birmingham, Bristol, the South Wales area and Liverpool. Early in September the burden of the German attack shifted to the hours of darkness and London became the chief target. On 7th September and during the following night London experienced its first 'blitz'. The bombing was widespread, ranging from the dock area, where the damage was most severe, to Woolwich Arsenal, East Ham, Poplar, Battersea, Bermondsey, Paddington, Bethnal Green, Waterloo Bridge, Westminster and Dagenham. On the night of 10th September Buckingham Palace itself was hit.[1]

London was, of course, very much more accessible to the *Luftwaffe* than was Berlin to the Royal Air Force. Nevertheless, on the first night after the initial German attack on London, Bomber Command carried out an attack against Berlin. This was on the night of 25th August. Mr. Churchill, like many other people in the country, was now anxious that the Germans should get as good as they were giving, and he suggested to Sir Charles Portal that Bomber Command should henceforth spread its bombs as widely as possible over the cities of Germany. This idea did not yet, however, appeal to the Air Staff, who continued to defend the policy of selective attack indicated in the directive, which they believed was producing precision results. 'I think there is little doubt', the Vice-Chief of the Air Staff, Sir Richard Peirse, told the Prime Minister, 'that the reason for the effectiveness of our night bombing is that it is planned; and relentless until the particular target is knocked out or dislocated, whereas German night bombing is sporadic and mainly harassing.'[2] These words were written before the major attacks on London began. Nevertheless, they reveal Sir Richard Peirse's continuing confidence in the policy of selective precision attack, and his fear that Bomber Command might be diverted to purely psychological attack, which the Air Staff had already told Sir Charles Portal could not 'in itself be decisive.'

When, therefore, the Fighter Command victory in the Battle of Britain gradually began to become apparent and the invasion threat showed signs of lifting, Bomber Command was not immediately

---

[1] Record of attacks on London, September–November 1940, and *Principal Events of the Second World War*, 1948, prepared by A. H. B.
[2] Letter Peirse to Churchill, 5th Sept. 1940.

launched on a furious assault against German towns. Indeed, according to a rather optimistic memorandum from the Plans Division of the Air Ministry, the idea of indiscriminate bombing had little appeal for the Royal Air Force, because its crews were adequately trained to find really important precision targets. This enabled Bomber Command, the memorandum claimed, to operate on a carefully thought out plan in which every bomb dropped was designed to make a direct contribution to victory.[1] Whether this view was widely shared among the members of the Air Staff or not, the directive of 21st September 1940 told Sir Charles Portal that the disruption of German oil supplies remained 'the basis of our longer term offensive strategy'. The attack on communications was now elevated to a position of new importance and was said to be 'one of the most important contributions that our bombing can make to Germany's economic disruption'. Here, then, were the two principal offensive aims upon which the Air Staff now seemed to have fixed their eyes. But there were still the pressing needs of defence to be considered. The attack on the German aircraft industry would have to go on, though it was no longer necessary to aim for such immediate results. The growing threat of German submarines called for attacks upon their organisation ashore and invasion counter-measures would have to continue. There was one concession to the new ideas which were growing strong. Berlin was said to contain no targets associated with the major strategic plans. All the same attacks were to be made with the object of causing 'the greatest possible disturbance and dislocation both to the industrial activities and to the civil population generally in the area'.[2]

At Bomber Command these plans were hardly felt to fit the circumstances and the Commander-in-Chief would have liked to go a good deal further towards meeting the suggestion for the widespread bombing of German towns which had been made to him by the Prime Minister. On 11th September 1940 Sir Charles Portal had told the Air Staff that he thought twenty German towns should be warned by wireless and that each indiscriminate attack by the *Luftwaffe* on a British town should be followed by an indiscriminate Bomber Command attack on one of them.[3] Each of these retaliatory raids would be carried out by between 150 and 160 aircraft and over 130 tons of bombs would be dropped on each occasion. If it was thought inadvisable to give the wireless warning and so to announce publicly this policy, Sir Charles Portal thought that the attacks might nevertheless be made 'on such a town as Essen, the whole of which

---

[1] Air Staff Plans Memo., 20th Sept. 1940.
[2] Dir. Douglas to Portal, 21st Sept. 1940, App. 8 (ix).
[3] He suggested Berlin, Bremen, Brunswick, Darmstadt, Düsseldorf, Essen, Frankfurt am Main, Hamburg, Hanover, Kiel, Coblenz, Leipzig, Magdeburg, Mainz, Mannheim, Munich, Münster, Nuremberg and Stuttgart.

can for practical purposes be regarded as a military objective'. Alternatively, Sir Charles Portal suggested that a similar scale of attack should be aimed at selected military targets in the other towns 'with the knowledge that the normal spread of such a heavy attack would inevitably cause a high degree of devastation in the town'.[1]

After the issue of the Air Staff directive of 21st September, Bomber Command continued to canvass this idea of diverting the attack from the enemy's means to fight to 'the will of the German people to continue the war'.[2] These suggestions, both from the Prime Minister and the Commander-in-Chief, Bomber Command, raised a number of questions connected with feasibility, desirability and morality as factors in the making of bombing policy. It had always been evident that any bombing attack, save against the most isolated targets such as warships at sea or troops on the battlefield, would inevitably cause damage outside the particular area of the target. Though the limitations in the accuracy of night bombing were still far from fully realised, it was obvious that the Germans, even if they wished to, could not execute an attack on Battersea power station without endangering numbers of civilians living in the area. Equally it was impossible for Bomber Command to attack the marshalling yards at Hamm without running the same risk. If there was to be any strategic bombing at all, civilians would be killed; hospitals, churches and cultural monuments would be hit. The Air Staff, as represented by its Vice-Chief, Sir Richard Peirse, believed that what was inevitable was also desirable only in so far as it remained a by-product of the primary intention to hit a military target in the sense of a power station, a marshalling yard or an oil plant. Bomber Command, as represented by its Commander-in-Chief, Sir Charles Portal, now believed that this by-product should become an end-product. He believed that the time had come to launch a direct attack on the German people themselves. He believed that this course had been justified by previous German action and that it would be justified as a strategy in the outcome.

Operational factors had clearly exerted considerable influence upon this strategic conclusion, and in the course of time, as they became more fully appreciated, their influence was to be greatly extended. Meanwhile, a most important change of roles occurred, for on 4th October 1940 Sir Charles Portal relinquished his Command to become Chief of the Air Staff and was succeeded as Commander-in-Chief, Bomber Command, by Sir Richard Peirse.

---

[1] Letter Portal to Air Min., 11th Sept. 1940.
[2] Bomber Cmd. Memo., 30th Sept. 1940.

1. Air Chief Marshal Sir Edgar Ludlow-Hewitt, G.C.B., G.B.E., C.M.G., D.S.O., M.C., Air Officer Commanding-in-Chief, Bomber Command, September 1937 to April 1940.

2. Air Chief Marshal Sir Richard Peirse, K.C.B., D.S.O., A.F.C., Air Officer Commanding-in-Chief, Bomber Command, October 1940 to January 1942.

3. Lord Thurso (The Rt. Hon. Sir Archibald Sinclair), K.T., P.C., C.M.G., Secretary of State for Air from May 1940.

4. Air Marshal Sir Robert Saundby, K.C.B., K.B.E., M.C., D.F.C., A.F.C., Senior Air Staff Officer, Bomber Command, November 1940 to February 1943, and subsequently Deputy Air Officer Commanding-in-Chief.

3. The oil plan and the Battle of the Atlantic October 1940–March 1941

On Sunday, 15th September 1940, the German air force delivered two major attacks on London in daylight. The damage was widespread and hits were secured on bridges, viaducts, railway stations, an electricity power plant, public and business buildings, and the Royal Army Ordnance Corps Headquarters at Barnet. Buckingham Palace was hit and the King and Queen, who were in residence, narrowly escaped injury. In the evening it was announced that 185 German aircraft had been destroyed and the country knew that a great victory had been won. Subsequent investigations have shown that, in fact, probably not more than fifty-six German aircraft were destroyed. Nevertheless, a great victory had, indeed, been won, for though it was not known in Britain at the time, Fighter Command had brought the Battle of Britain to a victorious conclusion. Operation *Sea Lion* was postponed *sine die*. Hitler's confidence in the *Luftwaffe* had been destroyed. Britain's 'finest hour', which was also the hour of her greatest peril, had passed. On 30th September the Air Ministry told Bomber Command that the immediate threat of invasion had receded.[1] The time had at last arrived when it seemed that Bomber Command might be able to turn its principal effort to the purpose for which it had been designed, the strategic offensive against Germany.

The hopes of what this offensive might achieve had always been high, but they now occupied a singular position in British strategy. The Navy, as Mr. Churchill pointed out on the first anniversary of the outbreak of hostilities, could lose the war. The Army, as the Chiefs of Staff observed on 4th September 1940, could not re-establish itself on the Continent until blockade and bombing had, by wearing down the German economy, 'secured conditions when numerically inferior forces can be employed with good chance of success'. Only the Air Force, said Mr. Churchill, could win the war.[2] This was the responsibility which lay on the Air Staff, who now, under their new Chief, Sir Charles Portal, turned once more to the consideration of bombing policy.

The impact of the experience of the first year of war and the modifications which it had imposed on the Air Staff's plans were shown in a draft directive which was sent to Sir Richard Peirse, now Commander-in-Chief, Bomber Command, on 25th October 1940.

---

[1] Dir. Air Min. to Bomber Cmd., 30th Sept. 1940, App. 8 (x).
[2] Winston Churchill: *The Second World War*, Vol. II, (1949), p. 405. C.O.S. Memo., 4th Sept. 1940.

This draft had been approved by the Chief of the Air Staff but it was thought desirable to show it to the Commander-in-Chief before it was sent to him officially. Now that the invasion danger was at least temporarily over, the time was 'particularly opportune', the draft directive said, 'to make a definite attempt with our offensive to affect the morale of the German people . . .' It was suggested that twenty or thirty German towns should be selected, taking into account their size and the importance of the objectives[1] they contained, and that one of these should be attacked by fifty to a hundred bombers every few nights. Thus, what had so recently been no more than a suggestion from Bomber Command, now became Air Staff policy. Hopes were still high that the oil offensive might prove decisive, and, though it had so long been delayed by the need to attack anti-invasion targets, it was now hoped that a sustained attack on oil targets might be launched, especially during the moon periods. Without demanding any particular geographical concentration, which the Chief of the Air Staff, at least, knew was impossible, the Air Staff wanted Bomber Command to concentrate against these two 'primary objectives', oil and morale. They felt that decisive effect could only be achieved in 'the material and moral spheres by a greater concentration of our offensive air attacks' than had hitherto been practised. They wanted to avoid as far as possible any diversion from the two target systems, but they said that a small effort should continue to be maintained against marshalling yards, that there would have to be an occasional attack on submarine yards and a limited effort against German aerodromes in France. Though the likelihood of invasion had considerably receded, they suggested that new crews might gain experience by attacking the invasion ports.[2]

Sir Richard Peirse felt that that the draft directive asked more of Bomber Command than it could fulfil. He feared that, if so many targets were to be taken on, the attacks would become mere 'nuisance raids'. He had come to the conclusion that on the longer range attacks only one out of every five aircraft which he despatched actually found the target. On the short-range attacks, he thought one in three found the target. Thus, the effective striking force, so far as the primary target was concerned, was very much smaller than it appeared to be. Sir Richard Peirse, therefore, suggested that the list of towns earmarked for morale attack should be reduced to twelve,[3] and he was prepared to attempt an attack against one of these almost every fourth night, fitting them in between precision attacks on

---

[1] This was originally written as 'military objectives', but the word 'military' is crossed out.
[2] Draft Dir. and Letter Douglas to Peirse, 25th Oct. 1940.
[3] He suggested these should be: Berlin, Hamburg, Cologne, Munich, Leipzig, Essen, Dresden, Breslau, Frankfurt and Düsseldorf with Hanover and Stuttgart as reserves.

THE OIL PLAN: BATTLE OF THE ATLANTIC 157

oil targets. Nevertheless, he pointed out, the attacks on northern Italy to which Bomber Command had for some time been committed, would compete with these oil attacks. Sir Richard Peirse asked the Air Staff to acquit him of pessimism, but, he added, 'with twice the force, I would gallop away with your directive'. To attempt too much, he suggested, would be 'to fail all round.'[1]

Writing 'demi-officially', Sir Richard Peirse had painted a somewhat more gloomy picture, particularly in that part referring to the numbers of bombers finding the target, than he might have been prepared to present in an official communication. The Air Staff had no alternative other than to reconsider their draft directive. Nevertheless, the official directive, issued on 30th October 1940, showed remarkably little change in form or emphasis. The primary aim of Bomber Command remained two-fold; the attack on oil and morale. Whenever conditions were favourable, oil targets were to be the first choice. When they were not, heavy attacks were to be launched against Berlin or towns in central and western Germany. It was left to Sir Richard Peirse to decide the frequency of these attacks on towns, but he was urged to adopt the German technique of opening the raid with a fire-raising attack. 'Successive sorties', the directive continued, 'should then focus their attacks to a large extent on the fires with a view to preventing the fire fighting services from dealing with them and giving the fires every opportunity to spread.' Thus, the fiction that the bombers were attacking 'military objectives' in the towns was officially abandoned. This was the technique which was to become known as area bombing.[2]

A series of reports from agents and neutrals had been arriving during the summer and autumn about the effects of the Bomber Command attacks. Many of these seemed to point to the value of dislocating civil morale, and the extent to which that aim was already being achieved. In particular, it was thought that the initial attacks on Berlin had created a great effect, and at the end of October a most encouraging report about the situation there was received from the British representative in Belgrade. Although the attacks were said to be only 'sporadic' they were reported to be causing a daily fall in the morale of the citizens. The 'cocksureness which every German felt after the victories in Holland, Belgium and France' was apparently 'steadily disappearing'.[3] This remarkable news excited the approbation of the War Cabinet, and it was hoped that Berlin might be bombed as often as possible.[4] Despite this, and much other evidence to support the policy which had now been adopted of

---

[1] Letter Peirse to Douglas, 28th Oct. 1940.
[2] Dir. Douglas to Peirse, 30th Oct. 1940, App. 8 (xi).
[3] From Campbell (Belgrade), 25th Oct. 1940.
[4] Letter Douglas to Peirse, 30th Oct. 1940.

attacking German towns as such, there was no question of abandoning the oil campaign. On 29th August Sir Archibald Sinclair, the Secretary of State for Air, had given Lord Hankey, its principal exponent, an assurance 'that we regard the destruction of Germany's oil sources as the foundation of our major strategy which aims at the reduction of the German war potential; and we shall continue to attack oil stocks in Germany on all possible occasions'. The crux of this assurance was, of course, contained in the words 'on all possible occasions'.[1] The number of these 'possible occasions' was limited by the strategic desirability of attacking other targets such as German towns, marshalling yards or targets in Italy. It was also limited by the operational consideration that it was not thought possible to hit precise targets like oil plants except in certain conditions of moonlight and weather. In case, however, the directive of 30th October might have created the impression that the Air Staff were imposing too great a strategic or voluntary limitation on the number of 'possible occasions', Air Vice-Marshal Douglas, 'to avoid possible confusion or misunderstanding', told Sir Richard Peirse on 10th November that his 'only primary targets in the strict sense of the term should be those in the Oil Plan. All other objectives should be regarded as secondary'. These secondary targets were only to be attacked 'when, for tactical or geographical reasons, you do not consider it is either possible or profitable to select objectives in the Oil Plan.'[2]

These 'tactical or geographical reasons' constituted the involuntary limitation upon the number of 'possible occasions' on which oil attacks could be made. On the other occasions, unless it was to be idle, Bomber Command would have to seek other and larger targets. The oil plan was, therefore, always something less than the whole design of the bombing offensive. That the oil plan might, nevertheless, be the most important part of that design had, in the strategic sphere, long been suggested by the intelligence about the German oil position presented to the Government and Air Staff by Lord Hankey and Mr. Geoffrey Lloyd. In the operational sphere, this conclusion was strongly supported by the estimates which were now being made of what had been achieved by the oil campaign since May 1940.

This campaign had extended over a period when there were many factors other than operational or geographical which tended to disperse the Bomber Command effort and reduce the concentration against oil plants. Nevertheless, the various experts on oil had apparently demonstrated the success of the attacks and also the precarious-

---

[1] Letter Sinclair to Hankey, 29th Aug. 1940.
[2] Dir. Douglas to Peirse, 10th Nov. 1940, App. 8 (xii).

ness of the German position. The amount of oil production thought to have been destroyed was not, in itself, great, but in relation to the effort devoted to the object it was impressive. Reporting for the War Cabinet in December, the Lloyd Committee made the point that a fifteen per cent reduction in synthetic oil output had been achieved by the expenditure of only 539 tons of bombs or, in other words, no more than 6·7 per cent of the total effort expended by Bomber Command against industrial targets, communications and invasion ports. In addition, however, to placing the estimated achievement of Bomber Command in the oil campaign in this light, the Lloyd Committee also pointed out that the oil position in Axis-controlled Europe was in any case deteriorating rapidly.[1]

This report made an immediate and a profound impression upon the Air Staff, and Sir Charles Portal lost little time in laying a memorandum before the Chiefs of Staff Committee outlining the part which he believed Bomber Command could play in establishing the 'quick death clinch' of which the report had spoken. In this memorandum the Chief of the Air Staff argued that if the seventeen major synthetic oil plants in Germany could be destroyed, then the Axis would, within six months, lose a potential production of nearly one and a half million tons of oil. Such a loss, even though it would leave the Rumanian supplies uninterrupted, would, in the context of the Lloyd report, be a heavy and possibly a fatal blow to Germany. Also, other means might be found of dealing with the Rumanian problem which was largely beyond the competence of Bomber Command. Sir Charles Portal thought that Bomber Command could, in fact, destroy these seventeen targets. 'Assuming that we can hope for an average of nine clear nights a month,' he told his colleagues, 'this entails the employment of a minimum of 95 sorties on each of these nights, i.e., 855 sorties per month and 3,420 sorties in four months. On the basis of the present strength of our bomber force this effort should be within our capabilities.'[2]

---

[1] Lloyd Committee 5th Report, 16th Dec. 1940. The Lloyd Committee referred to the estimate as 'very tentative and preliminary' but it accepted the figure of fifteen per cent as the reduction caused and said that 'on a conservative basis' it was not likely to be less. See p. 290.

[2] Memo. by Portal, 29th Dec. 1940. The conclusion was reached by the following calculation:

'1. Number of synthetic oil plants—17.

2. *Number of sorties required to destroy all 17 plants.*

(a) Number of *aimed* bombs calculated to be necessary to put one plant out of action for four months—400 × 500 lb. bombs.
(b) Average number of heavy bombers required to carry 400 × 500 lb. bombs—100 a/c.
(c) Number of sorties to be detailed for the attack of one plant, *assuming 50% of those detailed fail to attack their primary target*—200 sorties.
(d) Number of sorties to be detailed for the attack of all 17 plants—3,400 sorties.

3. Thus, every four months we must employ a total of 3,400 sorties in the attack of German synthetic oil plants.'

On the evidence of strategic desirability presented by Mr. Lloyd and that of operational feasibility presented by Sir Charles Portal, the Chiefs of Staff decided to press upon the Cabinet the adoption of the oil campaign as the sole primary aim of Bomber Command during the following six months. The secondary aim, they suggested, should be the destruction of German morale, which could be directly sought when the conditions for oil attacks were unfavourable. They agreed to suggest that the only diversions from this policy should be the attack on invasion ports in the event of invasion becoming again imminent, or naval forces when good opportunities occurred. Thus, the Chiefs of Staff, reporting on 7th January 1941, hoped that the Cabinet would give official sanction to the policy which the Air Staff had already substantially proclaimed in their supplementary directive of 10th November 1940.

Nevertheless, though the lines of bombing policy were beginning to emerge in some clarity, there were still many conflicting views, and, in their report, the Chiefs of Staff found it advisable not only to argue the case for the oil plan, but also to argue that against alternative plans, or a combination of them. The diversity of targets generally allotted to Bomber Command had, the Chiefs of Staff said, 'seriously diminished' the effectiveness of the offensive. They, therefore, strongly favoured the selection of one primary aim without material diversion from it. This brought them to a consideration of the various aims which might be adopted. The attack on the German aircraft industry seemed unprofitable because of the extent to which the targets were dispersed. The once hopeful prospect of affecting aircraft production by attacks on aluminium supply had been greatly reduced by the German acquisition of French resources. The best way of affecting the German air force was by attacking oil. Bombing as a counter-measure to invasion was not, the Chiefs of Staff pointed out, an offensive policy, and was only relevant when the danger of invasion was imminent, which was not the case in January 1941. They thought that transport offered an excellent target and that attack upon it might be one of the most important contributions which bombing could make to economic disruption. Marshalling yards would always be profitable alternative targets, but, in the opinion of the Chiefs of Staff, Bomber Command was not yet large enough to undertake a sustained attack on transport as its primary aim. Though industry in general might be brought practically to a standstill by selective attacks upon key points in the gas and electricity supply, these targets were not suitable for night attack and Bomber Command could not operate by day. German morale was, the Chiefs of Staff believed, weaker than British and they thought it possible that attacks on German towns might produce a quick collapse. On the other hand, they pointed out, this kind of attack might not be nearly so effective as expected. The Nazi government would be prepared for this kind of attack and its consequences, there was a very great area to cover and the effects were, in the British experience, liable to be only temporary. Bomber Command was not large enough to undertake as its primary aim such a big operation. Naval targets were very difficult to hit because they were either moving at sea or heavily defended in port. Submarine construction yards were widely dispersed and small in size.

Such were the arguments which could be marshalled in favour of concentrating on one primary aim and against selecting any alternative to oil as that primary aim. In favour of selecting oil, the Chiefs of Staff felt justified in concluding on the basis of the Lloyd report, that although the stoppage of Rumanian supplies would be the biggest single blow which could be struck at the enemy, 'the destruction of his synthetic oil plants in Germany alone would bring about a crisis'.[1] On the basis of Sir Charles Portal's memorandum, the Chiefs of Staff were justified in saying that the seventeen major synthetic plants in Germany could be destroyed in four months.[2]

A unanimous report of this kind by the Chiefs of Staff was certain to be extremely influential and it was endorsed by the Defence Committee of the War Cabinet on 13th January 1941.[3] Even so, some members of the Government and, notably, the Prime Minister himself were far from wholly satisfied with the policy which had been adopted. There was a growing feeling, inspired by what the *Luftwaffe* had done to British towns, that Bomber Command should become more ruthless in its reply to what was regarded as the German method of total war. Britain should give at least as good as she was getting. Bomber Command should turn the focus of its attack not on to specific targets, such as oil plants, but on to whole German towns. Moreover, the Prime Minister was sceptical of cut-and-dried calculations which showed how the war could infallibly be won. He still remembered the detailed arguments with which the Air Staff had supported the earlier Ruhr plan, and, though he was told that the new oil plan was based upon actual experience of war operations which had not been available when the Ruhr plan was made, he was still extremely doubtful whether its execution would lead to any significant success. He also regretted that oil plants were for the most part far removed from centres of population.

---

[1] This was, in fact, going further than the Lloyd report had done. In the Defence Committee discussion of this paper on 13th January 1941, Mr. Lloyd again made the point that the Royal Air Force alone could not carry the campaign to fruition. Sabotage in Rumania, he said, also vital. Defence Cttee. Mtg., 13th Jan. 1941.

[2] C.O.S. Memo., 7th Jan. 1941. App. 9.

[3] Defence Cttee. Mtg., 13th Jan. 1941.

The increasing insistence of the Prime Minister and of members of his government on a more ruthless bombing policy, and Mr. Churchill's surviving scepticism of precisely calculated bombing programmes, were soon to become factors of great importance in the development of the offensive, but in the meantime the Air Staff was empowered to write a directive of a much more restricted kind. On 15th January 1941 the Vice-Chief of the Air Staff, Sir Wilfrid Freeman, signed the most pungent directive which had yet gone to Bomber Command. Sir Richard Peirse was told 'that the sole primary aim of your bomber offensive, until further orders, should be the destruction of the German synthetic oil plants'. It was to be his 'principal object to ensure the destruction of these 17 plants[1] by concentrating your offensive against them to the greatest possible extent that tactical and weather conditions permit, giving such priority as may be tactically possible to the 9 larger plants'.[2]

When these 'tactical and weather conditions' made it impossible to attack the oil plants, Sir Richard Peirse was to direct the offensive 'towards harassing the enemy's main industrial towns and communications', and these attacks were to include 'periodically heavy concentrations against the former to maintain the fear of attack'. Even so it was hoped that this part of the policy might contribute to the oil plan, and it was suggested that Magdeburg, Hanover, Bremen and Oppau, towns associated with the oil industry, should be put on the list. As the Chiefs of Staff had agreed, the only diversions were to be against invasion ports, if the need arose, or against naval forces on special instructions.[3]

Thus, within three months of assuming the leadership of the Air Staff, Sir Charles Portal, who had so recently been arguing the merits of an offensive against the German people in their towns, and the inevitability and even desirability of a wide dispersion of the offensive, had put through a policy of concentrated precision attack against a target system many of whose targets were removed from centres of population. It is true that the plan for attack on German morale had not been abandoned. The destruction of towns was, in the terms of the directive, the tactical alternative to the bombing of oil plants. There would still be many occasions, therefore, when the main weight of the Bomber Command attack would fall on German towns as, on the night of 16th December 1940, it had fallen

---

[1] They were, in order of priority: Leuna, Pölitz, Gelsenkirchen (Nordstern), Zeitz, Scholven Buer, Ruhland, Böhlen, Magdeburg, Lützkendorf, Sterkrade Holten, Homberg, Kamen, Wanne Eickel, Bottrop, Dortmund, Castrop Rauxel and Brüx.

[2] These were the first nine on the list and, according to the Chiefs of Staff memorandum of 7th January 1941, they accounted for eighty-three per cent of home production. Later in the year, Lord Hankey observed that 'this figure is an exaggeration.' Memo. for C.O.S., 15th July 1941, App. 12.

[3] Dir. Freeman to Peirse, 15th Jan. 1941, App. 8 (xiii).

THE OIL PLAN: BATTLE OF THE ATLANTIC

on Mannheim in an 'area' attack carried out as a retaliation for German raids on Coventry and Southampton. It is also true that Sir Charles Portal had always been a strong believer in the oil policy. Nevertheless, these swift changes in the emphasis which was accorded to the selective attack on oil and other targets as compared with the 'area' attack on towns reflected something more than a changing strategic situation. They also reflected uncertainties about operational possibilities and indicated the extent to which the Air Staff still lacked actual experience of night operations to guide their decisions.

Now, on 13th January 1941, Sir Charles Portal had assured the Prime Minister that the oil plan, unlike the Ruhr plan, was founded on actual experience of night operations. On 17th January Sir Richard Peirse, speaking of the new oil directive, had told Sir Charles Portal that he was 'confident we shall be able to do what is necessary', and he added that he thought none of his crews would 'enjoy finding themselves one of a small minority who fails to get through to the target.'[1] Yet the evidence which was to hand about night bombing operations, though still far from complete and to some extent apparently conflicting, so far from according support to these extremely confident conclusions, seemed to suggest that they were largely baseless. The night attack against Hörnum carried out in March 1940 had yielded very disappointing and inaccurate results. Hörnum, being on a small island, was a great deal easier to find than the ordinary inland target. The moonlight attack against Mannheim in the middle of December 1940 had shown considerable inaccuracy and a failure to concentrate the bombs in the middle of the town. Mannheim was a very much larger target than any oil plant. The evidence about both these attacks was photographic. The difficulties associated with the identification of targets at night had been freely commented upon since October 1939 by Air Vice-Marshal Coningham and others. Sir Richard Peirse had himself told Sir Charles Portal as recently as October 1940 that he thought between one in three and one in five of the aircraft which he despatched found their primary target, depending upon the range. Yet in the oil plan it was assumed that fifty per cent of the bombers despatched would find the target. In the oil plan it was also assumed that an oil plant could be put out of action for four months by aiming four hundred 500-lb. bombs at it, and that this could be achieved by two hundred sorties. Yet, on 28th December 1940, a report by the Photographic Interpretation Section was circulated to Sir Charles Portal and Sir Richard Peirse. This report covered photographs which had been taken on 24th December of the two oil plants at Gelsenkirchen.

---

[1] Letter Peirse to Portal, 17th Jan. 1941.

According to the estimates, one of these plants had been attacked by 162 aircraft carrying 159 tons of bombs (exclusive of incendiaries); the other had been attacked by 134 aircraft carrying 103 tons of bombs (exclusive of incendiaries). The photographs showed that neither plant had suffered any major damage.[1] It is clear, however, that the significance of this report was not immediately appreciated. The report was circulated the day before Sir Charles Portal submitted his paper to the Chiefs of Staff on 29th December, ten days before the Chiefs of Staff issued their report on 7th January and sixteen days before Sir Charles Portal gave Mr. Churchill and the Defence Committee his assurance that the oil plan was based on actual experience of night operations.

Indeed, the scepticism with which the Prime Minister had greeted the oil plan and its 'cut and dried calculations' rested upon much more substantial evidence than he himself may have realised. Not long after they had issued the January oil directive and when the real implications of the Gelsenkirchen report came to be appreciated, the Air Staff began to view the whole question of operational possibility in an entirely new light. Significant changes in bombing policy were impending even before the oil offensive began to founder among other obstacles.

Of these obstacles, the most immediately insistent was the weather. By the end of February 1941 Bomber Command had, on account of bad weather, only been able to attack oil on two occasions.[2] In the first three months of the year only 221 sorties were flown against synthetic oil plants as compared with 425 in the last quarter of 1940,[3] and with the 3,400 sorties which, according to the plan, would be necessary to achieve the aim. Meanwhile, Britain was facing her third great defensive struggle of the war, the Battle of the Atlantic, and it was not to be long before once again Bomber Command was called away from the attack upon Germany to the defence of Great Britain. At the end of February, Sir Hastings Ismay told Sir Charles Portal that the Prime Minister was directing the attention of the War Cabinet to the need for further measures of defence at sea,[4] and at the same time Sir Archibald Sinclair warned Sir Richard Peirse that he might expect a naval directive before long. Despite the difficulties which he was experiencing in executing the oil plan, this news was most unwelcome to the Commander-in-Chief, Bomber Command, and he hastened to assure Sir Charles Portal, who he believed would be 'fighting to maintain our Directif as it stands at

---

[1] Photographic Interpretation Report, 28th Dec. 1940. The photograph, as well as the report, was sent to Sir Charles Portal and Sir Richard Peirse.
[2] Letter Portal to Ismay, 27th Feb. 1941.
[3] Air Ministry War Room Report.
[4] Letter Ismay to Portal, 27th Feb. 1941.

THE OIL PLAN: BATTLE OF THE ATLANTIC 165

the moment', that if Bomber Command had been given naval targets in January it would have made no more progress with them than it had done with oil targets.[1]

Sir Charles Portal was not, however, 'fighting' to maintain the oil directive. To a large extent he had already lost confidence in the oil plan. He knew there were 'serious doubts about the soundness of the calculations upon which our oil policy was based' and he thought 'that the next best policy to the attack on oil, if the latter is discarded, would be mass attacks on industrial areas. . . .'[2] He also thought it was 'no use pretending that we are not forced on to the defensive by the German attack on our seaborne trade', and he thought that, while this threat remained serious, the mass industrial attacks should be concentrated on areas where submarines and their accessories or Focke-Wulf aircraft were being built.[3] With these thoughts in mind, Sir Charles Portal, on 1st March 1941, broke the news to Sir Richard Peirse that 'A very high proportion of bomber effort will inevitably be required to pull the Admiralty out of the mess they have got into.'[4] Eight days later, following a ruling by the Prime Minister, an official directive was sent to Bomber Command. The Prime Minister's ruling, it said, enjoined 'that for the next four months we should devote our energies to defeating the attempt of the enemy to strangle our food supplies and our connection with the United States.' The directive continued with the Prime Minister's words, 'We must take the offensive against the U-Boat and the Focke Wulf wherever we can and whenever we can. The U-Boat at sea must be hunted, the U-Boat in the building yard or in dock must be bombed. The Focke Wulf, and other bombers employed against our shipping, must be attacked in the air and in their nests.' In somewhat less picturesque language the directive went on to say that 'operations should, therefore, be directed against submarine and long range aircraft activities whenever circumstances permit, until the menace has been dealt with.' This was not, however, entirely to exclude attacks on oil against which the Commander-in-Chief was to continue to employ a 'proportion' of his effort.[5]

Whether Sir Charles Portal really believed that this directive would get the Admiralty out of the 'mess' or not it was in effect the Admiralty which had got the Air Ministry out of the 'mess', for if Bomber Command had, at this stage, been left free to carry out the oil plan it would probably have done a great deal more damage to

---

[1] Letter Peirse to Portal, 28th Feb. 1941.
[2] It is impossible to believe that operational factors had not influenced Sir Charles Portal's views.
[3] Min. Portal to Directorate of Plans, 28th Feb. 1941.
[4] Letter Portal to Peirse, 1st March 1941.
[5] Dir. Freeman to Peirse, 9th March 1941, App. 8 (xiv).

its prestige than to its targets. As it was, the Air Staff were given an opportunity to reconsider their plans for the offensive, and when the conditions for resuming it once more returned very different counsels were seen to prevail.

4. The decline of selective attack and the coming of area bombing
March–November 1941

The Prime Minister's ruling in March 1941 had spoken of concentrating on the Battle of the Atlantic for a period of four months. This struggle was, however, to continue with fluctuating fortune throughout the war. The great crisis of early 1941 was only the first of many which threatened the very existence of Britain and frequently interfered with the course of the strategic air offensive against Germany. Moreover, even when at last the defensive aims of the Battle of the Atlantic had been achieved, the battle still had to be maintained with the offensive object of using sea communications to build up, supply and move the allied attacking forces. Bomber Command itself, indeed, depended upon this use of sea communications. Many of its crews received their early training overseas and all its fuel supplies had to be imported. Thus, even in its defensive phases, the Battle of the Atlantic had an ultimately offensive purpose. Nevertheless, the application of Bomber Command's principal effort to naval targets under the directive of 9th March was neither permanent nor exclusive. Four months later to the day a new directive carried Bomber Command back into the Battle of Germany, and at no time in the interval did the offensive against the heart of the enemy entirely cease.

Indeed, some ostensibly naval targets were whole German towns, and on 18th March 1941 the new Deputy Chief of the Air Staff, Air Vice-Marshal A. T. Harris, told Sir Richard Peirse that Mannheim would remain on, and Stuttgart be added to, the list. He explained that it was thought desirable that a limited number of targets should be 'selected geographically to allow for variations in weather and to impose A.R.P. measures over a wide area'.[1] Thus, at any rate to some extent, the offensive against Germany might continue *pari passu* with the defensive campaign against her sea power.

With this, however, Sir Richard Peirse was not satisfied, and on 15th April 1941 he complained to Sir Charles Portal that since 10th January he had been compelled to throw about 750 tons of high explosive into Brest harbour for the 'benefit' of the *Hipper*, the *Scharnhorst* and the *Gneisenau*.[2] He did not think he had much chance of destroying the ships and he was sure this tonnage of bombs would have been much better employed against Bremen or Mannheim. 'We

---

[1] Dir. Harris to Peirse, 18th March 1941, App. 8 (xv).
[2] Later corrected to 829 tons.

can', Sir Richard Peirse said, 'do more for the Battle of the Atlantic and, at the same time, use the bomber force in the manner for which it was designed by attacking targets in Germany.'[1]

Bomber Command had, however, been designed, as the Western Air Plans had shown, for the precision attack upon key industrial targets. If, as Sir Richard Peirse said of the attacks on the German battle cruisers at Brest, 'We are not designed for this purpose and we are not particularly effective in execution,' Bomber Command had not been much more effective in its execution of attacks on power stations or oil plants. The Air Staff agreed that Sir Richard Peirse might transfer his primary effort from Brest to Germany, but the question remained as to how and where this effort against Germany should be directed.[2]

If there was as yet very little evidence to show what Bomber Command could do, there was, since the Gelsenkirchen photographs, at least something to indicate tasks which it could not perform. The oil plan of January 1941 had been based upon the assumption that on an average of nine moonlight nights in the month it would be possible to bomb with an aiming error of not more than three hundred yards. Now, however, according to fresh Air Staff estimates, it seemed likely that this error was nearer one thousand yards, though it might be six hundred in the best conditions of moonlight and visibility.[3] This seemed to rule out further consideration of the oil plan, and later in the year Sir Charles Portal resisted heavy pressure brought to bear in favour of its resumption. On 14th July he told Lord Hankey, who was pressing for a renewed oil offensive, that, though the plan was 'strategically desirable', oil plants were not 'tactically vulnerable.'[4] Ten days earlier, Sir Charles Portal told Sir Archibald Sinclair, who was also advocating a return to the oil plan, that 'the most suitable object from the economic point of view is not worth pursuing if it is not tactically attainable.'[5] Though this elementary principle was not readily appreciated in certain quarters, for the Air Staff at least it did point imperatively towards a search for larger targets.

Now of these larger targets, that which exerted the greatest appeal was the largest of all, German towns. Sir Charles Portal himself, while he had been Commander-in-Chief, Bomber Command, had reached the conclusion that their destruction had not only been justified by German action, but that it might be one of the most

---

[1] Letter Peirse to Portal, 15th April 1941. Sir Richard Peirse asked that his views should be submitted to the Prime Minister. This was done by Sir Charles Portal.
[2] Air Min. to Bomber Cmd., 18th April 1941.
[3] B. Ops. 1 Memo., 5th April 1941.
[4] C.O.S. Mtg., 14th July 1941.
[5] Min. Portal to Sinclair, 4th July 1941.

profitable strategic courses which could be followed. Members of the Government, including the Prime Minister, were also strongly inclined to this opinion. A formidable quantity of intelligence reports from Germany and advice from people who claimed to know the country or to understand the Germans, ranging from President Roosevelt, who had studied in Germany,[1] to a member of the Staff of the London North Eastern Railway, who had studied at Bonn,[2] seemed to confirm this conclusion. 'All the evidence goes to prove', the Ministry of Information reported in December 1940, 'that the Germans, for all their present confidence and cockiness will not stand a quarter of the bombing that the British have shown they can take.'[3] From these and many other sources there emerged a picture of the German people, exhausted by the rearmament programme, unelated by Germany's military victories, being driven forward to further unendurable efforts, short of food and the comforts of life, fearful of bombing, eager to spring into revolt against the Nazi régime and, perhaps above all, in desperate need of a peaceful rest each night.[4]

This kind of advice and intelligence had been only of limited interest to the Air Staff while they believed that decisive results might be obtained by selective attack upon precision targets such as oil plants. As, however, that hope began to fade, so too the attitude to what had become a highly influential body, or at any rate large volume, of evidence began to change. Sir Robert Vansittart could scarcely have chosen a more appropriate moment than the end of February 1941 at which to send to Sir Archibald Sinclair a memorandum written by a former German staff officer and war pilot strongly urging an all-out attack on German morale,[5] and the same policy was urgently demanded by Lord Trenchard, who was at this time in close touch with the Air Staff, at the end of May. To him, the experience of two wars suggested that the Germans were peculiarly susceptible to bombing and it was against Germany that the Royal Air Force 'should strike and strike again'. If ships at sea were attacked, Lord Trenchard argued, then ninety-nine per cent of the effort would be wasted because ninety-nine per cent of the bombs would fall in the sea. If targets in occupied territory were bombed, then ninety-nine per cent of the effort would be more than wasted, for the bombs would kill and disturb old friends and allies. If, however, targets in German cities were attacked, then ninety-nine per cent of the bombs would contribute directly to the destruction

---
[1] Report on discussion with Mr. Roosevelt, Bowhill to Portal, 27th June 1941.
[2] Letter Murray to Sinclair, 11th Oct. 1940.
[3] Ministry of Information Report, 25th Dec. 1940.
[4] Letters and Reports to Air Min., July 1940 to Dec. 1941.
[5] Letter and Memo., Vansittart to Sinclair, 28th Feb. 1941.

of German morale. This form of attack should, Lord Trenchard believed, be mounted every night, even if on occasions it was only possible to send one bomber. The offensive should be carried to every corner of Greater Germany from the near West to Berlin, Munich, Stuttgart and eventually Vienna in the East. To achieve this, Lord Trenchard admitted, would be a costly adventure and would require an ultimately enormous force. He expected that casualties might at times mount to seventy per cent of the first line in a month and 400–500 per cent reserves would be necessary behind the front line. The production of long-range bombers and the provision of men to fly them would, therefore, have to enjoy an absolute priority. The diversion of the force to subsidiary targets such as invasion ports, oil plants or naval targets would have to be rejected. Lord Trenchard had little doubt that if the bombers went often enough and in great enough strength they could smash the morale of Germany. Meanwhile, the Army and the Navy would have to recognise that they could make no contribution to victory until this had been done.[1]

Strategic bombing, however, remained, relatively, an untried and certainly an unproved weapon. Not everyone shared Lord Trenchard's confidence about its eventual success. Considerations of defence, and, indeed, of survival, also weighed heavily upon those who were burdened with the responsibilities of office. Nevertheless, the Chiefs of Staff endorsed Lord Trenchard's principal diagnosis when they recorded their opinion 'that the most vulnerable point in the German nation at war is the morale of her civilian population under air attack. . . .'[2] But as to the means of exploiting this 'vulnerable point', they were not yet, and in the event never were, prepared to go as far as Lord Trenchard. To Sir Dudley Pound, the First Sea Lord, his memorandum seemed to be a 'complete over-statement'.[3] Both the First Sea Lord and Sir John Dill, Chief of the Imperial General Staff, pointed out that air co-operation in the Battle of the Atlantic would have to continue.[4] Sir Charles Portal observed that it would be impossible to afford the unconditional priority to the long-range bomber force which had been demanded by Lord Trenchard. It would still be necessary to maintain a strong Fighter Command and Fleet Air Arm. Nor would it be possible to concentrate the entire effort of Bomber Command exclusively against Germany.[5]

Thus, though the Chiefs of Staff accepted the strategic implica-

---

[1] Memo. Trenchard to Churchill, 19th May 1941, App. 10 (i). Circulated by the Prime Minister to the C.O.S., 28th May 1941.
[2] Min. C.O.S. to Churchill, 7th June 1941.
[3] Memo. by Pound, 2nd June 1941, App. 10 (ii).
[4] Memo by Dill, 2nd June 1941, App. 10 (iii).
[5] Memo. by Portal, 2nd June 1941, App. 10 (iv).

tions of Lord Trenchard's memorandum, they could not see their way towards providing the means to carry it out. Bomber Command could not be expanded at the rate Lord Trenchard wished, and many of the diversions against which he protested would still have to be accepted. Bomber Command would, therefore, remain, at any rate for some time, a force of limited strength and with a limited ability to achieve a functional concentration. Eventually, the Chiefs of Staff believed, Bomber Command could and should turn to the direct attack on German morale as its primary engagement. In the meantime, some rather less ambitious policy was required.[1]

These considerations had for some time been engaging the attention of the Air Staff, and in the Directorate of Bomber Operations, where the idea of selective attack died hard, a new plan was growing. This was for an attack on transport, by which all means of communication was meant, and it seemed to offer Bomber Command a policy which might at once contribute to the long-term aim of breaking German morale, be within the limited strength and accuracy of the force, and yet offer the prospect of securing decisive results in reasonable time.

The idea of attacking transport was not new. The Western Air Plans had indicated that in some circumstances it might be highly profitable, and since the outbreak of war belief in the idea had been growing stronger. Marshalling yards had always been popular alternative targets and transport in general had often seemed to be a desirable primary target. In the autumn of 1940 the Deputy Chief of the Air Staff had suggested that this form of attack might be 'one of the most important contributions' which could be made to the disruption of the German economy. In the following January the Chiefs of Staff had shown that they shared this view.[2] Now that Hitler had extended his activities over most of Europe and into Africa, and was compelled to shoulder heavy responsibilities in Italy, he was confronted with the 'most gigantic task of economic management ever attempted'. The interchange of goods from unaccustomed sources by unusual channels to peoples of varying degrees of hostility would, it seemed, tax German ingenuity and resources to the breaking-point. Transport might indeed prove to be one of 'the weakest links in the German economic chain.'[3]

Nevertheless, to attack German transport effectively would, as had also often been pointed out, be a gigantic operation; almost as gigantic as that postulated by the direct attack on morale. It would

---

[1] Min. C.O.S. to Churchill, 7th June 1941.
[2] Dir. Douglas to Portal, 21st Sept. 1940, App. 8 (ix) and Memo. by C.O.S., 7th Jan. 1941.
[3] J.P.S. Review, 12th June 1941.

also require a high degree of bombing accuracy, or at any rate a much higher degree than that required to hit a town. These were serious objections, which did not seem to be reduced by the substantially abortive attacks which had already been made against such famous targets at Hamm, Soest and Osnabrück in 1940. In the Directorate of Bomber Operations, however, it was felt that none of these objections could be sustained in the face of the plan now being made.

In and around the Ruhr there was an area of concentrated transport activity. The isolation of the Ruhr by the successful bombing of its railways would, in the view of the Directorate of Bomber Operations, have for Germany the same consequences that the severance of the Atlantic line would have for Britain. Thus, while the target remained potentially decisive, it was reduced to proportions which, it was thought, lay within the scope of Bomber Command. The new assumption that in conditions of good moonlight the bomb-aiming error should not exceed six hundred yards suggested that on the right nights it should be possible to hit large railway targets like marshalling yards. Thus, despite the knowledge that Bomber Command was not such a precise weapon as had been presupposed in the oil plan, it seemed reasonable to assume that it was precise enough to carry out the transport plan. The degree of destruction to be expected from these attacks should not, the Directorate of Bomber Operations thought, be compared to what had been achieved in the 1940 'harassing' attacks. On these occasions, it was now calculated with the six hundred yards aiming error, not more than eight bombs could actually have hit the target on the heaviest raids and on the average raids not more than 'about half a bomb'. In the new plan it was calculated that about a hundred bombs, amounting to twenty tons, would hit the target in each attack.[1]

---

[1] The calculation was as follows:

Assumptions: Attacks possible on seven clear moonlight nights per month: 120 aircraft with 180 tons of bombs despatched on each occasion: sixty-six per cent of these aircraft will attack the target (i.e. eighty aircraft with 120 tons): average bomb aiming error of these eighty aircraft will be six hundred yards. (These figures are changed in pencil to read seventy-five per cent will attack the target (i.e. ninety aircraft with 135 tons).)

Calculation:

Number of aircraft despatched	120
Number of bombs carried (H.E.)	900 (approx.)
,, ,, ,, ,, (incendiary)	6,000 ,,
Number of aircraft attacking target	80 ,,
Number of bombs carried to target (H.E.)	600 ,,
Number of bombs carried to target (incendiary)	4,000 ,,
Number of bombs hitting target (H.E.)	100 ,, } i.e. sixteen
Number of bombs hitting target (incendiary)	700 ,, } per cent

These estimates were thought 'conservative'. During the April moon period an average of 120 aircraft had operated for nine (not seven) nights and it was claimed that eighty per cent (not sixty-six per cent or seventy-five per cent) of them had attacked the primary target. Also, in a moonlight attack on the Focke-Wulf plant at Bremen, it was claimed that twenty-seven per cent (not sixteen per cent) of the bombs hit the target area.

There was, of course, no conclusive evidence as to what the effect of such an attack would be, for nothing on this scale had yet been attempted either by the *Luftwaffe* or the Royal Air Force. All the same, it was expected, according to what was described as the advice of British railway experts who had been observing the German raids, that such an attack would produce a result 'in the nature of complete stoppage for perhaps a week and very considerably limited operation for a much longer period'. In view of the fact that seven railway centres[1] were thought to be the key to the whole position, the Directorate of Bomber Operations was able to suggest that it should be possible to produce this result in one moon period.[2]

Such was the plan for a transport attack, which also was to include attacks on canals, made in the Directorate of Bomber Operations at the Air Ministry. Like the earlier oil plan, it contained a number of 'cut and dried' calculations of the kind which the Prime Minister mistrusted. Also like the oil plan, it was something considerably less than the whole design of the bombing offensive, for as the Directorate of Bomber Operations paper had said, 'It is accepted as a principle in this plan that the successful attack of a specific target at night can only be undertaken in clear moonlight. It follows therefore, that for approximately ¾ of each month it is only possible to obtain satisfactory results by the "Blitz" attack on large working class and industrial areas in the towns.' In the oil plan this had been a serious disadvantage and it had even led Sir Richard Peirse to attempt oil attacks on non-moonlight nights. In the case of the new transport plan it did not seem to be nearly such a serious disadvantage. Many bombs which were aimed at railway targets would, no doubt, fall in populated areas and reduce morale. Some, which were aimed at populated areas, might even hit railway targets. Thus, if as the Chiefs of Staff suggested to the Prime Minister on 7th June 1941, the long-term aim of Bomber Command should be the destruction of German morale and the immediate aim the dislocation of transport, then the two objects, which were in any case tactically complementary, would be also strategically complementary.[3]

This further attempt 'to formulate a policy expressed in terms of principle' did not appeal to the Prime Minister. He thought the plan of 'concentrating upon the marshalling yard business, in contradistinction to oil, enemy warships, U-boat and aircraft factories and residential districts in large cities' offered 'a very bleak and restricted policy.' He believed it would be found better simply to have

---

[1] They were: Hamm, Osnabrück, Duisburg-Ruhrort, Düsseldorf, Cologne (Kalk Nord), Schwerte and Soest.
[2] Memo. by D.D.B. Ops., 24th April 1941.
[3] Min. C.O.S. to Churchill, 7th June 1941.

a 'programme' for each month 'and carry it out as far as possible'.[1] Equally the suggestion that Bomber Command's operations should be conducted in this 'hand-to-mouth manner' did not appeal to the Chiefs of Staff. Bomber Command, they told the Prime Minister, should work to a 'definite strategic aim.'[2] This determination carried the day and the Air Staff were once more in a position to write a bombing directive.[3]

This directive, which was sent out on 9th July 1941, was the first of many written under the auspices of Air Vice-Marshal Bottomley, who had recently succeeded Air Marshal Harris as Deputy Chief of the Air Staff. The directive said that 'a comprehensive review of the enemy's present political, economic and military situation discloses that the weakest points in his armour lie in the morale of the civil population and in his inland transportation system. The wide extension of his military activities is placing an ever-increasing strain on the German transportation system, and there are many signs that our recent attacks on industrial towns are having great effect on the morale of the civil population.' The plan outlined by the Directorate of Bomber Operations was closely followed and Sir Richard Peirse was told to concentrate in moonlight against nine railway targets in the Ruhr area.[4] The choice of these targets had, the directive said, been governed not only by their importance to the railway system but also because of their proximity to industrial areas. 'These objectives', it continued, 'are therefore to be considered as suitably located for obtaining incidental effect on the morale of the industrial population.' If weather conditions made it impossible to attack one of these, other 'related' railway targets farther afield could be taken on. The direct attack on roads had been 'ruled out owing to their tactical unsuitability', but the destruction of the two principal synthetic rubber plants at Schkopau and Hüls was to be attempted as an alternative method of interfering with road transport. The Dortmund–Ems and the Ems–Weser canals with the River Rhine were also to be attacked. It was hoped to mine the river and to break down the raised banks of the canals. Such was the precision, or moonlight, part of the plan. It depended on the tactical assumption that on each occasion ninety bombers would actually attack the primary target and would bomb with an average aiming error of six hundred yards. On the other occasions, the attack was to centre on Hamburg, Bremen, Hanover, Frankfurt, Mannheim and Stuttgart.[5] Thus was the strategic desire

---

[1] Churchill to Ismay (for C.O.S.), 8th June 1941.
[2] Min. Sec. of C.O.S. to Churchill, 11th June 1941, App. 11.
[3] Defence Cttee. Mtg., 25th June 1941.
[4] To the seven suggested in the original plan, Duisburg (Hochfeld-Süd) and Cologne (Gereon) were now added.
[5] Dir. Bottomley to Peirse, 9th July 1941, App. 8 (xvi).

brought into line with the ruling conception of operational possibility.

This ruling conception was, however, to undergo another and more sweeping revision in the near future. Meanwhile, events in Europe had brought the Air Staff once more face to face with the problems of day bombing. The German spring campaign in the Balkans and, above all, the invasion of Russia on 22nd June 1941, presented Britain with new allies, new dangers and, perhaps, also with new opportunities. To sustain these operations it was obvious that the *Luftwaffe* would shift much of its strength from the West to the East. If Bomber Command could exploit any weakness in the air in the West it might either compel the Germans to bring back some of their squadrons from the East, or, if this was not done, it might inflict some severe strategic damage upon Germany. In co-operation with Fighter Command it might also bring the German air force to action on unfavourable terms to the latter and strike an important blow in the battle for air superiority. Now, since the night fighter was not yet a serious factor in the German air force, it was obvious that all or any of this could only be achieved by daylight attack.[1]

Nevertheless, Bomber Command's experience of day bombing so far had been extremely unhappy. The casualties had been prohibitive and the results very disappointing. The pre-war belief in the self-defending bomber formation and the surprise light attack had been dealt a shattering blow over the North Sea in 1939 and over France in 1940. The German experience in the Battle of Britain, even though they often escorted their bombers with fighters, had seemed to confirm the wisdom and inevitability of the British decision to confine Bomber Command mainly to night operations. If, however, the Eastern campaigns should make sufficient inroads on German air strength in the West the situation might change.[2] Also

---

[1] Air Staff Memo., 8th July 1941. Bomber Cmd. to 2, 3 and 5 Groups, 10th April 1941. Note by Saundby (S.A.S.O. Bomber Cmd.), 26th June 1941.

[2] The Directorate of Intelligence at the Air Ministry estimated that in the month before 22nd June 1941 and after further reinforcements up to the end of July, the Germans had built up the following force on the Eastern Front: 1,050 long range bombers, 230 reconnaissance bombers, 300 dive bombers, 800 fighters (including 700 single-engined) and 250 army co-operation aircraft. Since 22nd June they were thought to have sent further reinforcements from the west. By the end of July 1941 the force remaining in the west was estimated as follows:

Twin-engined fighters: Denmark, ten, Schleswig-Holstein thirty, N.W. Germany ninety, Holland 130, total 260.

Single-engined fighters: Norway twenty, Sylt ten, N.W. Germany ten, Holland twenty, Pas de Calais 150–160, Cherbourg and Brest thirty, total 240–250.

Twin-engined fighters (O.T.U.): Denmark twenty, Ruhr twenty.

Single-engined fighters (O.T.U.): N.W. Germany twenty, Holland thirty, N. and N.W. France forty.

The Commander-in-Chief, Fighter Command, thought there were rather more in the Calais and Brest areas. Mins. of Air Min. Conf., 29th July 1941. Owing to different methods of classifying aircraft, exact comparisons between British estimates and the real position are not possible. For the German figures see note at the end of this section, pp. 187–188.

Bomber Command's new four-engined aircraft, the Stirling and the Halifax, might prove more robust than the earlier twin-engined Wellingtons or single-engined Battles. At any rate the need was sufficient to justify the hope.

The Pas de Calais area lay within the operational range of Fighter Command and it was, therefore, possible for Bomber Command to make escorted attacks on this area. But, where Germany was concerned, Fighter Command could not go the distance. It was, therefore, part of the day bombing plan to concentrate on the Pas de Calais area with the threefold purpose of damaging 'valuable military objectives', affording the escorting fighters 'an opportunity of destroying the enemy's fighters' and of causing the Germans to concentrate their fighters in that area. If they could be persuaded to do this, then opportunities might arise for unescorted bombers to make daylight penetrations of Germany herself. These attacks could, however, be little more than 'Stunts', and it would not usually be possible to repeat them since they would depend for success upon an ability to take the enemy by surprise and, therefore, to evade such defending fighters as were available.[1]

Clearly this plan depended upon whether the Germans would react sufficiently to the Pas de Calais attacks. Despite an early success on 21st June, Sir Wilfrid Freeman, the Vice-Chief of the Air Staff, doubted if they would. He did not think they would be 'shamed into the air', but expected they would 'prefer to stop on the ground in spite of the jibes' of the French.[2] This was neither the first nor the last time that Sir Wilfrid Freeman sounded a note of warning in the Air Staff which events proved to be well founded. On 29th July 1941 Sir Richard Peirse told a conference held by Sir Charles Portal that the expectation of pinning down the German fighter force in the Pas de Calais area had been 'over-optimistic'.[3] It was now evident that in order to bring an opposing air force to action it was necessary to bomb something which the enemy was not prepared to leave undefended and to have there fighters capable of engaging the aircraft which he sent up to defend it. The difficulty was that the Germans were prepared to leave undefended the areas which could be reached by the Royal Air Force fighters and, where they had vital targets, there the Royal Air Force fighters could not go. Mr. Churchill was not slow to grasp, and, indeed, to anticipate, the implications of this situation, for, speaking of the day offensive, he told Sir Charles Portal on 2nd June 1941, 'For this the range of our

---

[1] Note by Saundby, 26th June 1941.
[2] Min. Freeman to Portal, 22nd June 1941.
[3] Mins. of Air Min. Conf., 29th July 1941.

fighters must be extended. If this is not done, you will be helpless in the West and beaten in the East.'[1]

Sir Charles Portal, however, was convinced that long-range fighters could never hold their own against short-range fighters and were suitable for 'regular employment only in areas where they will not be opposed by enemy short range fighters.'[2] This, in Mr. Churchill's words, closed 'many doors',[3] and it was a reaffirmation of the principle that evasion of the enemy air force was the only way to the target compatible with survival. The ultimate hope that the self-defending bomber formation might yet beat 'the German fighter in the air' was not abandoned, but it was found by Sir Richard Peirse to be as impracticable in 1941 as it had been by Sir Edgar Ludlow-Hewitt in 1939.[4] In the immediate future, at least, Bomber Command would remain a night force.

Doubts about the degree of precision which Bomber Command could achieve at night had been growing, and though the directive of 9th July 1941 still held out hopes of achieving important effects by precision attack, it was becoming increasingly obvious that if Bomber Command could not fulfil the role of the rapier it would have to undertake that of the bludgeon. It was also obvious that much more force would be required to deliver effective bludgeon blows than rapier thrusts. It was, indeed, this consideration which had impelled the Chiefs of Staff to refrain so far from recommending that the primary and immediate aim of Bomber Command should be the destruction of German morale by the all-out attack on German towns. Though this was the role for which Bomber Command seemed to be eventually destined both on tactical and strategic grounds, yet, unless it was given a greater share of the productive capacity of the nation, it seemed that it might never be powerful enough to carry the task to fruition.

The Air Staff was already demanding a force of 4,000 heavy bombers, but, as Sir Archibald Sinclair explained to Sir Charles Portal in June 1941, this programme was 'encountering heavy weather.' Ministers were 'reluctant to commit themselves to so big a concentration of effort upon one means of winning the war . . .' This, indeed, had been one of the reasons which had made it seem so desirable to attempt daylight bombing again.[5] Thus, Bomber Command seemed to be caught in a vicious circle. Because of the

---

[1] Churchill: *The Second World War*, Vol. III, (1950), p. 687.
[2] Min. Portal to Churchill, 3rd June 1941.
[3] Letter Peck (Private Sec. to Churchill) to Crawford (Private Sec. to Portal), 9th June 1941. Mr. Churchill made this comment on the 8th.
[4] Note by Saundby, 26th June 1941. Min. Portal to Sinclair, 6th July 1941. Bomber Cmd. Note on daylight attack on Brest and La Pallice on 24th July 1941 dated 28th July 1941. Mins. of Air Min. Conf., 29th July 1941.
[5] Min. Sinclair to Portal, 16th June 1941.

limitation upon its bombing accuracy, imposed mainly by darkness, it required an immense force to achieve decisive results by imprecise means. But because of doubts about its effectiveness, arising mainly from its inaccuracy, it might never be given the necessary force. It is possible that this situation had led the Air Staff to persist with the policy of precision attack at night for longer than they really judged it to be profitable. After all, Sir Richard Peirse had estimated in October 1940 that on the shorter range attacks one in three of the aircraft he despatched attacked the primary target and on the longer range flights only one in five.

Others outside the Air Ministry and Bomber Command also had doubts about the accuracy of bombing. They included Lord Cherwell, who had special facilities for the investigation of such problems, and it was on his initiative that a more searching enquiry into the question was undertaken. In the first half of August and on his behalf, Mr. Butt, a member of the War Cabinet secretariat, examined over six hundred photographs taken by night bombers during operational sorties flown between the beginning of June and the end of July. He also studied a large number of operational summaries and other documentary records. On the basis of this evidence Mr. Butt concluded that of all the aircraft recorded as having attacked their targets, only one-third had got within five miles of them. The percentage of successes, however, varied greatly with the geographical position of the target, the state of the weather and the intensity of the anti-aircraft defences. Over the French ports, for example, he calculated that two-thirds of the aircraft reported to have attacked the target had actually been within five miles. Over the Ruhr the proportion was reduced to one-tenth. A French port, he estimated, was more than twice as easy to find as a target in the interior of Germany, but a target in the Ruhr was four times as difficult to locate as one elsewhere in Germany. In full moon, two-fifths of the aircraft reported to have attacked their targets had, according to Mr. Butt's calculations, got within five miles of them. Without a moon the proportion fell to one-fifteenth.

These proportions only applied to those aircraft which claimed to have attacked their targets. If the total number of aircraft despatched was considered, the proportions would have to be reduced by another third. Moreover, even these proportions were only established to have dropped their bombs within the seventy-five square miles which surrounded the actual target. Thus, many of the aircraft which, by Mr. Butt's test, were now credited with successful attacks would in fact have dropped their bombs in open country.[1]

The Butt Report did not claim to be infallible. It was admitted

---

[1] Butt Report to Bomber Cmd., 18th Aug. 1941, App. 13.

THE COMING OF AREA BOMBING

that the photographs themselves might conceal errors caused by banking the aircraft at the time of exposure, delay in launching the flare and changes in speed, height and course at the vital moment. Several of the operational summaries were found to have been inadequately completed and, of course, some doubt had to remain about those photographs which could not be plotted. Finally, as Mr. Butt pointed out, nearly half of the photographs examined had not been taken simultaneously with the bombing attack. They were included in the analysis because the position which they showed could still be compared with that which the navigator had calculated at the time. Nevertheless, Mr. Butt felt confident that the broad picture which his report presented was correct.[1]

Sir Richard Peirse found it hard to believe this. 'I don't think at this rate', he wrote, 'we could have hoped to produce the damage which is known to have been achieved.'[2] The Air Officer Commanding 4 Group, Air Vice-Marshal Carr, thought that 'the lack of a photograph of the precise target should not be regarded as conclusive proof that the aircraft failed to attack its proper objective . . .'[3] The Senior Air Staff Officer at Bomber Command, Air Vice-Marshal Saundby, emphasised that the weather in June and July had been particularly unfavourable and that a sample of ten per cent of sorties flown could not be accepted as an entirely reliable means of assessing the results of the whole force. He emphasised the last point by suggesting that Squadron Commanders tended to give cameras to the crews in which they had the least confidence.[4]

Whatever may have been the force and explanation of these objections and qualifications expressed at Bomber Command, they neither delayed, nor did they blunt, the impact of the Butt Report in high places. As Lord Cherwell told the Prime Minister, 'however inaccurate the figures may be, they are sufficiently striking to emphasise the supreme importance of improving our navigational methods'.[5] The Prime Minister told Sir Charles Portal that the report was 'a very serious paper, and seems to require your most urgent attention'. He awaited the Chief of the Air Staff's 'proposals for action.'[6] Sir Charles Portal, though he thought that the figures

---

[1] The Report stated that the photographs (actually 633 in number but given as 650) which purported to show the target area were taken on 'over 500 different sorties'. This presumably meant that some of the aircraft had taken more than one picture of the 'purported target area'.

[2] Pencil annotation by Peirse on the Report.

[3] Carr to Bomber Cmd., 8th Sept. 1941.

[4] Note by Saundby, 21st Aug. 1941. In a different context, Sir Arthur Harris was later to express the opinion that Squadron Commanders gave the cameras to their best crews. *Harris Despatch*.

[5] Min. Cherwell to Churchill, 2nd Sept. 1941.

[6] Winston Churchill: *The Second World War*, Vol. IV, (1951), p. 250.

might be 'wide of the mark', agreed with what Lord Cherwell had said. He believed that the need to improve night bombing was 'perhaps the greatest of the operational problems confronting us at the present time'. The agencies of operational research, improved training, developed tactics and above all of science were to be brought to bear upon the problem.[1] Thus, for the first time in air force history the first and paramount problem of night operations was seen at the highest level to be not merely a question of bomb aiming, though that difficulty remained, but of navigation. While the bombers were still not within five miles of the aiming-point, it was a matter only of academic interest as to whether a bomb could be aimed with an error of 300, 600 or 1,000 yards. By showing the need for the development of scientific aids to navigation, the scientific study of navigation, and the development of revolutionary tactics, the Butt investigation, carried out under the auspices of Lord Cherwell, had rendered a service to Bomber Command which was second to none.

Nevertheless, the introduction of these tactical and technical devices, some of which were already in the later stages of development, would take time. Meanwhile, it was obvious that the part of the existing bombing policy which called for selective and precise night attack was impracticable. If, indeed, as was suggested, less than one crew in ten who claimed to have done so were dropping their bombs within five miles of the aiming-point of the Ruhr targets, then it was hardly possible that much damage could be done to the railway targets allotted in the directive of 9th July 1941. Thus, Bomber Command's last and only resort was the area attack on German towns. The knowledge that the 'interim' policy could not be carried out, therefore, brought Bomber Command immediately face to face with this gigantic task which was known to be beyond its existing strength and which had long been regarded as only its ultimate role when it had been greatly expanded. While the Air Staff worked out plans for this great area attack and while they demanded the 4,000 front-line heavy bombers which they conceived to be necessary, everything really depended upon the confidence which they could inspire in their superiors as to the ultimate outcome of this offensive.

One of the most convincing arguments which spoke in favour of the Air Staff plan was the lack of any alternative means of attacking Germany. In July 1941, after the entry of Russia into the war, the Chiefs of Staff had declared, 'We must first destroy the foundations upon which the [German] war machine rests—the economy which feeds it, the morale which sustains it, the supplies which nourish it

---

[1] Min. Portal to Churchill, 11th Sept. 1941.

and the hopes of victory which inspire it. Then only shall we be able to return to the continent and occupy and control portions of his territory and impose our will upon the enemy . . . It is,' the Chiefs of Staff continued, 'in bombing, on a scale undreamt of in the last war, that we find the new weapon on which we must principally depend for the destruction of German economic life and morale'. The Chiefs of Staff 'set no limits to the size of the force required, save those imposed by operational difficulties in the United Kingdom. After meeting the needs of our own security, therefore,' they said, 'we give the heavy bomber first priority in production, for only the heavy bomber can produce the conditions under which other offensive forces can be employed.'[1]

The new plan, which once more sprang from the Directorate of Bomber Operations at the Air Ministry, naturally signalled the end of precision attack and the coming of area bombing. Calculations based upon theoretical assumptions about bomb-aiming errors were abandoned and a new yard-stick was adopted. This was the scale and effectiveness of German air attacks on Britain. The *Luftwaffe* had bombed many towns, Coventry, London, Portsmouth, Birmingham and Liverpool among them. The material damage could be seen. The psychological effect could, or so at any rate it was supposed, be calculated. The scale of the German attacks could be approximately deduced. Thus, a relationship between effort and effect could be established and calculations for the Royal Air Force offensive against German towns could be attempted.

Working on these lines, an 'index of activity' in British towns after German bombing was compiled. Production at a factory might suffer because the gas, water or electricity supply had been cut off, or because the workers absented themselves owing to fear, fatigue or lack of food. The index, therefore, endeavoured to include psychological as well as material damage. An examination of the Coventry attack, carried out on the night of 14th November 1940, suggested that the weight of the raid had amounted to about one ton of bombs to every eight hundred of the population. The reduction in the index of activity had been calculated at sixty-three per cent on the morning of 15th November. Recovery had taken thirty-five days. These figures were thought to correspond proportionately with those for other towns which had been bombed. It seemed reasonable to suppose that, if repeated attacks were made, the level of the index of activity would become progressively lower after each, provided sufficient time for recovery to normal in the intervals was denied. After the fourth or fifth successive attack on the Coventry scale it was supposed that the index of activity would be reduced to nil, and after

---

[1] C.O.S. Memo, 31st July 1941.

the sixth attack that it would be 'beyond all hope of recovery'. The ideal would, therefore, be to deliver six attacks on the Coventry scale against a single town on six successive nights. Since this would be impracticable, an alternative would be to make the six attacks at regular intervals over a period of six months. Even this would limit very seriously the number of towns which could be attacked, and, in practice, it was thought it might be preferable to attempt the partial destruction of a larger number of towns rather than the total destruction of fewer. A compromise would be to deal with one particular area of towns at a time.[1] The idea of general area bombing had been born.

Eventually, the plan envisaged the complete destruction of forty-three selected German towns which included the majority with a population of more than 100,000 and which had a total population of some fifteen millions. Such an achievement, it was felt, would certainly prove decisive, but it would require 4,000 first-line bombers to carry it out.[2]

This plan met with Sir Charles Portal's approval, and on 25th September he sent it to the Prime Minister with the suggestion that if Bomber Command was given its 4,000 bombers it could break Germany in six months.[3] Mr. Churchill was, however, as he had been in the case of earlier Air Staff estimates, very doubtful about this. 'It is very disputable', he told Sir Charles Portal, 'whether bombing by itself will be a decisive factor in the present war. On the contrary, all that we have learnt since the war began shows that its effects, both physical and moral, are greatly exaggerated. There is no doubt,' Mr. Churchill continued, 'the British people have been stimulated and strengthened by the attack made upon them so far. Secondly, it seems very likely that the ground defences and night fighters will overtake the Air attack. Thirdly, in calculating the number of bombers necessary to achieve hypothetical and indefinite tasks, it should be noted that only a quarter of our bombs hit the targets. Consequently an increase in the accuracy of bombing to 100% would in fact raise our bombing force to four times its strength.

---

[1] The Ruhr, though not mentioned, may have been in mind.
[2] B. Ops. Memo., 22nd Sept. 1941. The calculation concerning the 4,000 bombers was as follows:
Tonnage to be dropped monthly on forty-three towns populated by 15,000,000 people, at one ton per 800 persons: 18,750 tons
Tonnage to be lifted from base, assuming twenty-five per cent of the aircraft despatched attack the target: 75,000 tons
Number of squadrons (sixteen I.E.) assuming each aircraft carries three tons and each squadron operates a hundred sorties per month: 250
Total number of heavy bombers: 4,000
These figures were supposed to be indicative and not precise. 'We certainly cannot do with less bombers,' the report said. 'We may well need more.'
[3] Min. Portal to Churchill, 25th Sept. 1941.

THE COMING OF AREA BOMBING 183

The most we can say is that it will be a heavy and I trust a seriously increasing annoyance.'[1]

This was something more than the Prime Minister's usual vote of no confidence in 'cut and dried' calculations. It seemed to be tantamount to a vote of no confidence in the whole Air Staff strategy of the war, and it appeared to be a direct contradiction of most of the utterances and directives which the Prime Minister had issued on the subject of the bombing offensive. Thus far had the new evidence about Bomber Command's ability apparently undermined Mr. Churchill's confidence in it and revived the note of caution which he had sounded as early as 1917.[2]

In a minute of 2nd October 1941, which the Secretary of State thought was 'masterly' and 'audacious', Sir Charles Portal sought to repair this damage. He reminded the Prime Minister that 'since the fall of France it has been a fundamental principle of our strategy that victory over Germany could not be hoped for until German morale and German material strength had been subjected to a bombing offensive of the greatest intensity'. He pointed out that this principle had been affirmed over and over again both by the Chiefs of Staff and by the Prime Minister himself. Production, he observed, had been planned to conform with this strategic conception and 'we are already', he said, 'deeply committed to it'. If the offensive was going to be no more than 'a heavy and growing annoyance' to Germany, then a new strategic conception would have to be thought out without delay. Having thus, so to speak, called the Prime Minister's bluff, Sir Charles Portal tried to convince him that there was in fact no need to revise the basic strategy of the war. 'I see no reason', he said, 'to regard the bomber as a weapon of declining importance'. He thought it was as easy to underestimate the 'consequences to Germany of a bombing offensive on the scale envisaged by the Air Staff' as it was to overestimate them. Light attacks, he admitted, might stimulate morale, but this he thought could 'scarcely be said of attacks on the Coventry model. Judging from our own experience,' he asserted, 'it is difficult to believe that any country could withstand indefinitely the scale of attack contemplated in the Air Staff plan'. German attacks on England had in the last year caused death or serious injury to 93,000 civilians. 'This result', Sir Charles Portal said, 'was achieved with a small fraction of the bomb load we hope to employ in 1943. Moreover,' he added, 'the consensus of informed opinion is that German morale is much more vulnerable to bombing than our own'.[3]

In view of the subsequent course which the policy underlying the

---

[1] Min. Churchill to Portal, 27th Sept. 1941.
[2] See above, pp. 45 and 47.
[3] Min. Portal to Churchill, 2nd Oct. 1941. Min. Sinclair to Portal, 30th Sept. 1941.

conduct of the bombing offensive was to take, the Prime Minister's reply to Sir Charles Portal, written on 7th October 1941, must be reproduced in full:

> 'C.A.S.
>
> We all hope that the Air offensive against Germany will realise the expectations of the Air Staff. Everything is being done to create the Bombing force desired on the largest possible scale, and there is no intention of changing this policy. I deprecate, however, placing unbounded confidence in this means of attack, and still more expressing that confidence in terms of arithmetic. It is the most potent method of impairing the enemy's morale we can use at the present time. If the United States enters the war, it would have to be supplemented in 1943 by simultaneous attacks by armoured forces in many of the conquered countries which were ripe for revolt. Only in this way could a decision certainly be achieved. Even if all the towns of Germany were rendered largely uninhabitable, it does not follow that the military control would be weakened or even that war industry could not be carried on.
>
> 2. The Air Staff would make a mistake to put their claim too high. Before the war we were greatly misled by the pictures they painted of the destruction that would be wrought by Air raids. This is illustrated by the fact that 750,000 beds[1] were actually provided for Air raid casualties, never more than 6,000 being required. This picture of air destruction was so exaggerated that it depressed the Statesmen responsible for the pre-war policy, and played a definite part in the desertion of Czecho-Slovakia in August 1938. Again, the Air Staff, after the war had begun, taught us sedulously to believe that if the enemy acquired the Low Countries, to say nothing of France, our position would be impossible owing to the Air attacks. However, by not paying too much attention to such ideas, we have found quite a good means of keeping going.
>
> 3. It may well be that German morale will crack and that our bombing will play a very important part in bringing the result about. But all things are always on the move simultaneously, and it is quite possible that the Nazi war-making power in 1943 will be so widely spread throughout Europe as to be to a large extent independent of the actual buildings in the homeland.
>
> 4. A different picture would be presented if the enemy's Air Force were so far reduced as to enable heavy accurate daylight bombing of factories to take place. This however cannot be done outside the radius of Fighter protection, according to

---

[1] This is the figure stated by Mr. Churchill in his original minute. In the reproduction of the minute in his memoirs Mr. Churchill gives the figure of 250,000. See Churchill: *The Second World War*, Vol. III, p. 451.

THE COMING OF AREA BOMBING

what I am at present told. One has to do the best one can, but he is an unwise man who thinks there is any *certain* method of winning this war, or indeed any other war between equals in strength. The only plan is to persevere.

I shall be delighted to discuss these general topics with you whenever you will.

(Signed) W. S. C.'

After a conversation with the Prime Minister, and after reading his minute, Sir Charles Portal felt reassured that 'the primary importance of our bomber operations and of building up the bomber force on the largest possible scale' was accepted by the Prime Minister.[1] This, indeed, was a not unreasonable interpretation to place upon what the Prime Minister had said. Nevertheless, the most urgent need for Bomber Command was now to achieve some outstanding success in the field of action. Deeds were required to lend confidence to predictions and calculations. Yet Bomber Command was still without the scientific aids necessary to improve the appalling inaccuracy which had been revealed in the Butt Report. For example, on the night of 1st October 1941, when the objectives of Bomber Command were Karlsruhe and Stuttgart, its aircraft were reported over Aachen, Eupen, Malmédy, Coblenz, Neuwied, Kreuznach, Frankfurt am Main, Wiesbaden, Limburg, Darmstadt, Mainz, Worms, Trier, Offenburg, Saarfels, Nuremberg, Erlangen, Bamberg, Bayreuth, Coburg, Pegnitz, Aschaffenburg, Schweinfurt, Würzburg, Regensburg, Weiden and Chemnitz.[2] The development of new devices and techniques gave grounds for very real hopes of improvement in the future, but nothing much could be expected in 1941.

The second primary requirement was for a larger and more powerful force. Here again the future held out great hopes. The four-engined bombers were coming into service and the flow of recruits was being converted into a force of trained aircrews. But the casualties of 1941 were making serious inroads upon the existing force and constituted a threat to its future. On the night of 7th November 1941 a force of 400 Bomber Command aircraft took off to attack Berlin, Mannheim, the Ruhr, Cologne, Boulogne and to carry out mining and intruder operations. Thirty-seven failed to return. Of the whole attacking force, 169 were sent to Berlin and twenty-one, or 12·5 per cent, failed to return. Fifty-five were sent to Mannheim and seven,

---

[1] Min. Portal to Churchill, 13th Oct. 1941. The Air Staff admitted, in a note sent to the Prime Minister on 13th October 1941, that their pre-war estimates had been largely 'crystal gazing'. They claimed, however, that the abandonment of Czechoslovakia had been due to bankers and economists who feared the consequences of rearmament upon the national economy. They denied that they had ever said that a German occupation of the Low Countries would be fatal.
[2] Min. A.I. 3 (c) to D.D.I.3, 23rd Oct. 1941.

or thirteen per cent, failed to return. Forty-three were sent to the Ruhr and to carry out mining operations and nine, or twenty-one per cent, failed to return. There were no losses among the remaining 133 aircraft which were sent to Cologne, Ostend and Boulogne.[1]

On the following night Sir Richard Peirse was at Chequers, where he found the Prime Minister deeply perturbed about these high casualties, which he did not believe could be afforded, especially as 'he did not think we had done any damage to the enemy lately.' Sir Richard Peirse tried to reassure Mr. Churchill, but the Prime Minister became 'very insistent' that Bomber Command should be conserved and built up for the future. Meanwhile, smaller forces should be sent out and they should be restricted to the nearer targets.[2] It was now, the Prime Minister told Sir Archibald Sinclair and Sir Charles Portal, 'the duty of both Fighter and Bomber Command to re-gather their strength for the Spring'.[3] This matter was discussed 'at some length' by the Cabinet, where it was decided that the Prime Minister's advice must be accepted.[4]

There were, of course, certain difficulties and dangers connected with a policy of conservation. As Sir Richard Peirse told Sir Charles Portal, 'there is always the very important psychological factor. I am', he said, 'always preaching to the Command that they have a man-sized job to do; a job on which all eyes are turned; a job on which too much care and preparation cannot be expended, and above all a job which must be pushed right through to the conclusion if results are to be obtained. If, therefore,' (there is) he continued, 'any breath that the Powers-that-Be did not consider this to be the case, or that there is any hesitation in the handling of the Force, doubt must immediately arise in the minds of air-crews, and doubt spells irresolution. In other words,' he suggested, 'it is darned hard to fight a force like the Bomber Command at a subdued tempo.'[5]

Nevertheless, everything pointed towards the unwisdom of frittering Bomber Command away in a series of indecisive and extremely costly blows against Germany. There was no question of abandoning the offensive completely, but there was sense in saving up for the future. Accordingly, Sir Richard Peirse was told on 13th November 1941 in an Air Staff directive that Bomber Command was to be conserved 'in order to build up a strong force to be available by the spring of next year.' It was recognised that 'in vital operations heavy losses must be faced,' but it was thought 'undesirable in present circumstances and in the course of normal operations that

---

[1] Bomber Cmd. Report to Air Min., 2nd Dec. 1941.
[2] Letter Peirse to Portal, 10th Nov. 1941.
[3] Churchill: *The Second World War*, Vol. III, p. 748.
[4] Letter Portal to Peirse, 13th Nov. 1941.
[5] Letter Peirse to Portal, 10th Nov. 1941.

attacks should be pressed unduly especially if weather conditions were unfavourable or if aircraft were likely to be exposed to extreme hazard.'[1]

This was no less than a formal expression of the belief that the results which Bomber Command was achieving were not worth the casualties it was suffering. At one time, 1941 had been looked to as the year in which Bomber Command would become a weapon of war-winning power. Now the hope was transferred to 1943, and in the meantime it had been rudely frustrated and the Government's confidence in strategic bombing had been seriously undermined. Nevertheless, it was still intended to create a bombing force 'on the largest possible scale', rapid progress was being made with the development of the Lancaster bomber, new and remarkable radar aids to navigation were about to be introduced, and an officer who was presently to prove himself as one of the great commanders of the war was soon to assume command of the force. Above all, Bomber Command still remained, as it had been since the fall of France, the only weapon with which Britain could strike directly at Germany, and remind Russia of an ally in the West. 1941 had, indeed, brought Bomber Command to the nadir of its fortunes, but its prospects were by no means extinguished.

Note on the strength of the German Air Force, July 1941

(See p. 175 fn.)

The contemporary German figures for 26th July 1941 are as follows:

Eastern Front	Strength	Serviceable
Close Reconnaissance	298	192
Re-equipping	56	38
	354	230
Long range reconnaissance	219	131
Single-engined fighters	621	401
Re-equipping	24	15
	645	416
Twin-engined fighters	69	34
Bombers	812	449
Re-equipping	22	—
	834	449
Dive bombers	311	179

[1] Dir. Bottomley to Peirse, 13th Nov. 1941, App. 8 (xx).

Western Front: Luftflotte Reich

Single-engined fighters	37	32
Night fighters (twin-engined)	203	134
Twin-engined fighters (*Zerstörer*)	42	26

Luftflotte 3 (France and the Low Countries including Fliegerführer Atlantik)

Long range reconnaissance	39	28
Single-engined fighters	238	181
Re-equipping	24	21
	262	202
Bombers	128	62
Re-equipping	67	12
	195	74

Luftflotte 5 (Norway)

Long range reconnaissance	19	11
Single-engined fighters	39	28
Bombers	65	36

Reserves: on Eastern Front:

Close reconnaissance	32	20
Long range reconnaissance	59	26
Single-engined fighters	50	37
Twin-engined fighters	22	10
Dive bombers	25	16

Unlocated (probably in Germany)

Single-engined fighters	237	125
Twin-engined fighters	54	31
Bombers	280	133
Dive bombers	77	46

(Returns made by Q.M.G. German Air Min.)

CHAPTER IV

THE OPENING OF THE OFFENSIVE:
BOMBER COMMAND IN OPERATION

September 1939–November 1941

1. Trial and error: The conversion of Bomber Command into a night force, September 1939–April 1940
2. Night precision bombing, May 1940–March 1941
3. The tactical foundations of area bombing, March–November 1941

> 'I foresee a never ending struggle to circumvent the law that we cannot see in the dark.'
> AIR COMMODORE CONINGHAM, 9th December 1939

> 'The most suitable object from the economic point of view is not worth pursuing if it is not tactically attainable.'
> SIR CHARLES PORTAL, 4th July 1941

1. Trial and error:
the conversion of Bomber Command into a night force
September 1939–April 1940

BY comparison with what later became the routine operations of Bomber Command, the initial activities of the force may seem almost paltry, but, by comparison with anything which had been attempted before they were of immense significance. In its first daylight attacks, which began on 4th September 1939, Bomber Command was confronted with modern high-speed fighters supported by radar early warning devices and concentrated anti-aircraft fire. More was learnt about the potentialities and limitations of the day bomber formation in a few months of war experience than had been gained from the previous twenty years of theorising on the basis of fragmentary and often obsolete evidence derived from the First World War, the Sino-Japanese War and the Spanish Civil War. The leaflet raids, which began on the first night of the war, saw Bomber Command ranging far and wide over Europe in the darkness, reaching even the extremities at Berlin, Prague and Vienna. Such flights had been envisaged for 1919, but never before had they been carried out.

The men of 1939 and 1940 who planned and executed these operations were the pioneers of a new method of warfare which had never before been seriously tested in the field of action. In important aspects, as will appear, the decisions reached as a result of their experiences proved to be binding and set the pattern of subsequent and more famous operations. In particular, the decision to make Bomber Command primarily a night force arose from these early experiences.

Before the war, as will have been seen in Chapter II, when most of the major air plans envisaged precision bombing and when there had been grave doubts about the accuracy of night attack, the bulk of Bomber Command had been intended mainly as a day force. While it was believed that in day attacks even from high level the average bombing error would not be greater than three hundred yards, it was not thought that night bombing could achieve 'appreciable results' against precision targets.[1] The policy of restricted bombing which set a premium upon accuracy made it inevitable that the first bombing attacks would be carried out in daylight. Yet these daylight attacks might be expected to be formidable undertakings. In Britain the most effective means of defence against day

---
[1] Mins. of Air Min. Conf. (A.C.A.S. in chair), 30th Nov. 1938.

attack were already being perfected. Radar early warning devices, high-speed multi-gunned fighters of the Spitfire and Hurricane type together with anti-aircraft guns, balloon barrages and the Observer Corps, were the bases of the hope that any German day-bombing offensive against the United Kingdom might be defeated. Yet, if this hope was justified, how then would the British bomber formations fare against the German air defences? When the principal air plan was for a major daylight attack on the Ruhr this was, indeed, an urgent question for Bomber Command.

In theory, there were three principal methods by which day bombers might hope to pass safely through the opposing air defences. Firstly, they might travel at such great speed that the opposing fighters and flak would seldom be able to get on terms with them. In this way they would also be able to exploit the element of surprise to the full. A 'speed bomber' did not, however, exist in 1939, and though Sir Edgar Ludlow-Hewitt was pressing for the development of an aircraft of this kind, he did not expect that it would be able to perform more than harassing activities because it would have to be light.[1]

Secondly, the bombers might be covered by a long-range fighter escort but, as in the case of the 'speed bomber', no long-range fighter existed in 1939, and the years which followed were to show the difficulties of producing one. It was possible that Spitfires might afford support in an attack on the Ruhr, if flight over the Low Countries was possible, but it was unlikely that any would be available for this purpose.[2]

Thirdly, and this was the only immediately practical proposition, the bombers might concentrate in tight tactical formations and rely for their protection upon collective fire power. The defensive strength of these formations might be increased by equipping some aircraft with more guns or guns of larger calibre and, possibly, by providing them with special armour plating.[3] 'Self-defending' bomber formations might also, of course, gain a certain advantage by surprise, or at times they might be protected by cloud cover.

The success of self-defending formation tactics would depend upon whether the necessary concentration of fire power could be generated and sustained. This, in turn, would depend upon whether the bombers could keep station in the face of enemy attack from the air and the ground and after manœuvring over the target. Any advantage to be gained from cloud cover might be a disadvantage to station keeping, and whether surprise could be achieved or not would largely depend upon the extent to which the Germans had

---
[1] Letter Ludlow-Hewitt to Air Min., 23rd Sept. 1939.
[2] Note by D.D. Plans (Op.), 18th Oct. 1939.
[3] Letter Douglas to Ludlow-Hewitt, 12th Aug. 1939.

developed a system of radar early warning.[1] These problems and many others such as the performance and armament of the German fighters, the accuracy and strength of their anti-aircraft fire and the comparative advantages and dangers of high- and low-level attack, were either unknown or untested when, on 4th September 1939, fifteen Blenheims and fourteen Wellingtons took off between three and four o'clock in the afternoon to attack German warships reported to be off Brunsbüttel and in Wilhelmshaven.

Rain and cloud caused most of the bombers to lose their positions in the formations. For this reason, and possibly also because of faulty navigation, five Blenheims and five Wellingtons returned home having been unable to find any targets. For the same reason most of the aircraft which did find targets made individual attacks, thus offering the German gunners good targets. Very heavy casualties were suffered by the Blenheims, which attacked from 500 feet or below and came under effective anti-aircraft fire. Five of them failed to return. Some of the Wellingtons were engaged by Messerschmitt 109 fighters. These attacked from astern and slightly below the bombers, and the Wellington crews reported that the 'slightest skid' seemed to upset the fighters' aim. Much tracer was seen to go wide. Two Wellingtons failed to return, but it was thought most unlikely that either of them had been shot down by fighters. Superficial damage was done to the German fleet.[2]

The principal hazard on this operation had been from anti-aircraft fire directed at low-flying aircraft. The principal difficulties had been formation keeping and target finding in poor weather. Nothing had happened to reflect upon the validity of the self-defending formation theory, for the German fighter attacks had been brushed aside. Opportunities for repeating the experiment were, however, rare and difficult to exploit, for the German fleet proved to be an elusive target. It was not until December that the Wellingtons were again involved in serious encounter with the German air defences and, from the point of view of the effect which they had upon subsequent operations, the three actions which were fought on 3rd, 14th and 18th December were among the most important of the war.

Shortly after nine o'clock in the morning on 3rd December 1939

---

[1] As was later to be discovered, the Germans had made substantial progress with the development of radar early-warning devices. At the beginning of 1936 an early form of the 'Freya' device had located aircraft at a range of twenty-eight km. An improved version of the 'Freya' detected aircraft at a range of ninety km. when it was demonstrated to military and political leaders at Eckenförde in July 1938. *History of Radar Technology in Germany with Special Reference to its Application to Radio Location.* Paper read by Dr. H. Diehl at the Radar Conference in Frankfurt, 1953.

[2] Bomber Cmd. O.R.B., 4th Sept. 1939. Reports on Operations, 5th, 6th Sept. 1939. German account (undated). The cruiser *Emden* suffered minor damage and the pocket battleship *Scheer* was hit by three or four 250-lb. bombs, none of which exploded. These results were achieved by the Blenheims. Captain S. W. Roskill, R.N.: *The War at Sea*, Vol. I, (1954), p. 66.

twenty-four Wellingtons led by Wing Commander R. Kellet took off from Marham and Mildenhall to attack German warships in the vicinity of Heligoland. A rendezvous was made at 2,000 feet over Thetford, and at 9.45 a.m., over Great Yarmouth, the formation, divided into tactical sections of three, was in position. Thence the bombers turned out to sea, climbing on course to 10,000 feet. The leading section drew ahead on reconnaissance and at 11.26 a.m. Heligoland, visible through gaps in the cloud, lay one mile to the East. A number of ships could be seen, and in particular two cruisers were lying in the roads between the islands. This intelligence was signalled by wireless to the following formation and when it had drawn up attacks were delivered in turn by the sections. Cloud prevented accurate observation of the results but it seemed that hits and near misses had been achieved.

As it ran up on the target, the formation came under heavy anti-aircraft fire and two Wellingtons were hit but the damage which they sustained had no effect on their flying qualities. Within ten minutes of the initial sighting of Heligoland, Messerschmitt 109 and 110 fighters began to appear. They delivered a number of attacks, coming in from astern of the Wellingtons, but usually breaking off at a range of from 400–600 yards. The bombers experienced some difficulty in station keeping during their manœuvres over the target area and one, which got separated, was attacked by four Messerschmitt 109s. Three of these, however, came no nearer than 600 yards, and the other, which closed in to 350 yards, appeared to have been hit by fire from the Wellington rear-gunner. The bomber itself was not hit.

On the return journey four of the Wellingtons got left behind and had to recross the sea behind the main formation, but all the aircraft arrived safely at their bases. Despite the fact that the Germans had obviously had early warning of the attack and despite the fact that the formation had tended to break up over the target and had never completely re-formed, the Messerschmitts had failed to claim a single victim. The flak also had failed to bring anything down. The German fighters had shown a notable reluctance to press home their attacks in the face of the Wellingtons' rearward defences.[1]

The second encounter was to be less encouraging. On 14th December 1939, just before 11.45 a.m., twelve Wellingtons led by Wing Commander J. F. Griffiths, took off from Newmarket to carry out an armed patrol of the Schillig Roads. The formation was again divided into sections of three, the first two of which flew in line astern with the other two, also in line astern, echeloned to their starboard. At Great Yarmouth the formation was at 1,000 feet and just beneath

---

[1] Bomber Cmd. Report, 20th Dec. 1939.

ten-tenths cloud. The weather got worse during the sea crossing, and when the Dutch coast was sighted at five minutes past one o'clock the Wellingtons were flying at 600 feet in fine rain. They turned towards Heligoland with the object of deceiving the flak ships which were thought to have provided the early warning of the attack eleven days earlier. The weather became still worse, and when, just before two o'clock, the formation altered course for the Schillig Roads, it was down to 200 feet and the visibility was half a mile.

At this height the Wellingtons could not make any attacks because they had been ordered not to bomb unless they could see their targets from 2,000 feet. Nevertheless, they continued on their course and presently they sighted a number of naval, merchant and flak ships which opened fire upon them. For more than half an hour the Wellingtons remained within range of these guns and were subjected to almost continuous fire. Messerschmitt 109s and 110s also appeared at this stage. The co-operation between the fighters and the anti-aircraft gunners seemed to be excellent, the latter ceasing fire each time the fighters came in. Once again the Messerschmitts attacked from astern, but this time they pressed their attacks much more vigorously. One fighter closed in to 250 yards before opening fire, and broke off at 150 yards when it was seen to dive in flames.

As a result of this action five Wellingtons failed to return and another crashed on landing at Newmarket. Thus, half of the formation was destroyed. Yet it seemed possible that these losses were due to the anti-aircraft fire and not to the fighter attacks. 'It is now by no means certain', Air Commodore Bottomley, the Senior Air Staff Officer at Bomber Command, reported, 'that enemy fighters did in fact succeed in shooting down any of the Wellingtons. Considering that enemy aircraft made most determined and continuous attacks for 26 minutes on the formation, the failure of the enemy must be ascribed to good formation flying. The maintenance of tight, unshaken formations in the face of the most powerful enemy action is the test of bomber force fighting efficiency and morale. In our Service', he continued, 'it is the equivalent of the old "Thin Red Line" or the "Shoulder to Shoulder" of Cromwell's Ironsides.' The Germans, however, as will presently appear, took a very different view of the British formations, and on this occasion they reported 'the German fighters shot down 5 British aircraft and another was probably shot down but not confirmed. One German aircraft was lost.'[1]

Whether or not Air Commodore Bottomley was justified in describing the attacks by the German fighters as a 'failure', the Group Commander, Air Vice-Marshal Baldwin, clearly thought that

---

[1] Bomber Cmd. Report and Note by Bottomley, 28th Dec. 1939. *Lagebericht West No. 115, Luftwaffe H.Q.*, 15th Dec. 1939. The German report correctly stated that there were twelve aircraft in the British formation.

5. A Blenheim, Mk. IV (2 Group).

6. Wellingtons, Mk. Ic (3 Group).

7. A Whitley, Mk. V (4 Group).

8. Hampdens, Mk. I (5 Group).

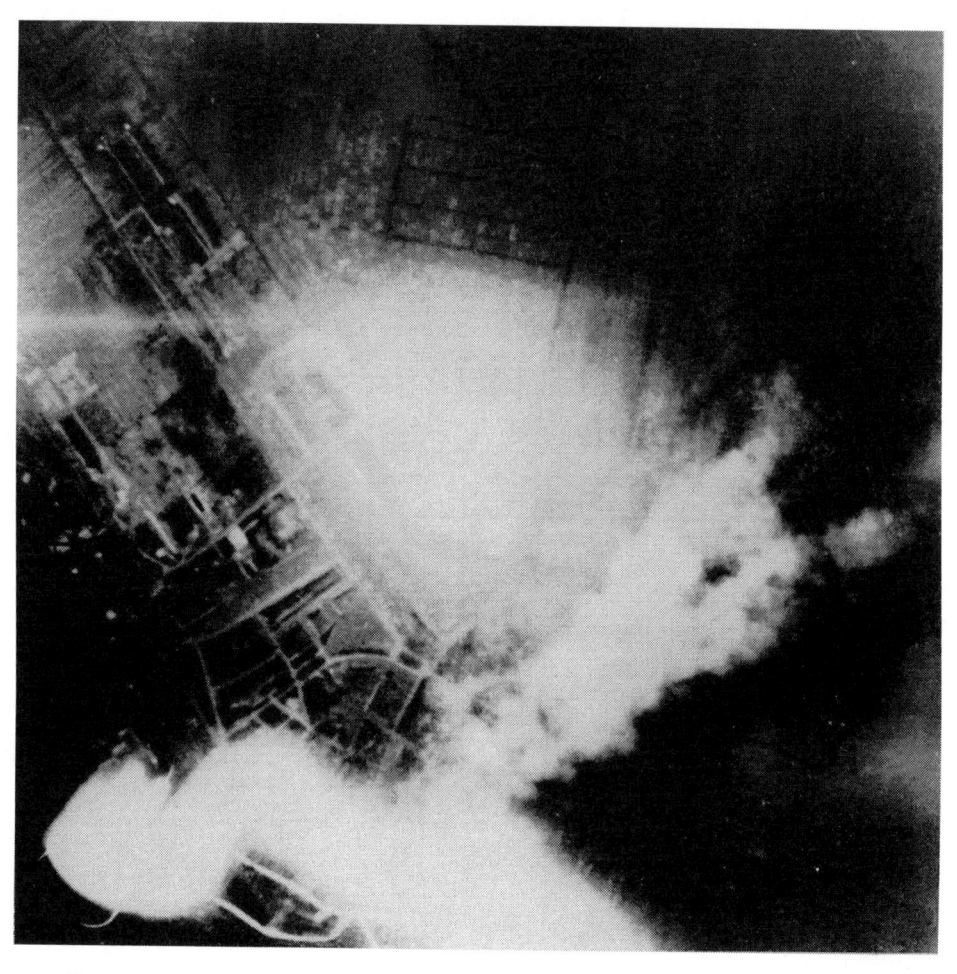

9. Emden, 31st March 1941. Bomber Command's first 4,000-lb. bombs. Night photograph of bombing.

10. A Wellington after returning from an attack on Bremen.

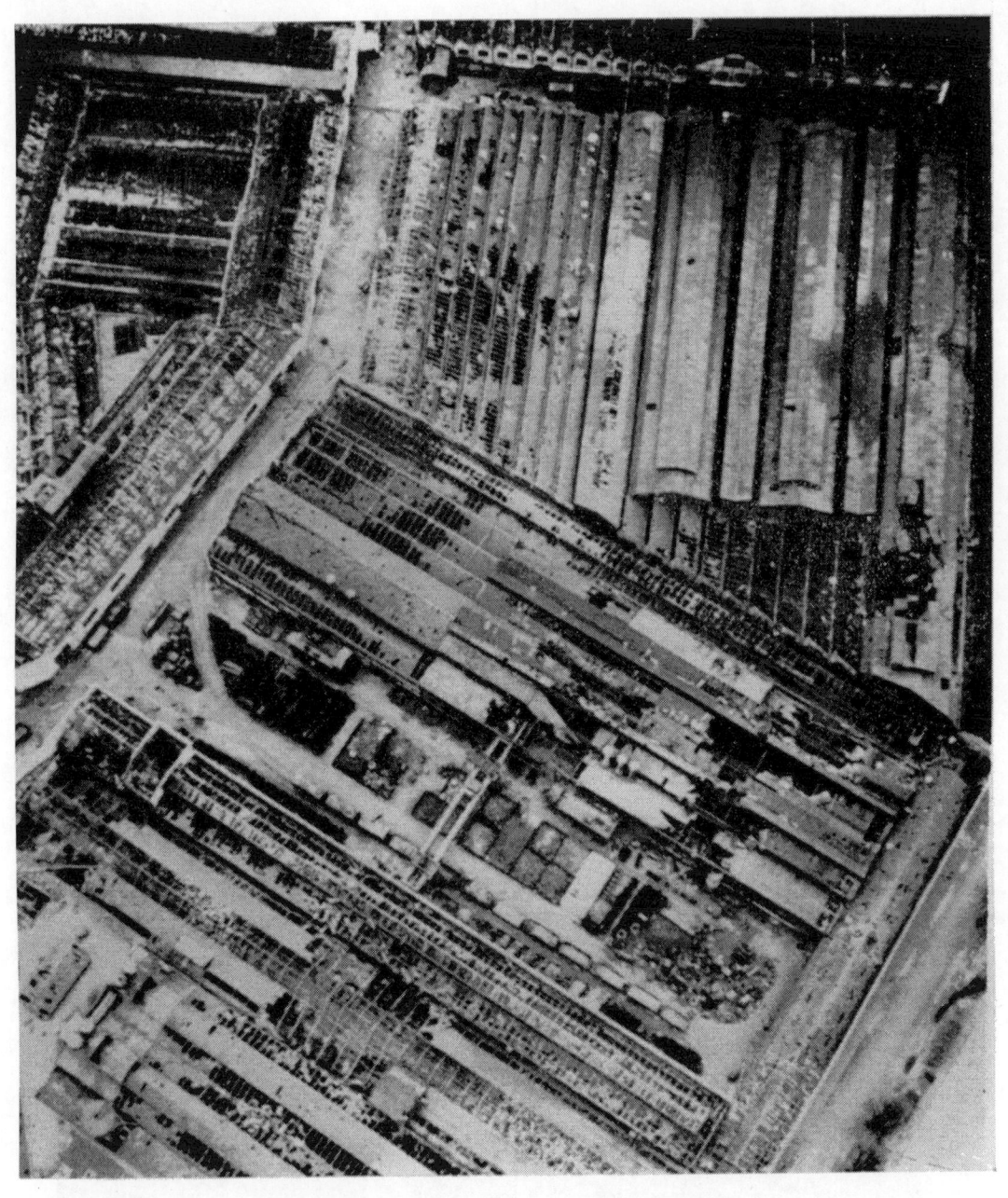

11. A section of the Renault Works after the attack on the night of 3rd March 1942, showing damage to the foundry and rolling mills.

someone had blundered, and he compared the attack to the charge of the Light Brigade. Sir Edgar Ludlow-Hewitt also felt that the leader of the formation should have had clear instructions to abandon the operation if the weather proved unsuitable. He was naturally loath to criticise the great gallantry which had been displayed by Wing Commander Griffiths, but he did feel it had been rash for the formation to trail its coat for forty-eight minutes in such hazardous circumstances.[1]

In the third operation of this series, carried out on 18th December 1939, twenty-four Wellingtons led by Wing Commander Kellet were despatched to patrol the Schillig Roads, Wilhelmshaven and the Jade Roads. They were ordered to attack with 500-lb. Semi-Armour Piercing bombs any warships which they sighted provided this could be done from a minimum height of 10,000 feet. Thus, the belief that previous disasters were due to the lethal effect of the flak at low level was written into the operational orders.

This time the Wellingtons were grouped into four formations each consisting of six aircraft, that is two sections of three. These formations were intended to provide mutual support, but were otherwise to act independently. About fifty minutes out from King's Lynn all the Wellingtons were in company, climbing to 14,000 feet into what became a cloudless sky with a visibility of about thirty miles. Two aircraft left the formation when it was about three-quarters of the way across the North Sea, and returned to base, the first because of engine trouble, and the second because of its captain's failure to receive an aldis lamp signal not to follow his leader. The remaining twenty-two Wellingtons continued towards Wilhelmshaven, making alterations of course to avoid the expected position of flak ships.

The first enemy fighters came in to attack when the formation was a few miles south of Heligoland, but the fighters broke off the engagement as the bombers came successively under anti-aircraft fire from ship and shore at Bremerhaven, Wilhelmshaven and the Schillig Roads. This flak caused some of the formations to open out somewhat, and when the bombers left Wilhelmshaven after aiming some bombs at warships there from about 13,000 feet, the fighter attacks were resumed with greater ferocity and they continued until what remained of the stricken formations were some seventy to eighty miles out to sea on the homeward journey.

Some German fighters were apparently using cannon at ranges of 600–900 yards, which was beyond the effective reach of the ·303 guns in the Wellingtons. Others pressed attacks in to close quarters, coming in one case to within fifty yards. Some attacks were delivered

---

[1] Letter Baldwin to Ludlow-Hewitt, 19th Dec. 1939. Letter Ludlow-Hewitt to Baldwin, 24th Dec. 1939.

from astern as before, but others came simultaneously from the two rear quarters. Yet others came from the beam where the Wellington had no defences. A desperate battle ensued. A bomber in the leading section was hit in a beam attack and its cabin burst into flames near the main spar. Another, having lost its station in a manœuvre, was heavily engaged, both the rear and the front gunners being wounded. When the ammunition in the rear turret had been exhausted, the captain of this aircraft dived to sea level, and though chased down by Messerschmitts, escaped to England. A Wellington was seen to break up in the air after a fighter attack; another went down with its port engine burning.

Of the six bombers in the rear formation which had been flying in pairs, only one returned, and this probably owed its safety to an accident. For the first fifteen minutes of the action this Wellington was at 15,000 feet. Then one of the crew who was going forward to the front turret accidentally operated the flap lever. The aircraft immediately lost its formation position. This captain also dived to sea level and got home. Wellingtons were seen heading for Holland with petrol streaming from their tanks. Of the twenty-two bombers which had been engaged, only ten returned.[1]

There was some comfort to be derived from the belief that the Wellingtons had given as good as they had got. It was estimated that they had destroyed no fewer than twelve of the attacking German fighters and that another twelve had probably been damaged beyond repair.[2] Nevertheless, though it could not at the time be known in Britain that these estimates exaggerated the actual German losses by at least three times,[3] the fact remained that the bomber losses were more than could be afforded. The loss of twelve Wellingtons with their valuable crews was a serious matter for the 1939 force, especially so when it happened so soon after other heavy losses. The loss of fifty per cent of the force despatched, and nearly fifty-five per cent of that engaged, was at least ten times the casualty rate which Bomber Command could ever afford as a regular drain on its crews and aircraft.

In the previous actions on 4th September and 14th December it had been assumed that the anti-aircraft fire, and not the opposing fighters, had caused the bomber casualties. The height of attack had accordingly been raised and the action of 18th December had been fought at high level around 15,000 feet. However much the anti-aircraft fire had contributed to the earlier results, there could be

---

[1] Bomber Cmd. Report, 22nd Dec. 1939.
[2] B.C.I.S., 4th March 1940.
[3] *Jagdgeschwader 1*, Battle Report for 18th Dec. 1939 (four aircraft lost and nine damaged), but another source, *Lagebericht West*, 19th Dec. 1939, admits the loss of only two aircraft.

no doubt that it was, on this occasion, the Messerschmitts which had achieved at least the majority of the kills. This raised issues of even greater significance than the actual loss of men and material which had been suffered. If this was the kind of punishment which daylight formations of bombers might expect to receive in general actions of the future, then clearly the whole conception of the self-defending formation, and with it, the most important among the Western Air Plans, particularly the Ruhr plan, had been exploded. If, on the other hand, it could be shown that the action of 18th December had been a freak, then it was possible that a gain in experience, a revision of tactics and the improvement of certain equipment might restore the balance before Bomber Command was committed to larger scale actions against targets of deeper penetration.

There were two matters of equipment to which the Group Commander, Air Vice-Marshal Baldwin, drew attention in a note accompanying the official report on the operation from his headquarters. The first was the inadequacy of the unprotected petrol tank in the port wing of the Wellington. The need for self-sealing tanks was now seen to be vital. Wellingtons were very gradually being equipped with armour plating on the port wing, but progress even with this *pis aller* was so slow that it would take three months to complete the modification of all the operational Wellingtons. Air Vice-Marshal Baldwin feared that if something drastic was not done, the morale of his crews might suffer. The second matter referred to defence against beam attack. Air Vice-Marshal Baldwin thought that a beam attack was unlikely to succeed. Nevertheless, he considered that at least one of his Wellingtons had been destroyed by this method. Certainly they had no defence against it, and he thought it was now necessary to site a gun centrally in the astro-hatch.[1]

The rest of the explanation seemed to lie in the failure of the aircraft to keep their stations in the formations. The 3 Group Report observed that on 18th December some of the Wellingtons had closed up and kept in very tight formation throughout the action. These, it was claimed, had suffered only one casualty. Others had opened out into loose formations as a result of the anti-aircraft fire and had, in consequence, it was suggested, suffered heavily when the fighters came in.[2]

This tendency for the bombers to split up when under pressure was disquieting when the crews had repeatedly been told that their safety depended on maintaining station in closely knit, mutually supporting formations. Air Vice-Marshal Baldwin feared it might be

---

[1] Report Baldwin to Bomber Cmd., 22nd Dec. 1939.
[2] 3 Group Report, 22nd Dec. 1939.

due to making over-severe demands upon pilots whose war experience was still inevitably very slight. He thought that 'raw' pilots 'would always experience a tendency to scatter when subjected to intense A.A. fire,' but he could think of no means of convincing them of the importance of avoiding this except by giving them an experience which was liable to be their last. In the First World War, he told the Commander-in-Chief, it had been found necessary to 'blood' the formations by sending them on very short raids on which they would encounter some opposition, but from which they could withdraw quickly before straggling became pronounced. In the case of the Wellingtons, he said that the formations were being sent out 'unaccustomed to the war issues, almost to the limit of the aircraft's endurance, and in to heavily defended areas, . . .' They were being exposed to 'a somewhat lengthy attack during which there is no possibility of assistance or respite, should straggling become apparent.'[1]

When he was preoccupied with thoughts of the full-scale daylight attack on the Ruhr, this argument must have had a disconcerting effect upon Sir Edgar Ludlow-Hewitt. He pointed out to Air Vice-Marshal Baldwin that the criterion of the severity and difficulty of an operation lay in the extent to which it involved penetration of enemy territory. In these December attacks the penetration had been practically nil, and it was for this reason that he had welcomed the German fleet as an initial target for his day squadrons. All the same, Sir Edgar Ludlow-Hewitt admitted that the opposition encountered had proved very much more formidable than expected, but he attributed this to 'crack' fighter squadrons with which he was convinced the Germans had reinforced their defences in the north before the actions of 14th and 18th December.

The Commander-in-Chief told Air Vice-Marshal Baldwin that he must personally get his unit and flight commanders together and 'rub into them the vital importance of good formation flying'. If necessary he was to go further and threaten disciplinary action against pilots who avoidably failed to keep station. Finally, he was suspicious of the standard of efficiency among the crews. Many of them were, he feared, ignorant of their equipment and many air gunners, he thought, did not understand the proper use of tracer ammunition. 'Now that we are actually at war,' he concluded, 'we must, I think, take drastic action to ensure that crews do actually understand what is required and do organise themselves efficiently for active operations.'[2]

The gist of all these comments seemed to display a surviving if

---

[1] Letter Baldwin to Ludlow-Hewitt, 19th Dec. 1939.
[2] Letter Ludlow-Hewitt to Baldwin, 24th Dec. 1939.

somewhat chastened confidence in the principle of the self-defending formation. They all showed that changes and improvements in equipment, training and briefing were necessary, and thereby they all expressed the hope that the action on 18th December 1939 had, indeed, been a freak which Bomber Command possessed the means to counter. The 3 Group report had even gone so far as to assert that 'There is every reason to believe that a very close formation of six Wellington aircraft will emerge from a long and heavy attack by enemy fighters with very few if any casualties to its own aircraft. A loose formation is however liable to suffer very heavy casualties under the same conditions.'[1] How far the Commander-in-Chief was prepared to test this confidence in further actions will presently appear. Meanwhile, it is instructive to consider the somewhat different view which the Germans took of the same action.

On 18th December 1939 the German fighter squadrons covering the north received radar early warning of the approaching British attack which was seen to be on a 'large scale'. The *Kommodore* was thus able to dispose his aircraft in good time and to divert to the battle area those which were already in the air.[2] The German fighter pilots had already experienced the formidable rearward defences of the Wellingtons, and on this occasion they had been ordered to attempt beam attacks. They found this tactic an effective means of breaking up the bomber formations, but they also thought that the rigidity with which the British pilots stuck to their courses and clung to their tight formations had facilitated their task. Only three British pilots had adapted themselves to the beam attacks by weaving, and this had proved effective against at least the Messerschmitt 109s which outnumbered the 110s. The German pilots, because of the greatly superior speed of their aircraft, were always able to choose their positions for attack. Even so some of them still made stern assaults, and these received many hits and two of them were shot down. Others found that they could put the Wellington rear turret out of action from ranges beyond four hundred yards and could then approach for the kill without opposition.

Once hit, the Wellingtons seemed to burn very easily. In one case the tail unit was seen to catch fire, and in several others the wings blazed up although, as the Germans thought, the petrol tanks had not been hit. To the Germans it seemed 'criminal folly' for the Wellingtons to approach in a cloudless sky with perfect visibility. They thought that the British had become over-confident as a result

---

[1] 3 Group Report, 22nd Dec. 1939.
[2] The experimental 'Freya' installation at Wangerooge picked up the Bomber Command aircraft at a range of 113 km. and direct control of the German fighters on the basis of cathode-ray readings was executed for the first time. Paper read by Dr. H. Diehl at the Radar Conference held in 1953 at Frankfurt.

of their success on 3rd December, but they did not suppose that their fighters would again be offered such easy targets. As a result of the combats they believed that thirty-four Wellingtons had been shot down by their fighters. They also reported that another had landed on the sea and that a thirty-sixth had been destroyed by naval anti-aircraft fire.[1]

This German report on the action, could he but have known it, confirmed Air Vice-Marshal Baldwin's suspicion that the beam attack was a serious danger and his belief that self-sealing petrol tanks were a vital necessity. It seemed to suggest that the British pilots had done all they could to maintain their formations, but it indicated that this was impossible and, perhaps, also unwise. Above all it showed that the German fighters enjoyed three cardinal advantages in a radar early-warning system, a greatly superior speed to that of the bombers, and an ability to shoot at greater range than the Wellington gunners. There was nothing to suggest that any 'crack' squadrons had been brought into the area before the engagement.

On the evidence of the German conclusions it might have been supposed that daylight formation bombing was no longer a practical proposition of war, that the action on 3rd December, and not that on 18th December, was the freak. On the evidence of the British conclusions, on the other hand, it might be supposed that tactical and technical adjustments of a relatively minor nature would enable the day bomber formations to withstand the battle. Yet, in 1940, it was the British who abandoned day bombing and the Germans who carried it out on a large scale. There was, however, the important difference that the German bombers could be accompanied by supporting fighters.

From the British point of view this apparent paradox is explained by the marked divergence between theory and practice which now appeared. For example, in a tactical memorandum of 29th December 1939, Air Commodore Bottomley continued to speak of the inviolability of a tight bomber formation and to attribute the recent losses to straggling. Yet, eleven days earlier, on the day of the heaviest losses, the Air Ministry had ordered Bomber Command to desist from reconnaissance in force of the Heligoland Bight estuaries until the armouring of petrol tanks had been completed.[2] On 2nd January 1940 Air Vice-Marshal Harris, Air Officer Commanding 5 Group, told the Commander-in-Chief that so long as three bombers were in company in daylight the pilots 'considered themselves capable of taking on anything'. At the same time it was decided that the Wellingtons of 3 Group and the Hampdens of 5 Group should join

---

[1] *Jagdgeschwader 1*. Battle Report for 18th Dec. 1939.
[2] Bomber Cmd. Memo., 29th Dec. 1939. Air Min. to Bomber Cmd., 18th Dec. 1939.

the Whitleys of 4 Group in leaflet raids to gain night-flying experience.[1] In any case, on the very day on which Air Vice-Marshal Harris expressed his confidence in the daylight section of three, a section of three Wellingtons was engaged over the North Sea by Messerschmitt 110s and two of them were shot down.[2]

Even more instructive was the difference in tone between what Sir Edgar Ludlow-Hewitt said in December 1939 to his Group Commander, Air Vice-Marshal Baldwin, and what he said in January 1940 to the Air Staff. On the former occasion most of his remarks were concerned with the need for better formation flying, better gunnery and greater crew efficiency as the means of successful daylight bombing. On the latter occasion he pointed to the December actions as strong evidence against carrying out the Ruhr plan.[3] In fact, the actions in December 1939 were taken as a powerful warning of the superiority of the day fighter over the day bomber, and the series of formation attacks was not continued after 18th December. Though neither the idea nor the practice of daylight bombing was entirely cast aside, and, indeed, were often to be revived in the future, immediate confidence in the theory of the self-defending formation, at least with the existing types of bomber, had been seriously shaken.

The factors which were driving Bomber Command towards a complete reorientation of operational policy were not, however, entirely negative. They arose not only from the actions fought in daylight over the North Sea, but also from the night flights of deep penetration which Whitleys of 4 Group had been carrying out over Germany since the first night of the war.

The German air defences by day had proved more formidable than expected. Very heavy losses had been inflicted upon the bombers even before they crossed the German coast. At night, however, there was no counterpart to the effective weapons which had been turned against the Wellington formations. By comparison with the developed state of daylight defence, the science of night defence, in Germany, as in England, was still in its early infancy. Indeed, the almost total lack of enemy opposition encountered by Whitleys on their night flights to Hamburg, the Ruhr, Münster, Osnabrück, Stuttgart, Mannheim, Nuremberg, Berlin and many other parts of Germany, came as rather a surprise to the Group Commander, Air Commodore Coningham. After three months' experience of directing these long-range leaflet raids, he told Sir Edgar Ludlow-Hewitt that 'Our views have undergone considerable change since the war started. The absence of enemy fighters' opposition at night, the

---

[1] Mins. of Bomber Cmd. Conf., 2nd Jan. 1940.
[2] Report by the surviving pilot.
[3] See above, pp. 198 and 139.

comparative ineffectiveness of their anti-aircraft fire even at middle heights, their doubtful searchlight efficiency' were all factors combining 'to lower in a surprising degree our opinion of the opposition we expected to meet.'[1]

This lack of enemy opposition did mean that the Whitley battle casualties were extremely light. Between 10th November 1939 and 16th March 1940, for example, there were none at all.[2] But it did not mean that the path of the Whitleys to their various targets was easy, nor was it by any means always certain that they had really got there. 'The real constant battle', the Group Commander pointed out, 'is with the weather. . . . The constant struggle at night is to get light on to the target', and he foresaw 'a never ending struggle to circumvent the law that we cannot see in the dark . . . '[3]

In these observations Air Commodore Coningham had epitomised two of the outstanding problems which confronted the night bomber throughout the war, but never more so than at its outset. It was obvious that a third would be added if the Germans developed any effective night air defences, but the fourth, which was, perhaps, the most elementary of all, that is navigation, was not yet recognised as a problem. All these problems had been grievously neglected in the years before the war and the early operations of the Whitley Group, which had been designed as a night bombing force, showed that both the crews and the aircraft were ill equipped for the tasks which they now had to attempt.

For example, on the night of 19th October 1939 a Whitley was returning from Hamburg at 18,000 feet. Possibly owing to icing it experienced engine trouble and came down to 1,500 feet before the engines recovered somewhat. During this descent the captain had ordered the crew to abandon the aircraft, but finding that they had remained on board owing to a misunderstanding, he decided to try and reach France. Static interference made it difficult to get loop bearings, but eventually a running fix in the neighbourhood of St. Omer was obtained. The aircraft came down through low cloud and rain in search of an aerodrome, but none was found. Eventually after driving away some cattle the pilot made a successful landing in a field between Abbeville and Arras.

Another illustration of the difficulties confronting these pioneers is provided by the operations carried out on the night of 27th October 1939. Whitleys were despatched with leaflets to Munich, Frankfurt am Main and Stuttgart. One of the aircraft engaged on the Munich operation experienced icing in cloud at 1,000 feet. It climbed to 20,000 feet, where it was still in cloud with severe icing conditions.

---

[1] Report Coningham to Bomber Cmd., 9th Dec. 1939.
[2] do. 16th March 1940.
[3] do. 9th Dec. 1939.

Crystalline ice formed on the leading edges of the wings, over the gun turrets and on the cabin windows. The front gun was frozen up and rendered useless. The aircraft's trimming tabs were jammed by ice and the 'dustbin' turret stuck about a third of the way down its travel. The ceiling of the bomber was reduced to 16,500 feet and it was forced to remain in cloud. After two and a quarter hours in the air the oxygen supply in the cabin was exhausted. Some of the crew occasionally banged their heads on the floor or navigation table as a relief from the feeling of frost bite and oxygen lack. On the return journey the icing became worse and the rear guns now also froze, lumps of ice flew off the airscrews, striking the sides and nose of the aircraft. Nevertheless, the Whitley successfully homed on a French base.

A second Whitley bound for Munich on the same night also encountered severe icing trouble. At 15,000 feet the temperature was −30° C. Soon after turning for home after dropping the leaflets, the starboard engine began to give trouble, but the Whitley managed to maintain its height till it crossed the German frontier. At this point a cylinder blew off and the engine failed. Despite the use of full power from the port engine the aircraft began to come down. At 2,500 feet opaque ice covered the instruments and windscreen. The remaining engine began to fail and the captain gave the order to abandon the aircraft. The rear gunner, whose intercommunication had failed, remained on board, unaware of the fact that he was alone. He escaped from the crash with a few bruises and burns convinced that his comrades were buried in the burning debris.

A third Whitley encountered similar difficulties on the return flight from Frankfurt am Main. Great discomfort and fatigue were felt by the crew. At one stage the captain collapsed but was revived by the wireless operator. The starboard engine caught fire and had to be stopped. The aircraft then sank into cloud and was covered with ice. Probably as a result it went into a dive, but the pilots managed to regain control at 7,000 feet. Even so, the bomber continued to lose height at the rate of 2,000 feet per minute. The port engine now also stopped and four inches of ice could be seen protruding from the cowling. The order was given to abandon the aircraft, but, on finding that both the front and the rear gunners were unconscious, the captain cancelled it. The Whitley glided down and broke cloud at about two hundred feet above the ground. All that could be seen by the crew was a black forest with a grey object in its centre for which they were heading. The aircraft brushed through the tops of the trees and came to rest in a field. The crew extinguished the fire and went to sleep in the fuselage.[1]

---

[1] Personal experience Reports.

These were examples of what Air Commodore Coningham meant by the 'real constant battle with the weather', and it was this battle which constituted the principal threat to the safety of the Whitleys. Even if these weather hazards could to some extent be overcome by the provision of de-icing equipment, cockpit heating and better weather forecasting, there were other difficulties associated with night operations which now began to disclose themselves.[1] Above all was the problem of night visibility. If these gruelling night flights were to be rewarded with any worth-while results, then, when they were allowed to carry them, the crews would have to succeed in hitting their targets with at least a proportion of their bombs.

Hitting a target was not simply a question of accurate bomb aiming, for before that, the target had to be found, and this presented the crew with a two-fold problem. Firstly, the aircraft had to be brought to the general area in which the objective lay. This was a question of navigation. Then, within that area, the particular target had to be located, and only after that could the bomb-sight come into action. Obviously the more accurate was the navigation, the smaller would be the final area of search and the quicker and easier the location of the target. Equally, unless the navigation was reasonably accurate the final area of search would be so large that the task of locating the target would become hopeless.

Before the war, as will have been seen, there was evidence to indicate the difficulties of navigation.[2] Navigation errors are, of course, cumulative, and the longer the flight the greater is the error to be expected. Nevertheless, despite the long-range attacks which were being planned from 1937 onwards, little or nothing was done to tackle the problem of air navigation, and on the outbreak of war Bomber Command was not far removed in its technique from the days of open cockpit flying when navigation was simply a question of instinct and map reading.

Apart from map reading, the only aids to navigation with which the night bombers of 1939 were equipped were the astro-sextant and directional radio, neither of which could be relied upon for accurate results and both of which required a high degree of skill in operation. The standard of navigation training did not justify the hope that such skill would often be forthcoming and, in addition, Whitley bombers had a tendency to 'wallow' at height which 'offered little

---

[1] There were frequent complaints about the inaccuracy of weather forecasts. There was not only the danger of aircraft running into impossibly bad weather but also that of good nights being missed because of bad forecasts. For example, for the night of 26th February 1940, Air Commodore Coningham reported, broken low cloud with a likelihood of mist was forecast for western Germany. In the event, visibility proved to be 'exceptional' and the three-quarters moon was only slightly dimmed by high broken cloud. Report Coningham to Bomber Cmd., 2nd March 1940.

[2] See, in particular above, p. 112.

CONVERSION TO A NIGHT FORCE

chance of success' with astro-navigation.[1] In fact, unless they could constantly pin-point their aircraft by direct observation, the night crews were seldom sure of their position.[2]

Thus, navigation remained largely a matter of observation, and by this means it was assumed that the majority of the night bombers would somehow or other arrive very close to their targets.[3] Dilatory discussions about the need for technical aids such as radar and the Air Position Indicator did take place from time to time,[4] but a general inertia overcame all significant progress until its serious consequences excited concern in Downing Street, and that did not happen until two years of war had passed.[5]

Somewhat more attention in the opening months of the war was devoted to the second stage of the problem, that is, the identification of the target once its general area had been reached. But before the war the problem of night vision, like that of navigation, had been largely neglected. Indeed, it was only in May 1939, when the majority of the Western Air Plans had already been made, that Sir Edgar Ludlow-Hewitt observed that it was important to know 'exactly what type of target was worthwhile allotting for attack by night. . . .' He suggested that one staff officer from each Group should do some night flying and then report on the possibilities to his Group Commander.[6] Nevertheless, the Bomber Command Operational Orders issued in August 1939 showed no clear appreciation of what the crew of an operational night bomber might be expected to see or not to see.[7] It was, therefore, left to the Whitley crews to find out on their early leaflet raids what they could see, and on the basis of their experiences the Group Commander was soon able to know that his operational orders were largely impracticable.

On 11th October 1939 Air Commodore Coningham reported to Bomber Command Headquarters on the problem of target location at night. He pointed out that the ability to see a target depended upon the state of the moon and weather, upon whether the objective was blacked out or self-illuminating, upon the height at which the

---

[1] Notes on Bomber Cmd. Conf., 6th Nov. 1939.

[2] For example, Coningham's report to Bomber Cmd., 2nd March 1940, dealing with operations on 26th Feb. 1940.

[3] Reports Coningham to Bomber Cmd., 11th Oct. 1939, 3rd Feb. 1940. Letter Coningham to Bottomley, 14th Oct. 1939.

[4] Notes on Bomber Cmd. Conf., 6th Nov. 1939. Mins. of Bomber Cmd. Mtg., 14th Nov. 1939.

[5] An example is provided by the Group Navigation Officers' Conference held on 12th November 1940. The Chairman, Wing Commander L. K. Barnes, announced his conclusion that only thirty-five per cent of the bombers despatched were reaching their primary targets. He also remarked upon the lack of items for the agenda and upon the fact that 'less than half of the Groups had replied to notification of the Conference . . .' For the Prime Minister's eventual intervention, see above, p. 179.

[6] Group Commanders' Conf., 22nd May 1939.

[7] B.C.O.O. 22nd Aug., 24th Aug. 1939.

aircraft was flying and upon the amount of searchlight dazzle encountered. In moonlight, which he thought would be effective for fourteen or fifteen days in each month, Air Commodore Coningham reported that areas of water became self-illuminating. Large rivers, canals and lakes could be seen from above 12,000 feet. Small rivers, however, could not be seen from above 6,000 or 8,000 feet. Railway lines were visible in certain angles of light from a 'surprising height'. Small towns could be seen from heights up to 4,000 or 6,000 feet. Separate buildings were not visible from above 3,000 or 4,000 feet.

On dark nights with no moon it was found that crews of low-flying aircraft could distinguish land from water. Otherwise all that they could see were self-illuminating objects like blast-furnaces. The glare of searchlights completely dazzled crews flying below 12,000 feet and Air Commodore Coningham, therefore, concluded that if the target had to be identified, then the only practical proposition for night attack was a self-illuminating objective. It did not, however, seem certain that to be destroyed a target had to be seen. 'Immediately the strictly visual limitation is waived,' Air Commodore Coningham suggested, 'the field of operations broadens. Targets can be bombed effectively and accurately by their known position in proximity to visible features . . . A tank farm, oil refinery, dockyard, or even a factory, can be sited exactly when in close proximity to a visible mark, and from a reasonable tactical height', he asserted, 'there is no reason why the bombing should not be as accurate as if the target itself were visible'.[1]

At the Air Ministry, however, this method of offset bombing was still regarded as illegal and it was thought necessary that the target should actually be identified before it was attacked.[2] The prospects of night bombing were, therefore, severely restricted by these revelations about the limitations of night vision. While confidence in the possibility of day bombing still remained high, this might not seem so serious,[3] but if day bombing failed, and in any case, if any precise results were to be got at night, then clearly something would have to be done to assist the crews to locate targets at night. This is what the Group Commander foresaw when he referred to the constant struggle to get light on the target and 'a never-ending struggle to circumvent the law that we cannot see in the dark.'

Sir Edgar Ludlow-Hewitt's immediate reaction was to adjust the night bombing plans to fit these newly realised operational limitations. Targets would have to be sought, he said, irrespective of whether their nature 'fits entirely the current plan or not'.[4] Evidence

---

[1] Report Coningham to Bomber Cmd., 11th Oct. 1939.
[2] Plans 5 comment on Coningham Report, 6th Nov. 1939.
[3] Plans 2 comment on Coningham Report, 6th Nov. 1939.
[4] Min. Ludlow-Hewitt to Bottomley, 15th Oct. 1939.

about the visibility of various targets was still far from complete. In particular, as the Air Ministry pointed out on 9th November 1939, it was important to find out whether railway marshalling yards could be bombed at night. These had not been mentioned in Air Commodore Coningham's report, but it was quite possible that a major bombing effort might eventually be turned against them.[1] Meanwhile, 4 Group would have the opportunity of making further observations, and Sir Edgar Ludlow-Hewitt suggested that they should constitute themselves into a sort of night flying investigation centre.[2]

At Bomber Command there were some doubts about the necessity for these investigations over enemy territory. In the case of the proposed reconnaissance of marshalling yards, for instance, Group Captain H. P. Lloyd thought that it was a waste of effort to go all the way to Germany to find something out which, it seemed to him, could equally well be learned by a flight over the railway yards at Basingstoke.[3] Air Commodore Bottomley, however, thought the blackout conditions might not be the same, and he thought that the reconnaissance of the Ruhr marshalling yards should be given to 4 Group as a 'primary task'. The Commander-in-Chief agreed and the orders were given on 11th December 1939.[4]

At the instance of the Air Ministry, further questions were put to 4 Group in February 1940 as to the visibility of cooling towers, rivers and canals.[5] By this time two Whitleys had been to investigate Hamm and Schwerte. Flying at between 1,000 and 5,000 feet they reported that there was no blackout in the marshalling yards and that 'accurate bombing attacks could have been carried out at any height up to 10–12000 feet.'[6] Weather interfered with other experiments and it was not until the night of 26th February that three Whitleys found excellent visibility over western Germany by the light of a three-quarter moon. Two of the crews reported the identification of various cooling towers at Ibbenbüren, Düsseldorf and Cologne, from heights varying between 4,000 and 9,000 feet. From 8,000 feet over Bielefeld, one crew said that the marshalling yards, faintly lit with blue lamps, were 'conspicuous'. Another found the Rhine between Duisburg and Cologne 'very distinctive'. The third Whitley got lost while the pilots were changing seats, and despite a square search at 2,000 feet, it failed to locate its position.[7]

---

[1] Letter Collier (for D. of Plans) to Ludlow-Hewitt, 9th Nov. 1939.
[2] Min. Bottomley to Groom (Ops.1.b.), 30th Oct. 1939.
[3] Min. Lloyd to Bottomley, 4th Dec. 1939.
[4] Mins. Bottomley to Ludlow-Hewitt, 7th Dec. 1939, Ludlow-Hewitt to Bottomley, undated. Bomber Cmd. to 4 Group, 11th Dec. 1939.
[5] Letter Air Min. (D.H.O.) to Ludlow-Hewitt, 2nd Feb. 1940. B.C.O.O., 8th Feb. 1940.
[6] B.C.I.R., 22nd Jan. 1940.
[7] B.C.I.R., 27th Feb. 1940. Report 4 Group to Bomber Cmd. sent under cover dated 2nd March 1940.

Air Commodore Coningham at once saw the danger of drawing general conclusions from particular evidence. The weather and visibility, he pointed out to Bomber Command, had been exceptionally good. He also thought it wise to assume that the German defences had not been working at full strength.[1] The Commander-in-Chief also saw the danger of over-optimism, and, though he was well pleased with the results of this reconnaissance, he warned the Air Ministry that the crews had only succeeded by 'meticulous and careful pin-pointing of their tracks.' Any attempt to use Dead Reckoning Navigation would, Sir Edgar Ludlow-Hewitt said, 'involve a real risk of failing to find their targets altogether . . .'[2] Thus, successful night precision bombing, it seemed, would depend upon the ability of the crews to see the ground in sufficient detail to enable them, for the purpose of navigation, to pass from one pinpoint to another and finally to make a visual identification of the target. This would mean flying fairly low, and certainly not above 12,000 feet, and it would also require good weather and reasonable moonlight. Increased German defences might soon drive the bombers above 12,000 feet and experience had already shown that the weather was often not only bad, but impossible. If all other things had been equal, the prospects of night precision bombing in the continued absence of any effective means of illuminating the target artificially and of any satisfactory aid to Dead Reckoning Navigation, might have seemed, as they had done before the war, extremely doubtful.

All other things were, however, far from equal. Sir Edgar Ludlow-Hewitt was becoming increasingly pessimistic about the prospects of daylight bombing, and after the experiences of December 1939 it is hardly surprising that he turned with some pleasure to the contemplation of night operations from which so few of his aircraft failed to return. If the crews were given the 'maximum experience of night reconnaissance plus training in the identification of night targets', then, Sir Edgar Ludlow-Hewitt believed, it might be possible to carry out 'the major destructive part of our plans by precision bombing at night'. In order to 'avoid loss of aircraft by day,' the Commander-in-Chief said, 'it is worth concentrating our maximum energies upon training all our heavy units up to the standard where they can do precision bombing on these targets at night'.[3]

Accordingly, the Hampdens of 5 Group and the Wellingtons of 3 Group which had already had some experience of the leaflet raids, were, on 6th March 1940, ordered to join the Whitleys of 4 Group on night reconnaissance flights over probable targets in Germany.[4]

---

[1] Report Coningham to Bomber Cmd., 2nd March 1940.
[2] Letter Ludlow-Hewitt to Air Min., 6th March 1940.
[3] Min. Ludlow-Hewitt to Bottomley, 6th March 1940.
[4] Bomber Cmd. to 3 and 5 Groups, 6th March 1940.

Bomber Command was rapidly becoming a night force, but it still had day plans for the destruction of small targets by precise attack.

Most considerations about how night bombing was to be achieved began with the assumption that the bombers had reached an area around the target measuring ten miles by ten miles, and that within that area they had succeeded in identifying some prominent landmark.[1] The question upon which attention was focussed was how the bombers, having found this landmark, would proceed and secure hits on the neighbouring target. The most hopeful solution seemed to lie in a timed run from the recognised landmark to the position of the target and the release of flares or flash bombs to illuminate the area. The 4·5-inch parachute flare with which Bomber Command was already equipped proved to be of limited utility. It would serve to confirm the position of the aircraft provided that it was already known, but it could not be used to illuminate a target unless there was an aircraft closely following that which dropped the flare.[2] In other words, if the navigator knew that he was about to pass over some feature he might, if he was lucky, confirm it by dropping a flare on it; if he was wrong in his expectation, he would hardly be able to act on the momentary illumination which would be shed. Over the target the aircraft dropping the flare would have passed before the illumination became effective, and by the time it returned the flare might well have gone out. In any case, and for either purpose, the flare would have to be placed with extraordinary accuracy.

The assumption made by Air Commodore Coningham that a timed run from landmark to target would result in bombing 'as accurate as if the target itself were visible'[3] was not borne out even under trial conditions. In exercises carried out in January 1940 the bombing errors after three runs at 6,000 feet from ten, fifteen and twenty miles away were respectively 1,200 yards, 4,840 yards and 5,280 yards.[4]

Ever since September 1938 Bomber Command had been pressing for improved illuminating equipment, but they had not yet succeeded in formulating a clear idea of what they wanted, or how they were going to use what they got. To the Navigation Officer at Bomber Command, Wing Commander Ivelaw-Chapman, the attitude

---

[1] Notes on Bomber Cmd. Conf., 6th Nov. 1939. Memo. Coningham to Bomber Cmd., 3rd Feb. 1940. At the Bomber Command Conference it was assumed that this degree of accuracy could be achieved by astro-navigation, but the note recording the discussion contains the following curious sentence: 'It was not considered unreasonable to assume that this size target area could be reached because it was felt that by the time the necessary illumination aids to precise bombing had been developed, improvements in navigation would enable a target area of the size indicated to be made good.'

[2] Memo. Coningham to Bomber Cmd., 3rd Feb. 1940.

[3] Report Coningham to Bomber Cmd., 11th Oct. 1939.

[4] Report on the trials on 18th, 20th and 26th Jan. 1940.

of the Air Ministry seemed to savour of 'defeatism'.[1] On 14th September 1938, for example, the Air Ministry had told Sir Edgar Ludlow-Hewitt that 'an early solution to the night bombing problem appears unlikely at the moment.'[2] On 7th July 1939 Bomber Command had enquired at the Air Ministry if any progress had been made with flares. They received no reply and wrote again on 15th August.[3] It was not until 17th September that they were informed that the existing 4·5-inch flare seemed to be adequate. Apart from an experimental electrically ignited flare to be towed behind the aircraft and a marker bomb which could be extinguished by the enemy and would in any case probably bury itself, there were, Bomber Command was told, 'no new scientific inventions known to the Air Ministry which could be used for illuminating target areas.'[4] Eventually a 5·5-inch flare was produced which, according to the Bomber Command Armament Officer, was 'almost impossible to handle' in the aircraft, which gave very little light and was very dangerous.[5]

The situation in October 1939 suggested to Air Commodore Bottomley that Bomber Command would be 'well advised to concentrate on astro-navigation and D/F positioning as the main aid to night bombing or rather position finding at night'.[6] He did not suggest how this would help in the actual location of the target for which the flares had been intended, and it was left to Wing Commander Ivelaw-Chapman to explain that astro and wireless navigation, even if perfected, would not 'give a pilot more than his target *area*'.[7] Thereafter the discussion turned to the possibility of a light flash bomb which could be carried in great numbers, but at length in June 1940 the Air Ministry told Bomber Command that this project had been dropped owing to the fact that it required magnesium.[8]

Such were the unhappy preliminaries to the night bombing offensive for which, what may be regarded as a dress rehearsal, was held on the night of 19th March 1940, when thirty Whitleys and twenty Hampdens were despatched to attack the German seaplane base at Hörnum on the island of Sylt. In striking contrast to the earlier activities of the Wellingtons by daylight in this area, only one of these fifty bombers failed to return. On the night of the attack the moon was two days past its first quarter and it was due to set just after half-past four (B.S.T.) the following morning. This left a

---

[1] Min. Chapman to Lloyd (G/C Ops.) and Bottomley, 20th Sept. 1939.
[2] Letter Air Min. (D.S.D.) to Ludlow-Hewitt, 14th Sept. 1938.
[3] Letters Bomber Cmd. to Air Min., 7th July and 15th Aug. 1939.
[4] Letter Saundby (D.O.R. Air Min.) to Ludlow-Hewitt, 17th Sept. 1939.
[5] Min. W/Cmdr. Armt. 2. to Lloyd, 1st Oct. 1939.
[6] Min. Bottomley to Ludlow-Hewitt, 6th Oct. 1939.
[7] Min. Chapman to Lloyd, 17th Oct. 1939.
[8] Letter Air Min. (D.O.R.) to Portal, 3rd June 1940.

CONVERSION TO A NIGHT FORCE

period of moonlit darkness of six hours during which the attack was to be carried out. The first four hours were allotted to the Whitleys of 4 Group and the remaining two to the Hampdens of 5 Group. 500-lb. and 250-lb. General Purpose bombs were carried and certain specially selected crews also carried incendiaries in the hope that fires would be started which would help in the location of the target. Some aircraft also carried flares. The Groups were ordered to send only 'experienced crews, and those with knowledge of the particular area in which the target was situated.'

Of the thirty Whitleys, twenty-six claimed to have recognised and attacked the target. One returned early with engine trouble, two failed to locate the target and one did not return. Of the twenty Hampdens, fifteen claimed to have attacked the target, three failed to locate it, and two returned early with engine trouble. The attacks were delivered singly at short intervals from heights varying between 1,000 feet and 10,000 feet. All the bomb-aimers reported that the target was easily recognisable and could be seen through the bomb-sight. They said that they had experienced no difficulty in aiming their bombs.

Many direct hits on the air station were reported, including hits on hangars, living quarters, a slipway and light railway. Two hangars were said to have been left on fire. Photographic reconnaissance of the island, carried out on 6th April, indicated, however, that all the buildings at Hörnum and elsewhere remained 'outwardly intact'. The supposition was that the damage had been either repaired or concealed.

Perhaps with another possibility in mind, the Bomber Command report concluded with 'a caveat against over-optimistic conclusions drawn from this operation as to the visibility of objectives at night, and the possibility of identifying them and bombing them accurately. The operation', the report went on, 'does not confirm that, as a general rule, the average crews of our heavy bombers can identify targets at night, even under the best conditions, nor does it prove that the average crew can bomb industrial or other enemy targets at night ... Our general opinion is that under war conditions the average crew of a night bomber could not be relied on to identify and attack targets at night except under the very best conditions of visibility, even when the target is on the coast or on a large river like the Rhine. Under the latter conditions about 50% of the average crews might be expected to find and bomb the right target in good visibility; if the target has no conspicuous aids to its location, very few inexperienced crews would be likely to find it under any conditions.'[1]

---

[1] Bomber Cmd. Reports, 10th April 1940 and 19th/20th March 1940.

S.A.O.—I—P

Within a month of this attack the new Commander-in-Chief, Bomber Command, Air Marshal C. F. A. Portal, received an Air Staff directive in which he was told that 'the operations of our heavy bombers are to be confined mainly to night action . . .'[1] The alternative possibility of large-scale daylight attacks by unescorted bombers was seen no longer to exist, if prohibitive casualties were to be avoided. If Bomber Command was to remain in the war it had no alternative but to fight in the dark.

Already many of the difficulties which beset night bombers had been recognised. Warning voices had intermittently been raised, but the full magnitude of the problem was still far from being realised. Indeed, much optimism continued to prevail and even Air Commodore Coningham, who had reported many unpalatable facts, seemed at times to speak with two voices. '. . . the accuracy of night bombing', he told Bomber Command in February 1940, 'will differ little from daylight bombing . . .'[2] So long as such optimism resisted realism, bombing policy was likely to remain out of touch with operational possibility and, perhaps, even more important, the need for technical devices to overcome the obscurities of the night was itself obscured.

---

[1] Dir. Slessor to Portal, 13th April 1940, App. 8 (i).
[2] Letter Coningham to Groom, 19th Feb. 1940.

2. Night precision bombing, May 1940–March 1941

The outstanding result of the first eight months of the war in the air was, then, the decision to confine the operations of heavy bombers mainly to night action. When, after the German invasion of the West, the experiments of those early months were succeeded by urgent and war-like operations, that decision was quickly shown to have been both wise, timely and inevitable. Between 9th May and 4th June 1940, operating exclusively by night, the Wellingtons, Whitleys and Hampdens of 3, 4 and 5 Groups flew some 1,696 sorties and lost thirty-nine aircraft. In the same period, operating by day, the Blenheims of 2 Group completed 856 sorties and lost fifty-six aircraft, in addition to which a further ten were damaged beyond repair.[1]

The Blenheim was not, however, as well armed as the Wellington, and in the 3 Group squadrons there were apparently still advocates of the self-defending Wellington formation who believed that they could withstand the Messerschmitt fighters.[2] Air Marshal Portal was less optimistic and he felt certain that these formations would be worn down by relays of fighters.[3] Air Vice-Marshal Baldwin agreed with his Commander-in-Chief. Later in the year, after he had taken over Sir Charles Portal's command, Sir Richard Peirse showed that he too did not believe in the Wellington as a daylight bomber. Writing to the Air Ministry on 19th October 1940, he described it as 'comparatively slow and unhandy'. He did not believe in its potentialities for evasive action in cloud any more than his predecessor had done in its defensive power in formation.[4] Until the introduction of new types, then, the heavy aircraft of Bomber Command continued to be committed only to night action.

All the same, there remained important tasks which could only be attempted in daylight, and these hazardous operations fell to the Blenheims of 2 Group. During the Battles of France and Britain it was not necessary to devise means of bringing the German air force to action, but it did become urgent to attempt some dispersal of its concentrated activities. Night bombing was not yet producing a fighter reaction, and on 3rd June 1940, 2 Group was, therefore, ordered to attempt daylight attacks on German targets with a view to breaking up the concentrations of German fighter strength in France and 'redressing the balance of air superiority in our favour'. It was also

---
[1] 3, 4, 5 and 2 Group Reports to Bomber Cmd. The 2 Group Report refers to the period 10th May–3rd June 1940.
[2] Letter from 3 Group Gunnery Officer shown to Portal, 20th June 1940.
[3] Min. Portal to Bottomley, 21st June 1940. Note by Bottomley of conversation between Portal and Baldwin, 23rd June 1940.
[4] Letter Peirse to Air Min., 19th Oct. 1940.

regarded as important that targets which had been bombed at night should be harassed by day to prevent repair and salvage. Reconnaissance photographs of these targets were also required to indicate the damage done.[1]

The Blenheims, with the Battles stationed in France, were also committed to the consuming demands of direct support to the hard-pressed allied armies.[2] After the fall of France, 2 Group had to undertake attacks against German aerodromes and invasion barges.[3] Thus, while the heavy bombers faced dangers and difficulties of a different sort, the Blenheims continued to run the gauntlet of the German air defences by day. They possessed neither the armament necessary to a slow bomber nor the speed necessary to an unarmed bomber, and, in consequence, they suffered heavily.

In formation the Blenheims were shown to be highly vulnerable by a grim encounter on 17th May. Twelve aircraft of 82 Squadron were approaching Gembloux at 8,000 feet. The first burst of anti-aircraft fire brought down one and the formation began to open out. Hostile fighters then closed in and only one of the original twelve Blenheims survived the battle, and even that one was heavily damaged.[4] The alternative to formation flying was the adoption of evasive tactics and the use of cloud cover. This left the Blenheims largely at the mercy of the weather, and on numerous occasions during the summer of 1940 they had to abandon their sorties because of the lack of cloud cover.[5] Once again experience told against the conception of the self-defending formation, and on the basis of the operations by Battles in France it was concluded that the only way in which daylight casualties could be reduced 'to some extent' was by the provision of fighter escort or the use of cloud cover.[6]

Escorting fighters might, however, have the opportunity of performing something more than a purely defensive role. When the Battle of Britain was over the thoughts of some Royal Air Force Commanders began to turn towards ways and means of bringing the *Luftwaffe* to action on terms favourable to themselves. Fighter Command had won a famous victory against the German air force over Britain, and if it could extend the field of its victorious operations to the Continent, then what had been impossible for the Germans in the autumn of 1940 might become possible for the British in the future. If the *Luftwaffe* was to be brought to action against its will, then clearly

---

[1] Dir. Bomber Cmd. to 2 Group, 3rd June 1940.
[2] do. 5th June 1940.
[3] do. 6th July 1940.
[4] Report Robb (A.O.C. 2 Group) to Bomber Cmd., 12th June 1940. Bomber Cmd. O.R.B., 17th May 1940.
[5] Bomber Cmd. O.R.B.
Report Advanced Air Striking Force to Bomber Cmd., 24th Sept. 1940.

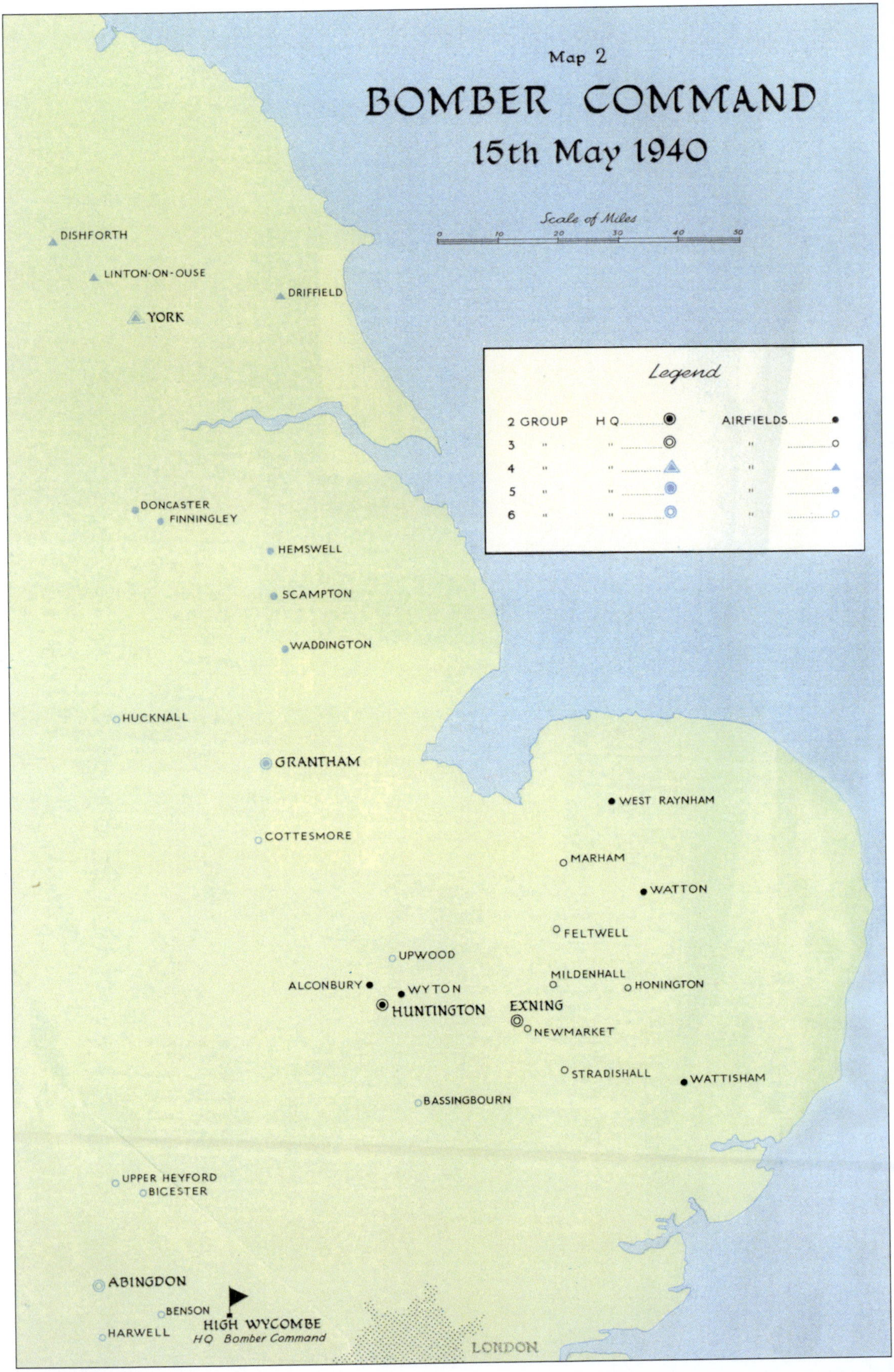

Map 2
BOMBER COMMAND
15th May 1940

Scale of Miles
0 — 10 — 20 — 30 — 40 — 50

Legend

2 GROUP	H Q	⦿	AIRFIELDS	●
3 "	"	◎	"	○
4 "	"	▲	"	▲
5 "	"	⦿	"	●
6 "	"	◎	"	○

- DISHFORTH
- LINTON-ON-OUSE
- DRIFFIELD
- YORK
- DONCASTER
- FINNINGLEY
- HEMSWELL
- SCAMPTON
- WADDINGTON
- HUCKNALL
- GRANTHAM
- COTTESMORE
- WEST RAYNHAM
- MARHAM
- WATTON
- FELTWELL
- UPWOOD
- ALCONBURY
- WYTON
- HUNTINGTON
- MILDENHALL
- HONINGTON
- EXNING
- NEWMARKET
- STRADISHALL
- WATTISHAM
- BASSINGBOURN
- UPPER HEYFORD
- BICESTER
- ABINGDON
- BENSON
- HARWELL
- HIGH WYCOMBE
  HQ Bomber Command
- LONDON

bombers as well as fighters would have to take part in the assault. The bombers would have to seek some target which the enemy felt compelled to defend and they would have to do 'sufficient damage to make it impossible for him to ignore them . . .' This, it was hoped, would force the Germans 'to give battle under conditions tactically favourable to our fighters.'[1]

With this object in mind, 2 Group was ordered on 23rd January 1941 to prepare for daylight attacks on Boulogne, Calais, Dunkirk and Cherbourg, in co-operation with fighters of 11 Group. This was the origin of what later became known as *Circus* operations, and it was the first essay in the co-ordinated offensive action of fighters and bombers. This conception was ultimately shown to be of great significance.

Meanwhile, what Sir Edgar Ludlow-Hewitt had described as 'the major destructive part of our Plans' was being attempted by the heavy bombers at night, and the strength and disposition of the German air force was, for the time being, the least of the problems confronting the Wellingtons, Whitleys and Hampdens.

The very circumstances which made it possible for these aircraft to carry bombs in place of leaflets also tended to draw them away from what was regarded as their true destination. Instead of concentrating their main weight of attack against oil plants or other strategic targets in Germany, the night bombers were compelled during the Battle of France to devote much effort to the destruction of military lines of communication and other tactical targets. During the Battle of Britain their first duty was to reduce the scale of German air attack by bombing aircraft assembly plants. The war at sea also made its claims on Bomber Command and particularly on 5 Group, whose Hampdens carried out extensive mine-laying operations. Whitleys and Wellingtons carried the war to Italy, at first from French bases and then after long flights from the United Kingdom.

Despite all these distractions, Bomber Command carried out as many strategic attacks on Germany as possible. Here the principal targets were oil plants and marshalling yards. On the night of 25th August 1940, Hampdens and Wellingtons attacked industrial targets in Berlin, and wherever the bombs may actually have fallen on this and other occasions, it was not until after the German attack on Coventry that Bomber Command was deliberately given the centre of a town as its target. This, the first 'area' attack of the war, was carried out against Mannheim on the night of 16th December 1940.

The great majority of these targets required, if they were to be reached, a high standard of navigating accuracy and, if they were to be hit, a high degree of precision bombing. Before the offensive began,

---

[1] Dir. Saundby to Robb (Copy to 11 Group), 23rd Jan. 1941.

optimism had been mingled with pessimism and there had been little certainty about what could be achieved. As the offensive developed this blend of hope and fear persisted, but invariably it was the more optimistic deductions which were used in the calculations made. In November 1940, for example, it seemed to be proved that no fewer than sixty-five per cent of the bombers despatched had been failing to find their targets.[1] Yet, in December 1940, Sir Charles Portal assured the Chiefs of Staff that fifty per cent of them would not only find but would also hit their targets even if they were as small and unilluminated as oil plants.[2]

Much of the experience gained in the first eight months of the war had tended to confirm the conclusion reached before the war that 'night attacks would not achieve appreciable results against "precision" targets,'[3] but in all this experience there had been a strong element of doubt. In the case of the night bombing trials of January 1940, for example, the conditions were thought to have been 'rather unfavourable' and the results 'not as good as were expected'.[4] In the case of the Hörnum attack, the reconnaissance photographs were extremely small, the scale being one mm. to 175 feet, and it was, therefore, thought to be 'difficult to ascertain the results of the raid'.[5] Whatever it might suggest, the evidence proceeding from these experiences was not conclusive, nor was it as compelling as the lessons which had been learnt about the vulnerability of day bombers. If precision targets were to be bombed at all, it may well have seemed preferable to rely on the possibility of accurate results at night rather than upon the certainty of crushing casualties by day. Perhaps for these reasons, the 'all important basis', as it was later described, of the calculations made was that in moonlight conditions the average night-bombing error would not exceed three hundred yards.[6]

This three hundred yards error was exactly the margin within which, before the war, it had been hoped that day bombing might be confined.[7] The appreciation of operational possibility throughout the offensive of 1940 was therefore based upon the assumption, voiced by Air Commodore Coningham at the beginning of the year, that 'the accuracy of night bombing will differ little from daylight bombing.'[8]

The night operations of Bomber Command between 9th May and 4th June 1940 produced somewhat conflicting opinions about this

---

[1] Mins. of Group Navigation Officers' Conf., 12th Nov. 1940.
[2] Memo. by Portal, 29th Dec. 1940.
[3] Mins. of Air Min. Conf., 30th Nov. 1938.
[4] Memo. Coningham to Bomber Cmd., 3rd Feb. 1940.
[5] Bomber Cmd. Report, 19th April 1940.
[6] B. Ops. 1 Review, 5th April 1941.
[7] Mins. of Air. Min. Conf., 30th Nov. 1938.
[8] Letter Coningham to Groom, 19th Feb. 1940.

assumption in the minds of the various Group Commanders. Speaking of the Hampden Group, Air Vice-Marshal Harris reported to Bomber Command that 'the standard of navigation achieved has improved considerably as crews have gained experience, and', he asserted, 'the majority of aircraft can be expected to arrive within a few miles of their objective on D.R. and W/T.' Air Commodore Coningham was scarcely less optimistic about the performance of his Whitleys. 'Navigation', he reported, 'has reached a high standard, and with the assistance of loop bearings, crews are enabled to navigate accurately to the neighbourhood of their targets, but', he continued, 'the final location of such targets depends on the ability of the crew to read their maps accurately'.[1]

It was left to Air Vice-Marshal Baldwin to sound a note of greater caution, and the experiences which Air Vice-Marshal Harris and Air Commodore Coningham had found so satisfactory, seemed to him to show 'that grave limitations are placed on night bombing of specific targets, particularly on moonless nights, owing to [the] inexperience of pilots and navigators in map reading by night'. Owing to the necessity for weaving to afford the gunners a better view, loops were not, he pointed out, of much use over enemy territory. The system of navigation adopted in the Wellingtons was, the Group Commander explained, to run on dead reckoning to the Dutch coast and from a pin-point there to calculate a wind for the run to a landmark near the target, which was also made by dead reckoning with the aid of map reading. From the landmark to the target map reading was 'resorted to', but considerable difficulties were encountered at this stage owing to the frequent failure of parachute flares and to searchlight dazzle.[2]

An obvious rider to these conclusions was added by Air Vice-Marshal Baldwin in the second report covering the Wellington operations between 5th and 16th June 1940. The great danger in relying almost exclusively upon dead reckoning navigation was that the wind might change. 'It is necessary, therefore,' Air Vice-Marshal Baldwin observed, 'that pilots and navigators of aircraft should be competent in map reading by night.'[3]

Apart, therefore, from the new-found confidence shown by Air Vice-Marshal Harris and Air Commodore Coningham in the loop aerial, it was obvious that successful navigation depended upon what Sir Edgar Ludlow-Hewitt had described in March 1940 as 'meticulous and careful pin-pointing'.[4] This, in turn, depended upon the extent

---

[1] Report Harris to Bomber Cmd., 1st July 1940. Report Coningham to Bomber Cmd., 24th June 1940.
[2] Report Baldwin to Bomber Cmd., 2nd July 1940.
[3] do., 22nd July 1940.
[4] Letter Ludlow-Hewitt to Air Min., 6th March 1940.

of night vision afforded to the crew and their ability to recognise what they saw. Yet the limitations of night vision, even in moonlight conditions, had been revealed by the leaflet bombers and recognised by Air Commodore Coningham almost from the outset of the war.

Nevertheless, the operational reports on Bomber Command's night activities during the summer and winter of 1940 seemed to indicate that a great deal more could be seen than might have been supposed on the basis of Air Commodore Coningham's earlier reports. For example, on the night of 2nd July 1940 sixteen Whitleys were sent to bomb the marshalling yards at Hamm. There was no moon, but ten of the aircraft claimed to have attacked successfully. '. . . bursts were seen to the north and south of the target. In addition the aerodromes at Brussels and Hingene were attacked, both targets being hit many times.' On the night of 4th July 1940, which was also moonless, ten Wellingtons claimed to have attacked an aircraft factory at Bremen where 'bursts were seen followed by large fires . . .' The airframe factory at Wenzendorf was also said to have been attacked and 'bombs were seen to straddle [the] target and cause fires.' Again without a moon, on the night of 7th July, Wellingtons claimed to have bombed the marshalling yards at Osnabrück. 'Hits were observed and fires started.'

On the night of 22nd July 1940, which was in a moon period, nineteen Hampdens were sent to bomb the synthetic oil plant at Gelsenkirchen. Eighteen of them claimed to have succeeded. '. . . bombs were seen to burst on the target, fires started and heavy explosions followed.' As the moon entered its last quarter on the night of 27th July, Wellingtons claimed hits on oil refineries at Hamburg. '. . . hits were observed on one oil refinery, followed by two fires and two explosions. Bombs straddled the second refinery and three fires were seen.'

Even against a target as distant and as large as Berlin, it seemed possible, even with little help from the moon, to distinguish precision targets. The report for the night of 7th October 1940 said:

'Forty two aircraft—thirty Wellingtons of 3 Group and twelve Whitleys of 4 Group were ordered to attack targets in BERLIN and vicinity. Thirty three aircraft completed the attack and seven attacked other objectives.

Six Wellingtons attacked the MOABIT Electricity power station, BERLIN. A large fire was started in the target area, visible for 70 miles and pinkish and greenish explosions were observed; other bombs fell among buildings to the S.W. of the target. Four Wellingtons attacked the West Power Station, BERLIN: bombs fell around the target and caused fires; large sheds to the East of existing fires were lit and big explosions followed with black smoke. Some bombs also fell to the west of the target and straddled a marshalling yard. Four Wellingtons attacked WILMERSDORF Electricity Power Station, BERLIN. Bombs were dropped in a stick along the railway straddling the target and on the marshalling yard at CHARLOTTENBURG causing fires which were visible for 21 minutes after aircraft left. Eight Whitleys attacked the Chancery in BERLIN: a fire was seen in a building adjacent to the target but other results were not observed. One Whitley attacked the War Office, BERLIN: results were not observed. Five Wellingtons attacked SCHONEBERG marshalling yards, a very large reddish fire was seen before arrival and large explosions followed by fires, one with blue and orange flames—were caused which were visible for 115 miles. Two Wellingtons attacked the Coal Gas Works, BERLIN. Bombs fell across the target causing some large and numerous small fires and explosions: two large fires were visible for 100 miles. Two Whitleys and one Wellington attacked RUMMELSBURG marshalling yard, the B.M.W. aero engine factory and SIEMENS cable works, BERLIN. Results were not observed. Seven Wellingtons attacked BAHRENFELD aerodrome the VIKTORIA chemical works, near the MOABIT Power Station, BERLIN, railways near XANTEN and at RUMMELSBURG, marshalling yards at SCHONENBURG, and an aerodrome probably GILZE-RITEN. Bursts were observed on all these targets. At BAHRENFELD a small fire was caused and lights extinguished; at VIKTORIA Chemical Works large fires and explosions were caused, one fire being visible for 65 miles, fires were also caused in the marshalling yards at SCHONENBURG and at the aerodrome believed to be at GILZE-RITEN, these at the latter target started with a white flame which gradually changed to red. CASUALTIES: One Wellington missing and one crashed.'[1]

These reports, which were typical of those made on operations throughout the year, made complete nonsense of the doubts and anxieties which had been expressed from time to time about night bombing. If they were reliable, it was clear that Bomber Command had achieved not only an astonishing standard of navigating accuracy but also an ability to distinguish a wealth of detail about its precision targets. It was very rarely that these reports indicated that there had been any difficulty in reaching and locating the target, whether it was an oil plant, a marshalling yard, an aircraft factory or even an individual building in a city.

Intelligence reports coming from Germany did nothing to deny and much to confirm the probability that this was so. A direct hit on one of the oil plants at Gelsenkirchen was reported on 3rd July 1940,

[1] Bomber Cmd. O.R.B., 2nd–3rd July, 4th–5th July, 7th–8th July, 22nd–23rd July and 7th–8th Oct. 1940.

increasing traffic jams 'in areas such as Hamm, Soest, Dusseldorf and Cologne' on 7th July, and on 25th July it was said that 'R.A.F. pilots display extraordinary skill and the accuracy of their bombing is good.' On 10th August the Scholven hydrogenation plant was said to have been hit and 500,000 litres of aviation petrol lost as a result. On 4th September a 'reliable source' spoke of the 'apparent ease with which the R.A.F. reach their objectives', and a direct hit on the oil plant at Leuna was reported on 30th September. On 10th October 'well informed industrialists' had estimated that some twenty-five per cent of 'the total productive capacity of Germany' had been affected by the bombing.[1]

This last report, in particular, caught the attention of Air Vice-Marshal Harris. He found it and many other intelligence reports 'very pleasant' reading and he was delighted to know of 'the accuracy with which our aircraft hit military objectives as opposed to merely browning the towns.' These reports, he told Sir Richard Peirse, were one of the few encouraging signs of the time, 'but,' he continued, 'amongst other matters which these summaries serve to impress upon one is the by now patent fact that the Air Ministry Publicity Department is half-witted.' He complained bitterly that reports of these events were not finding adequate space in the newspapers. 'What a riot of publicity would attend such results,' he said, 'had they been secured by the Army, and what a catastrophic spate of words if the Navy succeeded in doing a thousandth as much! Yet when the bombers begin to win the war—and we are the only people that can win it, and we are winning it—what happens? Nix!' As a final compliment to the effectiveness of bombing, Air Vice-Marshal Harris suggested that perhaps the members of the Air Ministry Publicity Department had themselves been bombed and 'are all long since dead, and nobody's noticed it. Naturally enough, nobody would!'[2]

This was a theme to which Air Vice-Marshal Harris, *mutatis mutandis*, was often to return in the future. Meanwhile, however, the Air Ministry publicists were, perhaps, not as half-witted as he supposed. There were already ominous cracks in the imposing edifice which Air Vice-Marshal Harris sought to have publicly unveiled, and within a few weeks much more serious ones were to appear. The era of delusion based upon the evidence of crew and intelligence reports was gradually drawing to an end. Photography was already beginning to work what eventually proved to be a major revolution in the appreciation of tactical possibility.

The evidence which had so greatly encouraged Air Vice-Marshal Harris, and upon which the Air Staff had evidently based their

---

[1] B.C.I.Rs., 3rd July, 7th July, 25th July, 10th Aug., 4th Sept., 30th Sept., 10th Oct. 1940.
[2] Letter Harris to Peirse, 11th Oct. 1940.

bombing policy, had arisen from certain theoretical assumptions about the accuracy of navigation and bomb aiming which both the crew and intelligence reports had tended to confirm. The authorities, confident of success and short of cameras, had for long been led to rest their judgment on these sources, rather than upon the meagre and almost invariably disappointing evidence of the camera.

Speaking of intelligence, Clausewitz wrote that a 'great part of the information obtained in war is contradictory, a still greater part is false, and by far the greatest part is of a doubtful character.' To assess it needed discrimination which 'only knowledge of men and things and good judgment' could give.[1] In dealing with the crew and intelligence reports of 1940 the air force commanders could not always rely upon their 'knowledge of men and things' because there were few precedents to guide their discrimination. The camera was really the sole reliable means of judging the accuracy or otherwise of the Bomber Command attacks. The day reconnaissance photograph would indicate the extent of the damage inflicted upon the target, and the night photograph taken by the bomber as it dropped its bombs would, if it could be plotted, give the position of the aircraft at the time which could be compared with that which the navigator had estimated at the same time.

The need for the reconnaissance photograph as a means of damage assessment had often been stressed,[2] and the Blenheims of 2 Group, which was the only part of Bomber Command engaged on day flying, were repeatedly told to photograph the targets attacked by night bombers whenever they could.[3] The difficulties encountered were, however, formidable. The Blenheims frequently failed to reach their targets and a large proportion of their efforts had to be devoted to the even more urgent task of recording the symptoms of German invasion preparations. The photographs which they did secure were invariably small both in number and size. The tendency was, therefore, to blame the photograph rather than the bomb aimer when no damage could be detected on the prints.[4] It was not until 16th November 1940 that a Photographic Reconnaissance Flight equipped with Spitfires was formed, and soon after this astonishing results came in.[5]

The camera carried in the bomber as a means of checking navigation was in extremely short supply and of indifferent quality. As late as January 1941, when the official establishment for night cameras

---

[1] Clausewitz: *On War*, Vol. I, (1949), p. 75.
[2] For example, Report Baldwin to Bomber Cmd., 25th Oct. 1939, letters Portal to Air Min., 4th May and 25th June 1940.
[3] Dirs. Bomber Cmd. to 2 Group, 23rd July, 11th Sept., 3rd Nov. 1940.
[4] As, for instance in the case of the Hörnum photographs and again in that of the oil plants 'bombed' in the summer of 1940.
[5] Bomber Cmd. O.R.B., Nov. 1940. Dir. Bomber Cmd. to 3 Group, 21st Nov. 1940.

was four per squadron and there should, therefore, have been 168 in service, there were actually only twenty-two available.[1] As in the case of the reconnaissance pictures, there was a strong tendency to neglect the few and ominous results which were obtained. During the period between 5th and 16th June 1940, for example, Wellingtons engaged on night operations took fifteen photographs. Three of these were 'successful', but the other twelve were described by the Group Commander as being 'not of much account', though one of the reasons given for their being unsuccessful was the 'failure of pilot to find targets'.[2]

These photographs, taken by night and day, did in fact constitute the writing on the wall, but as in the case of the reports about night vision based on the experiences of the leaflet bombers, it was still possible to entertain doubts about them. Writing to the Air Ministry on 28th July 1940, the Commander-in-Chief, Sir Charles Portal, applied for the services of an oil expert. He said that the services of such an adviser would be especially valuable in view of 'the lack of information of the results of our bombing attacks, and the very small number of photographs which it has been found possible to take of objectives which have been bombed.'[3] It was, however, not the lack of experts, but the lack of conclusive evidence, which now caused the Air Staff appreciation of tactical possibility to wander dangerously astray.

In considering the question of what was being achieved by the offensive against German oil plants, the Commander-in-Chief's new oil adviser, Mr. D. A. C. Dewdney, found that there was no clear direct evidence upon which to work.[4] In his first memorandum on 4th September 1940, he drew Sir Charles Portal's attention to the small number of reconnaissance photographs available. The small-scale prints which had been produced, he said, revealed 'disappointingly little apparent damage'. At the same time, he suggested that much larger-scale photographs of British targets bombed by the Germans showed much less damage than was known to have been caused. It therefore seemed unwise to accept the interpretation of the small photographs of German oil targets. Pilots' reports, Mr. Dewdney insisted, suffered from serious limitations. They only referred to a strictly limited time and the pilot was liable to be deceived by appearances. A very impressive oil fire might in fact involve only a small quantity of oil. Intelligence reports were likely not only to be exaggerated but also to be vague. Though he thought it hardly needed repeating to Sir Charles Portal, Mr. Dewdney stressed the

---

[1] Letter Peirse to Beaverbrook, 13th Jan. 1941.
[2] Report Baldwin to Bomber Cmd., 22nd July 1940.
[3] Letter Portal to Air Min., 29th July 1940.
[4] For Mr. Dewdney, see note on p. 473.

need for seizing 'every possible opportunity' of getting more photographs, and he was presently to make proposals designed to improve the content of the pilots' reports.

Meanwhile, though some information might be gleaned by comparative methods from an examination of targets in Britain attacked by the German air force, and also by the analysis of samples of oil taken from German aircraft, there remained only a theoretical means of solving the problem. Mr. Dewdney's method was to consider the weight of bombs aimed at each target and then, in order to calculate the effect, to apply certain assumptions regarding the destructive power of the bombs and the accuracy with which they were aimed. He assumed that each 500-lb. bomb would cause complete destruction within a radius of twenty-five yards from the point of impact, and he assumed that the average aiming error was three hundred yards. Thus, if the aim was to achieve seventy-five per cent destruction of each oil plant, the necessary weight of attack could be calculated. Mr. Dewdney estimated that 260 bombs would be required for a target measuring 10,000 square yards and 530 for one of half a million square yards. Similarly, he thought he could calculate the damage already achieved by comparing the weights of bombs dropped with these ideal figures. It was on this basis that he advised Sir Charles Portal that the results of the oil offensive, as far as it had proceeded in September 1940, were 'satisfactory'.[1] It was on this basis that in October he drew more specific and highly encouraging conclusions about the further conduct of the offensive. Evidently confident that the basic tactical assumptions were correct, Mr. Dewdney had said in September, 'However little damage appears in a photograph, an objective must have suffered damage in proportion to the weight of bombs dropped over it . . .'[2]

Yet the gulf between the assumptions and the reality, or even the probability, was clearly shown by the further information which Mr. Dewdney now asked for in the pilots' reports. In a questionnaire which he prepared for the crews and which was circulated by Air Vice-Marshal Bottomley on 8th September 1940, Mr. Dewdney enquired how the oil plant buildings ran and where the chimneys were in relation to the buildings. If the chimneys were hit, he wanted to know if they were those near the distillation columns, the concrete boxes or the power houses.[3]

Mr. Dewdney had not, of course, been appointed to Bomber Command as an expert in the operational and natural problems of night bombing, but it is, perhaps, surprising that Air Vice-Marshal Bottomley should have passed this questionnaire when, less than a

---
[1] Report and covering letter Dewdney to Portal, 4th Sept. 1940.
[2] Report Dewdney to Portal, 4th Sept. 1940.
[3] Memo. Bottomley to 1, 2, 3, 4 and 5 Groups, 8th Sept. 1940.

year before, he had forwarded to the Air Ministry, without adverse comment, Air Commodore Coningham's first report in which, speaking of oil plants, the 4 Group Commander had said, 'Being non-illuminating they cannot be seen at the light free tactical height that would be allowed.' In the same report, Air Commodore Coningham had enlarged upon the impossibility of seeing separate buildings, let alone their chimneys, from above three or four thousand feet.[1] On the other hand, the operational reports on the night attacks of the summer and autumn of 1940, and notably that on the Berlin raid in October, had suggested that these things, perhaps, could be seen.

As the year drew to its end, however, evidence was gradually accumulating which threw grave doubts upon the accuracy of the crew reports upon which these operational summaries were based. On the night of 7th November 1940 a force of Wellingtons, Hampdens and Blenheims was despatched to attack the Krupps armament works at Essen. According to the operational report, 'Six Blenheims attacked Krupp A.G. at Essen. Four flashes were seen and fires started'. Of the 3 Group force, 'Twenty Wellingtons heavily attacked Krupp A.G. at Essen. Aircraft of 214 Squadron reported many fires and explosions over the target area. Flames were seen to reach to a great height and then die down and recommence. Three large explosions turned into three good fires which were visible for 24 miles after leaving [the] target. One building was seen to be in a state of white heat. Aircraft of 9 Squadron reported many fires, including a chain of fires burning on arrival over [the] target area. Bombs from this squadron caused many various coloured explosions and the whole target area burst into fire, which spread rapidly. Fires were still seen burning 60 miles away. Some very bright explosions were also observed. Aircraft of 115 Squadron reported direct hits on a medium howitzer shed and a machine shop, also hits on other buildings. Bombs also fell on existing fires which could be seen 15 miles away. Continuous explosions could be seen over [the] target area for 45 minutes and there was a very large explosion near a steel works. As the aircraft of this squadron left the target, many existing fires were observed to merge into one long line of fire'.

From the 5 Group force, again according to the operational report, 'twenty-four Hampdens attacked Krupp A.G. at Essen. Bursts were seen but no other results observed, except by one aircraft which reported a large blaze on arrival at 2210 hours and which started further fire'.[2]

The Wellington attack had begun at ten minutes past eight and

---

[1] Report Coningham to Bomber Cmd., 11th Oct. 1939, forwarded by Bottomley to Air Min., 30th Oct. 1939. The 'light free height' means the lowest height at which the bombers would be above the searchlight dazzle.

[2] Bomber Cmd. O.R.B., 7th–8th Nov. 1940.

ended at twenty-six minutes past ten o'clock. The Hampdens began to arrive at twenty-six minutes past nine and left thirty-five minutes after midnight. The Blenheim attack lasted from a quarter past eleven until just after a quarter to midnight.[1] It, therefore, struck the staff at Bomber Command Headquarters as curious that the Wellingtons should have witnessed such a tremendous conflagration while the Hampdens and Blenheims had seen little or nothing.

Air Vice-Marshal Harris said he could never rely 'entirely' on crew reports, but he was 'reasonably confident' that some of his Hampdens at any rate had been over the Krupp works. 2 Group Headquarters were satisfied that their Blenheims had been there, but the Senior Air Staff Officer at 3 Group was equally sure that the Wellingtons really had started the conflagrations at Essen and he could only explain the 5 Group report by suggesting that it was in error. After further reflection he became more firmly convinced that the Hampdens had failed to reach Essen 'owing to clouds'. He thought fires in an armament works might blaze up and then die away quickly. He admitted that there were a 'few incidents where even experienced pilots are convinced that they have been over a certain locality when in fact they have been elsewhere', but, on the whole, he thought that 'the pilots of this Group are very open in their reports, and have no hesitation in saying that they have not found their target, or that they have wandered in their navigation'. In the case of the Essen attack he felt that their reports were 'substantiated'. The only photograph mentioned was one taken by a Wellington. This turned out to be of some woods and according to 3 Group was 'not operationally important'.[2]

It was obvious that errors very much smaller than those suggested by the evidence about this attack on Krupps works would cause many bombs to fall on objects which were other than 'legitimate'. Indeed, some recognition of this fact had already been afforded on 9th September, when captains of aircraft were reminded that 'in industrial areas there was invariably a very large number of targets'. They were told that 'In view of the indiscriminate nature of the German bombing attacks and in order to reduce the number of bombs brought home . . . every effort should be made to locate and bomb these.'[3] Whatever the inference of this instruction, the official intention was still clearly to hit 'legitimate' targets such as railways, but the orders for the attack on Mannheim, carried out on the night of 16th December 1940, showed a new departure.

The raid was to be opened by a fire-raising force of Wellingtons,

---

[1] Min. Airey (W/Cmdr. Controller) to Bottomley, 8th Nov. 1940.
[2] Bomber Cmd. Telephone Log, 8th Nov. 1940. Letter Good (S.A.S.O. 3 Group) to Bottomley, 8th Nov. 1940.
[3] Bomber Cmd. O.R.B., 9th Sept. 1940.

flown by the 'most experienced crews available' and armed with incendiary bombs. The following aircraft were ordered to take as their aiming points 'the fires raised in the initial attack.'[1] The object of the attack, as the Commander-in-Chief, Sir Richard Peirse, later explained, was 'to concentrate the maximum amount of damage in the centre of the town . . .'[2] Bomber Command received the War Cabinet's approval of this plan on 13th December 1940,[3] and three nights later in perfect moonlight conditions 134 aircraft were despatched to carry it out.[4]

Of this force, forty-seven Wellingtons, thirty-three Whitleys, eighteen Hampdens and four Blenheims claimed to have attacked Mannheim. All reports agreed in suggesting that the majority of the bombs had fallen in the target area. The centre of the town was said to have been left in flames and Sir Richard Peirse immediately sent a signal congratulating all concerned on the successful operations.[5]

On 21st December 1940, at the second attempt and after further light attacks on the town, a Spitfire of the new Photographic Reconnaissance Unit succeeded in photographing Mannheim in daylight.[6] From the mosaic, it was immediately apparent to Sir Richard Peirse that the operation had 'failed in its primary object . . .' Though 'considerable damage' had been done, the photographs showed 'a wide dispersal' of the attack. Some of the fires had evidently been started outside the target area, and this, Sir Richard Peirse told his Group Commanders, had led the following crews astray. He thought the operational orders had been too rigidly worded in telling the crews to aim at the fires, and he believed they should have been ordered to identify and aim at the target itself. In future attacks of this kind, he said, 'I count on the great majority of bombs hitting within half a mile radius of it' [the aiming point].[7]

Both Air Vice-Marshal Bottomley, who had recently assumed command of 5 Group in place of Air Vice-Marshal Harris, and Air Vice-Marshal Coningham agreed with the Commander-in-Chief about the danger of instructing crews to bomb fires. 'There is always the grave danger', Air Vice-Marshal Bottomley said, 'of acquiring the idea that a bomb dropped anywhere in Germany is of value.' Both Group Commanders also agreed that they were very much in the dark about what their bombers had been achieving. The Mannheim photographs were, according to Air Vice-Marshal Bottomley,

---

[1] B.C.O.O., 4th Dec. 1940.
[2] Memo. Peirse to 1, 2, 3, 4 and 5 Groups, 24th Dec. 1940.
[3] Air Min. to Bomber Cmd., 13th Dec. 1940.
[4] Bomber Cmd. O.R.B., 16th–17th Dec. 1940.
[5] do.
[6] do. 21st Dec. 1940.
[7] Memo. Peirse to 1, 2, 3, 4 and 5 Groups, 24th Dec. 1940.

'the first of any real evidence we have had as to the general standard of bombing accuracy which characterises our present night operations'. Air Vice-Marshal Coningham pointed out that 'the Groups have no way of telling whether their people are doing good bombing or not', and, he admitted, 'For my part, I have little idea of what the Whitleys do, and it causes me considerable anxiety.'[1] Such was the sobering result of the first effective photographic reconnaissance.

The question remained, however, as to whether these disappointing results at Mannheim, which was after all a very much larger target than those at which Bomber Command had previously been aiming, were due merely to injudicious orders on the night in question or to a basic inability in the crews and the inadequacy of their equipment. Air Vice-Marshal Bottomley clearly thought the former was the operative explanation. The plan for an initial fire-raising attack seemed to him to constitute 'an added risk of failure' because the fires might be in the wrong place, or they might be dummies started by the Germans. Apart from warning the captains that they were individually responsible for identifying their targets, the only suggestion he offered was that there should be more practice bombing in daylight.[2]

With a more intimate and longer experience of night operations, Air Vice-Marshal Coningham penetrated the problem somewhat further. He complained of the lack of bomb-sights and aircraft for bombing practice, but he thought that the principle of an initial fire-raising attack was sound. He was impressed with what the Germans had achieved by the use of picked crews and, he said, 'they have the right method'. He thought Bomber Command could do 'equally well, and better, if we pick our best units and specialise on similar lines.'[3] This, as will in due course emerge, was a most important conclusion, but of even greater importance was the fact that Air Vice-Marshal Coningham now realised that the problem of night bombing was not confined to bomb aiming. He had at length recognised that the existing methods of and facilities for navigation were inadequate. Radio navigation, in which he had previously reposed such faith, he now admitted to be 'unreliable'. Astro-navigation could only be used 'by a percentage of crews' and the very good conditions necessary only occurred on 'a small proportion' of the occasions on which Bomber Command had to operate. 'Something more definite is required', he told the Commander-in-Chief.

Meanwhile, the absence of the means of navigation was, Air Vice-Marshal Coningham thought, resulting in a great waste of effort

---

[1] Memos. Bottomley to Bomber Cmd., 26th Dec. 1940, and Coningham to Bomber Cmd., 29th Dec. 1940.
[2] Memo. Bottomley to Bomber Cmd., 26th Dec. 1940.
[3] Memo. Coningham to Bomber Cmd., 29th Dec. 1940.

'through crews not reaching the target area.' On this point, he now thought it unwise to rely upon the pilots' reports. There had been cases, he said, of navigation errors of up to a hundred miles, yet on these occasions 'the pilots, relying blindly on a Met. wind forecast and flying above 10/10 clouds have been convinced that the area bombed through the gap in the clouds was their target.' Crews who failed to find their bases on return, were 'nearly always' convinced that they had found their targets. Air Vice-Marshal Coningham had collected many such 'skeletons in the cupboard' during 1940, and, he said, 'they must not be added to in 1941. The waste of a Halifax bomb load is too serious a matter, equalling as it does four or five Whitleys.'

Even while Sir Richard Peirse was still looking at the photographs of Mannheim which had stimulated this new mood of realism, the photographic Spitfires were out again. This time, on 24th December 1940, excellent photographs were taken of the two oil plants at Gelsenkirchen, and four days later the interpretation report spread the news to those who had to know that neither had sustained any major damage. There was no sign of any important repairs having been carried out and few bomb craters could be seen in the vicinity. It was obvious that the majority of the crews of the 196 aircraft which claimed to have attacked these targets had been mistaken and that the greater part of the 260 tons of bombs, excluding incendiaries, which they reported as having fallen on them, had not done so, and, on the contrary, had missed by an immeasurable distance.[1]

It was, therefore, also obvious, as Mr. Dewdney immediately pointed out to Sir Richard Peirse, that the average bomb-aiming error was greater than three hundred yards on 'at least some of the sorties',[2] and forthwith Mr. Dewdney embarked on a tour of operational squadrons in Bomber Command to see what he could learn from the crews themselves. He found that 'opinions ranged from entire confidence in the ability to identify and accurately bomb all of the targets to grave doubts about the ability to identify and bomb any of the targets.' He formed the impression that the more experienced

---

[1] P.I.R., 28th Dec. 1940.

[2] Letter Dewdney to Peirse, 1st Jan. 1941. The 300-yard aiming error was the basis of Mr. Dewdney's previous calculations. He said he had taken it 'from an Air Ministry paper, in turn based on pre-war experiments.' This is curious. Reporting to the Bombing Committee in February 1939 on exercises carried out in 1938, Bomber Cmd. said, 'Only No. 3 Group has reported on night bombing. Practices with practice bombs are possible only on bombing ranges and here the targets are lighted. They consider, therefore, that the bombing results obtained are no guide to those which might be expected on an unfamiliar unlighted target after a long flight. Practice has been obtained using mobile camera obscurae, results have been disappointing.' The pre-war assumption had been that the average *day* error would be 300 yards. About night bombing the assumption had been that it would not 'achieve appreciable results against "precision" targets.' No evidence seems to exist to show that any other authoritative conclusion was ever reached on the basis of experiments before the war.

crews were the less optimistic. Mr. Dewdney found greater unanimity as to what he described as 'a general wish' for an improved flare which would ignite nearer the ground and burn longer. The crews he spoke to also seemed, in general, to believe that it was necessary to have the target marked by specially picked crews who could start fires as a guide to the following aircraft. Many of them, however, also admitted the dangers presented by German dummy fires. As a result of his conversations, Mr. Dewdney was convinced that it was the exception for the target to be visible to the bomb-aimer during the attack because of searchlight dazzle and the height to which the bombers were driven by flak. He gained the impression that the crews felt the need for more effective means of identifying their targets.

As to the crew reports on operations, Mr. Dewdney said that 'without exception' every station 'threw out dark hints about the inaccurate claims of the other squadrons'. He suggested that a great deal depended on the quality of the intelligence officers who carried out the interrogations. Finally, he referred to the fact that 'regret was expressed on several occasions that the Command Staff were so seldom seen at the stations.'[1]

The lessons which Mr. Dewdney had learned from the operational crews at the beginning of 1941 did little more than confirm the diagnosis made by Air Vice-Marshal Coningham at the end of 1940. The need for effective aids to navigation and target location was now obvious. The need for night cameras carried in the bombers as a means of detecting navigational errors was equally evident. All these matters had been brought to the point of recognition by the reconnaissance photographs taken by Spitfires of the Photographic Reconnaissance Unit.

The operational limitations of night bombing were still far from complete or universal realisation, but at least it was now clear that something would have to be done, that the bombers with their existing equipment could not battle through cloud and darkness to reach and hit small unmarked targets, that the crews, dazzled by searchlights and in the stress of action, could not report as accurately as the camera. The 'never ending struggle to circumvent the law that we cannot see in the dark' was now to begin, but the formidable legacy of previous neglect could not be overcome in a day. The need for further navigational aids was now 'fully understood' and the equipment was being developed 'on the highest priority'.[2] Lord Beaverbrook was urgently asked to accelerate the production of night cameras.[3] But these things could not be turned out at once, and the

---

[1] Letter Dewdney to Peirse, 1st Feb. 1941.
[2] Memo. Saundby to Coningham, 14th Jan. 1941.
[3] Letter Peirse to Beaverbrook, 13th Jan. 1941.

most important of them, the new navigation aid, to be known as *Gee*, was not to be ready for general use until the spring of 1942.

Meanwhile, Bomber Command was still committed to the battle, and if it could not find or hit its precise targets, the only immediate and realistic alternative was to look for larger and more easily recognisable objectives. In the opening months of 1941 it became a common practice to designate as the target the 'industrial centre' of a large German town, and a number of these attacks on the model of the Mannheim experiment were carried out against such places as Berlin, Düsseldorf, Hanover, Bremen, Cologne and Hamburg.[1] Thus, the new appreciation of operational possibility was beginning to exert an influence upon bombing policy.

Nevertheless, more evidence and the further consideration of that which had already accumulated was still required before this process was completed. Meanwhile, a tendency not to look facts in the face persisted and Sir Richard Peirse chose this moment to invite his Group Commanders to consider the possibility of achieving against oil plants in conditions of non-moonlight what they had already failed to achieve in moonlight periods.[2] What was, perhaps, more remarkable than the invitation was the series of replies which followed.

Writing on 27th January 1941, Air Vice-Marshal Coningham advised the Commander-in-Chief to go ahead with the oil plan when weather conditions were expected to be good even if there was no moon. He considered that all his 'pilots' were 'capable of operating under these conditions'. At the beginning of the war, he explained, 'we made a clear distinction between moonlight and moonless periods. In 1940, however,' he asserted, 'we all agreed that visibility and a clear sky were more important factors. This meant,' he said, 'that one could plan to attack almost any target irrespective of the moon, if conditions were good.' Air Vice-Marshal Coningham expressed the opinion that 'bombing on moonless nights generally means dropping a flare from a maximum height of 10,000 feet, whereas with moonlight an attack can be made from any height up to 12,000 or 15,000 feet without the need of flares.'[3]

As he explained, Air Vice-Marshal Coningham had changed his mind since the time when he had been reporting on the activities of the leaflet bombers. He did not explain why he had now also contradicted his own findings after the moonlight attack on Mannheim which had taken place as recently as December 1940.

Air Vice-Marshal Baldwin was not quite as confident, but he thought some of his crews, about twenty on the more distant and

---
[1] Bomber Cmd. O.R.B., Jan.–March 1941.
[2] Letter Peirse to Coningham, 23rd Jan. 1941. (Similar letters to Oxland, Robb, Baldwin and Bottomley.)
[3] Letter Coningham to Peirse, 27th Jan. 1941.

forty on the nearer targets, could take on some oil targets in non-moon periods. Those which he thought most suitable were at Gelsenkirchen, Leuna and Pölitz. One plant at Gelsenkirchen and that at Magdeburg he thought more suitable for moonlight attack.[1] Air Vice-Marshal Bottomley, however, was prepared to send all his crews to bomb the plant at Magdeburg and also those at Pölitz, Homberg and Leuna in dark periods.[2]

The consideration of range seems to have been the factor governing Air Commodore Oxland's advice, and he suggested that the two plants at Gelsenkirchen were the most suitable targets for dark periods.[3] These, of course, had been the subject of the photographic reconnaissance carried out on 24th December 1940, and they were the targets for which the operational crews had, according to Mr. Dewdney, expressed a 'universal dislike' because of the lack of leading marks.[4] Air Commodore Oxland may, however, have had the photographs in mind, and he may have guessed what Mr. Dewdney was finding out because one of his reasons for selecting these two targets was the prospect of achieving useful damage in the neighbourhood. In fact, he thought this district was worth bombing through ten-tenths cloud.

However this may have been, operations carried out in the middle of February did not lend much encouragement to the hopes which had been expressed. For example, on the night of 14th February only six of the twenty-two Hampdens despatched to Homberg even claimed to have attacked the oil plant there, though at the time there was 'good moonlight'. Of the forty-four Wellingtons sent to Gelsenkirchen on the same night, seven claimed to have accomplished their task. On the following night the claims were rather higher and, attacking Homberg before moonrise, fourteen out of thirty-three Hampdens claimed to have succeeded. Evidence other than the crew reports was lacking because at this time the photographic Spitfires were constantly impeded by cloud and condensation trails.[5]

On the basis of reports from the Blenheim crews, Air Vice-Marshal Robb concluded that attacks on oil targets were 'impracticable under conditions of no moon'. Air Vice-Marshal Coningham, on the other hand, still thought the task possible, but he blamed the weather for the disappointing results of the February attacks. Neither Air Vice-Marshal Baldwin nor Air Commodore Oxland had anything to add to what they had already said, but Air Vice-Marshal Bottomley said

---

[1] Letter Baldwin to Peirse, 25th Jan. 1941.
[2] Letter Bottomley to Peirse, 27th Jan. 1941.
[3] Letter Oxland to Peirse, 28th Jan. 1941.
[4] Letter Dewdney to Peirse, 1st Feb. 1941.
[5] Bomber Cmd. O.R.B., Feb. 1941. Letter Bottomley to Peirse, 1st March 1941.

that experience had 'not confirmed' his impression that Homberg could be attacked without moonlight.[1]

This episode was, however, of short duration and was really no more than a kind of anachronism from what was now almost a previous age. Doctrinaire assumptions and what was often little more than wishful thinking were giving way in the appreciation of operational possibility to empirical methods and notably the evidence of the camera. Already the revelations of December 1940 were gradually driving Bomber Command from precision to area attack. Further and even more startling discoveries were presently to complete the process.

---

[1] Memo. Robb to Bomber Cmd., 16th Feb. 1941. Coningham to Bomber Cmd., 17th Feb. 1941. Baldwin to Bomber Cmd., 17th Feb. 1941. Oxland to Bomber Cmd., 17th Feb. 1941. Memo. Bottomley to Bomber Cmd., 20th Feb. 1941.

3. The tactical foundations of area bombing, March–November 1941

The first phase of the war in the air, extending from September 1939 to April 1940, had sufficed to convert Bomber Command mainly into a night force. The second phase, from May 1940 to March 1941, had gone far to show that the night bomber was more a bludgeon and less a rapier than had been supposed, that the change from day to night attack meant not only a change in bombing technique, but also a change in bombing strategy.

In March 1941, however, these revolutions were by no means complete, nor were they final. There were yet to be many attempts to revive daylight bombing and the aim of precision bombing at night was never far from the thoughts of most of those who directed the offensive. Indeed, Bomber Command was ultimately to succeed both in carrying out daylight attacks in strength and depth and in achieving an astonishing degree of precision at night. For the greater part of the war from 1941 onwards, however, the overwhelming majority of its attacks consisted of area bombing at night.

In seeking the explanation of how this came to pass, there are many and various factors to be considered, but none was more important than the tactical conclusion that the only target on which the night force could inflict effective damage was a whole German town and that day bombing was not a practicable proposition of war against targets of penetration or as an operation of a sustained nature.

The operational experience which had accumulated by the end of 1940 had already pointed more than tentatively towards this conclusion, but it was only the further evidence arising from the operations of the spring and summer of 1941 which made it inescapable, though, of course, not necessarily permanently so. The revolutions set in motion by the experiences of the daylight Wellington forces in December 1939 and by the analysis of reconnaissance photographs of targets attacked by the night bombers in December 1940 had, by December 1941, become firmly established and widely recognised. It is this process which lends particular importance to the operations undertaken by day and night by Bomber Command between March and November 1941.

Nevertheless, in March and April 1941 tactical considerations were thrust into the background by grave strategic developments. Bomber Command was not diverted to naval targets in March because it was thought that they could be more effectively bombed than oil plants, but because, as in the case of air force targets during the summer of 1940, national survival seemed to depend upon the attempt. The rate of merchant ship sinkings, and not the Gelsenkirchen photographs, was the operative explanation of the changed policy. Similarly, the renewed attempts to carry out daylight bombing were inspired and nourished more by the desire to intervene in the campaigns which Germany undertook first in the Balkans and then in Russia than by any new-found confidence in the practicability of the operations.

From the point of view of the tactical opportunities which existed and also of the operational lessons which were learnt, the campaign following the Prime Minister's Atlantic Directive of 9th March 1941 was of no great significance. The night bombers had perforce to attempt the destruction of the German battle cruisers which lay in Brest and elsewhere, but their failure to do so came as no surprise to Sir Richard Peirse. The campaign also included attacks against other precision targets such as submarine bases and factories producing long-range Focke-Wulf Condors which were being used by the Germans against convoys in the Atlantic. On the other hand, a considerable number of the Bomber Command attacks were directed against towns such as Kiel, Emden, Hamburg, Wilhelmshaven and Bremen, which contained naval installations. On these occasions the Mannheim technique was employed and the selection of the targets was, perhaps, not greatly different from what it would have been if Bomber Command had already been primarily committed to an offensive against German industrial morale.[1]

This campaign against German warships, which also amounted to area attacks upon the ports in which they lay, and against 'naval' towns, absorbing as it was, did not prevent Bomber Command from attacking other German towns and, in particular, an increasing number of sorties were flown against Berlin. Thus, the Prime Minister's Atlantic Directive had little influence upon the trend of night bombing operations which was logically inevitable in the light of what had occurred during the offensive against oil plants. While Bomber Command continued to attempt precise night attacks from time to time, including some against oil plants, it was increasingly turning towards the aim of destroying areas rather than points.

This tendency contributed to the dissatisfaction which Sir Richard Peirse expressed with the policy of attacking the battle cruisers at Brest. The destruction of the area, much of which was in any case water, did not seem to be a profitable objective, and the destruction of the points represented by the battle cruisers, seemed to be highly improbable.[2] To those who began to understand the limitations of

---

[1] These attacks on towns associated with naval activities bear comparison with the later plan of attack on towns associated with the aircraft industry. They are an early example of the idea of harnessing the practice of area bombing to a selective purpose.

[2] Letter Peirse to Portal, 15th April 1941.

TACTICAL FOUNDATIONS OF AREA BOMBING

night bombing, the contribution of those bombs which would undoubtedly miss their 'point' targets now appeared to be a matter of the first importance. It seemed to be no more than common sense to select targets in profitable areas and the most obviously profitable areas were the large and congested industrial districts of western Germany.[1]

Nevertheless, the overriding urgency of the Battle of the Atlantic, proclaimed by Mr. Churchill and recognised by Sir Charles Portal, remained and it was not until July that the strategic situation became temporarily more free and, as far as the night offensive was concerned, more susceptible to the operational conclusions which had been forming since the turn of the year. By that time, however, the Balkans had been conquered and Russia invaded and, for the strategic reasons which have already been shown, Bomber Command once more turned some of its energies to the task of daylight attack.

The strategic situation which prompted this renewed attempt also created what seemed to be much improved tactical prospects of carrying it out successfully. It was a reasonable assumption, confirmed by intelligence reports, that German fighter strength in the West would be much reduced in consequence of the new campaigns in the South and East. What had during the previous twenty months been the front now became the back door, and Bomber Command now had the prospect of taking Germany in the rear. This was a better prospect than the German air force had enjoyed during the Battle of Britain.

On the other hand, Germany was considerably more distant from Britain than Britain was from German bases in France, and the key to the whole situation remained the lack of range of Fighter Command. Daylight attacks on Germany would have to be made by unescorted bombers, and as Air Vice-Marshal Saundby, no doubt in the light of experience, observed, 'it is not therefore worth while to expose a considerable force of bombers to the risk of being intercepted by the enemy fighters'.[2] Indeed, Air Vice-Marshal Baldwin had already protested strongly and successfully against any of his Wellingtons being exposed to this hazard. He reiterated his conviction that the Wellington, 'which lacks armament, speed and handiness and especially rate of climb is a most unsuitable type of aircraft for daylight operations . . .'[3]

Thus, a daylight entry to Germany, even by the back door, was seen to be a hazardous undertaking, but there did seem to be a way

---

[1] Cf. Trenchard's views expressed in May 1941. See above, pp. 169–170.
[2] Note by Saundby, 26th June 1941.
[3] Memo. Baldwin to Bomber Cmd., 11th April 1941. The Wellington Ia with which 3 Group had been equipped at the beginning of the war was 'considerably faster and lighter' than the Ic which was now in use.

in which the short-range aircraft of Fighter Command might help to make it possible. 'If we can succeed in concentrating the enemy's fighters in the Pas de Calais area', Air Vice-Marshal Saundby said on 26th June 1941, 'and containing them there by continuing our bombing attacks with strong fighter support, we ought to be able to create opportunities for the daylight attack of objectives in Germany and North-Western France.'[1]

These co-ordinated fighter and bomber operations in the Pas de Calais area, which had begun on 14th June 1941, were, therefore, the tactical hinge upon which the whole of the daylight bombing plan now turned. The Blenheims of 2 Group, by attacking industrial and military targets, were intended to provoke the desired German fighter reaction and the Spitfires of 11 Group were intended to engage and destroy these fighters and, at the same time, afford protection to the Blenheims. Thus, the triple aim of causing the Germans to bring fighter reinforcements from the East or suffer the consequences of not doing so, of extending the sphere of British air superiority across the Channel and of opening the way for unescorted daylight attack on Germany might be achieved.[2]

After rather less than a fortnight of these *Circus* operations, Air Vice-Marshal Saundby was encouraged to believe that the enemy was being forced to 'choose between allowing us to bomb without interference and engaging our fighters in circumstances in which he is certain to get the worst of it'.[3] Air Vice-Marshal Saundby had wisely qualified this comment with the words 'up to the present', and as time went on it became increasingly doubtful whether the Germans were always getting the worst of it. Indeed, as was presently seen, the German fighters, though numerically far inferior to the forces thrown against them, enjoyed certain tactical advantages over the Royal Air Force fighters committed to protecting the Blenheim formations and often flying at the limit of their petrol endurance.[4]

These tactical advantages were very similar to those which had been so effectively exploited by Fighter Command during the Battle of Britain. Apart from the fact that the Messerschmitt 109F had a slightly superior performance to the Spitfire V, the German fighters were generally in an advantageous position before the British attack developed. Their radar early-warning system, which appears to have been sluggish at the outset, had improved 'out of all recognition' by

---

[1] Note by Saundby, 26th June 1941.

[2] Dirs. Bomber Cmd. to 2 Group, 23rd Jan., 21st Feb., 30th June 1941. Dir. Bomber Cmd. to 4 Group, 28th June 1941.

[3] Note by Saundby, 26th June 1941.

[4] Air Vice-Marshal D. F. Stevenson, Air Officer Commanding 5 Group, estimated the British superiority at 'more than two to one in fighters alone'. Letter Stevenson to Peirse, 10th Sept. 1941.

September. By the time the British formations were only leaving the English coast on the outward journey the German fighters were already at considerable altitude over the St. Omer, Lille and Béthune areas. The limited range of the British escort fighters made it obvious, within a reasonably limited area, where the attack would fall. Thus, the German fighters could wait to attack until they had the advantage of height and sun. They were more likely to surprise the British fighters than to be surprised by them. Furthermore, the German fighters were always operating near their bases while the Spitfires, even if they were to penetrate only to the Lille-Béthune area, were near the limit of their petrol endurance. This meant that the British aircraft could not fight freely with the Messerschmitts. If they were outmanœuvred, the latter had only to dive to the south-east. They could not be followed for long. It was only on the raids of extremely short penetration that it was found possible to give a number of the Spitfire wings 'carte blanche to operate in loose formation with freedom to seek out and destroy the enemy'. But, of course, the enemy had no need to trail his coat within what was only a short motor journey of the coast, and he soon transferred his fighter bases from the coastal region to the areas around Amiens, Albert, Lille, Bruges and St. Omer. Despite these difficulties, however, Air Vice-Marshal Leigh-Mallory, the 11 Group Commander, claimed that between 14th June and 3rd September 1941, 437 German fighters had been destroyed and a further 182 probably destroyed for the loss of 194 British fighter pilots. Of the 520 bomber sorties covered by his fighters, Air Vice-Marshal Leigh-Mallory suggested that ten bombers had been lost to anti-aircraft fire and only four to the German fighters.[1]

Though Hampdens and Stirlings had taken part in the *Circus* operations, the great majority of the bomber sorties had been flown by Blenheims which Air Vice-Marshal Leigh-Mallory regarded as unsuitable for the task. '. . . unless the Bombers hit hard and well,' he pointed out, 'the enemy fighters are not forced to risk a direct and determined attack upon them in the face of the escort—but content themselves with pecking at our Fighters . . .' This they could do, as has already been shown, under tactical conditions generally favourable to themselves.

In order to force the Germans to fight at a disadvantage, by which he meant compelling them to attack the bombers rather than their escorts, Air Vice-Marshal Leigh-Mallory thought it was essential to

---

[1] Memo. by Leigh-Mallory, 5th Sept. 1941. Air Vice-Marshal Stevenson said he had lost seven bombers to German fighters. Letter Stevenson to Peirse, 10th Sept. 1941. Air Vice-Marshal Leigh-Mallory's claims of German aircraft destroyed vastly exceeded the actual figures. The actual number of German fighter aircraft destroyed over France and the Low Countries between 14th June and 3rd September 1941 appears to have been 128. A further seventy-six were damaged. Note compiled from Quartermaster General's Dept. (*Abt. VI*), German Air Ministry. Not all these casualties were necessarily sustained as a result of *Circus* operations.

put more weight into the bomber attacks. If, instead of the Blenheims, heavy bombers were sent, the formations would become smaller and, therefore, easier to protect. At the same time their attacks would be more formidable and the German fighters would, therefore, be more likely to take risks in order to bring them down. 'I realise,' Air Vice-Marshal Leigh-Mallory said, 'that the general policy of the Air Council is to utilise every available heavy Bomber for bombing Germany rather than occupied territory, but I believe that the diversion of even say 5% of our heavy Bombers to regular "Circus" operations would enable our Fighters to maintain such a high toll of enemy Fighter pilots as to embarrass his Eastern operations.'[1]

This belief may have been somewhat optimistic, for it must always have been doubtful if the German air force would risk its life in the defence of French industry, but to Air Vice-Marshal Stevenson it seemed also to be 'fantastic'. The 2 Group Commander thought that the German fighter reaction was already quite adequate and he also believed that 'every bomb we throw on French soil is a wasted bomb if it could have been thrown on Germany.' The fault in the *Circus* operations was, in Air Vice-Marshal Stevenson's view, attributable not to the bombers but to the fighters. Air Vice-Marshal Leigh-Mallory was, he said, 'fighting the same kind of battle as the G.A.F. fought in 1940 and since he is using similar equipment, he must not be surprised if the results are unfavourable'.

The fixed-gun interceptor fighter designed for the defence of Great Britain was, Air Vice-Marshal Stevenson believed, unsuitable for 'the protection of offensive bombing operations by close escort and support fighter Squadrons carrying out a purely defensive role.' He cited the 'monumental example' of what had happened to the *Luftwaffe* in the Battle of Britain to show that 'if an air defence system possesses the necessary fighter strength, is well organised and has a good warning system, successful continued bombing operations could only be undertaken if the enemy fighter force were overwhelmed and a high state of air superiority thereby established.' He was not entirely confident as to how far it would help, but he thought that the tactical position would be improved by the introduction of free-gun fighters among the escorts. In any event, as he foresaw that before the war was over 'we shall have to bomb in daylight, possibly on a wide scale', it was, in Air Vice-Marshal Stevenson's opinion, an urgent necessity that 'Fighter Command or someone else gets busy and thinks out the right kind of equipment and tactics to carry the bomber offensive safely through an enemy air defence system in daylight ...'[2]

---

[1] Memo. by Leigh-Mallory, 5th Sept. 1941.
[2] Letters Stevenson to Peirse, 10th Sept. 1941 and to Slessor, 14th Sept. 1941.

There was clearly much truth in both views, and it was clear that the Germans would hardly be driven to measures of desperate defence by bombers which, because of the limited range of their escorts, could not penetrate much beyond Lille. Similarly the British fighters could not count on manœuvring for favourable combat when they were often flying at the extremity of their petrol range and were tied as close escorts to the bombers. Finally, as the Battle of Britain had so clearly demonstrated, an immense advantage was conferred on the fighter force which had the operational initiative and could choose its moment for attack. In the *Circus* operations it was, as Air Vice-Marshal Leigh-Mallory had pointed out, only on the raids of extremely shallow penetration that some of the escorting fighters could be freed from the disadvantageous position of having to fly as close defensive escorts to the bombers, and given 'carte blanche . . . to seek out and destroy the enemy.'

Basically, therefore, the problem was one of range. Only increased range could drive the Germans to measures of desperate defence by bringing the attacks nearer their heart. Only increased range could confer the operational initiative upon the British fighters, but it was Sir Charles Portal's conviction that 'increased range can only be provided at the expense of performance and manœuvrability.' 'The long range fighter', he had told the Prime Minister in May 1941, 'whether built specifically as such, or whether given increased range by fitting extra tanks, will be at a disadvantage compared with the short range high performance fighter.' [1]

In this crucial judgment, which was supported by much experience, Sir Charles Portal was eventually shown to have been wrong.

Meanwhile, the incentive to grapple with the formidable technical problems involved in the production of an effective long-range fighter was, perhaps, blunted not only by the authoritative opinion that the task was impossible, but also by the suspicion that it was also unnecessary. The belief still lingered that heavy bombers might yet be cast into self-defending formations capable of carrying the war to the interior of Germany in daylight. Indeed, one of the objects of launching the *Circus* operations had been to create conditions favourable for this.

During the summer of 1941 small forces of the new four-engined heavy bombers were occasionally despatched to make unescorted daylight attacks on targets ranging from Kiel, where six Halifaxes were sent on 30th June, to La Pallice, where the *Scharnhorst* was allotted as the target for six Stirlings on 23rd July and for fifteen Halifaxes on 24th July. These attacks on La Pallice, which were carried out in conjunction with partially escorted attacks on the

---

[1] Memo. Portal to Churchill, 27th May 1941.

Gneisenau and *Prinz Eugen* at Brest, merit special attention because important conclusions were drawn from them.

The original plan was to carry out a surprise daylight attack on the *Scharnhorst* and *Gneisenau* while both were still at Brest. The comparative weakness of the German fighter forces estimated to be in the immediate vicinity of Brest and the fact that five squadrons of Spitfires were now being equipped with extra tanks which would enable them to operate as far as Brest encouraged the hope that the plan might succeed.[1] In order to give a reasonable chance of hitting the ships it was considered necessary to despatch between 140 and 150 heavy and medium bombers.[2]

The limited number of 'long range' Spitfires available would be inadequate to afford direct cover to the whole of such a large force of bombers, and in any case it was not thought possible to produce a sufficiently high standard of formation flying in the bomber pilots to allow all these aircraft to move in one tight formation. It was therefore decided to open the attack with unescorted Fortresses operating at a high altitude and to follow this fifteen minutes later with a force of eighteen Hampdens closely escorted by three of the 'long range' Spitfire squadrons. By these means it was hoped to attract the majority of the enemy fighters in the immediate vicinity and cause them to exhaust their ammunition and petrol before the main attack developed. The main force of Wellingtons and heavy bombers, numbering about 120 aircraft, was then to attack, without close escort, in the shortest possible time, which was estimated to be about forty-five minutes. The remaining two squadrons of 'long range' Spitfires were to be in the area at the time in order to deal with any hostile fighters which might already have refuelled and rearmed. To contain other German fighters around the Cherbourg area, Blenheims were to make a diversionary raid there under the protection of ordinary Spitfires of 11 Group. For about a month before the attack the Hampdens rehearsed their role.

Such was the plan. Its execution was seriously upset by the last-minute move of the *Scharnhorst* from Brest to La Pallice, where she lay beyond the reach of the specially equipped Spitfires. This resulted in the heavy bombers being taken out of the attack on Brest and diverted to La Pallice. Together with the loss of the Manchesters, which had to be withdrawn from the operation owing to technical failures, this meant that the main attack on Brest would be reduced in strength from 120 to seventy-eight bombers. It also, of course, meant that the

---

[1] It was estimated that there were thirty single-engined and nine twin-engined fighters in the immediate vicinity of Brest. A further sixty single-engined fighters in the Cherbourg and Channel Island areas might, it was thought, also intervene. The five Spitfire squadrons had been equipped with their tanks and were ready for operations by 15th July.

[2] 'Heavy Bombers' now meant Stirlings, Halifaxes, Manchesters, and Fortresses. 'Medium Bombers' were the old heavy bombers, i.e. Wellingtons and Hampdens.

heavy bombers had to operate against La Pallice without any fighter cover at all.

Apart from these serious reductions in strength, the Brest attack was carried out on 24th July more or less according to plan. The Hampden attack seemed to draw up the expected number of enemy fighters and the crews reported about twenty-four of them in the air at this stage. Two or three more were seen by the three Fortress crews who had preceded the Hampdens. The opposition was, however, by no means exhausted when the main force arrived and, in particular, these seventy-eight aircraft failed to swamp the anti-aircraft fire which was 'intense and accurate'. The diversionary attack at Cherbourg encountered little opposition and suffered no casualties. From the ninety-nine bombers which had attacked Brest eleven were shot down by fighters and flak. These casualties were evenly distributed between the Hampdens and all phases of the main attack. Two further aircraft crashed on the way home.

On the evening before this, six Stirlings had been sent to engage the *Scharnhorst* at La Pallice. Reports differed as to the number which succeeded in carrying out the attack, but one failed to return and the others reported combats with about half a dozen fighters. The next day, while the Brest attack was in progress, fifteen Halifaxes were sent to La Pallice. Fourteen of them reached the target and were met by what appeared to be between twelve and eighteen Messerschmitt 109s. Every one of these fourteen Halifaxes was hit by fire from the fighters or by flak. Five failed to return, five more were damaged to an extent which required about three weeks to repair. Two were damaged to a lesser extent and the remaining two were superficially damaged.[1]

These Halifax casualties were incurred in an attack upon a fringe target in the extreme west of France. They did not augur well for daylight attacks on the interior of Germany. Indeed, they showed, in the words of the Bomber Command report, 'that unsupported daylight attacks by heavies when faced by equal or slightly superior numbers of fighters are not a practical proposition'. Moreover, it was seen that the German fighter opposition had 'seriously interfered' with the bombing accuracy of the Halifaxes.[2]

Under these circumstances it seemed to Air Vice-Marshal C. R. Carr, the new Commander of 4 Group, to be 'questionable if attacks by daylight, carried out against intensive opposition by fighters and A.A. fire, will be any more effective than attacks at night when

---

[1] Bomber Cmd. Air Staff Note, 28th July 1941. Bomber Cmd. O.R.B., 23rd and 24th July 1941.

[2] Nevertheless, no less than five direct hits on the *Scharnhorst* were obtained. The resulting damage was serious. The *Scharnhorst* sailed for Brest that evening with three thousand tons of flood water inside her. See Roskill: *The War at Sea*, Vol. I, p. 487.

conditions are favourable'. Yet the casualties to be expected by day would be ten or more times as great as those suffered at night.[1]

Even at Brest, where the bombers had enjoyed the advantage of some fighter support, the casualties had exceeded ten per cent of the force engaged. Yet many of the German pilots appeared to be inexperienced and it seemed that a proportion of them belonged to operational training units. More thorough training of the Royal Air Force bomber pilots in formation tactics, though it might reduce their casualties against fighter pilots of this calibre, would offer no guarantee of immunity when the better German squadrons were encountered.[2]

Apart, however, from the possible ineffectiveness of such special training in formation tactics, it would result in a diminution of the night offensive, for, in order to carry it out, the chosen squadrons would have to be withdrawn from the line. As the Commander of 5 Group, Air Vice-Marshal Slessor, put it, 'this day bomber business ... is a terribly uneconomical business.'[3]

Successful day bombing, however, clearly called not only for special training but also for special equipment. Ceiling, speed, armour, armament and long-range fighter escort were, Sir Archibald Sinclair had suggested to Sir Charles Portal in June 1941, the factors upon which attention should be concentrated. 'The tactics of daylight penetration and the use of fighters with long range tanks in support of daylight raids are doubtless being considered,' he said. 'Would it not be a good plan, however,' he asked Sir Charles Portal, 'to remit the whole problem of daylight penetration for intensive study to a special Committee analogous to the Night Interception Committee?'[4]

Sir Charles Portal, however, saw no need for any special study of the problem in view of what he described as 'the progress that has already been made in studying all aspects of the tactics of daylight penetration and the use of fighters with long range tanks in support of daylight raids'. He did not, as he had already told the Prime Minister, believe that the long-range fighter was a practical proposition,[5] and he did not, as he now told Sir Archibald Sinclair, see any immediate prospect of producing a bomber capable of operating at high altitude. Nor was he hopeful about a 'speed' bomber. The

---

[1] Memo. Carr to Bomber Cmd., 26th Aug. 1941.

[2] Bomber Cmd. Air Staff Note, 28th July 1941. Memo. Carr to Bomber Cmd., 26th Aug. 1941. Min. G/C Ops. to Saundby, 27th Aug. 1941.

[3] Letter Slessor to Peirse, 12th Sept. 1941.

[4] Min. Sinclair to Portal, 16th June 1941. The progress now being made in the science and tactics of night interception was one of the reasons for which Sir Archibald Sinclair and other members of the Government were anxious to see the problem of daylight penetration tackled.

[5] See above, p. 239.

TACTICAL FOUNDATIONS OF AREA BOMBING

Buckingham would not be ready till 1943, but he thought Bomber Command might receive some Mosquitoes.[1] As to Sir Archibald Sinclair's suggestions about increasing the armour plating on day bombers, particularly with a view to protecting the rear gunner, he said that Bomber Command would be satisfied with more protection for the engines. Finally, on the question of putting cannon in the bombers, he said that this depended on the production of an efficient predictor sight which, he suggested, was still a long way off.[2]

Such were the apparently insuperable obstacles to the development of the equipment which even before the war had been recognised by some at least as necessary for day bombing. These difficulties were sufficient, even before the Halifax attack on La Pallice, to convince Sir Charles Portal that a day attack on the interior of Germany was virtually impossible. 'I am certain', he had told the Prime Minister on 3rd June 1941, 'that we shall be unable to carry out such attacks by day until we have so large a bomber force that we can bear for a time something like the scale of losses which we inflicted on the Germans last Autumn and which they could not prevent even by their short range fighter escorts'.[3]

In November, because of the extraordinary high casualties they were suffering, the Blenheims of 2 Group were diverted from day bombing and told to join the night offensive.[4] On 6th December 1941 Sir Richard Peirse reported that neither the Fortress I nor II were suitable as day bombers. They should, he advised, be fitted with exhaust flame dampers and committed to the night offensive.[5]

The operations of the summer and autumn of 1941 had served to confirm the lessons which had been learnt about day bombing in earlier phases of the war. They had again demonstrated the decisive superiority of the day fighter over the day bomber and the inability of the 'self-defending' formation to defend itself. They had shown some of the difficulties inherent in the conduct of fighter-escorted bomber operations and above all the impossibility of extending the sphere of air superiority without also extending the range of Fighter Command. These operations had shown that the force which had been designed for the defence of Great Britain could not effectively

---

[1] But he had already rejected Sir Richard Peirse's second and urgent demand for Mosquitoes, saying that it would take twenty-one days to convert them into bombers and that they should, in the first instance, be used for photographic reconnaissance. Letter Portal to Peirse, 26th June 1941.

[2] Memo. Portal to Sinclair, 6th July 1941.

[3] Min. Portal to Churchill, 3rd June 1941.

[4] Letter Stevenson to Peirse, 3rd Nov. 1941. Letter Peirse to Air Min., 8th Nov. 1941. Letter Bottomley to Peirse, 25th Nov. 1941.

[5] Letter Peirse to Air Min., 6th Dec. 1941. These Fortresses were not nearly so heavily armed as those later used by the United States Eighth Air Force. The American view tended to be that the British crews had not been operating the Fortresses correctly. See *The Army Air Forces in World War II* edited by W. F. Craven and J. L. Cate, Vol. I, (Chicago, 1948), pp. 600–604.

intervene in the offensive against Germany. They had also shown that a force which had already become predominantly committed to night action could not suddenly turn to day attack simply on account of strategic necessity or even considerable tactical opportunity. Day bombing was seen to be a specialised activity calling for specialised training and specialised equipment. If Bomber Command was to undertake large-scale day operations it could not also maintain a sustained night offensive. In any case, massive daylight operations against long-range targets would have to await the perfection of many devices ranging from cannons in the bombers to extra tanks in the fighters. Some of these things were prospects in the distant future, but others were still over the horizon.

Meanwhile, though small-scale efforts with small parts of Bomber Command might continue,[1] the bulk of the force was irrevocably committed to night action. The resources of science, industry and tactical ingenuity were to be mainly applied to the problems of night bombing and not those of daylight penetration. This, indeed, was almost inevitable, for, while its night technique and equipment were gradually improved Bomber Command, with however little effect, could always continue its war operations. If it had been committed to daylight attack it could, for much of the time, hardly have operated at all. The incidence of casualties is ultimately the most important of all operational considerations.

The virtual abandonment of day bombing was now seen to be a much more serious matter than had at one time been supposed. This was because of the growing realisation of the inaccuracy of night attack. The belief voiced by Sir Archibald Sinclair in October 1940 that 'our small bomber force could, by accurate bombing, do very great damage to the enemy's war effort, but could not gain a decision against Germany by bombing the civil population',[2] now had to be qualified in the light of the ascertained facts relating to operational possibility.

Already in April 1941 it was evident to the Air Staff that it was useless to attempt the destruction of specific targets on dark nights. It followed that for about three-quarters of every month 'it is only possible to obtain satisfactory results by the "Blitz" attack of large working class and industrial areas in the towns.' Even this was recognised to be 'a matter of the greatest difficulty' unless the selected areas were near water.[3]

---

[1] For example, 2 Group was to consider the use of Boston III's for day bombing, when it got them. The role of the Mosquito as a bomber was also to be day attack, again, when it became available. Letter Bottomley to Peirse, 25th Nov. 1941.

[2] Min. Sinclair to Churchill, 31st Oct. 1940.

[3] Appendix to paper on bombing policy by D.D.B. Ops., 24th April 1941. This appendix was attached to the Air Min. directive of 9th July 1941 with some minor modifications of wording, see App. 8 (xvi), for the directive.

TACTICAL FOUNDATIONS OF AREA BOMBING

Thus, the operational experience of late 1940 and early 1941 had sufficed to convert Bomber Command from a force which had previously been mainly devoted to the aim of precision attack to one which was now predominantly concerned with area bombing. Even so the idea of precision attack at night, like that of daylight bombing, died hard, and, as has already been shown, the Air Staff still hesitated to abandon it, if only because the destruction of German towns was such a gigantic undertaking. It was obvious that the original assumption of an average aiming error of three hundred yards even under the best conditions of moonlight had been unduly optimistic, but the Directorate of Bomber Operations was now prepared to suggest that under these conditions, and when the weather was also perfect, the average error would be six hundred yards. If this was so, there would still be occasions during about a quarter of each month when precision bombing could be attempted.[1]

This doubling of the expected average bomb-aiming error and the confinement of its application to those nights on which perfect conditions prevailed represented a considerable advance in the science of operational appreciation. It arose, the Directorate of Bomber Operations suggested, from the need of getting rid 'completely of ideas which we conceived before we had the chance to learn from experience', and the desirability of working 'on the data which we have been able to accumulate rather than on assumptions which approximate to wishful thinking'.

The extent to which previous assumptions, and notably the three hundred yards aiming error, had approximated to 'wishful thinking' had, of course, been indicated by the evidence, and especially the photographs, which came to hand in December 1940. The new assumption of the six hundred yards aiming error in perfect conditions was largely based upon an analysis of the results of a moonlight precision attack on the Focke-Wulf factory at Bremen carried out in perfect conditions on the night of 12th March 1941.

On this night fifty-four Wellingtons were ordered to bomb the factory while a further thirty-two Blenheims attacked the centre of the town. Thirty-three of the Wellingtons carrying 132 bombs and 840 incendiaries claimed to have executed their orders. The others joined the Blenheims in the attack on the town. This had been allotted as the alternative target. Photographic reconnaissance showed that twelve bombs had hit the factory and that a further twenty-eight had fallen within approximately six hundred yards of it.[2]

The fact that this and other unspecified evidence was taken to suggest that under perfect conditions the average aiming error would be

---
[1] B. Ops. 1 Review, 5th April 1941, see extract App. 45.
[2] B. Ops. 1 Review, 5th April 1941. Bomber Cmd. O.R.B., 12th/13th April 1941. For the effects of this attack, see below, pp. 301 and 303.

six hundred yards showed the extent to which assumptions still tended to approximate to 'wishful thinking'. In fact, somewhat less than one-third of the bombs aimed at it had fallen on or within six hundred yards of the Focke-Wulf factory. The other two-thirds had all fallen more, and perhaps very much more, than six hundred yards away. It was also significant that twenty-one of the Wellingtons had failed to locate the factory at all, even though the target was near the coast.

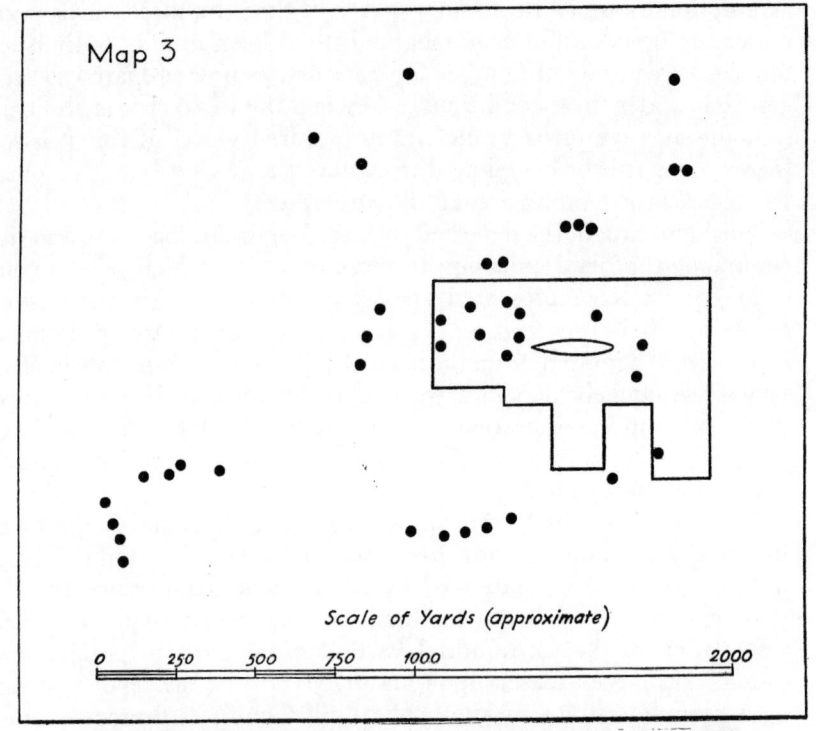

The Focke-Wulf factory at Bremen attacked on 12th March 1941. The points of impact of the forty bombs which fell within, approximately, 1,250 yards of the factory are shown thus..● An outline of the Scharnhorst ⬤ drawn to the same scale is superimposed on the centre of the factory.

Nevertheless, great concessions had been made to reality. The new estimates showed that it was not worth while to attempt precision bombing except when there was a coincidence of good moonlight and perfect weather. They showed that even on these occasions the targets would have to be larger than had often hitherto been the case. The plot of the Bremen attack, for example, showed that if the *Scharnhorst* had been lying in the centre of the Focke-Wulf factory she would not have sustained a single hit. The laws of probability showed how rapidly the number of direct hits on an oil plant would decline

TACTICAL FOUNDATIONS OF AREA BOMBING

as the aiming error was increased. Against a standard oil plant, for instance, the number of direct hits to be expected from four hundred shots would, with an aiming error of three hundred yards, be 30·8. If the aiming error was increased to six hundred yards the number of hits would decline to 13·6. With an error of a thousand yards 5·96 hits might be expected. If the aircraft dropped their bombs by dead reckoning, having reached an area around the target measuring three miles by three miles, the number of direct hits on the oil plant, again from four hundred shots, would be 0·87.[1]

Above all, the new estimates showed that nothing more than area bombing was operationally feasible on dark nights. Indeed, it was now feared that 'the limitations of the night bombing during the moonless period of each month are not yet fully appreciated by the War Cabinet and senior members of the other Services . . .' This, it was thought, might be 'partly accounted for by an unconscious lack of honesty on our part to recognise and admit our operational limitations under certain conditions'.[2]

These, then, were the tactical assumptions which dictated a change of bombing policy when, in July 1941, Bomber Command once more turned to the strategic attack on Germany as its first commitment. They were largely written into the bombing directive of 9th July which inaugurated the campaign against railway centres and town areas.[3] Yet the course of that campaign was now to show that even these assumptions were still greatly over-optimistic and that Bomber Command still had much progress to make before even the largest area targets could be hit with any certainty or regularity.

The Butt Report, which it will be recalled was based upon a statistical analysis of night photographs taken by Bomber Command in June and July, was sent to Bomber Command Headquarters on 18th August 1941.[4] It indicated that the majority of the aircraft despatched on night operations were failing to find their targets. It suggested that in all attacks about a fifth of the force was getting its bombs within five miles of the appointed targets. Thus, of the 6,103 aircraft sent out during the period reviewed by the report, from which 4,065 claimed to have attacked their targets, it now appeared that only about 1,200 had even bombed an area of seventy-five square miles around them. In the case of the Ruhr, where the defences were stiff and an industrial haze common, it seemed that only about seven out of every hundred bombers despatched got even this somewhat imprecise result.

---

[1] B. Ops. 1 Review, 5th April 1941. For other figures and reasoning used to support these conclusions, see App. 45.

[2] One of the principal objects of the report by B. Ops. 1 in which these words occur, was to point out the futility of continued night attacks on the *Scharnhorst* and *Gneisenau* at Brest.

[3] See above, pp. 174–175.

[4] For the Butt Report, see App. 13.

Despite the doubts which were entertained at Bomber Command about the soundness of this report, it is not surprising that Lord Cherwell found it 'depressing reading'. After discussing the situation with Sir Charles Portal and Sir Richard Peirse, he told the Prime Minister that it was proposed to institute a small branch at Bomber Command to continue this kind of research. He also suggested that immediate and vigorous measures should be taken to bring aid to a force which was obviously lost in the dark.

Lord Cherwell suggested that an investigation should be held to find out whether more value could not be extracted from astro-navigation. He wanted Bomber Command to 're-examine most carefully the possibilities of making specially expert navigators, or bombers equipped with special navigational aids, fly ahead of the main body to light fires in the right region for the rest to home on, as the Germans do. (It seems possible', he added, 'that means could be found of distinguishing these fires from decoys.)'

Lord Cherwell was also concerned with the rapid development of new equipment. 'The use of marker bombs dropped in daylight, made to light up or emit radio signals in the night is', he said, 'to be considered. The use of apparatus similar to A.S.V.[1] to tell when the bomber is above a built up area is to be examined and the design of apparatus by which a bomber could follow along the German high tension grid is to be reopened.' Finally Lord Cherwell referred to the so-called *Gee* apparatus 'by means of which a bomber can find his way in any weather within a couple of miles of any target up to a distance of 400 miles . . .'

This radar device was already in an advanced stage of development, and one experimental set had already been lost over Germany. *Gee* was susceptible to counter-measures and Lord Cherwell did not believe that it would have a useful life of much more than three, or at most six, months after the Germans got wind of it. For this reason, he was anxious that it should be pressed into operational service during the coming winter instead of waiting a year, as had been suggested, until the whole force could be equipped. By November 1941 he believed it would be possible to equip and maintain two hundred *Gee* bombers which would be a much larger force than the German fire-raising squadrons had ever possessed.[2] All these ideas were endorsed by Sir Charles Portal.[3]

---

[1] Air to Surface Vessel. This was a radar device for the detection of submarines on the surface. The apparatus, as modified for use in bombers, was known as *H2S* and its first operational use in this role was in the attack on Hamburg on 30/31st January 1943. *H2S* had, however, been under development for some time before Lord Cherwell made these recommendations. Air Chief Marshal Sir Hugh Lloyd has related to the authors, how, flying in a Whitley during 1940, he was able to detect coastlines and the Pennine Range on an experimental *H2S*. See Annex I.

[2] Min. Cherwell to Churchill, 2nd Sept. 1941.

[3] Min. Portal to Churchill, 11th Sept. 1941.

There was really little or nothing new in these suggestions. The devices and tactical expedients mentioned by Lord Cherwell had been under development for a long time. What was new about the situation in September 1941 was the realisation of the extreme urgency of bringing them to fruition. This was due to the impact of the Butt Report.

Nevertheless, the difficulties, dangers and controversies associated with these projects remained. In the case of the new equipment, the fear of placing dangerous weapons in the hand of the enemy was ever present. In due course, we shall see how the introduction not only of *H2S*, but also of other important devices, was delayed for this reason. There was also the consideration of how many sets of a new equipment it was expedient to have before risking showing the secret to the enemy. In the case of *Gee*, Lord Cherwell believed that one hundred sets would be enough to justify the introduction of the device.[1] The Air Staff, however, seemed to prefer to wait until they had enough equipment to supply twenty squadrons.[2]

This problem was closely connected with that of a special fire-raising or target-marking force. It was obviously in Lord Cherwell's mind that a relatively small proportion of the force, equipped with *Gee*, might communicate the precision of that instrument to the rest of the force, not yet so equipped, by some means of target indication. This in turn was connected with the development of a marker bomb, either pyrotechnic or radio. Such a bomb would clearly have to possess ballistic qualities which would enable it to be accurately aimed, and it would also have to possess characteristics which would make it difficult for the enemy to move, simulate or extinguish it.

In this matter the considerable technical difficulties, which had been encountered during the past four years, persisted. If the bomb was to fall quickly enough to allow of accurate aiming, it was likely to bury itself. If it was to fall slowly enough to avoid burial, it was impossible to aim it with accuracy.[3] In these circumstances, it is, perhaps, not surprising that Lord Cherwell agreed early in 1942 to the dropping of the projects both for the pyrotechnic and radio marker bombs.[4] Nevertheless, when eventually the special target-finding force was brought into being, the lack of a marker bomb and so of a reliable means of directing the main force was found to be a serious handicap. This, however, was a lesson of the future, for old fears joined with new prejudices to delay the establishment of the Pathfinder Force until August 1942.

---

[1] Min. Cherwell to Churchill, 2nd Sept. 1941.
[2] Notes Baker (Director of Bomber Operations) to Saundby, 5th Sept. 1941.
[3] do.
[4] Min. Sinclair to Churchill, 21st Jan. 1942. Min. Cox (Assistant P.S. to Portal) to Portal, 11th Feb. 1942.

The upshot was that none of the devices mentioned by Lord Cherwell came into general service during 1941. Many of them did not appear until 1943. Meanwhile, Bomber Command, though it had now received a charter of operational and technical development which eventually produced amazing results, was left to the cheerless task of continuing the offensive with its existing and wholly inadequate means. There were, after all, strict limits to what could be expected from astro-navigation under operational conditions and to pursue this line further was only to flog a dead horse.[1]

Nevertheless, Sir Richard Peirse now addressed his Group Commanders on the 'urgent need for improved navigation', and he exhorted them to take 'a very close personal interest in the investigation and remedy of navigational or other failures which result in crews failing to locate their targets.'[2] The first stage in solving a problem is to recognise it. This was the stage which had now been reached.

The immediate need, as had been pointed out in the Butt Report, was to obtain more evidence about the navigation error so that the conclusions already reached could be checked, expanded and kept up to date. The only reliable source from which this evidence could come lay in the night photograph taken by the bomber to record its position. It was by this means alone that individual navigation errors could be established and measured. An immediate increase in the number of cameras carried on night operations was needed.[3] Previous neglect coupled with a continuing tendency not to face the facts, however, raised formidable obstacles in the way of enlightenment.

At Bomber Command, and elsewhere, some difficulty was experienced in deciding whether the object of the night photograph was to provide evidence about the damage done to the target or merely to record the position of the aircraft. The former requirement necessitated a complicated camera which had not yet been satisfactorily developed. The latter requirement could be met by the 'simplified' camera which was now becoming available in substantial quantities. This confusion led to some delay in the fitting of cameras, and it was

---

[1] Improvements such as averaging gear for sextants and the Astrograph were not expected by the D.B. Ops. to produce fixes giving a circle of uncertainty of less than eight miles. Notes Baker to Saundby, 5th Sept. 1941. The Navigation Officer at Bomber Cmd. did not think that the hand-held sextant could produce results giving an error of less than five miles even if operated by a very experienced navigator in conditions of perfect straight and level flight. Bomber Cmd. Report, 19th Oct. 1941.

[2] Memo. Peirse to 1, 2, 3, 4, 5, 6 and 7 Groups, 13th Sept. 1941.

[3] On 25th April 1941 Bomber Command had 165 night cameras (eighty-eight automatic and seventy-seven simplified). Fifteen of these belonged to the two Operational Training Groups, 6 and 7. The official establishment for night cameras at the time was 693 (550 automatic and 143 simplified). Min. Heath (Air Photos Bomber Cmd.) to D.S.A.S.O., 25th April 1941.

not until 31st August 1941 that Bomber Command agreed to accept as many simplified cameras as could be provided.[1]

Even this, however, did not mark the end of the confusion. On 16th September 1941, 5 Group Headquarters officially expressed the opinion that 'the main object of night photography is to provide a means of raid and damage assessment. To abandon this main object which has been impressed on all concerned, will revive the prejudice amongst crews of regarding the camera as the official spy—a prejudice which we have been at such pains to kill'. For these reasons it was thought at 5 Group 'that it would be undesirable and impractticable to use photography as a means of obtaining navigational information'.[2] This attitude could no longer be tolerated and, on 19th September, the Group Commanders were told, 'for your information, the purpose of night photography in this Command can be defined as follows:

(i) To confirm the location of the bomber aircraft at the time of the attack.
(ii) To pin point the bomb bursts.
(iii) To provide general information.

It is not considered that night photography can provide a means of raid damage assessment'.[3]

The advantages which presently flowed from this clear directive were soon to become apparent to all concerned in the direction and the execution of the bombing offensive. In conjunction with the day reconnaissance photographs of targets which had been attacked, the night camera showed what happened to the bombs which were carried into the darkness over Germany. In the field of navigation it delineated the possible and the impossible, and it brought to an end the period in which the Commanders had been largely ignorant of what their crews were doing.[4]

It would, however, clearly have been inadequate merely to increase the volume and quality of the evidence by these and other means, if steps had not simultaneously been taken to provide for its constant digestion and interpretation. The appointment of Dr. Dickins as head of the now expanding Operational Research Section of Bomber Command was an event of scarcely less importance than the widespread introduction of night photography. Henceforth the scientific and empirical appraisal of operational problems was increasingly extended to matters which, in the past, had often been left

---

[1] Correspondence between Bomber Cmd. and Air Min., March–Aug. 1941. Letter Bomber Cmd. to Air Min., 31st Aug. 1941. Damage Assessment photographs were, of course, a task for the day Photographic Reconnaissance Unit.
[2] Memo. 5 Group to Bomber Cmd., 16th Sept. 1941.
[3] Dir. Bomber Cmd. to 1, 3, 4, 5 and 8 Groups, 19th Sept. 1941.
[4] Cf. Coningham's comment on 29th Dec. 1940. See above, pp. 227–228.

to chance, guess-work or the spasmodic investigations such as those carried out by Mr. Dewdney and Mr. Butt.

Thus, the Butt Report, though it did not start a revolution, consolidated one which had begun earlier. It did not result in the introduction of new ideas, but it did bring many plans to the point of action. Moreover, its effect was not confined to the field of technical development but, as has already been shown, also extended to that of strategy. Here again the Butt Report did no more than hasten the acceptance of a policy which had long been gaining ground and had, indeed, already been partially adopted. Nevertheless, the Butt Report marked the occasion on which Bomber Command virtually abandoned the aim of selective industrial attack and embraced that of general area bombing directed towards the reduction of German production and morale. The transition from precision to area attack which was thus entailed, necessitated a complete review of operational tactics.

The methods of bombing adopted for the destruction of the 'purely military objectives', which had been selected in the light of what the Air Staff had believed to be 'the right war-winning policy', were not necessarily the best methods of achieving the new aim. The destruction of residential and industrial centres and the spreading of the fear of death were tasks which called for a technique quite different from that needed for the destruction of a railway viaduct or even an oil plant. In the technique of area attack, it appeared to the Air Staff, the *Luftwaffe* was somewhat more expert than Bomber Command.

A comparative study of photographs of English and German towns which in each instance had, it was thought, been attacked by forces of approximately equal strength revealed 'considerably more widespread devastation in the English than in the German towns'. The British high-explosive bombs were thought to be at least as effective as the German, but the *Luftwaffe* had been carrying a higher proportion of incendiaries than Bomber Command. In the opinion of the Air Staff, the conclusion was irresistible 'that the greater damage achieved by the enemy is caused by incendiarism'.[1]

Moreover, not only did the Germans carry a larger number of incendiaries, but they also dropped them in a greater concentration than did the British. So far as could be ascertained, they seemed to open each attack with an exclusively incendiary force of from twelve to twenty-four aircraft. These started a conflagration into which the

---

[1] Air Staff Memo., 23rd Sept. 1941, sent to Bomber Cmd., 29th Sept. 1941. The proportion of incendiaries carried by German bombers was estimated to average thirty per cent and to rise on occasions to sixty per cent. That of Bomber Command averaged about fifteen per cent and rose occasionally to thirty per cent. The Vice-Chief of the Air Staff, Sir Wilfrid Freeman, did not entirely endorse the verdict. He thought the German fire-fighting services were better organised than the British. Min. Freeman to Bottomley, 27th Sept. 1941.

TACTICAL FOUNDATIONS OF AREA BOMBING

following aircraft aimed high-explosive bombs. The British practice, on the other hand, was to spread the incendiaries evenly through all phases of the attack.

Those who had to fight the fires in British towns, and notably 'responsible members of the London Fire Brigade', were of the 'unanimous' opinion that it was 'the great number of incendiaries dropped in a comparatively short space of time, say 20 minutes, that beats the fire-watcher, and, in turn, the fire-fighter'. It was, therefore, not unreasonable to conclude that the Bomber Command attacks were failing to saturate the German fire-fighting organisations either because not enough incendiary bombs were being dropped or because they were not being dropped within a short enough space of time.

In the light of these considerations, the Air Staff now suggested that each Bomber Command attack should include a minimum of between 25,000 and 30,000 incendiary bombs.[1] They suggested that this load should be carried irrespective of the effect it might have upon the number of high-explosive bombs which could also be lifted. They suggested that these incendiaries should be dropped in the opening phase of each attack within the shortest possible space of time. They also thought that German methods might be further and profitably imitated by the employment of a special fire-raising force to lead each Bomber Command attack. The role of the high-explosive bombs, in addition to spreading the fear of death, was to force the fire-fighters off the streets and burst the water mains. This would give the incendiaries a better chance of doing their work.[2]

Thus, instead of trying to blow up each building with high explosive, which was obviously an impossibly large task, the aim was to start a conflagration in the centre of each town, which, it might be hoped, would consume the whole. The success of these tactics clearly depended upon the concentration of each attack in time and space. Thus, area bombing was seen to demand not only a certain accuracy of aim but also a considerable precision in timing. It would not be enough if the aircraft arrived at the right place; they would also have to arrive at the right time.

The means of achieving this concentration did not yet exist; nor did the means of ensuring that the initial fires were started in the right place. It is not, therefore, surprising that Sir Richard Peirse was somewhat sceptical of the new plan. He had not forgotten the lesson of the Mannheim attack. He did not, however, appear to have any alternative tactical plan in mind and confined himself to claiming

---

[1] It was estimated that in their successful attacks the *Luftwaffe* had dropped approximately 20,000 incendiaries per night. It was thought that Bomber Command should improve on this. The German incendiary bomb weighed 2 lb., the British 4 lb., but it was the number and not the weight which was held to be the criterion.

[2] Air Staff Memo., 23rd Sept. 1941.

that the damage in Münster, Aachen and Kiel compared favourably with that in Coventry, Bristol and Southampton.[1]

A second and equally important consideration in the area bombing plan was the very large force, estimated by the Air Staff, it will be recollected, at not less than 4,000 bombers,[2] which would be required to carry it out. This introduced once more the perennial question of conserving Bomber Command as an investment for the future. It was now increasingly evident that Bomber Command, with its existing equipment, was unlikely to achieve decisive results. On the other hand, the imminence of new equipment offered much improved prospects in the spring of 1942. By then the force would not only be guided to its targets by the new radar aid to navigation, but the Lancaster would also be ready to begin its operational career.[3] The argument against frittering away the Bomber Command crews before these weapons could be put into their hands was overwhelming.

As the German anti-aircraft defences improved and the first improvised night fighters took the air, Bomber Command's casualties began to increase. The loss of 107 bombers in the first eighteen nights of August, for example, had been noted with concern by the War Cabinet.[4] It was, however, as has been shown above, the disastrous attacks carried out on the night of 7th November 1941 which brought the issue to a head and resulted in the conservation directive of 13th November.[5] Thus it was that, while it regathered its strength for the spring, Bomber Command ended the year, as it had begun it, with frequent night attacks on the German battle cruisers at Brest.

This, however, was not the only consequences of the ill-fated operations against Berlin, Mannheim, the Ruhr and elsewhere which, on the night of 7th November, had resulted in the loss of thirty-seven bombers from a force of 400. The conservation directive had not originally been intended, as Sir Charles Portal hastened to assure Sir Richard Peirse, to reflect upon the Commander-in-Chief's handling of the force.[6] Indeed, the first impression was, as reported by Sir Richard Peirse himself, that Bomber Command had been the victim of treacherous weather which the meteorologists had failed to forecast.[7]

---

[1] Letter Peirse to Air Min., 16th Oct. 1941.
[2] Min. Portal to Churchill, 25th Sept. 1941.
[3] Air Vice-Marshal Bottomley, when commanding 5 Group, had flown in a Lancaster as early as 1st February 1941 and had reported to Air Marshal Peirse that he was 'tremendously impressed with its performance'. Its four Merlin engines were 'beautifully smooth and I am sure', Air Vice-Marshal Bottomley said, 'that our crews will be most enthusiastic about the aircraft when it reaches them'. Letter Bottomley to Peirse, 1st Feb. 1941.
[4] War Cab. Mtg., 19th Aug. 1941.
[5] See above, pp. 185–187.
[6] Letter Portal to Peirse, 13th Nov. 1941.
[7] Report Peirse to Portal, 10th Nov. 1941. Min. Sinclair to Churchill, 14th Nov. 1941.

A second examination of the evidence, however, suggested to Sir Charles Portal that this was an inadequate explanation. By 23rd November, indeed, he had decided that Sir Richard Peirse's report could not be submitted to the Prime Minister because 'essential information is lacking and because there are certain inconsistencies...' Information given to the Air Ministry showed, Sir Charles Portal now told Sir Richard Peirse, that 'the probability of thunderstorms, icing and hail was generally included in the forecasts for the night of the 7/8th and that the advice offered by the Senior Meteorological Officer at your Headquarters included statements during the morning, and also as late as 4 o'clock in the afternoon, that over the southern North Sea there would be much convection cloud with tops rising to 15,000 to 20,000 feet and icing in cloud'. To Sir Charles Portal, it, therefore, seemed that 'the disproportionate losses during these operations were the result of failure to appreciate fully the extent to which icing conditions might affect endurance rather than to a faulty forecast in the weather'.

Nor was this all. 'I understand', Sir Charles Portal continued, 'that at least one Group Commander regarded the forecasted conditions as unsuitable for long-range operations and asked permission to attack the alternative objective of Cologne. Further, I have been told that one Station Commander allowed only his most experienced pilots to proceed on these operations in view of these same conditions, with the result that he sustained no losses though the amount of petrol left in the tanks proved that even these experienced pilots found that they were "near the bone".'

Finally, Sir Charles Portal was also 'concerned about the narrow margin of safety in petrol-ranges which may have been allowed, having regard to the high winds which were expected on this flight. Even had the cloud conditions[1] been somewhat less severe, the forecast winds were high enough to call into question the margin of safety over the long distance to Berlin and back'.[2]

Sir Richard Peirse sent in a revised report on 2nd December 1941 in which he again stated that he had been inadequately warned by the meteorologists. He also suggested that an important factor in the losses was the general level of inexperience which prevailed among his crews. His report contained the suggestion that the losses, 'though unusual, were no more than 50 per cent in excess of the average'.[3] In the opinion of Sir Wilfrid Freeman, the Vice-Chief of the Air Staff, Sir Richard Peirse was avoiding 'detailed analysis' of the losses, and he thought the new report was 'hardly less objectionable than its

---

[1] Which by causing icing and, perhaps, also navigation errors might be expected to increase petrol consumption.
[2] Letter Portal to Peirse, 23rd Nov. 1941.
[3] Peirse's second report, 2nd Dec. 1941.

predecessor . . .' To suggest that the losses were due to the inexperience of the crews seemed to the Vice-Chief of the Air Staff to be a 'damning admission'. If the crews were inadequately trained, it was, Sir Wilfrid Freeman thought, the duty of the Commanders to train them.[1]

In this last assertion, Sir Wilfrid Freeman had done less than justice to Sir Richard Peirse who had for long been the unwilling recipient of crews whose training was inadequate at all stages from elementary to advanced flying.[2] Moreover, for the Commander-in-Chief to continue the strategic air offensive without from time to time incurring the risk of heavy casualties was, of course, an impossibility. Equally, as Sir Richard Peirse had himself observed, it was 'darned hard to fight a force like Bomber Command at a subdued tempo.'[3] Nevertheless, it seemed to the Air Staff that very grave miscalculations had been made. Indeed, Sir Wilfrid Freeman thought, and Sir Charles Portal agreed, that it would be unwise to pursue the enquiry further for fear of a lack of confidence spreading to Sir Richard Peirse's subordinate commanders. For this reason they were unwilling to lay the various papers before the Prime Minister.[4] Sir Archibald Sinclair, nevertheless, judged that this should be done,[5] and on 4th January 1942, when both were engaged in the Washington War Conference, Sir Charles Portal submitted all the relevant reports to the Prime Minister.[6]

When these melancholy events took place Sir Richard Peirse had been Commander-in-Chief, Bomber Command, for just over a year. This had been a time of progressive disillusionment as the limitations which beset the night bomber were gradually and ruthlessly revealed. Many of the tactical judgments had been shown by events to have been remote from reality. The Commander-in-Chief's handling of the force had been called into question. Bomber Command had achieved no signal triumphs, but in its lone struggle against the enemy it had been paying a heavy price in the lives of its aircrews. In the view of some observers, the morale of the force and the confidence of its commanders in the success of their attacks was beginning to decline. There were indications that crews were becoming less eager to return for second operational tours.[7] As Air Vice-Marshal Baldwin put it at the end of the year, there was no 'concrete evidence'

---

[1] Min. Freeman to Portal, 4th Dec. 1941.
[2] Letter Peirse to Air Min., 2nd Dec. 1941.
[3] See above, p. 186.
[4] Min. Freeman to Portal, 5th Dec. 1941. Min. Portal to Sinclair, 6th Dec. 1941.
[5] Min. Sinclair to Portal, 8th Dec. 1941.
[6] Min. Portal to Churchill, 4th Jan. 1942.
[7] For example, letter Smyth-Pigott (Station Commander) to MacNeece Foster (A.O.C. 6 Group), 23rd June 1941.

TACTICAL FOUNDATIONS OF AREA BOMBING

as to the psychological effect of the bombing offensive and the 'material results obtained have been definitely disappointing'. It seemed to him that 'at the present moment the defences have the upper hand in so far as accuracy in bombing is concerned, either by day or night'.[1]

It is true that the Commander-in-Chief was not directly responsible for these misfortunes and disappointments. It was not he who ordered the reductions in standards of training for which the squadrons were now paying. It was not he who diverted large numbers of crews and aircraft from Bomber Command to the Middle East.[2] Nor had he by any means been alone in his misjudgment of operational possibility. Nevertheless, in the injustice of war, it is seldom permitted to a commander who has once become associated with failure to reap the benefits of the remedial actions which follow its acknowledgment. So it was to be in this case, and before radar navigation was introduced operationally and before the Lancaster bomber flew its first sortie, a change in the command had been made. Sir Richard Peirse was appointed Commander-in-Chief of allied air forces in the A.B.D.A. area and subsequently became Commander-in-Chief of the air forces in India and South-East Asia. A new commander stood ready to lead Bomber Command into a new era. This was Air Marshal Harris.

---

[1] Memo. by Baldwin, 7th Dec. 1941.

[2] 3 Group had sent Nos. 37, 38 and 40 Squadrons to the Middle East. Also half of 115 Squadron and the aircrews of 15 and 57 Squadrons were sent. A steady drain of reinforcing crews from O.T.U. followed. Air Vice-Marshal Baldwin referred to this as a 'running sore'. Letter Baldwin to Peirse, 11th Nov. 1941.

CHAPTER V

THE OPENING OF THE OFFENSIVE: APPRECIATIONS AND RESULTS
September 1939–November 1941

1. The machinery for target selection and appraisal of results
2. The nature of the German war economy and the British estimate of it
3. The nature of the target systems
4. The estimated and actual results, 1940-1941

'... their judgement was based more on wishful thinking than on a sound calculation of probabilities; for the usual thing among men is that when they want something they will, without any reflection, leave that to hope, while they will employ the full force of reason in rejecting what they find unpalatable.'

THUCYDIDES: *The Peloponnesian War*

'... in the course of action circumstances press for immediate decision, and allow no time to look about for fresh data, often not enough for mature consideration.'

CLAUSEWITZ, *On War*

1. The machinery for target selection and appraisal of results

AS has been seen, the British Government had with great foresight set up in 1929 an Industrial Intelligence Committee to collect information about foreign states, and it was this department which began to study the problem of Germany.[1] Its nucleus had been provided by a private organisation round which had been slowly brought together a number of experts in German industry and commerce or at least experts on various forms of industry and commerce who could apply their knowledge to the special problem of Germany. When war broke out this staff became the Intelligence Department of the Ministry of Economic Warfare as had been always designed.[2] It was naturally at first largely preoccupied with the most immediate task, the economic blockade of Germany carried out by the navy and by economic and political action in neutral states. The Economic Intelligence Department had been set up to supply the necessary information for that purpose, but it had also from the beginning been designed to provide information on other means of exerting economic pressure on Germany and in particular for the bombing offensive. It had already, as has been seen, provided much of the information on which the W.A. plans had been based. Indeed, this had always been regarded as one of the primary tasks of the Economic Intelligence Section by those who had planned it at a period when it was thought that British participation in a future continental war might be limited to naval and air action.

Moreover, it had been decided by the Committee of Imperial Defence that attack from the air would be most effective if it were co-ordinated with other forms of economic warfare, such as the blockade, and this view was held to give the M.E.W. a special position of authority. 'It must however be emphasized', ran the instruction, 'that air action against economic objectives, if employed at all, can be most effectively employed only if carefully related to

---

[1] See above, pp. 92–93.

[2] Complete histories of the work of the Ministry of Economic Warfare, the Ministry of Home Security and the Foreign Office have not been included in the series of the Cabinet Office. Professor Medlicott has described with meticulous care the system of economic pressure in *The Economic Blockade*, two volumes (1952 and 1959), but the problems discussed in this book are only briefly sketched. Many of the records of M.E.W. which bear most closely upon them have not been discovered and some appear to have been destroyed. Use has been made of some that have survived in other departments and of those of the department of the Ministry of Home Security which was also closely concerned with the assessment of damage in Germany as well as in this country. But it is recognised that further investigation of the records of the civil departments may add some significant detail to the information now available.

the development and effects of other forms of economic warfare . . . The Ministry of Economic Warfare will, therefore, keep a close watch on the enemy's supply position, and, acting on its information as to the distribution of enemy industry, centres of storage and sources of supply, and as to the key points of his transport system, will be responsible for advising the Air Ministry as to the selection of suitable economic targets.'[1]

But the exact relation of the new Ministry to the Air Ministry and other service departments could only be determined by experience. Service departments desire to have their intelligence as far as possible under their own control. They have large staffs for assessing that concerning the armed forces of the enemy. Round this, as has been noted, they tend also to develop machinery to determine his economic situation and the morale of the civil population, since the armed forces themselves are so powerfully affected by those factors. There was, indeed, in the First World War, considerable rivalry as well as co-operation between the intelligence departments of the different services and between those of the services and civilian departments.

It was partly to avoid a repetition of this experience that the Joint Intelligence Committee of the Committee of Imperial Defence was set up. Since there had long been a Joint Planning Committee of the Directors of Plans of the three services to work out the details of plans approved by the Chiefs of Staff Committee, this was an obvious development. In the J.I.C. the Directors of Intelligence of the three services combined together with a joint staff so that agreed appreciations could be supplied to the Chiefs of Staff and the Committee of Imperial Defence. They were to be reinforced where necessary by representatives of civilian departments but the committee remained a military one. The Directors of Intelligence also naturally relied mainly on their own staffs and, when a matter was urgent, often dealt directly, instead of as a committee, with the Joint Planners. There was dissatisfaction in Whitehall with this position and in July 1939 a Foreign Office representative was made a permanent member of the J.I.C. and presided over its meetings. Other departments, however, including the Industrial Intelligence Centre, were only consulted when the J.I.C. so decided.

Shortly after war broke out the Economic Intelligence Branch of M.E.W. of which Major D. Morton was the head, was divided into two departments. One, the Blockade Intelligence Department, was closely integrated with the operative departments carrying out the economic blockade of Germany, while the other, the more general Economic Warfare Intelligence Department, was placed under the

---

[1] Committee of Imperial Defence, *Handbook of Economic Warfare*. The handbook was prepared by the Advisory Committee on Trade Questions in Time of War and approved by the Committee of Imperial Defence on 27th July 1939.

direction of Professor Hall. After the fall of France the occupied territories were added to the field of study of this latter department which was entitled the Enemy and Occupied Territories Department and shortly after its reorganisation by Mr. C. G. Vickers, who succeeded Professor Hall in April 1941, it was given the name of Enemy Resources Department.

For some time this department failed to establish close co-operation with the Air Staff and to win their complete confidence. The Air Staff had other means of assessment of several target systems, notably oil, communications and the aircraft industry, the main ones of this period. Gradually action was taken, particularly by the War Cabinet Secretariat, to create closer contact between M.E.W. and the services. At an early date a liaison department for this purpose had been set up at M.E.W. and when some of its members returned to their own intelligence departments personal links were formed between them and their opposite numbers in M.E.W. By the end of 1940 it was admitted by all concerned that M.E.W. was at least an important factor in assessing the economic value of most of the target systems.

Meanwhile, also largely due to the influence of the War Cabinet Secretariat, the Economic Warfare Intelligence Department was brought into closer contact with the J.I.C. and in May 1940 M.E.W. was given a permanent representative on the Committee. As the staff of the J.I.C. was increased, staff of M.E.W. was incorporated in it. Professor Hall and his staff were also increasingly being consulted by the Joint Planners. All this machinery was, of course, being used more for appreciations of the general economic position of the enemy than specially directed towards strategic bombing which had hardly begun. It showed, however, that closer integration with the services was necessary and a plan had been put forward to second service officers to M.E.W. so that mutual confidence could be increased. This plan failed to earn final approval and it was left to Professor Hall's successor, Mr. Geoffrey Vickers, to find the solution.

So far as the J.I.C. was concerned the M.E.W. Intelligence Department with its permanent representative on the committee had, by the end of 1940, obtained the status that it required to exercise its due influence. It had also been constantly consulted as to the objectives of the strategic bombing offensive. 'Your Ministry', wrote Sir Archibald Sinclair to an official of M.E.W., 'are our principal advisers on the air offensive against Germany'.[1] Co-operation was made easier when a section of service intelligence officers, though still part of their own intelligence organisations, was established at Lansdowne House, one of the buildings occupied by M.E.W. The

---

[1] Letter Sinclair to Tennant, 29th July 1940.

M.E.W. Intelligence Department was also represented on the Bomb Targets Information Committee set up by the Director of Bomber Operations at the Air Ministry. It took time, however, and a good deal of discussion before their position was established. 'There is also, as you know,' Mr. Hugh Dalton, the Minister of Economic Warfare, told Sir Archibald Sinclair, 'a very close liaison between our two Ministries for studying the best economic targets for air attack and estimating the effects of raids. My officers have recently discussed with the Director of Bomber Operations ways and means of improving cooperation and preventing overlapping'.[1] This discussion appears to have met with success. It was established at any rate by the end of this period that M.E.W. should always be consulted on the economic aspects of bombing policy before a decision was taken. 'M.E.W. expresses its views on the importance of economic targets', Lord Selborne was told when he became head of the Ministry in 1942, 'and on the bombing policy which ought to be pursued both at the Bomb Targets Information Committee ... and in continuous and informal contact with the Air Staff. The liaison between M.E.W. and the Air Staff has not always been free from difficulty but is now satisfactory in this respect, both in theory and in practice, and is continually growing better. It may be taken that if any matter of policy is referred by A.C.A.S.(I) or D.B. Ops to their respective staffs, it will invariably be discussed and agreed with M.E.W. before recommendations are sent back'.[2]

The degree of integration and mutual confidence was, however, never as complete as it might have become if more service officers had been seconded to M.E.W. The Air Ministry always received economic advice from other quarters, and in some cases direct from commercial firms. On some questions, for example on the aircraft industry, it claimed to be the final authority and possessed information which for security reasons it did not share with M.E.W.[3] The different estimates of German aircraft production attracted the attention of the Prime Minister, who appointed a High Court Judge to investigate the problem. The result was to show that the more general knowledge of M.E.W. was a valuable check on the more specialised knowledge of aircraft production possessed by others and the effect was to increase the collaboration between M.E.W. and Air Intelligence.[4]

---

[1] Letter Dalton to Sinclair, 24th June 1941.

[2] Memo. by Lawrence, 4th Feb. 1942, App. 14.

[3] In some cases commercial firms might give to the Air Ministry information which they did not wish to reveal to M.E.W. lest commercial secrets should be compromised.

[4] Some of this information is derived from a memorandum written by Professor Hall after the war. Eventually the Air Ministry took full responsibility for assessing aircraft production. The estimates were not very accurate, but there is no reason to suppose that better results would have been attained by different machinery.

On the other hand, the planning and operations departments of the Air Ministry often went direct to M.E.W. rather than through their own intelligence department. There was sometimes disagreement between different departments of the Air Ministry on policy and each sought from M.E.W. intelligence which would support its own point of view. But gradually the information provided by M.E.W. became indispensable to the Air Ministry in planning the directives to Bomber Command though it might be given a somewhat different emphasis and interpretation in their hands.

This process was made easier by the reorganisation of the Enemy Branch of M.E.W. in 1942 when an Objectives Department was formed under Mr. O. L. Lawrence for the purpose of giving advice on bombing targets and ultimately to advise all three services on economic objectives. The Enemy Resources Department had been split into three separate sections for collating and appreciating all economic intelligence concerning the enemy. A services liaison department had been formed which included the representatives in the J.I.C. and personnel of Mr. Lawrence's Objectives Department. The Objectives Department, segregated from the intelligence departments from which it drew its information, could thus work more easily with the service departments in what were often highly secret matters and devote itself to understanding their needs and winning their confidence. While, therefore, the situation was always somewhat anomalous, a considerable degree of co-operation and mutual confidence did grow up, greater than existed, for example, between civilian departments and the services in the First World War. At a later date this machinery had to be adapted to the requirements of the Combined Bomber Offensive, and to work with the intelligence and operations departments of the United States Army Air Forces, as is described in a later chapter.[1]

During this period, therefore, the appreciations of the economic position of the enemy, on which all strategic plans, including the bombing offensive, partly depended, were based in the main on the information supplied by the M.E.W. intelligence department. It was also constantly asked for detailed information on many of the different target systems suggested for attack from the air. But it was not represented at the higher levels where the decisions were made as to the priorities of the various target systems. 'The part which M.E.W. has had to play so far', wrote one of its principal officers in May 1941, 'has inevitably been limited for the most part to advising on the selection of targets within the terms of reference handed down from above. The targets selected are inevitably for the most part not

---

[1] See the memorandum of Sir Geoffrey Vickers printed in W. N. Medlicott: *The Economic Blockade*, Vol. II, p. 675.

those which we should put forward if the bomber effort was being employed on the strategic-offensive in support of the general economic warfare effort'.[1]

Moreover, on two target systems of great importance, M.E.W. had only a subsidiary role. On oil, which had been recognised before the war as one of the weakest points in the German economy, the Cabinet had in 1939 appointed a special committee under Lord Hankey to keep in touch with the departments engaged in preventing oil from reaching Germany. It held a number of meetings for this purpose, and the Industrial Intelligence Centre, and after war broke out its successor in M.E.W., supplied estimates of production, imports and stocks. There was, however, a conflict of opinion on the subject and shortly after war had broken out a special intelligence committee was set up at the request of the Chief of the Air Staff to advise the Hankey Committee and prepare the estimates submitted to the Chiefs of Staff and the Defence Committee. It was headed by Mr. Geoffrey Lloyd, the Secretary for Petroleum, and representatives of the services and other departments served on it, including the head of the Economic Warfare Intelligence Branch of M.E.W. Throughout the war M.E.W. supplied the estimates of civilian consumption in Germany and much on production, stocks and other relevant factors, but the Lloyd Committee also drew its information from a variety of sources and was in close touch with the technical staffs of the great oil companies.

Some dissatisfaction was expressed by Professor Hall with this procedure and in June 1940 he threatened to withdraw from the committee. It was, he wrote, dangerous to discuss such delicate questions with representatives of the great oil companies, some of them with large foreign connections and possibly anxious about their own interests in the event of a German victory. The Director of Plans sent a soothing reply, but he pointed out that, while M.E.W. at the beginning of the war had been sceptical about oil as a target, many others, and especially the Hankey Committee, had urged it on the Air Ministry. The Lloyd Committee had been set up to resolve these differences of opinion. 'We always regard the M.E.W.', he continued, 'as being our responsible advisers on the selection of suitable targets and hope you are keeping the Lloyd Committee on the rails'. Meanwhile, meetings had been arranged between the staffs of the Air Ministry and M.E.W., which, he was sure, would in future 'do more than anything else to ensure that our plans for our action against [the] German war economy are well founded, and the Lloyd Committee reports will do no more than supplement these direct contacts which are worth any amount of long winded reports.'

---

[1] Memo. by Lawrence, 9th May 1941.

It was, however, the reports of the Lloyd Committee which were used by Lord Hankey and the J.I.C. and thus had the greatest influence on the decisions of the Chiefs of Staff and the Defence Committee.[1]

This system remained until March 1942 when acute differences arose as to the attack on oil between Lord Hankey and the Chiefs of Staff and Defence Committees. After a report from Colonel Stanley, the J.I.C. was given the task of making monthly reports on this subject, advised by a new committee under Sir Harold Hartley which took over the work of the Lloyd Committee. Mr. Attlee, as Deputy Chairman of the Defence Committee, was the Cabinet Minister specially in charge, Lord Hankey ceasing to belong to the Government at this time, and it was his duty to draw the attention of the Defence Committeee to any new aspect which needed their consideration. There was throughout a sub-committee of leading experts in the oil industry under Lieut.-Colonel S. I. M. Auld which took account of the analysis of the oil in crashed enemy aircraft and other captured enemy weapons and assessed the output of the enemy plants.[2]

A second target system, which was eventually to be of equal importance, was that of enemy communications. These had been under survey before the war both for tactical and strategic reasons. On this subject the main authority was the Railway Research Service which had been set up by the main railway companies in the inter-war period. It had advised the Air Ministry directly and had also supplied experts to M.E.W. who, however, remained under its own technical direction. The Inland Transport section of M.E.W. also largely drew its information from this source, supplemented later by photographic intelligence. This department was the main adviser on the earlier attacks on communications, but the development of the immensely important strategic attacks in 1944 arose later from the tactical approach and was only partially foreseen in this period.

The material on the target systems was organised with meticulous care. Files were prepared and kept up to date as new information was acquired. When photographic reconnaissance became the principal source of information aerial photographs could be used to complete the detailed maps of the different targets. The information sent to the Bomber Command stations became so great and so rapidly obsolete

---

[1] Letters Hall to Slessor and Slessor to Hall, 26th and 29th June 1940.

[2] *Oil as a Factor in the German War Effort, 1933–1945*, 8th March 1946, a report by the technical sub-committee of the C.O.S. on Axis oil. Memo. by Stanley, 16th April 1942. Sir Harold Hartley had been a member of the Lloyd Committee and advised it on the analysis of enemy oil. To Mr. Lloyd was left the task of endeavouring to deny oil to the Germans in the occupied countries, especially Rumania, while the Minister of Economic Warfare was to be responsible for giving advice on questions of policy affecting the denial of oil to the enemy, whatever that might mean. For the later developments in the machinery for assessing the enemy oil position, see below, Vol. III.

that its very bulk was a complication and it was realised that some simplification was necessary. Eventually the target books, known as *The Bomber's Baedeker*, were produced in which much of the information was put in a more convenient form.[1]

Just as important as the selection of the targets was the assessment of what injury had been done to them by the attack. And there was also the problem of how far present and potential production of German industry would be affected by the damage done. In this matter also M.E.W. naturally expected to have a major, if not a determining, influence.

Consequently, from an early date in 1940, it began to issue a fortnightly series of surveys of the damage done and the effects such damage might be likely to produce.[2] At this period the camera had hardly begun to be used and the information was derived from such news as leaked out in Germany, from reports of British representatives in neutral countries or from neutral representatives and business men in Germany and the usual secret sources of intelligence. These reports were highly unreliable and, together with those of the crews of the aircraft, were one of the reasons why it took so long to realise the failure of Bomber Command to inflict any appreciable damage on Germany. The Air Ministry Intelligence reports, using the same material, were even more optimistic and these estimates when translated into communiqués to the public were often entirely misleading.

At the beginning of the war, as has been seen, nothing had been found out by practical demonstration of the effect of bombs upon industrial buildings. But much new information of the effect of high-explosive bombs and incendiaries was obtained from the results of the German attack on Britain in the autumn and winter of 1940–41. The assessment of this damage was a function of the Ministry of Home Security and the special section set up for this purpose, the Research and Experiments Department, could be used to advise on the probable effects of bombing Germany. It could give expert advice, for example, on the right proportion of incendiaries and high-explosive bombs, the effect of different kinds of bombs on various kinds of buildings, and the manner in which an attack was most likely to render the task of the German Air Raid Precaution services more difficult and dangerous. Statistical analysis could be applied to the results in Britain, since the sample was a fairly large one, and its findings then used in the assessment of the damage to houses and factories in Germany. Sir John Anderson had foreseen the use of the Research and Experiments Department for this purpose when the

---

[1] In November 1941 it was calculated that 2,400 targets were in the German target books at the stations and that some had dossiers and maps for 1,500 of them. Min. Scott (A.I.3 (c)) to Baker (D.B. Ops.), 10th Nov. 1941.

[2] These were at first called Industrial Targets Reports and later Industrial Damage Reports.

Ministry was first set up. Its Director, Mr. Reginald Stradling, took up the problem with great energy and enthusiasm, but its work had hardly become significant by the end of this period.

Meanwhile, far too tardily, there had been established the most effective and scientific method for obtaining accurate information on this vital question—photographic reconnaissance. Both the cameras and suitable aircraft had been lacking at the beginning of the war, one of the gravest omissions of the Air Ministry in the preparation for a bombing offensive. Eventually, after repeated efforts to impress the agencies of supply, both the cameras and the special Spitfires and Mosquitoes were provided.[1] But at first neither the central agency set up in the Air Ministry nor that of Bomber Command itself was capable of interpreting the photographs. These were generally taken at a great height and special machines and special techniques were necessary before their full significance could be appreciated. It was only by bringing into the Air Ministry organisation a civilian firm, the Aircraft Operating Company, which had in vain been pressing its services for some time, that an efficient department was organised. By means of the Wild Automatic Plotting Machine which it owned and used, it was able to measure with considerable accuracy the evidence supplied by the photographs.[2]

This section was eventually made part of the Central Interpretation Unit and, in spite of protests, some of the skilled officers of Bomber Command were transferred to it as well as others who had acquired special experience of photographic reconnaissance during the campaign in France. The headquarters of the unit were finally established at Medmenham in 1941. There then was a highly skilled and effective machine which increased in efficiency and importance as the war went on.

Its surveys were not only indispensable in planning the attacks on the targets and in revealing the effects of the bombing, but it also gave invaluable information on new developments in German factories which were used by those engaged in making surveys of the enemy's production. 'Aerial photographs', writes one of those engaged in this work, 'began at this time to play an important part in these surveys as it was often the only means of detecting the increases of plant capacity'.[3] It could also ascertain when a plant was returning to production after bombing and thus played an all-

---

[1] The delay was partly due to the necessity of using the available resources to survey the invasion bases and ports. The Blenheims used in the earlier period with such cameras as existed were quite unsuitable for such work.

[2] A.H.B. Narrative: *Photographic Reconnaissance*, Vol. I. The Air Ministry, though ready to engage some of its personnel, had refused to take over the company as a unit. It was eventually made to do so by a letter from the First Lord of the Admiralty, then Mr. Winston Churchill, to the Secretary of State for Air informing him that the Admiralty would take over the unit if the Air Ministry did not do so.

[3] Memorandum of W. A. Burton, in charge of Enemy Resources Department in M.E.W.

important role in the precision bombing of later years, especially that on oil.

But in spite of the ingenuity and skill of those who interpreted them, the photographs were an imperfect source of information on the results of a bombardment. They revealed more accurately the damage to the buildings themselves than to their contents. They gave a fairly accurate picture of the effect of bombing on housing, but they were less useful in estimating the effects on industrial production, for in many, indeed in a majority of cases, the machinery might receive little or no injury when the roof of a factory was destroyed by fire produced by incendiaries or shattered by the explosion of a high-explosive bomb of moderate weight. The known effects in British towns were, of course, a valuable check on these estimates. But this calculation also depended on a number of assumptions which were by no means certain, such as the relative efficiency of German and British bombs. And this more cautious approach was not always taken by those who used these photographs to make an impression on important members of the higher direction of the war.

For it must be always kept in mind that the bombing directives were necessarily determined at the highest level, in this period by the British Chiefs of Staff and the Defence Committee of the Cabinet, who received the technical information on the economic possibilities and effects of strategic bombing in a highly concentrated form, mainly through the appreciations of the J.I.C. or Joint Planners. They had not only to take into consideration the general strategy of the war, operational possibilities and supply, but were also liable to receive advice on economic factors from sources other than those agencies specially equipped to give it. The method of warfare was so new that many people with no knowledge of aerial warfare and little claim to knowledge of Germany thought that they knew the most valuable point to attack. Some of these, because of their position in politics or industry, could not be ignored.[1] Few people except journalists ventured to advise the Army and the Navy on how to conduct the war. But a surprising number thought themselves competent to direct Bomber Command to its objectives. In some cases, of course, experts on a particular subject could draw attention to some aspect of the problem which might otherwise have been overlooked. But during this period the most important of these were either drawn into the intelligence departments or consulted by these latter in the ordinary course of business. The experts of the

---

[1] As an example, it might be noted that a prominent and highly respected member of the House of Commons asked the Secretary of State for Air to consider a memorandum on the bombing of Germany prepared by his greengrocer who had served in the Middle East in the First World War. A polite and reasoned memorandum had to be sent in reply.

intelligence departments had, of course, the opportunity of using the normal machinery on all occasions. Nevertheless the experts of M.E.W. were not satisfied that their views were given sufficient weight at the highest level. 'The danger', Lord Selborne was told, with the implication that he ought to do something about it, 'is not so much that proper co-operation will not be achieved between M.E.W., the Air Staff and Bomber Command in drawing up an effective and practicable plan for attacking economic objectives, as that a practicable plan when achieved at this level, will be rendered impracticable and ineffective by subsequent amendments at a higher Service or political level'.[1]

It must also be remembered that the Prime Minister had his own investigating agency under Lord Cherwell to supply him with criticism and analysis of the reports sent to him from the service and other departments.[2] The two previous chapters have shown the powerful influence that could thus be exerted on the estimates of the strategic offensive.

The damage done to its physical targets by Bomber Command was susceptible to some sort of measurement even if it was difficult to obtain the facts on which such measurement could be based. But there was also the much vaguer objective of German morale on which it was even more difficult to make any judgment. This question was the subject of report by the Foreign Office and its agents abroad while the Ministry of Information also claimed knowledge about it. The Political Intelligence Department of the Foreign Office made periodical references to it in its appreciation of Germany. The Air Ministry Intelligence Department circulated similar intelligence. Many others had views upon it and the kind of action that would be likely to affect it.

It is surprising, however, how rarely any precise definition was given to the conception even in the most official memoranda. This lack of analysis was no doubt one cause of some of the misleading estimates which were made about it. Here again the experience of Britain during the German bombing provided an opportunity to estimate the effect of the destruction of housing and amenities on the capacity or determination of the working people. But in this period judgment on this question tended to be based on more speculative reasoning which had a strong appeal to certain minds.

---

[1] Memo. by Lawrence, 4th Feb. 1942, see App. 14, para. 15.

[2] A short description of the functions and methods of the Prime Minister's agency is given by Sir Donald Macdougal, who was a member of it, under the title *The Prime Minister's Statistical Section* in *Lessons of the British War Economy* (1951), edited by D. N. Chester, pp. 58–68. Later the Operational Research Section of Bomber Command played an important part in providing analyses on which future action could be based, including the selection of the targets. That which worked for the Admiralty under Professor Blackett was also sometimes used to provide analysis of air operations. See *Operational Research: Recollections of Problems Studied, 1940–1945*, by Prof. P. M. S. Blackett, Brassey's Annual, 1953.

2. The nature of the German war economy and the British estimate of it

There is still much to be found out about the German economy in the pre-war and war periods. 'The historian', wrote Sir Keith Hancock, 'would like to make clear how the British Government gained its knowledge of the enemy's economic power and to what extent that knowledge was correct; what action the Government took—by blockade, by bombing, by sabotage and other means—to destroy the enemy's resources; what disappointments it suffered; what success it achieved. Before such a study could be completed, many things would be necessary—among them a knowledge, both comprehensive and exact, of the war economic history of the enemy powers. To seek this knowledge would employ a team of many historians for many years.'[1] However, the reports made by the United States Strategic Bombing Survey, if necessarily somewhat hastily completed, are based on a large body of statistics drawn from many sources, supplemented by visits to industrial areas, even while the war was going on, and interrogations of many of the principal members of the German Government, high officers of the services, officials and industrialists. The British Bombing Survey Unit has relied largely on materials collected by the United States teams, though some independent investigations were made.[2]

The conclusions of the two bodies, though agreeing on the main features of the German war economy, differ in some respects on the effect of the bombing upon it. No doubt much will become clearer when further comparative studies of the war economies of the two sides have been produced. Nevertheless, whatever changes may be made in emphasis of particular aspects, it is improbable that further investigation will materially alter the general picture of the German war economy.

The evaluation was all the more difficult because once the National Socialists had seized power, the situation in Germany became anomalous and unprecedented. Politically they were supreme and possessed in the Gestapo and the *S.A.* and *S.S.* the means of repressing all opposition both in the trade unions and in the general public. The Government could either legally or by strong-arm methods coerce its subjects, whether industrialists or workers, to do what it wanted. It was thus possible in the pre-war years to devote a much larger share of the rising production to armaments than was the case

---

[1] *The Economic Blockade*, Vol. I, p. ix (editor's note).
[2] For a more detailed review of the surveys, see **Annex V**.

in Britain and to produce more quickly large numbers of aircraft and tanks. While in Britain a war economy was not contemplated until 1938, in Germany, though, in spite of Goering's famous phrase, austerity of life was not really enforced on the German people, their standard of living was kept below that of the British during the pre-war period.

On the other hand, there was less unselfish co-operation among the industrialists than in Britain; there were at the highest level of direction men entirely ignorant of or with distorted ideas of economics such as Goering, Funk and Hitler himself: there was great rivalry between the new men who had come suddenly into power and between the departments, old and new, which they had attached to themselves: and finally the influence of the National Socialist Party, expressed through its Gauleiters and their assistants, was often exerted in a direction contrary to the interests of the state. Thus, while there was an amazing success in creating so rapidly a new army and air force, it was less than could have been accomplished with more skilful direction from above and more wholehearted co-operation from below. German propaganda magnified its results, great as these were, and the rest of the world accepted too easily these exaggerations. The effect of this propaganda endured well into the war period.

From the first Hitler not only planned war, but a particular kind of war, the exploitation of weapon superiority so as either to intimidate any opposition to his demands or to defeat the enemy quickly, and then with the extra advantages, political, strategic and economic derived from the conquest, to go on to the next objective. The German economy was designed to accomplish this strategic purpose, which in every case postulated a short and decisive campaign—a *Blitzkrieg*.

Thus, after Hitler came to power, it was decided to rearm Germany by a great effort so that in a comparatively short time her armaments on land and in the air would be much superior to those of her immediate neighbours. For this reason, as General Thomas, then the head of the Armaments Production Centre of the *Wehrmacht*, later said with emphasis, Germany rearmed 'in width' and not 'in depth'. By this was meant that a supply of weapons was to be obtained as soon as possible. Factories for the construction of aircraft, tanks, guns and ammunition were to be erected immediately, workers assembled and trained and the great industrial complex of coal, steel and chemicals, in which Germany had the pre-eminence in Europe, utilised to produce the materials for the intense effort necessary. There was not to be a preliminary concentration on the production of the materials on which the supply of armaments and their use depended, steel, coal, aluminium, oil and the rest, so that in a more distant future an even greater quantity of armaments could be obtained. That would give Germany's neighbours time to rearm likewise, thus making a quick decision in the war less probable.

General Thomas's phrase has often been quoted with approval by those explaining the German economy and, indeed, is true enough; but it needs some qualification. Germany did obtain immediate results, but in such a manner as partly accounts for the remarkable expansion of German armaments in the second half of the war.

In the first place considerable attention was given to the problem of ensuring a better supply of raw materials. Except for coal and the basis of all explosives, nitrogen, obtained largely by means of a synthetic process, Germany was dependent for these on outside sources, many of them outside Europe. The most important deficiency was oil, but iron ore, bauxite, chrome and nearly all minerals necessary to produce special steels came almost exclusively from abroad as well as natural rubber and cotton. The Four Year Plan was set up under Goering mainly to deal with this problem, though in the course of time many other things were placed under it. A great effort was made to expand the supply of oil, both crude oil and that produced by synthetic plants from coal, in spite of the fact that it was much more costly than the imported oil on which in peace time Germany depended and which came mainly from across the seas. Storage capacity was much increased and endeavours were made to fill it in the face of inadequate foreign exchange and Anglo-American efforts to prevent success. At the same time and, indeed, as part of the same process, the manufacture of synthetic rubber was increased.

Many other things were done. Primary aluminium capacity, of such great importance to the *Luftwaffe*, was nearly five times as large in 1939 as in 1933. New factories were also set up for synthetic fibres. Special attention was paid to agriculture, and, except in fats and oils, Germany had become nearly self-supporting as regards food by 1939. Care was taken to increase the stock of cattle and sheep. Large stocks of important minerals were laid in, insufficient, indeed, but more than could have been obtained by private enterprise.[1] General Thomas and others in the *Wehrmacht* have asserted that they expected that this process would go on until at least 1942 before war was risked, and there is other evidence that some such date was in the minds of many of those preparing for the future.

But Hitler had no such intention, nor was the Four Year Plan carried out in any very systematic way. There never seems to have

---

[1] It has been estimated, for example, that the reserve of bauxite, the raw material from which alumina and then aluminium is made, was one and a half million tons, enough for about two years at the rate of use at the time. *United States Strategic Bombing Survey (U.S.S.B.S.), Light Metal Industry* (No. 20), p. 10.

been a real overall plan made in order to calculate the necessary supplies and to apportion the effort in the most efficient manner possible over its several parts. To increase the synthetic oil industry, for example, on the scale originally suggested would have taken four and a half million tons of steel, for which there were many competitors. The rather grandiose plans laid down in 1936 and in 1938 at Karinhall (Goering's residence) had to be greatly curtailed. Nevertheless, much was done and more was planned to be done which bore fruit during the war itself.

One of the reasons given for the failure to do more was that steel was in demand for the construction of the West wall, the bridges of the autobahns and the navy, as well as for new steel works and armaments. The expansion of the synthetic plants for oil and rubber also meant that larger supplies of coal were needed. But little was done in Germany to increase the coal supply which it was assumed was sufficient since fifteen per cent was exported. The conquests of 1938–41 brought further coal under German control. The Czechoslovak and Polish-Silesian coalfields enabled new industrial plants to be set up, including those for the synthetic production of oil and rubber, in regions remote from the air power of the west.

There was also considerable expansion in the production of steel by 1941. When the industrialists refused to use the low-grade German iron to make steel because the cost was too great, the Hermann Goering Works were set up for that purpose. But the ore found in Austria and Czechoslovakia was more suitable and the main activity was transferred to the South. In one way or another by new construction and by controlling captured coal and steel works the Hermann Goering project did add a good deal to the total.[1] The conquests in the West added a great deal more. The production of Germany in 1939, including Austria, the Sudetenland and, in the final months, Upper Silesia, was about twenty-three million tons of crude steel. The full exploitation of Upper Silesia and that of the territory occupied in 1940–41 raised production to thirty-one million tons of crude steel in 1941 and to thirty-four million tons in 1943, the peak year. When the war began, in fact, the productive capacity of Germany alone was not far short of the combined capacity of the United Kingdom and the U.S.S.R.[2]

---

[1] A detailed account of the creation and expansion of the Hermann Goering Works is given in Special Paper No. 3 of the Overall Economics Effects Division of the *U.S.S.B.S.* Its capital at its height was estimated at 4,000 millions of R.M. Its total steel production at the end of 1944 was nearly six million tons, of which about half was due to the special efforts of the combine. It also constructed the great synthetic oil plant at Brüx in Czechoslovakia.

[2] *U.S.S.B.S. Effects of Strategic Bombing on the German War Economy* (No. 3), pp. 99–106, *B.B.S.U. The Strategic Air War Against Germany, 1939–1945*, pp. 88–89. See App. 49 (xx) and (xxi). There is considerable difficulty in establishing the exact figures, for the earlier German records are not explicit on the distinction between crude and finished

Naturally not all the steel and still less of the coal could be used for the manufacture of German armaments; the needs of the occupied countries themselves had to be considered. They were, indeed, supplying Germany with valuable materials such as aluminium and with finished armaments and components. She relied, for example, a good deal on France for motor vehicles and railway engines. It can be seen that the German base was extended considerably by the conquests made.

These conquests also gave control of or access to new sources of raw materials. Poland, Hungary and Austria had small supplies of oil and the last was vigorously exploited during the war. Rumanian oil for export could also be monopolised by the Axis and large quantities were sent to Germany, though less, perhaps, than might have been anticipated. The very existence of this alternative supply affected allied strategy to a considerable extent.

Similarly, Germany obtained the excellent iron ore of Lorraine while both Sweden and Spain could be expected to increase their exports to Germany if necessary. Before Russia was attacked, she provided many other raw materials, including a good deal of oil, and allowed others to be transported via the Trans-Siberian railway from Japan.[1] Stocks of many other raw materials, including much oil, were obtained in the West in 1940. The overthrow of France also meant that North African fats and vegetable oils could be obtained. In total, all this meant that Germany's raw material position showed no signs of deterioration during these years and seemed fairly well safeguarded for the future. It was, indeed, not until late in 1944 that the production of armaments was seriously threatened by the lack of raw materials and by that time other factors were of much greater importance. There were, of course, temporary shortages of various kinds, but these could always be overcome by a reduction in civilian consumption or the use of substitutes.

During the whole of the period 1938–41 at any rate, Hitler's method of warfare seemed to be eminently successful. Austria and Czechoslovakia had been absorbed without the necessity of firing a shot. The Polish, Danish and Norwegian campaigns, as well as the attacks in the West and the Balkans, had completely fulfilled Hitler's expectations. He had failed to conquer Britain, but it was not thought by Hitler himself or by his immediate circle that she would be able

---

steel. Under ordinary conditions there is a loss of roughly thirty per cent in converting steel ingots into rolling-mill products. The British team made a special survey of the steel production and their estimates do not exactly correspond with those of the *U.S.S.B.S.*, but the variations are of no great importance in assessing the general situation.

[1] A full list of German imports from and through the U.S.S.R. in 1939–1941 is given in Appendix III of Professor Medlicott's *The Economic Blockade*, Vol. I, pp. 667–671. They correspond closely with the estimates made during the war by the M.E.W. They include 279,499 metric tons of petroleum products, 234,145 of gas oil, 134,820 of fuel oil and 16,729 of lubricating oil.

S.A.O.—I—T

to do much to hinder his plans on the continent of Europe. Right down to the end of this period the attack on Russia seemed to be following the same pattern, if taking rather more time and effort than had been expected at the outset. There seemed to be no necessity to make any great sacrifices for the future and, in fact, none was made.

Secondly, though Germany prepared 'in width' the width was a large one. The demands for weapons were made by soldiers with no particular desire to conserve money or materials. They built lavishly and the machine-tool industry could with comparative ease provide the necessary machinery. They took more account than was possible in Britain of the dispersal of the new factories, especially ammunition and propellant factories and those for the construction of aircraft, though, as was to be seen, not sufficient account. In some cases, such as oil, rubber and nitrogen, such a course was not possible to any great extent for they had generally to be made in the midst of or close to the great centres of the chemical industry. They were in fact concentrated in large plants to conserve steel and make the maximum use of the existing facilities.[1]

But at any rate lavish factory space was provided, far more than Britain was able to construct in the pre-war period. At the outset of the Hitler régime Germany had large numbers of unemployed who could be used in construction, and though some of them were wastefully employed in making the autobahns, which were a luxury to a country so ill supplied with petrol, and some had to be diverted to constructing the West wall, yet much surplus labour remained. If all these things be taken into account as well as the new synthetic plants and other preparations under the Four Year Plan including stockpiling, it has been calculated that by 1938 Germany was devoting nearly a quarter of her national production to war preparation, while Britain at that time was expending less than seven per cent for the same purpose. Even so the actual amount of finished armaments, though adequate to its immediate purpose, was still small compared to that of later periods of the war. But preparation had been made which would result in much larger quantities within a year or two. Thus, Hitler's boast on the eve of the war that he had spent ninety milliards of Reichsmarks on armaments was no idle one.[2]

---

[1] Hitler publicly rebuked Dr. Krauch, of the *I.G. Farbenindustrie*, who, in 1937, became Commissioner General for the Chemical Industry, for concentrating ammonia and methanol production in a few large plants. Dr. Diekmann said after the war that the Wehrmacht had no appreciation of raw material requirements. *U.S.S.B.S. Oil Division Final Report*, (No. 109), p. 12, and *Powder, Explosives, Special Rockets and Jet Propellants, War Gases and Smoke Acid* (No. 111), pp. 4 and 14.

[2] Wagenfuehr ridicules Hitler's claim and it has been assumed that it was mere propaganda. It is true that statistics show that the value of the finished armaments was very much less than that figure. But Professor A. J. Brown has calculated that very nearly ninety milliards were spent on all preparations for war, including pay of the armed forces. A. J. Brown: *Applied Economics*, (1947), pp. 20 and 24. Dr. Rolf Wagenfuehr: *Rise and Fall of German War Economy, 1939–1945*, p. 5 (unpublished).

Moreover, the German machine-tool industry in 1939 was far bigger than that of Britain and a quarter of its production was exported. The factories could be supplied, therefore, with far more ease than was the case in Britain. There was, thus, a large reserve which was of great importance in maintaining production after destruction of factories by bombing. The plenitude of factory space and ample supply of machine tools made Germany's power of recuperation greater than that of Britain where the shortage of machine tools had been one of the greatest difficulties to overcome.

The third element in production, labour, was also not for a long time a limiting factor in the supply of armaments. The men called up to the armed forces were replaced by foreign labour and prisoners of war. This was, no doubt, one of the main reasons why Germany did not mobilise her labour for war production to the same degree as Britain. But foreign labour did not fill all the gap. Nearly twelve million men were mobilised for the armed forces in the course of the war, of which one million was supplied by the natural increase of the population. Seven and a half million foreigners and prisoners of war were incorporated in the labour force. There was thus a reduction of three and a half million during the war years. Some of the foreign labour was also less efficient than German labour. Yet surprisingly little effort was made to transfer labour from civilian production to war production, while, in contrast to Britain, female labour was never fully mobilised. In 1942 there was a registration of women between the ages of 17 and 45, but a comparatively small number was called up. The number of domestic servants was practically unchanged during the war, while in Britain it was reduced by two-thirds.[1] In the closing stages of the war Goebbels, who had often noted in his diary the necessity of total war, tried to organise an all-out effort, but it was then far too late.

The explanation of this surprising fact seems to arise from a number of causes. The non-employment of women no doubt was partly due to Hitler's principle of keeping women in the home in order to increase the number and quality of the race. German women themselves seem to have been much more averse to employment than British women. There was a fall in the number of women employed in the first two years of the war, which is generally attributed to the generous separation allowances. No doubt also there was a limitation of the use of unskilled labour by a limitation of skilled men, but that difficulty could have been met, as it was in Britain, by dilution and intensive training. But it does not seem that Germany's war production was much reduced by an overall labour shortage until late in the war, though particular industries such as

---

[1] There was also some increase of foreign female labour in domestic service, e.g. Ukrainian.

aircraft production might complain that they were not getting a proper share.[1] The hours of work were increased during the war and in some cases excessive hours were worked, but it was found in Germany, as in Britain, that this policy did not pay and the all-round increase was not exceptional. It seems clear, however, that by a better disposal of the labour force more men could have been obtained for the armed forces. It may be that it was decided that armaments could not be found for them, but these also depended on readjusting the supply of labour to essential needs. Yet until the last year of the war the fall in production of civilian goods was not as steep as in Britain.

A further factor which enabled armaments to be increased even when bombing had become very destructive was the organisation of military procurement and German industry. After the war Speer described it as extremely inefficient and showed that its inefficiency was much increased by the impossibility of criticising it without personal risk.[2] The pre-war plans were largely in the hands of serving officers who drew only second-rate industrialists into the military machine. German industry also for all its expansion and energy was in many respects organised in a wasteful and inefficient manner when war broke out. The industrialists had always made their demands for raw materials such as steel and copper as high as possible, partly from a natural tendency of enterprise, and partly that they might have a surplus to use in the more profitable sale of their products to private purchasers both at home and abroad. Nor did they apply mass-production methods to the same degree as was done in the United States or even in Britain. There was no efficient system of priorities which were often issued without due regard to the quantity of material available and the necessities of industries with less influence at the centre.

Thus, there was a large potential production not utilised in these earlier years which could be made to produce great results when it was at last realised that the war would be a long and hard one. This is the main explanation of the great increases in munitions, particularly in aircraft and tanks, in the later stages of the war.

The extension of German control over three-quarters of the European continent, though it gave a broader base for the supply of raw materials and labour, also raised special difficulties of which

---

[1] Milch and Speer accused Sauckel of failing to give them a proper labour supply and even of falsifying figures to deceive Hitler.

[2] Speer Interrogations, Aug. 1945, 'The Industrial Mobilization of Germany for War Production'. This is the most incisive of Speer's many criticisms of the military and industrial leaders. He even said that Germany would have been better off had there been no planning before the war. That, he thought, was the secret of the success of the United States in the First World War, which thus had to turn to men of real knowledge and capacity. This last remark, though characteristic, should not be taken too seriously.

the main one was that of communications. The German state railway system, the *Reichsbahn*, was one of the most efficient in the world. During its construction military considerations had always been given high priority so that there was more than the usual provision of alternate routes and servicing and repair facilities. It had also more than the normal supply of rolling stock. 'In brief,' reported the United States engineers, who inspected it after the war, 'the Reichsbahn was the sort of plant any railway man would like to have constructed had he been free from financial obligations'.[1] It incorporated in it the railway systems of Austria, Alsace-Lorraine, Luxembourg and part of Poland, thus extending its length from 33,804 miles to 48,968 miles. The whole was divided into a number of *Direktionen* or railway divisions. The occupied territories were left under their own administrations, but they could and did supply rolling stock at the expense of their own countries, as well as newly built railway engines and trucks.

The war strain on the German railways was, of course, an immense one. The cessation of so much sea traffic meant a great addition to the load to be carried. The extension of the front added much to the burden cast on the railways by the transportation of the armed forces and their supplies. But these difficulties were mitigated by the assistance obtained from countries outside Germany, by the reduction of normal passenger traffic and by increasing the load allowed per truck for which the pre-war margin of safety had been fixed at a high level.

In addition, Germany has a highly developed system of inland waterways. At the beginning of the war the fleet of vessels was old and ill-adapted to the different river systems which had only comparatively recently been linked together by canals. But here again Germany was able to obtain, through the conquest of France and the Low Countries, a large number of modern barges which increased the capacity of the fleet by twelve and a half per cent. It was thus possible to divert more of the traffic to the waterways, though because of the complexities of German administration, full use was hardly made of them.

Another consequence of the extension of Germany's fronts deep into the East and South of Europe was the necessity for greater stocks of munitions and oil, if local shortages were to be avoided. In the case of oil, it is true, new sources of supply were sometimes available near at hand, but still the total supply had to be distributed over a much wider area. The same is true of munitions and these stocks and depots were liable to be overrun by the enemy when the retreat came. For this reason Germany lost far more in the long run than she

---

[1] *U.S.S.B.S. The Effects of Strategic Bombing on German Transportation*, (No. 200), p. 6. *B.B.S.U. The Effects of Air Attack on Inland Communications*, pp. 177–179.

gained when the tide of battle was in her favour. These last difficulties were, however, mainly in the future. They were easily coped with down to the end of 1941 and it was hoped that the overthrow of the Soviet Union would relieve permanently such difficulties as existed.

In view of all these facts it is, perhaps, not surprising that but little was done in 1940–41 to intensify the war effort. There is no doubt that during these years there was but little increase in the total production of armaments in the pre-war Reich, though, of course, some additional supply was obtained from the occupied territories. By the end of 1941, war production in Britain was as great as that in Germany and even surpassed it in aircraft. There was, of course, a considerable increase in some things such as oil production and tanks. But no overall effort was made such as was proceeding in Britain. This comparative stagnation seems to have been accepted without protest by all those in high command in spite of the fact that by December 1940 it was known that a war with Russia was contemplated. In September 1941, after that war had broken out, Hitler ordered a reduction in the production of ammunition and, though the order was not fully obeyed, it had serious consequences later on.

Meanwhile, in London there was quite a different view of the German economy. The Ministry of Economic Warfare on whom the task of assessing it mainly fell, was well staffed with specialists of many kinds and had the means of consulting many more. It provided a large quantity of accurate and detailed information about particular industries in Germany. But it was less well supplied with economists. It had deliberately sought the assistance of practical men of affairs rather than that of theorists of repute. At any rate there was a failure in Britain to appreciate some of the basic facts of the German economy and thus hopes were raised of success by blockade and bombing which could not be fulfilled. It was for long thought that the German war effort was nearing its peak and that it would soon be reduced by lack of raw materials. The German people were considered already to be injuriously affected by the efforts of preparation for war and an austerity of life that bordered on privation. It was not realised that the German standard of living during these years, if lower than that of the British, was well above that of the Germany in the years of the economic depression. It was even thought at times that food would run short as in the First World War. It was pointed out that the control which Germany had obtained over two-thirds of Europe would bring many difficult problems of supply to its masters, but for a long time the advantages which accrued from it were underestimated.

Some of these facts could not be expected to be properly appreciated until some such investigation was made as was done in the post-war surveys. But some were sufficiently obvious to cause surprise that more attention was not paid to them. The German machine-tool industry, for example, was never accurately assessed in Britain. 'In England', it is stated in the British survey, 'the ratio of men to machine tools in 1943 was 5·7. The corresponding German ratio between 1939–44 fluctuated between the narrow limits of 2·26 and 2·44. The failure to recognise this very great reserve of machine tool capacity and machinery of all kinds was probably the major shortcoming of our economic Intelligence during the war'.[1]

It might also have been noticed that in almost all cases single shifts were being worked and the necessary conclusions have been drawn from that important fact. The resilience of German industry under bombing was thus greatly underestimated and the impression given that even a small reduction of her output by that means would cause great difficulties in the supply of armaments. Indeed, the prospect was held out that, in any case, by the second half of 1941 German production would be in serious straits for lack of raw materials. There were, of course, in many appreciations made during this period modifications of this position in one aspect or another as is usual in intelligence summaries. These qualifications and cautions, perhaps, sometimes lost some of their force when they came to be summarised in the papers of the J.I.C. The mistake was often one of emphasis. At any rate, the impression remained, not only in this period but in subsequent years, that Germany was so severely strained that an additional burden might well produce a complete breakdown in the national economy. This misconception was particularly important in considering the possible effects of area bombing.

This attitude was first shown in the estimates given to the Chiefs of Staff when, towards the end of May, they were asked to consider the prospects of Britain in the event of the overthrow of France. They were told by the representative of M.E.W. that by the winter of 1940–41 there would be widespread shortage of food in many European industrial centres including parts of Germany itself, that lack of oil would force Germany to weaken her control over her conquests and that by the middle of 1941, because of the shortage

---

[1] B.B.S.U. *The Strategic Air War*, p. 83.

Actual and estimated inventory of machine tools in Germany 1938–43

Year	Actual Inventory	M.E.W. Estimate
1938	1,327,000	658,000
1939	1,498,000	706,200
1940	1,664,000	746,400
1941	1,840,000	766,000
1942	2,007,000	838,300
1943	2,150,000	981,400

When in 1941 it was known that machine tools were still being exported it was suggested that this was 'propaganda' or due to a severe shortage of foreign exchange.

of raw materials, she would have difficulty in replacing her military equipment, while a large part of the industrial plant of Europe would be brought to a standstill, thus giving to the German government an immense problem of unemployment.[1] In August another review was prepared by the Joint Planning Sub-Committee for the Chiefs of Staff 'in close collaboration with the Ministry of Economic Warfare', which was almost equally optimistic, especially as regards the oil situation. 'Although', they concluded, 'the date by which deficiencies and distribution difficulties may make it impossible for Germany to maintain large enough armed forces to stave off defeat cannot be predicted, the effect of the oil situation alone on her military freedom of action may soon be far reaching'.[2]

This judgment was modified to some extent in the twelve months following the fall of France. But the precariousness of the German position was continuously over-estimated. Only as regards oil, which will be surveyed in the next section, was there any substance in these prognostications. Yet how long they persisted may be seen in the important report of the Joint Planners, written before the German attack on the Soviet Union, on which the bombing policy of transport and morale was based. 'It is impossible to estimate', it is there stated, 'at what point these difficulties will become so great as seriously to reduce the mobility, efficiency or size of Germany's armed forces. It would, however, appear certain that even if these qualities could be maintained in 1942 it could only be at the cost to the civilian populations not only in the occupied countries, but also in Germany itself, of such suffering as may well prove intolerable, and of difficulties rapidly becoming insuperable. . . . We believe that, even if nothing occurs to accelerate German collapse, the strains and shortages of 1943 could not be supported without a drastic reduction in the power of her armed forces, which would leave Germany highly vulnerable to an enemy still retaining power and vigour'.[3]

No doubt in the years when the means for a successful armed

---

[1] C.O.S. Memo., 25th May 1940. See J. R. M. Butler: *Grand Strategy*, Vol. II, pp. 212–215. It seems to be mainly on this paper that Professor Sir Keith Hancock based his harsh judgment: 'Germany's economy was immeasurably strengthened by her conquests and the Ministry of Economic Warfare's forecasts were sheer illusion.' W. K. Hancock and M. M. Gowing: *British War Economy*, (1949), p. 100. Professor Medlicott (*The Economic Blockade*, Vol. I, pp. 60 and 420–421), claims that this forecast was made on assumptions of action by the fighting services which were not in fact carried out. But this estimate was made when Russian supplies were still available to Germany and even when this source and French North Africa were closed to them the effects were not that which the Ministry's representative thought were likely to ensue. The report was drafted by a Committee of Four, but the work was considered so secret that the representative of M.E.W. was not allowed to disclose it to his subordinates. This advice had an important influence in the strategic conclusions reached at this time by the Chiefs of Staff. See above, pp. 146–147.

[2] C.O.S. Report, 21st Aug. 1940.

[3] J.P.S. Review, 12th June 1941.

attack on Germany seemed far out of reach it was natural to exaggerate her economic vulnerability. The error fortified the belief that Germany could be defeated even when her ascendancy in Europe seemed to be supreme and no certain military assistance was evident outside the Commonwealth. The psychological effect on those directing the war and through them on the British people during this trying period was, perhaps, important, and when it had been realised to some extent that these expectations had been too highly pitched, a new aspect had been given to the war by the resistance of the Soviet Union and the involvement of the United States.

3. The nature of the target systems

During this period all the principal target systems under attack in Germany during the whole war were at one time or another made the subject of a main directive to Bomber Command except one of which there was yet no knowledge—the V-weapon production and sites. Oil, communications, morale and area bombing of a selected number of industrial towns were to be the main targets of offence. Submarine construction and harbours, ports, naval vessels and invasion preparations were the main targets of defence. In this period the attack on the aircraft industry and aerodromes was also considered as a target of defence, though at a later stage it was held to be a necessary preliminary to offence. In addition, the mining of enemy waters was begun in this period and continued throughout the war.

All these target systems had been considered and surveyed, though sometimes in a most cursory fashion, in the Western Air Plans made before the war.[1] The apparent flexibility of air power now seemed to allow one after another to be chosen as the primary aim of Bomber Command and then to be removed to a lower position as another came into favour. Thus, during this period, the attack was never concentrated for long on any one target system, which naturally made it difficult to appreciate its results. At the end of the period when the Chief of the Air Staff suggested yet another objective, he was advised that no directive had been allowed to run long enough to obtain any cumulative estimate of its value or of the ability of Bomber Command to carry it out.[2]

This dispersal of effort, as has been shown, was due mainly to the recurring necessity of assisting the defence, to the need of alternative targets to suit the weather and the moon and to the operational limitations of Bomber Command. But the decisions also depended on the economic assessment of the target systems. The machinery by which these decisions were made has been outlined in the first section of this chapter. In this section the nature of the different target systems and the economic reasons for attacking them will be briefly described.

Of all those attacked none was more carefully considered than oil. Though not at first given great prominence in the W.A. Plans, its importance was soon recognised. By the beginning of the war oil had become one of the favourite targets of the Air Ministry.[3] Because of

---
[1] See above, pp. 94 ff.
[2] Mins. Portal to Bottomley, 28th Sept. 1941, Baker to Bottomley, 29th Sept. 1941.
[3] It was strongly advocated in the Planning Directorate. The Deputy Director of Plans, however, was inclined to prefer the Ruhr plan to it because he thought that Germany

some controversy about it, the Lloyd Committee had been set up at the Air Ministry's special desire to advise Lord Hankey's Cabinet Committee, the existence of which showed the exceptional interest in official circles concerning this target system. Before, however, considering the advice which was tendered on this subject, it is necessary to say something of the German sources of supply and the relation of the German oil industry to other parts of the German economy.

There were during the war three main sources of supply. There was first, though only a small part of the total supply, the crude oil of Germany itself and that of Austria and Poland which she controlled. Secondly, there was the crude oil of Hungary and the much larger supply of Rumania which, despite her armed strength, Germany was not able to dispose of as she would have wished. Until 1941, Russia also supplied Germany with considerable quantities of oil. Thirdly, there was the synthetic oil produced by the Bergius Hydrogenation and Fischer-Tropsch processes, of which the former was more extensively developed, and other synthetic oil and benzol produced by coal-tar distillation and carbonization and alcohol distilleries, also not susceptible of such great increase as the hydrogenation plants. Thus, the hydrogenation plants, owned by the great *I.G. Farbenindustrie*, were of special importance, and this was enhanced by the fact that they were the source of about ninety per cent of all the high-octane aviation spirit produced during the war.[1]

There was ample refining capacity for the crude oil, much of it being in Hamburg, Hanover and other parts of North-West Germany. More refineries were later available in Poland, Western Europe and Italy, while Rumania also had large ones; but facilities for obtaining high-octane aviation spirit by this means were almost entirely lacking in Germany. On the other hand, lubricating oil, of which, of course, all German industry had need, could only be obtained by refining crude oil. In addition to aviation spirit and lubricating oil, Germany needed motor petrol, diesel oil and fuel oil which could be obtained both from crude oil and synthetically.

Thus, the hydrogenation plants were a very important part of the oil complex. But there was also another aspect of them which was never fully taken into account in the plans for a strategic attack upon them. They were part of the complicated chemical processes by which not only aviation spirit and other petrol but other vital materials were obtained. The elements of coal were isolated, turned into gas and used under compression with air and water to make new substances, the principal ones, in addition to oil, being synthetic rubber, ammonia, the basic material of nitric acid, and methanol,

---

might obtain large stocks of oil by the conquest of the Netherlands. Min. Collier to Slessor, 21st Oct. 1939.

[1] For the output of the different sources during the war, see App. 49 (xxxiii).

the two last being the essential constituents of explosives.[1] Thus, by cutting off the gas supply through the destruction of the conversion plants, the gas purification plants or the compression plants, the production of explosives and rubber would have been much reduced as well as that of high-octane aviation spirit.

These facts were, of course, known to the technicians advising the oil committees. But they were never made the basis for an attack on the whole chemical industry. So far as the connection between oil and explosives was mentioned it was the supply of oil alone that was taken into consideration. The attack on oil did ultimately produce a great effect on the supply of explosives with an important influence on German resistance. But this was accidental, not designed. A few attacks were made on rubber-producing plants, but none on nitrogen production as such, partly, it would seem, because, as it was also the source for the large supply of agricultural fertilisers, it was considered that any losses would be absorbed by the civilian economy. This question will be further discussed in Chapter XIV, when the successful attack on oil production in 1944–45 is examined. Here it need only be pointed out that, whatever decision had been arrived at, it is curious that the attention of those directing the offensive was not called at an early date to this aspect of a target system so much discussed.[2]

Another small but indispensable constituent of high-octane aviation spirit and motor petrol is ethyl fluid which is composed of tetra-ethyl-lead blended with a corrective agent, ethylene dibromide. The plants of both processes are highly vulnerable. Only two tetra-ethyl-lead plants were in operation in Germany during the war, but the largest of these at Froese was not discovered until late in 1944. There were also three much smaller ones in France and Italy, but the location of these was not known until a late stage of the war. There was only one ethyl dibromide plant in Germany and one in France which was never used. No attacks were made on any of these plants, because by the time they were all discovered, it was considered that stocks would then suffice for all the aviation fuel that could be produced.[3]

---

[1] In the oil hydrogenation process hydrogen, made from coke in water-gas generators, is combined under very high pressure and at 800° F. with a paste of ground coal and heavy oil.

[2] The Fifth Lloyd Report, 16th December 1940, states, for example, that 'the destruction of the Nitrogen plants, such as those at Leuna and Oppau, has a special value in view of their potentialities for the output of substitute fuels.' An Air (Targets) Intelligence paper of 27th June 1939 pointed out that the processes of synthetic oil and synthetic nitrogen were interchangeable. When Sir Charles Portal, as A.O.C.-in-C. Bomber Command, suggested that chemical plants should be attacked instead of oil, the Air Ministry disagreed but neither seems to have appreciated the connection between the two targets. Letters Portal to Air Min. and Douglas to Portal, 16th and 24th July 1940.

[3] There is a division of opinion on this point between British and United States experts. The latter considered that an opportunity had been neglected (*U.S.S.B.S. Oil Division*

The chemical industry was dominated by the powerful *I.G. Farbenindustrie*, which from the first co-operated readily with the Hitler régime and supplied the technical direction for the synthetic oil industry. Stimulated by the special interest of the *Wehrmacht* and especially of the *Luftwaffe* and assisted by the funds and influence of the Four Year Plan, they accomplished a great deal in the pre-war years, even though they failed to produce anything like the quantities envisaged in the 1936 and 1938 plans. The whole industry was co-ordinated under the presidency of an official of the *I.G. Farbenindustrie* and two other officials from the same firm were at the head of the crude-oil and synthetic-oil sections of the Four Year Plan.

Most efficient arrangements were also made for the distribution of the oil to the armed forces, two special organisations being created for that purpose. That specially meant for the *Luftwaffe*, commonly called W.I.F.O.,[1] accumulated in the pre-war years stocks of about 640,000 tons and constructed large underground storage tanks and a few pipe-lines. During the war it distributed oil to the *Luftwaffe* with great efficiency and also helped the army. Much of the blending of other constituents of aviation spirit with petrol was done at the main depots of the W.I.F.O. Its success in storing safely large quantities of aviation spirit until the concluding stages of the war was a great contribution to the defence of Germany.[2]

The transport of oil within Germany and from Hungary and Rumania to Germany was also most efficiently handled until the closing stages of the war, Germany's own ample supply of tank waggons being supplemented by those captured in the West. There was less need, therefore, to keep large supplies in the forward areas instead of in the underground storage tanks in Germany.[3]

Thus, when war broke out, if German stocks of oil of all kinds were far below the minimum that might be regarded as necessary for prolonged operations, preparation had been made to increase the supply considerably by the end of 1941. New hydrogenation plants were under construction both at centres already established and at Brüx in Czechoslovakia. After the fall of Poland others were set on foot in Upper Silesia. The crude oil of Austria was being developed as rapidly as possible. Thus, German oil production increased

---

Final Report, No. 109, Appendix, pp. 14–16), the former that it had never existed (*Oil in the German War Effort*).

[1] *Wirtschaftliche Forschungsgesellschaft* (Economic Research Co.), a cover title.

[2] A detailed account of the distribution system was obtained after the war from *Oberstabsingenieur* Ahrens, who was in charge of it. He stated that there were ten large underground depots of 100,000 tons each and a number of smaller above-ground depots holding small quantities. He estimated the stock of aviation spirit at the beginning of the war at 500,000 tons.

[3] *Oil in the German War Effort*. In the opinion of its authors no great difficulty would have arisen if larger quantities had had to be transported by rail had the Danube route been more seriously injured. But this is a rather controversial question.

steadily from 1940 to the middle of 1944, that of the hydrogenation plants being more than doubled in that period.

It is clear that to appraise so widespread and complicated an industry and to estimate the amount of the different kinds of oil available to the enemy was a most difficult problem and one that could not be expected to be solved with complete accuracy.[1] The production of many different kinds of plants had to be assessed and account had to be taken of the fact that different kinds of oil as well as other products could be obtained from the same plants. Nor could there be absolutely certain information of how much oil reached Germany from Rumania and, until June 1941, from Russia. Consumption had to be estimated by calculating the amount of oil necessary for the tanks, ships, trucks and aircraft assumed to have been employed in a particular period of time and from the restrictions placed upon the civil economy and the substitute fuels used by it. If all these difficulties are remembered the estimates of the Lloyd Committee and its successors were as successful as could be expected.

Future calculations depended on the stocks which Germany possessed when war broke out. The appraisal of the Industrial Intelligence Centre made just before the war which placed them at the low level of three million tons was remarkably accurate and was adopted by the Lloyd Committee in its first reports. Because of different estimates made in the United States, France and Russia and for other reasons the British estimate was raised during this period to five million tons, and, though this included more provision for oil in process of distribution, it was, in fact, too high. The level of German stocks was for this reason always over-estimated.[2]

As has been seen, M.E.W. made a most optimistic forecast of the probable shortage of oil in Germany towards the end of May 1940. In March, the Lloyd Committee had estimated that stocks of oil had fallen to about 1,750,000 tons and that by the end of the year they would be down to as little as 510,000 tons. Thus, Germany appeared to be confronted with a critical oil position, a prospect which, as will have been seen, had an important bearing upon the making of bombing policy at this time.[3] But in May 1940, the Lloyd Committee

---

[1] 'Conjecture must play a large part in any estimate we make. The possible margin of error is—as has so often been demonstrated in the past—very considerable.' Memo. by Stanley, 13th April 1942.

[2] It is difficult to define exactly what is meant by 'stock'; how far, for example, oil in process of refining and that necessary to keep the pipe-line full should be included. Different rules were used by different people and varied from time to time. For this reason it is not possible to compare exactly the stocks estimated in London with those reported by the Germans after the war. But a trustworthy German document of July 1939 gives 2,084,000 tons as the total supply on 1st October 1939. *Oil in the German War Effort.* See App. 49 (xxxii). Whatever allowances are made, this is no greater than the first estimate of M.E.W.

[3] See above, p. 141.

revised these estimates and forecast that German oil stocks at the end of the year would amount not to 510,000 tons but to 1,350,000 tons. Disturbing factors in the calculations were the booty seized by Germany during her advance westwards and the unexpectedly short duration of the campaign.[1]

These estimates had then to be reconsidered in the light of Germany's conquests and her domination of Europe up to the Russian frontier. The task was not an easy one because in addition to estimating the totals of German production and consumption the result depended on how much oil could be extracted from Rumania, if, as was anticipated, it fell completely under German control, on the capacity of Germany to transport it and on the amounts she would allot to the subjugated countries. In July the Lloyd Committee came to the conclusion that Germany and Italy would need in the coming year at least eight and a half million tons of oil and that their share of the European oil supply would fall considerably below that figure. Consequently their stocks would decline until in less than twelve months there would be a breakdown. This breakdown would of course be accelerated by a successful attack on the industry and it was suggested that while the synthetic plants should be the main target, attacks should also be made on refineries in France and Italy and on the communications with Rumania by the Danube and by rail. It was even said that, while admittedly sufficient damage could not be done in a short time to prevent an invasion of England, yet Germany might well be diverted to the Middle East in order to secure her future oil supplies. This last point was, no doubt, made in order that the oil target system might be able to compete with others, such as the aircraft industry and Channel ports, which might be expected to be more important under the immediate threat of invasion.[2] Oil could not, however, be given an established priority until the threat of invasion was over. The Lloyd and Hankey Committees meanwhile turned their attention to the problem of reducing the amount of oil delivered by Rumania to Germany, whether by action in Rumania itself, by obstructing the Danube, or by bombing

---

[1] 1st, 2nd, 3rd Reports of the Lloyd Committee, 13th Oct. 1939, 15th March, 31st May 1940. The 2nd and 3rd Reports were placed before the Cabinet by the Hankey Committee which, on 4th June, recommended oil production as a main target system as well as action to stop Rumanian supplies. There was, however, much uncertainty at this period about the oil position. For the actual stocks, production and consumption of German oil during the war, see App. 49 (xxxiii) to (xxxv).

[2] Lloyd Committee 4th Report, 14th July 1940. Hankey Committee 5th Report, 16th July 1940. The large stocks of aviation spirit in the West meant that no immediate effect could be produced on the activities of the *Luftwaffe*. Germany's position as regards aero-engine fuels was held to be more satisfactory than her general oil situation, while lubricants were thought to be less so (C.O.S. Memo., 21st Aug. 1940). It may be noted that four days after the signature of the Armistice in 1940 the Office of the Four Year Plan produced a 'Petroleum plan for Europe' which foresaw a deficit of eighteen and a half million tons and suggested that this should be obtained from the Middle East. There was no reference to Caucasus oil. *Oil in the German War Effort*.

storage and refinery plants to which it came or the railways by which it was transported.[1]

Then in December the Lloyd Committee made a further report which had an immediate effect. While there was no evidence, it said, that the military effort of Germany and Italy was yet affected, total stocks would fall rapidly until the spring and then more slowly as supplies came in by the Danube and from the new synthetic plants then being constructed. The gradual accumulation of knowledge was shown by the fact that the different kinds of oils could now be discussed in more detail. Special importance was given to the Fischer-Tropsch plants because they produced diesel oil said to be in very short supply. But also for the first time the Defence Committee were informed that 'apart from any stocks which still remain, Germany will be almost completely dependent for high grade octane spirit upon the output of her hydrogenation plants.' Thus, as was noted in the report of the Chiefs of Staff, 'the destruction of the synthetic oil plants in Germany alone would bring about a crisis.' 'It is worth repeating', a covering note by Mr. Lloyd concluded, 'that the only way to get a quick death clinch on the whole enemy oil position is both to destroy the synthetic plants and to interrupt Rumanian supplies.' Meanwhile, he pointed out, Germany was working ceaselessly to increase her synthetic production and her means of transport from Rumania. Time, therefore, was the decisive factor.[2]

As will have been seen, this intelligence played an important part in securing for oil the primary place in the bombing directive of January 1941, but, as will also have been seen, the oil campaign did not last for many months.[3] Nevertheless, the Hankey and Lloyd Committees tried for a year to get oil back into the primary position. In their reports of early May 1941 they insisted that the basic position remained the same and that stocks were dwindling in spite of the fact that it was now known that the attacks of 1940 had inflicted much less damage than had hitherto been assumed and that Rumanian oil could be supplied direct to the German army on the Balkan front, in addition to that transported to Germany itself by the

---

[1] Letter Lloyd to Hankey, 20th Aug. 1940. The Air Staff when consulted were not very encouraging. Note by Newall, 28th Sept. 1940.

[2] Lloyd Committee 5th Report, 16th Dec. 1940. Hankey Committee 6th Report, 2nd Jan. 1941. C.O.S. Report, 7th Jan. 1941. The last pointed out that the effect on Germany's armed forces might even soon be apparent. See App. 9. 'This is particularly so, since a high proportion of the loss of oil we could inflict would fall on certain grades of oil which might then be almost unobtainable.' But the D.D. Plans (Op.) wrote on 25th October 1940: 'It is not possible—as A.I.3(b) imply—to divorce aviation fuel from other types of fuel. This is particularly true of the German Air Force which uses an ordinary high-grade petrol in its aero engines.' Min. Baker to Douglas. But most of this 'petrol' was also made in the hydrogenation synthetic plants.

[3] See above, pp. 159–160 and 163–165.

usual routes. Nevertheless, they insisted that important results could be achieved if the nearer synthetic plants were intensively attacked as the previous directive had intended they should be.

But these arguments now produced no effect on those directing strategy and the only concession made to them was that the Defence Committee did invite the Air Ministry to arrange one more heavy attack on the synthetic plants as soon as weather permitted. This apparently was to test the possibility of inflicting damage on them, but before the subject could be thrashed out the invasion of Russia altered the whole situation.

To the two committees this seemed to be a heaven-sent opportunity, for Rumanian oil could now be bombed from Russian bases, while they repeated their arguments as to the dangerous level of German stocks, all the more dangerous now that the attack on Russia would cause them to diminish at a more rapid rate. But the Chiefs of Staff were adamant for operational reasons, while the Prime Minister and the Foreign Office were foremost advocates of the attack on civilian morale in Germany. All that Lord Hankey could obtain by a 'final appeal', in a memorandum made after a personal presentation of his case to the Chiefs of Staff, was the promise of one more attack on the oil plants during the next moon period.[1]

It was in vain that the seventh report of the Lloyd Committee supported Lord Hankey's arguments with new estimates of the shrinkage of German stocks. All eyes were concentrated on the Russian front on whose resistance depended whether Germany would or would not obtain access to oil supplies which would give her all the oil she required. M.E.W. thought that any reduction of the oil output by less than 100,000 tons per month would be ineffective.[2] Thus, though the estimates of Germany's weak oil position were confirmed at the end of the year and the Hankey Committee continued to press for an attack, nothing was done. There was a fleeting hope that the more powerful bomber force and the new commander might alter that situation in 1942. But his directive had already been laid down and he was the last man to wish it to be altered.[3]

Finally, the pressure of the oil committee, other representations and the support of Mr. Attlee caused the Cabinet to direct Colonel Oliver Stanley, Secretary of State for the Colonies, to make a special

---

[1] C.O.S. Report, 15th July 1941, after the interview with Lord Hankey. Memo. by Hankey, 15th July 1941 (circulated by order of the Prime Minister on 20th July 1941).

[2] Air Min. Plans brief for C.A.S., 3rd March 1942.

[3] Lloyd Committee 7th and 8th Reports, 28th July and 1st Dec. 1941, monthly reports, 14th Jan. and 21st Feb. 1942. Hankey Committee 9th Report, 4th (revised 15th) Dec. 1941. Letter Lloyd to Hankey, 23rd Feb. 1942, admitting the lack of effect of previous attacks, but stating that he had wished them to be supplemented by sabotage and parachute attacks. 'Perhaps Air Marshal Harris could consider calling together his experts and review the tactics, which so far have been so unfruitful, and see whether they could not be reshaped to secure more decisive results.'

S.A.O.—I—U

enquiry, but his report confirmed the previous decisions. Neither the synthetic plants, the Rumanian refineries at Ploesti nor the communications from Rumania could be seriously damaged by the means available. No reference was made to aviation spirit for the *Luftwaffe* which does not appear to have been taken into consideration at this time.[1] Oil had to wait two years before further attacks on it were planned.

Thus, oil, in spite of the skilled advocacy of influential committees, had only been the primary target for a very short period. It was displaced by communications and morale which were to develop into area bombing—the main offensive target system of Bomber Command during the rest of the war. But before considering the nature of these target systems, something must be said of the others of this period. Most of them can be more briefly considered for none was attacked with any great persistence or confidence in success. One, however, the aircraft industry, had an important place in the directives and was to be the subject of special attacks at later stages of the war.

This target system was large and dispersed. There were alumina and aluminium processes which provided the material for the airframes, the assembly plants themselves where the airframes were made, the aero-engine plants which provided their power, the components such as ball-bearings or propellers indispensable to these, and finally the storage depots and aerodromes where the aircraft were finally deposited.

In the first place there was an immense development of alumina and aluminium production during the period 1933–39.[2] The alumina capacity was increased by 153 per cent and aluminium capacity by 375 per cent. This was by no means all utilised, but the production of aluminium increased ten-fold between 1933 and 1939. In 1941 less than half of this was used for aircraft production, but the rest was largely devoted to other war industries, only one-fifth being for civilian use.[3] At Hitler's orders the new plants were built well away from the Rhineland in central and eastern Germany so that the industry was well dispersed. Germany had no bauxite, but she was able to increase her supplies from Hungary and France as well as to obtain manufactured aluminium from these countries.[4] Transport and electric

---

[1] Memo. by Stanley, 16th April 1942, App. 16.

[2] Alumina is the conversion of bauxite by a chemical process. Aluminium is the conversion of alumina by means of cryolite and large quantities of electric power—about 25,000 kwh. to produce one ton of aluminium. The two processes were generally carried out in different localities and under different management. *U.S.S.B.S. Light Metal Industry of Germany* (No. 20) gives a detailed account of the industry.

[3] In 1943 aluminium was reserved entirely for military use.

[4] The import of bauxite from Hungary was doubled and from France quadrupled, in spite of some sabotage, but owing to effective resistance that from Yugoslavia fell by a

power were thus vital to the functioning of the industry, and it was, in fact, in later years reduced by injuries to them.

The aircraft industry had also grown up mainly since 1933. Then the aircraft construction companies, which had hitherto had to concentrate on civil aircraft and research, developed with the general direction and assistance of the Air Ministry into large and elaborately organised complexes for the production of military machines with numerous shadow factories and sub-contractors attached to them. Though the original factories were often situated in or very near large towns, the new ones were deliberately planned to reduce vulnerability to bombing. There was no concentration of production in a single region. The principal plants extended from Bremen to Munich and, after 1938, to Czechoslovakia and Vienna. Those built between 1934 to 1939 were in the open country, as far as possible from cities or towns, though few in this period were in forests which were in later years to be a refuge from bombing. Moreover, the buildings in the new plants were themselves dispersed. By an Air Ministry order, the total ground area of any one building was restricted to 7,500 square feet. Thus, the usual plant consisted of a number of buildings distributed over an area of thirty or forty acres with wide spaces in between them. The target system was thus made difficult, though, as will be seen, the dispersal had to be much increased when the great attack came on it in 1943–44. The buildings were substantially built with steel frames and in most cases all processes were duplicated. It is significant that there were few blackout buildings, showing that night shifts were not normally contemplated. But there was a great reserve of productive capacity, which, if one building was hit, could be kept up by working double shifts in another.

The aero-engine industry was concentrated in a much smaller number of factories and was not so widely dispersed, though later this course was also made necessary by the attack upon it. But the buildings were heavier and more substantial and the machinery less liable to be destroyed by the blast of bombs. The new factories were also built in separate blocks. They were less self-destructive than the airframe factories, though their machinery was vulnerable to fire in certain cases.

Then there were the specially manufactured components necessary for the functioning of an aircraft and its engines. A few of these and large proportions of others were made in a single factory. The *Vereinigte Deutsche Metallwerke A.G.* at Frankfurt am Main, for example, produced a considerable percentage of the metal propellers, landing gears, radiators and hydraulic components. Bosch of Stuttgart was practically the sole source of aircraft engine magnetos and

---

half. The large new plant for the production of alumina in Norway was destroyed by the U.S. Eighth Air Force before it came into operation.

certain other electrical equipment.[1] If such a target could have been destroyed it would have been a most economical method of dislocating production. But hardly any of these bottlenecks was known, and if they had been would have been hard to find and, in this period, impossible to hit, except by a lucky accident. At a later stage, when bombing became much more effective, these industries were also dispersed. In this period, though the idea was well to the fore, these 'panacea' targets were not much discussed. The exception was the ball-bearing plants at Schweinfurt on which discussion had already begun and which will be considered in a later chapter.

Finally, there were the depots and aerodromes where aircraft were stored or kept ready for action. But the aircraft were widely dispersed over the airfields and only a small proportion were in the depots. There were numerous small aerodromes in Germany and many were later made in France. One of the distinguishing characteristics of the *Luftwaffe* was its mobility. It could and did continually transfer *staffel* from one base to another with great speed.

This target system had been much studied before the war in plan W.A.1, with not very hopeful conclusions. The Air Ministry decided, and the decision was endorsed by M.E.W., that the attack on raw materials, alumina and aluminium, or components, such as propellers, was likely to be the most economical and effective method. But in 1940 there was much further controversy on the subject. Attention was, of course, concentrated on defence at this time and the principal problem was the reduction of the scale of attack on Britain. It was thought by some sections of the Air Staff that a quicker result would be obtained by bombing the aircraft assembly plants, and it was also suggested that the bombing of four of the principal maintenance and equipment depots would have a more immediate effect.[2] On the other hand, Sir Wilfrid Freeman, the Air Member for Development and Production, was of the opinion that the airframe plants could be re-established in two months, and in any case he believed that alternative factories would be ready for instant use. M.E.W. meanwhile continued to insist that aluminium was still the part of the target system most vulnerable to attack and this view was supported by the Deputy Director of Plans (Op.).[3] The uncertainty is reflected in the directives in which both airframe factories and aluminium works were

---

[1] *U.S.S.B.S. Aircraft Division Industry Report* (No. 4), pp. 107–109. Aero-pistons were made at only one plant in Britain and it was suggested that the same might be true of Germany, but there was little accurate information on such subjects.

[2] See above, p. 147. Min. Baker to Douglas, Slessor, D.H.O., and D.D.I.(3), 19th June 1940.

[3] 'If the Committee are still instructed to devote their main attention to reducing the German air striking force within 2 to 3 months (from the end of June), then alumina and aluminium remain the most hopeful line of attack.' Memo by Roskill (E. and O.T. Dept., M.E.W.), 13th July 1940. Min. Baker to Douglas, 18th Oct. 1940, which reviews the controversy.

included, as well as, in a lower position, some air stores, parks and depots. Attacks were even ordered on aluminium works after the fall of France, which it was known must have increased the supply. It was later proposed that aero-engine factories were a more economical target than airframe factories, even though they were deeper in Germany, but this also was strongly resisted at a higher level.[1]

Throughout the period the question of attacking aerodromes both in Germany and France had also been constantly under consideration. The German success in such an attack in Poland had been a notable one, but it was pointed out that this was due to an overwhelming superiority of force. The Prime Minister pressed for attacks on them in the hope of reducing the German bombing of Britain, but the Air Ministry remained of the opinion, held before the war, that these were unprofitable targets. Such attempts as were made in this period confirmed these views and little more success attended those made on the aerodromes of the fighters which attacked the British aircraft operating against submarines in the Bay of Biscay.

No other target system received any very prolonged trial, though many were discussed and some put into the directives. For a period before the war the power plants in the Ruhr held a high position and for a short time these, as well as coal and gas, were in the directives, but the impossibility of hitting such small targets was soon realised and they were displaced by the larger oil plants.

More attention was paid to the possibility of destroying German crops and forests by means of special incendiaries. This course was urged upon the Air Ministry by a surprising number of people of whom some had some knowledge of the subject. In June 1940 M.E.W. recommended that such attacks should at once be put into operation on the ground that the European harvest would be a bad one and further damage to it might be important. But tests on British crops showed poor results and it was not thought that much more had been accomplished in Germany.[2]

None of these targets made any great appeal to the Air Staff and oil was displaced by another target system, communications and morale. The two, however dissimilar in appearance, must be considered, to some extent, together because, as will have been noticed, they were so closely associated in the decision which made

---

[1] One of the arguments for attacking these was tactical, viz. that the Germans would withdraw fighters from the north of France to defend them, but as a penetration of 400 miles was necessary, the attack could only take place at night.

[2] The Black Forest was also often put forward as a most rewarding target and special incendiaries were devised to set the ground carpet of forests on fire. These were no more successful, and it was at last realised that the only great merit of these targets was that they could be easily found. The incendiaries came in useful when stocks were found to be short for the incendiary attacks on cities which began at the end of this period.

communications the primary and morale the secondary objective of the offensive. On communications the advice of the Railway Research Department was sought and, in the opinion of its branch in M.E.W., the efficient functioning of the German railway system depended on its marshalling yards. They were many in number, but one-third of the total capacity lay in three sets of yards in the Essen, Cologne and Wuppertal divisions of the *Reichsbahn*. If these could be successfully attacked an immediate effect, it was suggested, would be produced on the whole of the German transport system.[1] Other plans were put forward by other advisers such as those for attacks on locomotives and locomotive sheds or on the junctions of main lines, but the Railway Research Department of M.E.W. continued to insist on its point of view. Some attacks were made on the marshalling yards in the summer of 1940 and there was the usual optimism as to the results. It was said that even if no damage was done the alarm caused by a night raid over a yard seriously reduced its efficiency. It was even suggested that transport difficulties were among the causes of the delay in the invasion of Britain.[2]

The controversy as to which was the most vulnerable part of this target system continued throughout the rest of this year, evidence being sought in the assessment of the effect produced by German bombing of British railways. Since thirty per cent of German freight was borne by the elaborate river and canal system, this was also under continual review as an object of attack during the period. Special attention was paid to the Dortmund-Ems canal and the Mittelland Canal over the Ems. Studies were made as to the type of attack necessary and the nature of the bombs required. Plans were made for dropping specially constructed bombs in the canals to blow up barges and thus cause obstruction. The 1,000-lb. bomb was not ready in June 1940 when a gallant attack was made on the Dortmund-Ems canal, but considerable damage was done. In spite of this success the improbability of hitting such a target at night with the means available became more evident and inland waterways tended to recede into the background.[3]

As has been seen, the attack on communications was, in fact, closely linked with that on the morale of the civil population. Hitherto an attack on German morale as a primary target had always been resisted by the Air Ministry when it was advocated by civilian leaders. The fact that the German attack on Britain in the autumn of 1940

---

[1] M.E.W. Intelligence Dept. Paper, 16th Nov. 1939, circulated 22nd Nov. 1939. Min. V. B. Bennett (Plans 2) to D.D. Plans (Op.), 2nd Dec. 1939.

[2] Memos. by Sherrington, 26th July and 9th Aug. 1940. Though the evidence was admittedly slight, it was calculated that 10,000 wagon days had been lost in the period 16th June to 20th July.

[3] There is a large collection of memoranda dealing with the German inland waterways in great detail in A.H.B.

had produced little effect on British morale might have seemed to reinforce this view. But it was now believed in almost all quarters that German morale was much weaker than that of Britain. This view was put forward by the Joint Planners and endorsed by the Chiefs of Staff at the beginning of the year. 'The evidence at our disposal', they reported, 'goes to show that the morale of the average German civilian will weaken quicker than that of a population such as our own as a consequence of direct attack. The Germans have been undernourished and subjected to a permanent strain equivalent to that of war conditions during almost the whole period of Hitler's regime, and for this reason also will be liable to crack before a nation of greater stamina. It can be argued that concentrated attacks on the main centres of population in Germany, making the maximum use of damage by fire, continued with harassing action in the interval between the main attacks, might comparatively quickly produce internal disruption in Germany.'

As has been seen, the strain on the German people had been grossly overestimated in Britain, but other reasons in the opinion of the Planners made morale an unprofitable target, in particular, the control by the Nazi régime over public opinion, and the inability of Bomber Command to cover a wide enough and a deep enough area. 'Our own experience', it was suggested, 'indicates the local and transient effects of concentrated attacks on centres of population.'[1]

But meanwhile in the Air Ministry the linking of communications and morale as twin target systems had been more and more accepted, and on 13th May 1941 the Director of Bomber Operations had already placed them together. This view was reflected in the appreciation of the two target systems, now brought closely together by the Joint Planners, in a memorandum of 12th June. No new arguments were advanced to show that an attack on communications was more likely to achieve its object except that it was pointed out 'that every new extension of the area of German control means new strains of the system.' But emphasis was laid on the fact that 'the best railway targets . . . lie in the main, adjacent to workers' dwellings and congested industrial areas.' It is clear that it was this aspect of the communications target system which caused it to be accepted as the primary objective. It was added that morale might become the primary objective when the bomber force had been expanded and when German morale showed signs of weakening from other causes.

In all this discussion of morale, though there was some analysis of the conditions which were likely to affect it, there was hardly any consideration of what exactly was meant by the term. Civilian morale, it was said, depended on the cumulative effect of numerous factors,

---

[1] C.O.S. Report, 7th Jan. 1941.

but the two main ones were the deprivation of necessities and amenities and the fear of death. Thus, 'in order to get tangible moral effects it is essential that the attacks should be severe and frequently repeated. Unless the reality of air bombardment is worse than the anticipation, the attacks may defeat their own ends.'[1] But what exactly was meant by a breakdown of morale was not defined except in such vague terms as 'final collapse', 'general dislocation' or 'internal disruption'.

Only at the end of 1941 was any definition attempted. This course was made necessary by the criticisms of the United States Chiefs of Staff of morale as an objective. As a result, the Joint Planners informed the United States Special Observer Group in London that the attack on morale included 'the disruption of transportation, living and industrial facilities of the German population rather than the more restricted meaning.'[2] This definition implied that the attack was directed not so much to destroying the German worker's will to work as to deprive him of the means of working effectively. This distinction became more apparent in later stages of area bombing. It is obviously different from that put forward by Lord Trenchard and others who had supported the attack on morale earlier in 1941.

---

[1] J.P.S. Review, 12th June 1941.

[2] Conf. of J.P.S. and U.S. Special Observer Group, 21st Nov. 1941. J.P.S. Report, 11th Nov. 1941. The controversy is summarised and the quotation above given in Mark S. Watson: *U.S. Army in World War II: The War Department: Chief of Staff: Prewar Plans and Preparations*, (Washington, 1950), p. 409.

4. The estimated and actual results, 1940–1941

It is recognised by all those who have investigated the problem that the German war economy was but little, if at all, affected by the strategic bombing that took place during these years. Indeed, the whole period is dismissed with a few words expressing this view in both the British and United States post-war surveys of the results of the strategic bombing offensive. And though at first the estimates made in Britain as to what had been done were grossly exaggerated, towards the end of the period the truth, if not fully known, was to a certain extent realised. It was obvious that the light scale of attack and the errors in navigation and bomb aiming meant that no great damage had been done to Germany.

It is not necessary to quote at length from the earlier reports of the intelligence services of Bomber Command. They contained many wild statements such as reports that industrial output in the Ruhr-Rhine and Frankfurt-Main districts had fallen by more than thirty per cent owing to the lack of sleep among the workers and that bombing had affected twenty-five per cent of the total productive capacity of Germany.[1] Nevertheless, the Air Staff, though perhaps with less confidence, also at times showed the same kind of optimism.[2] By 1941 the tone had grown somewhat more sober and such exaggerations had never been admitted to the appreciations of the Joint Intelligence Committee or the Joint Planners. The Industrial Targets reports of M.E.W. constantly contained optimistic estimates but generally with a caution.[3] They were, indeed, often contradicted by later intelligence. Nevertheless, the total effect was very misleading and there was embarrassment when in 1941 photographic reconnaissance failed to confirm much of what had been stated about the damage done in various towns. For some time it was suggested that hasty repairs had been made by the Germans to conceal it, less important effects being allowed to remain in order to add to the deception. Gradually, however, photographic evidence was accepted as overriding all other sources.

---

[1] Bomber Cmd. Intelligence Reports, 24th Aug. and 10th Oct. 1940.

[2] Thus, '... it is considered that our attacks on the German aluminium plants have already resulted in a shortage of these products in Germany ... Evidence continues to accumulate that our sustained attacks against the enemy's railway and canal communications is having the anticipated effect of dislocating the enemy's supply systems both in the industrial and strategical spheres.' Dir. Douglas to Portal, 21st Sept. 1940, see App. 8 (ix), paras. 5 and 10.

[3] As late as 9th May 1941 Mr. Lawrence of M.E.W. could say 'Nevertheless, it is thought that some of the aircraft assembly plants were damaged sufficiently to reduce German aircraft output by about 10% over a period of, say, 2 months.' Memo. by Lawrence.

The most serious error of all this period was that concerning the 1940 attack on the oil plants. How far it went is seen in a letter of Mr. Lloyd to Lord Hankey at the end of September which said that Bomber Command had probably heavily hit sixty per cent of the Fischer-Tropsch plants.[1] It seems, however, to have been the theoretical calculations of Mr. Dewdney, then the oil adviser of Bomber Command, that led to the estimate that oil production had been reduced by fifteen per cent. This estimate found its way into the Industrial Targets Reports and the reports of the Lloyd Committee. It was reiterated as late as 9th March 1941 by Sir Archibald Sinclair to the Prime Minister after the latter had asked for comments on despatches from Washington which stated that United States observers on the spot had very different opinions.[2] But the next Industrial Target Report admitted that this estimate had been proved wrong. The Gelsenkirchen plants, on which a hundred tons of bombs had been thought to have been dropped in 1940, were shown by the photographs to be quite uninjured. The estimate was accordingly reduced in their report and in that of the Lloyd Committee to between five and ten per cent. This also was a gross exaggeration. Some damage had been done, especially to pipes and connecting lines, and in a later attack the Gelsenkirchen Nordstern plant, one of the largest in the Ruhr, was put out of production for three weeks by 4·7 tons of bombs dropped by five Wellington aircraft. But the total effect was of no great consequence. A reliable contemporary German report states that the total loss of oil caused by enemy action to the end of 1943 was 150,000 tons, a very small proportion of the total production of the period and much of this was oil in storage.[3]

This last estimate had no consequence for, as has been seen, the Air Ministry were by now convinced that Bomber Command was unable to inflict serious damage on the oil plants, but the first error no doubt contributed to the decision to make oil a primary target in January 1941. That decision was, however, based as much on calculations of Germany's future oil position as on an estimate of what had already been accomplished. These calculations were substantially correct and Germany's stocks touched almost their lowest point in 1941.

Perhaps the real estimate in responsible circles of the damage

---

[1] Letter Lloyd to Hankey, 25th Sept. 1940.

[2] Min. Sinclair to Churchill, 9th March 1941, commenting on three telegrams from Lord Halifax of 21st Feb., 26th Feb. and 5th March 1941. The last stated: 'German production of mineral oil up to the present has not been seriously disturbed.' The earlier telegrams were more optimistic as to what had been done. According to his own account after the war, Mr. Dewdney seems to have been somewhat sceptical of his own calculations, but Bomber Command eagerly accepted them. Lecture by Dewdney, Jan. 1948.

[3] I.T.R., 3rd April 1941. Previous reports (e.g. 23rd Jan. 1941) had thrown doubts on the estimate but had not been fully believed. The German report is that of the *Planungsamt* made on 29th June 1944 obtained by the Field Information Agency, Technical, of the Control Commission for Germany quoted in *Oil in the German War Effort*.

which had been done to German industry in 1941 is best shown in the appreciation issued in April 1942 by the Joint Intelligence Committee. This contained a comprehensive review of the whole period. It included the successful attacks on Billancourt and Rostock made early in 1942 and described in Chapter VII, but in the main it is based on the experience of this period. It concluded that the results were 'not important' or were 'inconclusive' or were 'not proportional to the increased weight of attack', thus indicating that not much had been accomplished. It stated, however, that submarine construction has been 'delayed' and that the Focke-Wulf factory had been transferred from Bremen to other towns farther east. Highly successful attacks had also been made on smaller cities such as Aachen and Münster.

But it was the indirect effects of the bombing which were considered to be of the greatest importance and these were mainly of three kinds, (1) the 'dislocation' of German industry by damage to houses, shops, communications and public utilities, which, as in Britain, would cause greater loss of output than direct damage; (2) the necessity for Germany to expend a large effort in defence which, it was claimed, had affected her front against Russia as well as reduced the aircraft that could be used against British shipping and (3) the effect on morale, which was 'beyond question', it was claimed, 'considerable' in the areas attacked, though it had fluctuated in the course of the period.[1]

Two estimates in this survey were substantially correct. The Focke-Wulf factory was in process of removal though not because of the loss of production which was supposed to have caused it, but because of the possibility of even more successful attacks in the future. Germany was also devoting a considerable amount of effort to passive defence, as she had done since the beginning of the war, and this effort was increased at the end of 1941, as a result of the British bombing. But no 'dislocation' of German industry had taken place to any appreciable extent, nor was the morale of the workers in any way significantly impaired. These claims rested on no tangible evidence.

Nevertheless, the estimate of the damage done was now based on the more scientific analysis of the evidence which had begun to be used more and more during 1941. The day photographs had revealed the small extent of damage in towns which it had been thought were heavily hit. But only a small number of night photographs which could check the position of the aircraft when the bombs were dropped

---

[1] J.I.C. Report, 6th April 1942. The economic appreciation was written in M.E.W. Mr. Vickers expressed his surprise that the task should be given to the J.I.C. rather than to the Air Ministry and M.E.W., but he added, 'a remarkable opportunity is offered to bring to the attention of the Chiefs of Staff and the War Cabinet all the relevant facts about our bombing policy'. Min. Vickers to Knight and Lawrence, 24th March 1942.

had yet been produced. The reports of the crews were thus still the only evidence available and it was inevitable that they should be constantly mistaken both as to where they had dropped their bombs and as to the effect which they had produced when dropped.

A considerable amount of damage of one kind or another had, of course, been caused in Germany since June 1940. In the fringe of towns along the coast and north-western Germany which had been attacked on many occasions, even if only with light forces, houses had been destroyed, some factories injured and their production temporarily reduced, railway stations and tramways put out of action for a short time and other communications occasionally injured. But most of the effect had been on the civilian economy and easily absorbed. Only in a few cases was there any loss to the war economy and this had been overcome. The German records of these years are incomplete and the post-war surveys made little attempt to give a statistical account of a period which they regarded as unimportant. But sufficient material is available to show the kind of damage inflicted and to compare it in some cases with the contemporary estimates. On towns difficult to find or where other similar towns were near at hand the number of bombs counted by the Germans was sometimes not more than a fifth of that claimed to have been dropped by the British. In other cases, such as Berlin, where the target was a large one, the figure might rise to thirty per cent. In many cases the bombs which were thought to have been dropped on one town were really dropped on another. The only general survey which we possess is that for the south-west part of Germany, which includes Mannheim, Cologne, Frankfurt and Nuremberg for the thirteen months May 1940–May 1941. In this area just under fifty per cent of the missiles dropped fell in the open country. Of the rest, twenty per cent fell in residential areas, 11·2 per cent on communications, 8·2 per cent on industrial objectives, 5·2 per cent on military objectives and aerodromes and 1·1 per cent on inland harbours and waterways. The proportion that fell in the open country varied considerably from month to month, but not apparently because of the weather, for the summer months are no better than the winter ones. On the whole, as might be expected, the proportion dropped in the open country grew less as the time went on.[1]

The kind of damage done may be illustrated by the results in towns of which we possess records extending over fairly long periods. Most damage was done to the ports of north Germany which were more easily found than other towns. The attack on Hamburg in November 1940 caused some slight damage to the ship-building works of Blohm and Voss, though far less than had been estimated in

---

[1] The compilation was made by *Luftgau XII/XIII*. It may not be very accurate, nor is it necessarily representative of other areas.

Britain.[1] In 1941 a number of other attacks were made especially in March and May. In March the showrooms and administrative buildings of Blohm and Voss were partially destroyed, but there was no loss of production. Further damage was done to these works in May and at last it was admitted that the destruction caused by fire in the yards, machine shops and boiler-house had resulted in some loss of production. There was also other damage in Hamburg, three small boats were destroyed and some factories injured, but these were of no great importance.

Kiel, the principal naval base, was also attacked frequently. Little damage was done in 1940, but the larger raids of March and April 1941 had a considerable effect on the building yards and, in addition, quantities of stores were destroyed and communications injured. Production was certainly delayed for a short period and in one case a total stoppage was necessary; but the effect on U-boat construction was not of much consequence. Hits were recorded on the main target, the naval vessels, but no important damage was done to them.[2] There was also some damage done at Wilhelmshaven which had an effect on the output of the port, though the main targets, the *Tirpitz* and the U-boat construction yards, were not hit. A number of attacks were also made on Emden, the nearest of the ports. No records exist as to the damage done, but it was not rated highly in Britain.[3] More effective than all these attacks was the minelaying campaign, some off the Biscay ports, but mainly in the Baltic and Kattegat. 118 ships were sunk, mostly of small tonnage, but amounting in all to over 100,000 tons.[4]

Bremen, however, was constantly attacked because, in addition to its port facilities, the Focke-Wulf works were situated at Bremen-Hemelingen where were produced not only the best German fighters but the long-range Condors which were doing damage to Atlantic shipping during this period. The attacks of 1940 did it little harm, but those of 1941 were perhaps the most successful of this period. A number of incendiaries and H.E. bombs, including some delayed action, fell on it; four buildings were completely destroyed and others severely damaged. This, according to the records, caused no loss of production since the parts for assembly could be obtained from stock, but further attacks reduced slightly the number of Condors produced and there must have been some dislocation caused by the partial gutting of the Drawing Office. At any rate, the Focke-Wulf directorate

---

[1] Where five partly built U-boats were reported to be damaged. I.T.R. No. 14, 12th Jan. 1941.

[2] S. W. Roskill: *The War at Sea*, Vol. I, p. 261.

[3] The I.T.R. No. 20, 21st April 1941, nevertheless, stressed from the evidence of night photographs the immense effect of the dropping of two 4,000-lb. bombs which were first tried out over Emden. See the photograph following p. 194.

[4] S. W. Roskill: *The War at Sea*, Vol. I, pp. 336, 510-511.

were convinced that their factories were in great danger and began to remove them gradually to Marienburg in East Prussia and the Posen district of Poland. The plant was thus dispersed as well as moved to a safer position, though, as will be seen, it did not escape devastating attacks in later years. No immediate loss of production was caused by this move since the factory was not working at full capacity and the necessary machine tools and jigs had been set up in the new buildings without the necessity of stopping work at Bremen. A plan for the dispersal of the whole aircraft industry was prepared by the Air Ministry, but the industrialists refused to carry it out. No other aircraft company followed the example of Focke-Wulf for more than a year, and little had been done when the great attack on the aircraft industry began in 1943.[1]

Some towns not on the coast were also heavily hit. Of the larger towns we have a comprehensive record of the bombing of Cologne over a nine months' period. From 1st June 1941 to February 1942, Cologne was a primary target of Bomber Command on thirty-three nights and 2,010 sorties were flown against it, of which however only 111 were by heavy bombers. 6,600 H.E. bombs and 147,000 incendiaries were carried by those claiming to have attacked the target, of which the German records registered only 1,100 bombs and 12,000 incendiaries, sixteen per cent and eighteen per cent respectively. This seems a small proportion and does not fit in with the percentages recorded over the larger area mentioned above. But no doubt many of the bombs were dropped on other towns and were not entirely wasted on the open country. Though 138 people were killed and 277 injured and 947 residences destroyed or seriously damaged, there was little loss to industrial production, only two or three small factories being put completely out of action for a longer period than a week, while others were working at a reduced rate for similar short periods. No doubt some small loss of production was also caused by the effect on the workers.[2]

This record may be compared with that of Berlin where we have the complete A.R.P. records for the period 2nd June to 8th November 1941. Berlin was much more difficult to reach, but it was a much larger target when found. Bomber Command despatched 630 sorties during this period, of which just over half claimed to have attacked the target with 1,086 H.E. bombs. The German record shows that about one-third as many bombs fell within the city area and these must have included some from the aircraft which failed to return and

---

[1] *U.S.S.B.S. Aircraft Division Industry Report* (No. 4), p. 23. The special study of the Focke-Wulf aircraft plant by the *U.S.S.B.S.* (No. 10) barely mentions the raids of 1940–1941, which caused the dispersal.

[2] Comparison between raids on Cologne June 1941 to February 1942 and the Thousand raid from British records and German A.R.P. records in R.A.F. Narrative, *The R.A.F. in the Bombing Offensive against Germany*, Vol. III.

report, sixty-two in number. 133 people were killed, 369 injured and 4,705 people made homeless. Though the damage reported was occasionally a serious nuisance, such as the destruction of an overhead tramway system, the closing of streets to traffic and injuries to the railway stations, no appreciable effect was produced on war production during this period.[1]

These examples give a measure of the other towns attacked of which no records are available and they are confirmed by the replies of industrialists and others to the enquiries made after the war. Such important damage as was done was often quite accidental. Thus, the *Lang Motorenfabrik* at Mannheim had its foundry heavily damaged by two bombs on 18/19th September 1941 which were probably those reported as having hit a marshalling yard, and on 20/21st October 1941 a department of Krupps manufacturing small gear-wheels was burnt out as the result of an incendiary attack from an aircraft whose primary target was Gelsenkirchen.

In such circumstances it was not to be expected that such targets as marshalling yards or railway junctions would often be hit and, in fact, hardly any damage was caused to the communications of the Ruhr or any other part of north-west Germany during this period. This target system was, as has been seen, really only a pretext for the attack on the towns, and the hopes and plans of the early period of the war had in effect long been abandoned. One gallant effort had, however, seriously injured the Dortmund-Ems canal, which had so long been high on the programme of the Air Ministry. Attacks in June caused little damage, but one by Flight Lieutenant Learoyd on 12th August 1940 resulted in so serious a block that no boats could be passed through it for ten days.[2]

Finally, though it is not part of the strategic offensive against Germany, it must be remembered that Bomber Command made a considerable contribution to the defence of Britain by attacking barges and other shipping in French and Belgian ports in 1940 and also an immense effort against the German warships at Brest in 1941. Four of their bombs did inflict considerable damage on the *Gneisenau* on 10th April, but she had already been hit by a torpedo aimed by an aircraft of Coastal Command and would in any case not have been able to take part in the operations with the *Bismarck*. The *Scharnhorst*, though undamaged, was engaged in a refit and also unable to take part. This ship was later hit by five bombs at La Pallice and in

---

[1] The A.R.P. record was kept by the *Oberbürgermeister* at the Berlin *Rathaus*. One raid was reported in it when it is known that no British aircraft was anywhere near the area and it would seem that this raid came from Russia.

[2] Flight Lieutenant Learoyd was awarded the Victoria Cross for this feat. Among the boats delayed were motor boats meant to take part in the invasion of Britain, but this can hardly have had much effect on the invasion plans as is suggested in *Royal Air Force 1939–1945*, Vol. I, p. 182.

December and January some not very serious damage was inflicted on the repaired *Scharnhorst*.[1] Possibly greater results would have been obtained if the bombs hurled into Brest harbour had been used against the submarine pens on the Atlantic coast of France, then not fully protected by the concrete which resisted almost all later attacks. But here again it may be doubted if such targets could have been successfully attacked by the aircraft and tactics available at that time.[2] The attacks on the submarine yards in north Germany do not suggest that very favourable results would have been obtained. It is, of course, true that, if a much greater proportion of the resources of Bomber Command had been devoted to the defence against the German naval attack, the task of the Admiralty and Coastal Command might have been rendered somewhat easier. It is also true that but little was accomplished by Bomber Command during this period. But, if less effort had been put into the offensive, Bomber Command would have been even further from discovering how successful attacks could be made on German industry and transport and the final victory certainly postponed, if not jeopardised altogether.

---

[1] See Basil Collier: *The Defence of the United Kingdom* (1957), pp. 224–225, 227; S. W. Roskill: *The War at Sea*, Vol. I, p. 487. *The Prinz Eugen* also received a direct hit on the night of 1st July.

[2] Captain S. W. Roskill (*The War at Sea*, Vol. I. p. 459) indicates that an opportunity was lost, but he does not discuss the operational difficulties though earlier recording that no substantial damage was done to the submarine yards in N.W. Germany, targets no smaller than the Biscay submarine pens.

PART III

The Mounting Offensive and the Impact of Experience
November 1941–December 1942

INTRODUCTION

DURING this period there was virtually no quantitative expansion in the available front-line strength of Bomber Command. In November 1941 the daily average of aircraft available with crews for operations was 506. In January 1943 it was 515. But the force of January 1943 had undergone an important qualitative improvement. In terms of aircraft available for operations, it included a daily average of 178 Lancasters and seventeen Mosquitoes. It did not include any Blenheims, Whitleys or Hampdens, which had been taken out of service between May and September 1942 and which, together, had accounted for more than half of the available force in November 1941. Moreover, the force of November 1941 had no radar aids to navigation and bomb aiming. That of January 1943 was extensively equipped with *Gee*, it had a small *Oboe* Mosquito element and some of its aircraft had been fitted with *H2S*.[1]

These developments, however, had more bearing upon the operations of 1943 than upon those of 1942. Apart from the introduction of *Gee*, which began in March 1942, they occurred towards the end, and, in the case of the introduction of *H2S*, after the end of the year. Though Lancasters came into operational service in March 1942, only an average of seven per night were available in that month and it was not until November that this figure rose above a hundred. Nevertheless, Bomber Command was an incomparably more effective weapon in 1942 than it had been in 1941.

The underlying reasons for this advance are analysed in the second of the chapters which follow. Among them was the performance of *Gee* which, at least until it was jammed in August 1942, had a great effect upon the ability of Bomber Command to concentrate. Also, and partly on the basis of *Gee*, important new bombing techniques were devised and tested in action. After August, these were elaborated by the Pathfinder Force which was created in that month. Another development of great significance was the reorganisation of the bomber crew which occurred early in the year. Second pilots were dropped and a single pilot policy was adopted throughout Bomber Command. Thus, higher standards could be achieved and more aircraft could be put into the air at the same time. This was a vital factor in making possible the 'Thousand' bomber attacks in the summer. The rest of the crew was also reorganised. A rational division of labour was introduced which made for greater specialisation and

---

[1] See pp. 316–317, where a short account of these devices is given and Annex I, for a more detailed description.

INTRODUCTION

much greater efficiency.[1] Thus, Bomber Command prepared itself for the new aircraft with their more complex equipment. In another way too it was prepared for a greater future. In February 1942 Air Marshal Harris became Commander-in-Chief.

The combination of these and other favourable developments was not, of course, sufficient to enable Bomber Command to exert decisive pressure upon Germany in 1942. The force was still much too small for that. Moreover, it was still regularly plundered in the interests of other theatres and of functions other than the strategic air offensive. Nevertheless, it was sufficient, in so far as it lay within the power of Bomber Command to do so, to surmount the crisis which beset the force in the first half of 1942. This crisis, of which the transfer of Bomber Command aircraft to Coastal Command and the Middle East Air Forces was one of the most obvious symptoms, raised the question of whether the force should be given the strategic impetus and the production and manpower resources to develop a sustained and long-term strategic air offensive against the heart of Germany.

It arose partly from the disillusioning experience of Bomber Command in the previous two years, which was reflected in the declining confidence of the Prime Minister, and partly from the generally desperate situation of the newly formed Grand Alliance. It led to criticisms of the Air Staff bombing policy, as it was restated in a directive of February 1942, on the grounds that it could not be carried out operationally and also that it was not strategically defensive. It would, after all, be no good laying plans for an ultimately effective air offensive if this involved, through neglect of defensive plans, the loss of the war in the meantime. In view of what Bomber Command had achieved in 1940 and 1941 there was some reason for fearing that the air offensive might not, even ultimately, be effective and, in view of what the Axis was achieving in Russia, in the Middle East, in the Pacific and in the Atlantic, there was also reason to fear that the war might be lost in the meantime. What was needed to lend substance to the Air Staff directive of February 1942 was neither promises nor calculations by partial or impartial minds. It was recognisable victories in the field of action.

These victories were won. They started with a remarkable precision attack on the Renault factory near Paris in March 1942. They continued with the successful area attacks on Lübeck and Rostock later in the month and in April. They culminated in the famous Thousand Bomber attack on Cologne at the end of May. By these crucial operations the destructive potential of Bomber Command was demonstrated. Confidence in the plan for the strategic air offensive

---

[1] See Annex III.

began to return and good reason was given for believing that it might ultimately be effective. The positive result was that the strategic offensive was given a prominent place in the grand strategy of the war when, as the Grand Alliance began to emerge from the straits to which it had been reduced by German and Japanese advances, more and more attention came to be focussed upon the means of achieving victory rather than upon those of averting defeat.

This place, due in large measure to the early victories of Sir Arthur Harris, was, however, less than he had hoped, for the grand strategy of the war was essentially conventional. Victory was to arise from the defeat of the enemy armies in the field. The strategic air offensive was to be developed, not as an instrument of outright victory, but as the means of softening Germany at the centre so that the armies could prevail from the edges.

The definition of this role for the bombing offensive, which was to be formally expressed at the Casablanca Conference in January 1943, did not, however, determine the bombing policy by which it should be sought, and it was this issue which produced another crisis for the strategic air offensive. To some extent, the Bomber Command operations of 1942 were a determining factor. Despite the great successes at the Renault factory, at Lübeck and Rostock and at Cologne, there were also a larger number of reverses and disappointments. Two subsequent Thousand bomber attacks went largely astray, persistent attempts to strike the middle of Essen produced scarcely any success and experiments in the use of heavy aircraft of Bomber Command in daylight were disastrously frustrated. Moreover, even the successes were due to special conditions which could not be expected on other occasions.

The operational lessons of the campaign were obvious. Against major targets and in major strength, Bomber Command could not operate in daylight, nor could it achieve precision results at night. Even for the purposes of systematic success in the area offensive at night it required not only radical expansion but also a further and great tactical development. Moreover, the German night air defences were rapidly improving in efficiency.

These limitations, however, were not necessarily permanent, nor, even if they were, did they determine whether the area offensive should be devoted to general or to selective purposes. There was thus a great deal of surviving scope for argument about bombing policy which was further complicated by the intervention of United States bombing forces.

The Americans had determined that their bombers should operate in daylight, and in the course of 1942 they adopted an elaborate plan for a selective precision offensive against what were regarded as key points in the German war economy. Though American bombers did not cross the German frontiers in 1942, it was obvious that, in numbers at least, they might eventually become the predominant element in the combined bomber offensive.

Thus the development of bombing policy, which is considered in the first of the chapters which follow, was, in the first half of the period, chiefly influenced by the need to establish a place for the strategic air offensive in the grand strategy of the war and, in the second half, by that of considering the requirements of a combined Anglo-American bomber offensive. Upon these considerations both the operational advances and the continuing operational limitations of the period, which are considered in the second chapter, exerted a profound and in some respects a decisive influence.

The period was, therefore, also one in which all the agencies concerned had to reconsider their views as to how the greatest economic damage could be inflicted on Germany by the immediate force available and the much greater weight of attack that would be forthcoming in the future. Clearly the best method of discovering what could and should be done would have been the closest co-operation between those who possessed the fullest information about German industry and the Air Ministry and Bomber Command. So far as the Air Ministry was concerned this co-operation which had already been established was maintained throughout this period. But this readiness to consider economic advice and to give in return the fullest possible information on operational possibilities did not extend to Bomber Command. The controversy which began in this period extended throughout the rest of the offensive.

The general appreciations of the German economy made by the Ministry of Economic Warfare and the Joint Intelligence Committee continued to repeat the error that it was so stretched that any damage to it would diminish war production. But a much greater realism was shown in this period in estimating the results of the bombing. In September 1941 the Operational Research Section was set up by Bomber Command and it began to make scientific surveys of operational results of each raid from the photographic evidence. This same material, after interpretation by the Central Interpretation Unit at Medmenham, was used by M.E.W. to estimate the economic effects of the damage done. Meanwhile, use was made of the scientific survey of the extent of the damage produced in Britain by the German raids of the previous twelve months which was undertaken by the Research Department of the Ministry of Home Security and the special organisation (R.E.8) which it proceeded to set up for this purpose. Thus, while the estimates of Bomber Command itself still continued to be influenced by the desire to show that it could, if sufficiently reinforced, play a deciding role in the war, the more considered appreciations of M.E.W. and R.E.8 provided a corrective.

Though morale had been specifically designated as a main objective, little reference was made to it by any of these agencies, but the Foreign Office still continued to believe that it was gravely affected by the attacks of this year.

In reality the damage inflicted on Germany up to the end of 1942, while by no means negligible, had but little effect on her war production or the morale of her population. The realisation that armaments production must be increased was caused more by the situation in Russia and the Mediterranean than by the attacks of Bomber Command, and priority was still given to those weapons most important to the fighting on land. While considerable effect was for a time produced at first on those concerned with morale and production, such as Goebbels, Milch and Speer, this anxiety does not seem to have extended except to a very limited degree to Hitler himself or the higher command. At the same time this limited experience provided an opportunity to organise the means by which the effects of the bombing could be reduced and immediate assistance be given to the inhabitants of the bombed cities. The experience prepared to some extent the German people and those directing their economy for the much greater ordeal of 1943.

Meanwhile, Speer had begun to reorganise German industry, and though his sphere was still limited the effects were already apparent. There was a great increase in war production and plans were made for a much greater advance in the next eighteen months. And though there was some decrease in the standard of living of the civilian population this was obtained without any excessive burdens being placed upon them.

CHAPTER VI

THE MOUNTING OFFENSIVE: THE CRISIS OF STRATEGIC BOMBING
November 1941–December 1942

Note on Bomber Command radar aids introduced between March 1942 and January 1943

1. The consequences of failure: Bombing policy assailed. November 1941–March 1942
2. An improving prospect: General and selective policies. April–September 1942
3. The American intervention and the strategic problems of a daylight policy. September–November 1942
4. The role of strategic bombing and the outlook for 1943. October to December 1942

'Victory speedy and complete, awaits the side which first employs air power as it should be employed.'
SIR ARTHUR HARRIS, 17th June 1942

'... a policy of bombing German towns wholesale ... cannot have a decisive effect by the middle of 1943, even if all heavy bombers and the great majority of Wellingtons produced are used primarily for this purpose.'
SIR HENRY TIZARD, 20th April 1942

Note on Bomber Command radar aids introduced between March 1942 and January 1943

The introduction in this period of *Gee*, *Oboe* and *H2S* wrought a great change in the operational abilities of Bomber Command and, therefore, also exerted an important influence upon the making of bombing policy. These devices, which had advantages and disadvantages, and others of later origin, are described in Annex I of Volume IV, but for the sake of convenience a brief note on *Gee*, *Oboe* and *H2S* is inserted here. A note on *G–H*, which was introduced in a later period, is given in the relevant place on p. 149, Volume II.

Gee, initially known as T.R. 1335 and sometimes referred to as 'G', underwent service trials and operational tests in 1941 and was introduced into general service in March 1942. The system, which was later extended to cover a number of different 'chains', depended, in each case, upon transmissions from three stations in Britain (one 'master' station and two 'slaves').

The pulses of these transmissions were displayed on a cathode-ray tube in the aircraft and, by measuring the time interval between their reception, the navigator was able to select the two *Gee* co-ordinates, which were drawn as lattice lines on a navigator's chart, on which his aircraft was placed. The position, as determined by the point of intersection, was then converted into longitude and latitude and transferred to the plotting chart. Thus, a 'fix' could be obtained, provided, of course, that the *Gee* transmissions were not jammed, which, after August 1942 and over Germany, they generally were.

By a reverse process, as a means of blind bombing or of homing to base, the navigator could set up the co-ordinates of the point which he wished to reach on the cathode-ray tube and then direct the pilot to steer in such a way that the pulses were brought into line. The aircraft would then, if the *Gee* was skilfully tuned, be over the required point. This method made it difficult to keep an air plot, which, in the event of *Gee* failure or German jamming, was needed.

Gee was not dependent upon radio echo and was therefore technically not a radar device. It was, however, generally referred to as such.

Oboe was a bearing and distance radar device for enabling an aircraft to fly down a radio beam until a predetermined point was reached. It was introduced into operational service in December 1942. The system depended upon transmitters and receivers in Britain which sent out directional signals and picked up the echo reflected by the aircraft. By this means the controller on the ground could direct the course of the aircraft and determine the moment at which it had reached its destination. The pilot received signals orally which indicated deviations to one side or the other of the correct path and also the point of arrival at his destination. *Oboe*, which had a higher degree of accuracy than *Gee*, could thus be used as a blind bombing or blind marking device.

It could be used with a strictly limited number of aircraft at one time and, because the transmissions went off at a tangent to the curvature of the earth, was limited in range by the ceiling of the aircraft using it.

H2S was an adaptation of the Coastal Command radar device known as A.S.V. which was used for detecting ships on the surface. It was introduced into general service in January 1943. The equipment was exclusively carried in the aircraft and consisted of a rotating transmitter, which 'scanned' the ground beneath the aircraft, and a receiver, which picked up the radio echo and displayed the result on a cathode-ray tube. Owing to the fact that different kinds of ground gave different responses and water and land gave different responses, it was possible for the navigator to trace the shape of coastlines, rivers and built-up areas and so on from the cathode-ray tube. By comparing these with *H2S* maps he was able to establish his position by the method of 'pin pointing' or the measurement of bearings and distances. Thus, *H2S* could be used for navigation and, when the image was sufficiently distinct, which often it was not, for blind bombing.

A high degree of skill was required in interpreting the *H2S* picture and the *H2S* transmissions disclosed the position of the aircraft to German early warning and airborne interception devices.

1. The consequences of failure: bombing policy assailed, November 1941–March 1942

By the end of 1941 Bomber Command was involved in a deep but not unrelieved depression. The high hopes which had been placed in it at the outbreak of the war had been frustrated by the first two years of the campaign. On the other hand, the lessons of experience had produced the prospect of better things to come. Nevertheless, the unpleasant fact remained that whatever successes Bomber Command might expect in the future, it could point to few in the past.

It is true that much of the optimism which had characterised the early plans for Bomber Command had been tempered by the knowledge that the force, with its initial war strength, was too small to mount a full-scale offensive of a kind which might be expected to produce decisive results against Germany. Those who were still optimistic could, with justice, point to the failure adequately to expand the force which, since the fall of France, had represented the sole means of striking offensive and direct blows against Germany.

The programme of expansion for Bomber Command had, indeed, been gravely retarded by the need to build up strength in other segments of air power and in other theatres of war. The priority which had, since 1938, been afforded to Fighter Command had, perhaps, saved the country from defeat in 1940, but it had also blunted the blow which Bomber Command could strike against Germany. The needs of Coastal Command and the Middle East Command had often been met even more directly at the expense of Bomber Command.

Nor were the effects of these and other requirements confined to the numbers of aircraft and crews passing to or remaining in Bomber Command. The situations which created them also frequently diverted the bombing offensive from its central theme. During the first two years of the war a high proportion of Bomber Command sorties were flown in support of the army during the Battle of France, of Fighter Command during the Battle of Britain and, above all, in support of the Navy during the continuing Battle of the Atlantic. Many sorties had also been flown against invasion barge concentrations.

The penalty of weakness in numbers and dispersal of effort was, as the Air Staff knew well enough, failure to make an impression on the German homeland. Nevertheless, these factors were not the operative explanation of the disappointments which had occurred. The fundamental and more disquieting explanation was the failure of the night bombers to find and hit their targets. This consideration was now uppermost in the minds of those who directed the force. It largely dictated the bombing policy which was about to be adopted, for it was evident that if Bomber Command was to lay claim to the great resources needed for its expansion, it would first have to give an effective demonstration of its potentially war-winning capabilities. At the end of 1941 no such demonstration had been given. 1942 was, therefore, seen to be a decisive year in the history of Bomber Command.

Meanwhile, astounding changes had taken place in the general war situation. Hitler's summer *Blitzkrieg* in Russia had failed. The wound had been deep, but not mortal. In the winter it was the turn of the German army to suffer deprivations and its first important defeats of the Second World War. While these gigantic events were being unfolded in Russia, Japan attacked the American fleet at Pearl Harbour and Hitler declared war on the United States of America.

These circumstances, which ultimately led to the downfall of Nazi Germany, had an immediately unfavourable effect upon Bomber Command. The strategic bombing offensive no longer seemed to represent the sole means of attacking Germany. As the Prime Minister was to put it, 'In the days when we were fighting alone, we answered the question: "How are you going to win the war?" by saying: "We will shatter Germany by bombing." Since then the enormous injuries inflicted on the German Army and man-power by the Russians, and the accession of the man-power and munitions of the United States, have rendered other possibilities open.'[1]

Not only, however, was one of the principal arguments in favour of the strategic bombing offensive somewhat blunted by these 'other possibilities', but the prospects of expanding Bomber Command to the formidable dimensions demanded by the Air Staff were rendered more distant. As Sir Charles Portal explained to Sir Richard Peirse, 'the entry of Japan into the war has caused the United States to place an embargo, total at present, on the export of munitions to the Allies. We, on the other hand are trying to fulfil our promise to Russia, to send reinforcements to the Far East and to maintain up to full strength the units which are in the forefront of the battle in the Middle East. Not only', Sir Charles Portal continued, 'are our liabilities heavier than ever before, but our expectations too have been seriously upset.'[2]

The total embargo on the export of American arms was, of course, temporary, but the policy that American aircraft should, whenever possible, be flown by American crews and commanded by American officers was permanent. Though Bomber Command was in the future to receive much material assistance from America, notably in the

---

[1] Churchill: *The Second World War*, Vol. IV, (1951), p. 783.
[2] Letter Portal to Peirse, 11th Dec. 1941.

supply of Packard-Merlin engines, the prospects of its ultimate expansion seemed to be much curtailed. Henceforth, the bombing offensive was no longer a purely British concern. The policy and efficiency of the United States Army Air Forces became factors of ever-increasing importance in its conduct.

At the Washington War Conference of December 1941 and January 1942 Britain and the United States had reaffirmed the strategic plan agreed between themselves in August 1941. Germany was to be regarded as the principal enemy and, until she had been defeated, only holding actions against Japan should be undertaken. Prominent in the plan of action against Germany was the wearing down of her war effort by bombing.[1] Nevertheless, the American Air Force was as yet an untried weapon of war, which many of the British tended to regard with some doubt. Thus, it was difficult to measure the consequences of the diversion of so large a production potential from the Royal Air Force to the United States Army Air Forces.

Despite all these difficulties and doubts the British Air Staff had, by the beginning of February 1942, come to the conclusion that the time had arrived for a resumption of the offensive against Germany. Since the conservation directive of November 1941, the attack on Germany had been restricted with a view to gathering strength for the spring of 1942 when more effective methods of attack would be available. Between 10th December 1941, when Bomber Command had been directed to focus its principal attack on the three German battle cruisers at Brest,[2] and 20th January 1942, no less than thirty-seven per cent of the total Bomber Command effort had been harnessed to this unrewarding task.[3] Such a state of affairs, though acceptable to the Air Staff before the *Gee* apparatus was ready for operations, became most irksome when they had enough sets to equip a reasonable porportion of the bomber force.

Accordingly, on 9th February 1942, Sir Archibald Sinclair presented the Air Staff case to his colleagues on the Defence Committee. 'The time has come,' he said, 'for a greater bombing effort to be made against Germany for the following reasons:

(i) This is the time of year to get the best effect from concentrated incendiary attack.
(ii) It would enhearten and support the Russians to resume our offensive on a heavy scale while they are maintaining so effectively their own counter-offensive against the German armies.

---

[1] Memo. by U.S. and British C.O.S., 20th Jan. 1942.

[2] Dir. Air Min. to Bomber Cmd., 10th Dec. 1941, App. 8 (xxi). Japanese successes had placed a premium upon the destruction of German warships which, by their mere existence, contained large British naval forces in home waters.

[3] Draft Air Memo., 4th Feb. 1942. The memorandum of the Secretary of State, 9th Feb. 1942, which is cited below, was based on this draft.

(iii) The coincidence of attacks with Russian successes would further depress German morale.
(iv) A new navigational aid is about to come into service. It is advisable to use it now to the full, both for the above reasons and because, once we start it, the device will probably only have a short life before the enemy provides effective counter-measures.'

This 'new navigational aid' by which, of course, Sir Archibald Sinclair meant *Gee*, covered north-west Germany and 'in particular the Ruhr and Rhineland'. He explained that the best way of exploiting the device was considered by the Air Staff to be firstly by 'concentrated incendiary attacks on the principal industrial areas in the Ruhr-Rhineland area and north-west Germany ... secondly when really favourable conditions occur by attacking precise targets of the most decisive economic character.'[1] In suggesting this policy, Sir Archibald Sinclair did not ignore the 'high importance' of attacking Brest. 'Our experience has, however, shown', he said, 'that there is little value in continuing to divert a large effort against this objective, since the target area is invariably obscured by smoke in a very short time after the arrival of the first few aircraft. Daylight attacks on Brest', he continued, 'are not, in the opinion of the Air Staff, justifiable, because the chance of securing a hit on one of the ships is extremely small and the casualties are certain to be very heavy.'

It was obvious that little headway could be made with the Air Staff policy which had thus been indicated to the Defence Committee until Bomber Command was freed, at least to some extent, from its heavy commitment of assisting the Navy in the Battle of the Atlantic. At the same time this battle was approaching yet another crisis, which was closely associated with Japanese naval triumphs in the Far East. It was obvious to all that the whole allied war effort depended upon the successful outcome of this gruelling and long-drawn-out maritime struggle. But it was also likely that there would be differences of opinion as to the division of effort which should be made between offence, that is the strategic attack on Germany, and defence, that is, in this case, participation in the Battle of the Atlantic.

Such differences of opinion were likely to be nourished not only by

---

[1] The targets suggested were:

Primary Industrial Areas: Essen, Cologne, Duisburg, Düsseldorf, Gelsenkirchen, Bremen, Wilhelmshaven and Emden.

Alternative Industrial Areas beyond Gee Range: Hamburg, Kiel, Lübeck, Rostock, Kassel, Hanover, Wetzlar, Jena, Frankfurt, Mannheim, Schweinfurt and Stuttgart.

Precise Targets: Hüls (rubber), Gelsenkirchen Nordstern (oil), Gelsenkirchen Buer (oil), Wesseling (oil), Remscheid (aero crankshaft forgings) and Krefeld (aero crankshaft forgings).

Precise Targets beyond Gee Range: Schkopau (rubber), Leuna (oil), Frankfurt-Heddernheim (airscrews) and Stuttgart-Feuerbach (Bosch). Memo by Sinclair for Defence Cttee., 9th Feb. 1942.

different views of the gravity of the situation at sea and the appropriate action to be taken, but also by varying degrees of confidence in the effectiveness of the proposed strategic bombing offensive. To those who believed that a sustained air attack on Germany would reduce her to a point at which she could no longer defend herself, the prospect of a continuing diversion in the Battle of the Atlantic was hard to justify except in dire emergency. To those, on the other hand, who had little faith in strategic bombing, or whose confidence had been shaken by the campaigns of 1940 and 1941, such a diversion was the more readily permissible.

Sir Charles Portal was under no delusions as to these probable differences of opinion and he expected that opposition from the Navy to the suggested bombing policy would develop into a 'general attack on the "Heavy Bomber" . . .' Nevertheless, seeing that the Air Staff case was 'really founded on "Gee",' he thought that it might therefore 'get through'.[1]

Any difficulties, however, which may have been anticipated from the presence of the *Scharnhorst* and *Gneisenau* at Brest were removed by the enemy. On 12th February these two famous warships, despite a series of most gallant attacks delivered by the Royal Air Force and Fleet Air Arm in appalling weather, made good their escape up the Channel.[2] The 'Brest question' had thus, in the words of the Prime Minister, 'settled itself by the escape of the enemy'. Mr. Churchill added that he was 'entirely in favour of the resumption of full bombing of Germany, subject always, of course, to our not incurring heavy losses owing to bad weather and enemy resistance combined.'[3]

Sir Archibald Sinclair took this to mean that the policy of conservation enforced by the directive of 13th November 1941[4] was at an end. 'The bomber offensive', he told Sir Charles Portal and the Deputy Chief of the Air Staff, Air Vice-Marshal Bottomley, 'should be resumed as soon as the weather experts give us the prospect of two or three fine nights in succession. Thereafter', he said, 'it should be sustained at the maximum intensity of which Bomber Command is capable. We are bound to accept big risks from enemy action; nor can Bomber Command expect perfect weather every night. Weather risks, must, however,' Sir Archibald Sinclair concluded, 'be measured against the importance of the contemplated operations.'[5]

The new bombing directive, which was issued on 14th February

---

[1] Min. Portal to Sinclair, 7th Feb. 1942.

[2] The *Gneisenau*, however, was badly damaged by mines previously laid from the air.

[3] Min. Maudling (Assistant Private Sec. to Sinclair) to Sinclair, Portal and Bottomley, 14th Feb. 1942, repeating Prime Minister's minute of same date. The Prime Minister had recently received the reports bearing on the costly operations of 7/8th November 1941. See above, pp. 254–256.

[4] See above, pp. 186–187.

[5] Min. Sinclair to Portal and Bottomley, 14th Feb. 1942.

1942, accordingly authorised the Commander-in-Chief[1] to employ his effort 'without restriction'. This, however, was not to be taken as a warrant to press attacks if the 'weather conditions are unfavourable or if your aircraft are likely to be exposed to extreme hazards'. The Commander-in-Chief was told that the Air Staff expected the introduction of *Gee* to 'confer upon your forces the ability to concentrate their effort to an extent which has not hitherto been possible,' and that during its effective life it would 'enable results to be obtained of a much more effective nature' than hitherto. Since, however, the effective life of *Gee* was not expected to exceed six months at most, the importance of exerting the greatest possible effort in this crucial period was stressed.

The directive laid down that the 'primary object' of these operations 'should now be focussed on the morale of the enemy civil population and in particular, of the industrial workers.' With this aim in view four industrial areas of the Ruhr and Rhineland, all lying within *Gee* range, were selected as the primary targets. They were Essen, which was regarded as the most important, Duisburg, Düsseldorf and Cologne. Three further area targets within range of *Gee* and also on the coast were chosen as alternatives. These were Bremen, Wilhelmshaven and Emden. A third list of area targets, situated beyond *Gee* range in northern, central and southern Germany, was added. These were to be attacked when conditions were 'particularly favourable'. Berlin was included in this list but the intention was to mount only a 'harassing' attack on the capital. In all other cases, the Commander-in-Chief was invited to concentrate on each target until 'the effort estimated to be required for its destruction has been achieved.'

Gee would, of course, be a considerable help to aircraft bombing beyond its range, for it would enable them to make an accurate start to their flights. It was also thought that it might make a resumption of precision bombing possible. For this event a number of oil, rubber and power plants were selected.

The directive concluded with the usual provisos about probable diversions notably against German warships and submarine building yards but also against French factories working for Germany which had already been allotted as targets in a directive of 5th February 1942.[2]

The lists of area targets given in the appendix to this directive had, in each case, included a mention of the industrial function which made the town important. Sir Charles Portal evidently felt that this

---

[1] Air Vice-Marshal J. E. A. Baldwin was acting Air Officer Commanding-in-Chief, Bomber Command. Sir Richard Peirse had laid down the command on 8th January 1942. Air Marshal Harris assumed it on 22nd February 1942.

[2] Dir. Bottomley to Baldwin, 14th Feb. 1942, App. 8 (xxii).

might cause confusion, and on 15th February 1942 he addressed the following minute to Air Vice-Marshal Bottomley:

> 'Ref the new bombing directive: I suppose it is clear that the aiming points are to be the built-up areas, *not*, for instance, the dockyards or aircraft factories where these are mentioned in Appendix A.
> This must be made quite clear if it is not already understood.'[1]

Air Commodore Baker, the Director of Bomber Operations, spoke to Air Vice-Marshal Baldwin about this and the point was recorded at Bomber Command so that it would be 'available to Air Marshal Harris when he arrives.'[2]

This directive of 14th February 1942 was not superseded until February 1943, and even then it was possible to argue that it had been no more than confirmed. As a general statement of bombing policy, especially when considered with Sir Charles Portal's explanatory note, it possessed, in some respects, considerable clarity. It was at least obvious that Bomber Command was to turn primarily to the attack on German civilian morale, particularly that of her industrial workers in the Ruhr. That other targets should be included was inevitable, if only to prevent a concentration of the German defences. All the same, the directive did not exclude other objects from the practice of area bombing. The inclusion of Schweinfurt, the centre of the German ball-bearings industry, in the list of alternative area targets was particularly significant. From this it might be inferred that area bombing, apart from seeking a general industrial dislocation, might be used to destroy a particular industrial complex, that it might, in other words, be harnessed to the purposes of selective attack.

Nor did the directive exclude the possibility of renewed precision bombing, which, if found practicable, would presumably be applied against what the Secretary of State had described as 'precise targets of the most decisive economic character.' Finally, the inclusion of such a relatively unimportant place as Lübeck, which happened to be especially inflammable, in the target lists, showed the extent, at any rate in the initial and experimental phase of the campaign, to which a town might become a target mainly because it was operationally vulnerable.

These considerations show that the February Directive did not make the objects of the bombing offensive as clear as a first glance might suggest. For the present it is sufficient to bear these points in mind. In due course it will be shown how the directive lent itself to

---

[1] Min. Portal to Bottomley, 15th Feb. 1942. The original of this minute is written in pencil by Sir Charles Portal.
[2] Min. Baker to Portal, 16th Feb. 1942.

various interpretations and how it permitted differences of opinion to grow within the Air Staff and more particularly between the Air Staff and the Commander-in-Chief Bomber Command. Meanwhile, it should be recognised that some uncertainty was inevitable in February 1942 when Bomber Command was about to embark on revolutionary operational methods. Nevertheless, while excessive rigidity is certainly a vice, clarity is also a virtue.[1]

Meanwhile, it is necessary to turn to broader matters concerned not with the alternative ways in which the strategic bombing offensive might be conducted but with the question of whether that offensive should be conducted at all, and whether there were not perhaps other employments for the heavy bomber which might prove more lucrative than the continued long-range assault on Germany.

The opposition to the Air Staff bombing policy which Sir Charles Portal had anticipated from the Navy did not, in the first instance, at any rate at responsible levels, seem to oppose insuperable obstacles in the way of its acceptance. Indeed, on 14th February 1942, which was a pregnant date in air history, the First Lord of the Admiralty said in a memorandum for the Defence Committee that there were 'no objections' so far as the Admiralty was concerned to the bombing policy which had been proposed by the Secretary of State for Air.[2] Nevertheless, the Admiralty's policy was going to make its execution difficult; for Mr. Alexander qualified this approval with the proviso that certain naval requirements of long-range General Reconnaissance aircraft should be met. His immediate requirements were, he explained, for the Battle of the Atlantic and for the Indian Ocean. As far as Bomber Command was concerned, this demand entailed the transfer of six and a half Wellington squadrons to Coastal Command and the despatch of two Bomber Command squadrons to Ceylon for long-range reconnaissance work.[3] 'It must be clearly understood,' the First Lord of the Admiralty further observed, 'that these Naval requirements are not final and are confined to those requirements that are considered to be immediate in order to deal with the increasing U-Boat attack and the extension of the Naval war to the Indian Ocean.' Finally, Mr. Alexander recorded the Admiralty opinion that

---

[1] In February 1940, while Air Vice-Marshal Bottomley was S.A.S.O., Bomber Command, a document drafted by a member of the Staff came before him and struck him as being 'full of uncertain meaning and lacking in clarity.' He suggested that 'We must be most careful that our memos and correspondence are clear and not subject to misunderstanding, especially in war. Our documents', he continued, 'should be without reproach in this respect and an example to subordinate formations. If we can't put out a useful clear helpful directive on this matter, it is better not to put anything out.' Min. by Bottomley. These admirable sentiments did not flourish in the confusion and controversy of war.

[2] And which, as has been seen, had already been communicated to Bomber Command.

[3] At the same time, the Admiralty demanded eighty-one Fortresses and Liberators for Coastal Command and the transfer of three Catalina Squadrons from Coastal Command to the Indian Ocean. These were to be followed by a fourth as soon as possible.

still further bomber squadrons should be 'thoroughly trained in homing on to a reconnaissance aircraft which is shadowing enemy forces at sea, and in the technique of bombing moving targets at sea.'[1]

Within a short time, the Admiralty formulated further demands. These included the institution of Coastal Commands overseas and the transfer to them and to the home Coastal Command of yet more long-range bombers.[2] It was questionable whether these suggested transfers of long-range bombers would produce good results. 'Our experience has clearly proved', Sir Archibald Sinclair explained to the Defence Committee in a note of 8th March 1942, 'that Long-Range General Reconnaissance duties can only be usefully undertaken by aircraft fitted with A.S.V. The installation of this equipment', the Secretary of State for Air continued, 'is a lengthy process and no squadrons from Bomber Command could be modified and put into operation for some months. By this time', he suggested, 'the planned expansion of Coastal Command in Long-Range G/R aircraft will already have made good the present weakness.' Meanwhile, 'the transfer of bomber squadrons without the necessary modification would', Sir Archibald Sinclair claimed, 'be a dispersion of our bombing resources in an attempt to contribute defensively to the control of sea communications over immense areas of ocean where targets are uncertain, fleeting and difficult to hit. Their efforts in this direction would be largely wasted.'

Sir Archibald Sinclair was not, however, only concerned with the probable ineffectiveness of the long-range bombers if they were applied to the purposes which the Admiralty demanded. He was also, of course, concerned with the effects which these deprivations would have upon the strategic attack against Germany. 'It remains the considered view of the Air Staff', he said, 'that squadrons of Bomber Command could best contribute to the weakening of the U-boat offensive by offensive action against the principal industrial areas of Germany within our range, including the main naval industries and dockyards. To divert them to an uneconomical defensive role would be unsound at any time. It would', he pointed out, 'be doubly so now when we are about to launch a bombing offensive with the aid of a new technique of which we have high expectations and which will enable us to deliver a heavy and concentrated blow against Germany at a moment when German morale is low and when the Russians are in great need of our assistance.'[3]

Nevertheless, none could deny the truth of the sentence with which Sir Dudley Pound had opened the last Admiralty memorandum. 'If

---

[1] Memo. by Alexander, 14th Feb. 1942.
[2] Memo. by Pound, circulated to Defence Cttee. by Alexander, 6th March 1942.
[3] Memo. by Sinclair, 8th March 1942.

we lose the war at sea,' he had said, 'we lose the war.'[1] The issue did not, however, turn upon an estimate of the actual gravity of the situation at sea. As Mr. Churchill has written, 'The Battle of the Atlantic was the dominating factor all through the war. Never for one moment could we forget that everything happening elsewhere, on land, at sea, or in the air, depended ultimately on its outcome, and amid all other cares we viewed its changing fortunes day by day with hope or apprehension.'[2] Neither at the beginning of 1942 nor in the years before did the Air Staff deny their responsibility to join in this struggle. Sir Archibald Sinclair had concluded his memorandum of 8th March 1942 with the statement that it was 'incumbent' upon the Air Ministry to do its utmost 'to meet Admiralty requirements as expeditiously as possible.'[3] A few weeks later Sir Charles Portal was to write in a further memorandum for the Defence Committee, 'the Air Ministry fully share the Admiralty view that the present situation at sea calls for substantially increased assistance from the Royal Air Force.'[4]

The real divergence of opinion revealed itself then not as to the state of the war at sea but as to the measures which should be taken to win it. The Naval Staff clearly thought that increasing numbers of long-range bombers should be tactically committed to the actual zones of encounter, and that this should be done regardless of the effect which it might have upon the strategic air offensive against Germany. Though the Air Staff was prepared to make considerable sacrifices to meet this naval argument, they naturally found it contrary to the basic doctrine which lay behind the creation of Bomber Command. They believed that the diversion and dispersal of heavy bombers to the struggle at sea should be kept to the absolute minimum consistent with survival. The real function of the heavy bomber, they argued, was to concentrate on strategic attacks against the heart of the enemy. Thus, by destroying Germany's war potential they would also destroy her naval power. Certainly the Air Staff could never have justified to themselves a policy of removing the heavy bombers from an activity in which they believed they could succeed, that is the strategic attack on Germany, and introducing them to another in which they thought they would fail, that is the destruction of surface and submarine vessels at sea.

These arguments had many ramifications and refinements, but enough has been said to show that the crucial point in dispute was an estimate of the value of the strategic air offensive. Arguments about what Bomber Command was going to achieve in 1943 or even 1944 were liable to appear to those who considered 1940 and 1941 as mere

---
[1] Memo. by Pound for Defence Cttee., 6th March 1942.
[2] Churchill: *The Second World War*, Vol. V, (1952), p. 6.
[3] Memo. by Sinclair, 8th March 1942.
[4] Memo. by Portal circulated to Defence Cttee. by Sinclair, 1st April 1942.

pious hopes. Especially was this so when so many crises pressed upon Britain in other fields of war activity.[1]

Indeed, it seemed not impossible that the Grand Alliance would be shattered at the moment of its conception. Following the destruction of so much of the American fleet at Pearl Harbour, the allied cause suffered a series of immeasurable disasters. On 10th December 1941 the *Prince of Wales* and *Repulse* were sunk off the Malayan coast by Japanese aircraft. On Christmas Day Hong Kong surrendered to Japanese forces. On 1st February 1942 the British army evacuated Derna in the Western Desert, and on 15th February Singapore capitulated, an event which the Prime Minister signalised as 'the greatest disaster in our history.'[2]

While Japan swept forward to the most rapid conquest of an Empire which the world has seen, while the German U-boats reaped a veritable harvest of allied shipping, while Rommel stood triumphant in Libya and while Russia prepared to receive a renewed onslaught from the German army, British public opinion became disturbed and perplexed. These feelings were reflected in Parliament and the Prime Minister found it necessary to reconstruct the Cabinet. The inclusion of Sir Stafford Cripps as Lord Privy Seal was presently to be the cause of some embarrassment to the Air Staff.[3]

In a speech to the House of Commons on 25th February 1942 when he was winding up a two-day debate on the war situation, Sir Stafford Cripps said, 'another question which has been raised by a great number of Members is the question of the policy as to the continued use of heavy bombers and the bombing of Germany. A number of hon. Members have questioned whether, in the existing circumstances, the continued devotion of a considerable part of our effort to the building up of this bombing force is the best use that we can make of our resources. It is obviously a matter which it is almost impossible to debate in public, but', Sir Stafford Cripps continued, 'if I may, I would

---

[1] It would be tedious and irrelevant to trace further the course of the dispute about the provision of long-range general reconnaissance aircraft for Coastal Command. There is a formidable volume of documentation upon the matter, but the dispute was never settled to the satisfaction of both sides. Mr. Churchill, to whom the matter was constantly referred, found himself in a dilemma. 'Just at the time when the weather is improving, when [the] Germans are drawing away flak from their cities for their offensive against Russia, when you are keen about our bombing U-boat nests, when the oil targets are especially attractive,' he telegraphed to President Roosevelt on 29th March 1942, 'I find it very hard to take away these extra six squadrons from Bomber Command in which Harris is doing so well.' Churchill: *The Second World War*, Vol. IV, p. 105. The Bomber Command attack on Lübeck had taken place the night before. In 1942 Bomber Command parted with six squadrons to Coastal Command (three Whitley, Nos. 51, 58 and 77, one Hampden No. 144 and two Wellington Nos. 304 and 311). War Room Manual of Bomber Cmd. Operations 1942.

[2] Churchill to Roosevelt, 5th March 1942.

[3] Sir Stafford Cripps, who at this time enjoyed considerable prestige in the country, had been appointed Lord Privy Seal and Leader of the House of Commons. For the Cabinet changes and the reasons underlying them, see Churchill: *The Second World War*, Vol. IV, pp. 65–80.

remind the House that this policy was initiated at a time when we were fighting alone against the combined forces of Germany and Italy and it then seemed that it was the most effective way in which we, acting alone, could take the initiative against the enemy. Since that time we have had an enormous access of support from the Russian Armies, who, according to the latest news, have had yet another victory over the Germans, and also from the great potential strength of the United States of America. Naturally,' the new Lord Privy Seal said, 'in such circumstances, the original policy has come under review. I can assure the House that the Government are fully aware of the other uses to which our resources could be put, and the moment they arrive at a decision that the circumstances warrant a change, a change in policy will be made.' [1]

Thus, growing doubts about the strategic bombing offensive, which had previously been largely confined to expert discussion within the secret conclaves of the Ministries and service staffs, were now being freely canvassed in the country and in Parliament. Sir Stafford Cripps' declaration had been guarded and somewhat vague. Nevertheless, it contained certain implications which, to the advocates of strategic bombing, were disquieting. In the view of these advocates, it was also likely to produce a bad effect in Washington where the crisis which assailed the whole conception of long-range bombing was even more acute than in London. There was, in fact, an instant reaction from the Royal Air Force delegation in Washington.

The delegation felt that the statement of Sir Stafford Cripps might be taken to mean that the British Government had lost confidence in the strategic bombing offensive as the principal means of 'wearing down and undermining German resistance,' which they had so recently expressed at the Washington War Conference. The *New York Times* had reported the speech and the Royal Air Force delegation feared that this publicity would strengthen the hands of those Americans who were pressing their Government to concentrate on the war against Japan in contradistinction to that against Germany. It might also, they thought, have an adverse effect upon the American production programme for heavy bombers. 'Unless authoritative reaffirmation of our belief in [the] Bomber offensive is supplied immediately,' the message from the Royal Air Force delegation ended, the 'effect both on strategical and production planning here may well be irremediable.' [2]

The Air Staff, however, remained reasonably confident. There was a growing feeling in 'unofficial circles', they told the Royal Air Force delegation, that heavy bombers should be directed more against naval

---

[1] Parliamentary Debates. Commons. Vol. 378, Cols. 316–317.
[2] R.A.F. Del. (Washington) to Air Min., 26th Feb. 1942.

targets and less against German industry.[1] Nevertheless, the Air Staff pointed out, the policy of strategic bombing, outlined in the directive of 14th February, had received the approval of the Government[2] and this, they said, held the field. In any case, the Air Staff was confident that it would now be impossible to reverse this policy without throwing the whole war production programme out of gear. Defensive bombing could, they observed, never win the war and they saw no reason to fear that it would be a serious threat to the offensive against Germany, especially as the Russian situation had produced one of the strongest arguments in favour of intensifying the latter. They hoped that the impending debate on the Air Estimates would provide the Secretary of State for Air with a suitable opportunity to provide the necessary 'authoritative reaffirmation.' [3]

This opportunity, which arose on 4th March 1942, was not missed by Sir Archibald Sinclair. It is, however, significant that in his speech to the House of Commons on that day, the Secretary of State for Air laid great emphasis upon the auxiliary co-operation which the Royal Air Force had been affording to the Navy in the Atlantic and to the Army in the Middle East. He spoke particularly of the part which Bomber Command had played and the numerous attacks made on the *Scharnhorst* and the *Gneisenau* provided him with some convenient statistics with which to illustrate his point. At length he came to the controversial question of the strategic air offensive. He spoke of the Stirlings, Halifaxes, Lancasters and also, unfortunately, of the Manchesters, which were coming into service, and he declared that it was intended 'to resume the bomber offensive against Germany on the largest possible scale at the earliest possible moment.' The Bomber Command crews were, he said, well armed and inflexibly determined, 'they are the only force upon which we can call in this year, 1942, to strike deadly blows at the heart of Germany.' [4]

---

[1] This feeling was not confined to 'unofficial circles'. For example, arguing for a greater concentration of air power on the naval war, Sir Dudley Pound, in a memorandum of 20th March 1942, asked of the bombing of Germany 'Are we sure that this is the best way of using our increasing strength in this arm? Is it right to employ a very large proportion of our heavy bombers doing to Germany this year little more than they did to us last year with such inconclusive results?'

[2] This was not strictly correct. The Prime Minister had sanctioned the resumption of the offensive (see Churchill to Sinclair, 14th Feb. 1942, cited above, p. 322), but the Government was not technically committed to any particular bombing policy. The Defence Committee had not pronounced upon the Sinclair memo. of 9th Feb. (cited above, p. 321) and it never did. This was because the Chiefs of Staff had been unable to agree upon their recommendations (C.O.S. Mtgs., 11th March 1942). As late as 16th March 1942 the Vice-Chiefs of Staff were officially unaware of the contents of the February Directive (C.O.S. Mtg.). The Defence Committee had, however, sanctioned the principle of area bombing in 1941. See above, pp. 173–174.

[3] Air Min. to R.A.F. Del. (Washington), 28th Feb. 1942.

[4] Parliamentary Debates. Commons. Vol. 378, Cols. 666–681. Sir Archibald Sinclair could, of course, make no mention of the most important consideration of all; the introduction of radar navigation. This fact serves to illustrate the limitations of the public discussion of war policies.

This last remark had great force. Nevertheless, the debate which provided Sir Archibald Sinclair with a platform also necessarily gave the 'opposition' a chance to voice their complaints and suspicions. They were able to suggest that little had yet been accomplished by Bomber Command and to claim that air power could be more profitably employed as an auxiliary to military and naval operations rather than as a force of independent strategic attack. Some peculiar operational arguments were deployed in the debate, but there was also the consideration that these views were not confined entirely to a group of irresponsible and ill-informed members of Parliament. They were also to some extent shared by others with more knowledge and more authority.

Thus, Bomber Command was in danger not only of being denied the resources needed for its expansion, but it was also existing under the threat of having its established squadrons taken away and, perhaps, even re-equipped for other purposes. It was also confronted, as it always had been, with the prospect of formidable diversions of its effort from what the Air Staff regarded as its central task.

There were many circumstances in early 1942 which, as has been shown, tended to make conditions unfavourable for those who advocated a renewed and increased strategic air offensive. These difficulties arose partly from the failures of Bomber Command in the first two years of the war which resulted in a reduction of confidence in the idea of an independent offensive. They also partly arose from the failures of other allied arms in theatres as far separated as the Atlantic and the Pacific, which resulted in an ever-increasing demand for the services which Bomber Command aircraft could, and in some cases could not, perform.

It was at this moment of the crisis of strategic bombing that Lord Cherwell intervened. On 30th March 1942, he addressed a minute to the Prime Minister in which he said:

> 'The following seems a simple method of estimating what we could do by bombing Germany:
>
> Careful analysis of the effects of raids on Birmingham, Hull and elsewhere have shown that, on the average, 1 ton of bombs dropped on a built-up area demolishes 20–40 dwellings and turns 100–200 people out of house and home.
>
> We know from our experience that we can count on nearly 14 operational sorties per bomber produced. The average lift of the bombers we are going to produce over the next 15 months will be about 3 tons. It follows that each of these bombers will in its lifetime drop about 40 tons of bombs. If these are dropped on built-up areas they will make 4,000–8,000 people homeless.
>
> In 1938 over 22 million Germans lived in 58 towns of over 100,000 inhabitants, which, with modern equipment, should be easy to find and hit. Our forecast output of heavy bombers

(including Wellingtons) between now and the middle of 1943 is about 10,000. If even half the total load of 10,000 bombers were dropped on the built-up areas of these 58 German towns the great majority of their inhabitants (about one-third of the German population) would be turned out of house and home.

Investigation seems to show that having one's house demolished is most damaging to morale. People seem to mind it more than having their friends or even relatives killed. At Hull signs of strain were evident, though only one-tenth of the houses were demolished. On the above figures we should be able to do ten times as much harm to each of the 58 principal German towns. There seems little doubt that this would break the spirit of the people.

Our calculation assumes, of course, that we really get one-half of our bombs into built-up areas. On the other hand, no account is taken of the large promised American production (6,000 heavy bombers in the period in question). Nor has regard been paid to the inevitable damage to factories, communications etc. in these towns and the damage by fire, probably accentuated by breakdown of public services.'[1]

Sir Archibald Sinclair and Sir Charles Portal found Lord Cherwell's calculations 'simple, clear and convincing.' They, however, drew the Prime Minister's attention to the four conditions which would have to be fulfilled if they were to be realised. Firstly, the necessary numbers of heavy bombers would have to be produced. Secondly, these bombers would, on the average, have to survive thirteen or fourteen operational sorties. Thirdly, Bomber Command would have to develop sufficient navigational and aiming accuracy to ensure that fifty per cent of the bombs found their targets. Fourthly, diversions from the bombing offensive against Germany would have to be avoided.[2]

The Cherwell minute, therefore, involved certain matters of high policy such as the production programme for heavy bombers and the concentration of the bombing offensive upon certain strategic objectives. It also involved calculations of probability such as the average life of an operational bomber in 1942 and 1943 and the effect of a certain weight of bombs upon a given number of German towns. Clearly the results which Lord Cherwell foresaw in consequence of his probability calculations would not be achieved unless policy decisions were taken in the sense which his minute suggested as necessary. On the other hand, these policy decisions could not be justified by the probability calculations themselves because the calculations seemed probable only to those who, in any case, believed in the

---

[1] Min. Cherwell to Churchill, 30th March 1942. Circulated by the Prime Minister to Defence Committee on 9th April 1942. The whole text of the minute is transcribed above.
[2] Min. Sinclair to Churchill, 6th April 1942.

policy. To those who did not, they seemed to be wholly improbable and, in this connection, one scientist could easily be answered, or at least questioned, by another. Sir Henry Tizard, for example, observed, that 'the risk entailed by this policy is so great that it is necessary to be convinced not merely that it has a chance of success but that the probability of success is very great.' [1]

To Sir Henry Tizard it seemed that Lord Cherwell's calculations contained certain important fallacies. He pointed out that the Ministry of Aircraft Production programme provided for the construction of 3,585 Wellingtons and 5,219 heavy bombers between the beginning of April 1942 and the end of June 1943. 689 of the Wellingtons were earmarked for Coastal Command. Thus, the bomber programme provided for 8,115 aircraft. Experience had taught Sir Henry Tizard 'that we cannot rely on more than 85% of the target programme' and he therefore estimated that Bomber Command would receive 7,000, and not 10,000 aircraft in the period reviewed by Lord Cherwell.

Even if this difficulty could be overcome, Sir Henry Tizard immediately saw another in the assumption that each of these aircraft would on the average complete fourteen operational sorties. This would mean that they would all be destroyed and that 'we should be left at the end of the period with a front line strength no greater than it is at present, which is surely quite unthinkable.' The two difficulties led Sir Henry Tizard to the conclusion that Bomber Command would be able to drop on Germany only half the tonnage which had been estimated by Lord Cherwell.

The next point which struck Sir Henry Tizard as 'much too optimistic' was the assumption that the '58 towns of over 100,000 inhabitants' would be easy to find and hit. He thought that Lord Cherwell had underestimated the difficulties which would confront the bomber crews operating at night in the face of heavy opposition. *Gee*, he pointed out, had a limited range and would have a limited life. New radar aids were not expected by Sir Henry Tizard to come into service until April 1943.[2] He, therefore, thought it unsafe to assume that more than twenty-five per cent of the bombs lifted would find their targets. Thus, he calculated that in the period reviewed by Lord Cherwell and on the assumption that all heavy bombers were concentrated exclusively on the task,[3] not more than 50,000 tons of bombs would fall on the built-up areas. If this was spread over the fifty-eight towns the effect might, on the average, be three or four times as great as that produced by the Germans in Hull and Birmingham.

---

[1] Memo. by Tizard, 20th April 1942.
[2] In which expectation he was not far wrong.
[3] Which concentration, Sir Henry Tizard thought, would be neither wise nor possible.

This, Sir Henry Tizard thought, 'would certainly be most damaging but would not', he said, 'be decisive unless in the intervening period Germany was either defeated in the field by Russia, or at least prevented from any substantial further advance, e.g. to the Russian or Iranian Oilfields.'

Thus, although Sir Henry Tizard had by no means fully realised the extraordinary resilience and determination with which the Germans were to meet both the bombing of their towns and the defeat of their armies in Russia, he had sounded a note of warning against the assumptions upon which the Cherwell minute was based and so against the policy into which Bomber Command was drifting. The concluding paragraph of his memorandum is worth quoting in full:

'I conclude therefore,' he wrote:
'(a) That a policy of bombing German towns wholesale in order to destroy dwellings cannot have a decisive effect by the middle of 1943, even if all heavy bombers and the great majority of Wellingtons produced are used primarily for this purpose.

(b) That such a policy can only have a decisive effect if carried out on a much bigger scale than is envisaged in . . . [the Cherwell minute]' [1]

Lord Cherwell clearly felt that his calculations had been taken too literally. 'My paper', he told Sir Henry Tizard, 'was intended to show that we really can do a lot of damage by bombing built-up areas with the sort of air force which should be available.' As to the size of the bomber force, he said that he had used 'the round figure of 10,000' partly because in March, when he wrote his minute, the Ministry of Aircraft Production had been somewhat more optimistic than it was in April when Sir Henry Tizard wrote his, and 'partly to save the Prime Minister the trouble of making arithmetical calculations.' Even, however, if Sir Henry Tizard's expectations proved to be more realistic than his own and, in the event, it was only possible to subject the leading German towns to a weight of attack three or four times as heavy as that which had fallen on Hull and Birmingham, Lord Cherwell remained convinced that the effects would be 'catastrophic'.[2]

Sir Henry Tizard had never denied this, but he had sought to show that there might be much difference between 'catastrophic' and 'decisive' results. 'I should like to make it clear', he told Sir Archibald Sinclair on 20th April 1942, 'that I don't disagree fundamentally with the bombing policy, but I do think that it is only likely to be decisive if carried out on the scale envisaged by the Air Staff, which,

---

[1] Memo. by Tizard, 20th April 1942. Sir Henry Tizard sent his note to Sir Archibald Sinclair and Lord Cherwell.

[2] Letter Cherwell to Tizard, 22nd April 1942.

if I remember rightly, contemplated a front line strength of 4,000 aircraft and a rate of reinforcement of 1,000 heavy bombers a month. We cannot achieve this', he continued, 'this year, or even until next year, so if we try to carry out the policy with a much smaller force it will not be decisive, and we may lose the war in other ways.'[1]

In other words, Sir Henry Tizard's objections were really founded upon the fear that by concentrating Bomber Command upon an offensive which, in view of its limited size and rate of expansion, he thought would not be decisive, the war might be lost by a failure to attend adequately to defensive measures. 'You know', he told Sir Archibald Sinclair, 'that I am very keen about the greater and better use of the Air Force against enemy ships of war . . .'[2] The differences between Sir Henry Tizard and Lord Cherwell were the same as those at issue between the Naval Staff and the Air Staff. The fact that Sir Henry Tizard had been able to point out fallacies in Lord Cherwell's calculations, fallacies which Lord Cherwell scarcely denied, was relatively unimportant. After all, these calculations, like those made by Sir Henry Tizard, were extremely approximate and were only used to make the case presented more graphic.

These calculations, indeed, depended upon factors which could not be measured and scarcely guessed. It was difficult to work out the numbers of bombers which the British aircraft industry could produce. It was still more difficult to estimate the speed at which the Germans would be able to shoot them down. The ultimate role and size of the American bomber force was still unknown. Even so these matters comprised the simpler parts of the calculations. The problem of trying to estimate the consequences to Germany of the offensive was infinitely more complex. It was still possible to arrive at widely different opinions as to the effects of the German attacks on British towns. It was impossible to know how much more effort the Germans would have had to make in order to produce decisive effects. Similarly, it was impossible to calculate the size and duration of attack which would be necessary to reduce Germany to the point of capitulation. It was possible only to guess. As Mr. Churchill wrote, 'experience shows that forecasts are usually falsified and preparations always in arrear.'[3] The difference of opinion between Lord Cherwell and Sir Henry Tizard was, therefore, really no more than an illustrative reflection, in somewhat more scientific terms, of the issues which divided the counsels of the Air and Naval Staffs.

Nevertheless, as the Prime Minister also remarked, 'there must be a design and theme for bringing the war to a victorious end in a

---

[1] Letter Tizard to Sinclair, 20th April 1942.
[2] do.
[3] Churchill: *The Second World War*, Vol. III, p. 583.

reasonable period. All the more is this necessary when under modern conditions no large-scale offensive operation can be launched without the preparation of elaborate technical apparatus.' Lord Cherwell's minute, despite its largely and inevitable fallacious 'forecasts',[1] had done no more and no less than to acknowledge a 'design and theme' for the air offensive, and Lord Cherwell exerted a much greater influence upon the Prime Minister than did Sir Henry Tizard.

The Air Staff, as has been shown, had already devised this theme towards the end of 1941 and Lord Cherwell had added little that was new. All the same, because of the position which he occupied and the time at which he submitted his minute, Lord Cherwell's intervention was of great importance. It did much to insure the concept of strategic bombing in its hour of crisis.

Nevertheless, the conflict of opinion which revealed itself over the acceptance of the February directive and the Cherwell minute was never resolved and was never far beneath the surface. The conduct of the bombing offensive was always either to a greater or less extent the product of compromise between the demands of offence and defence, of the strategic and tactical roles of the force and between the independent and auxiliary applications of bombing.

---

[1] There were, of course, many fallacies, some less inevitable than others, besides those remarked upon by Sir Henry Tizard. For example, Lord Cherwell had assumed that if one ton of bombs dropped on a built-up area made between a hundred and two hundred people homeless, then forty tons would make four thousand to eight thousand people homeless. This, however, did not necessarily follow.

2. An improving prospect: general and selective policies, April–September 1942

The Cherwell minute, despite the great influence which it exerted, settled nothing. It summarised the hopes and ideas of those who were working for the build up of the strategic bombing offensive. It did not convert those who were sceptical of the whole conception. The controversy continued unabated and it was decided by the Government that the problem should be referred to an independent judgment. Accordingly on 16th April 1942 Mr. Justice Singleton, who had previously conducted an enquiry into the probable strength of the *Luftwaffe*, was invited to undertake an enquiry with the following terms of reference:

> 'In the light of our experience of the German bombing of this country and of such information as is available of the results of our bombing of Germany, what results are we likely to achieve from continuing our air attacks on Germany at the greatest possible strength during the next 6, 12 and 18 months respectively?' [1]

Though such an enquiry did not cover the positive claims which the Admiralty was making for the more extensive use of heavy bombers in the naval war, it did, by enquiring what was to be gained by the Air Staff policy and so, conversely, what might be lost by the naval policy, strike at the root of the problem. A clear and independent opinion at this stage would have been of great value.

If such was the object of initiating the enquiry the hope was doomed to failure. Mr. Justice Singleton was unable to answer the question posed by his terms of reference. His report, which was submitted to the Defence Committee on 20th May 1942, enumerated the uncertain factors in the problem, but it did not seek to distinguish the probable from the improbable. It referred to various matters on which there was a conflict of opinion, but it did not attempt any judgment of the issues.

Mr. Justice Singleton failed to reach a conclusion as to what the effects of the German air attacks on Britain between August 1940 and June 1941 had been. He did not know which of the widely different estimates of lost war production was correct. He did not know whether the effect on morale had been serious or not. Thus, he had no yardstick against which to measure the effects of the forthcoming Bomber Command offensive against Germany.

---

[1] Letter Bridges to Singleton, 16th April 1942. The Prime Minister caused the invitation to be sent, but the idea seems to have originated in Sir Charles Portal's mind. C.O.S. Mtg., 10th April 1942.

The report recognised that much would depend upon the success with which Bomber Command could grapple with its operational problems, but, though he was somewhat doubtful about the effectiveness of *Gee*, Mr. Justice Singleton gave little or no indication of how this struggle was likely to develop. He also suggested that much would depend upon how the Russian armies fared in campaigns which were yet to come.

Taking into account the effects which the bombing offensive might have not only upon German industry and morale, but also upon the disposition of the German air force, 'by the hold-up' of fighter aircraft on defensive activities and 'by keeping occupied a large number of men and guns on anti-aircraft work and on searchlights and a very large number on Air Raid Precautions,' Mr. Justice Singleton thought that there was 'every reason to hope for good results from a sustained bombing policy'. In an attempt to define what was meant by 'good results' Mr. Justice Singleton amplified and qualified this remark with the following words:

> 'I do not think it [the bombing offensive] ought to be regarded as *of itself* sufficient to win the war or to produce decisive results; the area is too vast for the effort we can put forth: on the other hand, if Germany does not achieve great success on land before the winter it may well turn out to have a decisive effect, and in the meantime, if carried out on the lines suggested, it must impede Germany and help Russia. If Germany succeeds in her attack on Russia there will be little apparent gain from our bombing policy in six months' time, but the drain on Germany will be present all the time: and if Russia stands it will remain a powerful weapon on our hands. It is impossible to say what its effect will be in twelve or eighteen months without considering the position of Russia. If Russia can hold Germany on land I doubt whether Germany will stand twelve or eighteen months' continuous, intensified and increased bombing, affecting, as it must, her war production, her power of resistance, her industries and her will to resist (by which I mean morale).' [1]

The vague language of the Singleton Report so far from resulting in any firm conclusions merely tended to exacerbate the dispute about bombing policy which continued to divide the counsels of the Chiefs of Staff Committee. It was impossible to summarise the findings of the Report, but it was easy to draw quotations from it which could be used to illustrate almost any argument. This is precisely what the First Sea Lord did. In a memorandum for the Chiefs of Staff of 16th June 1942, Sir Dudley Pound sought to show that the allied reverses in the Far East, the increasing scale of German submarine and air attack on merchant shipping and the Singleton Report made the case

---

[1] Singleton Report, 20th May 1942, App. 17.

for his argument that the Air Force should play a larger part in the war at sea.[1]

To Sir Charles Portal this proposition seemed 'wholly unacceptable'. He believed that the construction of new shipping would soon overtake the rate of sinking and in any case he continued to believe that Bomber Command could make a bigger contribution by launching strategic attacks against submarine construction yards than by seeking out these vessels at sea. The Singleton Report, he observed, proved nothing because it reached no conclusions.[2]

Nevertheless, the Singleton Report did perform one valuable service. It showed that a decision about bombing policy could not be arrived at on the basis of academic investigations into the prospects of the strategic bombing offensive. Whether these investigations were statistical or juridical they could, because of the nature of the evidence, prove nothing. The solution of the problem did not lie in further research or in further argument. It lay in the field of action.

If in 1942, Bomber Command, with its limited and, indeed, diminishing resources, could win some notable victories then and then only might it be afforded the opportunity of fulfilling its destiny. This was realised by the Air Staff and it was realised by none more forcibly than by the new Commander-in-Chief, Air Marshal Harris.

Indeed, the resumed offensive was already beginning to yield results. In March and April Bomber Command carried out a series of impressive attacks against Lübeck, Rostock and the Renault factory in France. It is true that these were less difficult targets lying in lightly defended areas. Nevertheless, the success which was achieved, not only in terms of mass destruction in the two Baltic towns, but also in precision results against the Renault factory and the Heinkel works at Rostock, far surpassed anything which Bomber Command had previously achieved. These victories were favourably noticed in the Singleton Report.

The attacks on the Ruhr, and particularly those on Essen, which were initiated on the night of 8th March 1942, were meeting with less success. Events were to show that further technical aids and operational developments as well as an augmentation in the front-line strength of the Command were necessary before this formidable task, which lay at the core of the policy pronounced in the February directive, could be attempted with the prospect of success. Meanwhile, these disappointments over the Ruhr were, to a certain extent, mitigated by the gigantic achievement of the Thousand Bomber Raid on Cologne.

This attack was carried out on the night of 30th May 1942 and was

---

[1] Memo. by Pound, 16th June 1942.
[2] Memo. by Portal, 23rd June 1942.
S.A.O.—I—Z

made possible by summoning to the battle all available reserves, including large numbers of crews and aircraft normally engaged on training. The casualties were not unduly high and photographic reconnaissance showed that about a third of the total area of Cologne had been heavily damaged. This was an impressive demonstration of what Bomber Command might achieve if it was expanded. It was no more than that for, with a front-line operational strength which was, in 1942, seldom much in excess of and often much less than 400 aircraft, Bomber Command could not sustain such efforts without disrupting its whole training organisation and, therefore, its future. Only two more attacks of this size were made in 1942 and in neither case did the targets, Essen and Bremen, suffer as heavily as Cologne had done. Public opinion was naturally much uplifted by the Cologne success at a time of sore trial on other fronts. It expected, indeed, too much from Bomber Command and did not realise how exceptional the circumstances were.

Thus, in the spring and summer of 1942, Bomber Command, though it had suffered failure and disappointments, also won its first outstanding successes. These were not, and had not been expected to be, on a sufficient scale, in themselves, to exert a decisive effect upon Germany. They were rather a miniature demonstration in the field of action of what might be achieved on a much larger and more terrible scale in the future. As such, they exercised a decisive influence not only upon the making of bombing policy, but upon the existence of Bomber Command itself. To the new Commander-in-Chief, they were the proof and justification of his theory of strategic air power.

Sir Arthur Harris had established a close and direct contact with the Prime Minister and in a personal minute of 17th June 1942 he unfolded to Mr. Churchill his views on the conduct of the war. 'Victory, speedy and complete,' he began, 'awaits the side which first employs air power as it should be employed'. Germany, he observed, had missed victory through air power by a 'hair's breadth' in 1940. Subsequently she had entangled her air force in the meshes of vast land campaigns and could no longer disengage it for 'strategically proper application.' Britain, on the other hand, still had the freedom of choice, but she stood at the cross-roads. 'We are free, if we will,' Sir Arthur Harris said, 'to employ our rapidly increasing air strength in the proper manner. In such a manner as would avail to knock Germany out of the War in a matter of months, if we decide upon the right course. If we decide upon the wrong course, then our air power will now, and increasingly in future, become inextricably implicated as a subsidiary weapon in the prosecution of vastly protracted and avoidable land and sea campaigns.'

If Britain entered upon a continental land campaign, other than 'on a mopping up police basis,' she would, Sir Arthur Harris believed, 'play right into Germany's hand.' She would be inviting her enemy to take advantage of 'the one superior asset remaining to her, a vast and efficient army.' If Russia could hold her front and with the support of vast American armies and uprisings among the oppressed nations such a campaign might 'in the very long run' result in an allied victory. At best, however, Sir Arthur Harris feared, it would lead to the slaughter of the flower of the country's youth 'in the mud of Flanders and France' and, at worst, it might end in a second Dunkirk.

These considerations, which were also often in the mind of the Prime Minister, who had also lived through the years 1914–18, brought Sir Arthur Harris to the crux of his argument. 'It is imperative, if we hope to win the war,' he said, 'to abandon the disastrous policy of military intervention in the land campaigns of Europe, and to concentrate our air power against the enemy's weakest spots . . . The utter destruction of Lübeck and Rostock, the practical destruction of Cologne (a leading asset to Germany turned in one night into a vast liability), point the certain, the obvious, the quickest and the easiest way to overwhelming victory. The overstrained, far stretched and militarily compromised condition of Germany plays right into our hands—if we now employ our air power properly. The success of the 1,000 Plan,' Sir Arthur Harris continued, 'has proved beyond doubt in the minds of all but wilful men that we can even today dispose of a weight of air attack which no country on which it can be brought to bear could survive. We can bring it to bear on the vital part of Germany. It requires only the decision to concentrate it for its proper use.'

The decision for which Sir Arthur Harris called was for the immediate return to Bomber Command of all bomber aircraft in Coastal Command, which he regarded as 'merely an obstacle to victory,' the return of all Middle East bombers as soon as the battle there was stabilised, the return of all suitable aircraft and crews from Army Co-operation Command, the extraction of every possible bomber from America, an approach to Stalin to transfer his bomber force to Britain and the highest possible priority for the production of heavy bombers in Britain.[1]

Sir Arthur Harris was fired with a burning conviction that the strategic air offensive was the only means by which the war could be won in reasonable time and at bearable cost. In common with most other commanders, he did not believe in understating his case or underestimating his requirements. Inevitably he tended to view the war situation from the angle of his own Headquarters at High

---

[1] Min. Harris to Churchill, 17th June 1942.

Wycombe which he left only with reluctance and as seldom as possible. All other strategies could, it seemed to him, lead only to a Pyrrhic victory or even defeat. 'One cannot win wars,' he said in a second memorandum of 28th June 1942, 'by defending oneself.' Bomber Command was, he claimed, the 'only offensive weapon against Germany.' Yet, according to Sir Arthur Harris' calculation, Bomber Command had in its operational squadrons only about eleven per cent of the total first-line strength of the Royal Air Force and the Fleet Air Arm. Even of this eleven per cent only about half the effort was devoted to the strategic offensive against Germany. The rest was harnessed to 'Naval and Military targets.'

To Sir Arthur Harris this simply did not make sense, especially when he observed that 'whilst it takes approximately some 7,000 hours of flying to destroy one submarine at sea, that was approximately the amount of flying necessary to destroy one-third of Cologne, the third largest city in Germany, in one night . . .' [1]

In short, implicit in Sir Arthur Harris' argument was the suggestion that only Bomber Command could win the war and that Bomber Command, if it was given the resources and not diverted from its central and strategic task, could win the war alone. This was not a view which the Prime Minister could 'adopt or endorse' and he recognised that many of Sir Arthur Harris' arguments and claims were exaggerations.[2] Nevertheless, Mr. Churchill's view was far from unsympathetic and it was powerful. He was clearly impressed both by what Bomber Command had achieved in the spring and summer and by the need to rescue it from further deprivations and to increase its strength.

'We must observe with sorrow and alarm', the Prime Minister wrote in a War Cabinet memorandum on 21st July 1942, 'the woeful shrinkage of our plans for Bomber expansion.' This was due, he explained, to the needs of the Navy, the Middle East and India, to the wish of the Americans to fly their own machines and also to a short fall of British production. All these losses fell 'exclusively upon Bomber Command.' [3] On the need to build up Bomber Command, then, the Prime Minister was in sympathy, if not by any means in entire agreement, with Sir Arthur Harris. As to the role of Bomber Command, there was a more significant divergence of view.

'We must', Mr. Churchill said, 'regard the Bomber offensive against Germany at least as a feature in breaking her war-will second only to the largest military operations which can be conducted on the Continent until that war-will is broken. Renewed, intense

---

[1] Note by Harris, 28th June 1942. Circulated to the War Cabinet by Churchill on 24th Aug. 1942, App. 18. The comparison was not, perhaps, a fair one.

[2] Note by Churchill, 9th Sept. 1942.

[3] Churchill: *The Second World War*, Vol. IV, p. 783.

efforts should be made by the Allies', he continued, 'to develop during the winter and onwards ever-growing, ever more accurate and ever more far-ranging Bomber attacks on Germany. In this way alone can we prepare the conditions which will be favourable to the major military operations on which we are resolved.' [1]

Thus, the Prime Minister rejected Sir Arthur Harris' advice as to the major strategy of the war. In his view, the bombing offensive alone could not be regarded as an adequate means of victory. It could, however, reduce Germany to a condition in which it would be feasible to contemplate an effective invasion of the Continent by land forces. The Prime Minister had, in effect, defined a role for Bomber Command which after much further debate was eventually accepted at the Casablanca Conference in January 1943 as the mission of the combined Anglo-American bomber offensive. At the same time the Prime Minister, even at this early stage, suggested that provision should be made 'to ensure that the bombing of Germany is not interrupted, except perhaps temporarily, by the need of supporting military operations.' [2]

This showed the extent to which the Prime Minister regarded the bombing offensive as a contribution to victory which would be parallel with and not subordinate to that of the invading land armies. Even so this parallel role for Bomber Command was never agreeable to Sir Arthur Harris. By its very nature it would deny to Bomber Command that unconditional priority in production and allocation and that unqualified concentration of effort which the Commander-in-Chief regarded as the indispensable condition for the fulfilment of his promise of 'victory, speedy and complete.' Here was a divergence of opinion which should be focussed in the mind, for, in due course, it was to have great significance.

The consequences of this divergence were not, however, immediately apparent, for both views tended towards the expansion of Bomber Command and the greater concentration of its activities upon the strategic offensive against Germany. On 17th September 1942 the Prime Minister told Sir Archibald Sinclair that the strength of Bomber Command must be increased from its existing thirty-two operational squadrons to fifty operational squadrons by the end of the year. He promised to secure Cabinet approval of an Air Ministry plan to achieve this aim and he himself suggested that two squadrons might be transferred from Coastal Command and one from the Airborne Division. Two more might be obtained by restricting the flow of aircraft to the Middle East and India. The remaining thirteen, Mr. Churchill suggested, should come from increased output by the

---

[1] do.
[2] do. p. 784

Ministry of Aircraft Production and more speedy 'working up' in Bomber Command.[1]

This was not the scale of expansion for which Sir Arthur Harris had called and it did not correspond with Sir Henry Tizard's estimates of the expansion necessary to justify the policy of area attack on German morale.[2] Also it was not fulfilled on schedule.[3] Nevertheless, it marked an upward turn in the supply fortunes of Bomber Command and it did make possible some great achievements in 1943. This improvement in Bomber Command's prospects was due to returning confidence founded upon the achievements of the force in 1942. It was also due to the generally more favourable course which the war began to run as the year approached its end. The tide of German and Japanese conquest had flowed and begun to ebb. The argument that 'one cannot win wars by defending oneself' was gaining strength. The crisis of strategic bombing, though certainly not resolved, was relaxed.

These discussions about the role of Bomber Command, about the part it was to play in the major strategy of the war, and, therefore, about the scale on which and the rate at which it should be expanded were not directly concerned with the actual policy by which that role might best be discharged. Nevertheless, this was obviously a factor of the greatest importance to which it is now necessary to revert.

It might be inferred that the operational experiences of 1939–41 had settled the issue by giving a practical demonstration of the operational impossibility of attempting anything other than the destruction of town areas. To draw such an inference was, indeed, to form a just appreciation of the operational conditions under which Bomber Command had been operating in the first two years of the war, and this was the inference which had been drawn in the February directive and more specifically in the clarifying note which Sir Charles Portal wrote about it.[4]

This was, however, neither a complete nor was it a permanent solution. Even for those who believed that the attack on town areas was intrinsically the best policy which Bomber Command could pursue, regardless of developments which might increase its ability to hit smaller targets, it was not a precise guide to bombing policy. There might be differences of opinion as to the purpose for which towns should be destroyed, and, therefore, as to which towns should be

---

[1] Churchill: *The Second World War*, Vol. IV, pp. 793–794.

[2] i.e. a front-line strength of 4,000 aircraft with a reinforcement rate of 1,000 per month.

[3] On 31st December 1942 Bomber Command had only forty-four operational squadrons, and even this number included one on loan to Coastal Command and two which had detachments of twelve aircraft each in North-West Africa. Memo. Sinclair to Churchill, 1st Jan. 1943.

[4] See above, pp. 322–324.

attacked. Area bombing, as has been noticed, could be harnessed to the aim of causing general dislocation, terror and discomfort by the selection as targets of the largest towns. Alternatively, it could aim at particular dislocation by the choice as targets of towns associated with selected activities. Thus, for example, though it might be operationally impossible to bomb aircraft factories, this did not mean that the only alternative was to make a general attack on German national morale. It might still be possible to attack the aircraft industry by a selective attack on towns associated with it. Even within the framework of area bombing there was, therefore, the question of whether the attack was to be general, as might be inferred from the Cherwell minute, or selective as was postulated by later advices. The February directive, as will have been observed, did not answer this question.

Nor had the February directive, and more particularly the memorandum in which Sir Archibald Sinclair had prepared the way for it, closed the door on a resumption of precision bombing. There were, after all, those who accepted the policy of area bombing only as a temporary and an operational expedient. To these, the idea of returning to precision attack as soon as the means, tactical and technical, justified the attempt was ever present. In the course of 1942 some of those means were created and others were soon to follow.

Thus, the February directive, to some extent inevitably, had not clearly defined the objects of the bombing offensive. It had established certain emphases, dictated by the operational circumstances of the time, but it had mentioned many possibilities. Above all, it had shown, more clearly than any previous directive, how bombing policy had to be decided primarily on the grounds of its operational feasibility and secondarily on those of its strategic desirability. The decision, therefore, necessarily and to a large extent, devolved upon the officer charged with the execution of the offensive; upon the officer whose judgment of what could, and what could not, be done was most weighty; upon Sir Arthur Harris.

It is now possible to see how the Commander-in-Chief, Bomber Command, though theoretically only responsible for carrying out a policy decided by his superiors, was, in practice, in a very strong position to influence the making of that policy. If he had convictions of his own, he could always, or nearly always, rule out competing ideas on the ground that they were impossible. All the more would this be so if the direction from above was weak or uncertain.

Sir Arthur Harris was a man of strong convictions and unshakable determination. Moreover, he had already infused Bomber Command with a new spirit and he had directed it towards its first outstanding successes of the war. In support of his convictions he, therefore, had great prestige. He had a facility for concentrating on one side of a question, and of regarding the other as a mere obstruction. His presentation of the case for expanding Bomber Command and concentrating on the strategic offensive showed the mould in which his mind was cast. With equal persistence, and, perhaps, even greater determination, he was presently to advocate a continuous and general area attack upon Germany and it became his aim to see this carried out to the exclusion of all other possibilities.

It would be a mistake, nevertheless, to assume that Sir Arthur Harris was, in this matter, activated by some preconceived notion, or that he was himself responsible for the initial decision to adopt the methods of area attack. We have seen how, as Air Officer Commanding 5 Group, he had once boasted of 'the accuracy with which our aircraft hit military objectives as opposed to merely browning the towns.'[1] Later, as Deputy Chief of the Air Staff, he had played a part in the adoption of the policy of attacking oil, and even as late as April 1942, as Commander-in-Chief, he suggested to Sir Charles Portal that heavy area attacks should be made 'on convenient occasions' on Lorient, St. Nazaire, La Rochelle, Bordeaux and Brest in order to complicate the turn-round of submarines.[2] The Chief of the Air Staff's note clarifying the February directive had, of course, been written before Sir Arthur Harris arrived at High Wycombe.[3]

Though there were pointers to the direction in which his mind was moving, Sir Arthur Harris' views upon bombing policy were, perhaps, not fully crystallised before the end of 1942, and in any case the policy of general area attack was not seriously challenged in 1942. It was not until 1943 that his interventions became frequent, strongly expressed and, from his point of view, necessary.

Meanwhile, within the councils of the higher direction of the war there were some doubts about the course of events. Even on 2nd February 1942, when the Air Staff were about to present their case for the attack on German morale, Sir Archibald Sinclair suggested to Sir Charles Portal that the resumption of the offensive might be the moment 'for switching at least a substantial part of our bomber effort on to oil.'[4] Sir Charles Portal told him that even if all the ten plants within *Gee* range could be completely destroyed the total Axis supply of oil would decline by only 7·6 per cent. He added that in view of the operational difficulties he did not think that the production of these plants could be reduced by more than one per cent. He thought the

---

[1] Letter Harris to Peirse, 11th Oct. 1940.

[2] Letter Harris to Portal, 7th April 1942. Sir Charles Portal rejected the suggestion on the ground that a change of Cabinet ruling, which he thought improbable, would be required. When eventually these attacks were carried out, Sir Arthur Harris had for good reasons changed his mind.

[3] Sir Arthur Harris himself has rightly pointed out that he was not responsible for the adoption of this policy. See Harris: *Bomber Offensive*, p. 73.

[4] Min. Sinclair to Portal, 2nd Feb. 1942.

plan should be postponed at least until experience of *Gee* had been gained. Sir Archibald Sinclair agreed.[1]

Nevertheless, as will have been seen in Chapter V, intelligence bearing on the problem continued to emphasise that oil was, strategically, a most attractive target, but the Air Staff after finding that the Air Officer Commanding-in-Chief, Middle East, could not undertake an offensive against Ploesti, the Rumanian oil centre, which was regarded as a vital objective in the oil target system,[2] adopted the same curious expedient to which they had previously resorted in similar circumstances. On 3rd September 1942 they instructed Sir Arthur Harris to bomb the large oil plant at Pölitz.[3] Action did not follow.

Thus, as in the summer of 1941, the plans for a resumption of the oil offensive in 1942 did not prosper. The operational conclusion that there was little prospect of inflicting effective damage upon such small targets mingled with the assumption that the key to the whole Axis oil position lay in Ploesti sufficed to kill the idea without any intervention from Sir Arthur Harris. The experiences of 1940 and early 1941 were not easily to be forgotten. Nevertheless, the fate of the oil plan did not exhaust the possibilities of selective attack.

Intelligence appreciations had for some time been drawing attention to the importance and vulnerability of the German ball-bearings industry[4] and the Air Staff was impressed both by the strategic importance and vulnerability of Schweinfurt, where it was mainly concentrated. In order to persuade Sir Arthur Harris, who had been more doubtful, Air Commodore Baker, the Director of Bomber Operations, sent the Commander-in-Chief the Ministry of Economic Warfare appreciation and at the same time made the suggestion that Schweinfurt should be given 'the same sort of medicine as you gave Lubeck.'[5]

Sir Arthur Harris was not, however, easily to be convinced. He thought the Ministry of Economic Warfare appreciation which suggested that Schweinfurt produced two-thirds of all German ball-bearings, was 'somewhat vague and its information appears to be based on the pre-war situation prevailing in the industry.' He found it 'hard to believe' that Germany was still left 'with any dangerous bottle-necks particularly in the production of such important components as ball-bearings.' Even so, Sir Arthur Harris was prepared

---

[1] Min. Portal to Sinclair, 13th Feb. 1942, and Min. Sinclair to Portal, 14th Feb. 1942.

[2] Air Staff Memo., 1st May 1942.

[3] Dir. Bottomley to Harris, 3rd Sept. 1942, App. 8 (xxvi). The earlier occasion was in July 1941 when Sir Charles Portal, at the insistence of Lord Hankey, agreed to launch one big attack on Gelsenkirchen. Min. Portal to Sinclair, 4th July 1941.

[4] See below, pp. 466–467 and Chapter XI, Vol. II.

[5] Letter Baker to Harris, 7th April 1942.

to admit that 'the evidence points to Schweinfurt being an important target.'

Operationally, Sir Arthur Harris said Schweinfurt 'would be most difficult to locate.' However, he thought that some good crews from 3 Group who had been studying the problem, might be able to pick up the river Main on a moonlight night and use it as a lead in. The town did not, he observed, compare in inflammability with Lübeck. Although of similar acreage, he said, 'its population is only 40,000 against Lubeck's 123,000 . . .' In conclusion, Sir Arthur Harris said, 'I am keeping an open mind on this target and, given the right conditions, I might decide to burn the town and blast its factories.'[1]

This was an extremely significant letter. Sir Arthur Harris had shown that Schweinfurt would be a difficult target, but he had not suggested that the task was impossible. On the contrary, he had implied that, 'given the right conditions,' he could fulfil it. At the same time he had shown that his decision to launch the attack would not depend solely upon his operational judgment. He had made it clear that his view of the strategic importance of the target would also be a factor. He had also indicated that his strategic judgment might not, and in this case did not, correspond with that of the Ministry of Economic Warfare or of the Air Staff.

It was not, however, in this instance, the strategic factor which caused the plan for an attack to founder. By August 1942 the Air Staff had concluded that a successful attack would require some 500 bombers and they were not prepared to send these until some ground-marking system could be laid by agents.[2] Thus, it was on the operational issue that the plan was postponed. Nevertheless, the ball-bearing plan, from the operational point of view, was not such a forlorn hope as that for the attack on oil. The latter depended entirely on precision bombing and what was regarded as the key target in the system, that is, Ploesti, still lay out of effective reach. In the case of ball-bearings, the key target, that is, Schweinfurt, was within range and the execution of the plan did not depend entirely upon precision bombing. It was not impossible that the task could be largely accomplished by area attacks on the town of Schweinfurt to the accompaniment of smaller precise attacks upon the two ball-bearing plants themselves. This would be no more than a repetition, though admittedly against a much more difficult target, of what had already been accomplished against Rostock and its Heinkel Factory. The ball-bearing plan was, indeed, to be revived sooner and pressed harder than the oil plan, but both plans had an important future.

---

[1] Letter Harris to Baker, 11th April 1942, *The Bomber's Baedeker* (2nd ed., 1944, unpublished) put the population of Schweinfurt at 60,000.

[2] Min. Grierson (S.O.E.) to Gubbins (S.O.E.), 20th Aug. 1942. These ground markers were known as *Eurekas*.

These plans, like that for the general area attack upon industrial morale and activity, were all in correspondence with the central theme which lay behind the creation of Bomber Command. They all sought to destroy the enemy war machine by direct and offensive action. They all represented the idea of an independent and strategic air offensive; independent in the sense that they sought to contribute to victory regardless of the activities of the other services and strategic in the sense that they aimed at the destruction of the sources, and not the manifestations, of German armed strength.

Fundamentally, therefore, and in their origin, the disputes which these various policies occasioned were disputes about details and not principles, for all these ideas were simply variations on the same theme. They all conformed to the Air Staff doctrine of strategic air power. Nevertheless, the differences of opinion which were created by these various possibilities did raise important principles.

It was obviously a much smaller task to remove by a series of deft and selective attacks one vital segment of the German war economy than to attempt the destruction of the whole vast machine. This was the great appeal of the selective, or as Sir Arthur Harris called them, 'panacea' policies. Nevertheless, the selective policy called for greater skill and knowledge than the general policy. After all it is usually much easier to hit any town than to hit a particular town and it is always much easier to hit a town than an oil plant or a factory. There was also the consideration that the intelligence appreciation upon which the selection of the particular segment, or target system, had been based might be inaccurate. There was the possibility that important targets had been overlooked, or that accumulated stocks of or substitutes for the product in question might neutralise the effects on immediate production. There was also the disquieting consideration that a selective attack might enable the enemy to concentrate his defences, and his resources for repair or, indeed, to disperse the industry altogether. Apart, therefore, from the great operational difficulties, which in 1942 were still of a decisive character, the selective plan cast an immense responsibility upon those who framed the intelligence appreciations. No one could be certain they were right and Sir Arthur Harris, as he had indicated in the case of ball-bearings, had a growing conviction that they were wrong.[1]

These difficulties and disadvantages seemed to redound to the advantage of the general attack on towns. Indeed, the operational difficulties alone had, as we have seen, made such a policy temporarily inevitable. The damage caused by this kind of offensive would be much more widely spread and physically much greater than that

---

[1] The problems of the economic appraisal of general and selective bombing are considered in greater detail in Chapter VIII.

involved in any other policy. It was reasonable to suppose that it would be impossible for the enemy to repair all this damage. Nor could he disperse or evacuate all his leading towns. The importance of precise intelligence also seemed to be less because it might be supposed that in the general attack, what was vital would come down alongside of that which was not. In the plan for general area attack, however, the physical destruction of factories and so on was secondary and incidental. The primary aim was to dislocate production by destroying both the means of and the will to carry it on. Now this, as the Air Staff had often suggested, was likely to be a very large task. No one could say with any certainty how large it really was, but the answer obviously depended upon the Germans themselves, upon their organisation for repair and relief and ultimately upon their national spirit. If the German people were already weak in morale, liable to panic and eager to revolt then clearly a cancer of the national war will could be more easily established than if they were resolute, calm and obedient. Similarly, if the German war economy was already stretched to the limit it would obviously snap more easily than if it was cushioned by reserves and surplus capacity. Thus, after all, the responsibility thrown upon those who wrote the intelligence appreciations was, in the case of the general towns plan, just as great as in that of the selective plans. Indeed, in the former case, the task confronting the intelligence experts was also more difficult than in the latter. Though it is not easy to collect accurate evidence about enemy oil or ball-bearings production, it is, perhaps, generally easier than to present a clear picture of such an elusive subject as enemy national morale. It also is generally easier to get accurate facts about one industry than about a whole economy.

Here then were some of the considerations which bore upon the problem of bombing policy in the summer and autumn of 1942. Clearly the success of the offensive depended upon the choice of a target system which was vital and vulnerable and upon the ability of the force to cause and sustain sufficient damage for long enough. Various possible solutions to this simple proposition had already been mooted but the sovereign factor of operational ability had so far been decisive. The policy of general area attack reigned supreme. Nevertheless, though it is inevitable that existing operational means control contemporary policy, it is also true that projected policy influences future operational developments. To this extent the question was circular.

All these plans involved the common assumption that the opposing air force could be successfully evaded at night. Their execution was supposed to be a matter of range, navigation, bomb aiming, weight of attack and measures of evasion. They did not seem to involve a trial of strength, but only a trial of wits with the German air force.

All the operational experience of the war seemed to support this thesis. It was true that neither the British nor the German night defences had been able to inflict paralysing casualties on the forces of night bombers which had challenged them. Thus, the question of seeking the destruction of the enemy air force seemed, from the point of view of the British night offensive, to be irrelevant. Nevertheless, there were other reasons which from time to time suggested the importance of attempting the task.

It had been frequently argued that any effective attack on Germany would render assistance to Russia. This argument had been adduced in support both of the ball-bearings and the oil plans. Stalin himself attached great importance to the bombing of Berlin.[1] All the same, the 'Russian' argument had particular force in relation to any plan for the attack on the German air force, for the importance of air superiority in the area of a military campaign had been convincingly demonstrated on several occasions and in many theatres and it was widely appreciated.

It was largely for this reason and also on account of British combined operations in the West that the problem of attacking the German air force continued to occupy the attention of the Air Staff. *Circus* operations were still going on and, on 5th May 1942, an amendment to the bombing directive had been issued. This drew Sir Arthur Harris' attention to what intelligence sources suggested was a serious shortage of fighter aircraft in the *Luftwaffe*. It suggested that area attacks should be made on towns associated with the production of fighter aircraft and that, when and if possible, these should be accompanied by precision attacks on some of the factories themselves.[2]

As has already been seen, there were difficulties which Bomber and Fighter Commands had encountered in their attempts to get to grips with the German air force in the air during their *Circus* operations. As has also been seen, even if the inaccuracies of night bombing had been less, the strategic target of German aircraft production would still have been a very difficult proposition on account of its geographical distribution and its division into small units. Indeed, already in effect, Bomber Command, as a predominantly night force, and Fighter Command, as a short-range force equipped for the air defence of Great Britain, were virtually powerless to strike offensive and direct blows against the German air force. The most, it seemed, that Bomber Command could do was to contain parts, no doubt, even significant parts, of it, in western Germany for the air defence of the country. The most that Fighter Command could do was to repel it

---

[1] Churchill (in Russia) to Sinclair and Portal, 17th Aug. 1942. See also below, p. 492.
[2] Dir. Bottomley to Harris, 5th May 1942, App. 8 (xxiii).

when it offered battle over Britain herself, or those parts of France which lay closest to Britain.

So far as rendering assistance to the land campaign in Russia, this was seen to be a handicap. But in so far as the strategic air offensive itself was concerned it did not seem to be serious or even relevant. The directive amendment of 5th May 1942 was, therefore, concerned with a not very hopeful attempt to increase the auxiliary contribution which Bomber Command was making to the military war. Developments which were now impending and particularly those which were the consequence of the intervention of the United States Army Air Forces were presently to place an entirely different complexion upon the whole question of attack on the German air force. It is to these developments that we must now turn.

3. The American intervention and the strategic problems of a daylight policy, September–November 1942

The entry of America into the war, followed by the Presidential decision that American aircraft should be flown by American crews, had dealt a serious blow at the plans for the expansion of Bomber Command. Nevertheless, it was not unreasonable to suppose that this disadvantage would be more than offset by the active intervention of the United States Army Air Forces. From the point of view of the strategic air offensive the question of who flew the aircraft was not important. What mattered was how many long-range bombers the Americans would produce and to what purpose they would apply them.

The decisions in these matters were American decisions which the British might influence but could not control. Yet the sense in which they were taken was likely to have, and, in fact, did have, a profound effect upon the course of the British air offensive. After 1942 it is no longer possible to follow the history of the British air offensive without repeated reference to the policy, operations and achievements of the United States Army Air Forces. The two air forces acted and reacted upon each other to such an extent that to attempt a separate analysis of the history of either without frequent reference to the other would be to produce an incomplete and a misleading account.

The extent to which the strategic air offensive would be compensated for the loss to the Royal Air Force of many American-built aircraft, depended, then, upon the size and performance of the American bomber force, as also upon the speed with which it could be mobilised and put into effective operation over Germany. The answer to this riddle remained for long in a state of anxious suspension.

At the Washington War Conference of December 1941 and January 1942, it will be recalled, the new allies had confirmed their earlier decision to regard Germany as their first and principal enemy. Japan was to be contained and then attacked only after the downfall of Germany. Nevertheless, like most major decisions in war, this resolve was not founded upon unanimous support, and it was, perhaps, more difficult for the Americans than the British to assimilate the argument that the Germans were the first and principal enemy. It was, after all, the Japanese, and not the Germans, who had struck at the Americans the most wounding and humiliating blow which they had ever sustained. Moreover, the march of events in the Far East soon showed that the holding actions of the allies were not containing the Japanese. There was, accordingly, much force in the argument voiced by such authorities as General MacArthur and Admiral King,

354 THE CRISIS OF STRATEGIC BOMBING

that a greater effort should be applied to the war in the Far East, and, therefore, necessarily, a smaller one to that in Europe.

The general debate had a particular reference to the prospects of an American bombing offensive against Germany. The American Air Staff favoured a plan for building up a heavy strategic air force in the United Kingdom for the purpose of developing an attack upon Germany. Such a plan had received the approval of the Washington War Conference, but, according to information which reached London, it seemed that the American Naval Staff had different ideas. Their plan apparently envisaged the development of air and sea operations in the Far East, working north-west from a line through New Caledonia, Fiji and Samoa. The possibility arose that this naval plan would absorb all the available American heavy bombers for as long as eight months.[1]

In any case the particular question of the American bombing offensive was obviously and intimately related to the general question of the grand strategy of the war. Nevertheless, there was much that Britain could do to influence the situation. Apart from the unexampled prestige which Mr. Churchill had acquired, Britain had a longer experience of the war and she also had larger forces immediately available for operations. To that extent she was for the time being the senior partner in the new alliance and to that extent her influence was likely to be weighty.

This influence was cast into the scales in favour of maintaining the agreement reached at the Washington War Conference. It was British policy to enlist the American air force in the strategic offensive against Germany as soon, and on as large a scale as possible, but in the presentation of this policy there were difficulties and hazards which opposed almost insurmountable obstacles. The American Staffs 'as a whole' were extremely dubious about the efficacy of the night area bombing offensive.[2] They were 'fanatic' about the need for daylight bombing. So deeply were the Americans committed to the policy of daylight bombing that any condemnation of it by the British on operational grounds was likely to have far-reaching strategic consequences. It was certain to strengthen the American naval argument.[3]

---

[1] R.A.F. Del. (Washington) (Strafford) to Air Min. (Dickson), 20th Feb. 1942.

[2] Numerous reports on British and German night area bombing had been produced in the United States and by United States observers in Europe. The Air Warfare Plans Division, in a report of 11th September 1941, had suggested that this kind of attack would be useful only after enemy morale had begun to crack as a result of precision attacks upon key targets. A.W.P.D./1. R.S.I. 145·81–23. An Air Corps Tactical School report of 4th December 1941 said that the results of British and German bombing had been far from decisive and were unlikely to become so. do. 248·2209A–15. A Military Intelligence Division report of 23rd February 1942 said that the material and morale effects of British night bombing appeared to amount to little. do. 248·2209A–13.

[3] R.A.F. Del. (Washington) to Air Min., 20th Feb. 1942. It was a fact of considerable significance that the Americans had been able to observe the effects of the Bomber

The situation was further complicated by the President's desire that American troops should engage the enemy in 1942. The allied plan for an invasion of North Africa, known as Operation *Torch*, still further diminished, or at any rate delayed, the prospects of an effective American intervention in the strategic bombing offensive. Added to all this was the fact, which has already emerged, that the position of the British advocates of the strategic bombing offensive was by no means impregnable.

Despite all these difficulties General Arnold persevered with his plan for a daylight strategic bomber force to be based in the United Kingdom and, by 17th August 1942, he had succeeded far enough to allow the opening of operations. On that day twelve aircraft of the Eighth Bomber Command delivered a daylight attack on the marshalling yards at Rouen. They suffered no losses. Thereafter these operations were continued. They were partly designed to make a strategic contribution to the Battle of the Atlantic, for the majority of the targets attacked were submarine bases, but they were also and primarily intended as 'working up' for the coming attack on Germany. That attack did not, however, materialise until 1943. Meanwhile, these experimental and tentative daylight attacks on fringe targets were a beginning.[1]

They were not, however, a beginning which the Prime Minister found particularly impressive. In a message to the President of 16th September 1942, he said that the first operations of the Flying Fortresses had been 'most encouraging', but he observed that they had not yet struck 'very deep'. Meanwhile, Mr. Churchill said, 'in spite of the fact that we cannot make up more than 32 squadrons of bombers, instead of 42 last year, we know our night bomber offensive is having a devastating effect'. He wanted President Roosevelt to read Sir Arthur Harris' memorandum on the role and work of Bomber Command,[2] for, though he admitted that the Air Marshal had, 'out of zeal . . . no doubt overstated a good case', he thought that Sir Arthur Harris had 'almost unique qualifications to express an opinion on the subject,' and that his paper was 'an impressive contribution to thought on the subject.' 'If', Mr. Churchill continued, 'we can add continuity and precision to the attack by your bombers striking deep into the heart of Germany by day the effect would be redoubled.' He, therefore, hoped that the American bomber force in Britain would be built up so that 'together we might even deal a blow at the enemy's air power from which he could never fully recover. . . . I am sure we

---

Command night offensive through the eyes of their diplomats, journalists and business men in Germany during its most ineffective phase from 1939 to 1941.

[1] *The Army Air Forces in World War II*, Vol. II (1949), Appendix *Eighth Air Force Heavy Bomber Missions*.

[2] See above, p. 342.

should be missing a great opportunity if we did not concentrate every available Fortress and long range escort fighter as quickly as possible for the attack on our primary enemy'. Mr. Churchill noted with 'some concern' how the build-up of American air forces in Britain was falling behind schedule, especially as more than 800 British and American aircraft had been withdrawn from the United Kingdom for service in the North African campaign. He wanted the President to consider special priorities for aircraft production in America and he suggested that 'special emphasis should be laid on that of heavy bombers and pursuit aircraft'. For 'keeping up and intensifying the direct pressure on Germany', Mr. Churchill said, 'the Fortress and the long range fighter are indispensable.'[1]

This was exactly the argument calculated to strengthen General Arnold's position. It did not seek to question the validity of the American plan for daylight bombing. On the contrary, it supported it, but it did show the need for rapid and large reinforcement of the Eighth Air Force, for, to quote Mr. Churchill's message to the President again, in order to make an effective attack on Germany 'without prohibitive loss' the Eighth Air Force 'must have numbers to saturate and disperse the defences.' Moreover, it needed them quickly for 'a few hundred Fortresses this Autumn and Winter, while substantial German air forces are still held in Russia may well be worth many more in a year's time when the enemy may be able greatly to reinforce his Western air defences.'

Nevertheless, General Arnold's whole position, as also the argument which the Prime Minister had now advanced to President Roosevelt, turned upon whether in the event, when they had received their reinforcements, the American bombers would succeed in breaking into Germany in daylight and without prohibitive losses, adding 'continuity and precision' to the strategic air attack.

Sir Charles Portal was pessimistic about the prospect and he saw grave dangers in the attempt. It seemed to him that if the American day bombers suffered heavy casualties with five or six groups 'they will merely say that the job requires 15 or 20 Groups and by the time they have 20 Groups they will probably be committed to 40 or 50. In the end,' Sir Charles Portal thought, 'they may find themselves no more successful with 50 Groups than the Germans were with the same numbers in the Battle of Britain.' The danger was that by the time the Americans had learnt this lesson it would be too late for them to convert their offensive from day to night. Whereas he believed that a good night bombing force could be quickly turned into a day force, Sir Charles Portal thought it would be 'a long and difficult process to turn a day bombing force into a night bombing force.'

---

[1] Churchill to Roosevelt, 16th Sept. 1942.

The process would involve 'not only production but also training'. The Americans, he considered, would be unable to get a night bombing force by the beginning of 1944 unless they started before the end of 1942, and since he estimated that the American component of the eventual combined bomber force would account for two-thirds of its size, this was obviously a matter of the first importance.

For these reasons, Sir Charles Portal felt inclined to try to persuade the Americans 'to lay the foundations in aircraft production and in training for at least a substantial part of their offensive to be by night bombing.' Since neither the Fortress nor the Liberator appeared to be suitable for night bombing, it seemed to Sir Charles Portal that the Americans should build 'a very large number of Lancasters while we might build a corresponding number of Mustangs'.[1]

Thus, by building Lancasters, which had already demonstrated a claim to be considered the ideal night bombers, the Americans might insure themselves against the failure of their day plans. By building Mustangs, which were still an unknown quantity but which in time achieved the distinction of becoming the ideal long-range fighters, the British might help to secure the success of the day plan. This would, indeed, have been a curious solution, for it was the Americans who believed in day bombing and the British who disbelieved in it.

It was also a solution which was likely to encounter serious difficulties and, perhaps, endanger the bombing offensive to an even greater extent than Sir Charles Portal believed the American day plan had already endangered it. Air Vice-Marshal Slessor, the Assistant Chief of the Air Staff (Policy), who was consulted on this point and who in 1940 and 1941 had been in Washington, thought it certain that the Americans contemplated no plan for large-scale training in night bombing. He said they had not thought out what they would do if the day-bombing plan failed. 'They have', he added, 'hung their hats on the day bomber policy and are convinced they can do it'. He thought that to cast doubts on this policy 'would only cause irritation and make them very obstinate'. The impending election in America would, Air Vice-Marshal Slessor thought, make the Administration reluctant to admit limitations in their bombers especially as charges had already been made to the effect that their fighters were inadequate.[2]

Air Vice-Marshal Slessor's advice was not conditioned solely by his realistic view of what would be acceptable or unacceptable to the Americans, though there can be no doubt that he judged this matter aright. A more important factor was that he too believed that the American day bombers could 'do it.' The Americans, he explained to

---
[1] Memo. by Portal, 26th Sept. 1942. Sir Charles Portal sent this to Air Vice-Marshal Slessor with the question 'What do you think?'
[2] Min. Slessor to Portal, 26th Sept. 1942.

Sir Archibald Sinclair on 26th September 1942, 'intend to do precision bombing in Germany by daylight. This is the basis of their air policy in this theatre. They believe that with their good defensive armament they can do it when they get sufficient numbers. Their early operations', Air Vice-Marshal Slessor continued, 'lend some support to this belief—the B.17' (i.e. Fortress) 'has shown that it can defend itself and take an enormous amount of punishment. It has yet to be proved', he admitted, 'whether it is possible to carry the war deep into Germany by day. But they believe they will and I personally am inclined to agree with them *once they get really adequate numbers.*'

Air Vice-Marshal Slessor had been shown the detailed American plan. It assumed that Bomber Command would continue the area assault by night and it envisaged the American day bombers picking on selected 'vital war industrial targets one by one.' While in some respects the plan seemed to Air Vice-Marshal Slessor to be 'academic and unduly optimistic', it was, he told Sir Archibald Sinclair, 'a very impressive bit of work and always assuming it *is* possible to bomb Germany by day,' he thought it was a 'war-winner'. For the discharge of the plan the Americans had in mind a force of some 2,000 heavy bombers supported by a further 1,000 medium bombers. The first selected target was the German fighter aircraft industry.[1]

Sir Charles Portal remained unconvinced by these arguments. He agreed, he told Sir Archibald Sinclair on 27th September 1942, that a force of 3,000 heavy and medium bombers 'able to pick off small targets with precision in any part of Germany by day would enable us to win the war,' but he did not agree that the Americans would ever be able to do this. He pointed out that it was 'quite easy' to hit small targets by day when there was no serious opposition. He suggested that the proposition became entirely different when the day bombers were harassed by fighters and flak. So far, he said, 'the Fortresses have had virtually no opposition except at Rotterdam, where I believe none of them claimed to have bombed anywhere near the target.' Sir Charles Portal did not believe that the American day formations would be able to defend themselves. 'The Ruhr is 300 miles away and assuming', he said, 'that the American fighters can go in 200 miles the Fortresses would have 200 miles to fly unescorted. Berlin', he continued, 'is 550 miles and would involve 700 miles' unescorted flying . . .' He predicted that the Fortress gunners would be overpowered by constant German fighter attack. 'My own prophecy', he said, 'of what will actually happen is this: The Americans will eventually be able to get as far as the Ruhr, suffering very much heavier casualties than we now suffer by night, and going much more rarely. They will in effect do area bombing with the advantage of the

---

[1] Min. Slessor to Sinclair, 26th Sept. 1942.

THE AMERICAN INTERVENTION

absence of decoys. If it can be kept up in face of the losses (and I don't think it will be) this will of course be a valuable contribution to the war, but it will certainly not result in the elimination of the enemy fighter force and so open the way to the free bombing of the rest of Germany. I do not think', he continued, 'that they will ever be able regularly to penetrate further than the Ruhr and perhaps Hamburg without absolutely prohibitive losses resulting from being run out of ammunition by constant attack or from gunners being killed or wounded.'

Sir Charles Portal hoped he would be proved wrong in this severe judgment, but he did not think it would be possible to know until the beginning of 1943 at the earliest. Meanwhile, he reverted to his idea of enlisting the Americans in the night offensive. 'I have no doubt', he said, 'that if by the end of 1943 we had a force of 3,000 American heavy and medium bombers properly trained for night flying to our standards, we and they together could pulverise almost the whole of the industrial and economic power of Germany within a year, besides utterly destroying the morale of the German people'. The Chief of the Air Staff recognised that this great night offensive would involve considerable casualties but, though he thought that 'the battle of night defence versus night bomber will swing backwards and forwards all the time', he did not believe that night bomber casualties would ever become insupportable. 'The advantage of bombing for devastation', he added, 'is of course that the vast majority of the bombs have a direct effect on something—at best an important factory, at worst the morale of the German people—whereas the very high percentage of bombs which I expect to miss a small target will often do no good whatever.' [1]

This judgment by Sir Charles Portal was weighty and in many of its details it was also wise. It is, perhaps, in place here to mention that the prediction of the Fortresses' incapacity to defend themselves when beyond the range of fighter cover was fully justified by subsequent events. So also did subsequent events show that Sir Charles Portal had been right in suggesting that precision bombing by day would tend to develop into area bombing when the opposition was severe. The peculiar irony of the situation was, however, that Sir Charles Portal, who had no confidence in the future of a long-range fighter, was pressing for the development of the Mustang, which the Americans did not regard with favour. A further and, perhaps, even greater irony was introduced by the fact that Air Vice-Marshal Slessor, whose judgment of the prospects of the self-defending formation of Fortresses was almost as wrong as that of the Americans themselves, had, by his advice, rendered a service to the bombing offensive, which, as

---

[1] Min. Portal to Sinclair, 27th Sept. 1942.

will presently be shown, was of outstanding and, perhaps, even of decisive value.

In this somewhat curious situation, the Prime Minister inclined to the opinions which had been expressed by Sir Charles Portal. In a personal message to Mr. Harry Hopkins of 16th October 1942, he spoke of the necessity for the American Air Force to develop an effective night bomber and also of the urgency of producing Mustang fighters with Merlin and later Griffon engines. 'I must also say to you for your eye alone', he explained, 'and only to be used by you in your high discretion that the very accurate results so far achieved in the daylight bombing of France by your Fortresses under most numerous Fighter escort mainly British, does not give our experts the same confidence as yours in the power of the day bomber to operate far into Germany. We do not', he added, 'think the claims of the Fighters shot down by Fortresses are correct though made with complete sincerity, and the dangers of daylight bombing will increase terribly once outside Fighter protection and as the range lengthens.'[1]

Within the purely British circle of the Chiefs of Staff Committee, the Prime Minister went further and, addressing them on 22nd October 1942, he said that the American day bombers would 'probably experience a heavy disaster' as soon as they flew beyond the range of their escorting fighters. 'We must try to persuade them', he added, 'to divert these energies (a) to sea work, beginning with helping "*Torch*" (including bombing the Biscay ports), and (b) to night work.'[2]

This suggestion amounted to writing off the American day contribution to the bombing offensive against Germany and its conversion into a kind of Coastal Command. This was not an idea which appealed to the British Air Staff. Meanwhile, Air Vice-Marshal Slessor's advice had not been without effect and, on 23rd October 1942, Sir Archibald Sinclair made an important intervention. In a minute to the Prime Minister he said that 'with 4,000 to 6,000 bombers operating from this country we can pulverize German war industry and transport and bring the harvest of victory within the compass of such land forces as we shall have available in 1944'. The creation of such a force by the middle, or certainly the third quarter, of 1944 would be possible provided both Bomber Command and the American Bomber Command were supplied with the proper reinforcements. The prospect for both Commands was, in Sir Archibald Sinclair's estimation, conditional upon the attitude of the Prime Minister.

'According to our information', the Secretary of State for Air told Mr. Churchill, 'your pronouncement would be decisive in its in-

---

[1] Churchill to Hopkins, 16th Oct. 1942.
[2] Memo. by Churchill, 22nd Oct. 1942.

fluence upon American deliberations at this critical juncture. American opinion is divided;' he explained, 'some want to concentrate on the Pacific; others against Germany; some want an Air Force which would be mainly ancillary to the Army, equipped with Army Support aircraft and employed (no doubt in extravagant numbers) in the theatres of land operations; others want to build up a big bomber force to attack the centre of German power. It is in your power,' Sir Archibald Sinclair said, 'to crystallise American opinion and to unite it behind those schools of thought which want to attack Germany and want to do it by building up an overwhelming force of bombers in this country. Instead, however, of uniting those schools of thought which want to build up a big bomber force and want to use American power for a decisive attack upon Germany in 1943 and 1944, you will,' he warned Mr. Churchill, 'throw these forces into confusion and impotency if you set yourself against their cherished policy of daylight penetration.'

This policy of daylight penetration had, Sir Archibald Sinclair went on to say, 'in the opinion of the Air Staff, and my own inexpert opinion . . . a chance of success.' If it did succeed it would, he suggested, be possible 'in the earliest months of next year for us to send a thousand bombers over Hamburg one night, for the Americans to follow up with 5 or 600 bombers the following day and, if the weather is kind, for us to follow up with a large force of heavy bombers the next night—and then to go on bombing one city after another in Germany on that scale.' If it succeeded, he said, 'the Fortresses will be able to pin-point vital aircraft factories and to knock them out in a series of daylight attacks.' Moreover, even allowing for exaggerated claims, it seemed to Sir Archibald Sinclair that the Fortresses would shoot down a large and, perhaps, a crippling number of German fighters. If the Americans were not unduly impeded by diversions it was, Sir Archibald Sinclair reported, 'their firm intention to drop bombs on Germany in daylight next month. It would be a tragedy', he said, 'if we were to frustrate them on the eve of this great experiment.' [1]

Matters were now clearly approaching a crisis and Sir Charles Portal was placed in an extremely delicate position. If his influence was to be thrown into the scale of building up the American strategic bomber force, it seemed that he would have to support an American bombing policy in which he had little confidence. If, on the other hand, he was to persist with his objections to that bombing policy, he was likely to be instrumental in the diversion of the American strategic bomber force which he believed was necessary to victory. In these circumstances it is hardly surprising to discover that Sir Charles

---

[1] Min. Sinclair to Churchill, 23rd Oct. 1942.

Portal subjected his views upon daylight bombing to radical revision. On 7th November 1942 he told the Prime Minister that the small results which had, up till then, been achieved by the American bombers were due to lack of training, lack of numbers, lack of operational experience and diversions to the Pacific and North African theatres. He expressed his belief that 'fighter escort into Germany will prove impracticable and that the bombers must look after themselves', but he suggested that they might be able to do this if the formations were strengthened by some aircraft carrying ammunition at the expense of bombload. He did not think that the daylight plan ought to be abandoned if aircraft occasionally ran out of ammunition. This, he said, was liable to happen to anyone.

In order to decide the best course of action, Sir Charles Portal now said, it was necessary to balance 'the probability of success which may not be very high,[1] against the results of success if it is achieved. If success could only amount to a tour de force having no real military value, I should', he told the Prime Minister, 'be entirely with you in trying to ride the Americans off the attempt altogether. Actually, however,' he continued, 'success would have tremendous consequences.'

The most important of these consequences, it seemed to Sir Charles Portal, would be the effect on the German air force. According to his estimates, the Germans were already losing between fifty and seventy-five night fighters a month as a result of the Bomber Command night attacks. These losses were, he said, mainly due to crashes and were not, of course, a primary object of the offensive which cost Bomber Command an average of 140 aircraft a month. He estimated the total loss of all German fighters on all fronts at about 360 per month. Now if the Americans were prepared to lose the same number of bombers by day as Bomber Command was losing by night, and, if for each one destroyed in action three German fighters could be shot down, then the German fighter losses on the Western Front alone would rise from 125 to about 545 per month and their total losses on all fronts to roughly 780 per month. He estimated the German production of new fighters at 535 per month. 'The effect of this on all fronts', Sir Charles Portal said, 'needs no emphasis. Failing a great increase in fighter production and repair (which must be at the expense of something else and could not in any case be achieved very quickly) the German fighter force would within a few months be so weakened as to leave the whole country open to day bombing and air superiority on all land fronts in the hands of United Nations'.[2]

No doubt, Sir Charles Portal had been much influenced by the

---

[1] To which, at Sir Archibald Sinclair's suggestion, he added the words 'but is not negligible'.
[2] Min. Portal to Churchill, 7th Nov. 1942.

prospect of seeing the American heavy bombers take their departure for the Bay of Biscay, the Mediterranean, and the Pacific, or even of never being produced at all. His conversion to the idea of daylight bombing was far from wholehearted and it had not been encouraged by the experience of the daylight Lancaster attack which had taken place on 17th April 1942 against the M.A.N. factory at Augsburg.[1] Nevertheless, it is interesting to note that although he had once more decried the prospects of the long-range fighter, Sir Charles Portal had envisaged the possibility of the downfall of the *Luftwaffe* in consequence of battles in the air. He had also indicated the significance which the resulting air superiority might have, not only for the land campaigns, but also for the bombing offensive itself. The ultimate importance of these ideas was profound, especially in view of the fact that there was, as we have seen, a considerable body of opinion both within and without the Air Staff which accepted the American belief that, if it was possible, selective precision attack was a more effective policy than general area attack. This was, after all, the belief with which the British Air Staff had entered the war. Thus, as, with Mr. Churchill's powerful pronouncement still in doubt, the autumn turned into the winter the question of an attack on the German air force began to assume a new and different significance.

---

[1] See below pp. 441–444.

4. The role of strategic bombing and the outlook for 1943, October–December 1942

The differences of opinion which had revealed themselves between the British and American Air Staffs did not concern the major strategy of the air offensive. On this great issue General Arnold and Sir Charles Portal were united. Both believed in the long-range bomber as a weapon of 'independent' potential. Both believed that its true and main function was to strike at the heart of the enemy. Neither accepted the view which prevailed among their respective naval and military colleagues that air power was no more than an adjunct to conventional operations on the surface. Though the American air force was still a part of the American Army, the strategic thinking of its leaders was close to that which inspired the Royal Air Force Bomber Command.

The differences which separated the two Staffs, and to a less extent the individual members of each Staff, related, then, not to the major strategy, but to the bombing policy by which that strategy might be realised. They proceeded from different views of operational possibility and probability, from different interpretations of the previous course of the war and from the different types of aircraft with which the two air forces were equipped. These differences were important, for obviously the achievement of the strategic aim depended upon the selection of a bombing policy which was at once effective and possible. It also depended upon the measure of integration which could be achieved by the two forces. Nevertheless, these differences were not such as could be settled round a conference table and, in the circumstances which have already been discussed, any attempt to bring American policy into line with the British was liable to jeopardize the whole position of the bombing offensive in the grand strategy of the war.

Sir Charles Portal had realised this and he was accordingly willing to refer the issue of daylight bombing to the test of operations. Nevertheless, the doubts which inevitably persisted about what would actually happen to the American formations when they crossed the German frontier, as well as the various possibilities of change to which British bombing policy was increasingly subject, still made it impossible to envisage with clarity the pattern of the coming Anglo-American air offensive.

All the same, it was important and urgent to reach some general conclusions about the role which this air offensive was to play in the grand strategy of the war. The bombing offensive was no longer justified solely on the grounds that it was the only means of exerting offensive pressure against the enemy. At least in theory, other possibilities were already open. Nor, and for the same reason, was the production of long-range bombers necessarily entitled to all the resources which could reasonably be spared after the immediate needs of direct defence had been met. The survival of Russia, and above all the involvement of America in the war as well as the generally more favourable situation of the allied cause necessitated a re-definition of the role of the strategic air offensive. It was, indeed, only in the light of such a definition that calculated decisions could be taken about the size to which the long-range bomber forces should be expanded and the degree of priority which should be accorded to their production in the general scramble for armaments of all kinds. It was only in the light of such a decision that the strategic desirability of the various bombing policies could be judged.

The principal new possibility which had been introduced by the resistance of Russia and the involvement of America was the prospect of defeating Germany by the action of land armies, which had been such a forlorn hope for the British Commonwealth while it was fighting alone. Nevertheless, this was a prospect which remained formidable and, unless German strength could first be sapped by other means, perhaps, even hopeless. Yet it was generally agreed that the allies would ultimately have to occupy Germany with land forces.

The solution to this problem had been propounded in general terms at the Washington War Conference. The attack on Germany would have to be developed in two phases. In the first, she would be worn down by strategic bombing, blockade, subversive activities and propaganda. In the second, she would be attacked from the perimeter by invading armies.[1] Like most decisions which have to be acceptable to many divergent opinions, this proposition was, however, too general to have much meaning. The theory was that the preliminary weakening of Germany's heart would lead her limbs the more readily to succumb. The extent to which the heart could be weakened by the means proposed and the amount of force which would still be necessary to break through the surviving crust of resistance were controversial questions to which Admirals, Generals and Air Marshals or Air Generals were sure to give different answers.

There was, however, a great danger in the usual compromise by which such matters are normally adjusted. As Sir Charles Portal observed at the end of September 1942, the probability was that if a middle course was pursued between the policies of building up the land forces for the offensive from the perimeter and the bomber forces for that at the centre, neither would gain the necessary strength to achieve decisive results and the war might drag on for years. If,

---

[1] Memo. by U.S. and British C.O.S., 20th Jan. 1942.

however, Sir Charles Portal told his colleagues, a force of some four to six thousand heavy bombers could be brought to bear upon Germany by 1944, then, he said, in that year they would be able to create the opportunity for decisive action by a relatively small land force.[1]

About two-thirds of this bombing force would have to be American and it was partly with a view to attracting Americans to Europe and stimulating American aircraft production that Sir Charles Portal chose this moment to pronounce his views.[2] It was, perhaps, also for the same reason that the three British Chiefs of Staff were able, within a month, to agree upon a strategic review which embodied and expanded Sir Charles Portal's proposition.

This review, which was circulated on 30th October 1942, clearly reaffirmed that the allies must 'undermine Germany's military power by the destruction of the German industrial and economic war machine before we attempt invasion.' For this purpose, apart from the Russian military effort, the Chiefs of Staff said, 'The heavy bomber will be the main weapon,' and, they added, it must have 'absolute priority of Anglo-American production' subject only to the needs of allied security and the necessity of containing Japan. It was from the resources which remained after these commitments had been met that the forces of surface invasion were to be built up.

'The aim of the bomber offensive', the Chiefs of Staff now said, 'is the progressive destruction and dislocation of the enemy's war industrial and economic system and the undermining of his morale to a point where his capacity for armed resistance is fatally weakened.' In estimating the prospects of realising this aim, the Chiefs of Staff added, it was 'important not to be misled by the limited results attained in the past two and a half years.' Improvements in equipment and technique, both actual and prospective, meant that Bomber Command would 'attain far higher standards of efficiency and accuracy in night bombing in the future, than have been possible in the past.' Moreover, daylight bombing by the American Air Force was said to show promise, and, if it failed over Germany, it was hoped that it might join Bomber Command in the night assault.

It was not suggested that the bomber offensive would 'at once shatter the enemy's morale,' but it was claimed that an appreciable effect had already been achieved and that there would be ever-increasing effects on the German 'distributive system and industrial potential.' As to the size of the combined bomber force, the Chiefs of Staff said, 'We can now drop 6,000 to 7,000 tons of bombs a month on Germany. By the end of this year we hope, with the aid of the American air forces which should by then be operating in the United

---

[1] Memo. for C.O.S. by Portal, 30th Sept. 1942.

[2] Letter Portal to Brooke, 28th Sept. 1942, in which he said, 'you will realise that in writing this paper my eye has been mainly on American developments.'

THE OUTLOOK FOR 1943

Kingdom, to raise this to 10,000 tons a month. We should aim at dropping at least 20,000 tons a month on Germany by June 1943, and', they continued, 'at attaining a target force of the order of 4,000–6,000 heavy bombers by April 1944 with a monthly bomb delivery of 60,000–90,000 tons. With American co-operation', the Chiefs of Staff concluded, 'we believe this can be achieved.'[1]

This declaration by the Chiefs of Staff represented an extraordinary victory for the Air Staff point of view and it was a tribute not only to the persuasive powers of Sir Charles Portal but also to the prestige which Bomber Command had acquired in the course of 1942. It was, nevertheless, by no means a final victory. To become effective the document still required not only the approval of the British Government but also the endorsement of the United States Joint Chiefs of Staff, and, even if these sanctions could be obtained, the fact still had to be faced that between declaration and fulfilment men often change their minds.

In America the discussion about war production and allocation was running somewhat ahead of the debate on war strategy and it seemed to the British representatives in Washington that the British Chiefs of Staff memorandum should be communicated to the United States authorities as a means of injecting some strategic direction to the production plans. With this consideration in mind, the British Joint Staff Mission in Washington asked, on 5th November 1942, for full approval of the memorandum from London. Two days later Mr. Oliver Lyttelton, the Minister of Production, who was on a visit to Washington, asked the Prime Minister for authority to use it as the strategic basis of his impending discussions with the President, Mr. Harry Hopkins and the United States Chiefs of Staff.[2]

Matters were, however, developing so quickly that later in the day on 7th November and before any authority had been received from London, Field Marshal Sir John Dill, after consultation with Mr. Lyttelton, decided to give the United States Chiefs of Staff an 'unofficial' digest of the memorandum with the explanation that it had not yet been approved by the British Government.[3] The views of the British Chiefs of Staff which were thus conveyed to the United States Chiefs of Staff appeared, as Sir John Dill had expected, to meet with the approval of the latter, with the possible exception of Admiral King.[4] General Arnold, in particular, was well pleased, and Air Marshal Evill thought that the views expressed would help him

---

[1] C.O.S. Memo., 30th Oct. 1942.
[2] J.S.M. (Washington) to C.O.S. (London), 5th Nov. 1942. Lyttelton (Washington) to Churchill, 7th Nov. 1942.
[3] Dill (Washington) to C.O.S. (London), 7th Nov. 1942.
[4] Slessor (Washington) to Portal, 9th Nov. 1942. Of Admiral King's attitude, this message said that Sir John Dill thought that 'even he really agrees with it'.

to overcome the diversionary tendencies by which his plans were threatened.[1]

The Prime Minister was, however, unwilling to be rushed, and, without consulting the Chiefs of Staff, he instructed Mr. Lyttelton to withdraw the unofficial digest from circulation. He added that the memorandum was already out of date on account of the success which had been achieved in the invasion of North Africa. 'An entirely new view must be taken', he said 'of the possibilities of attacking Hitler in 1943.' In a second message he told Mr. Lyttelton that his authority did 'not extend to combined strategy.'[2]

This imposed a pause upon the swift course which affairs had been running, but before proceeding to an examination of the motives which prompted Mr. Churchill to this somewhat drastic intervention, it is necessary to see how brittle was the unity which the Chiefs of Staff seemed to have achieved in their memorandum of 30th October 1942.

This memorandum, it will be recalled, had envisaged an Anglo-American force of some four to six thousand heavy bombers in the United Kingdom by April 1944. It had also defined the general aim of the air offensive as 'the progressive destruction and dislocation of the enemy's war industrial and economic system and the undermining of his morale to a point where his capacity for armed resistance is fatally weakened.' The memorandum had not, however, concerned itself with the details of bombing policy by which this aim might be pursued nor had it attempted a precise analysis of how far the force which was envisaged might be able to achieve it.[3]

These more detailed considerations were, because of the many uncertainties which they involved, highly controversial, but they were also highly relevant and it was inevitable that the Chiefs of Staff should wish to examine them. On 5th October 1942 Sir Charles Portal had been invited by his colleagues to circulate a note 'setting out the facts and arguments which support the Air Staff view that a heavy bomber force rising to a peak of between 4,000 and 6,000 heavy bombers in 1944 could shatter the industrial and economic structure of Germany to a point where an Anglo-American force of reasonable strength could enter the Continent from the West.'[4]

This request, it will be noted, had been made more than three weeks before the Chiefs of Staff issued their strategic memorandum

---

[1] Evill (Washington) to Portal, 8th Nov. 1942.

[2] Churchill to Lyttelton (Washington), 9th and 10th Nov. 1942, and (showing that C.O.S. were not consulted) Portal to Slessor, 9th Nov. 1942. The Prime Minister, in adopting this attitude, was no doubt much influenced by the assurance which he had recently given to Marshal Stalin to the effect that a second front would be opened in Europe in 1943. See below, p. 375.

[3] C.O.S. Memo., 30th Oct. 1942.

[4] Memo. by Portal for C.O.S., 3rd Nov. 1942, App. 20.

on 30th October. It was not, however, until 3rd November that Sir Charles Portal complied with it. He claimed that the paper which he then laid before his colleagues was not a 'policy paper' but was merely an attempt to assess the effects of putting into practice a policy which they and he had already agreed upon[1]—this claim, however, was not strictly true, for any attempt to assess the effects of the offensive inevitably involved assumptions about the policy which would govern it, and these assumptions might not necessarily prove acceptable to the naval and military Chiefs of Staff. It was only upon a somewhat vaguely worded definition of the general aim of the offensive that the Chiefs of Staff had reached agreement. There was, therefore, no advance guarantee that the particular assumptions about bombing policy which Sir Charles Portal made would prove acceptable.

Nevertheless, it did seem that the Chiefs of Staff had endorsed the Air Staff hope of mustering four to six thousand British and American heavy bombers in the United Kingdom by 1944 and it was on the assumption that this plan would be realised that Sir Charles Portal based his calculations. In estimating the effects of the offensive which could be mounted by such a force, the Chief of the Air Staff was, of course, confronted with all the insuperable difficulties which Lord Cherwell and Mr. Justice Singleton had encountered earlier in the year. There was still insufficient evidence about the effects of Bomber Command attacks on Germany in the past to make them a satisfactory guide to those planned for the future and Sir Charles Portal was, therefore, thrown back upon the old method of taking the German offensive against Britain in 1940 and 1941 as the yardstick, and it was against this yardstick that he now sought to predict the consequences of the Anglo-American offensive in 1943 and 1944.

Assuming then that a monthly scale of attack amounting to 50,000 tons of bombs by the end of 1943 and rising to a peak of 90,000 tons by the end of 1944 could be delivered, then it would, in these two years, be possible to drop one and a quarter million tons of bombs on Germany. If it was also assumed that the effects of each ton of bombs dropped would be comparable to those of each ton which the Germans had dropped in 1940 and 1941 then, Sir Charles Portal concluded, the results would include the destruction of six million houses with a proportionate destruction of industrial buildings, means of transport and public utilities. Twenty-five million Germans would be rendered homeless, 900,000 would be killed and one million seriously injured. If these attacks were spread over the main urban areas of Germany, three-quarters of the inhabitants of all German towns with a population of more than 50,000 each would

---

[1] Undated Note by Portal (probably November 1942).

be left without homes, and they would, Sir Charles Portal said, 'destroy at least one-third of the total German industry.'

German industry was not, in Sir Charles Portal's view, in a condition to withstand such an onslaught. It was true, he admitted, that the German air offensive against Britain had 'produced no major interruption of the British war effort,' but apart from the fact that this offensive was many times less heavy and less efficient than that which he was considering, it seemed to Sir Charles Portal that there was another important factor. At the time of the German attacks, he said, the British war effort was running far below its potential maximum. In most cases alternative manufacturing capacity could be found to replace damaged factories. There were nearly a million builders available for repair work and these could be supplemented by soldiers. Britain also had had the resources of America behind her and she was not engaged upon any great land campaign. The British people were comparatively fresh, well fed and well clothed. 'They were braced by the ordeal of Dunkirk and sustained by the triumph of the Battle of Britain.'

In Germany, on the other hand, Sir Charles Portal expected the situation to be quite different. 'The heavy drain of the Russian war, the campaign in Libya, the existing air offensive and the blockade are', he said, 'all contributing to a progressive attrition. Damaged resources, plant and stock [sic] of materials cannot now be adequately replaced; structural damage can no longer be adequately repaired; replenishments obtainable from the stocks of occupied countries are a waning asset. The output of German labour is falling through war weariness, food difficulties and other domestic problems, while that of foreign labour—whether in Germany or in the occupied territories—falls with Germany's diminishing prospects.'

Thus, Sir Charles Portal saw the German war economy as a much more brittle structure than that which had existed in Britain at the beginning of the war and he saw coming against it a bombing offensive very much heavier and more effective than that which had fallen on Britain. He concluded that 'an Anglo-American bomber force based in the United Kingdom and building up to a peak of 4,000–6,000 heavy bombers by 1944 would be capable of reducing the German war potential well below the level at which an Anglo-American invasion of the Continent would become practicable. Indeed,' he added, 'I see every reason to hope that this result would be achieved well before the combined force had built up to peak strength.'[1]

In so far as it depended upon a diagnosis of the German war economy, this estimate was based upon a judgment of the situation

---

[1] Memo. by Portal for C.O.S., 3rd Nov. 1942, App. 20.

inside Germany which completely failed to comprehend the economic, industrial and moral resilience of the country. It was not, however, on this account that it found disfavour with the naval and military staffs. Nor did Sir Charles Portal's colleagues confine their criticisms to the detailed assumptions which had been made about bombing policy. On the contrary, they decided to forget that they had ever subscribed to the memorandum of 30th October and the whole strategy of the air offensive was once more assailed.

Sir Dudley Pound now observed that the bomber strength which was envisaged in Sir Charles Portal's estimate, and also, of course, in the memorandum of 30th October, would involve the import to the United Kingdom in 1944 of five million tons of aviation fuel, in addition to the existing need for one and a quarter million tons. He thought it was 'virtually certain' that this could not be done unless American tanker production was 'immensely increased'. Moreover, he was also somewhat doubtful of the labour and general supply implications of the proposed bomber programme and he suggested that the Ministers of Labour and Supply should be consulted. Finally, he was unwilling to accept Sir Charles Portal's estimates of the effects of the offensive and he wanted what he described as an 'objective scientific analysis' to be made by a committee consisting of Lord Cherwell, Sir Henry Tizard, Professor Bernal, Dr. Cunningham, Sir Charles Darwin and Professor Blackett.[1]

Sir Charles Portal was, however, most unwilling to reopen the strategic aspects of the question which he regarded as settled by the memorandum of 30th October. His reaction to Sir Dudley Pound's suggestions was, therefore, of a somewhat cavalier nature. He considered that the supply problem was relevant to and had been taken into consideration in the decisions which had been embodied in the October memorandum. Furthermore, he was not agreeable to the First Sea Lord's idea of an 'objective scientific analysis.' He thought that the proposed members of the committee 'would probably roam about over a very wide field,' and he doubted 'whether they would agree with one another or we with them.' He merely foresaw that 'their deliberations would certainly cause much further delay.'

Sir Charles Portal had clearly recognised the limited usefulness of 'objective' analyses of matters which involved much uncertain data, especially if they were to be conducted by experts who were known to hold irreconcilably different views of the probabilities. He, therefore, felt that, if the Chiefs of Staff really wanted further scientific advice, 'Lord Cherwell should be asked to give or obtain an authoritative opinion.'[2]

---

[1] Memo. by Pound, 15th Nov. 1942.
[2] Undated Note by Portal.

S.A.O.—I—BB

Nevertheless, the disquiet which existed in the Admiralty appears to have been more deep-seated than had appeared in the comments made by the First Sea Lord. Naval opinion, indeed, found it difficult to accept the strategic doctrine which was basic to the thought of the Air Staff. This doctrine seemed to be pessimistic and defeatist because it appeared to assume that 'we cannot even then hope to win the war by defeating the enemy armed forces . . . but only by dehousing the German population and destroying industry.' At the Admiralty the plan of day bombing seemed more attractive than that of night bombing because if 'the well armed day bomber squadron can, in fact, hold its own against fighters, then the possibility of effectively destroying the enemy fighter force by a day bombing programme becomes possible.'[1]

These ideas really amounted to an attempt to relate the principles of sea power as enunciated by Mahan, to the uses of air power, but they were neither clearly expressed nor logically developed. It was obvious that the defeat of the enemy fighter force, or any other of his armed forces was no more than a means to an end; the end being the defeat of Germany. The real question was whether this was, in fact, the only means to that end. The Air Staff thought not and their policy was to pursue the 'end' directly. The past conduct and future plans for Bomber Command showed the Air Staff conviction that the long-range bomber force could operate effectively against the heart of the enemy even while the opposing fighter force and armed forces generally remained intact. They believed that this strategic attack would ultimately become so devastating that the armed forces themselves would disintegrate in the general debacle. Thus, even if the enemy did not actually capitulate at this stage, it would, by then, be a relatively simple matter to force him to do so by land and sea operations. In other words, the Air Staff believed that the victory could be won before the battle whereas the Admiralty inclined to the view that the battle itself would be decisive. It was because the plan for daylight bombing almost certainly involved a battle with the opposing air force that the majority of the British Air Staff tended to regard it as impossible or at least unnecessary.

The immediate significance of Sir Dudley Pound's criticisms, which were presently to be reinforced by the Chief of the Imperial General Staff, Sir Alan Brooke, was, however, to show that the agreement, which had seemingly been reached in the October memorandum, was really no agreement at all. Indeed, when at last he did speak, Sir Alan Brooke's views showed that in supporting the October agreement Sir Charles Portal was left in a minority of one.

In a note of 26th December 1942, Sir Alan Brooke showed that

---

[1] Undated Admiralty Min. to V.C.N.S. sent to Portal.

he sympathised with Sir Dudley Pound's anxieties about supply. He feared that the programme of bomber construction would compete with the requirements of the army from 'cranes to tent pegs' and he argued that the whole strategy would be self-defeating, if the bomber programme, which was intended to pave the way for a continental invasion, prevented the creation of an army and supporting tactical air force adequate to carry out that invasion. In other words, the Chief of the Imperial General Staff was not prepared to put much faith in the theory that the bombing offensive could create conditions in which the action of the army would become little more than a police operation. He was inclined to believe that Sir Charles Portal had been unduly optimistic and that he had, perhaps, overestimated the success of radar bombing devices. He also drew attention to the more important fact that a large part of the offensive would be American and that it was still an open question whether they would succeed with day bombing or be able to go over to night attack. As to the import of aviation fuel which had troubled Sir Dudley Pound, he did not think the difficulties would be 'insuperable', though he maintained that they would be considerable.[1]

Such pressure could not be ignored and Sir Charles Portal was compelled to reopen the whole strategic argument and also, as was shown in a second Chiefs of Staff memorandum of 24th November 1942, to give much ground. In this the proposed allied offensive policy was re-defined as being firstly, rendering material assistance to Russia, secondly, preparing for the invasion of Europe and thirdly, softening up north-west Europe by bombing. As to this last measure, the Chiefs of Staff suggested, 'From now onwards we must strike with ever-increasing strength at Germany's industrial and economic system, submarine construction, source of air power and, last but not least, the morale of the German people. Plans must be laid immediately for the assembly in the United Kingdom of a bomber force strong enough to ensure, in combination with the Russian assault from the East and the Allied offensive in the Mediterranean, that the German war effort is weakened as soon as possible to an extent which will permit a successful invasion of Western Europe by Anglo-American land forces. The size of this bomber force', the Chiefs of Staff continued, 'should be fixed as a matter of urgency. Until such

---

[1] Memo. by Brooke, 26th Dec. 1942. The question of petrol imports had been the subject of a report by the Principal Administrative Officers Committee on 16th December 1942. In this, the Chiefs of Staff were told that the problem was insuperable from the purely British point of view, but it seemed to be indicated that, if treated as a United Nations problem, it could be overcome. Sir Charles Portal wrote in pencil on his copy, 'We shall get this [the 100 octane petrol] all right if they [the Americans] send their bombers.' Sir Charles Portal presently wrote to Sir Alan Brooke in a memorandum that 'It cannot be seriously suggested that the United Nations could not conduct the strategy they consider best for winning the war because of 350,000 tons of petrol.' Memo. Portal to Brooke, 1st Jan. 1943.

time', they, however, said, 'as this force is assembled, the necessary priorities in shipping, man-power and munitions production should be accorded to it, second only to the minimum needs of security ... In particular American Air Forces should have priority of transportation over the American Army.'[1]

The changes of emphasis, wording and content which this memorandum showed by comparison with that of 30th October were most significant. The plan for a force of 4,000 to 6,000 heavy bombers by the beginning of 1944 was revoked, or at least thrown open to a future decision. The possibility of a continental invasion before 1944 was recognised and the importance of military campaigns in Russia and the Mediterranean area was stressed. Finally, the aim of the bombing offensive itself was significantly diversified. The influence of the criticisms which the Prime Minister had made about the October memorandum, and also those which Sir Dudley Pound had offered in reply to Sir Charles Portal's bombing estimate, was patently obvious.

Nevertheless, even this new review did not meet the objections which had caused Mr. Churchill to disavow Sir John Dill's use of the previous memorandum in America. The Prime Minister had, since the early disappointments of the war, been somewhat sceptical of 'cut and dried' projects for victory through air power. He had always placed a high value upon the bombing offensive and he had done much to nourish it, but he did not subscribe to the view that bombing alone could win the war and that it substantially invalidated other methods of attack. He was concerned to preserve a balance between the various possibilities and, perhaps, above all, he was anxious to preserve a freedom of choice. Though he did not deny the necessity for long-term planning, he was also ever watchful for opportunities which might be exploited in unexpected ways. He, therefore, tended to be cautious about doctrinaire strategies which might result in over-specialised production and mobilisation, and might, therefore, in turn, destroy, or at any rate reduce, the freedom to exploit unforeseen opportunities. It is, perhaps, because these thoughts were constantly in his mind that the Prime Minister's attitude has so often been misunderstood and misrepresented. He, had to examine many sides of many questions and more often than not his rulings and advice were addressed to subordinates who were often and necessarily considering only one side of one question.

It is clear that, at this stage and in spite of the many and significant changes that had been made in the memorandum of 24th November as compared with that of 30th October, Mr. Churchill still felt there was a danger of the bombing offensive assuming an importance in

---

[1] C.O.S. Report, 24th Nov. 1942.

THE OUTLOOK FOR 1943

strategy, and, therefore, also in supply, man-power and transport which might be out of proportion not only to the results which it was safe to assume would be achieved, but also to the other possibilities and obligations which existed.

The particular opportunities which the Prime Minister had now in mind were the Russian successes in the east and the Anglo-American victories in the Mediterranean area. These had been specifically referred to by the Chiefs of Staff in their memorandum of 24th November, but it was evident that the Prime Minister doubted whether they had been adequately related to the particular obligation which he also had in mind. This was the assurance which he had given in August 1942 to Marshal Stalin that a 'second front' would, if possible, be opened in 1943. Mr. Churchill thought that the possibility of carrying out the invasion of France in July, or at any rate August or September 1943, should be given more serious consideration.[1]

Such a consideration might have a most important effect on the long-term plans for the build up of the strategic bombing forces and in any case as the Prime Minister had said earlier in connection with the prospect of a force of four to six thousand bombers in the course of 1944, he was not willing to give way to the 'pleasures of megalomania' until he knew more clearly what effect such a plan might have on the other possibilities of attack.[2]

There was, however, another important factor in Mr. Churchill's thought. This was his deep and abiding mistrust of the possibility of a successful attack on Germany by the American bomber force. Sir Charles Portal's 'conversion' in this matter was not, as has been shown, shared by the Prime Minister. He still thought it unwise to give priority 'to the arrival in this country of masses of American Air groundsmen, while the United States Air Force have not shown themselves possessed of any machines capable of bombing Germany either by night or by day.' He thought it was 'the greatest pity to choke up all our best airfields,' and, 'surely', he suggested, 'it would

---

[1] Min. Churchill to Ismay (for C.O.S.), 29th Nov. 1942. Note by Churchill, 3rd Dec. 1942. The Prime Minister, Air Vice-Marshal Slessor observed, had given his assurance to Marshal Stalin 'without consulting his military advisers.' Min. Slessor to Portal, 11th Dec. 1942. In his memoirs, Sir John Slessor records of Mr. Churchill that 'At the meeting in Moscow as recently as August, he had committed himself to Stalin to open up a second front on the Continent in 1943 . . .' See *The Central Blue*, (1956), p. 440. Referring to the afternoon meeting of the Chiefs of Staff on 3rd December, Lord Alanbrooke says in his *Notes on My Life* that Mr. Churchill mentioned the promise which 'we' had given to Stalin, to which he replied, 'No, *we* did not promise.' Lord Alanbrooke adds that the Prime Minister 'stopped and stared at me for a few seconds, during which I think he remembered that, if any promise was made, it was on that last evening when he went to say good-bye to Stalin and when I was not there.' See Arthur Bryant: *The Turn of the Tide*, (1957), p. 530. This last evening has been described by Sir Winston Churchill who shows that, in addition to himself and Stalin, only Molotov, the interpreter Pavlov, and, for part of the time, Stalin's daughter and Sir Alexander Cadogan were present. But he makes no mention of any promise about the second front. *The Second World War*, Vol. IV, pp. 581–591.

[2] Min. Churchill to Ismay (for C.O.S.), 18th Nov. 1942.

be much better to bring over half a dozen extra American divisions, including armour, and to encourage the American Air effort to develop mainly in North Africa.'[1]

There were, of course, obvious risks in heavy investment in the bombing offensive while the operational prospects of the American air force, which would ultimately account for two-thirds of its strength, were still so doubtful. Nevertheless, there was, as the Chiefs of Staff observed to the Prime Minister, also the danger that, if these risks were not accepted, the Americans might turn their major effort away from Europe and towards the Pacific.[2] The fate of the bombing offensive seemed to hang somewhere between the need to bring military help to Russia by a large and timely intervention in the continental campaign, and the need to sustain American interest in Europe by countenancing their plan for the daylight strategic air attack on Germany. Expressed in another way, the decision depended upon the extent to which the allied offensive from the west was going to depend upon a strategic air attack on the centre of Germany and the extent to which it was going to depend upon military action against her perimeters.

It now seemed to Air Marshal Slessor that a compromise between these two courses was imminent, with the attendant danger that neither the bomber forces nor the allied armies would gain sufficient strength to achieve decisive results. In this situation he feared that either the Russians would win the war singlehanded and that Britain would, in consequence, dispose a very weak hand at the peace conference, or that Stalin would reach an agreement with Hitler and leave Britain and America 'to face another two or three years of possibly inconclusive war.' Air Marshal Slessor, like Sir Arthur Harris, saw great danger in attempting a major continental intervention and he also thought it was quite unnecessary. Stalin would be likely to seek peace with Hitler if his allies 'sit and do nothing for the next nine months, preparing for a *ROUND-UP*[3] that we shall anyway not be strong enough to launch.' On the other hand, Air Marshal Slessor believed, Stalin would be well contented if an 'all out bomber offensive' was maintained against Germany and allied military operations were meanwhile confined to the Mediterranean. Air Marshal Slessor, again like Sir Arthur Harris, had advanced views upon the state of disintegration which the allied military forces would find when, after the air offensive, they entered Europe, and also on the speed and ease with which they would be able to overcome any remnants of the German army.[4]

---

[1] Min. Churchill to Ismay (for C.O.S.), 29th Nov. 1942.
[2] Min. C.O.S. to Churchill, 1st Dec. 1942.
[3] The invasion of France in 1943.
[4] Min. Slessor to Portal, 11th Dec. 1942.

Sir Charles Portal was also well aware of, and had earlier drawn attention to, the dangers of a compromise,[1] and he agreed with Air Marshal Slessor about the folly of returning to '1918 ideas' by which was meant a frontal attack on the German army before it was undermined from the rear. At the same time he also saw a danger of going 'too far in the other direction,' and he predicted that 'the German fighting services will retain their discipline to the last . . .'[2]

Although he believed that the strategic air offensive was the essential preliminary to a successful military invasion of Europe, Sir Charles Portal's note to Air Marshal Slessor showed that he did not believe that it was a preliminary which would necessarily render the invasion purely formal. On the contrary, this invasion might well be something much more formidable than a mere police action or, as Air Marshal Slessor had suggested, an operation for light flying columns. To this extent Sir Charles Portal was, in fact, favourably disposed towards a compromise between the strategic air offensive and the military invasion in the task of defeating Germany. To this extent he could agree with Sir Alan Brooke that the bombing offensive would be self-defeating if, in order to build it up, the allies were left without an army adequate to exploit its success.[3]

Both Sir Charles Portal and Air Marshal Slessor agreed that it would be necessary for allied armies to advance into Germany and Sir Alan Brooke agreed that the bombing offensive was the necessary, or at least the expedient, preliminary to this operation. Thus, the generally accepted theory was that the bombers would discharge at least something of the function which in the war of 1914–18, despite the blockade, had largely devolved upon the armies during their long-drawn-out and vastly costly ordeal in the trenches; that is, the wearing down of the enemy's war potential and his will to war until the conditions for a break-through had been created.

It would, nevertheless, have been a colossal strategic gamble to assume that the bombing offensive would be completely successful in carrying out this wearing-down process, and since the means of raising large allied armies did exist it would also have been an unnecessary gamble. Even if the bombing offensive was likely to achieve all that Sir Arthur Harris or Lord Trenchard claimed for it, it was still only simple wisdom to prepare for the event of it not doing so, even if these preparations did to some extent reduce the chances of a completely decisive air offensive. This had now been recognised by Sir Charles Portal and this was the fundamental motive behind the Prime Minister's interventions.

---

[1] See above, pp. 365–366
[2] Min. Portal to Slessor, 13th Dec. 1942.
[3] Memo. by Brooke, 26th Dec. 1942.

Apart from the effect which it might have upon the supply prospects of the bomber forces, the real significance of the 'compromise' which Sir Charles Portal had now recognised to be necessary was the modification in the object of the bombing offensive. The object was, and in some minds for long had been, to make the invasion possible and successful. Now the pursuit of this object might, of course, result in the collapse of Germany before the invasion took place, but, even if this did happen, the object was nevertheless not the same as that which Sir Arthur Harris had in mind when he spoke of 'victory, speedy and complete' through air power. Moreover, the two different objects might well involve the pursuit of different objectives because targets selected for their value in insuring the success of the invasion might be quite different to those chosen with a view to the outright defeat of Germany by bombing alone.

Inherent in this problem, there was also the question of how far the long-range bomber forces might be withdrawn from the strategic sphere and harnessed to the direct and tactical needs of the army, either by way of preparation for its landing or in support of its operations after it was on the Continent. This was similar to the constantly recurring question which arose in the Battle of the Atlantic as to whether Bomber Command should make tactical attacks on vessels at sea, or strategic attacks upon industrial centres which produced them, or even general attacks upon the country which employed them.

As far as the invasion was concerned the problem of the strategic or tactical application of air power was not, however, an immediate issue because the invasion itself was not an immediate prospect. The Chiefs of Staff, in a third memorandum of 31st December 1942, were, therefore, able to revert to the words they had used in October when they defined the aim of the bombing offensive as 'the progressive destruction and dislocation of the enemy's war industrial and economic system, and the undermining of his morale to a point where his capacity for armed resistance is fatally weakened.' Indeed, in so far as it dealt with the bombing offensive, this memorandum of 31st December was remarkably similar in wording to that of 30th October which had caused so much trouble. Certain passages were changed so as to appear more generally acceptable, but the actual content remained very much the same. For example, instead of speaking of four to six thousand bombers by 1944, the new memorandum referred to three thousand by the end of 1943. There were also references to the small effect which this build up would have upon imports into the United Kingdom and to the relatively light demands which it would make on shipping space.[1]

---

[1] C.O.S. Report, 31st Dec. 1942, App. 21. In substantially unchanged form this was laid before the Casablanca Conference in January 1943.

THE OUTLOOK FOR 1943

The three memoranda which the Chiefs of Staff had produced on 30th October, 24th November and 31st December 1942, and the debates which intervened, showed the difficulties which were experienced in trying to reach agreement even on the general strategy which ought to govern the bombing offensive. Still more they showed the much greater difficulty which was encountered as soon as the debate touched any detailed considerations. In many cases these difficulties were no less than the impossibility of predicting the effects of the air offensive, the uncertainty which prevailed about the operational prospects of the American air force and, indeed, also the problem of trying to decide whether the general area attack at night was desirable and inevitable, whether it was only inevitable, or whether it was neither.

Agreement could only be reached by a compromise stated in such general terms that it could later be interpreted by those taking part in it according to their particular and generally conflicting predilections. Nevertheless, the time had now come when these matters would have to be opened to Britain's American ally. Such solutions as could be produced would then have to receive the supreme approval of the American and British Governments. This was a task which lay before the allied conference which was about to assemble in North Africa at Casablanca. Even before the President and the Prime Minister and their Staffs arrived it was, however, clear that as far as the bombing offensive was concerned such agreements as were reached would be far less important than the way in which they were interpreted.

CHAPTER VII

THE MOUNTING OFFENSIVE: ADVANCES IN THE FIELD OF OPERATIONS
November 1941–December 1942

1. The introduction of *Gee* and the development of night bombing tactics, November 1941–May 1942
2. The Thousand bomber raids, May–June 1942
3. The creation of the Pathfinder Force, and the further development of bombing tactics, July–December 1942
4. Daylight bombing in 1942

'... the scientist can render his most significant assistance in meeting a practical requirement only when he is given the fullest information about the way in which the need itself has arisen and been identified...'
    SIR EDWARD APPLETON, Reith Lectures 1956

'The aim was to send 1,000 aircraft in one attack against a single objective ... The organisation of such a force—about twice as great as any the Luftwaffe ever sent against this country—was no mean task in 1942.'
    SIR ARTHUR HARRIS, *Despatch*

1. The introduction of *Gee* and the development of night bombing tactics, November 1941–May 1942

REVELATIONS about the inaccuracy of night bombing, which, in the course of 1941, had led to a serious loss of confidence in Bomber Command, had also acted as a spur to the development of new tactical ideas and the production of new equipment. The impending introduction of *Gee*, a radar aid to navigation,[1] the idea, borrowed from the Germans, of sending a force of picked crews ahead of the main attack to light the target and make it a beacon for those who followed and the plan of general incendiarism, also borrowed from the Germans, formed, as we have already seen, the basis of a new optimism about the prospects of Bomber Command.

These ideas had all been simmering for a long time. For example, the principles of *Gee* were explained to two officers from Bomber Command on 14th October 1940.[2] To some extent they had even been tried in practice. A form of the beacon plan had been employed against Mannheim in December 1940[3] and on the night of 11th August 1941 two aircraft equipped with *Gee* had attacked München-Gladbach.[4] Nevertheless, it was not until the inadequacy of the old methods was fully and widely enough recognised that these possibilities were brought into a sharper focus and seen to be matters of the utmost urgency. Indeed, before the end of 1941, it was obvious to the watchful that, unless they could be quickly and effectively brought into action, the future of Bomber Command would certainly be bleak and possibly even non-existent.

The foundation of the new hope was the radar aid known originally as T.R.1335 and later as *Gee*. All the tactical plans depended upon the ability of at least a proportion of the force to find the target with reasonable accuracy and regularity. Without some revolutionary aid, such as *Gee* showed itself to be during its service trials in 1941, it was clear that this ability could not be guaranteed and that, except against the most simple targets in the rare conditions of perfect weather and bright moonlight, it could scarcely be hoped for. Thus, the prospects of Bomber Command had to wait upon the many delays in production and introduction which *Gee* encountered between 1940 and 1942.

---

[1] Though it is generally (and in these volumes) referred to as such, *Gee* was not, strictly speaking, a radar device. See p. 316.
[2] Bomber Cmd. Memo., 31st March 1942.
[3] See above, pp. 225–226.
[4] Bomber Cmd. Memo. cit. above.

Meanwhile, there was no escape from the depressing state of affairs which had come to light in the autumn of 1941, notably as a result of the Butt Report. Sir Richard Peirse was naturally reluctant to repeat the experiment of sending crews in advance to make a beacon of the target because he feared the beacon was likely to be at the wrong target, or in open country. Bomber Command was, in fact, for the time being defeated by 'the law that we cannot see in the dark', and this had been recognised in the conservation directive of November 1941.

Nevertheless, even if it was possible to reduce the intensity of Bomber Command's operations, and there were certain dangers in doing this,[1] it was not possible to withdraw the force from the line. The war in the air was necessarily continuous and through the dreary winter of 1941-42 Bomber Command continued to engage the enemy as best it could.

In the last three months before the introduction of *Gee*, from December 1941 to February 1942, Bomber Command operated against targets in Germany and German occupied Europe on forty-three nights. On the evidence of the night camera, which was examined by the new Operational Research Section at Bomber Command, the results of these attacks were substantially the same as those calculated in the Butt Report for the previous June and July. In the winter attacks, it seemed that under all weather conditions, except those of thick haze or cloud, about forty per cent of those claiming to have attacked, or twenty-six per cent of those despatched to the target, actually got within five miles of it. Under conditions of thick haze or cloud it seemed that only about five per cent of the aircraft despatched reached the target area. Owing to the great size of the ground assumed for the purposes of the argument to be the 'target area' it followed that a large number of bombs technically within the target area would actually fall in open country. It was also true that some bombs falling outside the target area would, in fact, strike built-up areas. If, however, any built-up area rather than the particular territory within five miles of the aiming point was taken as the criterion even less encouraging results were obtained. On this basis it emerged that under all conditions, except those of thick haze or cloud, only twenty-four per cent of those claiming attack, or sixteen per cent of those despatched, had dropped their bombs on fully built-up areas. A further fifteen per cent of those claiming attack, or ten per cent of those despatched, had dropped their bombs in the vicinity of built-up areas or villages. In thick

---

[1] One of the principal ones which occurred to Sir Richard Peirse was the possibility of the air crews losing confidence and becoming irresolute. Letter Peirse to Portal, 10th Nov. 1941.

haze or cloud four per cent of those despatched had apparently hit built-up areas.[1]

These conclusions, though depressing, were not, in view of the earlier analyses, shocking. They merely served to emphasise once again the urgency of introducing *Gee* and the complementary tactical methods which it was hoped would bring about a radical improvement. It was, as had already been shown, principally upon this hope that the Air Staff founded their case for the full-scale resumption of the strategic offensive against Germany. On the other hand, as has also been made apparent, those who advocated the diversion of Bomber Command to other and largely auxiliary activities could find some support for their arguments in the scepticism of the Air Staff opinion which, having been nourished by previous setbacks, was growing strong in some quarters.

In the previous chapter we have seen how the operations which, with the aid of *Gee*, were now about to be undertaken, were themselves the decisive factor in the great strategic debates of 1942. It has been shown how, by the end of the year, Bomber Command had regained much of the confidence which, by the end of 1941, it had lost. Here we are concerned with the mechanism of that achievement; with the operations themselves.

In the somewhat precarious situation of late 1941 and early 1942 it was, perhaps, inevitable that the Air Staff should herald the advent of *Gee* with the most flattering prophecies and it was probably for this reason that there arose, both within and without the Air Staff, a certain tendency to confuse what was, after all, no more than a remarkable scientific advance, with a miracle. To some minds it seemed that though Bomber Command had been able to achieve little without *Gee*, it would, with this device, be able to achieve practically anything. The new Commander-in-Chief, Air Marshal Harris, did not share this delusion and within a month from the start of *Gee* operations he sounded a note of vigorous warning against it.

The occasion of this warning, the first of many, was a suggestion which came from the Foreign Office to the effect that a list of twenty selected German towns should be proclaimed over the wireless as doomed, and that Bomber Command should then progressively destroy them. It was hoped that the broadcast would lead to a general exodus from the named towns.[2]

Sir Arthur Harris, however, had the 'strongest objections' to dealing ' "progressively" with anything.' The weather, he pointed

---

[1] O.R.S.(B.C.) Report, 22nd April 1942. It is important to remember that night cameras were still in short supply and the figures were therefore derived from a 'sample'. Also some of the percentages were calculated on rather small quantities. For the most important figures used, see App. 46.

[2] Correspondence between Eden and Sinclair, April 1942.

out, was much too fickle to make the necessary concentration possible. Furthermore, the force at his disposal was 'far too small to enable such threats to be carried out at present.' He explained that he had to spread his attacks over Germany in order to prevent the enemy from concentrating their defences in one area, notably the Ruhr. The Foreign Office suggestion was, he said, 'the direct negation of this policy.' It was, of course, as Sir Arthur Harris also observed, physically impossible to knock out twenty towns. 'With the present size of force I feel', he said, 'that if we can knock out pretty seriously two or three really worth while towns in the most vital parts in Germany, and, at the same time, by our other attacks in France and elsewhere in Germany and our mine-laying efforts make the maximum possible contribution to the War as a whole we shall be doing well indeed.'[1]

This warning, coming as it did a few weeks after the first *Gee* operations, showed that Sir Arthur Harris was expecting no miracles. He clearly recognised that the operational problems confronting his Command were still formidable. He knew that the German air defences were growing stronger while Bomber Command, at least in actual numbers of operational aircraft, was still growing weaker. He did not neglect the elementary but fundamental factor of the weather. He realised that the task of making Bomber Command into the war-winning weapon which he believed it could become would be long and gruelling. His mind tended to reject simplified ideas which seemed to offer quick or easy solutions, and from the early days of his command he adopted towards the question of operational feasibility an attitude of stark realism amounting at times almost to pessimism.

There were, indeed, good grounds for Sir Arthur Harris' caution, for the introduction of *Gee* did not, in fact, produce such immediate, nor such far-reaching improvements as had at one time seemed possible. The bombing offensive still remained a compound of trial and error. Nevertheless, some remarkable successes were achieved and March 1942 marks the time from which Bomber Command began decisively to advance towards an ultimate operational efficiency which was astonishing. There were certainly times during this advance, particularly towards the end of it, when Sir Arthur Harris was led to underestimate what his bombers were operationally capable of achieving. On the other hand, there were also many occasions when the Air Staff and its advisers continued to overestimate these capabilities. Between these extremes there were to be many disputes which, as will in due course emerge, had important consequences.

In the view of the Air Staff, the principal limitation from which

---

[1] Letter Harris to Bottomley, 9th April 1942.

Gee suffered was the probable brevity of its effective life. They knew that the Germans would not be slow to devise the means of jamming the new equipment and even under the most fortunate circumstances they did not think that it would take more than six months for this to happen.[1] In the period before jamming, however, the Air Staff, encouraged by the operational trials, expected *Gee* to go a long way towards the solution of the problems of navigation, target location and even bomb aiming. Thus it was hoped not only that area bombing would become effective but also that a resumption of precision bombing would become feasible.[2]

There would, however, be a period during which only a proportion of Bomber Command was equipped with *Gee* and during this time, if the greatest advantage was to be gained, some means by which the *Gee* aircraft could guide their less-fortunate companions would have to be employed.[3] A system, subsequently known as the *Shaker* technique, was devised to meet this need. According to a general instruction, which Bomber Command sent out on 21st February 1942, the force was to be divided into three sections known as the illuminators, the target markers and the followers. The illuminating section, consisting of twenty Wellingtons fitted with *Gee*, was intended to arrive over the target in five waves with three-minute intervals between each. In the first wave there were to be eight aircraft and in each of the succeeding four waves there were to be three. Each bomber was to carry twelve bundles of triple flares and was to run along the up wind side of the target, dropping them at ten-second intervals. The bomb load was to be completed with high explosives. Thus, it was hoped to illuminate the target at zero hour with lanes of flares approximately six miles long which would drift over the target and to keep it so illuminated for twelve minutes.

Meanwhile, two minutes after the first wave of the illuminators had reached the target, the target markers, also equipped with *Gee*, would begin to arrive at the rate of two per minute. These would drop the maximum load of incendiary bombs. Thus, it was hoped that there would be a concentrated area of fire into which the followers, not yet equipped with *Gee*, could aim their high-explosive bombs. These followers were timed to start arriving fifteen minutes after zero hour.[4]

---

[1] Apart from the 1941 experiments, *Gee* was introduced operationally on the night of 8th March 1942. It was first jammed five months later in August. Nevertheless *Gee* continued to have considerable value until the end of the war.

[2] Dir. Bottomley to Baldwin, 14th Feb. 1942, App. 8 (xxii), cited above, pp. 322–324. See particularly paras. 2, 3, 8 and 9. For the history of *Gee* prior to March 1942, see Annex I.

[3] During March (after the 8th), twenty-seven per cent of the sorties were *Gee* equipped. By the first half of August the figure had risen to eighty per cent. In January and February 1943 it became one hundred per cent. O.R.S.(B.C.) Report, 20th May 1943.

[4] Dir. Bomber Cmd. to 1, 3, 4 and 5 Groups, 21st Feb. 1942. In practice the number of illuminating aircraft tended to be steadily increased.

MIDDLETON ST. GEORGE
CROFT
LEEMING
DALTON
DISHFORTH
LINTON-ON-OUSE
DRIFFIELD
YORK
POCKLINGTON
BREIGHTON
SNAITH
ELSHAM WOLDS
LINDHOLME
GRIMSBY
FINNINGLEY
BINBROOK
BIRCOTES
BAWTRY
HEMSWELL
SCAMPTON
WIGSLEY
SKELLINGTHORPE
WADDINGTON
WOODHALL SPA
CONINGSBY
BOTTESFORD
GRANTHAM
SALTBY
TATENHILL
COTTESMORE
LICHFIELD
WOOLFOX LODGE
NORTH LUFFENHAM
BRAMCOTE
UPWOOD
BITTESWELL
WARBOYS
ALCONBURY
WYTON
BRAMPTON GRANGE
HUNTINGTON
OAKINGTO
BOURN
WELLESBOURNE MOUNTFORD
GAYDON
STRATFORD
CHIPPING WARDEN
PERSHORE
BASSINGBOU
DEFFORD
EDGEHILL
STEEPLE MOR
HINTON IN THE HEDGES
MORETON IN THE MARSH
CROUGHTON
WINSLOW
UPPER HEYFORD
BICESTER
WING
CHEDDINGTON
STANTON HARCOURT
ABINGDON
LONDO
HIGH WYCOMBE
HQ. Bomber Command
HARWELL
HAMPSTEAD NORRIS
A.E.K

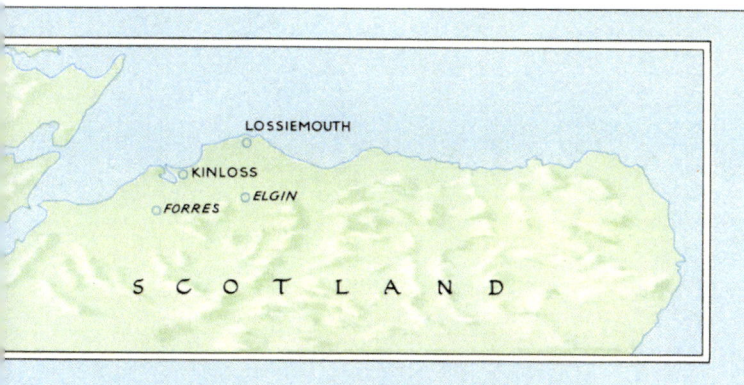

Map 4
BOMBER COMMAND
5th March 1942

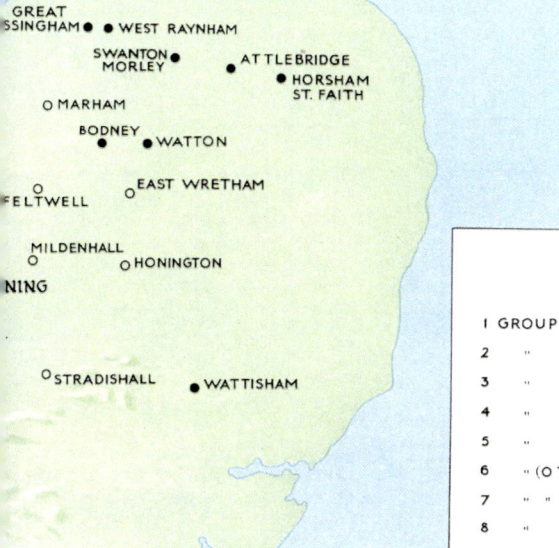

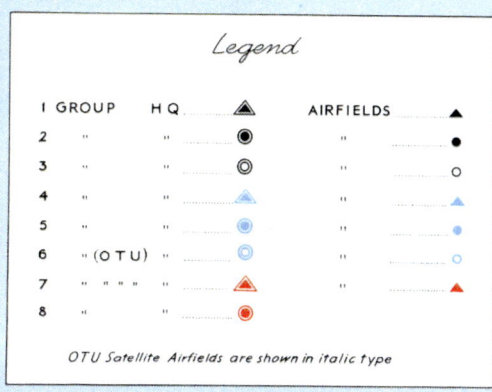

LOSSIEMOUTH
○ KINLOSS
○ ELGIN
○ FORRES

SCOTLAND

GREAT ○
SSINGHAM● ● WEST RAYNHAM
SWANTON ● ● ATTLEBRIDGE
MORLEY   ● HORSHAM
○ MARHAM   ST. FAITH
BODNEY
● ● WATTON
○   ○ EAST WRETHAM
ELTWELL
MILDENHALL
○   ○ HONINGTON
NING

○ STRADISHALL ● WATTISHAM

Legend

1 GROUP	HQ	▲	AIRFIELDS	▲
2	"	"	●	"	●
3	"	"	◎	"	○
4	"	"	▲	"	▲
5	"	"	●	"	●
6	"(OTU)"	"	○	"	○
7	" " "	"	▲	"	▲
8	"	"	●	"	

OTU Satellite Airfields are shown in italic type

Scale of Miles
0   10   20   30   40   50   60   70   80   90   100

Such was the general plan. The exact capabilities of *Gee* under operational conditions were not yet known and, therefore, its exact function was not yet defined. It remained to be seen whether the device would be sufficiently accurate and the navigators well enough versed in its operation to achieve the necessary degree of navigational accuracy which was now a question of getting not only to the right area but of getting there at the right time. The plan would not avail if the initial flares were dropped in the wrong place and equally it would not avail if they were dropped at the wrong time, perhaps after the followers had abandoned a fruitless search in the dark, or bombed by 1941 methods. It also remained to be seen whether *Gee* could be effectively used as a means of locating and attacking the target once the general area had been reached, whether, in fact, its fixes would be accurate enough to warrant 'blind' bombing. The effectiveness of incendiary saturation tactics against enemy targets still had to be demonstrated and, finally, it still had to be shown whether the flare technique would in fact produce sufficient illumination for long enough to make accurate visual bombing possible.

It was this last point which was the first to be tested in action. The War Cabinet had already decided that certain factories in occupied France, which were known to be working for Germany, should be attacked by Bomber Command. Among these was the Renault motor and armaments factory at Billancourt near Paris, and it was against this target that the Air Staff invited Bomber Command to carry out the first 'full-scale trial of the flare technique.' The object of the attack, it was explained, was to achieve the total destruction of the factory, while at the same time causing the minimum loss of life among French civilians. The defences at the target were expected to be weak and it was, therefore, hoped that both these aims might be facilitated by attacking from a low level.[1]

The Bomber Command operational order, which was issued on 6th February 1942, ordained that the attack was to take place in three waves. The advance force, consisting of Stirlings, Manchesters and Halifaxes flown by reliable crews, was to identify the target by the use of flares and then to bomb it visually with 1,000-lb. General Purpose bombs. Subsequently it was to drop the remainder of its flares on the windward side of the target. This, the first part of the attack, was to be delivered from between 1,000 and 4,000 feet and was to take place within the first fifteen minutes after zero hour. The main force, also carrying flares and 1,000-lb. bombs, was to follow immediately. It was hoped that the flares dropped by the advanced force would indicate the target to the leading aircraft of the main force, but in order to continue the illumination for the following

---

[1] Dir. Bottomley to Baldwin, 5th Feb. 1942.

S.A.O.—I—CC

aircraft each bomber was to drop its flares on the upwind side of the target after attacking. The main force was also to bomb from between 1,000 and 4,000 feet and its attack was to take place within the half-hour between zero plus fifteen minutes and zero plus forty-five minutes. Finally, the rear force, carrying 4,000-lb. bombs, was to complete the destruction within fifteen minutes after the main force attack. These last aircraft, being Manchesters, Halifaxes and Wellingtons equipped to carry 4,000-lb. bombs, were to attack from between 4,000 and 6,000 feet. Thus, it was hoped that, if good time-keeping could be achieved, the target would remain constantly illuminated throughout the attack after its initial identification by the experienced crews of the advanced force.[1]

This was not the *Shaker* technique. *Gee* was not yet available, and the target was not considered suitable for incendiary tactics. It was designed simply as a trial of the flare aspect of the new tactical plan, and as such it produced the most encouraging results.

On the night of 3rd March 1942, 235 aircraft of Bomber Command were despatched to carry out this attack on the Renault factory, and 223 of them claimed to have executed the task. Only one, a Wellington of 3 Group, failed to return. The evidence of the night camera was of limited value because it had been decided that cameras should be used only by the aircraft in the rear force in case the flashes interfered with bomb aiming. Furthermore, proper records of the photography were not kept and it was impossible to tell afterwards which photographs had been taken simultaneously with bombing. Nevertheless, fourteen aircraft did take forty-one photographs and thirty-eight of these showed enough ground detail to enable them to be plotted. Of these thirty-eight photographs, thirty-five, including at least one from each aircraft, were within one mile of the centre of the Renault factory. This was a good sign.

An even better sign was provided by a photographic reconnaissance sortie carried out immediately after the attack on 4th March. Photographs showing the whole area indicated that 'very great devastation of the target' had been achieved. Very few buildings had escaped damage and it was estimated that forty per cent of the Renault machine tools had been destroyed. From the limited evidence available, it seemed that the concentration had been excellent. Excluding two aircraft, one of which attacked early and the other late, the raid lasted for an hour and fifty minutes, and the average concentration in time appeared to be at the rate of 121 aircraft an hour. In one period of ten minutes, fifty-nine aircraft attacked, giving an average concentration of 354 aircraft an hour. The greatest previous concentration in time was at the rate of about eighty air-

---

[1] B.C.O.O., 6th Feb. 1942.

craft an hour.[1] In all, rather over 470 tons of high explosives were dropped from between 1,200 and 4,000 feet. The largest previous attack was thought to have been carried out by some 505 German bombers, but it was estimated that they had only dropped about 440 tons of bombs on London.[2]

On this evidence, which was, of course, somewhat incomplete, it seemed that the flare technique had more than justified itself. Heavy damage had been done to a precise target and Bomber Command had achieved an undoubted and outstanding success which was to be long remembered. All the same, the Renault attack had special features which were not likely to be common. The weather had on the whole been helpful. Throughout the attack there was a moon at ninety-nine per cent of full and, though there was slight ground haze in the target area, there was no cloud below ten or twelve thousand feet. Above all, the weak defences had made low-level attack both possible and inexpensive. Under these conditions, as had been shown even in the First World War, night precision bombing was by no means impossible. They were, however, conditions which, over the important targets in Germany, seldom prevailed, and, over the Ruhr, never.

Yet the Ruhr was the primary target which had been given to Bomber Command in the February directive and it was against this hazy and heavily fortified industrial area that the force was now to direct a great part of its effort. In this formidable campaign Bomber Command could expect to enjoy few, if any, of the advantages which it had so brilliantly exploited against the Renault factory. On the other hand, there were now between one hundred and a hundred and fifty aircraft equipped with *Gee* standing by for operations.[3] The time to bring these into action was ripe, and on the night of 8th March 1942 the first major attack with *Shaker* technique was launched against the supreme target: Essen.

This was the first of eight major attacks, each involving more than one hundred and some more than two hundred bombers, which were aimed at Essen during March and April. In all these attacks either the *Shaker* technique, or a variation of it, was used, but in none was any substantial success achieved. During these raids some 212 photographs showing ground detail were taken by bombers at the time of attack. Only twenty-two of them proved to be within five miles of Essen.

Some of the attacks were made in bright moonlight and others in dark periods. On some occasions there was much cloud. On others

---
[1] O.R.S.(B.C.) Nt. Raid Report, 18th March 1942. One of these photographs is reproduced following p. 194.
[2] Bomber Cmd. O.R.B., 3/4th March 1942.
[3] Min. Baker (D.B. Ops.) to Bottomley, 3rd March 1942.

there was none, but always the Bomber Command crews encountered stiff opposition from searchlights and flak and always they found visual identification of the target impeded by varying amounts of industrial haze. Many of them had evident difficulty in operating the new and unfamiliar *Gee* apparatus and not infrequently even the more experienced crews of the illuminating force, who were always instructed to drop their flares blindly on *Gee* fixes, reported that they had done so by visual aim.[1] It was also strongly suspected that the Germans had begun to shoot up dummy flares from the ground and this was believed to be the explanation of some seen over Hagen on the night of 12th April.[2]

Thus, the flares were seldom, if ever, concentrated at the right place, and even when the experiment was tried of giving a few specially selected crews red flares, which were to be launched only when the target had been unmistakably identified, it was found that these too were widely scattered.[3] The incendiary attack was, therefore, invariably dispersed over a large area, or concentrated at the wrong places, as, for instance, in the second attack on 9th March when Hamborn and Duisburg were effectively hit while Essen escaped.[4] A further complication was the prevalence of ingenious decoys, and one of these at Rheinberg drew off the brunt of the attack on 25th March.[5]

Essen was one of the most difficult targets in Germany and it was not until 1943 that Bomber Command found the means of breaking effectively through its natural and artificial defences. Meanwhile, rather more encouraging results were achieved against other important targets in Germany. On the night of 13th March 1942, for example, 134 aircraft, fifty of which carried *Gee*, were despatched to Cologne. On this occasion the *Shaker* technique produced a much better result than would have been possible before the introduction of *Gee*. Photographic evidence indicated that over fifty per cent of the crews claiming to have attacked the target area had actually done so. Since there was no moon during the attack and the target was partly obscured by drifting medium cloud and ground haze, it was thought that without *Gee* only ten per cent of the crews claiming success would, in fact, have achieved it.

The tactical plan seemed to have worked reasonably well. Twenty

---

[1] For example, in the first attack on 8/9th March 1942, eleven of the twenty illuminating crews dropped their flares on *Gee*. On the next night only nine out of twenty-three did so. O.R.S.(B.C.) Reports, 12th and 13th March 1942.

[2] O.R.S.(B.C.) Report, 3rd May 1942.

[3] On the night of 25th March 1942. O.R.S.(B.C.) Report, 4th April 1942.

[4] Photographic evidence suggested that on this occasion the Thyssen works at Hamborn received a direct hit from a 4,000-lb. bomb. O.R.S.(B.C.) Report, 13th March 1942.

[5] O.R.S.(B.C.) Report. A summary of the eight attacks which has been used here, is in an O.R.S.(B.C.) Report, 15th May 1942.

of the twenty-four illuminating aircraft appeared to have reached the target and seventeen of these launched their flares blindly by *Gee* as ordered. The first flares went down within half a minute of the correct time and, with one short break, the illumination lasted for more than half an hour. Of the twenty-six aircraft in the incendiary force, it seemed that nineteen had reached the target area. Several night photographs showed fires within the target area and others suggested that about half of the main force had got their bombs within five miles of the aiming point. Furthermore, six crews who made blind *Gee* attacks brought back simultaneous photographs. Four of these were plotted and all four were within the boundaries of Cologne at points varying between three and five miles from the aiming point.[1]

This attack on Cologne was a great deal more effective than anything achieved at this time against Essen. It was, nevertheless, far from having been an unqualified success and it was becoming apparent that the introduction of *Gee* and the development of the *Shaker* technique were not, in themselves, adequate to overcome the formidable difficulties associated with the destruction of major German targets. Before, however, continuing to examine further the evidence which led to this conclusion and the consequences which followed, it is necessary to pause and consider how the need to test another aspect of the new tactical plan resulted in two brilliant feats. These were the concentrated incendiary attacks on Lübeck and Rostock carried out at the end of March and the end of April.

It will be recalled how the Air Staff had, during the autumn of 1941, reached the conclusion that saturation incendiary tactics were likely to prove far more destructive than the conventional high-explosive attacks.[2] This belief, which was largely based upon the experience of German attacks on Britain, was reaffirmed in the February directive, but, towards the end of March 1942, the theory still remained to be tested in the field of action by Bomber Command.

Lübeck was chosen as the first target for this test because, to quote the words with which Sir Arthur Harris subsequently described it, the town was 'built more like a fire-lighter than a human habitation.'[3] At its centre lay the *Altstadt*, which was largely of medieval construction so that the buildings were inflammable and the streets narrow and tortuous. This part of Lübeck was also densely populated and within the central area of no more than 2·3 square kilometres

---

[1] O.R.S.(B.C.) Report, 25th March 1942. Thirty-one aircraft took successful photographs with their bombs or flares. Nineteen of these were plotted and eighteen showed the target area.

[2] See above, pp. 252–253.

[3] Letter Harris to Freeman, 29th April 1942. Extract quoted in D.B. Ops. Memo., 10th May 1942.

there lived more than thirty thousand people. In the larger suburban area of about forty-four square kilometres there were another ninety thousand inhabitants.[1]

Though Lübeck was beyond the range of *Gee* it was an easy target in the sense that it lay on the coast and was known to be only lightly defended. These factors made it 'a particularly suitable target for testing the effect of a very heavy attack with incendiary bombs . . .'[2]

On the night of 28th March 1942, 234 aircraft of Bomber Command were despatched to Lübeck. The moon was nearing full and the weather was excellent. The attack was divided into three phases. The first wave, consisting of ten *Gee*-equipped Wellingtons manned by specially selected crews, was ordered to drop flares for the first fifteen minutes after zero hour. The second wave, consisting of fifteen Stirlings and twenty-five Wellingtons carrying maximum incendiary loads and ten more Wellingtons carrying maximum high-explosive loads, was to attack between two minutes and twenty minutes after zero hour. All these aircraft were also equipped with *Gee*, which, though it would not be operative over the target, would give the opportunity for accurate navigation on the approach. Finally, in the last wave, which was timed to attack between sixty and 140 minutes after zero hour, there were to be forty-seven Wellingtons and eighteen Manchesters carrying maximum high-explosive loads including as many 4,000-lb. bombs as possible. The remaining 109 aircraft of this wave were to carry maximum incendiary loads. All the attacks were to be delivered from the lowest possible height.[3]

The night photographs left no doubt that the raid had been 'a first class success.' Thirty-two photographs taken at the time of bombing were subsequently plotted. Seventeen of them showed parts of the island town. Eleven more were within two miles of it and nine further photographs, taken independently of bombing, were all within three miles of the target. Moreover, several of these photographs showed great fires raging in the target area. The photographic evidence fully supported the claims of 191 aircraft to have attacked the target.

Photographic reconnaissance carried out in daylight on 12th April revealed 'large areas of total destruction amounting to probably 45–50% of the whole city.' More important still, it appeared that most of the damage had been done by fire. It was estimated that some 200 acres of Lübeck had been devastated and that in addition heavy damage had been caused in the suburbs. Two thousand

---

[1] *U.S.S.B.S. A detailed Study of the Effect of Area Bombing on Lubeck* (No. 38).

[2] O.R.S.(B.C.) Nt. Raid Report, 11th April 1942.

[3] Bomber Cmd. Executive Orders to 1, 3, 4 and 5 Groups, 28th March 1942. Bomber Cmd. O.R.B., 28th March 1942. O.R.S.(B.C.) Nt. Raid Report, 11th April 1942.

houses appeared to have been destroyed or damaged beyond repair. The central electric power station and four factories were destroyed or heavily damaged. The main railway station and workshops were damaged and a number of warehouses were damaged or destroyed. The cathedral, the Reichsbank and the Market Hall were destroyed.[1]

Lübeck was singularly vulnerable to a fire-raising attack and its light defences had enabled many of the bombers to come down as low as two thousand feet, before attacking. Nevertheless, the outstanding success of 28th March 1942, which far exceeded anything previously attained by Bomber Command, was a convincing demonstration of what could be achieved by the tactics of concentrated incendiarism, provided, of course, that the necessary concentration could be achieved.

A second demonstration of the same conclusion was provided almost exactly a month later by the four incendiary attacks made by Bomber Command against Rostock on four consecutive nights. As a target, Rostock had much in common with Lübeck. It lay beyond *Gee* range but it was a coastal town. It also was inflammable because it contained many medieval buildings, and, again like Lübeck, it was only lightly defended. Joined to the southern suburbs of Rostock was the Heinkel aircraft factory at Marienehe and in each of the attacks the factory was allotted as the precise target for a part of the force. This practice of accompanying the general area attack against the town with a rapier thrust against a particular target within, or near, that town was now becoming the standard procedure of Bomber Command. It had been tried at Lübeck where a machine tools works had been singled out, and it had, as will be remembered, been attempted with some success in the Bremen attack on the night of 12th March 1941.[2] Thus, while Bomber Command was striving to perfect the tactics of concentrated incendiary area attack, it was simultaneously striving to test the possibilities of high-explosive precision attack which it had already so successfully demonstrated in the Billancourt Renault raid. As landmarks in the development of both these techniques, the Rostock attacks were of considerable significance.

On neither of the first two nights was any spectacular success achieved. In the first attack on 23rd April the majority of the night photographs were found to be between two and six miles to the south-east of the old town. None showed the Heinkel factory which

---

[1] One of the reconnaissance photographs is reproduced following p. 410. O.R.S.(B.C.) Nt. Raid Report, 11th April 1942. Post-war surveys have amply confirmed these contemporary estimates which were based upon photographic evidence. This attack was, in fact, the first to cause serious alarm and even panic, not only in the target area, but also in high quarters in Berlin. See below, pp. 483–484.

[2] See above, pp. 245–247.

had been the target for eighteen aircraft of 5 Group. The second attack went rather better. Eighty-three of the ninety-one aircraft despatched to the town claimed to have attacked it and twenty-nine of the thirty-four 5 Group aircraft detailed for the factory claimed to have succeeded. Of the fifty-nine night photographs which could be plotted, twenty-one showed the town area, three the Heinkel factory and a further twenty-seven were within five miles of the aiming point. The concentration in time was good and all except five of the aircraft claiming to have attacked did so within one hour. Eighty-four of these bombed within half an hour. Nevertheless, the resulting fires were somewhat scattered and the main buildings of the Heinkel factory appeared to have escaped damage.

On the third night, when 128 aircraft were despatched, including eighteen to the factory, an outstanding success was achieved. 110 aircraft, including sixteen of the 5 Group precision force, claimed to have attacked. Seventy-one night photographs which could be plotted were taken simultaneously with bombing. This, incidentally, was a larger number of successful photographs than on any previous night. Thirty of these showed the centre of Rostock. Thirty-four were within five miles of the centre of the town and three showed the factory. The concentration in space and time was better than on the previous nights. Ninety-nine aircraft bombed within thirty-five minutes and both the night photographs and a daylight photographic reconnaissance showed that heavy damage had been done.[1]

It was, however, the last attack which, though it was on a slightly smaller scale, proved to be the masterpiece. Fifty-two bombers from 1 and 4 Groups were sent to the town and fifty-five from 3 and 5 Groups to the factory. Forty-six aircraft from each force claimed to have attacked and of the fifty-two photographs taken with bombing every single one showed the target area. Thirteen of them showed the Heinkel factory. The precision attack had been delivered from below six thousand feet and, in the case of four aircraft from 5 Group, from below two thousand feet. The whole attack was completed within an hour and the daylight photographic reconnaissance showed that Bomber Command had won another great victory.[2]

Thus, by the end of April 1942, Bomber Command under the vigorous leadership of Air Marshal Harris had shown, not only to Britain's allies, but also to her enemies, the tremendous potential power of the long-range heavy bomber force. Nevertheless, the

---

[1] One of these reconnaissance photographs is reproduced following p. 410.

[2] O.R.S.(B.C.) Nt. Raid Reports, 20–24th May 1942. It must not be forgotten that 'in the target area' still meant within five miles of the aiming point. Thus not all of the photographs showing the 'target area' also showed Rostock. In the last attack, for example, fifty-two photographs showed the 'target area', thirteen showed the Heinkel Works, eighteen showed Rostock town, and the remainder were off the target but within the 'target area'.

tactical situation was still far from satisfactory and Bomber Command had yet to win a major victory against a major target.

The introduction of *Gee* and the *Shaker* technique had, it is true, brought about a marked improvement in the performance of Bomber Command. If the attacks which had been made in bad weather were omitted, it was estimated from photographic evidence that, in March and April 1942, some forty per cent of the despatched sorties had attacked the target area. The corresponding figure for the previous three months had been twenty-six per cent. In the Ruhr area it was estimated that the average success achieved in conditions of moderate weather during March and April 1942 had been nearly twice as great as previously. In the case of the Cologne attack on 13th March the success was thought to have been about five times greater than the previous average. Furthermore, in March and April 1942, thirty per cent of the night photographs taken during attacks on the Ruhr showed some built-up area. In the period from June 1941 to February 1942 only twenty per cent had done so.[1]

These figures were indicative rather than precise for they were based upon evidence which tended to be imperfect and incomplete. Moreover, the calculations could not fully take into account all the variations of weather, hostile defences, and so forth, which occurred from target to target, from night to night and from season to season. Even so, there could be no doubt that the introduction of *Gee* had made Bomber Command into a more accurate force than it had ever been before. As an aid to navigation, which involved not only getting to the right area but getting there at the right time, *Gee* was already a proven success. As an aid to actual target location and blind bombing, it had, however, been most disappointing. The outstanding successes at Billancourt, Lübeck and Rostock had all been achieved when the Bomber Command crews had been able to identify and aim at the target visually. The ability to do this, of course, depended upon the location and the nature of the target and its defences, the phase of the moon and the state of the weather.

Gee had not proved itself to be an adequate substitute for visual identification and, in particular over Essen, it had failed to surmount the difficulties created by an ever-present industrial haze, the lack of prominent landmarks in the neighbourhood, the proximity of other and sometimes similar looking industrial towns, the extensive and artful use of decoys and, perhaps above all, the truly formidable searchlight and flak defences.[2]

This meant that the new bombing technique, which *Gee* had made possible, had already shown itself to be less effective than had been

---

[1] O.R.S.(B.C.) Report, 15th May 1942.
[2] do. 21st June 1942.

hoped. It was possible that the crews were not yet making the best use of *Gee*, it was possible that the *Shaker* technique was not yet sufficiently developed and refined, and, finally, it was also possible that *Gee* itself was fundamentally incapable of producing sufficiently accurate results to make blind bombing possible.

Gee was still relatively new to many of the crews who had to use it and it was clear that some of them had much difficulty in operating it. Furthermore, there was still some confusion as to how it might best be used. There were, at this time, few trained bomb aimers in the squadrons and this meant that if any form of visual bombing was to be attempted it generally had to be done by the navigator. Thus, when the aircraft began to run up on the target, the navigator had to leave the *Gee* set and go forward to the bombing hatch. In these circumstances, it was naturally impossible to locate the target by a combination of *Gee* homing and visual identification. The alternative, when there was no bomb aimer, was to attempt blind bombing. In this case, the navigator would remain in his seat and determine the moment to drop the bombs purely by lining up the *Gee* pulses.

Against difficult targets like Essen, it seemed that this blind method might in any case produce the best results because *Gee* would not be impeded as the human eye was by darkness, cloud, haze or searchlight dazzle. Also, it would not be distracted, as the bomb aimer was likely to be, by decoys. Blind *Gee* attacks had already been attempted, notably on the night of 22nd April 1942, when eighty aircraft were sent to Cologne with orders to attack by *Gee* alone. On that occasion nine successful photographs were brought back. Four of them showed only cloud, two were within five miles of the aiming point, two more were just outside this area and one showed open fields of unknown position. The inconclusive evidence suggested that this attack had been dispersed over an area between five and ten miles from Cologne.[1]

These blind attacks were normally only attempted when the target was covered with cloud and for this reason the night photographs gave little or no indication of where the bombs had fallen. Even so, it was obvious that the results were very much less accurate than those obtained in trials over home territory. It was estimated that the bomb density at Essen likely to be achieved by blind attack would be only about ten per cent of that achieved in the *Gee* trials. Thus, about five to ten per cent of the bombs dropped would hit Essen.[2] Even if this estimate was not optimistic, it was not in any case very encouraging.

---

[1] O.R.S.(B.C.) Report, 8th May 1942.
[2] do. 21st June 1942.

The cut of the *Gee* lattice lines was much less acute over the Ruhr than it was over England and this was an important explanation of the reduced accuracy. Moreover, it was quite a different proposition to home on *Gee* through the heavily defended area of the Ruhr by comparison with the same undertaking in calm conditions over Britain.

There were, of course, ways in which some improvement might be brought about. More intensive training in *Gee* homing, more careful briefing and modifications to the *Gee* set to make it easier to operate, might eliminate some of the elementary mistakes. Also a greater concentration of aircraft in the target area might, by reducing the effectiveness of the defences, give more bombers an uninterrupted run up to the aiming point.[1] All these measures, and in particular the last, were, as we shall presently see, duly tried, but there was a growing belief that the difficulties went deeper, and could only be solved by the creation of a specialised Target Finding Force.

This idea was not, however, a simple proposition and it aroused powerful opposition from Bomber Command, the Groups and the Squadrons. It was thus not until August 1942 that what then became known as the Pathfinder Force was created.[2] Meanwhile, when these old problems of navigation and bomb aiming at night still beset Bomber Command, another and an even more serious danger was beginning to disclose itself. This was the rise of the German night fighter force and the increased efficiency of the other defences against the night bomber.

Radar was, indeed, a double-edged weapon. In the form of *Gee*, as has just been shown, it was coming to the aid of the night bombers and, to some extent at least, it was enabling them to see in the dark. On the other hand, in the form of early warning devices, it had already made an important and, perhaps, even decisive contribution to the defeat of the German day bombers over England in the Battle of Britain. Earlier still, in 1939, it had also played a big part, as will be recalled, in the destruction of British plans for a day offensive against Germany. Now, and to a rapidly increasing extent, it also threatened the night offensive.

In the early stages of the war the main danger to Bomber Command operating at night came from the weather. The German defences at that time were, to quote the word used in Sir Arthur Harris' despatch, 'rudimentary.' They consisted mainly of gun-defended searchlight areas sited around the most important targets. These were controlled by sound locators. Such night fighters as were in the air had to rely upon purely free-lance methods of intercepting

---

[1] do. 21st June 1942.
[2] See below, p. 432.

the bombers. These imprecise methods allowed Bomber Command to carry out night operations without effective opposition from the enemy.

After the occupation of France and the Low Countries in June 1940 the Germans began to develop a much more elaborate system of night fighter defence. An early warning radar system was installed along the coasts of Denmark, Holland, Belgium and France. A belt of Ground Controlled Interception stations was built extending through Denmark and Holland and down the western frontier of Germany. This was backed up by a searchlight belt covering the Ruhr. By the end of 1941 a great part of this system was in operation.

Each Ground Controlled Interception station worked with a single night fighter which operated in a 'box' and all the 'boxes' in a belt were contiguous. Thus, the chances of intercepting bombers became much greater, especially when the force was scattered and several different 'boxes' were entered. During 1942, the Germans steadily extended the system and improved its efficiency until it became practically impossible for Bomber Command to cross the German frontier without passing through a Ground Controlled Interception box. At the same time radar control was increasingly displacing the much less precise sound locator as a means of directing anti-aircraft fire and searchlights.[1]

The mounting casualties which Bomber Command suffered after the resumption of its full-scale offensive in March 1942 established the reality of the new danger. Symptomatic of the changed situation was the greatly increased activity of German night fighters and the improved accuracy of the flak. From the Lübeck attack, for example, though the defences at the target were light, twelve Bomber Command aircraft failed to return. Anti-aircraft fire was intense on the route and particularly so in the Kiel and Hamburg areas. From the observations of returning crews, it was estimated that flak had brought down seven of the missing aircraft. It was also noticed that night fighters were 'unusually active.' No fewer than fifteen attacks and thirteen interceptions were reported. In these encounters ten bombers were damaged and it seemed likely that at least three more were destroyed.[2]

The missing rate in this attack on a particularly easy target was, therefore, rather more than five per cent of the sorties despatched and this was a casualty rate which Bomber Command could not afford to sustain for many months if it was to remain an effective fighting force. If total losses, including not only the missing aircraft but also those which crashed in the United Kingdom and the crews

---

[1] *Harris Despatch.*
[2] O.R.S.(B.C.) Nt. Raid Report, 11th April 1942.

which were posted, were sustained at seven per cent of the sorties, then, out of every hundred men who started a tour of thirty operations, only ten could survive. The experienced crews would thus be quickly lost and thereafter the efficiency of the force and the survival rate of the crews might be expected to decline further and steeply.[1]

It was naturally difficult to collect accurate statistics about Bomber Command casualties, which, for the greater part were incurred over Germany at night. For this reason it was difficult to measure with precision the effectiveness of the German defences. All the same it was evident that Bomber Command losses were gradually increasing and that they were approaching the dangerous level which towards the end of 1941 had temporarily checked the offensive.[2] In 1941 it was clear that the weather and certain mistakes in the handling of the force were primary factors in the losses which were sustained, but, in 1942, one of the most significant trends was the undoubted increase of bomber losses due to German night fighter action. At the beginning of 1942 it was estimated that night fighters destroyed about one per cent of the bomber sorties.[3] By the summer of 1942 this estimate had risen to over three and a half per cent. Over the longer period from August 1941 to October 1942 it seemed likely that the losses to night fighters had approximately doubled.[4]

'A bomber commander' Sir Richard Peirse had remarked in February 1941, 'has to be a meteorologist first and a strategist second.'[5] But now the increasing severity of the battle in the night air over Germany meant that, though he still had to be a meteorologist,

---

[1] Note by Bufton, 16th March 1945.

[2] The figures for night attacks in the first five months of 1942, from which only limited deductions should be drawn, were as follows:

January: 2,200 sorties, 2·4 per cent missing, 3·6 per cent damaged by flak and 0·4 per cent by fighters.
February: 1,157 sorties, 1·9 per cent missing, 2·4 per cent damaged by flak and 0·3 per cent by fighters.
March: 2,224 sorties, 3·5 per cent missing, six per cent damaged by flak and seven per cent by fighters.
April: 3,752 sorties, 3·7 per cent missing, 10·2 per cent damaged by flak and 1·1 per cent by fighters.
May: 2,699 sorties, 4·3 per cent missing, seven per cent damaged by flak and 0·8 per cent by fighters.
O.R.S.(B.C.) Reports. A further indication is given by figures calculated for the main German targets in an earlier and a later period. They are:
August–October 1941: 3·2 per cent of sorties missing, 1·4 per cent attacked by fighters.
August–October 1942: 5·3 per cent of sorties missing, 2·9 per cent attacked by fighters.
O.R.S.(B.C.) Report, 13th Jan. 1943. All the above figures of aircraft damaged or attacked by fighters refer, of course, to bombers which succeeded in regaining the United Kingdom.

[3] O.R.S.(B.C.) Report, 12th April 1942.

[4] do. 13th Jan. 1943.

[5] Text of speech to the Press by Sir Richard Peirse, 3rd Feb. 1941 (dictated 1st Feb.).

Sir Arthur Harris also had to be a supreme tactician. In order to know best how to handle the force the Commander-in-Chief clearly had to know in detail the methods and the equipment which the German defences were adopting, and he had to be ready and able to adapt his tactics to the particular situation which confronted him.

Already by the beginning of 1942 the existence of the German night fighter control system was known to the British Air Staff. Thereafter, the method of its operational working was gradually deduced. In the famous combined operation against Bruneval, which was carried out during the last night of February 1942, a small *Würzburg* apparatus of the kind used for plotting bombers and directing fighters was captured. By May 1942 the picture was almost complete.[1]

It was immediately obvious that the routing of Bomber Command attacks which had previously been haphazard, was now a matter of the first importance. It was also clear that concentration both in time and space was vital, not only over the target, but on the route as well. If large numbers of bombers passed through the same Ground Controlled Interception box at the same time, the probability of fighter interception would be much less than if small numbers passed through several boxes at different times. 'The tactical aim of Bomber Command in this period', Sir Arthur Harris subsequently wrote, 'can be described in the one word "concentration".'[2] The object of the experimental Thousand bomber raids which were about to be launched was, therefore, not only to test the theory that a mass attack would cause greater devastation than a series of smaller attacks but also to demonstrate the probability that it would result in fewer casualties.

Meanwhile, the possibility also existed of direct interference with the radar upon which, to an increasing extent, the German defences were known to depend. Experiments had shown that the dropping of metallised strips of paper in quantity produced a reaction on radar screens operating on certain frequencies and prevented accurate measurements being made on them. These metallised strips, which subsequently came to be known as *Window*, had the great advantage of being cheap, easy and quick to produce, and it seemed that their immediate introduction would confer upon Bomber Command an important advantage in the air battle which was now joined. For these reasons the Air Staff suggested in April 1942 that the use of

---

[1] *Harris Despatch*. This was perhaps optimistic. In August 1942 it still was not known whether German searchlights were radar controlled or not. At the same time it was only surmised that 53-cm. gun laying was used to direct unseen A.A. fire. O.R.S.(B.C) Report (which is quoted in the *Despatch*). As late as 1943 it was not certain whether the small *Würzburg* was used for fighter or flak control. O.R.S.(B.C.) Report.

[2] *Harris Despatch*.

Window should be authorised at once and the Chiefs of Staff had little difficulty in agreeing to the request.[1]

Nevertheless, the American representative at the discussions had asked that the matter should be put before the Combined Chiefs of Staff because he feared that the introduction of this device which favoured the offensive at the expense of the defensive might endanger the safety of the Panama Canal. This was an aspect of the problem which had not been overlooked by the British Chiefs of Staff. They had considered the probable effects of *Window*, which the Germans could, of course, use as easily as the British, on their own defences, but at this stage *Window* was thought of mainly as a counter to radar gun-laying and little account was taken of its possible effect on radar night-fighter devices. British radar gun-laying was working on a frequency which was regarded as 'practically immune' to *Window*, and though the introduction of more precise equipment, which would also be more vulnerable was planned, the Chiefs of Staff had reached the conclusion that the immediate advantage of disrupting the German defences would outweigh the possible future disadvantage of having to abandon an improvement of their own.[2]

It was at this stage, however, that Lord Cherwell intervened with the pertinent suggestion that *Window* might also disrupt night-fighter radar interception and after a meeting which he held with Sir Archibald Sinclair and Sir Arthur Harris early in May 1942, it was decided to defer the introduction of *Window* until these possibilities had been investigated.[3]

Thus, at a time when the Bomber Command offensive was rapidly gaining momentum in the face of heavy and increasing casualties and at a time when the German air offensive was diminishing to negligible proportions, a cardinal weapon, favouring the bombers and hindering the defences, was cast aside for more than another whole year. It was not until the night of 24th July 1943 that Bomber Command was able to use *Window* for the first time and the sensational success which it then achieved in the famous Battle of Hamburg is, indeed, a grave verdict on the many decisions to defer its earlier introduction.

In the meantime there were many other operational developments which also contributed to the eventual victory over Hamburg. Not the least significant of these were the Thousand bomber raids carried out in May and June 1942.

---

[1] Report of Radio Policy Sub-Committee circulated to Chiefs of Staff on 24th April 1942. Discussed by Chiefs of Staff on 27th April 1942.
[2] Report of Radio Policy Sub-Committee and C.O.S. Mtg., cit. above.
[3] Min. Portal to Bottomley, 5th May 1942.

2. The Thousand bomber raids, May–June 1942

Experience of the first three months of the resumed full-scale bomber offensive had all pointed to the vital importance of concentration in time and space both on the route and over the target. It seemed highly probable that concentration would diminish the effectiveness of the hostile defences. It was already certain that concentration greatly increased the damage at the target, particularly, as had been shown at Lübeck, in the case of incendiary attacks.

Concentration was partly a question of navigation and partly one of numbers and both these factors were interdependent. However large the attacking force might be, concentration would be lost if the bombers spread out over a wide area or a long time. Conversely, the effects of concentration would be lost, however good the navigation might be, if the force was too small to saturate the defences and, in the case of an area attack, to cover the target with a carpet of bombs. A number of isolated incidents would not devastate or even dislocate a great city. This could only be done by a major conflagration.

The science of navigation, though still far from perfect, was, as we have just seen, making significant progress, and on various occasions in March, April and May 1942, Bomber Command had achieved an impressive concentration. The size of the force was, however, still a seriously limiting factor and Air Marshal Harris' vigorous efforts to get Bomber Command expanded were not yet meeting with success. In March 1942 the average number of bombers which the Commander-in-Chief could mobilise for operations was 421. In May 1942 it was 416.[1] This front-line strength was inadequate to fulfil the great tasks which had been allotted to Bomber Command, and it was becoming more and more evident that against large and heavily defended targets a force of 250 to 350 aircraft was simply not large enough to achieve the concentration 'in time and space necessary to swamp the enemy's radar controlled guns and fighters, and to produce mass destruction around the aiming point.'[2] Air Marshal Harris was, nevertheless, determined that the theory of mass concentration should be tested in action and the famous 'Thousand Plan' began to take shape.

On 18th May 1942, Air Marshal Harris mentioned to Sir Charles Portal his idea for launching a thousand bombers against a single target in a single night. In order to realise this seemingly impossible

---

[1] *Harris Despatch*. Figures of this kind are never precise and different sources usually give different versions. In the case of the May figures, Bomber Cmd. O.R.B. gives the daily average of operational aircraft as 449. See also App. 39.

[2] *Harris Despatch*.

plan, Air Marshal Harris proposed to commit not only the whole of his front-line strength, but, by mobilising as many aircraft as possible from the Operational Training and Conversion Units, a large part of his second line as well. By these means he thought he might raise some 700 aircraft. The remainder he hoped to produce by canvassing other Commands. This audacious conception met with the warm approval of the Prime Minister, and Sir Charles Portal immediately authorised Air Marshal Harris to go ahead with the arrangements.[1]

The response to the Bomber Command appeal for aircraft to take part in this great operation was prompt and enthusiastic. Sir Philip Joubert, Commander-in-Chief, Coastal Command, offered no fewer than 250 aircraft, consisting of the two Wellington and two Whitley Squadrons which had been detached from Bomber Command, four squadrons of Hampdens, two of Beauforts and an assortment of Hudsons and Operational Training Unit aircraft.[2]

Sir William Welsh, Commander-in-Chief, Flying Training Command, had fewer aircraft suitable for operations, but he thought he could put up thirty Wellingtons, Whitleys and Hampdens which, he said, were or 'should be in every way fit for operations' though they would need checking over by operational groups.[3] Every exertion was also naturally made by the Bomber Command Groups including the two, 91 and 92, which consisted of Operational Training Units.

It was, however, only the efforts from within Bomber Command itself which had any real substance. An Admiralty intervention resulted in the complete withdrawal of the Coastal Command contingent,[4] and the Flying Training Command contribution proved to be almost totally ineffective. It amounted in the end only to four Wellingtons, one of which failed to return from the operation. None of the Hampdens or Whitleys could operate owing either to technical defects or because their crews lacked the minimum training and experience. Indeed, one of the Hampdens crashed near Doncaster while on the way to its operational base at Syerston.[5] Aircraft of Fighter and Army Co-operation Commands helped the 2 Group Blenheims of Bomber Command to carry out intruder operations against enemy aerodromes, but of the great force of 1,046 bombers

---

[1] Letters Portal to Harris, 19th May 1942, and Harris to A.Os. C.-in-C. Coastal, Flying Training, and Army Co-operation Cmds. and to A.Os. C. 1, 2, 3, 4, 5, 91 and 92 Groups, 20th May 1942.

[2] Letter Joubert to Harris, 21st May 1942.

[3] Letter Welsh to Harris, 21st May 1942.

[4] Min. Churchill to Portal, 15th June 1942. Letter Harris to Portal, 17th June 1942.

[5] This disappointing result was not due to a lack of enthusiasm, as was amply shown in a report on the 25 Group Detachment for operation 'Thousand', a further report of 14th July 1942 by the A.O.C. (Air Vice-Marshal E. D. Davis) and the O.R.S.(B.C.) Night Raid Report of 15th July. Two navigators and a wireless operator of Flying Training Command flew as members of Lancaster and Manchester crews in the great attack.

S.A.O.—I—DD

which was despatched to Cologne on the night of 30th May every single aircraft, with the exception of the four Training Command Wellingtons, was put up by Bomber Command itself.[1]

This effort extended Bomber Command as never before. One of the Operational Training Groups, No. 91, provided no fewer than 259 aircraft. The other, No. 92, sent out 108. The four operational groups put forth their full strength, which included many aircraft from their Conversion Units. Thus, although the auxiliary effort largely failed, the exertions of Bomber Command itself exceeded the original expectation of Air Marshal Harris and the thousand-bomber attack became possible.[2]

Despite their great importance and despite the formidable difficulties of achieving the magical figure of a thousand, sheer numbers were by no means the only problem raised by the Thousand Plan. Indeed, because of them, the importance of the planning for this attack and the responsibility which the Commander-in-Chief assumed in launching it were greater than ever before. 'The dangers', Air Marshal Harris subsequently wrote, 'were many and obvious.' He was committing not only his entire front-line strength, but also absolutely the whole of his reserves in a single battle. Such a bold action might produce a great triumph, but, if anything went wrong, the disaster might well be irremediable. The whole programme of training and expansion might conceivably be wrecked.[3]

The marshalling of the great force, of course, took some days. Many of the Operational Training Unit aircraft had to be moved from their normal bases, and once the force had been assembled, suitable weather had to be awaited. During this time the progress of operational training was necessarily dislocated. A large proportion of these aircraft were manned by instructor crews who had themselves previously completed tours of operations. The future of Bomber Command was in their hands and heavy losses among them would have had a paralysing effect.

Obviously the thousand-bomber force could not be kept standing by indefinitely, but to mount the operation in bad weather was to risk at best its failure and at worst a major disaster. The decision could only be taken by a Commander endowed with exceptional courage and resolution. The operation of such an enormous force was likely to produce considerable congestion over the target area and the possibility of collisions or the destruction of aircraft by falling bombs had also to be considered.

---

[1] O.R.S.(B.C.) Nt. Raid Report, 15th July 1942.

[2] 'The organisation of such a force—about twice as great as any the Luftwaffe ever sent against this country—was', Sir Arthur Harris modestly remarked in his *Despatch*, 'no mean task in 1942.'

[3] Harris: *Bomber Offensive*, pp. 108–109.

Air Marshal Harris saw his way clearly through all these difficulties. He determined that the attack would take place in bright moonlight or not at all, and he ordered that the bombers should be routed through the target area 'on a definite circuit' so as to reduce the risk from collision and falling bombs. At the same time he still aimed to achieve a high concentration in time and space which, by dislocating the defences, would, he believed, counterbalance the risk of collision.[1] The Commander-in-Chief also decided that the plan should embrace two targets so that good weather over either could be exploited in the final decision. The first choice was Hamburg and the second Cologne. The attack was planned to take place on the night of 27th May or on the first suitable occasion thereafter before the end of May.[2]

This was a moon period, and for that reason no flares were to be dropped. The bomb loads were to be predominantly incendiary, but, where high explosives had to be carried to make up economical loads, they were to consist of the largest possible bombs. In the case of Cologne being chosen as the target, the whole attack was to take place within ninety minutes. It was to be opened by *Gee*-equipped aircraft of 1 and 3 Groups carrying the greatest possible proportion of incendiary bombs. It was to be concluded by an attack starting an hour and a quarter later by all the available heavy bombers of 4 and 5 Groups.[3] The remainder of the force was to spread its attacks throughout the intervening period. Such was the plan for concentration in time. In order to achieve an even coverage of the target area three separate aiming points in Cologne were allotted to various parts of the force. The height from which attacks were to be delivered was left to the discretion of the Group Commanders, but it was to be from not lower than 8,000 feet. To avoid the danger of stragglers being left over Germany in daylight, all aircraft were to turn for home ninety minutes after zero hour whether they had bombed or not. Crews who could not find Cologne were ordered to bomb any built-up area in the Ruhr, and preferably in Essen.[4]

These orders, with similar ones for the contingency of Hamburg being the target, were issued on 26th May and they brought the Thousand Plan to the point of culmination. The great armada now lay poised and ready for action, but the weather still had to make its final arbitrament. For three days the operation had to be postponed, but on 30th May, when time was already running perilously short, a somewhat more promising situation was seen to prevail. The

---

[1] Letter Harris to Joubert, 23rd May 1942.
[2] B.C.O.O., 26th May 1942.
[3] This was subsequently changed to an hour later. Bomber Cmd. Executive Order May 1942.
[4] B.C.O.O., 26th May 1942.

weather forecast given to Bomber Command at twenty minutes past nine that morning said 'Germany: Much thundery cloud with some breaks over the North West, decreasing southwards and dispersing in the middle Rhine to relatively small amounts during the night.' For the home bases the forecast said 'convection cloud decreasing; local thundery showers.' [1] This was by no means ideal, but at twenty-five minutes past midday the executive order 'Thousand Plan Cologne' was given.[2]

Almost immediately afterwards, at one o'clock, a second forecast was received at Bomber Command; it said 'Cologne: Residual cloud tending to clear, but probably only to about 7/10. North-West Germany: More cloud probably 8/10. Home Bases: 1 Group may have 50% of their bases unfit but in general only a few stations unfit owing to ground fog.' By five o'clock, this weather drama had come full circle. The forecast then said, 'Cologne: Broken cloud with some large breaks. Route: much cloud and occasional thunderstorms going out improving somewhat for return. Home Bases: Conditions at take off generally very good but local interference owing to thunderstorms possible. On return local visibility troubles possible, particularly in 1 and 5 Groups but even then no more than 25% of the bases will be affected.' [3]

These predictions did not further delay the attack and during the night 1,046 bombers set course for Cologne.[4] The greatest attack yet made in aerial warfare was now under way, but it still remained to be seen whether the disaster would fall upon Germany or upon Bomber Command.

The force ran into dirty weather as it crossed the North Sea. There was much cloud and some cumulo-nimbus in which icing conditions and considerable static prevailed. Inland from the Dutch coast the conditions improved markedly and over Cologne there were only small amounts of cirrus cloud. The moon was above the horizon and ninety nine per cent of full throughout the operation and the visibility was good both for the Bomber Command and the German night fighter crews.

Reports from the leading aircraft indicated that *Gee* worked well on the approach to Cologne and the crews said they had no difficulty

---

[1] O.R.S.(B.C.) Nt. Raid Report, 15th July 1942.

[2] Bomber Cmd. Executive Order to 1, 3, 4 and 5 Groups, repeated 2 Group, 30th May 1942. This, as was usual in the case of these Executive Orders, confirmed earlier telephone messages.

[3] O.R.S.(B.C.) Nt. Raid Report, 15th July 1942.

[4] Sir Arthur Harris gives the number as 1,047 (*Harris Despatch*), as also does the Operations Record Book, but the total figure, including the four Training Command Wellingtons, amounted to 1,046 according to the Operational Research Section Nt. Raid Report, 15th July 1942. In addition to the bomber force, fifty Blenheims of 2 Group and Army Co-operation Command, together with thirty-seven fighters of Fighter Command, took part in associated intruder operations.

THE THOUSAND BOMBER RAIDS

in recognising the target when they arrived. Crews from the following aircraft reported that by the time they arrived considerable fires were burning in Cologne and that these easily enabled them to recognise the target. The last crews to attack said that 'large and growing fires were raging' and some reported that these could be still seen after 150 miles of the return journey had been covered. From the original force of 1,046, 898 of the returning crews claimed that they had attacked the target area. They had dropped some 1,455 tons of bombs.[1]

The evidence of the night camera was, as had so often been the case before, 'somewhat scanty'. Only 246 night cameras were carried. Forty-five photographs showing ground detail were brought home and thirty-two of them were plotted within five miles of the central aiming point. About another hundred photographs showed large fire tracks strongly suggesting that they had been taken over Cologne. An examination of this evidence suggested to the Operational Research Section that at least 600 of the bombers had attacked the target area and that the average density of bombs which had fallen upon it was about thirty-one tons to the square mile.[2]

Subsequent daylight reconnaissance brought more reliable evidence which fully confirmed the surmise that an amazing success had been achieved. The first report came from a Mosquito pilot who looked down on Cologne from 23,500 feet at five o'clock on the morning after the attack. He saw a pall of smoke rising to 15,000 feet and looking like a great cumulo-nimbus cloud. He could also see many fires still burning, both in the centre and the suburbs of the city.[3]

Then, when at last this smoke had cleared away, came the daylight photographs. They showed that the damage was 'heavy and widespread' and that it was 'on a much larger scale than any previously inflicted on a German city.' Six hundred acres of Cologne, including about three hundred acres right in the centre of the city, appeared to have been completely destroyed. There was no 'considerable' part of Cologne which these photographs showed to be free of damage.[4] Bomber Command had at last won a major victory against a major target.

Moreover, this victory had been achieved without insupportable losses. Forty bombers, representing 3·8 per cent of the original force, failed to return. A further 116 returned in a damaged condition. Twelve of these were beyond repair and another thirty-three

---

[1] 540 tons of H.E. and 915 tons of incendiaries.
[2] O.R.S.(B.C.) Nt. Raid Report, 15th July 1942.
[3] Bomber Cmd. Intelligence Narrative of Operations, 1st June 1942.
[4] O.R.S.(B.C.) Nt. Raid Report, 15th July 1942. These estimates were strictly realistic. See below, pp. 485–486. Two of these photographs are reproduced following p. 410.

were 'seriously' damaged. Considering that the visibility on the night of the attack presented the German night fighter pilots with perfect conditions for 'cat's eye' interception, that a proportion of the British crews were inexperienced[1] and the fact that no one had any previous experience of handling such a large force, this outcome was far from unsatisfactory.

There were, nevertheless, some disquieting features about the first thousand bomber raid and the most serious of these was the evident failure even of this enormous concentration of bombers to swamp the German defences. The timing of the attack was on the whole fairly accurate, and though the first bombs went down thirty-eight minutes after midnight, which was seventeen minutes early, and the last at ten past three, which was forty-five minutes late, only thirty-eight of the 898 aircraft claiming attack, bombed outside the planned time limit of ninety minutes. Even so the anti-aircraft defences at Cologne succeeded in bringing down a bomber every seven or eight minutes. Some of the crews thought the flak was unusually weak, but this impression was probably created because the guns and searchlights tended to concentrate upon single aircraft. It, therefore, seemed that the large numbers of aircraft over the target had not prevented the German location system from selecting and following individual targets. It was, however, possible that the searchlights had picked up their targets fortuitously and followed them visually.

The German night fighter effort was larger than usual and particularly so in the coastal area. The fighters were concentrated around the coast and in the neighbourhood of the target. The numbers in the air seemed to increase on the bombers' return journey. An examination of crew observations suggested that twenty-two bombers had been destroyed over Cologne. Of these, it seemed that flak had accounted for sixteen, fighters for four and a collision for two. Outside the target area it was, however, probable that fighters had shot down twice as many bombers as had the flak.

Of the 116 aircraft damaged, eighty-five had been hit by flak and twelve by fighters. The remaining nineteen, including two destroyed in a collision over England, were not damaged by enemy action. In all, thirty of the returning crews reported that their aircraft had been attacked by German fighters.[2]

The overall loss rate was slightly higher than the previous average for attacks on Cologne, but it was considerably lower than the previous average for attacks on Western Germany in conditions of

---

[1] Some being O.T.U. pupils.

[2] These were revised figures. The original estimates given in an O.R.S.(B.C.) Night Raid Report were 113 damaged, eighty-two by flak and twenty-nine attacked by fighters.

moonlight and no cloud.[1] The evidence about the effect of concentration upon casualties, though somewhat inconclusive, did, therefore, seem to confirm the expectation that there would be a reduction. A further indication in support of this belief was provided by a study of the missing rate in the various waves of the attack. From the first wave 4·8 per cent of the sorties failed to return. From the second wave, the missing rate was 4·1 per cent, but from the third wave it was only 1·9 per cent. The third wave was, in time, the most concentrated of the whole attack, though the number of casualties per minute over the target remained fairly constant all the time. The increased concentration factor in the third wave appeared to have reduced its percentage of casualties.

Even this evidence was, however, inconclusive because the third wave consisted of four-engined aircraft, which, it was thought, were, in any case, somewhat less vulnerable to fighter attack than their twin-engined companions.[2] Finally, it is interesting to note that the two Operational Training Unit Groups suffered lighter casualties than the four front-line Groups. 3·3 per cent of the sorties flown by 91 and 92 Groups failed to return. 4·1 per cent of the sorties flown by 1, 3, 4 and 5 Groups failed to return. The majority of the Operational Training Unit aircraft were flown by instructor pilots who had, of course, had previous operational experience, but in some cases pupil pilots operated and it is curious to find that the latter suffered more lightly than the former. From 91 Group, for example, 208 aircraft were flown by instructor pilots and seven, or 3·4 per cent, failed to return. A further forty-nine aircraft were flown by pupil pilots and only one failed to return.[3]

---

[1] The figures were:

Cologne	Sorties	Percentage Missing	Flak damaged	Attacked by fighters
30/31 May 1942	1,046	3·8	8·1	2·8
Aug. 1941 to April 1942	1,364	3·5	8·6	2·3

The average missing rate for attacks on west Germany in conditions of moonlight and no cloud during the period June 1941 to March 1942 was 4·6 per cent.

[2] The figures were:

	Sorties	Missing	Attacked
Four-engined aircraft	292	6 (2·1 per cent)	10 (3·4 per cent)
Two-engined aircraft	754	34 (4·5 per cent)	19 (2·5 per cent)

O.R.S.(B.C.) Nt. Raid Report, 15th July 1942.

[3] O.R.S.(B.C.) Nt. Raid Report, 15th July 1942. In connection with the last fact, the report drew attention to the small numbers involved and suggested they were too small to warrant any significance being attached to them.

Whatever conclusions might be drawn about the effect of concentration, types of aircraft and the experience of crews upon casualties—conclusions which had much importance for the future—the clear fact was that the Thousand Plan had been carried out without crippling losses. Moreover, there was no doubt whatsoever that the 1,046 sorties despatched to Cologne in a single night had done vastly more damage to the target than the 1,364 sorties which had been sent against it in the previous nine months. The exertions and the risks to which Air Marshal Harris had exposed his command had been justified by the event. Furthermore, a convincing and practical demonstration had been given of the argument for a great and speedy expansion in the front-line strength of Bomber Command.

Air Marshal Harris did not, however, rest on these laurels. Two days later, on 1st June 1942, while the moon was still up and the great Cologne force was still in being, the executive order for a second edition of the Thousand Plan was sent out. This time the target was Essen, the primary objective of the February directive and one which had so far eluded an effective blow from Bomber Command.

For this attack the normal *Shaker* technique was to be used. Twenty specially selected crews flying in *Gee*-equipped Wellingtons of 3 Group were to initiate the raid with sticks of illuminating flares dropped on *Gee* co-ordinates. A powerful incendiary force was to follow and its leading aircraft were to be manned by the best crews from each Group. The main force, also carrying a high proportion of incendiary bombs, was to open its attack fifteen minutes after the first flares had gone down and at the moment when the last of the incendiary force would be attacking.[1]

The plan was thus, in most respects, similar to that adopted in the previous *Shaker* attacks on Essen. The difference lay in the numbers of aircraft despatched and in this respect the attack corresponded to the Cologne raid. For the second time within forty-eight hours almost the entire strength of Bomber Command's first and second lines was committed to battle, and during the night of 1st June 1942, 956 bombers set course for Essen. Once again Flying Training Command participated, but this time it was only able to put up two Wellingtons. All the other aircraft came from Bomber Command, though as before a few of the aircrews were provided by Training Command.[2]

---

[1] Bomber Cmd. Executive Order to 1, 3, 4 and 5 Groups, 1st June 1942. O.R.S.(B.C.) Nt. Raid Report, 9th July 1942.

[2] O.R.S.(B.C.) Nt. Raid Report. In addition forty-eight Blenheims of 2 Group and Army Co-operation Command, together with some Fighter Command aircraft again went out on Intruder Operations. One of the Flying Training Command crews, captained by Wing Cmdr. H. R. A. Edwards, flew a Hampden of 408 Squadron in the Essen attack and had an eventful trip. While in the target area at 11,000 feet one engine failed. Wing Cmdr. Edwards crossed the Dutch coast home at 1,000 feet but after jettisoning all

12. Lübeck after the attack on the night of 28th March 1942.

13. Rostock after attacks in April 1942.

14. Cologne five days after the Thousand Bomber Raid on the night of 30th May 1942.

15. Marshalling yards at Cologne before and after the Thousand Bomber Raid.

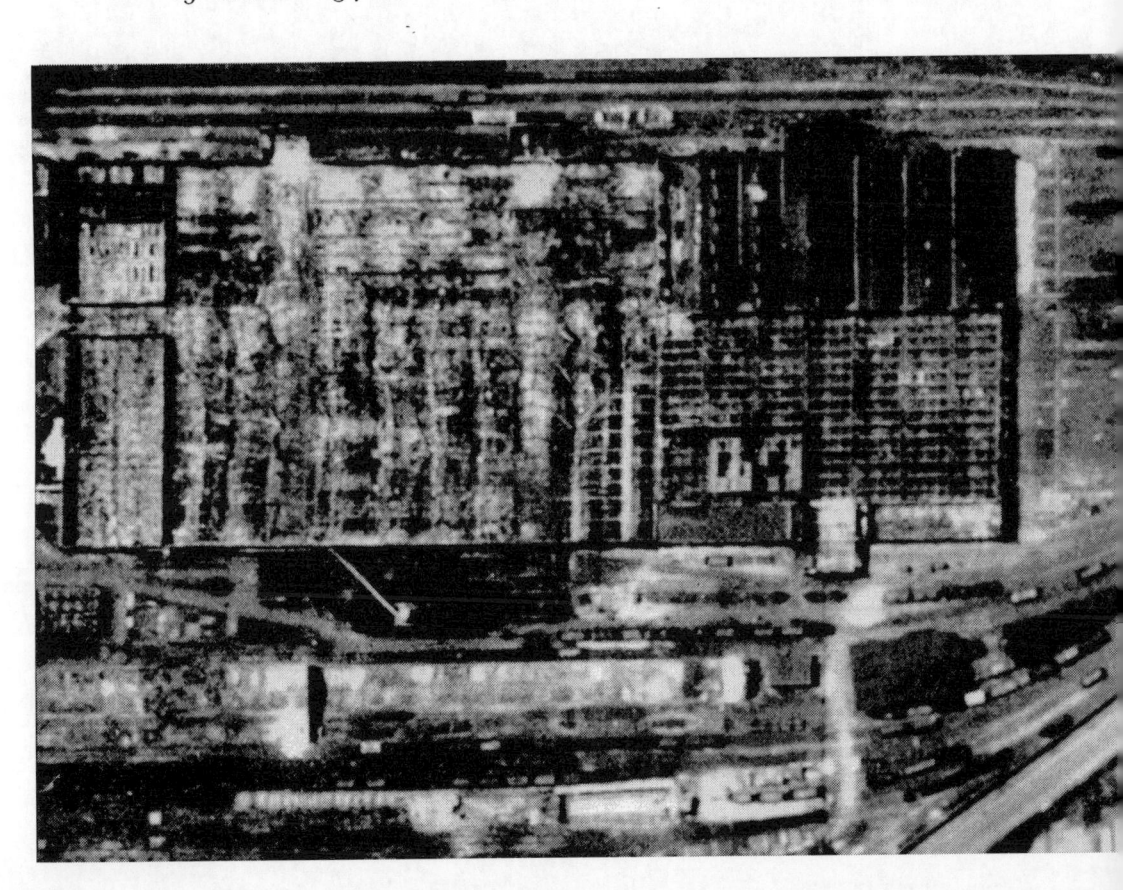

At this point the parallel with the Cologne raid ended and the results of this thousand attack on Essen were more or less similar to the earlier and smaller efforts which had been exerted against that important and difficult target. Most of the returning crews reported that in the area of Essen there was five- to ten-tenths cloud at 8,000 feet. Some said there was another layer of cloud at 3,000 to 5,000 feet, but a few said there was no cloud at all. As usual, Essen was veiled in a ground haze. The moon was eighty-nine per cent of full and visibility was reported as being between one and five miles.

A large number of crews believed that they had been over the target and 767 of them claimed that they had dropped their bombs in or near Essen. Very few crews were, however, prepared to assert with certainty that they had identified the target. Several of them aimed at fires which they sighted at their expected time of arrival over Essen. Others bombed blindly from *Gee* fixes and some made timed runs from pin-points on the Rhine. There were several reports of fires being scattered throughout the Ruhr.

Photographic evidence confirmed this last suggestion. Of the seventy-three night photographs which showed ground detail, none showed the target and only eight were within five miles of it. A number were plotted in the Duisburg-Hamborn area. One of the flare sticks fell near Oberhausen. The flares were not effective and some of them evidently illuminated the lower cloud layers and made ground identification even more difficult.

Daylight photographic reconnaissance carried out on 2nd, 3rd, 5th and 6th June showed little damage in Essen and none to the Krupp works. About thirty or forty houses, mostly in the southern and south-eastern suburbs of Essen, were destroyed or damaged and a few railway coaches to the west of the station were burnt out. Severe damage was seen at Oberhausen and it was clear that some of the attack had fallen on Mülheim and Duisburg.[1]

The communiqué of the German High Command spoke of 'widespread raids over W. Germany, especially Duisberg and Oberhausen where damage was done to residential quarters causing some casualties.'[2] The second thousand attack had failed to achieve any worthwhile concentration in space on the target area.

Thirty-one aircraft, representing 3·2 per cent of the original Essen force, failed to return. A further ninety-nine or 10·3 per cent were

---

removable and dispensable equipment he climbed to 2,000 feet and reached Norfolk where the other engine failed. Wing Cmdr. Edwards made a belly landing on the obstructed runway of a partially completed aerodrome at East Harling. No one was injured.

[1] O.R.S.(B.C.) Nt. Raid Report.
[2] Bomber Cmd. Intelligence Narrative of Operations, 2nd June 1942.

damaged to various extents, including five which were totally destroyed. Seventy-eight of the damaged aircraft had been hit by flak and thirteen by enemy fighters. The ratio of casualties between four- and twin-engined bombers was, by comparison with the Cologne attack, reversed. From the Essen attack 4·6 per cent of the four-engined sorties and 2·6 per cent of the twin-engined sorties failed to return. In the Cologne attack the four-engined aircraft had attacked in the last wave. In the Essen attack they went in early. It, therefore, seemed that the larger aircraft were not necessarily more robust, as had been supposed, but that the 'enemy's defences decrease in efficiency considerably during the progress of these very heavy raids.'[1] This was yet further confirmation that the theory of mass concentration was well conceived.

Immediately after the Essen attack and the waning of the moon, the thousand force was disbanded. The operational groups continued, as always, their attacks on Germany, but the operational training groups had to revert to their normal and indispensable role of producing reinforcements for the front line.

This was not, however, the end of the Thousand Plan and Air Marshal Harris was now beginning to think that it might be profitable to make it a permanent feature of the bombing offensive. It was apparent to him that if a force of this size could get on to its target it could achieve 'the most colossal destruction'. He reckoned that from two to four consecutive thousand attacks on a city the size of Cologne 'would have the effect of virtually destroying the objective to the extent of putting it out of action for any foreseeable duration of the war'. Moreover, he also thought that these great attacks would involve fewer casualties 'in proportion to those on small raids'. He concluded that the German night fighters would 'bag their quota, within limits, whatever the size of force we employ', and he, therefore, thought that the larger was the force of bombers despatched the smaller would be its percentage of casualties.

For these reasons Air Marshal Harris suggested to Sir Charles Portal that the Thousand Plan might become the normal scale of attack by Bomber Command. His idea was that the necessary armada of aircraft might be mobilised twice a month, and that, if possible, two raids should be launched on each occasion. During the rest of the month intensive efforts would be devoted to training, for which purpose more of the resources of the operational groups would also be used. It would be necessary to set aside a minimum force from the operational squadrons during these training periods to 'keep the pot boiling, to fill ad hoc requirements and to carry on with the mining.' Air Marshal Harris had 'a strong feeling' that four

---

[1] O.R.S.(B.C.) Nt. Raid Report, 9th July 1942.

thousand attacks each month 'might prove to be very much more effective than one Thousand Plan a month plus ordinary everyday hum-drum operations in the interim.'[1]

Meanwhile, Air Marshal Harris was, in any case, planning a third thousand attack to be carried out during the moon period which was due towards the end of June. This time, and for obvious reasons, he decided to make no approach to Flying Training Command, but he hoped that Coastal Command would make a solid contribution, especially as the destruction of the target he had in mind would have 'a direct effect on the Naval War.'[2]

Bomber Command had, of course, in the past made considerable diversions of its effort to contribute to the war at sea. It had also parted with many of its squadrons on detachment to Coastal Command. This had been done despite the belief of the bomber commanders, and often of the Air Staff as well, that many of the naval tasks allotted to Bomber Command had been tactically inappropriate and not infrequently operationally impossible. Nevertheless, there were always difficulties about securing the loan of Coastal Command aircraft for bomber operations, and we have already noticed the inglorious fate of the Coastal Command contingent which, it had been hoped, might take part in the first thousand attack.

This time, however, Air Marshal Harris had taken the precaution of invoking the early support of the Prime Minister, who asked the Admiralty 'to make sure that they do not prevent Coastal Command from playing its part'.[3] In these circumstances the First Sea Lord, Sir Dudley Pound, said that he would allow about a hundred of the Coastal Command Hudsons to take part in the proposed attack. He also offered the services of a Polish Wellington Squadron with the proviso that it should later be exchanged for another from Bomber Command. He thought that the Poles were unsuitable for Coastal Command work.[4]

This offer was less than Air Marshal Harris had hoped for. It was also less than he understood Sir Philip Joubert, Commander-in-Chief, Coastal Command, was willing to make.[5] Nevertheless, it was all that could be extracted.[6]

The plan was not, however, disrupted and once more Bomber Command rose to the occasion. The resources of the operational

---

[1] Letter Harris to Portal, 20th June 1942.
[2] do. 14th June 1942.
[3] Min. Churchill to Portal, 15th June 1942.
[4] Letter Portal to Harris, 16th June 1942.
[5] Letter Harris to Portal, 17th June 1942.
[6] Coastal Command eventually despatched 102 Wellingtons and Hudsons to Bremen in the third thousand attack. Five of them failed to return. Narr. *R.A.F. In Maritime War*, Vol. III, by Capt. D. V. Peyton-Ward, R.N.

training groups were for the third time put into the front line and on the night of 25th June 1942, in addition to the Coastal Command force of 102 aircraft, Air Marshal Harris was able to despatch 904 bombers to Bremen. Five of these were Blenheims from Army Co-operation Command, but all the rest, including 198 Wellingtons and Whitleys from 91 Group and 106 Hampdens, Whitleys and Wellingtons from 92 Group, came from Bomber Command.[1]

As in the previous thousand attacks, the plan was to achieve a high concentration in time and the Bremen attack was to be compressed into sixty-five minutes, starting at twenty minutes past one in the morning of 26th June, and it was to be carried out in three waves. The advance force, led by fifty Stirlings and fifty Halifaxes, was ordered to attack the centre of Bremen. The hundred four-engined aircraft were to do so within the first ten minutes after zero hour and they were to be immediately followed within the next ten minutes by 124 *Gee*-equipped Wellingtons of 1 and 3 Groups. The second wave, or main force, which included the Coastal Command and Operational Training Group aircraft, was to attack between zero plus twenty and zero plus fifty-five minutes. Various aiming points were allotted to this part of the force. 1 Group was ordered to bomb the southern end of the docks, 3 Group the centre of the town, 5 Group the Focke-Wulf aircraft factory, 91 Group the south-eastern part of the town, 92 Group the southern end of the docks and Coastal Command the Deschimag submarine building yards. The third wave, or rear force, consisting, like the advance force, of Stirlings and Halifaxes, was to conclude the assault, the Stirlings taking as their aiming point the town centre and the Halifaxes the area between the docks and the south-eastern edge of the town.

The bomb loads were adjusted to these various tasks. The Coastal Command Hudsons carried 100-lb. anti-submarine bombs and the Coastal Command Wellingtons 500-lb. high-explosive bombs. The 5 Group force detailed for the Focke-Wulf factory carried loads made up of fifty per cent heavy high-explosive and fifty per cent incendiary bombs. The remainder of the force carried maximum incendiary loads, made up as necessary by the larger high-explosive bombs. The minimum height from which attacks were to be delivered was 8,000 feet and all aircraft were to turn for home not later than two-thirty in the morning whether they had bombed or not.

Before the attack was launched a reconnaissance was made of the target and the up-wind area. Though Bremen was not then clear of cloud, the conclusion was that it would be before one-twenty in the morning. At nine o'clock in the evening the weather forecast sub-

---

[1] O.R.S.(B.C.) Nt. Raid Report, 15th Aug. 1942. In addition, forty-four Bostons, Mosquitoes and Blenheims of 2 Group and fifteen of Army Co-operation Command took part, with Fighter Command, in intruder operations.

mitted to Bomber Command said 'Bremen: Chance of less than 5/10 cloud is 50/50. The strong wind in the target area will favour a comparatively rapid passage of strato-cumulus across the target.'[1]

All long-range bomber sorties involved a gamble on the weather, but on this night the gamble was not successful. The wind over Bremen abruptly changed, the weather did not clear and the sky, both at the target and on the route, was covered with a layer of cloud in which only occasional breaks were seen. Bremen, which in good conditions was an easy target, now became a very difficult one. Very few crews saw the ground and those that did only caught glimpses of it. The advance force largely relied upon *Gee* fixes as a means of bombing and 117 of these aircraft bombed completely blindly on *Gee*. The main force aimed at the resulting glow and thirty-four of the crews in the rear force reverted to blind *Gee* bombing. In spite of orders to the contrary, one Halifax went down to 3,000 feet, at which height it broke cloud, and was able to bomb visually. The crew reported that considerable fires were burning in the target area. Only two of the night photographs showed any ground detail and neither of these could be plotted.

Photographic reconnaissance carried out the following day did, however, show that the attack had not been a complete failure. The damage was limited but 'useful'. Most remarkable of all was the fact that severe damage had been done to the Focke-Wulf factory about which the 5 Group crews had been diffident in their reports. A large block of this factory measuring 340 by 250 feet had been almost completely wrecked, probably by a 4,000-lb. bomb. Other buildings in the factory were also damaged.[2] Considerable parts of the town had also been damaged, mostly by fire, but the docks appeared to have escaped any injury. Such success as had been achieved, though it did not bear comparison with the major victory at Cologne, was, in the circumstances, remarkable. Since the target was constantly and more or less completely covered by cloud this success was attributed to the initial blind *Gee* attacks by the advance force. These had started fires, some of which were evidently in the right place and which were sufficient to produce a glow which could be distinguished through the cloud by at least some of the crews which followed.

This limited success was achieved at a cost in casualties which was higher than that incurred on either of the previous thousand attacks. Forty-four, or 4·9 per cent of the Bomber Command aircraft

---

[1] O.R.S.(B.C.) Nt. Raid Report, 15th Aug. 1942.

[2] This photograph, which was clear and satisfactory, was reproduced in the first number of the *Bomber Command Quarterly Review*, April–June 1942. The physical damage done to the factory did not, however, according to the post-war report of the U.S.S.B.S., have much effect on production.

failed to return and five of the Coastal Command aircraft were also reported missing. In addition, sixty-five of the returning Bomber Command aircraft were damaged. Forty-three of these had been hit by flak and ten by fighters. The other twelve, including one Lancaster hit by incendiary bombs dropped by a friendly aircraft, were damaged in accidents.

The brunt of these higher casualties was borne by the operational training aircraft of 91 Group. Four, or 12·5 per cent, of the thirty-two Whitley sorties and seventeen, or eleven per cent, of the Wellington Ic sorties flown by this group failed to return. Nearly all these aircraft had been flown by pupil crews.[1] It seemed that the difficult conditions experienced had been too severe a challenge to these inexperienced crews. The abrupt change in the wind had not been forecast, and there were few opportunities for sighting the ground. Navigation was, therefore, difficult and especially so for the crews who, like those from the Operational Training Units, did not have *Gee*. Inaccurate navigation would not only lead to some aircraft running out of petrol, as was known to have happened in the cases of two aircraft from 91 Group, but it would also lead them away from the main stream of bombers and expose them to the individual attention of the German defences. The Whitleys and Wellingtons Ic were also obsolescent aircraft.

The Halifaxes of 4 Group also suffered disproportionate casualties and 6·4 per cent of them failed to return. If the 91 Group casualties were excluded, the missing rate for the rest of the force was found to be 3·2 per cent, and if the Halifax casualties were excluded, the missing rate for the other heavy bombers was only 2·6 per cent. These were significant facts.[2]

This was the last thousand attack on a single target in a single night until 1944. Bomber Command was not inexhaustible, but because the public and the 'official critics' now tended to regard anything smaller than a thousand raid as 'chicken food' Air Marshal Harris had to explain his difficulties to the Prime Minister. He reminded Mr. Churchill that Bomber Command was not increasing in numbers and that in the first half of the year it had lost nineteen squadrons to Coastal Command, the Middle East and Army Co-operation Command. Only three had been returned. He pointed out that he had only thirty operational night bomber squadrons and

---

[1] Eleven Wellington Ic sorties provided by 91 Group but controlled by 1 Group were excluded from the calculation, but as one of them failed to return, the percentage would not have changed by their inclusion. The report says that '21 of the 24 aircraft of 91 Group which were missing for this attack had 100% pupil crews'. The same report, however, elsewhere indicates that the total number of aircraft missing from 91 Group was twenty-two (eighteen Wellingtons and four Whitleys). O.R.S.(B.C.) Nt. Raid Report, 15th Aug. 1942.

[2] O.R.S.(B.C.) Nt. Raid Report, 15th Aug. 1942.

the operational training units behind them with which to mount the offensive.[1] The number of sorties which he could despatch was limited by the number of casualties which he could afford to sustain, and he estimated that the most he could do was to send out between four and five thousand sorties each month. Air Marshal Harris also reminded the Prime Minister of the many activities which Bomber Command was expected to undertake in addition to its strategic attacks on Germany. These included the laying of about one thousand mines per month. He was also, as always, at the mercy of the weather, and in the summer his range was limited by the shorter hours of darkness. Even so, he hoped, as he had earlier mentioned to Sir Charles Portal, to mount from three to five thousand raids per month sending between six hundred and a thousand aircraft on each occasion.[2]

This hope was not, however, to be realised in 1942 and after the Bremen raid, the largest attack in the rest of the year was made by 630 bombers including many from the Operational Training Units. This was against Düsseldorf on the last night of July and it was a scale of effort which was not again exceeded until the Dortmund attack on the night of 23rd May 1943. By that time the front-line strength of Bomber Command had grown appreciably greater. Perhaps it would not have done so if, in the meantime, it had not been judged wiser to continue to regard Bomber Command as an investment for the future and to refrain from doing violence to the training organisation upon which that future so largely depended.

The thousand bomber raids of May and June 1942 did not, therefore, usher in a new and regular scale of Bomber Command attack. On the contrary, they long remained unsurpassed records, but they were not the less important for that reason. In a gigantic step they carried Bomber Command far along the painful road from doctrine to experience. The thousand raids taught incomparably valuable lessons about the administrative control and tactical handling of the great force of aircraft which Bomber Command was eventually destined to have in its front line. But they did more than that, for the Cologne attack had also demonstrated the immense devastation which could be achieved, even against a heavily defended target, by the tactics of mass concentration. The great and outstanding problem was to find the means by which that concentration could be achieved with more regularity in the varying conditions imposed by an alert enemy and variable weather.

---

[1] The weight-lifting capacity of the force was, however, increasing as the heavier bombers and particularly the Lancasters were introduced.
[2] Min. Harris to Churchill, 18th July 1942.

3. The creation of the Pathfinder Force and the further development of bombing tactics, July–December 1942

The introduction of *Gee* and the *Shaker* technique had brought about an improvement in the operational performance of Bomber Command, but the attacks carried out since March 1942 had shown that the night bombers were still largely a 'fair weather' and an 'easy target' force. Two of the thousand raids and many of the smaller attacks, including all those aimed at Essen, had gone astray in difficult conditions. Most of the successes had been achieved in the rare conditions of ideal weather and bright moonlight. More often than not they had also been achieved against targets which were easy to recognise because of their geographical positions and because, owing to their light defences, they could be approached at relatively low altitudes. Such successes, though they included the great victories at Lübeck, Rostock and Cologne, the last of which was not, of course, an 'easy' target, were by no means completely reassuring. Good weather and moonlight were not only rare but they were also helpful to the German night fighters. 'Easy' targets were not as a rule vital targets. These considerations acted as a stimulus to the idea, which had for sometime been strong, that the natural and indispensable corollary to the introduction of specialised devices like *Gee* and specialised tactics like the *Shaker* technique, was the creation of the specialised target-finding force.

Indeed, some form of target-finding force had become inevitable from the moment that *Gee* was introduced. For some months after March 1942 only a part of Bomber Command had been equipped with *Gee* and it was obvious that this part had a better chance of finding the target than the other part which was still navigating by the old methods. It followed that some method by which the *Gee*-equipped crews could communicate their observations to their less fortunate companions had to be evolved. In due course, it is true, the whole of Bomber Command was to be equipped with *Gee*, but the unbalance would be restored each time a new device such as *Oboe*, *H2S*, the Air Position Indicator, or the averaging sextant was introduced. Moreover, *Oboe* was a projected radar aid which, owing to its nature, could never be operated in more than a very few aircraft at one time. Thus, it was certain that some parts of Bomber Command would always be better equipped than others for target finding.

It had also long been recognised that the ability of bomber crews varied. Some had greater operational experience than others, some had greater powers of endurance and determination than others and,

CREATION OF THE PATHFINDER FORCE

in consequence, some had more success in finding the target than others. These facts all pointed to the conclusion that it was profitable to give some of the best crews the latest equipment and charge them with the special task of finding the target and indicating it to the main force. The Germans had been quick to grasp this principle and their bombing operations against Britain had profited from its application.

The British had, however, been more reluctant, partly because before March 1942 there was no specialised navigation equipment in service and partly because the Royal Air Force distrusted the idea of building up 'crack' squadrons much in the same way as it distrusted the continental habit of building up official air 'aces'. Nevertheless, when *Gee* did come into service the *Shaker* technique provided for the despatch of specially selected *Gee*-equipped illuminating and incendiary forces which were intended to reveal the target to the main force which followed. Thus, the introduction of *Gee* had automatically led to the adoption of a target-finding and a target-indicating technique.

This technique had, however, often failed because the flares had been dropped at the wrong place or because they had in other ways been ineffective. By the summer of 1942 it was already growing apparent that the equipment which Bomber Command had was still inadequate to its increasingly difficult tasks. If better results were to be got something more accurate than *Gee* and something more effective than the existing parachute flare was needed. It was also arguable that the best tactics had not yet been evolved and there were those who believed that they never could be evolved until a separate target-finding force had been created.

This idea had been in the process of development for some considerable time and, it will be remembered, Lord Cherwell had shown his approval of it in September 1941.[1] At that time all plans for the future tactics of Bomber Command naturally tended to hang fire while the introduction of *Gee* was awaited and it was not until March 1942 that the plan for a separate target-finding force was seriously pressed upon Bomber Command. By that time the idea had found a convinced and courageous champion in Group Captain S. O. Bufton, who, since November 1941, had been Deputy Director of Bomber Operations at the Air Ministry.

Group Captain Bufton, who spoke from considerable operational experience,[2] did not make proposals about the tactics which would

---

[1] Min. Cherwell to Churchill, 2nd Sept. 1941. Earlier still, in February 1941, Mr. Dewdney had reported on the general belief among operational aircrews that a special target-finding force was necessary. Letter Dewdney to Peirse, 1st Feb. 1941.

[2] He had commanded 10 Squadron (Whitley) from July 1940 to April 1941, 76 Squadron (Halifax) till the end of May 1941. He was Station Commander at Pocklington

have to be adopted if adequate and accurate concentrations of flares were to be placed over the target. He was convinced that these tactics could only be evolved by operational aircrews themselves, but, as he reminded Air Marshal Harris on 17th March 1942, Bomber Command had no squadrons specifically responsible for this task. He suggested that six squadrons should be put in 'close proximity' with each other and given the 'sole responsibility' for this work. He was sure that this six-squadron target-finding force would eventually develop effective tactics, even if it was manned by the normal crews who happened to be in the six squadrons at the time of its creation. To this extent he believed that the 'proximity' and the responsibility of the squadrons were the crucial factors.

Group Captain Bufton, however, also believed that the urgency of obtaining 'immediate results, both for strategical and political reasons' was such that the target-finding force would initially require some reinforcement by specially efficient crews. He, therefore, suggested that the new force should be strengthened by the posting to it of forty of the best crews from all Bomber Command. The other two-thirds of the aircrew strength of the target-finding force would be made up from the ordinary crews in the six selected squadrons. One of the principal objections to the plan which had already been voiced by Bomber Command would, therefore, be largely met, for, to fulfil Group Captain Bufton's scheme, it would only be necessary for each main force squadron to contribute about one crew. Group Captain Bufton did not think that this would amount to a serious dilution of the ordinary squadrons, and he claimed that it would in any case be non-recurring because the target-finding force could subsequently be reinforced directly from the Operational Training Units.[1]

If he did not already know it, Group Captain Bufton soon discovered that his proposals were viewed with extreme disfavour by the Bomber Group Commanders. Nevertheless, as he told Air Marshal Harris on 11th April, he was convinced 'that our present machinery is such that the correct doctrines are not automatically evolved in the squadrons, transmitted by Groups, and sifted, collated and applied at Command.' He thought that the Squadron and Station Commanders were 'too busy' and had little opportunity of examining the results of bombing or of applying their operational experience to the tactical problems of the force as a whole.[2] As he later also pointed out to Air Marshal Harris, it was quite possible

---

(405 R.C.A.F. Squadron, Wellington) until Nov. 1941. At the Air Ministry he was Deputy Director of Bomber Operations from Nov. 1941 till March 1943 and Director from then until June 1945.

[1] Letter Bufton to Harris, 17th March 1942.
[2] do. 11th April 1942.

that the advice received by the Commander-in-Chief about new tactical ideas might come 'through a non-operational Station Commander, a non-operational S.A.S.O., and the A.O.C., and on the way it is possible that its real implications or the supporting arguments are lost and, like so many, the idea is still-born.'[1]

Having thus confessed to Air Marshal Harris his distrust of the Bomber Command official channels, Group Captain Bufton also confessed that he had circulated the target-finding force proposals among some of his own operational friends, and that the replies that he and two other members of his Directorate who had done the same thing had received had all been favourable to the scheme.[2]

These vigorous proposals and somewhat unorthodox measures did not make much impression upon Air Marshal Harris and though, on 17th April, the Commander-in-Chief told Group Captain Bufton that he had 'a fairly open mind on the subject of the Target Finding Force,' he made it perfectly clear that he had no intention of creating one.

Air Marshal Harris' objections were not directed towards the principle of target finding by picked crews, which was, of course, a fundamental part of the already accepted *Shaker* technique, but he was utterly opposed to the plan for forming these picked crews into an individual force which he said would constitute a *corps d'élite*. The raising of such a force would, he was convinced, have a demoralising effect on the ordinary main force squadrons and it would also, he thought, reduce their efficiency. Moreover, he claimed to be reasonably well satisfied with the success which was being achieved by the existing tactical methods and without the services of a specialised target-finding force. 'I am convinced now,' he told Group Captain Bufton, 'after the last two months experience, that generally speaking the target when it can be seen at all is being correctly found ...' He attributed Bomber Command's continuing limitations not to tactical defects but to inherent difficulties and he said that 'where the heavily defended areas such as the Ruhr are concerned the difficulty persists of bombing a precise pin point in the face of searchlight glare which makes it physically impossible to see the pin point or to use the sight.' He had not the 'least doubt' that the *Shaker* technique had led to 'the majority of our bombs landing usefully in built up areas of the Ruhr reasonably close to the intended target ...'

Air Marshal Harris thought that, when his aim of universal photographs of bomb-aiming points at night had been achieved, and it was, therefore, possible to determine at the end of each month which were the best squadrons in the Command, it might be profitable to

---

[1] do. 8th May 1942.
[2] do. 11th April 1942.

allow all the squadrons to compete each month for the honour of being the target-finding force in the following month. This was as far as he was prepared to go and he was 'not prepared to accept all the very serious disadvantages of a Corps d'Elite in order to secure possibly some improvement on methods which are already proving reasonably satisfactory . . .'[1]

It was thus apparent that at this stage Air Marshal Harris not only regarded a separately organised target-finding force as undesirable but also as unnecessary. He thought it was undesirable because he feared the effects on the main force squadrons which might follow from creaming off their best crews and concentrating them in the target-finding force. He thought it was unnecessary because, though he admitted it might bring about 'some improvement on methods,' he believed that the existing tactics were proving 'reasonably satisfactory.' Whatever the final judgment might be about the effect on the main force squadrons, and Group Captain Bufton did not share Air Marshal Harris' apprehensions, the case for the target-finding force had now really come to depend upon a determination of whether or not the existing techniques really were proving 'reasonably satisfactory.'

This in turn raised the question of what Bomber Command was intended to achieve. Air Marshal Harris was evidently content if the 'majority of bombs' landed 'usefully in built up areas . . . reasonably close to the intended target.' Group Captain Bufton, on the other hand, was one of those who read the February directive, the first draft of which he had written himself, as an invitation to strive towards the aim of eventual precision bombing at night.[2] In March 1942 he had expressed to Air Marshal Harris his hope that the creation of a target-finding force would make it possible 'to consider attacks upon specific targets such as the Buna plant at Huls, or even special targets outside the range of "G", such as the other Buna plant at Schopau and the vital ball bearing town of Schweinfurt.'[3]

The real difference of opinion between Air Marshal Harris and the Air Staff view, in so far as it was represented by Group Captain Bufton, therefore, related to the value and the purpose of area bombing. Air Marshal Harris, of course, regarded area bombing as an end 'in itself', and, if vigorously enough pursued, as a means of winning the war. Group Captain Bufton thought it was only a preparatory phase through which Bomber Command would inevitably have to pass before it could perfect the technique of precise attack. The whole future tactical development of Bomber Command hung between these two extremes of opinion, for it was, of course,

---

[1] Letter Harris to Bufton, 17th April 1942.
[2] Bufton's comments on *Harris Despatch*, 28th Dec. 1946.
[3] Letter Bufton to Harris, 17th March 1942.

CREATION OF THE PATHFINDER FORCE

the ultimate aim which conditioned the processes of design, scientific investigation and production which resulted in the equipment, and of training which resulted in the operational aircrews.

Meanwhile, however, Group Captain Bufton was convinced that Bomber Command still had a long way to go before it could be said to have perfected the technique of area attack. He did not accept Air Marshal Harris' claim that the results being achieved were 'reasonably satisfactory.' He calculated that in eight attacks on Essen between 8th March and 12th April 1942, some ninety per cent of the aircraft had dropped their bombs between five and one hundred miles away from the target. He reckoned that seventy-eight per cent of the effort had been wasted in the first attack on Rostock and he pointed out that in the raid on Gennevilliers which was lightly defended and during which there was perfect weather and a full moon many fires wide of the target had been bombed.[1]

These failures, Group Captain Bufton told Air Marshal Harris, were due to the lack of an 'initial unmistakable conflagration,' which he thought could 'never be achieved when second class crews are mixed with first class ones in the initial phase of the attack. Even the first class crews will not be successful', he continued, 'unless they are co-ordinated in one body and develop the specialised technique.'

This insistence upon the co-ordination of the target-finding force was fundamental to Group Captain Bufton's proposals, and it led him to advise against Air Marshal Harris' competitive plan under which the best among the ordinary squadrons were to be selected at the end of each month for target finding. Such a force would, Group Captain Bufton said, lack cohesion through its geographical separation and there would be no organic growth of tactical methods because its composition would be constantly changing. There was also, he observed, the danger of a relatively poor squadron being

---

[1] Letter Bufton to Harris, 8th May 1942. These figures were scrutinised at Bomber Command and compared with those compiled by the Operational Research Section. According to Wing Commander Marwood-Elton of the Bomber Command Operations Branch, Group Captain Bufton was 'obviously biassed and has in certain cases given the percentage of successful photographs as the percentage of successful attacks. This', he continued, 'is misleading as some aircraft take more than one photograph and others take them at a different time to the time of release of their bombs.' Nevertheless, Wing Commander Marwood-Elton was not able to break down Group Captain Bufton's argument on this score. In the Essen attacks he found that the Operational Research Section placed 109 out of 131 plotted photographs between five and a hundred miles from the target. (Group Captain Bufton's figures were 110 out of 122.) In the Rostock attack he found that the Operational Research Section placed nine out of fifty-eight photographs in the target area. (Group Captain Bufton's figures were sixteen out of seventy-two.) On the Gennevilliers attack the Operational Research Section said twenty per cent of the photographs (six out of thirty) showed the target. (Group Captain Bufton's figure was twelve per cent—eleven out of ninety-one photographs taken by eighty-five aircraft.) Wing Commander Marwood-Elton concluded that, 'if some means is devised to lessen the difficulties of locating the target, a very large proportion of the wasted sorties would find and bomb their primary objective.' Min. Marwood-Elton to Saundby, 11th May 1942.

carried to success in the competition by the target-finding and marking abilities of a much better squadron. Moreover, there was the likelihood that even the best squadron would contain a number of bad crews. These would vitiate the efforts of their more competent companions.

Group Captain Bufton was not convinced that the difficulties of accurate attack against heavily defended targets at night were inherently insuperable. Searchlights, he pointed out to Air Marshal Harris, only seriously affected those aircraft upon which they were focussed. He was confident that a properly constituted target-finding force would devise the means of overcoming these difficulties. Nor did he believe that the creation of a target-finding force would have a demoralising effect on the main force squadrons. On the contrary, he believed it would raise their morale for they would all be ambitious to be selected for the new force themselves. Furthermore, he reminded the Commander-in-Chief of the demoralising effect upon the crews of constant failures to find the target. As to the effects which the reduced chances of promotion consequent upon entry into the target-finding force might have,[1] Group Captain Bufton thought that to raise this as an objection to the scheme[2] was to do an injustice to 'the spirit and idealism of the crews.' The majority of them held temporary ranks and were not concerned with making careers in the Royal Air Force. Moreover, during the five or six months of their operational tours they did not know, as Group Captain Bufton pointed out, 'from one day to the next which will be their last' and promotion did not, he suggested, 'enter largely into their calculations.'[3]

Air Marshal Harris remained unconvinced, but he was, in fact, far less complacent about the performance of Bomber Command than might be inferred from his correspondence with Group Captain Bufton. In spite of the victories at Billancourt, Lübeck, Rostock and Cologne, he found much to criticise. These criticisms and the generally pessimistic and at times even defeatist responses which they evoked from the Groups had an important bearing upon the eventual formation of a target-finding force.

Writing to his Group Commanders on 22nd May 1942, for example, Air Marshal Harris complained that the results of the recent attack on Mannheim had been 'most disappointing'. Photographic reconnaissance had shown that practically no damage had been done in the town or its suburbs. It appeared that 'almost the

---

[1] In each target-finding squadron there were likely to be many officers who, if they had remained distributed throughout the main force, would have become Squadron Commanders.

[2] Which had often been done.

[3] Letter Bufton to Harris, 8th May 1942.

whole effort of the raid was wasted in bombing large fires in the local forests, and possibly decoy fires.' Air Marshal Harris attributed this failure to 'the easy manner in which crews are misled by decoy fires or by fires in the wrong place,' and he asked the Group Commanders to impress upon them 'the fearful waste of effort which is occasioned if, after all the labour in providing them with training and with aircraft, their operations are rendered nugatory owing to lack of skill or carelessness in pushing home their attacks to the correct objectives.'

Air Marshal Harris fully appreciated the 'immense difficulties which the crews face up to with such extraordinary courage,' but he was determined that 'somehow or other we must cure this disease, for it is a disease, of wasting bombs wholesale upon decoy fires.' Referring to the attacks on Rostock, the Commander-in-Chief said that the bombing on the first night was 'hopelessly wild' and that most of the energy of the force, misled by the efforts of a few early arrivals, was expended 'in burning down inoffensive villages, in some cases many miles from the target area.' The size of the force sent against Rostock should, he said, 'have enabled it to have been reduced to its final state of ruin with one attack only.' It was, he added, 'only by effective attacks that the Bomber force is justified.'[1]

These remarks did not readily accord with Air Marshal Harris' claim made to Group Captain Bufton that Bomber Command's methods were proving 'reasonably satisfactory.' On the contrary, they were extremely close to the arguments which Group Captain Bufton was himself using. Nor, when he was addressing his Group Commanders, did Air Marshal Harris suggest that these failures were largely inevitable. He clearly showed that he believed in remedies.

In the case of the Mannheim attack he thought that the majority of the crews had failed to take the trouble, or to come low enough, to 'make certain of the nature of the fires.' Yet he thought that a forest fire should be distinctive and 'comparatively easy to recognise.' He detected a certain lack of bombing discipline in the force which he thought was encouraged by the frequent failures of the Groups and the Stations to 'take the trouble to compare the evidence of air photographs with the pilots' reports.' He had even received a recommendation for an immediate award to a pilot in which 'in the most glowing terms, a detailed report of the precise and extensive damage which had been done to a small objective was given.' Nevertheless, the photographic reconnaissance, which had been available both to the Station and the Group concerned, 'showed no trace whatever of any damage on this particular target.'[2]

---

[1] Letter Harris to Oxland, 22nd May 1942.
[2] do.

The question of bombing discipline was a most sensitive problem and it was by no means always a case of encouraging the crews to run greater risks. On the night of 1st April 1942, for example, Bomber Command's operations had included some attacks upon railways in north-western Germany. From a force of forty-nine aircraft despatched to Hanau and Aschaffenburg, thirteen had failed to return.[1] The weather on that occasion had been extremely dangerous and orders had been given that the bombers were not to fly above five hundred feet. In the event conditions had made low-level flying very difficult and in their enthusiasm to reach the target many crews had climbed 'into the danger zone, or continued under local weather conditions unsuited to the operation'. The situation had, Air Marshal Harris told his Group Commanders, 'not only justified but rendered imperative the abandonment of the operation . . .' The crews had, he said, been too 'full out' in conditions 'where discretion would certainly have been the better part of valour.'[2]

Nevertheless, it was clear to Air Marshal Harris, as it also was to Group Captain Bufton, that 'while a considerable percentage of resolute and skilful crews attain the objective whenever conditions make it reasonably possible, there are others who consistently fail to get anywhere near the target.'[3] Bomber Command's night operations were an individual test of the skill and courage of each crew for the aircraft were seldom visible to each other and there was virtually no communication between them. The only arbiter between the skilled and the unskilled, and between the strong and the faint of heart was, therefore, the night camera, which, in the cold light of the next morning, showed where the bombs had been dropped.

One of the early objections to the use of night photography for this purpose had been that it would 'revive the prejudice amongst crews of regarding the camera as the official spy . . .'[4] Nevertheless, as Air Marshal Harris clearly saw, this was the very function of the night camera which was most valuable. 'There is no doubt', he told his Group Commanders in August 1942, 'that we can improve our results hundreds per cent by adopting measures which will ensure that all crews do their utmost on all occasions to achieve what is required of them.' The principal measure which the Commander-in-Chief had in mind was that 'photographic proof' should alone be 'accepted as evidence that a crew has bombed its objective.' At the same time he

---

[1] Bomber Cmd. O.R.B.

[2] Letter Harris to A.Os.C. 1, 3, 4 and 5 Groups, 3rd April 1942. The case of the Halifax which, in the thousand attack on Bremen, bombed from 3,000 feet may also be recalled. See above, p. 415. Many other instances of gallant indiscipline occurred.

[3] Letter Harris to A.Os.C. 1, 3, 4 and 5 Groups, 4th Aug. 1942.

[4] Note 5 Group to Bomber Cmd., 16th Sept. 1941. This was an official Note signed on behalf of Air Vice-Marshal Slessor by W/Cmdr. Whitehead. It also suggested that the night cameras then in use were not accurate enough to produce statistics on navigation.

CREATION OF THE PATHFINDER FORCE

was considering the possibility of changing the basis of an operational tour in Bomber Command from that of hours flown to one of sorties completed, the majority of which would have to be photographically proved.[1]

Air Marshal Harris believed that these measures would tighten the bombing discipline of his Command and that by narrowing the gap in performance between the bad and the good crews would produce much improved results. Subsequently developments were to show that these ideas were well conceived and that the remedies were both necessary and effective. All the same, Bomber Command was never distinguished by an unwillingness to run calculated and uncalculated risks, and the question of bombing discipline in the shape of hesitancy on the brink of the target did not lie at the root of its problem. Blindness in the face of darkness, haze and searchlight dazzle were more important factors than reluctance in the face of intense opposition from ground and air. The question remained as to how this major problem could be overcome.

On the whole the Bomber Group Commanders, some of whom had a long experience of being asked to perform the impossible, were pessimistic about the prospects which existed for improvement. Most of them took the somewhat defeatist view that better results depended upon easier conditions or easier targets. Thus, when he was asked if he could think of any effective means of attacking Essen, Air Vice-Marshal Baldwin, Air Officer Commanding 3 Group, had to tell his Commander-in-Chief that his mind was a 'blank'. He suggested that it would be desirable to avoid 'anything like routine raids into the Ruhr valley,' and, in the meantime, still further to 'spread our attacks on towns hitherto not attacked, or only attacked infrequently . . . ' He thought this would 'hearten up' the crews and he hoped it would also dilute the German defences and, perhaps, 'open up areas which at the present moment are so strongly defended as to be expensive when attacked.' Attacks on the Ruhr, he believed, should only be contemplated when 'really maximum raids' were possible and when the weather seemed promising.[2]

Air Vice-Marshal Baldwin's views proceeded from the belief that Bomber Command was being driven too hard and that quality was being sacrificed to quantity. He favoured a return to the old idea of graduating the new crews on 'nursery slopes' and he complained that 'unfledged' crews were being pitted against heavy and well-exercised defences too early in their careers. Through lack of experience they either became casualties or emerged with shaken morale. Air

---

[1] Letter Harris to A.Os.C. 1, 3, 4 and 5 Groups, 4th Aug. 1942.
[2] Letter Baldwin to Harris, 9th June 1942. It is, perhaps, appropriate here to recall that the Air Vice-Marshal had personally accompanied his crews in the thousand attack on Cologne.

Vice-Marshal Baldwin also believed that the Command was operating at an intensity which was too great for its health. 'After four nights out in five,' he said, 'crews are definitely below par and the percentage of abortive sorties increases by leaps and bounds.'[1]

These considerations, which incidentally had not been absent from Air Marshal Harris' mind, were only palliatives.[2] They were no solution to the problem of how to achieve successful attacks on Essen or other targets which were similarly formidable.

If Air Marshal Harris had taken the view that the only method of avoiding failures over the most important targets was to avoid attacking them except when he could muster a thousand force and count on good weather, it is extremely unlikely that Bomber Command could have long survived the onslaught of its critics, actual and potential. Yet this was approximately what Air Vice-Marshal Baldwin had advised and it was exactly what his Senior Air Staff Officer recommended. 'It must not be thought that our crews are unprepared to face heavy fire,' this officer said in a memorandum which Air Vice-Marshal Baldwin forwarded to the Commander-in-Chief, 'and that this is the reason why they do not fly low to find and hit the target. The real reason', he continued, 'is that over a well defended town such as Hamburg, with its 80 to 100 searchlights, if they fly below 7 or 8,000 feet they are blinded by the searchlights and light flak and consequently the identification of the aiming point is impracticable. Their best chance, therefore,' he suggested, 'when engaging such a target is to fly high—10/16,000 feet—where they are out of the worst of the searchlights and light flak, but even here the glare of searchlights is considerable and they are, in any case, too high to identify the aiming point except under ideal conditions, and even at that height they experience heavy flak, making a steady bombing run on to the target extremely difficult.'[3]

Advice reaching Air Marshal Harris from other Groups was not much less discouraging. Air Vice-Marshal Oxland, Commander of 1 Group, for instance, was convinced that 'a few heavy attacks on fine nights' would be much more effective than the constant offensive. Air Vice-Marshal Oxland was also, if only by implication, an advocate of the easier targets solution. The Renault attack had, he said, brought up the morale of his crews to 'an astonishing extent, and', he added, 'they are simply longing for the time when they can have a repetition of this sort of work.'[4] Air Vice-Marshal Carr of 4 Group,

---

[1] Letter Baldwin to Harris, 16th May 1942.

[2] For example, letter Harris to Baldwin, 3rd June 1942, in which, among other things, he pointed out that 'nursery slopes' were not only a 'great waste of bombing effort' but were also of limited value as a preparation for the real thing. Air Marshal Harris thought that new pilots would gain much more from flying as passengers on major operations.

[3] Memo. by S.A.S.O. 3 Group sent to Harris by Baldwin, 9th June 1942.

[4] Letter Oxland to Harris, 8th March 1942.

writing on 5th July 1942, suggested that owing to the difficulties of visual identification of the target all attacks should be carried out by the *Shaker* or *Sampson* techniques.[1] These, of course, were the techniques which Bomber Command had been employing on most of its attacks, including those on Essen, throughout the spring and summer.

Thus, despite its notable victories, Bomber Command was in danger of sliding back into the frame of mind from which it had so recently been rescued by the advent of *Gee*. This alone might appear to have been a powerful argument in favour of the institution of a target-finding force which, in spite of its possible disadvantages, did at least, as Air Marshal Harris himself had admitted, promise 'some improvement on methods.' The target-finding force, however, continued to evoke singularly little enthusiasm at Bomber Command and none at all among the Group Commanders. The Commander-in-Chief himself was, it is true, constantly seeking the means by which he might exploit the advantages of having the best crews in the lead, without incurring what he deemed to be the disadvantages of forming them into a collective unit. He told Air Vice-Marshal Baldwin, for example, that he was sure 'we will increase our effectiveness if Groups invariably use specially selected crews to lead off the operations both for dropping flares and for starting fires.'[2] A few days later, on 12th June 1942, he told Sir Charles Portal that he was ready to institute regular 'Raid Leaders' within the ordinary squadrons. He was even prepared to distinguish these crews by giving them special insignia, which he suggested should take the form of the Royal Air Force 'eagle' worn below medal ribbons.[3]

These concessions, Air Marshal Harris justly claimed, provided 'all the requirements of the Target Finding Force fanatic, bar living together in special Units.' This 'living together in special Units' was, however, as Group Captain Bufton had sought to show, fundamental to the whole plan. It was, he believed, only by doing so that the selected crews would be enabled to receive special training and briefing, to develop special and empirical tactics and to be equipped with special devices which, for one reason or another, could not be supplied to the whole force. Nevertheless, the Commander-in-Chief and all his Group Commanders were still 'decisively and adamantly' opposed to this aspect of the proposals, and, after three months of debate during which nearly half of the spring and summer, and fully half of the expected life of *Gee* had passed, the situation was still one of deadlock. It is, therefore, important to analyse the grounds for the

---

[1] Letter Carr to Harris, 5th July 1942. *Sampson* was the code name for blind *Gee* attack.
[2] Letter Harris to Baldwin, 3rd June 1942.
[3] Letter Harris to Portal, 12th June 1942. This was the insignia eventually adopted for the Pathfinder Force.

continued resistance to the target-finding force from Bomber Command.

These were still, broadly speaking, that the special force was unnecessary, undesirable and would be ineffective, but the various emphases accorded to these points had changed somewhat and the supporting arguments were defined in ever greater detail. The contention that a target-finding force was unnecessary now rested less on the supposition that the operational performance of Bomber Command was already proving 'reasonably satisfactory' and more upon the claim that alternative measures of a less objectionable kind would meet the case equally well. In particular, Air Marshal Harris made this claim for his 'Raid Leader' scheme which he had outlined to Sir Charles Portal in his letter of 12th June. He said that he had even 'persuaded' his Group Commanders to hold an 'inter-Group Raid Leaders Conference' once or twice a month, so that the various techniques could be discussed, compared and improved upon.

As to the undesirability of the scheme, Air Marshal Harris now suggested that owing to 'restrictions on Foreign and colonial personnel and the technical attributes . . . of some types of aircraft' the choice of the six target-finding squadrons would practically have to be confined to the thirteen Wellington III and Stirling Squadrons. If six of these were withdrawn for the new force, the effect on the remaining seven would, he said, be 'disastrous'.[1] This consideration led the Commander-in-Chief to his last ground for objection, which was the probable ineffectiveness of the target-finding force. If it was drawn from such limited sources, it would, he said, be 'below rather than above the general standard of the present Raid Leader Scheme'. In any case, Air Marshal Harris could not understand why a 'target finding expert' should have any greater chance of or ability to see the target under the usual conditions of haze and searchlight glare, than anyone else. This was presumably an objection which could also have been applied to the raid leader scheme, for in Air Marshal Harris' view, and that of his Group Commanders, the real difficulty was not *'finding'* but *'seeing'* the target. This was why he believed that attacks

---

[1] Letter Harris to Portal, 12th June 1942. Letter Harris to Air Min., 13th June 1942. In the latter Air Marshal Harris excluded for the purpose of target finding:
(1) Six daylight squadrons.
(2) Seven Polish, Czech, Canadian, Australian and Rhodesian Squadrons on the grounds that the crews were unsuitable or proscribed from posting to 'mixed' units by the wish of their governments.
(3) Four Hampden and two Manchester Squadrons because the aircraft were unsuitable.
(4) Four Lancaster Squadrons because two were specialising for other purposes and the supply of these aircraft was uncertain.
(5) Two Wellington Ic Squadrons owing to the lack of *Gee* trained navigators.
(6) Four Wellington IV Squadrons owing to lack of range.
(7) The Halifax Squadrons because they could not carry an economical load of incendiaries.

on difficult targets, such as those in the Ruhr, would inevitably result in area bombing except under the most unusually favourable conditions of weather and visibility. He could foresee no advance on this 'until the force is so large that major conflagrations, even in the wrong objective, result from the effort of the first part of any attack.'[1]

These arguments, some of which had considerable substance, would, no doubt, have concluded the debate if Group Captain Bufton had been alone at the Air Ministry in championing the cause of the target-finding force. It was not possible for the Deputy Director of Bomber Operations or any other junior staff officer to dictate to the Commander-in-Chief, Bomber Command and, contrary to the view which Air Marshal Harris subsequently expressed, it was not by this method that the Pathfinder Force was imposed upon Bomber Command.[2] Group Captain Bufton was, however, not alone in holding the views which he had been laying before Air Marshal Harris. They had become Air Staff doctrines which enjoyed the support of the supreme officer, Sir Charles Portal. On 14th June 1942 the Chief of the Air Staff wrote a lengthy and carefully reasoned letter to Air Marshal Harris in which he made this perfectly clear. He referred to the inadequate and inaccurate results which Bomber Command was achieving by its 'present rule-of-thumb tactical methods by segregated crews' and he said that 'the problem confronting us is clearly so great that nothing less than the best will do.' Sir Charles Portal showed that he appreciated the difficulties which attended the scheme but he did not believe that any of them were insuperable. He also showed why the various compromises which had been suggested by Air Marshal Harris were unacceptable and he firmly stated that it was 'the opinion of the Air Staff that the formation of a special force with a role analogous to that of the Reconnaissance Battalion of an Army Division would immediately open up a new field for improvement, raising the standard and thus the morale which could not fail to be reflected throughout the whole force.'[3]

Though Sir Charles Portal was reluctant to 'impose' the Air Staff proposal on Air Marshal Harris while he objected so strongly to it, this intervention proved decisive and the Commander-in-Chief, Bomber Command, presently emerged as the courageous champion of the right to special promotion which he not unjustly believed

---

[1] Letter Harris to Portal, 12th June 1942. The significance of the words 'even in the wrong objective' should not be overlooked.

[2] In his *Despatch*, Sir Arthur Harris refers to the creation of the Pathfinder Force as 'yet another occasion when a Commander in the field was over-ruled at the dictation of junior staff officers in the Air Ministry'. In a personal minute to the Prime Minister of 6th July 1942, however, Sir Arthur Harris, speaking of the Pathfinder Force, said, 'I have been overborne by C.A.S. and the Air Staff'.

[3] Letter Portal to Harris, 14th June 1942.

ought to belong to the members of the Pathfinder Force.[1] This and the other administrative difficulties which arose caused further delay and it was not until 11th August 1942 that Air Marshal Harris was officially directed to proceed with the establishment of the new force.[2]

Thus, the Pathfinder Force, under the command of Group Captain D. C. T. Bennett, came into being. It operated for the first time on the night of 18th August 1942 when the target was Flensburg. About six nights earlier the German jamming of *Gee* had, for the first time, become effective. Neither *H2S* nor *Oboe* were yet in service and there were still no target-indicating marker bombs. The Pathfinder Force, therefore, began its operational career without any special equipment which was not carried by the main force. Indeed, while they were over Germany, neither the Pathfinders nor the main force now had any aids other than those which had been available to the 1941 force.[3]

These circumstances were not favourable, but before proceeding to study the way in which the Pathfinder Force confronted them and the effect which its efforts had on the night offensive during the remainder of the year, it is necessary to pause to consider three fundamental factors which controlled the new force, not only in the initial stages, but throughout its career. These factors were firstly, the personality of the Commander of the Pathfinder Force and the relations which he established with the main force Group Commanders, secondly, the quality of the crews which were posted to the Pathfinder Force, and thirdly, the extent to which it enjoyed real priority in the provision of the latest and the best equipment.

Group Captain Bennett was an Australian officer of vast experience and knowledge. He had an understanding of the many problems of long-range flying which was probably unique in the service. He had completed some sorties as a pilot in Bomber Command. He was an acknowledged expert on the subject of air navigation and he knew intimately the job which each member of a bomber crew had to undertake. These exceptional qualities and qualifications fitted him admirably and uniquely for the command which he had been given, but despite them and, perhaps, to some extent because of them, Group Captain Bennett did not always find it easy to establish har-

---

[1] The proposal was that each member of the Pathfinder Force who made good should, on the recommendation of his Commanding Officer and Air Officer Commanding, be entitled to one step up in promotion regardless of establishment. The men in question were to be asked to complete sixty operations without a break. Ordinary Bomber Command crews suffered much heavier casualties than those in Fighter or Coastal Command, but in addition to the extended tour and, therefore, the much reduced chance of survival, the Pathfinder Force crews were expected to suffer more heavily than those in the main force on a raid-for-raid basis, because they would be the first to reach the target area. This was the justification for the privilege asked. It took much argument to overcome the resistance of the Treasury presided over by Sir Kingsley Wood.

[2] Dir. Bottomley to Harris, 11th Aug. 1942.

[3] O.R.S.(B.C.) Report undated.

CREATION OF THE PATHFINDER FORCE

monious relations with the main force Group Commanders who, in rank, were his superiors. Like Group Captain Bufton, he was not easily convinced by the arguments of senior officers who, as he put it in another connection, had not been 'fortunate enough to be permitted to operate themselves.' He did not hesitate to apply his own operational experience to the problems which confronted him and he emphasised that in his associations with aircrews he had been of sufficiently junior rank to learn 'some of their characteristics from the inside.'[1]

These qualities did not tend to disperse the atmosphere of suspicion which had been created in the Headquarters of the main force Groups by the establishment of a *corps d'élite*. The natural reluctance of the main force squadrons to part with their best crews was, perhaps, increased, and in the case of one of the Groups in particular the tendency to compete rather than co-operate with the Pathfinder Force was soon to become pronounced. The Pathfinder Force crews were, as will be shown in due course, to perform many wonderful feats and they always earned the respect of all Bomber Command because their operational tours ended only with disaster or after they had completed sixty sorties without intermission. Nevertheless, it remains doubtful whether they were always the best crews which Bomber Command had to offer. It is not without significance that 617 Squadron, which was to become the most famous squadron in the Command, was formed, not in the Pathfinder Force, but in 5 Group. The three greatest bomber pilots of the war, Wing Commander Gibson, V.C., Wing Commander Cheshire, V.C., and Squadron Leader Martin belonged not to the Pathfinder Force but to 617 Squadron.[2]

In the matter of equipment the Pathfinder Force was perhaps more fortunate, but it was never more than a powerful competitor for what was available and it certainly never enjoyed absolute priority. One of the most valuable aids to target indicating, V.H.F. radio, was to come to 5 Group before it reached the Pathfinder Force, and it was, perhaps, significant that the directive introducing the Pathfinder Force laid it down that 109 Squadron, which was the first being equipped with *Oboe*, was to be 'associated with the force but established independently of it.'[3]

Thus, at the outset, the Pathfinder Force was confronted with

---

[1] Letter Bennett to Harris, 18th April 1943. Air Vice-Marshal Bennett has published his own account in *Pathfinder* (1958).

[2] In September 1943 Air Commodore Bennett complained to Sir Arthur Harris that he was 'not getting the very best of the crews.' Letter Bennett to Harris, 25th Sept. 1943. After the war Group Captain Bufton commented, 'I do not think 8 Group ever succeeded in obtaining the best crews from the other Groups, and at times it struggled with a deadweight of ex O.T.U. crews.' Comments on *Harris Despatch* by Bufton, 28th Dec. 1946.

[3] Dir. Bottomley to Harris, 11th Aug. 1942.

many formidable difficulties, both operational and otherwise, and it is not entirely surprising to find that its introduction did not bring about any marked or immediate improvement in Bomber Command's results.[1] It was not until 1943, when new radar aids and effective target-indicating bombs became available, that important changes in Bomber Command's ability and accuracy began to occur.

These later successes did, however, owe much to the experiments which were carried out in the second half of 1942. As Sir Arthur Harris himself said, 'Although no immediate improvement in the overall results of our night bombing was discernible as a result of the introduction of Pathfinder methods, a very definite advance in technique had in fact been made.'[2]

The chief and immediate result of the 'Pathfinder methods' was a marked increase in the concentration of bombing. In the period immediately before the introduction of the Pathfinder Force from March to August 1942 some thirty-five per cent of Bomber Command night photographs were plotted within three miles of the centre of the bombing concentration. In the period immediately following from August 1942 to March 1943 this percentage rose to fifty. Thus, it was shown that even with such inadequate substitutes for marker bombs as salvoes of 30-lb. and 250-lb. incendiaries, and 4,000-lb. incendiaries[3] the Pathfinder Force had achieved considerable success in concentrating the main force attacks on a single point.

This was, of course, a most important advance, for it had long been evident that it was only by heavy concentration in space that effective damage could be done to major targets. Nevertheless, concentration was not everything. Accuracy was quite as important, for it was evident that concentration would avail little unless its centre coincided with the aiming point. In the matter of accuracy the Pathfinder Force produced much less impressive results. In the period from March to August 1942, thirty-two per cent of Bomber Command's night photographs were plotted within three miles of the aiming point. In the period from August 1942 to March 1943 this percentage rose only to thirty-seven though, of course, the winter weather may have made a difference.

The gap between the improvement in the concentration and that in the accuracy of bombing was largely explained by a new difficulty associated with the Pathfinder technique, known as the systematic error. The old tactics, including to a large extent the *Shaker* technique, had generally left it to each crew to identify the aiming point for itself. The result had generally been a poor concentration and on many

---

[1] O.R.S.(B.C.) Report undated.
[2] *Harris Despatch.*
[3] Known as 'Pink Pansies'.

CREATION OF THE PATHFINDER FORCE

occasions the bombs had been widely scattered around the aiming point. Nevertheless, the mean point of impact of all these bombs had generally coincided with the aiming point. In the seven months directly preceding the introduction of the Pathfinder Force only about fourteen per cent of the attacks showed any appreciable displacement of the mean point of impact from the aiming point. In the seven months immediately following this percentage rose to about sixty-seven. Misplaced Pathfinder Force markers were much more potent in drawing attacks away from the aiming point than German decoys. The major problem which remained, therefore, concerned the reduction of the systematic error or, in other words, the distance between the centre of the bombing concentration and the aiming point. The chief factor in this problem was to find the means of enabling the Pathfinder Force to lay its markers more accurately.[1]

Effective marker bombs might be expected to produce a further improvement in concentration for they would be more easily recognised by the main force. The systematic error could, however, only be reduced by more accurate navigation and bomb aiming by the Pathfinder Force itself, and this was largely a question of new and better radar aids for, as Sir Arthur Harris had expected, even the best navigators and bomb-aimers were largely helpless in the conditions of cloud, industrial haze and searchlight glare which they so often encountered.

Oboe was first brought into operation on the night of 20th December 1942 when Lutterade was the target. Target indicator ground markers were first used in the attack on Berlin on the night of 16th January 1943 and *H2S* saw its first war service against Hamburg on the night of 30th January 1943. With these devices, to quote the words of Sir Arthur Harris, 'a new era in the technique of night bombing was initiated.'[2]

Thus, through the trials, the tribulations and the victories of Bomber Command in 1942, the operational tactics of night area bombing were brought to the verge of maturity and the foundations of the full offensive, which was to follow in 1943 and to embrace the Battles of the Ruhr, of Hamburg and of Berlin, were laid. This full offensive, like the foundations on which it rested, was mounted almost exclusively by night and the experiment of attempting a major daylight offensive against Germany was left, with little hope of success, at any rate in the estimation of Sir Charles Portal, to the United States Eighth Air Force.

That this should be so had been made largely inevitable by the operational experiences of Bomber Command in daylight even before

---

[1] *Harris Despatch.*
[2] do.

the end of 1939. Subsequent undertakings in 1940 and 1941 had merely served to reinforce the view of the British Air Staff that massive and sustained operations by unescorted bombers against defended areas were not, in daylight, feasible propositions of war. Indeed, such operations were not undertaken by Bomber Command until after the ultimate collapse of the German day fighter force had made daylight somewhat safer than darkness. Nevertheless, the limited and tentative experiments in daylight bombing which occurred in 1942 merit some attention if only because of the negative influence which they exerted.

4. Daylight bombing in 1942

Bomber Command's experience of daylight operations in 1941 had been neither happy nor encouraging. *Circus* operations, whose primary object had been to destroy German fighters in the air, had failed to bring the German air force to battle on terms favourable to Fighter Command. This, in the view of the Group Commander responsible for the bomber element, was attributable to the faulty tactics and unsuitable equipment of the covering fighters. In the view of the Group Commander directing the fighter operations, it was due to the inadequate striking power of the bombers. While, of course, there was some truth in both these opinions, the operative cause of the disappointing results obtained, was the limited range of Fighter Command. This meant that the *Circus* operations could not be carried beyond the fringe of France and, as was not surprising, it proved impossible to force a battle for air superiority on the issue of bombing targets whose destruction was of more concern to the French than the Germans. This, in turn, also meant that the way was not opened up, as Air Vice-Marshal Saundby had hoped that it might be, for unescorted daylight attacks by heavy bombers on targets in Germany and north-western France. Such attacks had, in the event, proved to be not only prohibitively expensive but by no means effective. By the end of the year it certainly seemed that these efforts amounted to little more than an unwarrantable and most costly diversion of strength from the main night offensive or, to quote the words of Air Vice-Marshal Slessor, to show that 'this day bomber business' was 'a terribly uneconomical business'.[1]

This, however, was not an adequate reason for the complete abandonment of daylight operations by Bomber Command, nor, as we shall presently see, was it taken as such. The failure of the *Circus* operations to achieve their primary object in 1941 did not mean that nothing was achieved. On the contrary, these activities did have two consequences which were of considerable importance. Though the Germans were not compelled to divert air forces from the east or the south to the west, they were forced to maintain a considerable day fighter strength covering northern France. This force contained a high proportion of the *Luftwaffe's* best fighters, the Focke-Wulf 190's which, in the absence of the daylight threat provided by *Circus* operations, might have been employed elsewhere. Certainly the Germans were left with the freedom to choose the terms upon which they would

---

[1] Letter Slessor to Peirse, 12th Sept. 1941. The Group Commanders directly responsible for *Circus* operations in 1941 were Air Vice-Marshal Stevenson, A.O.C. 2 Group, Bomber Command, and Air Vice-Marshal Leigh-Mallory, A.O.C. 11 Group, Fighter Command.

engage the *Circus* operations, but they were not in a position to ignore them. If they had done so then, indeed, the way would have been opened for daylight attack on Germany.

The second important consequence was that *Circus* operations were gradually leading to Royal Air Force superiority over the nearer parts of France. In relation to the strategic bombing offensive against Germany this was of little consequence, but in relation to the allied plan for an eventual military invasion of the Continent air superiority over these coastal regions was to be of far greater importance. The abandonment of daylight bombing in 1942 would have resulted in the sacrifice of both these important advantages. Clearly the German fighters would not rise to the bait of Fighter Command patrols unless Bomber Command was also there. *Circus* operations were, therefore, continued, with varying degrees of intensity in 1942.

They, nevertheless, continued to be a discouraging experience for all concerned with them. The appearance of Bostons in 2 Group to replace the hard-pressed Blenheims, provided the bomber crews with a somewhat better aircraft, but throughout the year there was no significant extension of the range of Fighter Command. For that reason, *Circus* operations continued to be confined to the same vicious circle which had marred their effectiveness in 1941. The Germans could still decide, purely on the grounds of tactical advantage, when and whether to come up. By June 1942, the Commander-in-Chief, Fighter Command, admitted that the balance of casualties had turned against him and in favour of the Germans.[1]

Even this, though it led to a reduction of the *Circus* effort, did not exhaust the case for daylight bombing. The primary role of 2 Group was to afford tactical support to military operations. In this capacity it had, with its inadequate equipment and in the face of hopeless odds, done its best, at an appalling cost, during the Battle of France. The fall of France and the repulse of the German threat to invade Britain amounted, for 2 Group, to a deliverance which left the mutilated force without an immediate task. Yet clearly this was a temporary state of affairs which could last only as long as the Channel lay between the German army and the allied armies. Eventually 2 Group would once more find itself confronted with its primary role and this was a role which, at any rate to a large extent, would clearly have to be performed in daylight. Night action is a poor school for day bombing and this was one of the good reasons for resisting the temptation to re-equip 2 Group with heavy bombers and commit its future to the main night offensive against Germany. The decision at the end of 1941 to confine 2 Group mainly to night action was not a

---

[1] Dir. Douglas to 10, 11 and 12 Groups (Fighter Command), copies to Bomber Command and 2 Group, 17th June 1942. The C.-in-C. Fighter Command attributed this to the technical superiority of F.W.190's over Spitfires.

surrender to this temptation. It proceeded not from an intention to change the role of the Group but merely from a recognition of the obsolescence and extreme vulnerability of the Blenheim. Its effect lasted only until better aircraft were available.

These, as has been mentioned, began to come into operation during 1942. By the beginning of March 1942, 2 Group had four operational squadrons and elements of two more which had detachments overseas. Three of these squadrons were equipped with Bostons and the rest still had Blenheims. Another squadron was working up on Mosquitoes. By the middle of September 1942 the Group had four operational squadrons, three of which were equipped with Bostons and the other with Mosquitoes. The remaining squadrons were working up or re-equipping with Bostons, Venturas and Mitchells.[1] The operational career of the Blenheim which had so long been the nightmare of day flying crews had come to an end as far as 2 Group was concerned.

Such were the developments which had made it possible to resume *Circus* operations in 1942. Unemployment, however, notoriously breeds the worst kind of inefficiency and frustration and, though 2 Group continued to play some part in the night offensive,[2] it began, after the diminution of *Circus* operations, to undertake an increasing number of unescorted low-level precision attacks in daylight upon widely separated targets in German-occupied territory. In this way, when the intensity of *Circus* operations was reduced, the Group avoided the dangers of unemployment and continued to enlarge its experience of daylight operations which was to be invaluable when, later in the war, 2 Group became a component of the Second Tactical Air Force. Some of the operations carried out in 1942, such as the Mosquito attack on the *Gestapo* headquarters in Oslo on 25th September,[3] were most audacious and highly spectacular, but they were mostly on a small scale and, in relation to the mounting night offensive, of strictly limited importance.

One significant exception was, however, provided by the more massive attack, carried out on 6th December 1942, against the Philips Radio Works at Eindhoven in Holland. This factory was thought to be responsible for about one-third of Germany's supply of radio components. It consisted of two groups of fairly closely packed

---

[1] Orders of Battle on 6th March and 18th Sept., 1942. Bomber Cmd. Narr. All the squadrons had an establishment of sixteen plus four aircraft, but the September return showed that some were below strength. On that date 88 (Boston) Squadron had only twelve aircraft and 105 (Mosquito) Squadron had seventeen.

[2] It was, for example, at this time that Mosquitoes began their career of light harassing actions at night.

[3] This operation was carried out by four Mosquitoes, one of which failed to return. The crews bombed from heights of between fifty and one hundred feet but, by great misfortune, most of the damage fell on a house on the opposite side of the street to the *Gestapo* headquarters. O.R.S.(B.C.) Day Raid Report, 8th Oct. 1942.

buildings and covered an area of about seventy acres. The surrounding district consisted mainly of open fields, broken only here and there by lightly built-up residential areas. The lack of housing concentrations around the target was a great advantage to Bomber Command since there was, of course, an extreme reluctance to inflict injury upon the friendly people of Holland.

The force despatched amounted to ninety-three aircraft, all of which were found by 2 Group. It was made up by thirty-six Bostons, ten Mosquitoes and forty-seven Venturas. The intention was that the force should approach the target almost at ground level in three compact groups, the first consisting of the Bostons, the second of the Mosquitoes and the third of the Venturas. The attack was to be divided between the two main groups of factory buildings and in each case was to be initiated by Bostons dropping their bombs from the lowest possible altitude and opening fire with machine-guns at the same time. The following Bostons and Mosquitoes were meanwhile to have climbed to between a thousand and fifteen hundred feet and were to attack from those heights. Finally, the Venturas were to come in at two hundred feet or less with bombs and machine-gun fire. The aircraft were then to re-form into their three compact groups and return to England at the lowest possible height.

This plan was, in any case, complicated, but the widely differing performances of the three different types of aircraft involved made it more so. Nor in spite of special preparations and training was it by any means perfectly executed in the event. The approach to the target was somewhat ragged and the Boston and Mosquito components were constantly harried by German fighters. The bulk of the Bostons were somewhat late at the target and, therefore, tended to interfere with the Mosquito attack. The formations failed to link up again after the attack and most of the returning aircraft came home separately or in small groups.[1]

Nevertheless, it appeared that about eighty-three per cent of the force attacked the target and dropped rather over sixty tons of bombs on it. Subsequent reconnaissance photographs showed that severe damage had been done to the factory.[2]

The cost of this impressive achievement was, however, very high. Thirteen of the despatched aircraft failed to return and two more were completely destroyed on the way home, one in the sea and the other in England. Thus, sixteen per cent of the force was lost, but this was not all. Another fifty-three bombers, representing nearly fifty-seven per cent of the force, were damaged.[3] Among the lost

---

[1] The Venturas, which were not attacked by fighters, had more success in re-forming and maintaining their formation on the homeward journey.

[2] One of these photographs is reproduced following p. 442.

[3] Among these, seven had sustained serious damage.

bombers were nine Venturas, five Bostons and one Mosquito. Among those damaged were thirty-seven Venturas, thirteen Bostons and three Mosquitoes.

The United States Eighth Air Force attack on Lille probably drew off some of the German fighters, but though the latter certainly had some success against the Eindhoven force, most of the 2 Group losses and the bulk of the damage were not due to German fighters. Indeed, the low-flying bombers, and especially the Mosquitoes, showed themselves to be elusive targets even for the best of the German fighters,[1] but this low flying exposed the force to other hazards. At least thirty-one of the aircraft returning in a damaged condition had collided with birds, and, though most of the resulting injury was of a minor nature, this form of interception was seen to be a very real danger and not only to the birds. A few other aircraft had hit trees and it was more than likely that several of the Venturas, attacking from roof-top height when smoke was drifting across the target, had crashed into unseen buildings. Light flak must have claimed some and it certainly damaged others.[2]

Despite the damage done to the Philips Radio Works, the casualties suffered by the bombers were too high to inspire much confidence in the future of this kind of operation. Moreover, Eindhoven, notwithstanding the great strategic importance which it was supposed to have, was no more than a fringe target. The task of extending low-level daylight precision attacks across the Rhine and into the heart of Germany by the use of heavy bombers was a much more formidable proposition. Indeed, the extent to which this was so had been demonstrated nearly eight months earlier on 17th April 1942 by the famous 5 Group Lancaster attack on the M.A.N. Works at Augsburg.[3]

This operation, involving a round trip of some 1,250 miles, mostly over enemy territory, was among the most audacious actions ever undertaken by Bomber Command. From the point of view of precision, both in navigation and in bomb aiming, it was also one of the most ambitious tasks ever attempted. The target was a single building, the engine assembly shop, which lay in the midst of the complex of factory buildings comprising the M.A.N. Works. The twelve Lancaster crews who were to take part received special training in the technique of low-level flying and bombing and they were also

---

[1] One of the Mosquitoes was attacked by a F.W. 190 as it approached Eindhoven. After fifteen minutes of successful evasive action, its pilot was compelled to abandon his intention of bombing the target. He set course for England at an indicated air speed of 330 m.p.h. The Focke-Wulf followed as far as Flushing and then gave up the chase. *Bomber Command Quarterly Review*, Oct.–Dec. 1942.

[2] O.R.S.(B.C.) Day Raid Report, 3rd Jan. 1943.

[3] The letters M.A.N. signify *Maschinenfabrik Augsburg–Nürnberg Aktiengesellschaft*. The choice of the particular objective was afterwards severely criticised by the Ministry of Economic Warfare which had not been consulted about its selection. The resulting dispute is discussed below, pp. 463–464.

thoroughly briefed in the recognition of the particular building whose destruction was their task.[1]

The outward flight was to be made in formation at the lowest possible altitude. The attack was also to be delivered from low level with 1,000-lb. general purpose high-explosive bombs fused with a delay action of eleven seconds. The return flight, most of which would be after darkness had fallen, was to be made individually and at a more customary altitude.

The low-level approach was designed to delay the appearance of the bombers on the enemy early warning radar screen and also, in the event of interception, to make the task of the German fighters more

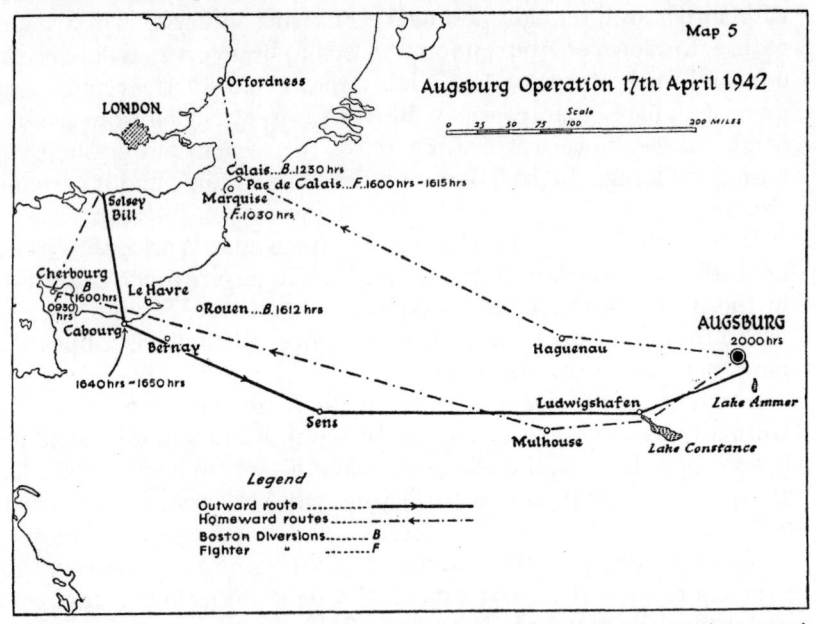

Map 5 — Augsburg Operation 17th April 1942

difficult. It was also thought to be the best defence against anti-aircraft fire. No fighter escort was provided at any stage, but thirty Bostons and over five hundred Fighter Command sorties went out over northern France in an attempt to distract the attention of the enemy. Nevertheless, whatever may have been the effect of these measures, the Lancaster force could scarcely have suffered more heavily without being completely exterminated. Of the twelve aircraft which set out, only five returned and all of these were damaged.

The selected route lay across France from between Le Havre and Cherbourg to Sens and then, in an almost due easterly direction, passing to the north of Mulhouse, and so to Augsburg. Squadron Leader J. D. Nettleton led the formation, subdivided into sections of three, across the French coast soon after half-past four in the afternoon.

---
[1] The force was provided in equal proportions by 44 and 97 Squadrons.

16. Mainz after attacks in August 1942.

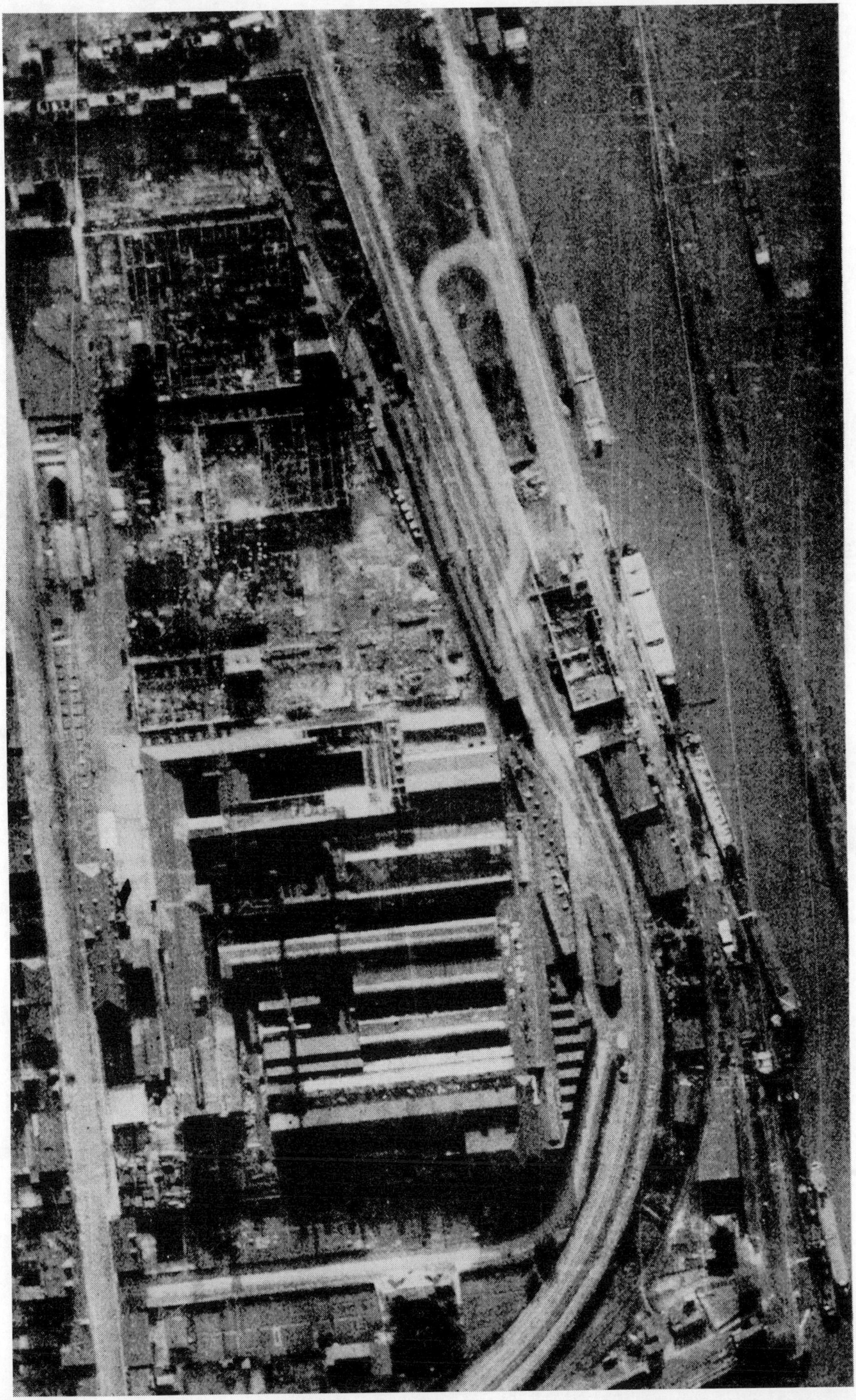

18. The Philips Radio Works at Eindhoven after the daylight attack of 6th December 1942. This reconnaissance photograph was taken half an hour after the attack had ended.

17. *Opposite*. Duisburg after attack on the night of 20th December 1942.

19. M.A.N. Works, Augsburg, after the daylight attack led by Squadron Leader Nettleton, V.C., on 17th April 1942.

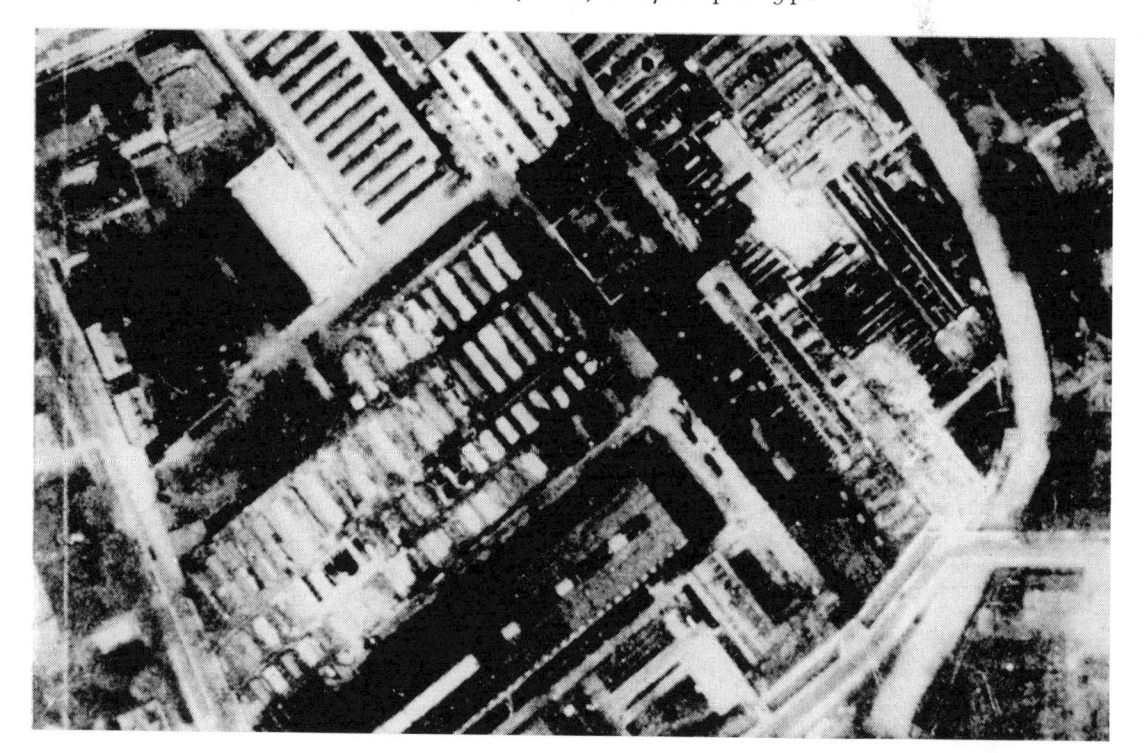

20. Air Vice-Marshal D. C. T. Bennett, C.B., C.B.E., D.S.O., Commander of the Pathfinder Force.

There was unbroken cloud at about a thousand feet and a little low cloud underneath it, but the visibility was about ten miles and the Lancasters dropped down to not much more than twenty feet above ground level and started on their spectacular journey across half of Europe. For a third of their number, this did not, however, last long.

When the neighbourhood of Sens was reached about twenty or thirty Messerschmitt 109's appeared and, within fifteen minutes, shot down four of the Lancasters. The remaining bombers flew on with Squadron Leader Nettleton still in the lead, and all of them eventually reaching Augsburg without further trouble from fighters but not without excitements of other kinds. The attack was pressed home with the utmost gallantry and considerable accuracy in the failing light at the end of the day. After it, only five Lancasters climbed into the gathering darkness for an uneventful journey back to England. In the course of the bombing, which was carried out from between fifty and four hundred feet, intense light flak had been encountered and three of the surviving eight Lancasters had been destroyed. By the chances of war, Squadron Leader Nettleton was among those who returned and his deeds on this day were recognised by the award of the Victoria Cross.[1]

Reconnaissance photographs showed that the main assembly shop, as well as some other buildings in the factory complex, had been hit and damaged, but even the *Bomber Command Quarterly Review*, which rightly boasted of this as 'one of the outstanding raids of the war', did not claim for the results more than that there was 'no doubt that work must have been very seriously delayed'. The report of the Operational Research Section was even more conservative and said simply that there was 'little doubt that work has been delayed'.[2]

However this may have been, there was much less doubt that the action had convincingly demonstrated that this type of operation was not a feasible proposition of war for Lancasters in 1942. The low-level tactics, which undoubtedly made the problems of interception and engagement difficult and dangerous for the German fighters, had not prevented them from shooting down a third of the force in a single and a short encounter. Moreover, these tactics had exposed the Lancasters to the perils of light flak and the other hazards of hedge-hopping. Though Squadron Leader Nettleton and his gallant companions had shown that an attack of this kind could be carried to a technically successful conclusion, the losses suffered by his force had

---

[1] This account adds little to the graphic description of the operation given in W. J. Lawrence: *No. 5 Bomber Group R.A.F.*, (1951), pp. 64–68, upon which it is largely based. Additional information has, however, been taken from B.C.O.O., 8th April 1942, and O.R.S.(B.C.) Day Raid Report, 5th May 1942. Squadron Leader Nettleton was killed in action on the night of 12th July 1943 during the Bomber Command attack on Turin.

[2] *Bomber Command Quarterly Review*, April–June 1942, and O.R.S.(B.C.) Day Raid Report, 5th May 1942. The actual results of the attack are recorded below, p. 464 fn. One of the photographs is reproduced following p. 442.

shown with equal clarity that such operations could not possibly be sustained. In fact, Lancasters of Bomber Command were never again despatched in daylight on a task of comparable ambition and hazard. As will be seen in a succeeding chapter, the development of specialised precision-bombing techniques was henceforth to be pursued by Bomber Command not in daylight but at night.

Nevertheless, 1942 did see further, though much more cautious, experiments in the daylight employment of Lancasters. On 11th July 1942, a force of forty-four Lancasters was despatched from 5 Group to attack the submarine building yards at Danzig. This endeavour was particularly notable for two reasons. In the first place it was the heaviest attack which Bomber Command had hitherto attempted against a German target in daylight. Secondly, Danzig was the most distant target which home-based bombers had ever tried to reach. The operation on 11th July involved a round flight of no less than 1,500 miles. That such an undertaking could be contemplated was remarkable, but the fact that it could be carried out with the loss of only two of the Lancasters was much more remarkable.

This astonishing achievement did not, however, in any way reverse the verdict of the Augsburg operation, for the conditions and the tactics of the two attacks were quite different. On 11th July, the Lancasters set off in formation at a very low level in the direction of Denmark, but they did not have to penetrate the German defences in this condition. They were soon able to break formation and climb into the enveloping cover of cloud which extended over the whole route. They encountered no German fighters and, flying nearly all the way over the sea, they were seldom troubled by flak until they reached the target. These conditions were a great safeguard but they also, of course, made navigation exceedingly difficult. For that reason about a third of the crews failed to find Danzig and most of those who did arrived there somewhat after the pre-arranged time. Since the attack, like that on Augsburg, had been planned to take place at dusk, this meant that most of it, in fact, took place in darkness. At any rate it was late enough for the Germans to use searchlights. The flak defences at Danzig proved to be formidable and they probably accounted for both the aircraft which failed to return. They also damaged eight of the other Lancasters. The losses were not greater because most of the bombers did not operate at a low level. Some, it is true, bombed from six hundred feet, but others were as high as fifteen thousand feet when they delivered their attacks. Thus, for many of the crews the operation assumed the characteristics of a standard night attack and the result was an area assault on the town of Danzig and not a precision attack on the submarine yards.[1]

---

[1] *No. 5 Bomber Group R.A.F.*, pp. 80–81, and O.R.S.(B.C.) Day Raid Report, 19th July 1942.

Another, and in many ways a potentially more dangerous, daylight action was undertaken, again by Lancasters of 5 Group, on 17th October 1942. On this occasion ninety-four aircraft from eight squadrons were despatched to attack the great Schneider Armaments Arsenal at Le Creusot and the associated switching and transformer station at Montchanin, a few miles to the south-east. The targets, of course, lay much nearer to England than Danzig, but the outward route was, as is shown in the diagram, by no means direct. The operation, in fact, involved a round flight of about 1,700 miles, and after

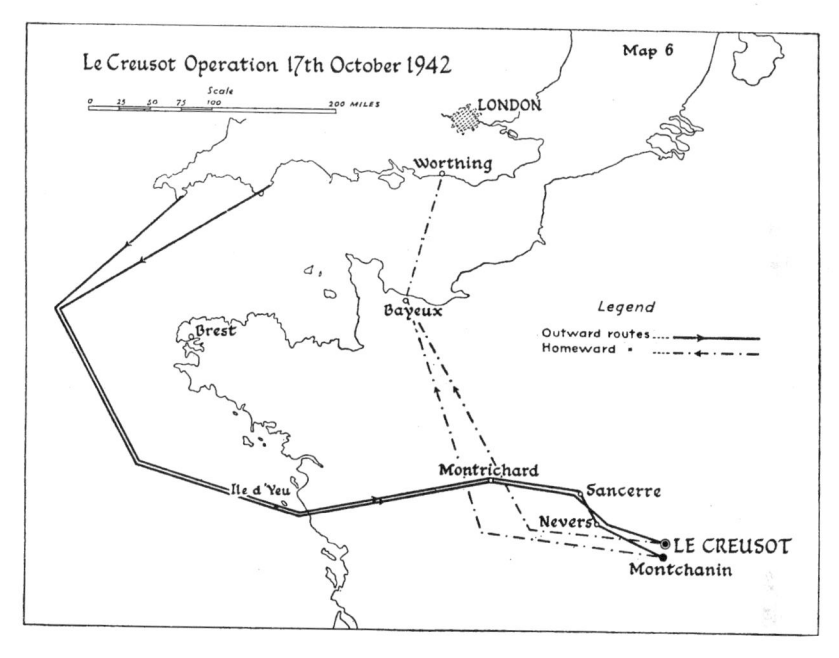

Le Creusot Operation 17th October 1942 — Map 6

crossing the French Atlantic coast just south of the Ile d'Yeu, the bombers had to penetrate inland for some 330 miles. Moreover, this was not an individual cloud-cover flight like that to Danzig, but a low-level formation operation similar, except in the numbers involved and the amount of enemy territory to be crossed, to that which had been led by Squadron Leader Nettleton exactly six months earlier.

The crews involved were given some special training in low-level flying and there had been a dress rehearsal of the operation in which Fighter Command had co-operated by making dummy attacks on the formation. Nevertheless, it was, of course, impossible for the Bomber Command crews to achieve in a few days the standard of formation flying which was characteristic of the United States Eighth Bomber Command. Nor was it the intention that they should do so. The aim was simply that the formation should be kept as compact as possible except in the actual neighbourhood of the target, when it was to open out to avoid congestion on the bombing runs. All the same, no one could be sure of what would happen under battle conditions, for the handling and navigation of such a large force of aircraft in a low-level formation was entirely without precedent in the operational experience of Bomber Command.

As always, plans were made to avoid fighter interception, but it could never be certain that they would succeed. Fortunately, however, on this occasion the force was not intercepted. If German fighters had intercepted the attack, there is little reason to doubt that disastrous casualties would have been suffered by the Lancasters and their comparatively inexperienced crews. This, however, did not happen and the only aircraft which met any fighters at all were a few which had been compelled to abandon their missions and were homeward bound. Moreover, the flak defences at the targets were almost negligible. The result was that from the original armada which set forth, only one Lancaster failed to return.

The attacks were delivered in good visibility just before nightfall. Eighty-one Lancasters discharged over a hundred tons of high explosive and nearly forty tons of incendiary bombs at Le Creusot. They attacked from between 2,500 and 7,500 feet. Five Lancasters dropped nearly ten tons of high-explosive bombs at Montchanin from between 150 and 800 feet. One of the latter, the one which attacked from a hundred and fifty feet, was damaged by the blast of its own bombs, but it was flown safely home by its pilot, Flight Lieutenant J. V. Hopgood, who thus survived to take part in and to die in a yet more famous Bomber Command operation seven months later.[1]

The results of the operation were, however, extremely disappointing. Reconnaissance photographs showed that hits had been obtained on both the targets, but it was also evident that the greater part of the Schneider Works had been left standing. Much of the bombing had overshot and fallen on suburban houses lying to the east of the target.[2] After further reflection, the Operational Research Section at Bomber Command came to the conclusion that the accuracy of the bombing had been far less than was expected. They thought this was partly attributable to the failing light and the smoke which soon began to drift across the target, but they also thought that the tactics adopted had been inappropriate and that the bomb-sights had not been properly used. They suggested that the outcome was the

---

[1] This was the attack on the Möhne Dam which is described in Vol. II. Wing Commander Gibson also flew on the Le Creusot operation.

[2] *No. 5 Bomber Group R.A.F.*, pp. 82–90, O.R.S.(B.C.) Day Raid Report, 18th Nov. 1942, Bomber Cmd. Report, 26th Oct. 1942. The author of *No. 5 Bomber Group* appears to have been misled as to the accuracy of the attack. He states, on p. 90, 'But the crews' impression that it was an extremely successful attack was amply confirmed by subsequent photographic reconnaissance and by intelligence reports.'

penalty of employing night crews in complex daylight operations without giving them more than a few days' training.[1]

Bomber Command was, indeed, more than ready to admit the shortcomings in daylight of its night force. There were, however, three powerful reasons which led Bomber Command to resist the apparently logical steps to remedy this situation. The intensive training necessary to convert even experienced night crews into efficient daylight crews would necessarily mean their withdrawal from night operations and the scale of the main night offensive would thus be reduced even more than it already had been by the diversion of reinforcements to the Middle East, to Coastal Command and elsewhere. Secondly, the modification of heavy bombers to make them a little more hardy for daylight activities would inevitably make them less effective as night bombers. In particular, the fitting of armour plating or increased armament would reduce the bombload which could be carried. Thirdly, and most important of all, it did not seem to Bomber Command that, even if these sacrifices were made, the employment of heavy bombers in daylight against important targets on a sustained basis, would, in the face of the existing German defences, become a practicable proposition of war.

Quite apart from the experience of daylight operations which Bomber Command had painfully gained in 1939, 1940, and 1941, the evidence of 1942 was the strongest possible support for this scepticism. Of nineteen Lancaster sorties which had been despatched to attack Augsburg and Montchanin at a low level, fourteen had succeeded in delivering attacks, eight had been destroyed and five more had been damaged.[2] Thus, the missing rate was forty-two per cent of the despatched force, and the total casualty rate was sixty-eight per cent. When the Lancasters attacked from somewhat higher levels the losses became much less, but so too did the accuracy of the bombing. Moreover, the two principal examples of this, the attacks on Danzig and Le Creusot, in which the casualties were very low, were scarcely a reliable guide. The attack on Danzig was more like a night than a day operation and the opposition mounted by the Germans in the Le Creusot operation was almost negligible.

This evidence bore eloquent testimony to the doubts which existed at Bomber Command as to the wisdom, and, if any substantial or sustained scale of attack was contemplated, the possibility of employing heavy bombers for precision attacks in daylight. If the conditions for accurate aiming existed, or were created by extremely low-level approach, the casualties were liable to be annihilating. If, on the

---

[1] O.R.S.(B.C.) Report, 20th Jan. 1943.

[2] These attacks were all made from below eight hundred feet and several of them from much less.

other hand, the bombers sought safety in greater altitude or in cloud cover, they were unlikely to be able to make precision attacks.

The last point was illustrated by a somewhat wider experience than existed in the case of the former. Between the beginning of December 1941 and the end of July 1942, Bomber Command despatched 190 'cloudcover' bombing sorties in daylight. Seventeen of these sorties were briefed to attack specific targets in Holland, 126 set out to bomb specific targets in Germany and the remaining forty-seven sorties were directed to make area attacks in Germany. These activities involved the despatch of seventy-nine Hampdens to various targets in north-west Germany and Holland, and eighty-eight Wellingtons, mostly to Essen and Bremen. The remaining twenty-three sorties were flown by Lancasters and Mosquitoes. On each occasion the intention was that the target should be approached under continuous cloud cover at high altitude and that the attacks should be made either from beneath the cloud or through gaps in it.

A measure of the efficiency of these tactics was provided by the fact that twenty-nine per cent of the sorties dropped bombs on enemy territory. Twenty-seven per cent of those despatched to German targets dropped bombs on German territory. Only five crews, or three per cent of the total despatched to make specific, as opposed to area, attacks, succeeded in identifying and bombing their targets. In all, no less than sixty per cent of the sorties were abandoned for the single reason that cloud cover was found to be inadequate. Seven bombers failed to return. This represented 3·7 per cent of the sorties despatched, 7·2 per cent of the aircraft reaching enemy territory and twelve per cent of those making attacks of any sort.

A somewhat more efficient form of daylight attack was made possible by the Mosquito performance. From seventy-four sorties against German targets carried out in daylight by Mosquitoes in which reliance was placed, not on cloud cover, but purely on speed and altitude, the missing rate was, however, eight per cent. Moreover, though seventy per cent of the despatched sorties reached Germany, only twenty-six per cent of them succeeded in identifying and bombing their primary and specific targets. Though the Mosquitoes, which operated at between eighteen and twenty-six thousand feet, were usually in clear air, their crews often found that patches of cloud lay between them and their targets.[1]

The evidence of 1942 indicated, as far as the experience of Bomber Command was concerned, that the only way in which daylight bomb-

---

[1] O.R.S.(B.C.) Reports, 29th Oct. 1942 and 27th Sept. 1942. An earlier appreciation had suggested that, as far as daylight cloud-cover operations were concerned, there was 'nothing to indicate that in the long run these raids would be any more efficient than the average night raids as regards the percentage of total bombs falling in a given target area.' O.R.S.(B.C.) Report, 28th July 1942.

ing could achieve reasonably accurate results without at the same time incurring prohibitive casualties, was by the provision of fighter cover. *Circus* operations carried out in the first six months of the year had 'shown conclusively', the Operational Research Section of Bomber Command reported, 'that adequate escort can render fighter defences ineffective against small raiding forces and that such forces can direct their bomb-load on to comparatively small targets with fair accuracy from a high altitude . . .' Though surprisingly large numbers of bombers taking part in these *Circus* operations were hit by flak, only two per cent of those making attacks failed to return.

'Unfortunately,' the same report observed, 'the area of operation of such raids is limited by the range of the fighter escort and their scale by the fact that so many fighters are required to protect each small formation.' These handicaps seemed to be insuperable and they led to the conclusion that it was 'improbable' that bomber operations with fighter cover 'can ever form a major part of any daylight bombing programme aimed at the heart of the enemy's war effort.'[1]

This conclusion, when related to the experience of Bomber Command in unescorted attack either at high level, in cloud cover or at low level, and whether carried out by Lancasters, Wellingtons, Hampdens, Bostons, Venturas or even Mosquitoes, was of fundamental importance. It made the prospects of daylight bombing appear to be bleak in the extreme and, in effect, it virtually killed the practice of daylight attack in Bomber Command. There is no doubt that it also underlay the pessimism with which some members of the British Air Staff, and especially Sir Charles Portal himself, greeted the American plan for a major daylight offensive against Germany.

The clear realisation of the limited offensive potential of Fighter Command did not result in efforts to extend the range of that force. Indeed, Sir Charles Portal was convinced that the production or modification of an aircraft with the range of a heavy bomber and the performance of an interceptor fighter was a technical impossibility. Nor was much consideration given to the problem of how the ratio of protecting fighters to attacking bombers might be reduced so that the scale of escorted bomber operations might be increased. In the case of the Royal Air Force this reaction, or lack of reaction, was, perhaps, not very surprising. The main offensive of Bomber Command had long since been committed to the cover, not of fighters, but of darkness. If the results of the night offensive had hitherto been somewhat meagre, they were already becoming more impressive and high hopes of their efficacy in the future were still entertained. Fighter Command had, of course, been designed and equipped primarily for

---

[1] O.R.S.(B.C.) Report, 28th July 1942.

the role which it had so brilliantly discharged in 1940, namely, the air defence of Great Britain. Its justification as a short-range, high-performance interceptor force lay in the decisive victory which it had won in the Battle of Britain, but its design made it impossible for Fighter Command to seek further victories at longer range, at any rate for so long as range and performance were considered to be irreconcilably opposing factors. For the two separately commanded forces the task of daylight bombing, or the support of it, therefore, tended to acquire a certain aspect of irrelevance to the major roles with which they were concerned. To Bomber Command, day attacks still seemed to be a 'terribly uneconomical business' and to Fighter Command the support of them seemed, at short range, to be tactically unsound and, at long range, technically impossible.

The position of the United States Army Air Forces was, however, quite different. There was no prospect of an American bombing offensive against Germany by night and the United States themselves were not even remotely threatened by an enemy bombing attack. The tradition and design of the Army Air Forces were, therefore, quite different from those governing the Royal Air Force. Throughout 1942 the Eighth Air Force was built up on English bases with the evident and declared intention of undertaking a major offensive against Germany in daylight. The build-up of the bomber component, the Eighth Bomber Command, fell behind schedule, but the preparation of the fighter component, the Eighth Fighter Command, was much more grievously neglected. All the P-38 Lightnings, which had initially been intended for the role of long-range fighting in the Eighth Air Force, were diverted to the North African theatre. Nothing was done to extend the range of the P-47 Thunderbolts, which, when they arrived, could go little further than Spitfires. No attention was paid to the potentialities of the P-51 Mustang, which was being developed by the Royal Air Force.

Thus, the Eighth Air Force came into being and went into action without the provision, or even the prospect, of any kind of long-range fighter support. Nor was the gravity of the omission properly appreciated until, in the summer and autumn of 1943, disaster began to overtake the valiant but unsupported efforts of the Eighth Bomber Command in its endeavour to strike at the heart of Germany. This situation was primarily the product of a revived and most strongly expressed confidence in the self-defending qualities of daylight formations of heavily armed, tightly packed and high-flying bombers. Certainly the B-17 Flying Fortress was the most heavily armed and the most high-flying bomber to be found in Europe. Moreover, the skill of the Eighth Bomber Command pilots in forming and maintaining large tactical formations was unequalled in any air force. Nevertheless, the principle of the self-defending formation had been disastrously exploded on each occasion that it had been tested by the Royal Air Force in serious combat with the main enemy defences. Equally it had tended to be resuscitated by each important development in the speed, altitude and armament of the latest bombers. It was an idea which died slowly and seldom took much cognisance of the scientific and tactical developments to which the opposing fighter forces were also subject. In fact, the relative superiority which the day fighter established over the day bomber at the very outset of the war endured with little relative variation throughout the whole war.

At the end of 1942, the Eighth Bomber Command had not yet been engaged in serious combat with the main German defences because it had not yet crossed the German frontier. Its operations up to that time had been restricted to fringe targets in France and other occupied countries. Often they had been carried out within the range of friendly Spitfire cover. At the end of the year the American confidence in the efficacy of the self-defending daylight formation was, therefore, largely theoretical. Even so, General Eaker wrote to General Arnold at the beginning of December 1942 saying that 'the B-17 has demonstrated that it is the best daylight bomber which has flown in this theater, because it is the only one which has completely demonstrated its ability to defend itself from enemy fighters and to fly at an altitude where it does not suffer losses from anti-aircraft.' [1]

It may seem curious that General Eaker felt able, for whatever reason, to make such a statement and that the United States Air Staff found it possible to digest it. It is, however, still more curious that earlier in 1942, the idea of the self-defending daylight formation was not quite dead in the minds of the British Air Staff and that even the Augsburg operation on 17th April 1942 had not killed it, at least in the view of the Vice-Chief of the Air Staff. Indeed, less than six weeks after that event, Sir Wilfrid Freeman informed Sir Arthur Harris that twelve specially armoured Lancasters would shortly be delivered to Bomber Command. He suggested that they should be allocated to a special squadron which should be released from night bombing and 'told to devote its whole attention to a technical and tactical study of daylight raiding'. Sir Wilfrid Freeman then imparted an even more startling piece of news. He told Sir Arthur Harris that an order for a further hundred of these specially armoured Lancasters had already been placed and that delivery would begin in the following September. 'I know you do not like the specially armoured Lancasters,' he said, 'but I want you to give them a really thorough trial. The lessons which we hope to learn from them about

---

[1] Letter Eaker to Arnold, 6th Dec. 1942. R.S.I. 168–491, Vol. I.
S.A.O.—1—GG

daylight attack may be of enormous value and affect the whole range of tactical doctrine.'[1]

This suggestion of exchanging the substance for the shadow did not recommend itself to Sir Arthur Harris. The specialisation of a Lancaster squadron and its consequent divorce from the night offensive would, he pointed out, reduce the Lancaster contribution to that offensive by no less than twenty-five per cent, for, at that time, Bomber Command had only four operational Lancaster squadrons. Moreover, the bombload of the day Lancasters would be reduced by 2,000 lb. on account of the armour plating which was to be carried, and Sir Arthur Harris did not, in any case, believe that these Lancasters would be able to attack anything other than 'second or third rate targets'. Such, in the view of the Commander-in-Chief, would be the loss to the striking power of Bomber Command.

This negative objection was, however, by no means the only one which occurred to Sir Arthur Harris. He did not believe that this further experiment in the use of unescorted heavy bombers in daylight had even a remote chance of success. If the experiments were to be carried out in the face of the enemy, he did not think the crews would 'survive long enough to develop anything.' If a formation of Lancasters met a large number of enemy fighters in daylight there was no doubt, Sir Arthur Harris suggested, 'that very few, whether armoured or unarmoured, would survive. Their fate', he said, 'would depend therefore, on chance—not armour.'[2]

Sir Arthur Harris was, therefore, being invited to sacrifice a significant, and, perhaps, an increasing, proportion of the best element in his night striking force to the interests of an experiment which, he firmly believed, would be highly expensive and totally ineffective. He was being asked to do this at a time when the night potential of Bomber Command had already been seriously diminished in the interests of the reinforcement of Coastal Command and the Middle East, at a time when the consequently limited efforts of Bomber Command were under public attack, and soon after the official approval of a mounting area bombing offensive against the principal German cities by night. In these circumstances, his discouraging reception of Sir Wilfrid Freeman's suggestions seems to be readily understandable. Moreover, Sir Arthur Harris' views on the prospects of heavy bombers in daylight were substantially supported by the whole operational experience of Bomber Command up to that time.

Nevertheless, Sir Wilfrid Freeman was exasperated by the recep-

---

[1] Letter Freeman to Harris, 26th May 1942. The letter was accompanied by a note dated 21st April 1942 in which the proposed armouring modifications to the Lancaster II were described. This note also showed the assumptions, both tactical and technical, upon which the modifications were based.
[2] Letter Harris to Freeman, 1st June 1942.

tion which his proposals had received and he sought to set them not in the context of suggestions, but of orders. The plan for armouring the Lancasters had been made, the Vice-Chief of the Air Staff explained, at a time when 'it was considered that a return to daylight raiding would be necessary and that every effort should be made to reduce casualties to the minimum.' The consequent reduction in bomb-lifting capacity had been considered and accepted and 'why not,' Sir Wilfrid Freeman asked, 'if the weight of bombs reaching the target is greater than it would otherwise have been?' Though Sir Wilfrid Freeman mentioned that the losses on the Augsburg raid 'might have been 50% less if the additional armour had been carried by our aircraft,' he does not seem to have taken into account the fact that, even if this had been so, they would still have accounted for more than a quarter of the force despatched. Nor did Sir Wilfrid Freeman make any reply to Sir Arthur Harris' not unreasonable assertion that the fate of a Lancaster formation in daylight would depend not upon armour but upon chance. Nevertheless, and in spite of the implication in an earlier part of his letter to the effect that a return to daylight bombing might no longer be regarded as necessary, Sir Wilfrid Freeman concluded with this abrupt phrase:

> 'I should now be glad if you would carry out the orders given to you in the letter dated 26th May.' [1]

Sir Arthur Harris, who was often reluctant to accept the advice of Air Staff Officers particularly when it tended towards a diminution of the main night offensive, was no more enthusiastic about Air Staff 'orders' when he considered that the latter impinged upon his own power of operational decision. In the case of the daylight armoured Lancasters, his attitude was governed by these considerations and by the following September the Air Staff had made little progress towards achieving the fulfilment of Sir Wilfrid Freeman's 'orders'. Indeed, on 22nd September 1942 the Assistant Chief of the Air Staff for Operations, Air Vice-Marshal Bottomley, had to report to Sir Charles Portal that Sir Arthur Harris 'had no wish even to try' the armoured Lancasters in daylight action. Air Vice-Marshal Bottomley admitted that his discussion with Sir Arthur Harris 'was not very profitable' and he added that it was 'clear that the C.-in-C. objected strongly to what he described as Air Ministry interference in the tactical handling of his forces.' [2]

This kind of attitude on the part of Sir Arthur Harris was, in due

---

[1] Letter Freeman to Harris, 3rd June 1942. The letter was marked *'Strictly Personal to be opened by addressee only'*. In the Air Ministry it was circulated only to A.C.A.S.(O), A.C.A.S.(T) and D.B. Ops. It is, perhaps, surprising that it was not shown to Sir Charles Portal, with whom Sir Arthur Harris had, however, discussed the matter earlier.

[2] Min. Bottomley to Portal (through V.C.A.S.), 22nd Sept. 1942.

course, to cause Sir Charles Portal much trouble, but, in this particular case, it is doubtful whether it disturbed him at all. In any case, it is more than evident that, as far as day bombing with heavy aircraft was concerned, the expectation of the Chief of the Air Staff was the same as that of the Commander-in-Chief, Bomber Command. It was, after all, at this very time that Sir Charles Portal was painting such a gloomy and such a realistic picture of what would happen to the day bombers of the United States Bomber Command when they attempted to penetrate beyond the range of protective fighter cover towards the interior of Germany. This picture did not refer only to the prohibitive casualties which were likely but also to the limited accuracy of the bombing which would be possible. What appeared to Sir Charles Portal to be unprofitable for the Fortresses can scarcely have been regarded by him as profitable for the Lancasters, whether armoured or not.

Though the idea of attempting to penetrate the German defences in daylight did recur from time to time it was not again seriously and authoritatively pressed upon Sir Arthur Harris until after the virtual collapse of the German day fighter force in the closing months of the war.[1] By that time the accuracy of night attack was generally greater than that of day attack, but the cover of darkness provided somewhat less security than the command of the air in daylight. Until that time, the issue of daylight attack by Bomber Command ceased to have any significant bearing upon the strategic air offensive against Germany and this state of affairs was no more than a logical development on the basis of the operational experience of Bomber Command and the technical limitations of Fighter Command in the first three years of the war.

In this development, the operations of 1942 had done little more than to confirm the impressions and the lessons of earlier phases in the war, but they had done this with much greater finality than had been possible in 1940 and 1941. The failures in daylight of the Wellington, Hampden, Blenheim, Halifax and Stirling could all too easily be attributed to the limitations of the aircraft themselves and assigned the label of provisional lessons to be revised when better aircraft came into service. In 1942 both the Lancaster and the Mosquito were tested in daylight action. No better aircraft than these came into service with Bomber Command during the war and the lessons taught by their performances were, therefore, permanent.

---

[1] One of these recurrences took place in May 1943 when Air Vice-Marshal D'Albiac, then A.O.C. 2 Group, invited Sir Arthur Harris' approval of his plan for the armouring of Lancasters for the role of daylight bombing. It was not forthcoming. 'Such radical alterations in design, equipment and training', Sir Arthur Harris wrote, 'would take years, rather than months, to put into effect.' Letters D'Albiac to Harris, 6th May 1943, and Harris to D'Albiac, 21st May 1943. Almost immediately after this 2 Group was detached from Bomber Command to become the nucleus of the new Tactical Air Force which was placed under the Command of Air Vice-Marshal D'Albiac.

Henceforth, it was left to the Americans to explore the daylight air over Germany as the medium of a major bombing offensive. But for the greater part of 1943 the United States Bomber Command was to suffer the consequences of disregarding the logic of British operational experience. Indeed, it was not until after the Americans had made a sustained test in daylight action with their own aircraft of the theory of the self-defending bomber formation, that they came to accept this logic which, in the process, had become more American than British. The solution then sought was, however, quite different from that which had been adopted by the Royal Air Force Bomber Command. Day bombing was not abandoned, but the range of fighter cover was extended until eventually it equalled the limit of the bombers' endurance. This technical development, proceeding from a tactical crisis, was to be one of the principal factors in the ultimate neutralisation of the *Luftwaffe*. It was, however, a development which, in 1942, was scarcely envisaged.

CHAPTER VIII

THE MOUNTING OFFENSIVE: APPRECIATIONS AND RESULTS
November 1941–January 1943

1. The economic appraisal of area and precision bombing
2. The estimated and actual results

'The submarine is just as an effective instrument of war for us as the air force is for the English; it enables us to strike the enemy at his weakest point.'
The Goebbels Diaries, 13th December 1942

'There was, however, one strong argument in favour of this heavy air offensive which had not yet been mentioned. Piecemeal devastation of German cities would bring the horrors of war home to the German people in a way that had not hitherto been possible. They might in this way be made to realise that aggression did not pay.'
SIR ALAN BROOKE, 18th November 1942

1. The economic appraisal of area and precision bombing

BY 1942 the machinery of economic advice and its relation to the Air Staff had been stabilised. The enemy branch of the Ministry of Economic Warfare had now five departments engaged in the collection, classification and analysis of economic information, two concerned with the dissemination of intelligence and two whose duty it was to supply to the services the economic advice necessary to appreciate the situation in Germany and to determine what were the most profitable economic objectives for Bomber Command and other services. The first of these last two departments was that which supplied the information and analysis for the representative of M.E.W. on the Joint Intelligence Committee, the body which was responsible for advising the Chiefs of Staff and the Defence Committee as to the general position of the German economy necessary for broad strategic appreciations. By the end of 1942 there were three interdepartmental teams working on this subject under the general direction of the J.I.C. in which M.E.W. had the predominant role. In addition, there was the special sub-committee of the J.I.C. on oil and others were subsequently set up, including one on German and Japanese manpower. Thus, in the general economic surveys of the enemy, M.E.W. had a determining voice. Its appreciations were accepted as authoritative though they might on occasion be challenged on details.

Secondly, there was the Objectives Department under Mr. Lawrence which advised the Air Ministry on the targets for the strategic offensive against the enemy and occupied territories. It also played a similar role with the other services and was eventually divided into three divisions dealing with air, sea and land forces. But in this period its main work was with the Air Ministry and it was in continuous and close communication with the Air Intelligence and Bomber Operations Directorates. Two committees had been established by the latter, one a Bombing Committee to consider tactical aspects on which M.E.W. was not represented, the other the Bomb Targets Information Committee on which M.E.W. had a place. This Committee met once a fortnight, reviewed the targets in detail and made suggestions for additions or alterations. But neither of these bodies dealt with the general strategy of the bombing offensive. That was decided at a higher level by the Chiefs of Staff and the Defence Committee and their economic information and advice came to them mainly from the J.I.C. or the departments of the Air Ministry advising the Chief of the

Air Staff.[1] In spite of its connection with the Air Ministry, M.E.W. was dissatisfied with the position for two reasons. Its advice was filtered through other bodies before it reached the higher direction of the war and it was not in close contact with those engaged in assessing the operational possibilities of Bomber Command.[2]

The directive of 14th February 1942, which designated as the primary objective of Bomber Command 'the morale of the enemy civil population and in particular, of the industrial workers', obviously made a good deal of difference to the nature of the advice as to the targets. Hitherto M.E.W. had considered mainly more precise targets or at least particular industries and weighed the economic advantages of concentrating on one or other of them. The rival claims of oil, the aircraft industry, the transport system and many others had been discussed with the Air Ministry and the advice and information provided by M.E.W. had had a considerable influence on the decisions taken. But a general area attack was in a different category. It no longer depended on particular industries or factories but on the general effect produced on the towns selected for attack. Such attacks would cause a reduction in the output of many different forms of production and the nice calculations which had been made as to the supply of oil or aluminium or the result of destroying marshalling yards or electric power plants were no longer relevant.

Nevertheless, both M.E.W. and some of the departments of the Air Ministry still thought that economic considerations should determine to a considerable degree what towns should be attacked. More immediate damage would be done if a town contained industries producing armaments than if it was mainly concerned with consumer goods. Moreover, if the production of an important material of war was concentrated in one or a very few towns, the damage done there was likely to be much more effective than if it was spread over a large number of industries none of which would be seriously crippled. Finally, neither the Air Ministry nor M.E.W. had abandoned the principle that war production could be most effectively reduced by the bombing of targets which contained industries essential to the production of all kinds of armaments or the functioning of the whole industrial process. Synthetic oil had been such a target system and attention was already being directed to others with a smaller number of targets than that of synthetic oil, the destruction of which, it was thought, would have a paralysing effect. Such targets would, it was

---

[1] Memo. by O. L. Lawrence, 17th July 1942.

[2] The Objectives Department had sought to have direct contact with Bomber Command, but there had been little except on the Bomb Targets Information Committee on which both were represented. In February 1942 it was hoped that a reorganisation of the staff would result in the appointment of an officer who would include in his duties that of liaison with M.E.W., but this plan, made at Bomber Command Headquarters, did not materialise. Memo. by Lawrence, 4th Feb. 1942, App. 14.

claimed, give much greater results than if the same weight of bombs were distributed indiscriminately over a number of towns without any calculation as to what the total effect would be on the production of armaments. There were also bottlenecks in the communications system whose obstruction would disrupt the means of transport to a far greater degree than the damage that might be inflicted on depots, railway stations and marshalling yards in a general area attack.

M.E.W. began to study this problem at the end of 1941 at the request of the Air Ministry, but it was nearly twelve months before a comprehensive scheme could be evolved. The Objectives Department recognised that operational considerations were now predominant and that the attention of both the Air Ministry and Bomber Command had been so occupied with solving them that they had had little time to consider what should be the targets of the new aircraft assisted by new directional aids. But they hoped that this was a passing phase, and, if not, that it could be corrected at a higher level by their new Minister, Lord Selborne. They wished to be kept better informed about the operational problems and the possibilities of the improved methods of attack so that they could adjust their economic objectives to the operational necessities of Bomber Command. They desired, therefore, the closest co-operation between M.E.W. and both the Air Ministry and Bomber Command. They were aware of the intention to use *Gee* and that it might be neutralised by German jamming at a comparatively early date. They hoped, therefore, that it might be used for a concentrated attack on a specific industry which 'might be catastrophic to the enemy at this stage of the war' rather than gradually introduced as a device to assist general area bombing.[1]

It was, of course, recognised that precision attacks could at the time only be carried out by Bomber Command in specially favourable circumstances which very rarely occurred. There was thus needed as a basis of the whole attack a plan for area bombing which should determine the priorities among the cities and towns to be attacked. For this it was necessary to make a comprehensive review of the whole of German war production and its geographical distribution over the Reich, and this work was not completed until the autumn. Meanwhile, advice was called for and M.E.W. had the duty to give the best possible at its command.

It is significant that the first request of the Air Ministry was directed towards discovering what specific industries were the best targets as well as what towns should be the primary objects of area bombing. M.E.W. took into account, as regards the first, varying degrees of vulnerability and accessibility, the concentration of the

---

[1] Letter Selborne to Sinclair, 4th Feb. 1942.

THE ECONOMIC APPRAISAL

industry in a small number of targets and its importance to the war effort. The result was a paper which recommended six target systems, electric power, synthetic rubber, some special components of air and armament industries, oil and substitute fuels, alumina plants and soda ash plants, and, be it noted, given the lowest category of advantage, the manufacture of diesel engines and accumulators for submarines. For general area bombing, on the other hand, it was necessary to choose large built-up areas, surrounded by a larger industrial area so that bombs which missed the main target were likely to do some damage. But, in addition, for moonlight nights there might be what has been termed in previous chapters 'selective area bombing', the choice as targets of towns where the industries were mainly concentrated such as Schweinfurt, Jena or Stuttgart.[1]

For area bombing proper the first choice could not be in doubt. M.E.W. naturally advised that it should be concentrated on the Ruhr. 'On economic grounds', a subsequent report advised, 'there is no target to compare with the Ruhr for this type of attack since it is without parallel as a heavy industry centre and is of absolutely vital importance to the German war effort despite efforts to develop alternative capacity elsewhere'. Moreover, it was superior to all other areas 'owing to the continuous urban development. It has been calculated that a bomb dropped at random in the Ruhr has an even chance of hitting some work of man'. Accordingly, M.E.W. listed the seven chief towns of the Ruhr together with the surrounding or adjacent smaller towns, forty-nine in number. They already had in mind a more comprehensive plan for examining the economic priorities of all the larger towns within the operational range of Bomber Command, forty in number as listed at that time, and thus indicating those which had the most important war industries and those where there was a highly specialised industry producing some important component of war material. These latter might be comparatively small towns like Schweinfurt or Jena, specialising in ball-bearings or optical and precision instruments respectively, or larger cities such as Stuttgart and its satellite towns which was a main centre of precision engineering of all kinds and might be termed 'the Coventry of Germany'. Hanover had also strong claims, if rubber was to be attacked, because it was the largest rubber-manufacturing centre. The first attempt of M.E.W. to work out such principles was admittedly incomplete. In particular, no key industries could be found in the northern area except the shipyards in Hamburg, Bremen and Kiel. But in

---

[1] M.E.W. Report, 8th Jan. 1942. Memo. and Appendices Lawrence to Morley (B. Ops. 1), 7th Feb. 1942, especially its App. 2. The term 'semi specific' targets was used. This was referred to at a Target Committee by D.B. Ops. as a 'most valuable paper', and he stated that the targets suggested were being graded from an operational point of view so that a more definite list could be sent to Bomber Command.

the central area outside the Ruhr they already had a number of suggestions.[1]

This memorandum was the foundation of that which the Secretary of State for Air submitted to the Defence Committee.[2] This listed only five towns in the Ruhr–Rhineland district with a very general description of their economic importance, while the only other primary targets were the naval ports. Nine more precise targets were also listed, taken from the various proposals of M.E.W. When this plan was approved the primary targets were accepted as suggested, but Berlin was substituted for two of the secondary targets, no doubt because of the desire of the civilians and particularly of the Prime Minister for Berlin to be attacked. It is to be noted that in the Directive the list of precise targets was increased and more emphasis was laid on oil targets and electric power. This was an indication that it was still hoped in the Air Ministry that such targets could be successfully attacked when *Gee* was in use, but they were as concerned, of course, to find as many as possible within *Gee* range, as to estimate their economic importance.[3]

Meanwhile, another list of precise targets had been made for the attacks on production in the occupied territories. Here precision was necessary, for, except at a later date on the submarine ports of the Bay of Biscay, there never was any authorisation of area bombing in France or other occupied countries. It was necessary to have worthwhile targets large enough to be easily recognised so that the loss of civilian life through bombs missing the target would be small. There had also to be incontrovertible evidence that the factories were working for the enemy. It was not easy in these circumstances to find suitable targets, but M.E.W. in conjunction with the Air Ministry drew up a list which took all these considerations into account and was the foundation of the directives to Bomber Command and towards the end of 1942 was also used by the Eighth Air Force.[4] Even then there was great reluctance in the War Cabinet to sanction such attacks and stringent rules were drawn up as to how they were to be made. The assent of the Governments in exile had also to be obtained for targets outside France and these sometimes had their own views on their economic importance. But consent was obtained more easily than might have been expected and both information and encouragement

---

[1] Memo. and Appendices Lawrence to Morley, 7th Feb. 1942, especially its App. 1. The synthetic rubber plant at Hüls was also included.

[2] See above, pp. 320–321.

[3] Memo. by Sinclair, 9th Feb. 1942. For the directive of 14th February 1942 which gives the towns finally selected, see App. 8 (Annex A of xxii).

[4] Min. Baker to Portal, 30th Jan. 1942. The targets were to be few in number. The most obvious was the Renault works at Billancourt near Paris. The others were the Ford Matford works at Poissy, the Gnome and Rhône works at Gennevilliers, the aircraft works at Villacoublay and the Gien tank depot. Much information had come through the French resistance movement about these factories.

to attack was supplied in most cases. The raids on Italy, on the other hand, could be made by area bombing and, as they were largely aimed at morale during the attack in the Mediterranean, the economic advice of M.E.W. played little part in determining them.

In addition to these attacks on industries in France and other occupied countries, Bomber Command had taken some account of precise objectives in Germany by detailing a portion of the force engaged in an attack on a town to aim at some particular factory. And, when in the spring the losses in the Atlantic grew menacing, Sir Arthur Harris decided to make the experiment of a daylight attack in southern Germany on a factory manufacturing engines for submarines. He had requested information on such towns from the Air Ministry, who had sent him the objectives already indicated by M.E.W. among their list of precision objectives, but put by them at the bottom of the list for economic reasons.[1] Sir Arthur Harris did not inform either the Air Ministry or M.E.W. of his intention or consult them as to what target would be likely to be most profitable from an economic point of view in the area which he had selected for attack.

The heroic raid on the M.A.N. Diesel engine factory at Augsburg was the result and it immediately drew an emphatic protest to the Prime Minister from Lord Selborne against the total disregard of the economic advice of his Ministry.[2] A precision attack in the south, it was claimed, could have been directed against far more profitable targets in Stuttgart or Schweinfurt. The Air Ministry had long ago been informed that the vulnerability of the M.A.N. plant was low and that there would be no sensible effect on the supply of engines even if it were destroyed completely. Surely the experts should have been consulted before the raid was made so that the sacrifice could have produced corresponding results.

This attempt to assert the rights of M.E.W. turned out to be misguided. The Chief of the Air Staff to whom the Prime Minister referred the letter defended the action of Sir Arthur Harris in every particular, including the concealment of his intentions which was necessary to preserve secrecy. The only concession was that he agreed that in the future a confidential check on the economic importance of a target should be made by Bomber Command. This enabled Lord Selborne's advisers to counsel that a soft answer should be returned, though they were anxious to challenge the assertion of the Chief of the Air Staff that M.E.W. was not necessarily the best judge of the vulnerability of a target. This Lord Selborne did in a conciliatory minute to the Prime Minister, but he was also led by other advice to express surprise that Sir Arthur Harris should take account of such a

---

[1] This target had been first specified on 9th March 1941, and, though subsequently deleted, it had been included in M.E.W.'s list of 8th January 1942. See above, p. 461.

[2] The description of the raid is given above, pp. 441–444.

question as the Battle of the Atlantic without a special directive from the Defence Committee on the subject. This last reference seems to have nettled Mr. Churchill, who sent back a revealing minute. 'I see these officers every week,' he wrote. 'We often talk these things over together.' This was a warning, whether so meant or not, that Sir Arthur Harris had a special position in relation to the Prime Minister.[1]

Sir Arthur Harris himself was naturally invited to make his comments, and his reply which dwelt on the tactical reasons for his decision and the necessity for secrecy was extremely convincing. He also had his own ideas on the vulnerability of targets and, as he implied, on economic matters also, but he too concluded with a conciliatory sentence which recognised the advice of M.E.W. as the '*first* factor in the consideration of any operation on economic targets', however much the decision had to be taken on other grounds. This answer the Prime Minister termed an excellent reply and suggested that Lord Selborne should invite Sir Arthur Harris to lunch and 'knit up afresh the close relations between the two Departments'. This Lord Selborne did, while still upholding the claim of M.E.W. to be a judge of the vulnerability of economic targets; but, though the invitation was cordially accepted, its object was not obtained.[2]

Henceforward, as his book reveals, Sir Arthur Harris had the greatest distrust of any economic advice emanating from M.E.W. The latter had, indeed, fought its battle on unfavourable ground. Tactical reasons alone were sufficient justification for not attacking the two places which M.E.W. had rashly suggested. Sir Arthur Harris was also completely in the right when he said that such a light attack on Schweinfurt, even if it could have been delivered, would have been more than useless. It might, indeed, have caused the dispersal of the ball-bearing industry at an early date and removed the opportunity altogether. Thus, though M.E.W. was entirely correct when it claimed that the target chosen was not worth the sacrifice demanded, the case had been so put that Sir Arthur Harris was left in triumphant possession of the field.[3]

---

[1] Letter Selborne to Churchill, 27th April 1942, Min. Portal to Churchill, 29th April 1942, Min. Selborne to Churchill, 2nd May 1942, Min. Churchill to Selborne, 3rd May 1942, App. 15 (i) to (v).

[2] Letter Harris to Churchill, 2nd May 1942, Min. Churchill to Selborne, 3rd May 1942, App. 15 (vi) and (v). Letter Selborne to Harris, 6th May 1942.

[3] M.E.W. subsequently claimed that as a result of interrogation of a prisoner of war it was found that the sketch map provided by M.E.W. and used on 17th April 1942 had placed the engine works in the wrong position. It does not appear, however, that they knew this fact before the raid took place, though they suggested that if they had been consulted they would have found it out. Min. Lawrence to Vickers, 8th May 1942. Two post-war reports were made on the damage done to the M.A.N. works in this and subsequent raids. Five of the bombs accurately dropped failed to explode. The others did substantial damage to two buildings, one where machine tools for making diesel engines were stored, and the other a forging shop where two furnaces were demolished and the structure damaged. Eight machine tools were completely destroyed, sixteen heavily damaged and fifty-three lightly out of 2,700; five cranes were completely destroyed and

If Sir Arthur Harris distrusted M.E.W., that department had no very favourable view of the direction of Bomber Command, while it wished to strengthen its own position in the hierarchy of advisory committees. An opportunity was given to Mr. Vickers to express these views when he was invited by Mr. Justice Singleton to give his opinion about the methods by which bombing policy was formulated and implemented. While deprecating any desire to go outside his own sphere, he intimated in his reply that the Air Ministry had not sufficient control over Bomber Command, that those directing Bomber Command had not sufficient contact with its operational squadrons, that both the Air Ministry and Bomber Command were susceptible to outside influence and finally that a committee in which tactical and economic considerations could be weighed against one another should be set up to advise the Defence Committee before directives were issued. 'To assess the probable effect on Germany's war effort of different degrees of damage to different parts of her economy', he concluded, 'is both difficult and essential in the framing of an effective bombing policy. Whatever the authority responsible for the proper strategic use of the bomber force, it is essential in my view that it should understand and give due weight to the difficult economic considerations involved. If a committee such as I have suggested were set up this should be borne in mind in determining its constitution'.[1] Such a committee would have, of course, enabled M.E.W. to exercise an influence on the strategy of Bomber Command at a higher level than it had yet been able to do.

This opinion was not without its effect on the Singleton report in which, in a mild way, the main point of Mr. Vickers was endorsed and some of the wording of the above quotation adopted. This sentence does not, however, seem to have attracted any attention when the report was considered by the Prime Minister and the Chiefs of Staff who showed no disposition to give M.E.W. any more important position in the advisory machinery than it had previously possessed.[2]

Nor for the moment was the controversy with Bomber Command continued. The Thousand raid on Cologne opened up new prospects for area bombing and more precise objectives were only in the background. They were, however, never out of the minds of the staffs of

---

six heavily damaged out of 558. The effect on production was slight. *U.S.S.B.S., MAN Werke Augsburg, Augsburg, Germany* (No. 164), p. 58. But even if production had been completely stopped the effect on submarine engine building could hardly have been important at that time: 'The decision for the operationally difficult R.A.F. attack of 17 April 1942 appears unfortunate, since at that time there were more than five of the firm's licensees building submarine diesel engines throughout Europe.' *U.S.S.B.S. Maschinenfabrik Augsburg-Nurnberg A.G., Augsburg, Germany* (No. 93), p. 2.

[1] Letter Vickers to Singleton, 2nd May 1942. The latter was also sent a number of M.E.W. papers so that he could see the kind of intelligence sent to the Air Staff and a special note on the technique of damage assessment. Letter and list of enclosures, Lawrence to Robertson (Secretary of Singleton Enquiry), 11th May 1942.

[2] Report by Singleton, 20th May 1942, App. 17.

the Air Ministry and M.E.W. These latter were constantly engaged in trying to discover bottlenecks, the destruction of which would, they thought, exert a far more paralysing effect on German industry than the indiscriminate damage by general area bombing. The Augsburg raid had proved, if it needed proving, that daylight attacks on precise objectives in Germany such as a particular factory were far too costly to be repeated. But selective area bombing, the concentration of night bombing on towns which were the main producers of some vital component, was not impossible and to this aspect M.E.W. turned its attention. The most obvious example was Schweinfurt, and by the autumn, M.E.W. had convinced the Bomber Operations Directorate of the Air Staff that its destruction might have devastating effects on German industry. The Minister of Economic Warfare had also convinced the Government of the wisdom of spending large sums of money in pre-empting the only possible considerable external supply of ball-bearings in Sweden. The project was thus designed for the close co-operation of Bomber Command with M.E.W. as originally prescribed by the Defence Committee. The effect might be so great that some people claimed that the war could be won by a successful attack on this same industry. Others whose hopes were not so high thought that such an attack would pay higher dividends than any other. But Sir Arthur Harris remained completely sceptical, and, while his opinion on the economic results likely to be obtained could not be considered authoritative, he had the last word on the operational possibilities. This dispute began in the autumn of 1942, but, as it was brought to a head in the succeeding year with the intervention of the United States Eighth Air Force, consideration of the economic factors involved is deferred to Chapter XI.

Meanwhile, many other bottlenecks were under consideration. A number of those engaged in the higher direction of the war began to believe that better results could be obtained by concentration on some specific part of German industry. The United States bombing force was designed for precision bombing and attention was called from time to time to the targets which it might attack. The review of the whole of German industry which was being made in M.E.W. naturally included consideration of this aspect of it. Consequently, in November 1942, M.E.W., in response to a request from the Air Ministry, were able to make a comprehensive review of German bottlenecks.

The qualifications necessary for any industry to be designated a bottleneck, as has been described in Chapter I, were importance to armaments production, concentration in a few plants, absence of spare production elsewhere, and limited possibilities of economy in its use. M.E.W. now sought to discover industries in Germany which possessed these qualifications. Such bottlenecks obviously were more likely to occur in manufacturing and processing industries where it was necessary to make the best use of limited numbers of highly skilled workmen. There was evidence that for this reason Germany had in some cases and to some extent reversed the earlier policy of dispersal. Synthetic oil and rubber, alumina, and soda ash had claims for consideration, though oil had been considered at times to be too dispersed to qualify. Many others were considered amongst the components of aircraft, submarines and other weapons. A rather long list of ten target systems was thus obtained, but eventually the covering note to the report reduced them to five industries of which a large percentage was situated in no more than ten towns, eight in Germany, one in Italy, and one in France. It was recognised that these recommendations were only provisional and would have to be dovetailed in to the more general recommendation for general area bombing for which the final draft was being prepared. The real preference of M.E.W. amongst the bottlenecks was shown in the draft of a letter to Sir Archibald Sinclair from Lord Selborne when the first list was sent in, which emphasised (a) the tremendous importance of the ball-bearing factories at Schweinfurt, (b) the large concentration of precision engineering factories in the Stuttgart district and (c) the large concentration of tyre manufacture in Hanover. 'It is a pity', the letter went on, 'that the two former towns are so inconveniently situated and I realise that their destruction raises operational problems of quite a different order from attacks on such places as Cologne and Mainz. But I believe the prize to be so large that a very great effort to do this would be justified'. Of these three the ball-bearing industry was much the most obvious bottleneck and could be dramatically presented as such, and in the coming year attention was concentrated on it for a long period.[1]

But meanwhile the general area attack had continued and throughout the year 1942 M.E.W. had also continued to investigate the possibility of the effort being directed in a more selective manner than had so far been pursued. A new survey was made of all German industry which was divided into fourteen categories. The density of the population of the towns in which each was situated was also estimated. A new appraisal was made of the importance of each industry in the German war economy. Towns could then be classified in an order of importance based on the probable reward of the bombing just as the Ministry of Home Security had assessed the claims of British towns

---

[1] M.E.W. Memo., 23rd Nov. 1942, Draft Letter prepared for Lord Selborne to send to Sir Archibald Sinclair (undated, but prepared at the end of November 1942), Air Min. Report, 24th Dec. 1942, with covering note. The five target systems in the covering note were ball-bearings, synthetic rubber, alkali, fuel injection pumps and electrical equipment, and optical and laboratory glass and instruments. The ten towns were Schweinfurt, Stuttgart, Schkopau, Hüls, Hanover, Bernburg, Rheinberg, Rosignano (Italy), Dombasle (France) and Jena.

to protection by anti-aircraft guns during the German air attack in Britain in 1940–41.

Though the work had not yet been completely finished it was on this basis that M.E.W. chose the fifty-eight towns which appear in the appendix to the paper on the Combined Bomber Offensive which was laid before the Defence Committee by the Chief of the Air Staff in preparation for the discussions at the Casablanca conference. Eighteen were large towns of more than 250,000 inhabitants, twenty with between 250,000 and 50,000 inhabitants and twenty small towns of under 50,000 inhabitants. When Sir Charles Portal saw this list, he observed that he presumed the towns had only been given as illustrations and wished he knew by what criteria the selection of those to be bombed would be determined. In fact, he was told, the fifty-eight towns were selected in consultation with M.E.W. as the best estimate of those that should be first attacked, based on such factors as location, population, degree of congestion of the populous districts, the key industries contained in them and the importance of these from the standpoint of economic bottlenecks.

Thus, as had been explained by M.E.W., some cities were commercial more than industrial, some specialised in an industry of little importance to the war effort, some specialised in an industry which was carried on in equal amount elsewhere. For one or more of these reasons seven major towns of over 250,000 inhabitants had not been included in the list. The lists of the smaller towns were, it was admitted, a preliminary selection and were liable to be altered. But these towns had been chosen either because they contained the major portion of some highly specialised industry or part of some industry which might be made the principal object of attack in one of the large towns. Thus, if rubber were chosen as the industry to be destroyed, Hanover would be the main target, but the small towns of Hanau and Fulda produced much of the rest of that commodity. The aircraft industry, likewise, could only be attacked with success if a number of smaller towns were included in the target system.[1]

In general, the selection had been made, it was asserted, so as to include the maximum amount of industry essential to war, such as steel, aircraft, mechanical transport and special components. Thus, though only one-third of German industry was included in the fifty-eight towns, the Chief of the Air Staff was able to claim that 'the method of selection employed ensures that they are the most important third of the German economy'.[2]

---

[1] *The Bomber's Baedeker* (Guide to the Economic Importance of German Towns and Cities), First Edition, 2nd Jan. 1943. M.E.W. Memo., 22nd Oct. 1942. Note by Portal on Anglo-American Bomber Offensive, 3rd Nov. 1942. Memo. M.E.W. to D.B. Ops., 4th Nov. 1942, and Min. Baker to Crawford (Private Secretary to Portal), 5th Nov. 1942.

[2] Note by Portal, 3rd Nov. 1942.

The Bomber's Baedeker, issued by the Enemy Branch of M.E.W. in January 1943, was based on these principles. It was meant to provide a guide both for area bombing and for precision attacks against specific objectives. The economic effects of an attack, its preface explained, could (apart from casualties inflicted which in most cases were negligible) be divided into direct and indirect effects. The direct effects were (a) the destruction of and damage to buildings and homes and (b) the destruction of and damage to factories and commercial properties and the interruption of utility services and communication. The indirect effects were (a) the loss of working time due to the general dislocation of economic life and (b) the expenditure of manpower and materials in rehabilitation. In the existing circumstances, it was thought, the greatest effect was produced by the first and last of these categories.

It then went on to make a point which weakened the effect of some of its other arguments. For it stated that, as the major part of production had always to be devoted to the civilian economy, and only the surplus could be used for the armed forces and the manufacture of their weapons, the devastation of cities by night bombing tended to increase the proportion of the national resources devoted to the civilian economy. This argument seemed to lead to the conclusion that it was immaterial what town was destroyed since all destruction would reduce war production. But, of course, much depended on the amount of the consumer goods destroyed which could be done without altogether and not replaced. It was just on this point that M.E.W. made a major error. As will be seen in the next section it continually insisted that the German economy was so stretched that such losses must be replaced.

It was on more solid ground when it claimed that more immediate results would be obtained by the destruction of factories, communications and public utilities and that the workers could thus be prevented from working for a considerable period. It was one of the main objects of *The Bomber's Baedeker* to point out the towns where the maximum effect on war production could be obtained in this manner so that the attacks could be concentrated on them.

In addition, information was given on specific industries, indicating their economic importance, vulnerability and the possibilities of repair, of substitute articles and of replacement from stocks. It was intended to show by all this information how area attacks by night could supplement precision attacks on selected industries. Though no reference was made to the United States, the idea of a combined offensive in which the Eighth Air Force would take part with precision attacks and the advantage of directing the two forces to a common target system was, no doubt, in the minds of those preparing the information.

Moreover, in following this plan, M.E.W. were able to classify the various towns giving to each a rating for its economic importance, known as the 'key point ratio' (K.P.R.) and also for its economic importance in relation to its size, known as the 'key point factor' (K.P.F.). There was also a large section which gave detailed information on every town in Germany together with a list of its factories, utilities and communications, each being given a priority number.[1]

It was clear that this survey, which had been prepared with the greatest care, might make a major contribution to the planning of the strategic offensive. It supplied information which enabled those directing the attack to consider how far, when operational possibilities had been given their due weight, an industry could be so destroyed as to cause the greatest possible disturbance in the German war economy. But the plan was based on many indeterminate factors. It was never absolutely certain that the industry did not also exist in other places. Nor did the Air Ministry admit, as has been seen, that M.E.W. was the final or the most reliable authority on the vulnerability of the targets to an attack by high-explosive bombs or incendiaries. The rate of repair of an industry was largely a matter of guess-work and clearly partly depended on how great was the importance which the Germans attached to it and how ready they were to divert labour and materials for that purpose. M.E.W. did not realise also that machine tools were in abundant supply, so that even if many were destroyed they could be replaced more quickly than had been possible in Britain. Similarly, as most factories were working single shifts, if some were destroyed, output might be maintained by working double shifts in those that remained. The amount of stocks in the possession of the consumers and the pipe-line supplying them was also not susceptible to precise estimation.

In addition, as Sir Arthur Harris frequently pointed out, the attack depended on the weather. In general it might be expected that anything less than the destruction of the major part of an industry in a comparatively short period of time would not have a decisive effect. Even if a successful attack were made on some part of an industry, it might be weeks before another part of the same target system could be attacked and meanwhile that already injured could be repaired. For this reason he preferred the cumulative effect of attacks on major cities without much notice being taken of the theoretical estimates of where the damage would be greatest.

---

[1] *The Bomber's Baedeker*. Priority was based on the categories of (1) factories of leading importance in the German war effort, (2) minor plants in major industries and (3) factories of small importance. In later editions five categories were used and maps issued for the towns concerned. The information was kept up to date so far as possible, especially as to the effects on the targets if the bombings took place: 'I hope it will provide you with a basis for planning either blitz attacks or precise attacks and that it will show how far the two can be coordinated in order to follow a common theme.' Min. Lawrence to Morley, 31st Dec. 1942.

THE ECONOMIC APPRAISAL

But the other partner in the Combined Bomber Offensive, which was to begin in 1943, was the United States Eighth Air Force which had been designed for precision bombing in daylight. Whatever doubts existed as to its ability to do so successfully against German targets, it was clear by the end of the year that it would make the attempt. All this information, especially that on bottlenecks and precise targets, would be available for its use. During 1942 it had no targets in Germany and not even specific directives. General Eaker, as he trained his force, worked closely with Bomber Command, attended its morning consultations and discussed his targets with Sir Arthur Harris. But already the United States had begun to make its own appreciations of the German economy.

The machinery set up for this purpose in Washington and London was analogous to that in Britain. The Air Staff of the United States had been prevented by the influence of other branches of the Army from setting up their own intelligence directorate before the war. But after war had broken out a Board of Economic Warfare with an Enemy Objectives Unit had been organised to perform the same functions in Washington as M.E.W. did in London. The two bodies worked closely together and in 1941 a liaison department of M.E.W. had been set up in Washington. Much information was thus supplied to the United States department by M.E.W. but the former began to supplement it from its own resources, especially by the help of business firms which had connections with Germany and in some cases had constructed plants there. The Eighth Air Force had also its own target intelligence section in London under Colonel Hughes and this used the London office of the Board of Economic Warfare which also was in very close liaison with M.E.W.

Thus, both in Washington and London the United States Army Air Forces were at first largely dependent on M.E.W. for information about the German economy. The question of its interpretation and application to policy was, however, a different matter. In August 1942 the President, through General Marshall, had directed General Arnold to submit an estimate of the number of combat aircraft of all types necessary to air ascendency over the enemy. This appreciation, which had to be made by his officers in a very short time, necessitated some consideration of the targets to be attacked. It was based on the principle that the United States Army Air Force would 'concentrate its effort upon the systematic destruction of selected vital elements of the German military and industrial machine through precision bombing in daylight'. A number of objectives were indicated with first priority given to the German air force and aircraft manufacture. Submarine construction, transportation, electric power, oil, alumina and rubber followed in that order of priority with some rather naïve calculations as to the weight of bombs necessary to destroy them. From this paper came the demand for the immense number of aircraft which the United States ultimately produced but these calculations depended on no very scientific appraisal of the unknown factors involved.[1]

In December 1942 General Arnold, therefore, appointed a special Committee of Operations Analysts to make a new survey of the whole problem. He was determined that in this, as in all other matters, the Eighth Army Air Force should have the machinery necessary to determine its own policy, though he seems to have paid but little attention to the subject until the end of 1942. 'Arnold insists', noted Mr. Hopkins at Casablanca, 'that the targets from England are selected by the British, but he seemed to me to be a bit vague on this point, and I am sure that this needs to be settled definitely, so that the Admirals and the Navy can't continue to say that Arnold is picking out some soft targets and is not making an adequate attack on the submarine bases and factories making submarine supplies'.[2]

The Committee of Operations Analysts drew up a new appreciation which was one of the main foundations of the plan for a Combined Bomber Offensive. There can be no doubt that the information supplied by M.E.W. either directly or through the intelligence departments of the Air Ministry was a main source for the estimate of the extent and location of the targets. Thus, if Bomber Command itself was sceptical of the value of the advice given by M.E.W., the latter's work in 1942 described in this section had a considerable influence on the economic appreciations of the Combined Bomber Offensive in 1943–44.

---

[1] Requirements for Air Ascendancy, 9th Sept. 1942. A.W.P.D.–42. See *The Army Air Forces in World War II*, Vol. II, pp. 277–278, 288–289.

[2] Robert E. Sherwood: *The White House Papers of Harry L. Hopkins*, Vol. II, (1949), p. 679. Note dictated by Hopkins on 19th January 1943.

2. The estimated and actual results

In 1940–41 the damage inflicted on the German economy by Bomber Command had been negligible. In 1942 some substantial damage was done if not such as had any appreciable effect on war production. The estimates made about it in Britain were, however, much more realistic than those made in the previous period. As a result of the analysis of the photographic records, the inaccuracy of former estimates had now been to a great extent realised and new machinery had been set up to make more exact assessments in the Central Interpretation Unit at Medmenham. The Operational Research Section of Bomber Command also began, in September 1941, to introduce in the Command itself a more accurate appreciation of what had been accomplished.

The photographs revealed the extent to which houses and factories had been destroyed or injured. How far the machinery of the factories had been destroyed or the effect of the destruction of housing on production were still, however, matters of dispute. In this problem the assessors now began to be assisted by the surveys made by the Ministry of Home Security of the damage done by the German bombing of Britain in 1940–41. The task was first essayed by Squadron Leader Dewdney when he realised the delusive nature of the methods which had been applied to the assessment of the damage done in 1940–41 to German oil plants.[1] He tried to obtain from the various departments of Government concerned with industry, housing and amenities, accurate figures of the total damage done to them and so construct a kind of index of damage in proportion to the weight of the attack; but he found that none of the departments had attempted the task.

Clearly some such survey would be most valuable and the Research Department of the Ministry of Home Security began, therefore, to tackle the problem in the autumn of 1941 by making intensive studies of particular towns. Later the special department R.E.8 under Squadron Leader Dewdney himself not only surveyed the damage in Britain but made special assessments of that done to German towns. But these studies were intricate; much information had to be collected and complicated statistical analysis applied to it which was only in the embryonic stage. Moreover, the bomb census of the attacks on Britain was far from complete and steps were taken in the course of this year to improve it. The first attempt, which concerned only two

---

[1] Lecture by Dewdney, January 1948. Mr. D. A. C. Dewdney was an oil expert who, as has been seen (p. 222), was sent to advise Bomber Command on that subject. He became head of R.E.8, which remained part of the Ministry of Home Security but was under the direction of the Operations Branch of the Air Ministry, Mr. Dewdney being given the rank of Squadron Leader.

towns, Hull and Birmingham, took four months.[1] When R.E.8 applied their technique to the assessment of the damage to German towns their reports could generally only be produced several months after the attacks had taken place. This time lag was a considerable disadvantage since in the meanwhile the tactical situation might alter a great deal. For this reason, in the autumn of 1943, preliminary reports were issued which were produced in a shorter time by more rough-and-ready methods. But these also tended to be six or seven weeks after the attack and they were not necessarily more accurate than other immediate reports.[2]

These studies, however, provided a better basis for the assessment of the damage done than any previously made, and in time the evaluation made by the Air Ministry of what had been accomplished was to some extent determined by them. They were supplemented by many other studies, based on British experience, of the effects of bombs on various kinds of different structures such as oil storage plants, aircraft factories or various kinds of housing. They could thus provide information as to what kind of bombs were most likely to achieve the best results and this information was to be of considerable use in later stages of the bombing offensive.

These methods could also be used to assess the success of a particular raid on a town or factory. But since R.E.8 studies took much time the estimates were first made by the Operational Research Section of Bomber Command and the Intelligence Directorate of the Air Ministry. Both relied a good deal on the reports of the Central Interpretation Unit. There was at the outset some disposition to challenge its interpretations of the photographs of German towns and a check was made on them by comparing the actual results on British towns with British photographs taken immediately after the raids.[3]

M.E.W., with a more detailed knowledge of German industry, gave in its Industrial Damage Reports an estimate of the effect of the damage on the German economy, but its reports generally took about six weeks to two months and were affected in some degree by intelligence reports reaching it during the period. The skill shown by the technical experts in calculating from the photographs exactly

---

[1] Ministry of Home Security Report, 8th April 1942. One of the surprising conclusions was that 'dwelling houses are destroyed by high explosive bombs and not by fire.' Factories, on the other hand, suffered more injury from fire than bombs. The calculations Lord Cherwell used were based on these researches. (See above, pp. 331–332.) The Intelligence Department of the Air Ministry, while admitting the value of the report as a 'check' on its own estimates of the effects of German bombing on a number of British towns made in the previous year, maintained that both German and British towns were more 'sensitive' to bombing in 1942 and that the estimate of loss was consequently now too small. Memo. by A.I.3c (Air Liaison), 25th April 1942.

[2] The series Preliminary Raid Assessment (R.E.8/P) begins with a report dated 26th November 1943 on the attack on Hagen of 1/2nd October 1943.

[3] Min. of Home Sec. Report, 14th Sept. 1942. Min. Morley to Baker, 23rd Sept. 1942.

how many houses had been destroyed was a high one and grew in accuracy with practice. The assessment also necessitated much exact information as to the topography of the towns and the situation of the factories but there had been a great deal published on that subject in Germany and further information could be found in the records of firms who had had dealings there.[1]

The Ministry of Home Security also began to make estimates of the loss of production in Britain due to absenteeism after heavy raids. At first these were rather tentative but by the end of 1942 a detailed study of the effects of the German 'Baedeker' raids had been completed. This contribution had, however, hardly progressed so far as to affect very much the estimates made during this period.[2]

Meanwhile, it was necessary to make estimates of what had been accomplished in order to decide future policy and, if these appraisals were more restrained and accurate than those of the previous period, they still tended to exaggerate the achievements of Bomber Command and to make unjustifiable deductions from British experience. The advocates of strategic bombing were, as has been seen in Chapter VI, facing considerable opposition. It was only natural that they should interpret what was at best very imperfect information in the manner most calculated to support their views.

One major error in the general assessment shared by all was not in any way due to wishful thinking but based on the radical misconception of the German economy already pointed out. Throughout the year all appreciations were based on the theory that the German economy was already strained to the utmost so that any injury to it would be felt throughout the whole structure. At the beginning of the year M.E.W. in a special memorandum strongly upheld the view that German production was already out of balance as a result of the failure to overcome Russia. 'Germany's economic situation', it insisted, 'is likely to be inelastic and vulnerable to a much greater extent than ever before'.[3] In its report on the German economy in the first six months of 1942 it suggested that unless the loss of food, housing and clothing could be made up by further looting in the occupied

---

[1] Squadron Leader Dewdney obtained the services of Mr. Dickinson, who had been a lecturer in urban geography at London University and studied the town planning of Germany. It was he who first divided German towns into zones, the central zone, the old core of the town, a residential zone round it of fairly high density of population and a factory zone outside that. In the central zone which sometimes dated back to medieval times, many houses were often old, highly inflammable and the open spaces were few. Zone maps were issued by a department of the Air Ministry Intelligence Directorate.

[2] Min. of Home Security Report, 19th Oct. 1942. The 'Baedeker' raids of April–May 1942 were on Exeter, Bath, Norwich, York and Canterbury. Hull, Poole and Grimsby were also attacked in this period. Two reports were also circulated on Bootle and Merseyside in February and March 1943; 2nd Feb. and 22nd March 1943. A more comprehensive one which included Clydebank and Greenock as well as the two above was then made. Min. of Home Security Report, 1st July 1943.

[3] Memo. by Selborne, 21st March 1942.

territories, the efficiency of the German labour force was bound to decline.[1]

This point of view was faithfully reflected in the reports made to the Chiefs of Staff during the consideration of the future bombing offensive. 'So long as the Allies maintain their pressure on Germany', it was laid down, 'she will not be able to arrest the decline in her industrial output'.[2] The doctrine was stated in its most extreme form in the memorandum of the Chief of the Air Staff when he asked for the construction of a 4,000–6,000 bomber force: 'A certain minimum proportion of the industrial effort of any country must always be devoted to maintaining a minimum standard of subsistence throughout the country as a whole. In Germany it is believed that this minimum has already been reached. It follows that any large scale damage inflicted on industry as a whole cannot be absorbed evenly but must be borne to an ever-increasing degree by that part of industry which is maintaining the armed forces'.[3]

The final estimate of the year by M.E.W. was somewhat more sober. It recognised that Germany had had some success in reorganising her industrial system. But it still insisted that war production was being reduced by the necessity of diverting resources to the civil population. 'Economically', it concluded, '[Germany] will not be able to support in 1943 a military effort as great as that of 1942, still less that of 1941'.[4]

These judgments represented the exact reverse of the real situation in Germany. So far from resources being diverted from the war production to the civil economy the latter was at last being reduced in order to increase war production. The decline in consumption was not, indeed, yet so great as that which had occurred in the United Kingdom since the beginning of the war and it was still being fiercely resisted by some sections of the National Socialist machine. The number of persons employed in the consumer goods industry steadily, if slowly, declined during 1941 and 1942.[5] All kinds of goods which could easily be dispensed with were still being made in large numbers. But Speer had managed to get more of the skilled workers transferred to the armaments industry. They were replaced by women, foreign workers and prisoners of war who were not so efficient, so that there was a decline in the amount produced.[6] But these reductions were

---

[1] M.E.W. Intelligence Weekly, 30th June 1942.

[2] C.O.S. Report, 30th Oct. 1942.

[3] Note by Portal, 3rd Nov. 1942, App. 20.

[4] M.E.W. Intelligence Weekly, 24th Dec. 1942. Thus, it concluded that since it was known that the production of aircraft, ships and motor vehicles had increased, that of tanks, guns and ammunition must have decreased. In actual fact they had been greatly increased. See App. 49 (i) to (iii).

[5] See the tables in App. 49 (x) and (xi).

[6] Wagenfuehr: *Rise and Fall of German War Economy, 1939–1945* (unpublished).

easily borne by the general economy together with the destruction of civilian goods by bombing. So far from the German economy being tightly stretched it was still very resilient and had a large cushion not only of stocks but of industrial capacity devoted to semi-luxuries and other goods of no real necessity to the welfare of the people.

Meanwhile, Speer, who on the death of Todt in an air accident was made Minister for Weapons and Munitions in February 1942, had begun to produce considerable results by his reorganisation of German industry. He had as yet limited powers. The military procurement authorities had still great influence in the direction of armaments. Neither the Navy nor the Air Force accepted the necessity for his services. In March 1942, by a decree of Goering, there was set up a Central Planning Committee to control the allocation of raw materials consisting of Speer himself, Milch representing the *Luftwaffe* and Koerner representing the Four Year Plan. Speer did not obtain a decisive position in it until some time had elapsed and meanwhile temporary bottlenecks occurred in the autumn. But Speer had made great progress by setting up the committees and rings of business men to overhaul production in their several industries. He forced them to abandon some of their self-seeking habits and to combine together. He got younger men into positions of control and got mass production under way. He put some curb on the demands of the services for modifications and changes which slowed up production by getting the Regional Armament Offices transferred from the Army High Command to his Ministry. He also succeeded Todt as Commissioner-General for armaments duties in the Four Year Plan organisation, but this office, subordinate to Goering, he never used to supplement his other means of control.[1] More and more foreign workers were brought in to increase the labour supply and, as has been seen, more skilled workers were obtained from the industries working for civilian production though the co-operation of Sauckel, the Minister of Labour, was no more than lukewarm.

Not all the increase of production in this year can be attributed to Speer. Some of it was due to the fact that after the failure in Russia it was at last being realised in all informed circles that the war was likely to be much longer and harder than had previously been imagined. But the effect was considerable. Production increased by eighty per cent and the total production of the year was fifty per cent higher than that of 1941. And this rise in production went entirely into the war effort, for civilian production had decreased. In addition there was an increase in the amount derived from the occupied territories as well as the increase in foreign workers. The percentage of

---

[1] *The Trial of German Major War Criminals, Proceedings of the International Military Tribunal Sitting at Nuremberg, Germany*, Pt. 17, pp. 4 and 6.

loss was, therefore, insignificant when the fact that armaments production had increased during the year by fifty per cent is remembered.[1]

If, however, British estimates of the total production were very wide of the mark their assessment of the loss produced on it by British bombing was much more realistic. Optimism was expressed about the future rather than the immediate present. There were occasionally a few wild speculations about the effect on particular industries, but it was realised that the total effect on production was not great. The report of Sir Arthur Harris at the end of June was an exception, but this was written at a time when the future of Bomber Command was still in doubt. 'The towns of Rostock, Lübeck, Emden and Cologne', he wrote, 'have all been destroyed to or beyond the point where they can be counted as a liability rather than an asset'.[2] In fact, the first three were in full production and Cologne was rapidly recovering from the devastating effects of the Thousand raid. Later, this facility for rapid recovery was recognised by Sir Arthur Harris himself as well as by the organisations assessing the effects of the raids, but that important fact was not fully realised in this period. As will be seen when statistics of particular towns are examined, those which were bombed were generally able to get back full production in a very short space of time.

That the total loss, however, was considered to be only small was indicated in the M.E.W. survey made at the end of the year, though they exaggerated the indirect effects of the raids on the general economy. 'It is clear', concluded the report, 'that the direct damage to plant and equipment though substantial has been a less potent factor in the reduction of industrial output than the general influence of transport dislocation, absenteeism, loss of working hours and increased fatigue due to nights spent in shelters and difficulties of workers' travel'. They also made some quite unsubstantiated estimates of particular loss such as that the coal output in the Ruhr, Aachen and Saar fields had declined by twenty per cent in the summer owing to continuous raids. But their main mistake was in thinking that even a comparatively slight loss, such as two per cent of the housing of Germany, (ten per cent of that of the cities raided), which was a fairly accurate estimate, would affect war production to any great extent.[3]

The effect of the limited attack of 1942 on such an economy was not likely to be very great. Some substantial damage was done to a

---

[1] For the figures, see App. 49 (i) and (ii).

[2] Note by Harris, 28th June 1942, App. 18.

[3] M.E.W. Intelligence Weekly, 24th Dec. 1942. During the year March 1942–March 1943 the production of bituminous coal increased in the Ruhr by 1·55 per cent, in Aachen by 2·77 per cent and in the Saar by six per cent, and of brown coal in the Rhineland by seven per cent. *U.S.S.B.S. Effects of Strategic Bombing*, Tables 55 and 56, pp. 92–93.

few towns and minor damage to a much greater number. The two post-war surveys have calculated the total effect on production during the year. By including the measures necessary to replace and provide substitutes for housing and civilian goods the United States survey estimated the loss of production of the Reich in 1942 as 2·5 per cent of the total. The survey of the B.B.S.U., based on the comparison of production in bombed and unbombed towns, if the figures of the iron and steel processing groups are included in it, reduced this estimate to as little as 0·7 per cent of total production and 0·5 per cent of war production.[1]

There were also the special estimates of the four great target systems which were always in the minds of those endeavouring to plan an attack, those of oil, aircraft, submarine construction and transport. It has been shown that the Stanley report of April 1942 had helped to prevent any attack on oil being planned for the immediate future.[2] Nevertheless, the situation was carefully watched by the new committees then set up and regularly reported on to the Chiefs of Staff and Defence Committee. 1942 was a critical year in the German supply of oil. The attack on Russia had increased consumption by the armed forces and the supplies of German-produced oil and imports from Rumania were not sufficient to meet it. Production of synthetic oil was, indeed, nearly a million tons more than in 1941 and more was obtained from Rumania, though that country still absorbed half of its total production while the rest of Axis Europe had meagre rations. Meanwhile, stocks in Germany were diminishing and by the end of the year were about 1,250,000 tons of all kinds of oil, while that of aviation, motor and diesel oil had sunk to about 800,000 tons. This was not sufficient to ensure an efficient distribution system to all parts of the German economy and local shortages occurred at times. How far this shortage affected the German strategy in the campaign against Russia is a matter of some dispute, but it was probably an element in the decision to direct the main attack to the South.

The British appreciation correctly estimated the serious position in Germany and rightly said that the stocks were below the necessary minimum for distribution. This conclusion was based on two errors which cancelled each other out. As has been seen, the German stocks of oil were over-estimated. But German consumption and that in Axis Europe was also over-estimated.[3] Thus, when at the end of the

---

[1] *B.B.S.U. Report on the Effects of Strategic Air Attacks on German Towns*, p. 80. App 49 (xii). The B.B.S.U. rejects these figures and, leaving out the two groups referred to, reaches the still smaller figures of 0·56 per cent and 0·25 per cent respectively. The basis of the survey calculations is discussed in Annex V.

[2] See above, pp. 291–292.

[3] For the figures, see App. 49 (xxxiii to xxxv) on German stocks, production and consumption and (xli) on the distribution of Rumanian oil. There is a difficulty in making a comparison between the estimated and actual stocks because of the problem

year, the J.I.C. insisted that even a moderate amount of damage done to the synthetic plants might make the situation really acute, it was entirely right.[1] The decision of the Air Staff not to try to take advantage of this opportunity was due to the belief that little damage could be done with the means then available, and, so it was said, though the case as represented by the J.I.C. hardly warranted the conclusion, that it was unprofitable to attack German oil unless the Rumanian refineries could also be seriously injured.[2]

This was also a critical year in German aircraft production now under the direction of General Milch, who inherited a situation which had caused his predecessor Udet to commit suicide. He began a reorganisation of the industry along similar lines to those of Speer and much increased production. He met with considerable resistance in the aircraft industry itself where firms were still too much concerned with their own interests to co-operate as effectively as possible. He was also prevented from increasing as much as he would have wished the supply of fighter aircraft which he already rightly foresaw would be needed. Hitler's whole attention was concentrated on the war with Russia and the aircraft and training of the *Luftwaffe* served well enough for that purpose. Only when Russia had been defeated was the *Luftwaffe* to be built up for the attack on the West. Germany had not successfully developed new types of aircraft. She had no prototypes that could compare with the Lancaster or Mosquito. Milch had to rely mainly on production of modified versions of the older types and the new Ju.88 which could be used both as a night fighter or a medium bomber. The result was that the great potentialities of aircraft production in Germany were still imperfectly utilised. Nevertheless, Milch increased production in 1942 by nearly 4,000 aircraft. The percentage of fighters, however, was only increased by five per cent, while that of dive-bombers increased also and other bombers remained about the same. Programmes and directives were still being constantly changed as the year came to an end and no one was very happy about the future.[3]

Hardly anything of this situation was due to the effect of British bombing on the aircraft industry. Some small reduction was caused

---

as to exactly how much of the transit and operating stocks the German figures comprised. The United States estimate was considerably higher than the British. *U.S.S.B.S. The German Oil Industry, Ministerial Report Team 78,* (No. 113), p. 82, January 1947. *Oil as a Factor in the German War Effort, 1933–1945,* Report of Technical Sub-Committee of the C.O.S. Cttee. on Axis Oil, 8th March 1946.

[1] J.I.C. Report, 16th Dec. 1942.

[2] C.O.S. Mtg., 14th Jan. 1943. The Chief of the Air Staff had said in a previous meeting that half-measures would be useless.

[3] For the figures, see App. 49 (xxii) and (xxiii). Address of Reichsmarschall Goering to representatives of the German Aircraft Industry, 13th Sept., 1942. 'Aircraft which were to be capable of a great deal, and for which much was promised, failed to live up to those promises . . . Gentlemen, will you at long last let the interests of your own firms take second place?'

THE ESTIMATED AND ACTUAL RESULTS

in the production of the Heinkel works at Rostock and the Focke-Wulf works at Bremen. There was, however, an indirect effect, for, though only one or two small enterprises followed the example of Focke-Wulf and began to disperse their works and move them to the East, others began to make plans to do so and were thus better prepared to face the far heavier attack on the industry by the United States Army Air Forces in 1943–44 when such dispersal became imperative.

Some part of the attacks on Bremen and Rostock was specially directed at the aircraft works there, and later the industry was specially mentioned in a separate directive. It was essential in any case to estimate the amount of production and as far as possible to determine the distribution of the aircraft to the several fronts. The British estimates of aircraft production went seriously wrong throughout the war. For three years the numbers were exaggerated and they were then much underestimated. But these mistakes had but little effect on the bombing offensive at this time since the attack on the aircraft industry was of no great importance during this period.[1]

Little need be said of the other two target systems. Submarine construction continued to rise and the effect of the large number of attacks on the ports concerned was negligible. That this was the case was realised by M.E.W., whose estimates of the number of submarines built in the year and the gradual rise of the monthly average was very accurate. The claim of Bomber Command that it could do more to help the Battle of the Atlantic by bombing submarine construction yards rather than the ports from which they set out was not substantiated.[2]

As to transport, there was considerable deterioration in the position in Germany in the spring and summer of 1942. In April, for example, there was not a sufficient number of wagons to convey urgently needed supplies to the Eastern front. Reports of these difficulties reached Britain and there was a natural tendency to attribute some part of them to the effects of bombing. They were, in fact, entirely due to other causes, especially the failure to adapt the *Reichsbahn* quickly enough to the new demands made upon it by the extension of the front in the East. But by the end of the year these difficulties had been overcome and the system was functioning with great efficiency as, indeed, was recognised in the final report of M.E.W.[3]

---

[1] For the figures, see App. 49 (xxv). In May some members of the Air Staff strongly urged that the aircraft industry should be put at the top of the list of directives and this was done. Min. Slessor to Bottomley, 1st May 1942. See also above, pp. 351–352.

[2] A memorandum of the Objectives Department, M.E.W., 21st July 1942, gave estimates of the numbers which closely corresponded to the actual figures. It exaggerated the damage done in 1941 and in the spring of 1942, but finally concluded that bombing can only have played a minor role in such delay in the programme as had occurred.

[3] *U.S.S.B.S. A Brief Study of the Effect of Area Bombing on Berlin, Augsburg, Bochum, Leipzig, Hagen, Dortmund, Oberhausen, Schweinfurt, and Bremen* (No. 39), p. 21. M.E.W. Intelligence

In addition to the attacks on Germany itself there were the precision attacks on factories working for Germany in the occupied territories. Some of them were very successful, such as that on the Renault factory at Billancourt. Of these the photographic information could be supplemented by reports received from the resistance movements. No general estimate of the total effect on French production for Germany could be made either then or later. There was evidence that these raids discouraged night working and thus slowed up production. But the effect was not yet important nor was it exaggerated in Britain.

The general estimates of damage done to production in Germany are confirmed by the surveys of particular towns made by the United States teams after the war and by the reports of the Police Presidents or Gauleiters made at the time. It will be seen also that the estimates made in Britain by the special organisations reporting on the raids were on the whole reasonably accurate and were couched in much more moderate and objective language than those of the previous period. The photographic record of the destruction of housing provided a basis which has been found to be essentially sound. The assessment of damage done to factories was apt to be exaggerated. And where the damage appeared much too small there was a tendency to look for reasons for the discrepancy such as hasty camouflage by the Germans. This was especially so concerning the Ruhr, where the industrial haze often made it impossible to obtain clear photographs of the towns attacked until a considerable period had elapsed, if at all. The real effect on the Ruhr, the Objectives Department once said, will not be known until after the war. 'In an enemy country, accurate assessment is well nigh impossible.' Occasionally, indeed, wildly optimistic statements were made about the Ruhr, such as one in October, that six of the seventeen steel plants there had been seriously damaged. But on the whole there was little illusion as to the small effect produced.[1]

The increase in the weight and efficiency of the attacks in 1942 for the first time really tested the effectiveness of German civil air defence. This had been set up under Goering and there had been developed between 1935 and 1939 a system of training not unlike that used in Britain but more highly organised. The system functioned locally

---

Weekly, 24th Dec. 1942. The attacks by Goebbels on the Minister of Transport, Dorpmüller, were clearly due to the dislike and jealousy of a good public official who was, however, rather old. He was given a capable second in Ganzenmüller. The Director of Transportation, War Office, thought that the locomotive position in Germany was critical and urged attacks on locomotive works at Kassel and in France. Letter and memo. McMullen to Baker, 1st. Dec. 1942.

[1] M.E.W. Industrial Damage Reports, 25th April and 3rd Oct. 1942. In actual fact the production of steel increased steadily in 1942 and hardly any loss was caused by bombing. U.S.S.B.S. *The Effects of Strategic Bombing on the German War Economy*, (No. 3), p. 104.

under the air-raid police and these were under the command of the Police Presidents of the towns and closely integrated with the ordinary police. The fire service was nationalised before the war, so that it was easy to send help from one town to another. The basis of the system was self-protection (*Selbstschutz*). The individual was taught to protect himself and his property and to join with others under a warden for mutual help. This training was very successful and, in the judgment of those who investigated the subject after the war, 'in no small measure, was responsible for the fact that the home front did not collapse'.

The party organisation played a considerable part in civil defence, its local network being used alongside the state machine. It was given the responsibility for relief and evacuation. When the Reich authorities during the Lübeck raid failed to act with sufficient energy in sending the materials for assistance, Goebbels obtained from Hitler a general control of relief all over the Reich, using the party organisation for that purpose. On the whole the task was well carried out. It varied in effectiveness, of course, with the energy and efficiency of the Gauleiters and their assistants in different parts of Germany. As 1942 went on the problems were more clearly seen and necessitated a number of new regulations and numerous notices, warnings and exhortations in the German Press. There was a tendency in Britain to interpret these as a sign that the civil protection measures and those of relief and rehabilitation were inadequate and that the confidence of the people in the party leadership was failing. There was, of course, much friction and grumbling, but on the whole the people rightly felt that they were being taken care of. The most difficult and controversial activity was evacuation, which the German people resisted even more than the British did and which in some areas was complicated by the not unjustified suspicion that the party was using it to obtain undue influence over the children of non-party members, especially the Catholics.[1]

The raid on Lübeck opened the new attack. The shock was a great one, as the reports from the town show, and much damage was done to the centre of the ancient city. 1,425 houses were completely destroyed, 1,976 heavily damaged and 8,000 more injured to some extent. The *Drägerwerke* factory, which made oxygen apparatus for submarine crews, was completely destroyed with eight others of less importance, while others were severely damaged by fire. 312 people

---

[1] A more detailed description of the civilian air defence and relief organisation is given in Vol. II, Chapter XI. In the Chief of the Air Staff's memorandum of 3rd November 1942 supposed breakdowns in relief at Cologne and Karlsruhe were featured and used to show that the organisation was inadequate. There was great dissatisfaction at Cologne with the new reception areas necessary after the Thousand raid, but a false impression was given when exhortations to the people of Karlsruhe to increase self-protection was taken as an indication of a general failure of the Reich authorities to perform their part.

were killed, 136 seriously wounded and 648 lightly wounded out of a population of 160,000. There was also considerable destruction of food and consumer goods in shops and warehouses. The port, not yet free of ice when the raid occurred, received considerable damage to cranes and warehouses and the whole area had to be shut up for ten days.

But this damage was soon remedied by the vigorous action taken. Factories resumed work in other buildings. Production had reached eighty to ninety per cent of normal within a week. The total decline in production as estimated by the post-war survey was only 0·03 months, though this is a case where war material suffered more heavily than civilian and had a decline of 0·12 of a month. No doubt there would have been some increase but for the raid. The transition to full activity of the port was also slightly delayed, but the delay was unimportant.[1]

There was naturally much jubilation in London over the operational success of this raid, but the considered estimates were not very wide of the mark. It was thought that 2,000 houses had been made uninhabitable, which was about the right number. The damage to the *Drägerwerke* factory was known. The total effect on production was, however, a good deal overestimated. Relying on the experience of British towns, M.E.W. reported that it probably did not reach more than '50% to 60% of normal for two weeks after the raid and total recovery would probably take six to seven weeks'. They also exaggerated the effect of what was called 'general dislocation' of life on the opening of the port.[2]

That the recovery was so rapid was largely due to the energetic steps taken by the party organisation spurred on by Goebbels and Hitler himself. Help was also generously given by nearby towns, for this was the first time that such help was asked for. The initial shock both locally and at Berlin was severe, but the situation was soon got in hand with excellent results. The threat to German towns was not nearly so great as it seemed to be in Britain and to many in Germany at the first news of the raid.[3]

---

[1] *U.S.S.B.S. A Detailed Study of the Effects of Area Bombing on Lubeck*, (No. 38).

[2] M.E.W. Industrial Damage Report, 9th May 1941 [*sic*]. The photographic reconnaissance had failed to cover the northern part of the area and the port so that the accuracy of the estimate of destruction is all the more notable. The number of killed was not of course known, but a later report, 22nd June 1942, stated that a good source had given the death roll as 2,600. This is an example of the kind of information which produced a misleading impression, though the accuracy of the report was not, of course, guaranteed.

[3] The telegraphic reports of the acting Gauleiter Carstens to Goebbels of 8 a.m. and 8 p.m. on 29th March give also the steps taken to get outside help. They were sent also to Bormann and Hitler's aide so that Hitler himself was kept fully informed from the outset and gladly agreed to Goebbels taking over a duty which the Berlin authorities seemed unable to carry out sufficiently promptly. *The Goebbels Diaries*, pp. 108, 113. Lübeck was under Gauleiter Kaufmann of Hamburg, who also kept the party informed.

The successful raids on Rostock also aroused great enthusiasm in Britain and were widely publicised. The estimates of M.E.W. were affected by a similar emotion to some extent. 'It seems little exaggeration to say', one report ran, 'that Rostock has for the time being ceased to exist as a going concern'. The judgment was a natural one and Goebbels himself had remarked after the final raid that 'community life there is practically at an end'. But the British estimate of the damage done to the aircraft and shipbuilding works was realistic. It was true that seventy per cent of the old city in the centre of the town had been destroyed as the British photographs had shown, communications had been interrupted and many public buildings including churches destroyed. Large numbers of people fled from the city into the surrounding villages and towns. But the panic was soon over and the people hastened back to work, took energetic measures themselves to put the streets in order, much helped by the vigorous action of the Mecklenburg Gauleiter Hildebrandt. He could report on 29th April that the principal war factories, including the Arado aircraft works and Neptune works, were nearly back to hundred per cent production. The special attack by 5 Group on the Heinkel aircraft factory at Warnemünde on the mouth of the river had been successful, but this works also made a brilliant recovery, one of the few things on which Goering could congratulate the aircraft industry in September.[1]

After the Lübeck and Rostock raids the Thousand raids were the most important. Here again the estimate of the effect was realistic, even if as regards Cologne the rate of recovery was rather underestimated. The attack did, of course, do a great deal of damage, more than in all the previous seventy raids on Cologne, though in total these had brought nearly twice as many aircraft to the city and dropped 400 more tons of bombs. 474 people were killed and over 5,000 were injured of which, however, only 565 were admitted to hospital. 3,330 houses were destroyed, 9,510 damaged in some way and 45,132 people rendered homeless, though many only for a short period. A large number of factories was destroyed, a figure of 1,500 being given in one report. But most of these were very small and of the 328 with A.R.P. organisations, presumably all the larger factories, thirty-six ceased production altogether, seventy lost fifty per cent and 222 a lesser amount, the length of time of the decrease not being stated. Clearly this loss had a considerable effect, but the major factories on the outskirts of the city were not so seriously hurt. The

---

[1] M.E.W. Industrial Damage Report, 6th June 1942, Reports to Goebbels, 29th April, 2nd May 1942. Address by Goering to Representatives of the German Aircraft Industry, 13th Sept. 1942. Goebbels' diary (*The Goebbels Diaries*, p. 146) gave 100,000 as the number that had to be evacuated. The final report of 2nd May estimated at 135,000–150,000 the number who fled the city. It added that they were returning almost as quickly as they went, once the worst panic was over. The figures given are fantastically high and were probably a rather emotional guess.

railway traffic from the station in the centre of the city was discontinued for a number of days.[1]

The British estimates were based on excellent photographs and the actual damage was determined with considerable accuracy. Thus, it was estimated that 3,000 houses had been destroyed and 50,000 people rendered homeless. No attempt was made to give the actual number of factories destroyed but a number of those actually destroyed were described correctly. The final conclusion of M.E.W. was that two months' production in Cologne had been lost. No post-war estimate has been made of the total loss in this case but it was probably a good deal less as regards war production since the major war factories suffered least. The assessment made by R.E.8 of the loss as one month's production was a good deal nearer the truth. Where M.E.W. tended to go wrong was in underestimating the rapidity of recovery of the general economy of the city which it thought would be prolonged because of the general shortages and the unforeseen demand for materials, labour and transport. It is true that the magnitude of the attack gave a great shock to the district and resulted in some panic and the usual crop of exaggerated rumours. But after a short interval the population faced the disaster with the same stoicism that the British had borne their ordeal in 1941. Help was brought from outside and the administration took measures to assist and speed up the recovery. Within two weeks the life of the city was functioning almost normally.[2]

There is not material available to give the actual results of the Thousand raids on Essen and Bremen. Such small damage as occurred in the former was forgotten in later raids and documentary evidence has not been found. It was, however, realised in London that this raid was a failure owing to the inability to concentrate over the city. Some consolation was found in the thought that towns in the Ruhr lay so close together that the bombs that missed Essen probably did damage elsewhere. This is in fact what occurred. The Germans were not even aware that a great raid on Essen had been attempted,

---

[1] The statistics are taken from the Police President's Report and the Report of the Cologne Office of the Ministry of Public Information and Propaganda. One of the factories completely destroyed made accumulators and a number of firms making uniforms suffered heavy damage. Seventeen water mains, thirty-two electrical cables, twelve telephone cables and five gas mains were so severely damaged as to be put out of action. Hitler stated in a Fuehrer conference that 9,000 houses had been destroyed. Conf. of 12th Dec. 1942. There were only 138 killed and 277 injured seriously in all the previous raids and the material destruction was much less, showing the immense increase in damage brought about by concentration.

[2] M.E.W. Industrial Damage Report, 4th July 1942. Min. of Home Sec. Report, 19th July 1943. The rapidity of the repair was to some extent realised later. It was known, for example, that joiners, plumbers and other artisans had been sent from other towns to assist it. M.E.W. Industrial Damage Report, 18th July 1942. As usual the number of killed was much overestimated, being put at some figure between 1,000 and 6,000, M.E.W. refusing to put any credence on the first official report of 411 of the numbers then known which was no doubt accurate.

but a number of cities all over the Ruhr and the Rhineland received bombs.[1]

The raid on Bremen also did comparatively little damage and this was also known, the poor weather being held to be the main reason. It was also pointed out that Bremen was harder to destroy than the close-packed districts of the Ruhr. The claim was also made that great damage had been caused to the Focke-Wulf factory at which a special attack had been aimed, but the estimate made of the effect on production there was a conservative one. In actual fact not very much harm was done to the factory by this attack and a later one in September did more damage.[2]

Towns in the Ruhr were difficult to find because of the industrial haze and difficult to photograph afterwards. But closely connected with them was Düsseldorf, a city of 450,000 inhabitants on the Rhine, which was not only like Essen and Duisburg a centre of armament and engineering industry, but was the third largest inland port in Germany and the seat of the administration of nearly all the important steel, iron and engineering works in the Ruhr. Three heavy raids were made on it, two of them having operational training units incorporated in them. These raids did a large amount of damage, thirty-three plants being destroyed and fifty-six seriously damaged. In addition, twenty-six public buildings were destroyed and thirty-three heavily damaged. Large numbers of others were slightly injured. 428 dwellings were destroyed and 1,921 seriously damaged, while about 18,000 others received some injury. 379 people were killed and 1,464 injured. No estimate was made in the post-war survey of the total loss of production, but it is interesting to note that a very detailed and carefully considered estimate of the last two raids by R.E.8, which was not produced until March 1943, assessed it as three days' loss with, perhaps, as much again for indirect loss through absenteeism. The production of Düsseldorf in the last six months of the year exceeded that of the previous six months by 1·8 per cent, but the rise is smaller than that in some other cities, and it is possible that R.E.8 underestimated the total loss. The M.E.W. surveys while showing with considerable accuracy the extent of the material damage, both as to factories and public buildings, tended as usual to

---

[1] M.E.W. Industrial Damage Report, 18th July 1942. Casualties were reported from Recklinghausen, Bochum, Wanne Eickel, Oberhausen, Duisburg, Mülheim, Geldern, Dinslaken, Walsum, München-Gladbach, Cologne–Aachen district. While Essen had only eight dead and thirty injured, Duisburg had forty dead and 108 injured, and Mülheim fifteen dead and thirty-five injured. German Raid Reports.

[2] M.E.W. Industrial Damage Report, 5th August 1942. *U.S.S.B.S. Focke Wulf Aircraft Plant, Bremen, Germany*, (No. 10). This report is mainly concerned with later raids by the U.S. Eighth Air Force and takes pains to show how much more effective these precision raids were. The industry had already been dispersed to a considerable extent as a result of the 1941 attacks. M.E.W. also suggested that damage to a woolcombing plant and jute factory was important, but this loss, such as it was, had no appreciable effect on the total supply.

exaggerate the general effect. 'As a whole', one asserted, 'the damage is [on] a scale sufficient to produce serious and prolonged dislocation in all public business, industry and commerce and to require the expenditure of a very large amount of labour and material for rehabilitation'. This sentence, of which the first part was reproduced in the memorandum of the Chief of the Air Staff of 3rd November, could mean different things to different people, but it was of the kind which created a too optimistic view of what had occurred amongst those who took their information only from such reports. By the time the report of R.E.8 appeared attention was turning to other phases of the attack which had by then entirely altered in character.[1]

Though the Police President records are often inadequate and the United States surveys tend to pass rather perfunctorily over 1942, a period in which the attack of the United States strategic forces on Germany had not yet begun, yet other studies confirm the impression produced by those of which some account has been given. The damage, while considerable, was in no case of significant extent. It was spread over so many different industries that in a period of rising production the loss was hardly felt. The rate of recovery was rapid and only in the case of Cologne was the effect felt for a considerable period, and that to a rapidly diminishing degree. The heavily bombed northern ports and the cities of the Ruhr and Rhineland recovered very quickly. Even Lübeck and Rostock, specially vulnerable to incendiary attack, only lost a few days' full production. Meanwhile, though not without some hitches in places, the civil defence service and the machinery of relief were working well and were gaining experience which enabled them to cope with the much heavier raids of 1943. The number of deaths was so small compared with British experience that the official figures were not believed in Britain, though, when given, they were accurate enough. But on the whole, though quite misleading conclusions were at times made from doubtful data, the British technical estimates of the results of the bombing were but little exaggerated. If they had been as near the truth in their estimate of the general situation of the German economy the task of the combined bomber offensive in 1943 would have been more clearly understood.

In addition to the special assessments of the raids on German towns, it was necessary also to appraise what had been done by

---

[1] *U.S.S.B.S. A Detailed Study of the Effects of Area Bombing on Dusseldorf* (No. 34), pp. 13a and 12b. Report by Min. of Home Sec. and Min. of Economic Warfare on 15th/16th Aug. and 10th/11th Sept. raids on Düsseldorf, 23rd March 1942. M.E.W. Industrial Damage Reports, 7th Sept. and 21st Oct. 1942. Note by Portal, 3rd Nov. 1942. The R.E.8 study was made partly to estimate the efficiency of equal loads of high explosives and incendiaries and its findings were highly favourable to incendiaries. Its estimate of the dead was as usual far too high, being nearly double the actual figure.

attacks on French targets. These precision attacks were in several cases very successful and perhaps the most successful of all was that on the Renault works at Billancourt, a suburb of Paris, on the night of 3rd March. These works were a prime example of collaboration, and though not working at full capacity were producing about 18,000 military trucks a year of which 13,000 to 14,000 went to the German armed forces. A study by a United States team provides a detailed account of the result.

According to this report, in the attack 11·08 per cent of the factory buildings were injured, 6·73 of them being completely destroyed or heavily damaged. Out of 14,746 machine tools, 721 were destroyed and 578 seriously damaged. Two assembly lines were destroyed but these were not in use and this fact to some extent deceived the assessors in Britain. The loss of personnel in spite of the unexpectedness of the attack was insignificant. It is difficult to say exactly what the loss of production was since it was partly continued by transference of machines to unused buildings which might, however, have been used to increase production later on if these machines had not then been required. After four months, production was higher than before the raid. But one and a half weeks of the total man hours of the plant had to be devoted to clearance of debris and half as much to reconditioning damaged vehicles. The final estimate of the survey was a loss of 2,272 trucks.[1]

The final estimates in Britain when fully completed were very accurate. They suggested that 2,000 trucks had been lost. At first there was a tendency to exaggerate the result and even to think that the factory would be abandoned and the personnel and machinery transferred to Germany. This plan was in fact considered for a moment, showing the shock administered by a raid far more accurate than had hitherto been experienced. There were also intelligence reports from French sources, no less than forty-three being received by the end of 1943. These tended to repeat much gossip and exaggerate the result so as to make M.E.W. doubt their own conservative estimate, but by and large the appreciation was as accurate as could ever be expected to occur.[2]

These assessments of damage, whether general or special, did not

---

[1] *U.S.S.B.S. Renault Motor Vehicle Plant at Billancourt*, (No. 80). Two later daylight raids in 1943 by the U.S.S.A.F. were also reported which produced losses estimated at 3,072 and 1,877 trucks respectively, and the number of aircraft employed was only one-third of that of the R.A.F. raid. There is also a report from the files of the French Ministry of the Interior.

[2] M.E.W. Industrial Damage Reports, 11th April 1942, 9th May 1942 and 23rd Feb. 1943. The *U.S.S.B.S.* survey (p. 12) condemns their assessment as 'far in excess of actuality'. It was true that at first it was thought that it might take 'years' for the plant to be got in full working order whereas it did so in four months. But by the end of the year M.E.W. had a fairly good idea of the recovery which had taken place and that production was above the pre-raid level.

take into account an indirect effect which became larger in this year and later grew into considerable importance. For the *Luftwaffe*, which was responsible for the armed defence of the Reich, had to turn more and more of its attention to that problem and use more and more of its weapons in defence rather than in attack. It is difficult to appraise with any exactness what the total effect was, for by the end of 1942 the *Luftwaffe* was fighting on three fronts. As has been pointed out, the diversion of production to defence had hardly begun but there was undoubtedly a diversion of fighters destined for the other fronts to the defence of the Reich against the attacks of Bomber Command. The *Luftwaffe* records show that the day fighters in the West grew during the year from 292 to 453, reaching, however, as many as 574 in September and staying above 500 for the next two months. The night fighter force increased from 162 in January to 349 in December, the increase steadily continuing during the year. Meanwhile, the strength of the fighters on the Eastern front, 449 single-engine and 110 twin-engine in January 1942, fluctuated a good deal, being highest in the middle of the year while by the end of it it was about the same as at the beginning. During the same period 272 day fighters and 97 night fighters were destroyed on the Western front and 85 and 189 respectively damaged. Not all these aircraft, of course, neither the increase in strength nor those lost in operations, would have gone to the Russian front. Some would have been stationed in any case in the West and others might have gone to the Mediterranean front. But it is probable that the bulk of them would have been sent there and there was thus a diversion in favour of Russia such as had been designed and was said at the time to have occurred. Though the claim by the Chief of the Air Staff in November 1942 that fifty per cent of the German fighters had been left on the Western front is exaggerated, if all the fronts be taken into account, it is true that the number of fighters on the Eastern and Western fronts tended to become about equal as the year went on, and this must have had a sensible effect on the fighting on the Eastern front where the *Luftwaffe* was used almost exclusively for army co-operation.[1]

In addition to the aircraft diverted to the active defence of the Reich there was a considerable increase in personnel and material devoted to the anti-aircraft organisation. The numbers employed in it increased by nearly 100,000 in the course of the year over that of

---

[1] *Luftwaffe* strength and serviceability tables, Aug. 1938–April 1945. *Luftwaffe* strength on the Eastern and Western fronts. Fighter losses of *Luftflotte 3* and Reich Defence 1942. Note by Portal, 3rd Nov. 1942. It was the Me.110 which supplied the bulk of the night fighters in this period, but Goering expressed dissatisfaction with their performance and the new Ju.88 designed as a medium bomber was also used. Only sixty-five Ju.88s were thus used, however, out of a total of 780. Goering also said that the best aircraft were needed in the West while those of inferior performance were adequate against the Russian forces. Nearly all the Focke-Wulf 190s were kept on the Western front.

THE ESTIMATED AND ACTUAL RESULTS

1941, which had already seen a similar increase over that of 1940.[1] The extension of the attack to the South was one of the causes of this increase, while more heavy flak guns were needed to protect the Ruhr and the Rhineland. An increase in production of these had already been planned and there was in fact a large increase during the year, though far from the fantastic figure which Hitler demanded at a time when he was cutting down other armaments. The monthly production of light guns was increased from 795 to 1,526 and of heavy from 199 to 348, and the resources at the disposal of the armed forces grew steadily larger.[2]

It is not possible to estimate from the studies made the exact number of anti-aircraft guns on the various fronts. There were, of course, frequent adjustments. Anti-aircraft guns, for example, had to be sent to Italy in the autumn when the cities of North Italy were attacked. But the great majority of the heavy guns were used in the Reich itself and the estimates made in Britain during the war are probably fairly accurate in that respect, though the information about other fronts may be more suspect. There was also a considerable increase in light flak. The searchlight concentrations needed a much larger number than before and a new programme was set on foot. The new chain of radar stations absorbed a number of highly skilled technicians and much material and many workers were used to prepare the decoys and camouflage which were often elaborate. All this was a considerable addition to the demands on German manpower and production at a time when the reverses in Russia showed that a great deal more effort would be needed there if victory was to be won.[3]

---

[1] The numbers were: 1940, 255,200; 1941, 344,400; 1942, 439,500. This last number had doubled by the end of 1944. *B.B.S.U. The Strategic Air War*, p. 97.

[2] *U.S.S.B.S. Ordnance Industry Report* (No. 101), p. 17. The numbers were:

Monthly Average of Pieces by Years

	1941	1942	1943	1944	1945 Jan. and Feb.
2 cm. flak	695	1,350	1,817	2,273	
3·7 cm. flak	100	176	387	636	
8·8 cm. flak	156	280	446	545	387
10·5 cm. flak	43	60	101	88	35
12·8 cm. flak	—	8	24	49	49

[3] The British estimate of the numbers of anti-aircraft guns and searchlights on the different fronts was as follows:

	Anti-aircraft guns	Searchlights
Jan. 1941		
Germany and Western Front	12,476	2,520
Other fronts	624	36
Jan. 1942		
Germany and Western Front	12,068	3,276
Other fronts	4,526	108

Harris Despatch.

Finally, there was the question of what effect had been produced on German morale which had been laid down as one of the main objectives in the February directive. This is not susceptible to exact measurement, since absenteeism, the decline in production and other symptoms of its existence can be due to physical causes rather than to the lack of will to work. The heavy raids in the spring certainly caused the German Government to fear that an important effect would be produced on morale. But the measures taken to prevent this from happening were found to be adequate to their purpose and Goebbels expressed more anxiety concerning the shortages of fats and potatoes than about bombing.[1] It is clear, indeed, that a people that could withstand the assault of 1943 cannot have been very much disturbed by the much lighter attack of 1942.

British estimates also ceased to dwell on this aspect of the attack as the year went on. In April the J.I.C. had thought that it was likely to contribute substantially to the demoralisation of Germany.[2] But Mr. Justice Singleton was uncertain, while in the Chiefs of Staff memoranda of October and November little was said about it. The whole argument rested on the physical effects likely to be produced by the attack on German industry.[3] The Foreign Office, it is true, took a rather different view. They continued to issue papers about the subject on which they were supposed to be the principal authority. As late as October it was suggested that the German authorities were afraid that grave unrest in the areas affected by bombing might seriously prejudice the war effort. Two months later the emphasis was placed on the 'nervous strain' rather than on morale. When morale would break, they confessed, they did not know, but when it did the crash would come suddenly. This was at least an admission that the effect could not be measured.[4] In view of this trend, it is perhaps a little surprising that morale was given such a prominent place in the Casablanca directive of January 1943.

---

[1] *The Goebbels Diaries*, pp. 154 and 169.

[2] J.I.C. Memo., 6th April 1942.

[3] Report by Singleton, 20th May 1942, App. 17. Note by Portal, 3rd Nov. 1942. C.O.S. Report, 30th Oct. 1942. Marshal Stalin, on the other hand, expressed his desire that workers' homes should be bombed to Mr. Churchill in August 1942. Mr. Churchill replied that while civilian morale was a military objective the destruction of the homes of the workers was only a by-product of near misses on the factories. Soon, however, according to the report of Mr. Averell Harriman who was present, the two together had destroyed most of Germany's cities and this mutual desire did, as Mr. Churchill himself says, do much to ease the tension between them. *The White House Papers of Harry L. Hopkins*, Vol. II, p. 617. *The Second World War*, Vol. IV, p. 432.

[4] Foreign Office Memos., 23rd Oct. and 24th Dec. 1942. The service departments were the authority on the morale of the armed forces which, it was admitted, was as yet unimpaired.

Principal Staff and Command Appointments, 1918–42

SECRETARIES OF STATE FOR AIR

	Date of Appointment
Lord Rothermere	3rd Jan. 1918
Lord Weir of Eastwood	27th April 1918
Mr. Winston S. Churchill	14th Jan. 1919
Captain F. E. Guest	5th April 1921
Sir Samuel Hoare	2nd Nov. 1922
Lord Thomson	23rd Jan. 1924
Sir Samuel Hoare	7th Nov. 1924
Lord Thomson	8th June 1929
Lord Amulree	18th Oct. 1930
Marquess of Londonderry	9th Nov. 1931
Viscount Swinton	7th June 1935
Sir Kingsley Wood	16th May 1938
Sir Samuel Hoare	5th April 1940
Sir Archibald Sinclair	11th May 1940

CHIEFS OF THE AIR STAFF

Major-General Sir Hugh Trenchard	18th Jan. 1918
Major-General Sir Frederick Sykes	15th April 1918
Marshal of the Royal Air Force Sir Hugh Trenchard	31st March 1919
Marshal of the Royal Air Force Sir John Salmond	1st Jan. 1930[1]
Marshal of the Royal Air Force Sir Edward Ellington	22nd May 1933
Air Chief Marshal Sir Cyril Newall	1st Sept. 1937
Marshal of the Royal Air Force Sir Charles Portal	25th Oct. 1940

VICE-CHIEFS OF THE AIR STAFF

Air Marshal Sir Richard Peirse	22nd April 1940
Air Chief Marshal Sir Wilfrid Freeman	5th Nov. 1940
Air Vice-Marshal C. E. H. Medhurst	19th Oct. 1942

DEPUTY CHIEFS OF THE AIR STAFF

Rear Admiral M. Kerr	3rd Jan. 1918
Air Vice-Marshal J. M. Steel	1st Aug. 1922
Air Vice-Marshal C. L. N. Newall	12th April 1926
Air Vice-Marshal C. S. Burnett	6th Feb. 1931
Air Marshal Sir Edgar Ludlow-Hewitt	1st Feb. 1933
Air Vice-Marshal C. L. Courtney	26th Jan. 1935

[1] Air Chief Marshal Sir Geoffrey Salmond was Chief of the Air Staff from 1st to 27th April 1933.

494 STAFF AND COMMAND APPOINTMENTS

Date of Appointment

Air Vice-Marshal R. E. C. Peirse	25th Jan. 1937
Air Vice-Marshal W. S. Douglas	22nd April 1940
Air Vice-Marshal A. T. Harris	25th Nov. 1940
Air Vice-Marshal N. H. Bottomley	21st May 1941[1]

ASSISTANT CHIEFS OF THE AIR STAFF
(Operational Requirements and Tactics)[2]

Air Vice-Marshal W. S. Douglas	17th Feb. 1938
Air Vice-Marshal R. H. M. S. Saundby	22nd April 1940
Air Commodore J. O. Andrews	18th Nov. 1940
Air Vice-Marshal F. J. Linnell	4th Feb. 1941
Air Commodore R. S. Sorley	5th June 1941

(This office was then changed to A.C.A.S. Technical Requirements.)

ASSISTANT CHIEF OF THE AIR STAFF (OPERATIONS)

Air Vice-Marshal N. H. Bottomley	5th May 1942

ASSISTANT CHIEF OF THE AIR STAFF (POLICY)

Air Vice-Marshal J. C. Slessor	6th April 1942

ASSISTANT CHIEFS OF THE AIR STAFF (INTELLIGENCE)

Air Vice-Marshal C. E. H. Medhurst	1st March 1941
Air Vice-Marshal F. F. Inglis	24th March 1942

DIRECTORS OF PLANS

Air Commodore J. C. Slessor	22nd Dec. 1938
Air Commodore C. E. H. Medhurst	21st Oct. 1940
Group Captain W. F. Dickson	1st March 1941
Air Commodore W. Elliot	26th April 1942

DIRECTOR OF BOMBER OPERATIONS

Air Commodore J. W. Baker	25th August 1939

BOMBER COMMAND

AIR OFFICERS COMMANDING-IN-CHIEF, BOMBER COMMAND

Air Chief Marshal Sir John Steel	14th July 1936
Air Chief Marshal Sir Edgar Ludlow-Hewitt	12th Sept. 1937
Air Marshal Sir Charles Portal	3rd April 1940
Air Marshal Sir Richard Peirse	5th Oct. 1940 to 8th Jan. 1942[3]
Air Chief Marshal Sir Arthur Harris	22nd Feb. 1942

---

[1] The title of D.C.A.S. lapsed from May 1942 to July 1943.

[2] At the beginning of Air Vice-Marshal Douglas' tenure of this appointment it was known as simply 'Assistant Chief of the Air Staff'.

[3] Air Vice-Marshal J. E. A. Baldwin was Acting Air Officer Commanding-in-Chief from 9th Jan. 1942 to 21st Feb. 1942.

STAFF AND COMMAND APPOINTMENTS

SENIOR AIR STAFF OFFICERS, BOMBER COMMAND

	Date of Appointment
Air Commodore N. H. Bottomley	17th Nov. 1938
Air Vice-Marshal R. H. M. S. Saundby	21st Nov. 1940

OPERATIONAL BOMBER GROUPS

AIR OFFICERS COMMANDING 1 GROUP[1]

Air Commodore S. W. Smith	7th Jan. 1937
Air Vice-Marshal P. H. L. Playfair	17th Feb. 1938
Air Vice-Marshal A. C. Wright	3rd Sept. 1939
Air Commodore J. J. Breen	27th June 1940
Air Vice-Marshal R. D. Oxland	27th Nov. 1940

AIR OFFICERS COMMANDING 2 GROUP[2]

Air Commodore S. J. Goble	1st Sept. 1936
Air Commodore C. H. B. Blount	2nd Dec. 1937
Air Vice-Marshal C. T. Maclean	16th May 1938
Air Vice-Marshal J. M. Robb	17th April 1940
Air Vice-Marshal D. F. Stevenson	12th Feb. 1941
Air Vice-Marshal A. Lees	17th Dec. 1941
Air Vice-Marshal J. H. D'Albiac	29th Dec. 1942

AIR OFFICERS COMMANDING 3 GROUP

Air Vice-Marshal P. H. L. Playfair	1st May 1936
Air Commodore A. A. B. Thomson	14th Feb. 1938
Air Vice-Marshal J. E. A. Baldwin	29th Aug. 1939
Air Vice-Marshal The Hon. R. A. Cochrane	14th Sept. 1942

AIR OFFICERS COMMANDING 4 GROUP

Air Commodore A. T. Harris	12th June 1937
Air Commodore C. H. B. Blount	25th May 1938
Air Vice-Marshal A. Coningham	3rd July 1939
Air Vice-Marshal C. R. Carr	26th July 1941

AIR OFFICERS COMMANDING 5 GROUP

Air Commodore W. B. Gallaway	17th Aug. 1937
Air Vice-Marshal A. T. Harris	11th Sept. 1939
Air Vice-Marshal N. H. Bottomley	22nd Nov. 1940
Air Vice-Marshal J. C. Slessor	12th May 1941
Air Vice-Marshal W. A. Coryton	25th April 1942

AIR OFFICER COMMANDING 6 GROUP ROYAL CANADIAN AIR FORCE

| Air Vice-Marshal G. E. Brookes | 25th Oct. 1942 |

---

[1] Re-formed in June 1940.
[2] In May 1943 2 Group was detached from Bomber Command.

STAFF AND COMMAND APPOINTMENTS

AIR OFFICER COMMANDING 8 GROUP (PATHFINDER FORCE)

	Date of Appointment
Air Vice-Marshal D. C. T. Bennett	13th Jan. 1943[1]

HEADS OF ROYAL AIR FORCE DELEGATION WASHINGTON

Air Vice-Marshal A. T. Harris	1st June 1941
Air Vice-Marshal Sir Douglas Evill	24th Jan. 1942

---

[1] Air Vice-Marshal Bennett (then Air Commodore) had been appointed to command the Pathfinder Force in August 1942 before it was formed into 8 Group.

Abbreviations

A.A.	Anti-aircraft
A.A.F.	Army Air Forces (U.S.)
A.B.D.A.	American, British, Dutch, Australian (Command)
a/c	aircraft
A.C.A.S.	Assistant Chief of the Air Staff
A.C.A.S.(I)	Assistant Chief of the Air Staff (Intelligence)
A.C.A.S.(O)	Assistant Chief of the Air Staff (Operations)
A.C.A.S.(T)	Assistant Chief of the Air Staff (Technical)
A.D.G.B.	Air Defence of Great Britain
A.H.B.	Air Historical Branch (Air Ministry)
A.I.	Air Intelligence
A.M.P.	Air Member for Personnel
A.M.S.R.	Air Member for Supply and Research
App.	Appendix
A.R.P.	Air Raid Precautions
Armt.	Armament
A.O.C.	Air Officer Commanding
A.O.C.-in-C.	Air Officer Commanding-in-Chief
A.S.V.	Air to Surface Vessel (Radar device)
A.W.P.D.	Air Warfare Plans Division (U.S.A.)
B.B.S.U.	British Bombing Survey Unit
B.C.	Bomber Command
B.C.I.R.	Bomber Command Intelligence Report
B.C.I.S.	Bomber Command Intelligence Summary
B.C.O.O.	Bomber Command Operation Order
B. Ops.	Bomber Operations (Air Ministry)
C.A.S.	Chief of the Air Staff
C.-in-C.	Commander-in-Chief
C.I.D.	Committee of Imperial Defence
Cmd.	Command or Command Paper
C.O.	Commanding Officer
C.O.S.	Chiefs of Staff
D. of Plans	Director (or Directorate) of Plans (Air Ministry)
D.B. Ops.	Director (or Directorate) of Bomber Operations (Air Ministry)
D.C.A.S.	Deputy Chief of the Air Staff
D.C.O.S.	Deputy Chiefs of Staff
D.D.	Deputy Director
D.D.B. Ops.	Deputy Director of Bomber Operations (Air Ministry)
D.D.H.O.	Deputy Director Home Operations (Air Ministry)
D.D.I.	Deputy Director of Intelligence (Air Ministry)

ABBREVIATIONS

D. of Org.	Director of Organisation (Air Ministry)
D. of Ops.	Director of Operations (Air Ministry)
D.D. Plans (Ops.)	Deputy Director of Plans (Operations) (Air Ministry)
D.D.S.D.	Deputy Director Staff Duties (Air Ministry)
Del.	Delegation
D/F	Direction Finding (Radio navigation)
D.H.O.	Director of Home Operations (Air Ministry)
Dir.	Directive
D.O.I.	Director of Operations and Intelligence (Air Ministry)
D.O.R.	Director of Operational Requirements (Air Ministry)
D.P.(P)	Defence Plans (Policy) Sub-Committee
D/R	Dead Reckoning (Navigation)
D.S.D.	Director (or Directorate) of Staff Duties (Air Ministry)
E. and O.T.	Enemy and Occupied Territories Department (Ministry of Economic Warfare)
F.W.	Focke-Wulf
G.A.F.	German Air Force
G/C	Group Captain
G.R.	General Reconnaissance
H.E.	High Explosive
I.E.	Initial Equipment
I.T.R.	Industrial Target Report
J.I.C.	Joint Intelligence Committee
J.P.C.	Joint Planning Committee
J.P.S.	Joint Planning Staff
J.S.M.	Joint Staff Mission
Ju.	Junker
Me.	Messerschmitt
M.E.W.	Ministry of Economic Warfare
Narr.	Narrative
Ops.	Operations
O.R.B.	Operations Record Book
O.R.S.(B.C.)	Operational Research Section (Bomber Command)
O.T.U.	Operational Training Unit
P.F.F.	Pathfinder Force
P.I.R.	Photographic Interpretation Report
P.R.U.	Photographic Reconnaissance Unit
P.S.	Private Secretary

ABBREVIATIONS

R.D.F.	Radio Direction Finding
R.E.	Research and Experiments Department (Ministry of Home Security)
R.S.I.	Research Studies Institute (U.S.A.)
S.A.S.O.	Senior Air Staff Officer
S.O.E.	Special Operations Executive
U.S.S.A.F.	United States Strategic Air Forces
U.S.S.B.S.	United States Strategic Bombing Survey
V.C.A.S.	Vice-Chief of the Air Staff
V.C.N.S.	Vice-Chief of Naval Staff
V.H.F.	Very High Frequency (radio)
W.A. Plan	Western Air Plan
War Cab.	War Cabinet
W/Cmdr.	Wing Commander
W.T.	Wireless Telegraphy

Code Names

Circus operations	Fighter escorted daylight bombing attacks against short-range targets with the aim of bringing the enemy air force to battle
Eureka	Ground radio transmitter for guiding bombers to their target
Gee	Radio aid to navigation and target identification
H2S	Radar aid to navigation and target identification
Oboe	Blind bombing radar device
Sampson	Blind *Gee* bombing attack
Sea Lion	German plan for the invasion of Britain
Shaker	Method of illuminating and marking a target with the aid of *Gee* equipped aircraft
Torch	Allied invasion of French North Africa in 1942
Window	Tinfoil strips designed to confuse German radar

Index

INDEX

A.S.V.: mentioned, 20; similar to *H2S*, 248, 317; in G.R. aircraft, 326
Aachen: 301
Abyssinia: 66, 71
Advanced Air Striking Force: 92
Admiralty: *see also* Naval Staff: abandon naval air wing, 34; control Fleet Air Arm, 83; on role of Coastal Command, 83fn; and attack on German fleet, 105; requests reconnaissance, 122; and the war at sea, 165, 320, 321, 325–327, 337; and Thousand bomber raids, 403, 413
Aerodromes: *see* Airfields
Aeroplanes: *see* Aircraft
Ahrens, Oberstabsingenieur: 287fn
Air Armament School: 115
Air Board: 36
Air Committee: 36
Air Council: brief description of, 62; those under, 82; and *Circus* operations, 238
Air Defence Development Establishment: 102
Air Defence of Great Britain Command: set up, 62; mentioned, 64; rearmed, 67
Air Defences:
 British: in First World War, 34 ff., 44–45; against day bombing, 190–191
 German: in First World War, 45fn; against day bombing, 190–192, 194, 195, 196–197, 199, 201, 214; against night operations, 201–202, 242fn, 311, 350–351, 359; improvement in, 254, 311, 385, 397–399; gain upper hand, 257; in early stage of war, 397–398; effect of on British tactics, 400; counter-measures against, 400–401; in Thousand bomber raids, 408; effect of 1942 air attacks on, 490–491
Air Gunners: shortage of, 72; training of, 116
Air Member for Development and Production: *see* Freeman
Air Ministry: *see also* Air Staff: and development of air force, 52; meetings at, 94, 100, 122, 139, 143; and propaganda leaflets, 105–106; and training, 108–109, 119–120; and navigation, 111, 112, 113; relations with Committee for Air Offence, 114fns; and reconnaissance, 121–122, 200; and target identification, 206, 207, 208, 210; relations with M.E.W., 261, 263–264, 265; and photographic interpretation, 268; and expansion of Bomber Command, 343
Air Ministry Intelligence Department: *see* Directorate of Intelligence
Air Ministry Publicity Department: 220
Air Officer Commanding I Group: *see* Oxland (from Nov. 1940)

Air Officer Commanding 2 Group: *see* Robb (from April 1940), Stevenson (from Feb. 1941); D'Albiac (from Dec. 1942)
Air Officer Commanding 3 Group: *see* Thomson, Baldwin (from Aug. 1939)
Air Officer Commanding 4 Group: *see* Coningham (1939), Carr (from July 1941)
Air Officer Commanding 5 Group: *see* Harris (from Sept. 1939)
Air Officer Commanding 8 Group (Pathfinder Force): *see* Bennett
Air Officer Commanding 11 Group, Fighter Command: *see* Leigh-Mallory
Air Officer Commanding - in - Chief, Air Defence of Great Britain: 82
Air Officer Commanding-in-Chief, Bomber Command: *see* Ludlow-Hewitt (to April 1940), Portal (to Oct. 1940), Peirse (to Jan. 1942), Harris (from Feb. 1942)
Air Officer Commanding-in-Chief, Fighter Command: *see* Dowding, Douglas
Air Officer Commanding-in-Chief, Middle East: 347
Air Parity Committee: 70
Air Position Indicator: 205, 418
Air Raid Precautions:
 British: views on in inter-war years, 45–47, 62–63, 88
 German: attempts to disrupt, 253, 267; effect of bombing on, 301, 313, 338; short description of, 482–483; experience gained in, 488
Air Raid Precautions Committee: 45, 62–63
Air Service Training: 109fn
Air Staff: on role of air force, 13, 42, 50, 63, 73–74, 77–78, 79, 80–81, 86–89, 91–92, 96–97, 102–104, 130, 144, 364, 367, 372; plans air force, 54; on aircraft industry, 57, 481fn; and disarmament, 58, 59fn; and lack of research, 60; relations with A.D.G.B., 62; on expected casualties, 63; and expansion and rearmament, 67, 68, 70–75, 80, 84, 107, 177, 254; estimates size of German air force, 69, 76; and Mosquitoes, 72; on role of Coastal Command, 83fn; on choice of targets, 93, 95, 96–97, 124, 284, 286fn, 414; and bombing policy, 99, 103–104, 118fn, 130, 135, 139, 141, 142, 143, 145–146, 147–169, 171, 174, 178, 180, 182–184, 220, 244–245, 252, 284, 290, 291, 294–296, 310, 318, 320–328, 329–331, 334–336, 337, 347–351, 384, 391, 422, 436, 449, 451, 466, 480, 481fn; realise limits of Bomber Command, 101, 125; and priority for Fighter Command, 102–103; and demarcation of responsibility, 103, 149;

503

INDEX

Air Staff—*cont.*
 views of on protection of bombers, 116; on bomb aiming, 118; and operational capability of Bomber Command, 222, 385, 413; and *Gee*, 249, 384, 385–386, 462; on technique of area attack, 252–253; relations with M.E.W., 262, 263, 458, 470; and results of bombing, 299; and relations with Bomber Command, 312, 325, 348; realises need for action, 339; and the American daylight plan, 360–361, 363; and attack on French factories, 387; and German air defences, 400; and *Window*, 400; and target finding force, 422, 431; and Pathfinder Force, 431fn

Air Superiority: discussed, 20–23; in First World War, 42–44; through longe-range fighters, 117; as preliminary to invasion of England, 137, 147; through day bombing, 175, 213, 236, 438; through defeating the enemy fighter force, 238, 362–363; connection with range, 243

Air Targets Sub-Committee: 93, 97, 98
Airborne Division: 343
Aircraft: specialisation in, 56; progress in, 65; inadequacy of, 79
 American: policy for, 319, 342, 353; production of, 366, 472
Aircraft Industry:
 British: (inter-war) small size of, 57; excellence of, 65; expansion of, 71, 72, 78; and heavy bombers, 76; (war years) exceeds German, 280
 German: attack on discussed, 14, 95, 293–294, 468; expansion of, 72, 480; proposed attack on, 145, 147–148, 149–150, 151, 153, 160, 165, 294–295, 351, 358, 373, 471, 481; attack on, 215, 218, 234; intelligence about, 263, 351, 481; description of, 293–294, 480; estimated effects of attacks on, 299fn; dispersal of, 304, 481; effects of attack on, 480–481
Aircraft Operating Company: 268
Airfields:
 British: (in First World War) attacks on, 48; (inter-war) location of, 61–62, 84, 109; increase in, 73, 84; (in Second World War) attacks on, 152
 German: (in First World War) attacks on, 48; (inter-war) location of, 95; (in Second World War) attacks on, 148; suggested attacks on, 156
Alexander, Rt. Hon. A. V.: 325
Aluminium Plants: *covered by* German Industry
Anderson, Sir John: 267–268
Anti-Aircraft Guns:
 British: location of, 62
 German: increase in, 491; location of, 491
Anti-Comintern Pact: 72
Armament: of bombers, 61, 115–116, 191, 242, 243, 358; training and research in, 110, 115
Armament Industry, German: expansion of, 271–280, 313, 476–478
Armament Training Camps: role of, 115; number of, 115; trials in, 117; mentioned, 118fn

Armaments Production Centre (German): 272
Armstrong Whitworth, Ltd.: 109fn
Arnold, Lieut.-General H. H.: final despatch of, 31; succeeds in basing day bombers in U.K., 355; Churchill's arguments help, 356; views of, 364; pleased with British strategy paper, 367; makes target appreciation, 471; appoints Committee, 472
Army: *see also* General Staff: and expansion, 74, 80, 86, 88; responsible for anti-aircraft, 87; role of, 90, 155
Army Co-operation: rearmament of squadrons, 67, 80; war plans for, 91
Army Co-operation Command: set up, 84; Harris demands return of aircraft from, 341; and Thousand bomber raids, 403, 406fn, 410fn, 414; Bomber Command aircraft for, 416
Ashmore, Major-General E. B.: 37, 44–45fns, 45
Assistant Chief of the Air Staff: *see* Douglas (to April 1940)
Assistant Chief of the Air Staff (Intelligence): *see* Medhurst
Assistant Chief of the Air Staff (Operations): *see* Bottomley
Attlee, Rt. Hon. C. R.: 266, 291
Augsburg: *for attack on M.A.N. factory, see that heading*
Auld, Lieut.-Colonel S. I. M.: 266
Austria: conquered, 79, 275
Australia: and air training scheme, 110
'Auxiliary' Aims: discussed, 6–9, 13; never settled, 336

'Baedeker' Raids: 475
Baker, Group Captain G. B. A.: 120
Baker, Air Commodore J. W.: links communications and morale, 297; and bombing policy, 324; and attack on ball-bearings, 347; on M.E.W. appreciation, 461fn
Baldwin, Air Vice-Marshal J. E. A.: and daylight actions, 195–196, 197–198, 200, 201, 213, 235; on navigation at night, 217; on attack on oil, 230–231; on results of bombing, 256–257; on aircraft and crews for Middle East, 257fn; receives directive of 14th Feb. 1942, 323, 324; views of on attacking Essen, 417; views of on night operations, 427–428; goes on Thousand attack on Cologne, 427fn; receives Harris' views on target finding force, 429
Baldwin, Rt. Hon. Stanley: and 'parity', 66; and rearmament, 67fn, 68–69, 70; announces bombing policy, 99, 104
Ball-bearings Industry: proposed attack on, 294, 324, 347–348, 463, 464, 466, 467; intelligence about, 347
Barnes, Wing Commander L. K.: 205fn
Barratt, Sir Arthur: 143
Battle of Berlin: 435
Battle of Britain: air superiority in, 21, 147; Heinkels in, 59fn; mentioned, 83, 151, 213, 370, 450; effect of on bombing policy, 130, 147–148, 175, 215, 318; short description of, 151–152, 155; plans after, 214–215, 235 ff.;

INDEX

Battle of Britain—*cont.*
compared with conditions of *Circus* operations, 236–237, 238, 239; Portal compares with American daylight plan, 356; role of radar in, 397
Battle of France: effect of on bombing policy, 130, 144–146, 215, 318; mentioned, 213; 2 Group in, 438
Battle of Hamburg: 401, 435
Battle of the Atlantic: Condors in, 59fn; effect of on bombing policy, 130, 164–166, 167, 215, 233–235, 318, 325–327; best way to help, 168; disagreement about air effort for, 321–322, 325–327, 378; American attacks help, 355; and attack on M.A.N. works, 463, 464; and bombing submarine yards, 481
Battle of the Ruhr: 435
Battles: obsolescent, 73, 95–96, 129fn; number in Bomber Command, 81; refuelling bases for, 84; for France, 100, 214; mentioned, 176
Beauforts: 403
Beaverbrook, Lord: 229
Belgium: threat to, 87, 92; refuelling bases in, 92
Bennett, Air Vice-Marshal D. C. T.: 432–433
Berlin: attacked, 152, 215, 218–219, 305fn, 435; on night 7th Nov. 1941, 185, 254; reports of attack of 7th Nov. 1941, 254–256; mentioned in directives, 153, 323, 462; supposed results of attacking, 157, 218–219, 224; results of attacking, 302, 304–305; Stalin wants bombed, 351; Churchill wants bombed, 462
Bernal, Professor J. D.: 371
Biggin Hill: 101
Billancourt: *see* Renault Factory
Birmingham: analysis of raids on, 474
Bismarck: 148, 305
Blackett, Professor P. M. S.: 114fn, 270fn, 371
Blenheims: converted to fighters, 80, 100; number in Bomber Command, 81; refuelling bases for, 84; capabilities of, 95, 96fn, 129fn; for reconnaissance, 122, 221, 268fn; for French army, 138; against German fleet, 192fn; on day operations, 213–214, 243, (*Circus*) 236 ff.; on night operations, 224 ff., 245 ff.; replaced, 438, 439; and attack on German warships, 240; taken out of service, 309; and Thousand bomber raids, 403; not suitable for day operations, 454
Blitzkrieg: planned, 272; fails in Russia, 319
Blockade: *see* Naval Blockade
Blockade Intelligence Department, M.E.W.: 261
Blohm and Voss: 302–303
Board of Economic Warfare, U.S.A.: 471
Board of Trade: 92
Boeings: 75
Bowhill, Air Chief Marshal Sir Frederick: 109fn
Bomb Aiming: *see also* Targets, identification and location of: training and research in, 117–121; assumption about, 172, 174, 216, 221, 223, 228, 245; beliefs in after attack on F.W. factory, 245–247

Bomb Sights: *for more detail see Annex IV*: 121, 227
Bomb Targets Information Committee: M.E.W. representative on, 263, 458, 459fn; set up, 263; work of, 458
Bomber Command: *for Bombing Policy, Directives, Targets, Navigation etc., see individual headings:* foundations of, 54; size and composition of (inter-war), 65, 67–80, (on outbreak of war), 81, (war years) 129, 309, 340, 342, 344fn, 355, 402, 416–417, 452; established, 73, 82–83; no role in defence, 79, 102; state of (inter-war), 79–81, 91, 95–97, 99–101, (on outbreak of war) 125–126, (war years) 129, 134, 318; first line reduced, 80; war plans for, 91–92, 94–106, 129–130, 318; location of, 92; makes appreciation of German industry, 97; and effect of separation from Fighter Command, 101fn; and effect of priority to Fighter Command, 102–103, 318; forced landings in, 112fn; hours flown in (1938), 113fn; relations with Committee for Air Offence, 114; exercises with Fighter Command, 115, 116; operational limitations of, 131, 149–150, 351–352; first land target of, 140; first mainland target of, 141fn; begins strategic offensive, 144; place in strategy, 170–171, 326–327, 329–331, 340–343, 365–379; expansion policy for, 177–178, 180–181, 182, 184, 185, 187, 254, 310, 318, 319–320, 334–335, 342–344, 353, 360, 365–370, 371, 373–374, 375, 476; relations with M.E.W., 270, 348, 459, 460, 463–465, 466, 472; relations with Air Staff, 312, 325; effect on of U.S. entry into war, 319–320, 365; and reinforcement of other theatres and commands, 257, 310, 318, 325–328, 342, 344fn, 413, 416, 447, 452
Bomber Command Headquarters: 85, 103; and Essen attack, 225; Harris' attachment for, 341–342
Bomber's Baedeker: produced, 267; on Schweinfurt, 348fn; contents of, 469–470
Bombers: *see also specific types:* protection of in First World War, 43–44; role of discussed inter-war, 54 ff., 65; defence against, 75; expected casualties in, 77; protection for (*see also* Armament), 96, 116–117; in self-defending formations (*for more detail see* Bombers, Day British), 175, 177, 243
Day American: plan for, 311–312; when on deep penetration, 358–359, 360; in 'self-defending' formations, 450–451, 455
Day British: casualties when unescorted (*for more detail see* Casualties), 54, 56, 61, 212, 216, 235; in 'self-defending' formations, 191–201, 213, 214, 239, 436, 450–453
Dive German: 480
German: no increase in, 480
Heavy American: production plans for, 329, 332, 353, 356
Heavy British: first plans for, 40, 68, 71, 72, 89; lack of, 60, 68; final decision for, 74–76, 79; threatened, 76–77; reserves for, 78; rearmament with reduced, 80–81; weakness of, 95; second pilot for, 111; when unescorted in daylight, 141, 239 ff.,

INDEX

Bombers: Heavy British—*cont.*
241–242, 311; during Battle of France, 146; wanted for *Circus* operations, 238; definition of changed, 240fn; role of challenged, 329–330; production of, 331–332, 333, 341, 365–370; average life of, 331, 333; role of, 366, 377; difficulties of in turning to day operations, 447
Light British: predominance of, 67, 79; obsolescent, 72; future of, 72; plea for, 76; bases for, 87
Medium British: in expansion plans, 71; plea for, 76–77; predominance of, 79; location of, 84, 92; refuelling bases for, 87, 92; weakness of, 95; second pilot for, 111; definition of changed, 240fn
Night British: for leaflet raids, 100
Bombing: attempts to limit, 50–51, 99; belief in accuracy of, 60; lack of training in, 61
Area: discussion of, 13–14, 349–350; early memo. on, 118; coming of, 130–131, 157, 163, 168–171, 232; arrival of, 180–185, 215, 225–226, 230, 233 ff., 245, 247, 252, 323–324; technique for, 252–253, 311; differences of opinion about, 344–345, 422–423; advocated by Harris, 346 (*now see* Harris); effect of *Gee* on, 386; economic advice for, 459–462; not allowed in France, 462; new prospects in, 465
Day: belief in preponderance, 100; impossibility of, 130, 212, 311, 435–436, 450; dangers of, 138–139, 141; desirability of after invasion of Russia, 175, 234, 235; early unhappy experiences of, 175–176, 192–201, 240–242, 447; plan for, 175–176, 213–215, 235–236 (*now see Circus* operations); Churchill's views on, 184–185, 355–356, 360; partial abandonment of, 200, 201, 244, 449; accuracy of, 216, 228fn; necessary conditions for, 242–243, 244; American plan for, 354, 357–358; first American operations in, 355; British views on American plan for, 355–363, 375–376, 454; Admiralty views on, 372; left to Americans, 435, 455; in 1942, 439 ff.; analysis of Dec. 1941–July 1942, 448–450; fighter cover for difficult to provide, 449; attempt to revive, 451–454; no longer significant, 454
Dive: suggested, 119
Night: in First World War, 47–48; estimated effectiveness of, 100–101, 118, 354; coming of, 130, 139–140, 143, 208–209, 212, 213, 233, 243, 244; accuracy of, 140, 177–180, 185, 190, 216, 220–232, 228fn, 244–248, 318–319; not indiscriminate, 145; problems of not realised, 212, 229; first operations in, 218 ff.; most economical use of, 234–235; limitations of, 247, 311
Precision: discussion of, 13–14; in First World War, 47–48; early memo. on, 118; training for, 119; still preferred, 141, 152–153, 177–178, 233, 245, 345, 363, 465–466; now impracticable, 180, 181, 230, 233; necessary conditions for at night, 208, 246, 389; still attempted

Bombing: Precision—*cont.*
at night, 234; difficulties of at night, 244, 311; American plan for, 311–312, 358; and the use of *Gee*, 323, 386–387; tendency to become area, 358–359; development of at night, 444
Selective: discussion of, 13, 349; early example of, 234fn; abandoned, 252; area bombing used for, 324, 345; M.E.W. searches for targets for, 466
Bombing Committee: role of, 117, 458; delegates work, 118; discusses flares, 123; reports to on accuracy, 228fn
Bombing Development Unit: 119–120, 124
Bombing Policy: *see also* Strategic Air Offensive: discussions on in inter-war years, 54 ff.; announcements in Parliament on, 99, 104, 328–329, 330–331; conservation decreed, 100, 103, 130, 134–136, 186–187, 254; confined to 'military objectives', 99, 104, 105, 130, 134–135, 190; 'military objectives' abandoned, 157; early course of summarised, 130–131; 1941–1943 course of summarised, 310–313; when to change to offensive, 136–138, 142–143; French views on, 137, 141–142, 145–146; Ruhr plan discarded (*for more detail see* Ruhr), 139, 141; oil plan favoured (*for more detail see* Oil), 139, 141, 158 ff.; the change to night bombing (*for more detail see* Bombing: Night), 139–140, 143, 190, 212, 213, 233 ff., 243, 244; concentration ignored, 142, 148, 284, 318; strategic attacks allowed, 144; during Battle of France, 145–146, 318; during Battle of Britain and possible invasion, 147–152, 318; concentration sought, 148–149, 160–161; effect on of isolated targets, 150; effect on of 'dispersal' argument, 150; 'morale' raids suggested (*for more detail see* Morale), 153–154, 156–157, 160, 162, 323–324; after end of invasion threat, 155–162; affected by Battle of the Atlantic, 164–168, 318, 325–327; returns to industrial targets April 1941, 168; communications plan favoured (*for more detail see* Communications), 171 ff.; day plan revived (*for more detail see* Bombing Day), 175–176, 213–215, 235 ff., 451–454; the change to area bombing (*for more detail see* Bombing: Area), 180 ff., 225, 230, 232, 245, 252; economic advice for, 262 ff.; tendency of people to advise on, 269; effect of U.S. entry into war on, 319–320; on the introduction of *Gee* Feb. 1942, 320–325; doubts about in 1942, 328–336; effect of 1942 victories on, 340, 344; Harris' position to influence, 345; the beginnings of the ball-bearings plan (*for more detail see* Ball-bearings Industry), 347–348
Bombing Policy Sub-Committee: 117fn, 118–119
Bombs: in First World War, 49; inter-war, 61; trials in, 124–125; limitations of, 129; assumptions about, 159fn, 223, 369–370; effects of on different buildings, 267, 474, 488fn; for canals, 296; in Thousand bomber raids, 407, 414

INDEX

Bombs—*cont.*
   100 lb. Anti-Submarine: 414
   500 lb.: 414
   1,000 lb.: not ready, 296; used against Renault factory, 387; used against M.A.N. works, 442
   4,000 lb.: first used, 303fn; used against Renault factory, 388; on Thyssen works, 390fn; against Lübeck, 392; on F.W. factory, 415
   Incendiary British: experiments with, 124fn; for fire-raising technique, 157, 225–226, 227, 252–253, 320-321, 382, 391–393; proportion carried, 252fn; weight of, 253fn; for crops and forests, 295; in *Shaker* technique, 386, 419; in Thousand bomber raids, 405, 407fn, 410, 414; 30 lb., 434; 250 lb., 434; 4,000 lb., 434; R.E.8 favours, 488fn
   Incendiary German: in First World War, 49; used for fire-raising technique, 252–253; proportion carried, 252fn; weight of, 253fn; effects of examined, 267
   Marker and Target Indicating: beginning of, 248; project dropped, 249; not yet available, 432, 434; first use of, 435
Bordeaux: 346
Bormann, Martin: 484fn
Bostons: (Mk. III) for day operations, 244; and Thousand raid on Bremen, 414fn; for 2 Group, 438, 439; in attack on Philips Radio Works, 440, 441; and attack on M.A.N. works, 442
Bottlenecks: definition of, 28, 466; difficulties of, 349; search for, 465–467, 468
Bottomley, Air Vice-Marshal N. H.: on night attacks, 101, 140; and directive of 9th July 1941, 174; becomes D.C.A.S., 174; on early daylight attacks, 194, 200; on night reconnaissance, 207; on navigation and bomb aiming, 210, 226–227; circulates crew questionnaire, 223; on attack on oil, 231; comments on Lancaster, 254fn; and bombing policy, 322, 324; praises clarity, 325fn; and specially armoured Lancasters, 453
Bremen: (*for the attacks on the Focke-Wulf Factory see* Focke-Wulf Factory): attacked, 245; in directive of 14th Feb. 1942, 323
   Thousand attack on: 340, 413–416; results of, 415, 486–487; mentioned, 426fn
Brest: harbour attacked, 167, 168, 234, 241, 242, 254; attack on planned, 240; percentage of sorties against, 320; Air Staff against attacking, 321; warships leave, 322; proposed attack against, 346
British Bombing Survey Unit: *for a detailed description see Annex V*: short description of, 271
British Expeditionary Force: (in First World War) mentioned, 34, 43; releases fighters, 36; (in Second World War) decision for, 104; at Dunkirk, 145
Brooke, Field-Marshal Sir Alan: and role of strategic air offensive, 372–373, 377; and petrol shortage, 373fn; (as Lord Alanbrooke) on second front, 375fn

S.A.O.—I—KK*

Brown, Professor A. J.: 276fn
Browning Machine Gun: 115
Bruneval: combined operation against, 400
Buckingham Palace: hit, 152, 155
Buckinghams: 243
Bufton, Group Captain S. O.: and target finding force, 419–426, 429, 431; career of, 419fn; views of on area bombing, 422–423; analyses success of raids, 423fn; mentioned, 433; on quality of crews for Pathfinder Force, 433fn
Butt, Mr.: report of on bombing accuracy, 178–180, 185, 247–248, 249, 250, 252, 383

Cabinet: *for war years see* War Cabinet: on air raid precautions, 45; approves air force plans, 53, 54, 71, 79, 81; and Ten Year Rule, 57; mentioned, 62; and 'parity', 66, 69, 70, 73; accept Inskip view, 77–78; and air threat, 88; receive future strategy report, 89; appoint oil committee, 265
Cadogan, Sir Alexander: 375fn
Cameras: lack of, 61, 122–123, 221, 268; importance of, 121; significance of, 232
   Night: *see also* Photographs, Night: numbers of, 221–222, 250fn; need for, 229, 250; evidence of, 383–384, 388; shortage of, 384fn; in Thousand bomber raids, 407; sole arbiter of success, 426
Canada: and air training scheme, 110
Canals: *covered by* Communications
Carr, Air Vice-Marshal C. R.: on photographic evidence, 179; on day bombing, 241–242; on night operations, 428–429
Carstens, Gauleiter: 484fn
Casablanca Conference: decides role of bombing offensive, 311, 343; memo. for, 378fn; about to assemble, 379; preparatory memo. for, 468; mentioned, 472
Casualties, Civilian and Military:
   American: forecast from day plan, 356, 358–359, 362, 454; forecast from possible night operations, 359
   British: bearable rate of, 18, 20, 244, 398–399, 417; in First World War, 34, 35, 38, 41, 45, 49; expected in Second World War, 46, 63, 89, 95, 97, 184; of aircraft, discussed inter-war, 54 ff., 77–78; inevitable, 50–51; Trenchard's views on, 55, 170; expected in attack on German air force, 95, 99; in attack on German air force, 95–96; and bombing policy, 99, 105, 125, 134, 137, 138–139, 140, 186–187, 216, 321, 322, 400, 447–448; connection of with accuracy, 119fn, 447–449; in daylight actions, 175, 192, 194, 196, 197, 199, 200, 201, 213, 214, 241–242, 243, 444, 447, 448; from bombing, 183; on night 7th Nov. 1941, 185–186, 254–256; in other night actions, 202, 210, 213, 219, 254, 362, 398 399, 401; in *Circus* operations, 237, 438, 449; in Thousand raid on Cologne, 340, 403, 404, 407–410, 412; in attack on Renault factory, 388; in attack on Lübeck, 398; in Jan.–May 1942, 399fn; in Aug.–Oct.

INDEX

Casualties, Civilian and Military: British—*cont.*
1941, 399fn; in Aug.–Oct. 1942, 399fn; in attacks on Cologne, 409fn; in west Germany June 1941–March 1942, 409fn; in Thousand raid on Essen, 411–412; in Thousand raid on Bremen, 413fn, 415–416; expected in Pathfinder Force, 432fn; in attack on Philips Radio Works, 440–441; in attack on M.A.N. works, 442–443, 453; in Le Creusot attack, 446, 447

French: through attacking factories, 387

German: in First World War, 34, 35, 38fn; in Battle of Britain, 152; in daylight actions, 196, 199, 490; from attacks on Cologne, 304, 486fn, (Thousand) 485; from attacks on Berlin, 305; estimated in day actions, 360; estimated in night actions, 362; forecast in day actions, 362; forecast from Anglo-American offensive, 369; from Thousand raid on Essen, 411, 487fn; from attack on Lübeck, 483–484; from attacks on Düsseldorf, 487; in night actions, 490

Catalinas, 325fn

Cave-Browne-Cave, Air Vice-Marshal H. M.: 114fn, 115fn

Central Flying School: 60, 108

Central Interpretation Unit, Medmenham: beginning of, 268; role of, 312, 473; work of challenged, 474

Central Planning Committee (German): 477

Chamberlain, Sir Austen: 57

Chamberlain, Rt. Hon. Neville: 81, 87

Chancellor of the Exchequer: and rearmament, 67, 73, 79, 81fn, 87

Chemical Industry, German: not attacked, 286; organisation of, 287

Cherwell, Lord: and the Butt report, 178, 179–180, 248; and aids to navigation and target location, 248–250, 419; position of, 270, 336; calculates effect of bombing, 331–336, 337; his minute referred to, 345, 369, 474fn; suggested that he undertake new analysis, 371; delays *Window*, 401

Cheshire, Wing Commander G. L.: 433

Chief of Naval Staff: *see also* Pound: 10

Chief of the Air Staff: *see also* Trenchard (Jan.–April 1918, 1919–1929), Sykes (1918–1919), Ellington (from May 1933), Newall (from Sept. 1937), Portal (from Oct. 1940); views on air power, 10; equal to other services, 53; on accuracy of bombing, 60fn; duties of, 82–83

Chief of the Imperial General Staff: *see also* Robertson, Brooke; views on air power, 10

Chiefs of Staff Committee: views on air power, 10, 180–181; created, 53; receive Trenchard paper, 63; discuss size of German air force, 69; mentioned, 86, 87, 103; receive J.P.C. paper, 89; draw up war plans, 90–91, 136–137; and 'worst case', 146; draw up plans after fall of France, 146, 281, 282fn; on long-term strategy, 155, 174, 183, 366; and attack on oil, 159–161, 162, 164, 216, 266, 290, 291; and attack on morale, 170–171, 173, 177, 180–181,

Chiefs of Staff Committee—*cont.*
297, 330fn., 366, 378, 492; and attack on communications, 171, 173; relations with J.I.C., 261, 458; and oil intelligence, 265, 266, 282; and bombing directives, 269; and Singleton report, 338; and the American daylight plan, 360; and role of strategic air offensive, 366–367, 369, 371–374, 378–379; and *Window*, 401; and German economy, 476

Churchill, Rt. Hon. Winston S.: views on air power, 10; (as Minister of Munitions) on air superiority, 43; on air raids, 45, 47; (as Sec. of State for Air and War) and organisation of air force, 53; (as Chancellor of the Exchequer) and Ten Year Rule, 57; (as an M.P.) and 'parity', 66fn, 70fn; (as First Lord of the Admiralty) and photographic interpretation, 268fn; (as Prime Minister) forms government, 144; on plans after fall of France, 146; on Battle of Britain, 152; and bombing policy, 152, 153, 154, 161–162, 163, 164, 169, 173–174, 182–186, 291, 295, 310, 322, 462; on naval strategy, 155; on air strategy, 155, 342–343; and the war at sea, 164, 165, 167, 168fn, 234, 235, 327, 328fn; and day bombing, 176–177, 243; and the Butt report, 179, 248; and casualties, 184, 186; and long-range fighter, 239, 242; and actions of night 7th Nov. 1941, 255, 256; and estimates of German air production, 263; uses Lord Cherwell, 270, 336; and results of attack on oil, 300; and grand strategy, 319, 341, 342–343, 368, 374–377; on fall of Singapore, 328; reconstructs War Cabinet, 328; and Cherwell's calculations, 332, 334; on forecasts, 335; on necessity for plans, 335–336; and Singleton report, 337fn; relations with Harris, 340, 464; and expansion of Bomber Command, 342–343, 375; views of on American daylight plan, 355–356, 360, 375–376; attitude of important to American daylight plan, 360–363; and withdrawal of C.O.S. strategy paper, 367–368, 374; and Stalin, 368fn, 375, 492fn; at Casablanca Conference, 379; and Thousand bomber raids, 403, 413, 416–417; and Pathfinder Force, 431fn; and attack on M.A.N. factory, 463–464

Circus operations: *for other day operations see* Bombing, Day: beginning of, 214–215; aim of, 236; description of, 236–239; short summary of difficulties of, 351, 437; achievements of, 437–438; in 1942, 438–439; conclusion from, 449

Civil Defence: *see* Air Raid Precautions

Coal Production: German expansion in, 274, 478fn; estimated losses of, 478

Coastal Command: set up, 83; and war plans, 91, 94; directs bombing operation, 141fn; attacks *Gneisenau*, 305; Bomber Command aircraft for, 310, 318, 325–326, 328fn, 344fn, 413, 416, 447, 452; more demanded, 326; Wellington production for, 333; Harris' views on, 341; aircraft from for

INDEX

Coastal Command—*cont.*
  Bomber Command, 343; and Thousand bomber raids, 403, 413–414, 416
Coking Plants: *covered in* German Industry
Cologne: results of attacks on, 302, 304; in directive of 14th Feb. 1942, 323; attacked night 13th March 1942, 390–391, 395; attacked night 22nd April 1942, 396
  Thousand attack on: 310, 339–340, 403–410, 412, 417; mentioned, 311, 418; effect of, 340, 407, 465, 478, 485–486, 488; relief following, 483fn; Harris' views on, 341, 342, 478; estimated effect of, 485, 486; recovery from, 486
Combined Bomber Offensive: and M.E.W., 264, 468, 472; beginnings of, 311–312; referred to, 471; foundation of plan for, 472
Combined Chiefs of Staff: 401
Comet: 72
Commander-in-Chief, Home Forces: *see* French
Commander-in-Chief, Royal Flying Corps: *see* Trenchard
Commander-in-Chief for Defence of London: *see* Ashmore
Committee for the Scientific Survey of Air Defence: 114
Committee for the Scientific Survey of Air Offence: set up, 114; on bomber armament, 115fn; on need for research, 121fn; advise on bombsight, 121
Committee of Imperial Defence: mentioned, 54, 86, 87, 108; receive future strategy report, 89; and assistance to Poland, 105; on M.E.W., 260–261; relations with J.I.C., 261
Committee of Operations Analysts: 472
Commonwealth Training Scheme: 108, 110
Communications: target system discussed, 28–29; proposed attack on, 94, 98, 142, 143, 146, 148, 149, 150, 153, 156, 160, 171–174, 247, 295–298, 482fn; reconnaissance of, 207; attack on, 215, 218; estimated effect of attacks on, 296, 299fn, 481; intelligence machinery for, 266; problems of in Germany, 279, 481; linked with morale, 297; effect of attack on, 305, 481
Coningham, Air Vice-Marshal A.: on night operations, 140–141, 163, 201–202, 204, 205–206, 207, 208, 209, 212, 216, 217, 218, 224, 226–228, 229, 230, 231; on weather forecasts, 204fn
Conversion Units: 403–404
Corps D'Élite: dislike of, 119, 419, 421–422, 433
Coventry: attack on examined, 181–182, 183; reprisal for, 215; attack on mentioned, 254
Crews: *see also individual members:* shortage of, 72; training of, 107–116, 255–256, 257; morale of, 197, 256; reports of on bombing, 220–221, 222–223, 224, 225, 228, 229, 231, 267, 302; views of on target identification, 229; dislike Gelsenkirchen, 231; reorganisation of, 309–310; Sinclair comments on, 330
Cripps, Sir Stafford: 328–329
Crops: suggested attack on, 295
Crowe, Sir Edward: 93fn

Cunliffe-Lister, Sir Philip: *see* Swinton
Cunningham, Dr.: 371
Czechoslovakia: annexed, 80, 104, 275; air force of, 87; threatened, 99; desertion of, 184, 185fn

D.H.9s: 44fn
D'Albiac, Air Vice-Marshal J. H.: 454fn
Dalton, Rt. Hon. Hugh: 263
Danzig: attacked, 444, 447
Darwin, Sir Charles: 371
Davis, Air Vice-Marshal E. D.: 403fn
De Havilland: 72
Defence Committee: and attack on oil, 161, 164, 266, 290, 291; and oil intelligence, 265, 266; and bombing directives, 269; and bombing policy, 320–321, 330fn, 462, 468; and the war at sea, 325–327, 464; and the Singleton report, 337; relations with J.I.C., 458; and relations between M.E.W. and Bomber Command, 466
Defence Plans (Policy) Committee: 74
Defence Policy and Requirements Committee: 67fn
Defence Programmes and Acceleration Committee: 81
Defence Requirements Committee: 67fn
Defences: *see* Air Defences
Denmark: invaded, 141
Department of Aircraft Production: 36
Department of Overseas Trade: 93
Deputy Chief of the Air Staff: *see* Peirse (1937–1940), Douglas (from April 1940), Harris (from Nov. 1940), Bottomley (from May 1941)
Deputy Chiefs of Staff: 92
Deputy Director of Bomber Operations: *see* Bufton
Deputy Director of Plans: *see also* Slessor, Harris: and attack on oil, 290fn; and attack on aircraft industry, 294
Deutschland: 148
Dewdney, Squadron Leader D. A. C.: on results of oil attacks, 222–223, 300; visits crews, 228–229; on crews' dislike of Gelsenkirchen, 231; mentioned, 252; on crews' belief in target finding force, 419fn; works on damage assessment, 473; note on, 473fn; employs Dickinson, 475fn
Dickins, Dr. B. G.: 251
Dickinson, Mr.: 475fn
Dill, Field-Marshal Sir John: 170, 367, 374
Directives: For Bomber Command: of 13th April 1940, 142, 212; of 4th June 1940, 146–147; of 20th June 1940, 147–148; of 4th July 1940, 148; of 13th July 1940, 149–151; of 24th July 1940, 151; of 21st Sept. 1940, 153, 154, 171, 299fn; of 25th Oct. 1940 (draft), 155–157; of 30th Oct. 1940, 157, 158; of 10th Nov. 1940, 158, 160; of 15th Jan. 1941, 162, 164, 290; of 9th March 1941, 165, 167, 234; of 18th March 1941, 167; of 9th July 1941, 174, 180, 244fn, 247; of 13th Nov. 1941, 186–187, 254, 320, 322, 383; background of 13th Nov. directive, 269; of 14th Feb. 1942, 310,

Directives—*cont.*
 322–324, 330, 344–345, 346, 391, 422, 459, 462, 492; of 5th Feb. 1942, 323; of 3rd Sept. 1942, 347; of 5th May 1942, 351, 352; Casablanca, 492
Director of Armament Development: *see* G. B. A. Baker
Director of Bomber Operations: *see also* J. W. Baker; 263
Director of Operational Requirements: *see* Freeman
Director of Plans: *see* Slessor
Director of Training: *see* Tedder
Director of Transportation, War Office: 482fn
Directorate of Bomber Operations: plan attack on communications, 171–173, 174; plan area offensive, 181–182; on bomb aiming error, 245; relations with M.E.W., 458; and attack on ball-bearings, 466
Directorate of Intelligence: on size and location of German air force, 175fn; relations with M.E.W., 263, 458; and supposed results of bombing, 267; on German morale, 270; on German chemicals and oil, 286fn; on damage assessment calculations, 474; issues zone maps, 475
Directorate of Operational Requirements: 68
Directorate of Plans: 100, 284fn
Disarmament: 58–59
Don, Group Captain F. P.: 94
Dorniers: Mk. 17; 125
Dorpmüller, Fritz: 482fn
Dortmund: attack on referred to, 417
Dortmund–Ems Canal: proposed attack on, 174, 296; attack on, 296; results of attacks on, 305
Douglas, Air Vice-Marshal W. S.: on co-operation between Fighter and Bomber Commands, 101fn; on superiority of Fighter Command, 101–102; on position of observer, 111fn; on bombing policy, 143, 158, 171; on Bomber Command's co-operation in land battle, 145; on *Circus* operations, 438
Dowding, Air Chief Marshal Sir Hugh: faith of in Fighter Command, 78, 101; on command organisation, 82; helps tactical problems, 108; navigation no problem to, 112fn; asks about armour for bombers, 116; views on Ruhr plan, 138; on location of German air force, 175fn
Dresden: attack on mentioned, 10
Duisburg: in directive of 14th Feb. 1942, 323; attacked in error, 390
Düsseldorf: in directive of 14th Feb. 1942, 323; attacked night 31st July 1942, 417; results of attacks on, 487; estimated results of attacks on, 487–488

Eaker, Major-General I. C.: 451, 471
Economic Intelligence Department, Ministry of Economic Warfare: 260, 261–262
Economic Warfare Intelligence Department, M.E.W.: set up, 261; relations with J.I.C., 262; relations with services, 262–263; relations with Lloyd Committee, 265

Eden, Rt. Hon. Anthony: 69
Edwards, Wing Commander H. R. A.: 410fn
Effects of Bombing: *see* Results of Bombing
Eindhoven: *see* Philips Radio Works
Electricity Plants: *see* Power Plants
Ellington, Sir Edward: 69, 82, 87–88
Emden: results of attacks against, 303, 478; in directive of 14th Feb. 1942, 323; Harris refers to, 478
Emden: 192fn
Ems–Weser Canal: proposed attack on, 174
Enemy and Occupied Territories Department, M.E.W.: 262
Enemy Branch, M.E.W.: 264, 458, 469
Enemy Objectives Unit, U.S.A.: 471
Enemy Resources Department, M.E.W.: 262, 264
Essen: suggested attack on, 153; attacked (night 7th Nov. 1940), 224–225, (March–April 1942) 389–390; failure of attacks on, 311, 339, 389–390, 395, 396; in directive of 14th Feb. 1942, 323; attacks on mentioned, 396, 429; making attacks on more effective, 427, 428
 Thousand attack on: 340, 410–412; failure of, 411, 418, 423, 486; effects of unknown, 486
Eurekas: 348fn
Evill, Air Vice-Marshal C. S.: 136, 367–368

Farbenindustrie, I.G.: 285, 287
Fighter Command: *see also* Fighters: and beginnings of radar, 75; role of, 79, 449–450; priority of, 80, 102, 318; set up, 82–83; effect of separation from Bomber Command, 101fn; superiority of, 101–102; state of, 107–108; relations with Committee for Air Defence, 114; exercises with Bomber Command, 115–116, 445; in Battle of Britain, 147, 151–152, 155, 214, 236; need for, 170, 450; and daylight operations with Bomber Command, 175, 176, 214–215, 236, 351, 437–438; to be conserved, 186; range of, 235, 243, 437, 438, 449–450; need for new equipment and tactics, 238; operational limitations of, 351–352, 437, 454; and Thousand bomber raids, 403, 406fn, 410fn, 414fn; and attack on M.A.N. works, 442
Fighters: (in First World War) do not protect bombers, 44; role of discussed inter-war, 54 ff., 88; plea for more, 76; expected casualties in, 77; priority for, 79, 92; superior to day bomber, 451
 British Day: *see also specific types:* need for, 214; in *Circus* operations, 236–239; free-gun suggested for, 238
 British Night: in First World War, 48
 German: little increase in, 480; on Eastern front, 490
 German Day: *see also specific types:* armament of, 195; tactics of, 199; advantages of, 200; superior to day bomber, 201, 243, 451; estimated strength of, 235; in *Circus* operations, 236 ff.; estimated number of at Brest, 240; protect German warships,

INDEX

Fighters: German Day—*cont.*
241–242; estimated shortage of, 351; estimated losses of, 360; collapse of referred to, 436, 454; number of in West, 490; losses of, 490

German Night: not yet serious factor, 175, 201, 397–398; efficiency of increase, 397–399; in Thousand bomber raids, 408; number of in West, 490; losses of, 490

Long Range: none, 44, 54, 116–117, 126, 191, 450; suggested, 96, 116, 176–177, 242; disadvantages of, 239; indispensable, 356; development of, 455

Fighting Committee: 102
Fire-Raising: *see* Bombs, Incendiary
First Lord of the Admiralty: *see* Alexander
First Sea Lord: *see* Pound
Flares: early trials and discussions of, 123–124, 209–210; early models of, 210; improvement in wanted, 229; in *Shaker* technique, 386–387, 419; in attack on Renault factory, 387–389; use of dummy, 390; in attacks on Essen, 390, (Thousand) 410, 411; in attack on Cologne, 390–391; in attack on Lübeck, 392; not used in Cologne Thousand raid, 405
Fleet Air Arm: rearmament of, 67, 80; Admiralty controls, 83; need for, 170; attack enemy warships, 322
Flensburg: attacked, 432
Fleurus, Battle of: 6
Flying Fortresses: *see* Fortresses
Flying Training Command: set up, 84; and Thousand bomber raids, 403–404, 406fn, 410, 413
Flying Training Schools: description of, 108; increase in, 109–110; navigation training in, 112; night flying facilities in, 113
Foch, Marshal: 40, 41, 64
Focke-Wulf Condors: in Battle of the Atlantic, 59fn, 234; attacks against, 234; results of attacks against, 303–304
Focke-Wulf Factory, Bremen: estimated results of attacks on, 172fn, 301, (Thousand) 487; attacks on, 245–247, (Thousand) 414; results of attacks on, 245, 301, 303–304, 481, (Thousand) 415, 487
Focke-Wulfs: (190s): effect of *Circus* operations on, 437; superiority of, 438fn; in attack on Philips Radio Works, 441; for Western front, 490fn
Forbes Adam, Colonel R.: 90fn
Ford Matford Works, Poissy: 426fn
Foreign Office: on Inskip's air plans, 77; and propaganda leaflets, 105; relations with J.I.C., 261; on German morale, 270, 291, 313, 492; suggests naming targets in advance, 384–385
Forests: suggested attack on, 104fn, 148, 295
Fortresses: armament of, 115, 243fn, 358, 450; in attack on German warships, 240, 241; not suitable for day operations, 243, 454; for Coastal Command, 325fn; Churchill comments on, 355–356, 360; not suitable for night operations, 357; not self-defending, 359, 450; Sinclair's expectations of, 361; Eaker's views on, 451

Four Year Plan: 273–274, 276; and *I.G. Farbenindustrie*, 287; on oil shortage, 289fn; referred to, 477; Speer's position in, 477
Fowler, Professor: 114fn
France: inter-war friction with, 54; friction relaxed, 57; refuelling bases in, 84, 92; staff conversations with, *see that heading*; capitulation of, 145, 146–147; supplies goods to Germany, 275, 279; area bombing of not allowed, 462
Franco-Prussian War: 6
Frankfurt: results of attacks on, 302
Freeman, Air Chief Marshal Sir Wilfrid: importance of, 68; favours twin-engines, 75; mentioned, 121fn; and directive of 15th Jan. 1941, 162; on daylight operations, 176; on use of incendiaries, 252fn; on losses night 7th Nov. 1941, 255–256; and attack on aircraft industry, 294; and Lancasters for day operations, 451–453
French, Lord, 35
French Air Force: subordinated to army, 54fn; size and composition of, 54; estimated bombload of, 62–63; obsolescent, 87, 126
French factories: as targets, 323, 387, 462
'Freya' Devices: 192fn
Funk, Walter: 272

G–H: 316
Gambetta: 6
Gamelin, General: 136, 137, 143
Ganzenmüller, Herr: 482fn
Gas Works: *covered in* German Industry
Gauleiters: position of, 272; reports of, 482, 488; and A.R.P., 483
Gee: for a detailed description *see* Annex I: not yet available, 230, 383; referred to by Lord Cherwell, 248; beginnings of, 248, 382; introduction of, 249, 316, 382–386, 395, 418; proportion of Bomber Command equipped with, 309, 320, 386fn, 389; performance and range of, 309, 321, 333, 346–347, 392, 395–397; short description of, 316; life of, 316, 321, 323, 333, 385–386, 429; effect of on bombing policy, 320–323, 462; mentioned in Singleton report, 338; first uses of, 382, 386fn; in *Shaker* technique, 386–387, 390–391, 410; M.E.W.'s views on, 460; in attacks on Essen, 390, 395, 396, (Thousand) 410–411; in attacks on Cologne, 390–391, 396, (Thousand) 405, 406; in attack on Lübeck, 392; over Ruhr in general, 397; in Thousand raid on Bremen, 414, 415, 416; necessitates target finding force, 418–419; situation after introduction of, 429; jammed, 432
Gelsenkirchen: results of attack on oil plants at, 163–164, 228, 300; oil plants at attacked, 218, 231; estimated results of attack on, 219; proposed attack on, 347fn
General Reconnaissance Aircraft: 67, 325–326
General Staff:
British: (in First World War): on air superiority, 43; (inter-war): views on air warfare, 51, 63, 88, 89, 96–97; oppose

INDEX

General Staff: British—*cont.*
  separate air service, 53; and war plans, 91; on assistance to Poland, 105
  French: on future course of war, 96; on bombing policy, 104, 136–137, 141–142, 143, 145–146; on assistance to Poland, 105
  German: (in First World War): and strategic bombing, 37, 50; (inter-war); on size of German air force, 70fn
Gennevilliers: *see* Gnome and Rhône Works
German Air Force: *see Luftwaffe*
German Economy: *for the results of bombing on the German economy see* Results of Bombing *and* German Industry: believed state of, 135, 280–283, 312, 370–371, 469, 475–476, 488; general description of, 271–280; American appreciation of, 471–472; true state of 1941–1942, 476–478
German Fleet: proposed attacks on, 105, 160, 162; attacks on, 134–135, 192–201, 234, 240–241, 254; percentage of sorties against, 320; Air Staff against attacking, 321
German Industry: proposed attack on (*for more detail see* Ruhr, Oil, Aircraft Industry, *etc.*), 91, 94, 97, 145, 147, 151, 160, 294–295, 370, 373, 461, 466–468, 471; intelligence about, 93, 280–283; less vulnerable than French, 137; expansion of, 271–280, 313, 476–477; description of aluminium in, 292–293; estimated results of attack on, 299fn, 300–301, 478; results of attack on, 301, 478–479; mentioned in Singleton report, 338
German Railways: *see Reichsbahn*
Germany: and disarmament, 58–59; rearms, 60, 66, 67, 68 ff., 86, 272–280; main enemy, 67, 320, 353, 366; threat from, 72, 74, 82, 86–87, 122; reconnaissance over, 122
Gestapo Headquarters: attacked, 439
'Giants': 38, 40, 49
Gien Tank Depot: attack on proposed, 462fn
Gibson, Wing Commander Guy: 433, 446fn
Giffard: 6
Gneisenau: attacked, 167; attack on planned, 240; futility of attacking, 247fn; results of attacking, 305, 322fn; escape of, 322; mentioned in House of Commons, 330
Gnome and Rhône Works, Gennevilliers: 423, 462fn
Goebbels, Josef: tries to organise labour, 277; and effects of bombing, 313; attacks Dorpmüller, 482fn; controls relief organisation, 483; helps Lübeck, 484; and state of Rostock, 485; worried about food shortages, 492
Goering, Hermann: no idea of economics, 272; runs Four Year Plan, 273, 274, 477; sets up Central Planning Committee, 477; appeals to aircraft industry, 480fn; sets up A.R.P. organisation, 482; on location of fighters, 490
Gosport Training School: 60
Gothas: 34–35, 38, 44
Government:
  British: accepts Roosevelt appeal, 134; and

Government: British—*cont.*
  early bombing policy, 145–146; lacks confidence in bombing, 187
  German: welcomes Roosevelt appeal, 134fn
Griffiths, Wing Commander J. F.: 193, 195
Griffon engines: 360
Ground Controlled Interception: 398, 400
Groups:
  1: in attack on Rostock, 394; and Thousand bomber raids, 405, 406, 414, 416fn
  2: and attack on airfields, 148, 214; and attacks on invasion barges, 149, 214, 221; on day operations, 213, 243, 244fn, 439, (*Circus*) 215, 236, 438–439; and reconnaissance photographs, 221; and attack on Essen, 225; and Thousand bomber raids, 403, 406fn; for night operations, 438–439; composition of in 1942, 439; joins 2nd Tactical Air Force, 439, 454fn; in attack on Philips Radio Works, 440–441
  3: reports on daylight actions, 197, 199; takes up night flying, 200, 213; takes up night reconnaissance, 208; in attack on Essen, 224, 225; reports on night accuracy, 228fn; type of Wellington in, 235fn; sends squadrons to Middle East, 257fn; in attack on Renault factory, 388; in attack on Heinkel factory, 394; and Thousand bomber raids, 405, 409, 410, 414
  4: leaflet operations of, 140, 201–205; to investigate conditions at night, 207; night operations of, 213; in attack on Rostock, 394; and Thousand bomber raids, 405, 409
  5: takes up night flying, 200, 213; takes up night reconnaissance, 208; mine-laying of, 215; in attack on Essen, 224, 225; Bottomley commands, 226; views of on night photographs, 251; in attacks on Rostock, 394, 485; and Thousand bomber raids, 405, 406, 409, 414, 415; relations with Pathfinder Force, 433; attacks Danzig, 444; attacks Le Creusot and Montchanin, 445
  6 (Operational Training Group): 250fn
  7 (Operational Training Group): 250fn
  8 (Pathfinder Force): 433fn
  9: 224
  11 (Fighter Command): and *Circus* operations, 215, 236, 237; and attack on German warships, 240
  25 (Armament): 403fn
  91 (Operational Training Group): and Thousand bomber raids, 403–404, 409, 414, 416
  92 (Operational Training Group): and Thousand bomber raids, 403–404, 409, 414
Guns: *see* Armament, Anti-Aircraft Guns, Air Defences

H2S: *for a detailed description see Annex I:* mentioned, 20, 316, 418; beginnings of, 248fn; introduction of delayed, 249; introduction

INDEX

H2S—*cont.*
  of, 309; short description of, 317; not yet available, 432; first use of, 435

Hague Rules: 14

Haig, Field-Marshal Sir Douglas: releases fighters, 36, 37; opposes separate air service, 37; loses Trenchard, 38; on strategic bombing, 39; on air superiority, 43

Halifaxes: beginnings of, 75; number of, 129; robustness hoped for, 176; in attacks on La Pallice, 239–241, 243; coming into service, 330; attack French targets, 387–388; in Thousand raid on Bremen, 414, 415, 416, 426fn; unsuitable for target finding, 430fn; unsuitable for day operations, 454

Hall, Professor: 262, 263fn, 265

Hamborn: attacked in error, 390

Hamburg: results of attacks on, 302–303; first Thousand choice, 405; attacked, 435

Hamm: attacked, 218

Hampdens: not available, 71; beginnings of, 72; role of, 75; number in Bomber Command, 81, 129; only one pilot in, 111; night operations of, 200, 208, 210–211, 213, 215 ff., 231; in *Circus* operations, 237; in other day operations, 448; in attack on German warships, 240, 241; taken out of service, 309; for Coastal Command, 328fn; and Thousand bomber raids, 403, 410fn, 414; not suitable for day operations, 454; unsuitable for target finding, 430fn

Hancock, Sir Keith: 271, 282fn

Handley-Page Bomber: 40, 49fn

Hankey, Lord, (*formerly Sir Maurice. See also* Hankey Committee*)*: chairs targets committee, 93fn; and incendiary bomb experiments, 124fn; and attack on oil, 158, 168, 266, 291, 300, 347fn; oil committee under, 265

Hankey Committee: set up, 265; Lloyd Committee advises, 265, 266, 285; disagreements with, 266; and attack on oil, 289–291

Hanover: proposed attack on, 461, 467fn, 468

Harriman, Averell: 492fn

Harris, Air Chief Marshal Sir Arthur: views on air power, 10; mentioned, 28, 90fn; on light bombers, 72fn; on flare trials, 123, 124fn; sends directive of 18th March 1941, 167; no longer D.C.A.S., 174; on use of cameras, 179fn, 426–427; and daylight actions, 200–201, 452–454; on navigation, 217, 435; on results of night bombing, 220, 225, 346, 421, 424–429; leaves 5 Group, 226; becomes Commander-in-Chief, Bomber Command, 257, 310, 323fn; and attack on oil, 291fn, 346, 347; effect of victories of, 311, 340, 394; and the note on the directive of 14th Feb. 1942, 324, 346; Churchill praises, 328fn, 355; realises need for action, 339; views of on strategy, 340–343, 346, 376, 377–378; relations with Churchill, 340, 464; on diversions from Bomber Command, 341, 416; on attack on Lübeck, 341, 348, 391, 478; on production and expansion for Bomber Command,

Harris, Air Chief Marshal Sir Arthur—*cont.*
  341, 344, 402; in position to affect policy, 345, 348; character of, 345–346; advocates area attack, 346, 422, 470; and the war at sea, 346; not responsible for area bombing, 346; and attack on ball-bearings, 347–348, 349, 464, 466; relations with M.E.W., 348, 463–465; relations with Air Staff, 348, 453–454; and 'panacea' targets, 349; and attack on aircraft industry, 351; on *Gee*, 384, 385; objects to naming targets in advance, 384–385; on minelaying, 385, 412, 417; views of on operational feasibility, 385, 464, 466; and German air defences, 397, 400; and *Window*, 401; and the Thousand bomber raids, 402–406, 410, 412–414, 416; on size and composition of Bomber Command, 416–417; on casualties, 417; on weather factors, 417, 470; and target finding force, 420–424, 429–431; on attack on Mannheim, 424–425; on attacks on Rostock, 425, 478; and Pathfinder Force, 431–432, 433fn, 434; and Lancasters for day operations, 451–453, 454fn; and attack on M.A.N. factory, 463–464; relations with Eaker, 471; on Emden, 478; on Cologne, 478; recognises speed of recovery in bombed towns, 478

Harrows: 71, 79

Hartley, Sir Harold: 266

Harts: 71

Hawkers: 71

Heinkel Factory, Rostock: attacked, 339, 393–394; attack on mentioned, 348; results of attack on, 481, 485

Heinkels: Mk. III: 59fn, 125

Henderson, Sir David: 35, 39

Hermann Goering Works: 274

Heyfords: 71

Higgins, Air Marshal Sir John: 109fn

Hildebrandt, Gauleiter: 485

Hinds: 71

Hipper: 167

Hitler, Adolf: on size of German air force, 69, 70fn; on German bombing policy, 136fn; victorious position of, 146, 275–276; and Battle of Britain, 155; and transport problems, 171; no idea of economics, 272; plans *Blitzkrieg*, 272, 273; on armament production, 276; likes women at home, 277; and supply of labour, 278fn; orders ammunition reduction, 280; and aluminium production, 292; and effects of bombing, 313; declares war on U.S.A., 319; and aircraft industry, 480; gives Goebbels relief organisation, 483; helps Lübeck, 484; and Thousand raid on Cologne, 486fn; demands anti-aircraft guns, 491

Holland: collapse of, 144

Homberg: oil plant at attacked, 231, 232

Hong Kong: surrender of, 328

Hopgood, Flight Lieutenant J. V.: 446

Hopkins, Harry L.: 360, 367, 472

Hörnum: attacked, 140, 210–211; results of attack on, 163, 211, 216, 221fn

House of Commons: Baldwin's statements in,

House of Commons—*cont.*
66, 68–69, 70, 99; priority to fighters revealed in, 102; statements on bombing policy in, 328–329, 330–331
Hudsons: 403, 413
Hughes, Colonel: 471
Hull: Cherwell analyses raids on, 331–332; R.E.8 analyses raid on, 474
Hüls: proposed attack on, 462fn, 467fn
Hurricanes: superiority of, 71, 96, 101; for Fighter Command, 80

Independent Air Force: established, 39; size and composition of, 39, 43, 45fn; raids of, 40, 41, 47, 48; losses of, 41; used photographic reconnaissance, 121
'Independent' Operations: discussed, 8 ff., 13; issue never settled, 336; related to targets, 349
Industrial Damage Reports: 267fn, 474
Industrial Targets Reports: 267fn, 299, 300
Industrial Intelligence Centre: set up, 93; relations with J.I.C., 261; supplies information to Hankey Committee, 265; on oil stocks, 288
Industrial Intelligence Committee: 92, 260
Inland Transport Section, M.E.W.: 266
Inskip, Sir Thomas: 45, 74, 76–77
Intelligence: discussion of, 11, 23 ff.; organisation of, 92–93, 261–262, 260 ff.; on results of early attacks, 145, 157, 219–221, 267, 299 ff.; on oil (*for more detail see* Oil), 151, 158, 222, 282, 347; on German morale (*for more detail see* Morale), 169, 297, 350; on German air strength, 175fn, 235, 263, 351; indispensable from M.E.W., 264; on communications, 266; on German industry generally, 93, 280–283; on ball-bearings, 347; relative importance of in selective and area attack, 349–350
Invasion Barges: proposed attack against, 148, 149; attacked, 318
Invasion of England: necessary conditions for, 147; possibility affects bombing policy, 148, 153, 160, 162, 318; threat of recedes, 152, 155–156, 160; estimated effect of bombing on, 305fn
Island of Sylt: *see* Hörnum
Ismay, Sir Hastings: 164
Italian Air Force: 57, 87, 125–126
Italy: as potential enemy, 65; threat from, 74; enters war, 146; attacks on, 157, 215, 463
Ivelaw-Chapman, Wing Commander R.: 209–210

Jade Roads: daylight operations in, 195–201
Japan: air force of, 57; threat from, 60, 65, 72, 74, 86; attacks Pearl Harbour, 319; policy for waging war against, 320, 353, 366; entry into war affects Bomber Command, 325–327; victories of, 328; threats to agreed policy for waging war against, 329, 353–354, 376
Jena: proposed attack on, 461, 467fn
Joint Intelligence Committee: set up, 261;

Joint Intelligence Committee—*cont.*
relations with M.E.W., 262, 264, 458; relations with Lloyd Committee, 266; reports on oil, 266, 480; and bombing directives, 269; reports on German industry, 281, 299, 301; reports on German economy, 312, 458; committees under, 458; on effect of air attacks on morale, 492
Joint Planning Committee: established, 87; report on air threat, 89–90; mentioned, 97; on bombing policy, 99; and assistance to Poland, 105; workings of, 261; and bombing directives, 269; on German oil situation, 282. *Now see* Joint Planning Staff
Joint Planning Staff (previously Joint Planning Committee): on situation in Germany, 282; on German morale, 297; on attacks on communications, 297; on estimated effects of bombing, 299
Joint Staff Mission, British: 367
Jones, Professor Melvill: 114fn
Joubert, Air Chief Marshal Sir Philip: 83fn 403, 413
Jourdan, General: 6
Junkers (88): 125, 480, 490fn

Karlsruhe: relief measures for, 483fn
Kaufmann, Gauleiter Karl: 484fn
Kellet, Wing Commander R.: 193, 195
Kiel: 148, 303
Kiel Canal: 105
King, Admiral E. J.: 353–354, 367
King, Rt. Hon. W. L. MacKenzie: 110fn
King of Spain: 50
Kitchener, Lord: 17
'Knock-Out Blow': fear of, 76–78, 80, 88–90, 134; Bomber Command useless against, 96
Koerner, Hans: 477
Krupps Works: attacked night 7th Nov. 1940, 224–225; results of accidental attack on, 305; in Thousand attack, 411

La Pallice: daylight attacks against, 239–341, 243; results of attacks against, 305
La Rochelle: proposed attack against, 346
Labour, German: not fully mobilised, 277–278
Lancasters: beginnings of, 75; coming into service, 254, 330, 417fn; Bottomley comments on, 254fn; numbers of, 309, 452; suggested that Americans build, 357; ideal bomber, 357; in Thousand bomber raids, 403fn, 416; not available for target finding, 430fn; in attack on M.A.N. works, 441–444; attack Danzig, 444; attack Le Creusot and Montchanin, 445–446; on day operations, 448, 454; no equal in Germany, 480 Mk. II: specially armoured, 451–454
Lang Motorenfabrik: 305
Lawrence, O. L.: position of, 264, 458; on estimated effects of attacking aircraft industry, 299fn; on *Bomber's Baedeker*, 470fn
Le Creusot, Schneider Armaments Arsenal: attacked, 445–446, 447; results of attack on, 446
Leaflets: *see* Propaganda
League of Nations: 58–60

INDEX

Learoyd, Flight Lieutenant R. A. B.: 305
Lehrdivision: 120fn
Leigh-Mallory, Air Vice-Marshal T. L.: 237–238, 239
Leuna: 220
Liberators: 325fn., 357
Lightnings, P-38s: 450
Lille: attacked, 441
Lindbergh, Colonel: 108
Lloyd, Group Captain H. P.: 207, 248fn
Lloyd, Geoffrey: *see also* Lloyd Committee: and attack on oil, 158, 160, 161fn, 290, 291fn, 300; committee under, 265; concentrates on occupied countries, 266fn
Lloyd Committee: estimates results of oil attack, 159–161, 300; set up, 265, 285; influence of, 266; end of, 266; on German chemical industry, 286fn; estimates of successful, 288; on oil stocks, 288–289; and attack on oil, 289–291
Lloyd George, Rt. Hon. David: 37, 38
Locarno, Treaties of: 57, 67
Lockheeds: 122
London: (in First World War): attacked, 34, 35, 36, 37, 38; mentioned, 46, 47; size of, 50; (inter-war): air threat to, 88, 89, 90, 99, 100; (in Second World War): attacked, 152
London Conference: 59
Londonderry, Lord: 70
Longbottom, Flying Officer M. V.: 122
Lord Privy Seal: *see* Cripps
Lords-Lieutenant: 109
Lorient: proposed attack on, 346
Lübeck: attacked, 310, 328fn, 339, 391–393, 398; vulnerability of, 324, 391–393; Harris' views on, 341, 348, 391, 478; attack on referred to, 347, 395, 402, 418, 424; estimated results of attack on, 392–393, 484; results of attack on, 393fn, 478, 483–484, 488; aid for, 483, 484; recovery of, 484
Ludlow-Hewitt, Air Chief Marshal Sir Edgar: on bombing policy, 79–80, 99–101, 140; on state of Bomber Command, 95–96, 100, 125; on protection for bombers, 96, 116; suggests leaflet dropping, 100, 105; fears effect of fighter priority, 102; on demarcation of responsibility, 103; on state of navigation, 112, 115, 217; on state of armament training, 115, 116; on bomb aiming, 117fn, 118–119; suggests harassing bombing, 118fn; presses for Bombing Development Unit, 119–120; on need for photographic reconnaissance, 122; on realistic exercises, 124; views on Ruhr plan, 138–139, 201; and night operations, 140–141, 201, 206–207, 208, 210, 215; leaves Bomber Command, 141; and self-defending bomber formations, 177, 198, 199; wants 'speed bomber', 191; and daylight actions, 195, 201; and target identification, 205, 207, 208
Luftwaffe: (*includes all references to German air force*): and air superiority, 21; abolished, 53; role of, 66, 68; estimated size of, 69–70, 71fn, 73, 86, 175fn, 235, 337; estimated plans of, 77; incapable of knock-out blow,

Luftwaffe—cont.
78; as first target, 90, 91, 94, 95; estimated potentiality of, 99, 104; position of pilot in, 112fn; designed for army co-operation, 125, 490; loses opportunity, 126; superior in strength, 134, 143; and restricted bombing, 134–135; Hitler instruction for, 136–137fn; in attack on Low Countries, 144; in Battle of Britain, 147, 151–152, 155, 238; effect on of attack on aircraft industry, 147–148; effect on of attack on oil, 149; and reprisal raids, 153, 161; and invasion of Russia, 175; attacks of affect British plans, 181, 252–253; attempt to bring to battle (*Circus* operations), 175, 214, 437–438; technique of in area attack, 252–253; mentioned, 273, 477; and oil, 287, 292; mobility of, 294; and necessity to destroy, 350–351, 352, 362–363; estimated shortage of fighters in, 351; suggested attack on, 471; German policy for, 480; effect on of increased British air attack, 490
Lutterade: attacked, 435
Lyttelton, Rt. Hon. Oliver: 367–368

M.A.N. Factory, Augsburg: attacked, 363, 441–444, 447; results of attack on, 443, 464–465fn; attack on referred to, 451, 453; dispute about attack on, 463–464; attack on cannot be repeated, 466
MacArthur, General Douglas: 353–354
Machine-Tools, German: plenty, 276, 277; industry inaccurately assessed, 281, 470
Maintenance: lack of, 84
Maintenance Command: 83
Malkin, Sir William: 99, 105
Manchesters: beginnings of, 75; numbers of, 129; fail, 240; coming into service, 330; attack French targets, 387–388; attack Lübeck, 392; and Thousand bomber raids, 403fn; unsuitable for target finding, 430fn
Mannheim: attacked, 163, 215, 225–226; results of attack on, 163, 226–227, 302, 305, 424–425; attack on mentioned, 230, 253, 382; attack on discussed, 424–425
Manual of Air Tactics: attack on forests in, 104fn; bomb aiming in, 117, 118; types of bombs in, 124
Marshall, General G. C.: 471
Marshalling Yards: *covered by* Communications
Martin, Squadron Leader H. B.: 433
Marwood-Elton, Wing Commander N. W. D.: 423fn
Medhurst, Air Vice-Marshal C. E. H.: 70fn, 263
Merlin engines: 360
Messerschmitts: in early daylight actions, 196, 197; in *Circus* operations, 237
109s: in early daylight actions, 192, 193, 194, 199, 241; Mk. F superior to Spitfire, 236; in attack on M.A.N. works, 443
110s: in early daylight actions, 193, 194, 199, 201; as night fighters, 490fn
Meteorological Office: 61
Middle East: air power in, 53; Bomber

Middle East—*cont.*
  Command aircraft and crews for, 257, 310, 318, 342 344fn, 416, 447, 452; Harris demands return of aircraft from, 341; and return of aircraft to Bomber Command, 343
Milch, General Erhard: on size of German air force, 73; on lack of labour, 278fn; and effects of bombing, 313; on Central Planning Committee, 477; work of, 480
Milne, Sir George: 64
Minelaying: in directive of 20th June 1940, 148; in directive of 13th July 1940, 149; by 5 Group, 215; results of, 303; mentioned, 385
Minister for the Co-ordination of Defence: *see* Inskip
Minister for Weapons and Munitions, Germany: *see* Speer
Minister of Economic Warfare: *see* Dalton, Selborne
Minister of Labour, Germany: *see* Sauckel
Minister of Munitions: *see* Churchill
Minister of Transport, Germany: *see* Dorpmüller
Ministerial Committee on Disarmament: 67fn
Ministry of Aircraft Production: 334, 343–344
Ministry of Economic Warfare: absorbs intelligence organisation, 93, 260; work and organisation of, 260–267, 312, 458 ff.; relations with Air Ministry, 261, 262, 263–264, 265, 270, 459, 460; relations with J.I.C., 262, 458; relations with services, 262, 263, 458; subsidiary role in oil, 265; subsidiary role in communications, 266; produces damage assessment reports, 267, 299, 465fn, 474–475; relations with Bomber Command, 270, 348, 459, 460, 463–465, 466; views of on German economy and target selection, 280, 281–282, 288, 291, 294, 295, 296, 301fn, 312, 347, 459–462, 466–470, 475–476; and attack on M.A.N. works, 441fn, 463–464; little part in offensive against Italy, 463; advisory role of, 465; relations with U.S.A., 471; and Combined Bomber Offensive, 472; estimates number of German submarines, 481; recognises German transport efficient, 481; estimates results of attack on Lübeck, 484; estimates results of attacks on Rostock, 485; estimates results of Thousand attack on Cologne, 486; estimates effect of Thousand attack on Bremen, 487fn; estimates effect of attacking Düsseldorf, 487–488; estimates effect of attack on Renault works, 489
Ministry of Home Security: works on damage assessment, 267–268, 473; assesses need for A.A. guns, 467–468
Ministry of Information: 270
Ministry of Munitions: 36
Mitchell, Brigadier-General: 61
Mitchells: 439
Mittelland Canal: proposed attack on, 296
Möhne Dam: suggested attack on, 98; attack on mentioned, 446fn
Molotov: 375fn
Montchanin: attacked, 445–446, 447; results of attack on, 446

Montgomery-Massingberd, General Sir Archibald: 87
Morale: estimated effect of attacks on, 45–47, 63–64, 150–151, 152, 183, 184, 297, 301, 313, 332, 354fn, 366, 492; as bombing target, 156–157, 160–161, 162, 168–171, 174, 177, 180–185, 234, 252, 291, 295–298, 323–324, 345, 350, 359, 366, 368, 373, 378, 459, 492; attack on connected with communications, 173; of Bomber Command crews, 197, 256; assessment of British, 270; definition of, 297–298; German weaker than British, 297; effect of attacks on, 301, 313, 492; mentioned in Singleton report, 338
Morton, Major D. F.: 93, 261
Mosquitoes: origins of, 72; and harassing bombing, 118fn, 439fn; for reconnaissance, 243 fn, 268; for day bomber, 244fn; numbers of, 309; the *Oboe* force, 309; and Thousand bomber raids, 407, 414fn; in 2 Group, 439; attack *Gestapo* H.Q., 439; in attack on Philips Radio Works, 440, 441; on day operations, 448, 454; no equal in Germany, 480
München Gladbach: attacked, 382
Munich Crisis: 79, 80, 94, 99, 100, 103, 105
Münster: 301
Mustangs: beginnings of, 126; suggested that British build, 357, 359, 360; ideal, 357; engines of, 360; (P-51) neglected, 450

Napoleonic War: 9, 50
National Socialist Party: 272
Naval Blockade: 50, 260
Naval Staff: oppose separate air service, 38, 53; views on air warfare, 51, 89, 124, 372; and expansion, 74; and war plans, 91; and requirements for the war at sea, 325–327, 337
Naval Targets: *see also* German Fleet, Submarines: proposed attack on, 148, 161, 164–165, 346; attacks on, 167–168, 234, 355; results of attacks on, 303, 305–306
Naval Wing: 34
Navigation: difficulties not appreciated, 47–48, 60–61, 110–112, 202, 204; training and research in, 110–115, 204; state of, 112, 115, 129, 204–205, 383–384, 402; problem first realised, 180, 205, 227, 229, 250, 382; in night precision bombing, 208, 217, 219–221, 224–232; beginnings of aids to (*for more detail see* Gee, H2S, Oboe), 248–250
Navigation Officer, Bomber Command: *see* Ivelaw-Chapman
Navigators: need for recognised, 111; shortage of, 112; duties and training of, 112–113; problems of, 114; and using *Gee*, 396, 430fn
Nettleton, Squadron Leader J. D.: 442–444, 445, 443fn
New Zealand: and air training scheme, 110
Newall, Air Chief Marshal Sir Cyril: on expected aircraft casualties, 77, 119fn; on mobilisation of Bomber Command, 80; on command organisation, 82; on role of Bomber Command, 101; and division of responsibility, 103; mentioned, 121fn; discards Ruhr plan, 139; and oil intelligence, 265

INDEX

Night Flying: training in, 113
New York Times: 329
Norway: invaded, 141
Nuremberg: results of attacks on, 302

Objectives Department, Ministry of Economic Warfare: work of, 264, 458; relations with Bomber Command, 459fn; realise operational conditions predominant, 460; estimates effect of bombing submarines, 481fn; on effects of bombing Ruhr, 482
Oboe: for a detailed description see Annex I: Mosquitoes equipped with, 309; short description of, 316–317; introduction of, 316; only few aircraft can use, 418; not yet available, 432; squadron equipped with, 433; first use of, 435
Observers: 72, 111, 116
Oil: proposed attack on, 103–104, 139, 141–143, 145, 146–147, 148, 149, 151, 153, 156–165, 230–232, 266, 289–292, 346–347, 461, 480; estimated results of attack on, 158–159, 168, 219–220, 300, 473; results of attack on, 163–164, 168, 221fn, 222–224, 228, 290, 291fn, 300; sorties flown against, 164; attack on resisted, 168, 291, 480; disadvantages of attack on, 173; attack on, 215, 218, 231, 234; aiming error in attacks on, 247; intelligence machinery for, 265–266; supply in Germany expanded, 273–274, 275, 280; intelligence about, 282, 288–292, 347, 480; general description of industry, 285–288; stocks of estimated, 288–289, 300, 479; effect of invasion of Russia on, 291, 479; situation of in 1942, 479
'Operational' factors: discussed, 17 ff.
Operational Research Section, Bomber Command: set up, 251, 312; work of, 270fn, 383–384, 407, 423fn, 473, 474; on attack on M.A.N. works, 443; on Le Creusot operation, 446; on *Circus* operations, 449
Operational Training Groups: *see* 6, 7, 91 and 92 Groups
Operational Training Units: send crews to Middle East, 257; in Thousand bomber raids, 403–404, 408fn, 409, 414, 416; in attacks on Düsseldorf, 417, 487; to reinforce target finding force, 420
Oxland, Air Vice-Marshal R. D.: 231, 428

Packard-Merlin engines: 320
'Panacea' Targets: *see* Bottlenecks
Parity: aim of announced, 66; with German air force, 68–81, 107
Parliament: *see* House of Commons
Pas de Calais area: proposed daylight operations in, 176; daylight operations in, 236 ff.
Pathfinder Force: *see also* Target Finding Force: creation of, 249, 309, 397, 431–432; insignia of, 429fn; promotion in, 431–432; first operation of, 432; quality of crews in, 432, 433; equipment of, 432; results following, 433–435
Pavlov: 375fn

Pearl Harbour: 319, 328
Peirse, Air Marshal Sir Richard: mentioned, 103; on harassing bombing, 118fn; on possible casualties, 119fn; discusses flares, 123; and attack on oil, 141, 163, 173, 230; and bombing policy, 143, 152, 154, 186; becomes Commander-in-Chief, Bomber Command, 154; and draft directive of 25th Oct. 1940, 155–157; receives directive of 30th Oct. 1940, 157; receives directive of 10th Nov. 1940, 158; receives directive of 15th Jan. 1941, 162; and finding the target, 156, 163, 178, 220, 228, 383; and the war at sea, 165, 167–168, 234; receives directive of 9th March 1941, 165; receives directive of 18th March 1941, 167; allowed to return to industrial targets, 168; receives directive of 9th July 1941, 174; on day bombing, 176, 213; comments on Butt report, 179; and operations of night 7th Nov. 1941, 186, 254–257; receives directive of 13th Nov. 1941, 186; and attack on Mannheim, 226, 228, 254; asks for Mosquitoes, 243fn; says Fortress unsuitable for day work, 243; on navigation, 250, 383; sceptical of area technique, 253–254; and the Lancaster, 254fn; assessment of, 256–257; leaves Bomber Command, 257, 323fn; and training, 256; and expansion of Bomber Command, 319; speech of, 399
Philips Radio Works: attacked, 439–441; results of attack on, 440
Phillips, Captain T. S. V.: 90fn
Photographic Interpretation: machinery for, 268–269
Photographic Interpretation Section: 163–164
Photographic Reconnaissance: *see also* Photographs, Cameras: importance of, 25, 30; role of, 29–30; beginnings of, 121–123, 268, 299; in Hörnum attack, 140, 211, 216, 221fn; of Mannheim, 226–227, 228, 424–425; of Gelsenkirchen, 228, 231, 234, 300; of F.W. factory, 245; of Cologne, 340, (Thousand) 407, 486; of Renault factory, 388; of Lübeck, 392–393, 484fn; of Rostock, 394, 485; of Thousand raid on Essen, 411; of Thousand raid on Bremen, 415; of Philips Radio Works, 440; of Le Creusot operation, 446
Photographic Reconnaissance Unit: formed (as Flight), 221; takes Mannheim photographs, 226; takes oil photographs, 228; results of forming, 229; weather impedes, 231; tasks of, 251fn
Photographs:
  Day: need for, 214, 221, 223; role of, 221; quality of, 221, 222; interpretation of, 268–269, 474–475; defects of, 269; evidence of, 301, 473
  Night: analysed in Butt report, 178–179, 247; role of, 221, 250–251, 426–427; significance not realised, 222, 225; shortage of, 301–302; of attack on Renault factory, 388; of attacks on Essen, 389, 423fn, (Thousand) 411; of attacks on Cologne, 390–391, 396, (Thousand) 407; of attack on Lübeck, 392; of attacks

INDEX

Photographs: Night—*cont.*
  on Rostock, 393–394, 423fn; of Ruhr, 395; of Thousand raid on Bremen, 415; of attack on Gennevilliers, 423fn; analysed after creation of Pathfinder Force, 434
Pilots: shortage of, 72, 79; more needed, 108–109; increase in, 110; as navigators, 110–111; second introduced, 111; captain aircraft, 112fn; second dropped, 309
Ploesti: cannot be attacked, 347, 348
Poland: air force of, 87; guarantees to, 105; German attack on, 134–135
Police Presidents: *see* Gauleiters
Political Intelligence Department, Foreign Office: 270
Pölitz: proposed attack on, 347
Portal, Marshal of the Royal Air Force Sir Charles: becomes Commander-in-Chief, Bomber Command, 141; and attack on oil, 141, 145, 151, 159–161, 162–165, 168, 216, 222, 223, 346–347, 480; receives directive of 13th April 1940, 142–143, 212; mentioned, 145; receives directive of 20th June 1940, 147; receives directive of 4th July 1940, 148; and directive of 13th July 1940, 149–151; receives directive of 24th July 1940, 151; receives directive of 21st Sept. 1940, 153; and retaliatory raids, 153–154, 168; becomes C.A.S., 154; and draft directive of 25th Oct. 1940, 155–156; and the war at sea, 164–165, 235, 322, 325, 327, 339, 346fn; on priority for Bomber Command, 170; and day bombing, 176, 213, 242–243, 453–454; views on long-range fighters, 177, 239, 242, 359, 363, 449; and expansion of Bomber Command, 177, 182, 185, 319, 365–370, 476; and the Butt report, 179–180, 248; and bombing policy, 182–185, 186, 322–324, 344, 346, 359, 368–372, 458–459, 468; asks for oil expert, 222; and 'speed' bomber, 242–243; and armament for bombers, 243; and aids to navigation and target location, 248; and actions of night 7th Nov. 1941, 254–256; suggests attacking chemical plants, 286fn; comments on Cherwell calculations, 332; and the Singleton report, 337fn, 339; views of on American daylight plan, 356–357, 358–359, 360, 361–363, 364, 375, 435, 449, 454; views of on German night defence, 359; strategic views of, 364–370, 373–374, 377–378; views of on German economy, 370, 476; on petrol shortage, 373fn; and Thousand bomber raids, 402–403, 412, 417; and target finding force, 429–431; relations with Harris, 454; and attack on M.A.N. factory, 463; and target selection, 468; and German civil defence, 483; and estimates of effects of attacks on Düsseldorf, 488; claims diversion of fighters to west, 490
Pound, Admiral of the Fleet Sir Dudley: and attack on morale, 170; and the war at sea, 326–327, 338–339; on role of heavy bomber, 330fn; on role of strategic air offensive, 371–372, 374; and Thousand raid on Bremen, 413

Power Plants: *see also* Ruhr: proposed attack on, 98, 461, 471; result of attack on, 168
Prime Minister: *see* Lloyd George, Baldwin, Neville Chamberlain, Churchill
Prince of Wales: 328
Prinz Eugen: 240, 306fn
Propaganda: as war weapon, 100; leaflets prepared, 105–106; leaflets dropped, 135, 140, 190, 201–205; exaggerates German rearmament, 272
Pye, Dr.: 114fn

R.D.F.: 101
R.E.8: *see* Research and Experiments Department, Ministry of Home Security
Radar: *see also* Gee, H2S, Oboe
  British: beginnings of, 74, 205; in Battle of Britain, 397
  German: *see also* Air Defences, German: early use of, 191–192, 199; in *Circus* operations, 236–237; against night bomber, 398
Railway Research Service: 266, 296
Railways: *covered by* Communications
Rearmament: of Germany, 60, 66, 67, 68–70, 86, 272–280; of Britain, 66, 67 ff.
Reconnaissance: *see also* Photographic Reconnaissance: at night, 207–208; of Bremen, 414
Reichsbahn: 279, 481
Renault Factory, Billancourt: attacked, 310, 339, 387–389, 489fn; attack on mentioned, 301, 311, 393, 395, 424; results of attack on, 388–389, 482, 489; attack on improves morale, 428; attack on proposed, 462fn; estimated results of attack on, 489
Repulse: 328
Research: need for, 52; lack of, 60
Research and Experiments Department, Ministry of Home Security: work of, 267–268, 312, 473–474; position of, 473fn; estimates effect of Thousand attack on Cologne, 486; estimates effect of attacking Düsseldorf, 487, 488
Reserve Command: 83, 110
Results of Bombing: *for more detail see individual targets and target systems:* appreciation of discussed, 29–31; first World War experience of, 49; disappointing, 131–132; early beliefs in, 145, 157, 158–159, 219–220, 267, 280–281, 299–301; first evidence of, 163–164, 168, 222, 226–227, 299–306; machinery for assessing, 267–269, 312–313, 473–475, 482; up to end of 1942, 313, 473, 478–492; discussed in *Bomber's Baedeker,* 469
Robb, Air Vice-Marshal J. M.: 231
Robertson, General Sir W. R.: 37
Roe, A. V. Ltd.: 109fn
Rommel, General: 328
Roosevelt, President: appeals for restricted bombing, 134–135; views of on German morale, 169; receives messages from Churchill, 328fn, 355–356; and *Torch,* 355; and Oliver Lyttelton, 367; at Casablanca Conference, 379; and air superiority, 471
Rostock: estimated results of attacks on, 301,

INDEX

Rostock—*cont.*
485; attacked, 310, 339, 393–394; attacks on mentioned, 311, 348, 395, 418, 424; Harris' views on, 341, 425, 478; Bufton's views on, 423; results of attacks on, 478, 485, 488
Rothermere, Lord: 38–39
Rotterdam: attacked, 144
Rouen: attacked, 355
Round-Up: 376
Rowe, A. P.: 75, 114fn
Royal Air Force: and air superiority, 21; origins of, 35, 37–38; birth of, 38; main role in First World War, 41; state and composition of inter-war, 52 ff., 57, 59–60; 65–81; independence of threatened, 53; strategy for, 54 ff., 62–81, 86, 88–92; organisation of commands in, 82–83; funds for, 88; training in, *see* Training.
Royal Air Force Delegation, Washington: 329
Royal Air Force Volunteer Reserve: 84
Royal Flying Corps: reinforced, 34; merged in R.A.F., 35; role of, 35–36; mentioned, 37
Royal Navy: *see also* Naval Staff: rearmament of, 80; vulnerability of, 86; role of, 90, 155
Royal Naval Air Service: merged into R.A.F., 35; role of, 36; night flying of, 47–48; attacks Zeppelin sheds, 48
Rubber: proposed attack on, 461, 467fn, 468, 471
Ruhr: proposed attack on, 94, 97–98, 100, 136–140, 141, 142, 143, 191, 197, 201, 284fn, 461; first attacks on, 144; first attacks on affect Prime Minister, 161; in attack on communications, 172, 174; difficulty of finding targets in, 178, 247; reconnaissance of marshalling yards in, 207; results of attack on, 482; estimated effects of attacks on, 482
Rumania: supplies oil for Germany, 275, 479; transport of oil from, 287, 290; unknown supplies from, 288; suggested action against oil from, 289–291; invulnerable, 292; importance of attacking oil in, 347, 480
Russia: possible threat from, 86; invaded, 175, 234, 235, 276, 291; provides Germany with raw materials, 275; *Blitzkrieg* fails in, 319
Russian Air Force: 126, 341

St. Nazaire: 346
Salisbury Committee: 53
Salmond, Sir John: 39, 44fn, 57–58fn
Sampson Technique: 429
Sauckel, Fritz: 278fn, 477
Saundby, Air Vice-Marshal R. H. M. S.: and Committee for Air Offence, 114fn; on photographic evidence, 179; on day bombing, 235; on *Circus* operations, 236, 437
Scapa Flow: 140
Scharnhorst: proposed attack on, 148, 239–240; attacked, 167, 241; moves to La Pallice, 240; moves to Brest, 241fn; compared with attack on F.W. factory, 246; futility of attacking, 247fn; results of attacking, 305–

Scharnhorst—cont.
306; escapes from Brest, 322; mentioned in House of Commons, 330
Scheer: 192fn
Schemes A: 67, 108; C: 70–71; D: 71fn; E: 71fn; F: 70–71, 72, 73, 74, 76; G: 73; H: 73, 74; J: 73, 74, 76fn; K: 77; L: 79; M: 80
Schillig Roads: daylight actions in, 193–200
Scholven oil plant: 220
School of Photography, Farnborough: 121, 122
Schneider Armaments Arsenal: *see* Le Creusot
Schweinfurt: proposed attack on, 294, 324, 347–348, 461, 463, 464, 466–467; population of, 348
Sea Lion: 155
Second Front: 368fn, 375
Second Tactical Air Force: 439
Secretary of State for Air: *see* Rothermere (Jan.–April 1918), Weir (to end of 1918), Churchill (1919), Londonderry (from Nov. 1931), Swinton (from June 1935), Wood (from May 1938), Sinclair (from May 1940)
Secretary of State for War: *see* Churchill
Selborne, Lord: briefed on M.E.W., 263; briefed on M.E.W.'s influence, 270; hopes of influence of, 460; and attack on M.A.N. factory, 463–464; and attack on ball-bearings, 466, 467
'Self-defending' bomber formations: *see* Bombers, Day
Senior Air Staff Officer, Bomber Command: *see* Bottomley (from Nov. 1938), Saundby (from Nov. 1940)
Shaker Technique: description of, 386–387; in attacks on Essen, 289–390, (Thousand raid), 410; in attack on Cologne, 390–391; success following, 395, 418; limitations of, 396; target finding principle follows, 419, 421; recommended by Carr, 429; mentioned, 434
Simon, Sir John: 69
Sinclair, Sir Archibald: and attack on oil, 158, 168, 300, 346–347; and the war at sea, 164, 325–327, 335; and attack on morale, 169; and expansion of Bomber Command, 177, 343; and bombing policy, 186, 244, 320–322, 324, 345, 462, 467; on day bombing, 242, 243; and relations with M.E.W., 262, 263; statements of in House of Commons, 330–331; and Cherwell's calculations, 332, 334; and the American day plan, 358, 360–361; and *Window*, 401
Singapore: fall of, 328
Singleton, Mr. Justice: reports on bombing, 337–339; his report referred to, 369, 465; asks advice from M.E.W., 465; on morale, 492
Slessor, Air Vice-Marshal J. C.: on fear of air raids, 45fn; and choice of targets, 94; on co-operation between Fighter and Bomber Commands, 101fn; asks about ability of Fighter Command, 101; and division of responsibility, 103; on bombing policy, 135, 137; on day bombing, 242, 437; and

INDEX

Slessor, Air Vice-Marshal J. C.—*cont.*
intelligence on oil, 265; views of on American daylight plan, 357–358, 359–360; and 'second front', 375fn; on grand strategy, 376–377; on use of night cameras, 426fn

Smuts, General: 10, 37–38

Sorpe Dam: 98

Speer, Albert: on lack of labour, 278fn; criticises industry, 278; and effects of bombing, 313; reorganises industry, 313, 476–477; appointments of, 477; mentioned, 480

Spitfires: superiority of, 71, 96, 101; for Fighter Command, 80; for reconnaissance, 122, 221, 268 (*now see* Photographic Reconnaissance Unit); operating with Bomber Command, 191, (*Circus*) 236–237; Mk. V inferior to Messerschmitt, 236; and attack on German warships, 240; range of, 450; operate with Americans, 451

Squadrons: 10: 419fn; 15: 257fn; 37: 257fn; 38: 257fn; 40: 257fn; 44: 442fn; 51: 328fn; 57: 257fn; 58: 328fn; 76: 419fn; 77: 328fn; 82: 214; 88: 439fn; 97: 442fn; 105: 439fn; 109: 433; 115: 224, 257fn; 144: 328fn; 214: 224; 304: 328fn; 311: 328fn; 405 (R.C.A.F.): 420fn; 408: 410fn; 617: 433

Staff Conversations: with France, 87, 92, 105fn, 136–137

Stalin, Marshal Joseph: Harris wants bombers from, 341; wants Berlin bombed, 351; and second front, 368fn, 375; Slessors's views on, 376; wants German towns destroyed, 492fn

Stanley, Colonel Oliver: 266, 291–292, 479

Stavanger: 141fn

Steel: German expansion in, 274; estimated effect on of attacks on Ruhr, 482; effect on of attacks on Ruhr, 482fn

Steel, Sir John: 82

Stevenson, Air Vice-Marshal D. F.: 236fn, 237fn, 238

Stirlings: beginnings of, 75; potentialities of, 100; numbers of, 129; robustness hoped for, 176; in *Circus* operations, 237; in attacks on La Pallice, 239–241; coming into service, 330; attack French targets, 387; in Thousand raid on Bremen, 414; suggested for target finding force, 430; unsuitable for day operations, 454

Stradling, Sir Reginald: 268

Strategic Air Offensive:
British: moral aspect of, 14–17, 50–51, 63–64, 130, 154; in First World War, 34 ff.; economic intelligence for, 93, 262 ff., 458 ff.; beginning of, 144; after fall of France, 147; confidence restored in, 310–311; role of in overall strategy, 311, 312, 319–320, 329–331, 340–342, 364–367, 371–379; versus the war at sea, 320–321, 325–327, 335, 338–339
German: no plans for, 26, 50, 78, 80, 88, 125; in First World War, 34 ff.; Hitler instruction on, 136fn

Stuttgart: proposed attack on, 461, 467

Submarines: proposed attack against, 153, 156, 161, 165, 373, 461; attack against, 234, 444; estimated results of attacks

Submarines—*cont.*
against, 301, 303fn, 481fn; results of attacks against, 303, 306, 481; intelligence about, 481

Sweden: pre-emption of ball-bearings in, 466

Swinton, Lord: chairs Air Committee, 70; becomes Sec. of State for Air, 70; expands aircraft industry, 71; mentioned, 76; resigns, 78

Sykes, Major-General Sir Frederick: 38, 46

Target Area: size of, 178, 247, 383, 394fn

Target Finding Force: beginnings of idea of, 227, 229, 248, 382, 397, 418–419: necessary equipment for, 249; in *Shaker* technique, 386–387, 419; in attack on Renault factory, 387–388; proposal for and opposition to, 419–424, 429–431; *now see* Pathfinder Force

Target Systems: definition of, 13; choice of, 23–29, 350; assessment of, 262, 264–267

Targets: *see also* Bottlenecks: 'tactical' discussed, 7–8, 13; 'strategic', discussed, 7–8, 12 ff.; 'strategic' related to targets, 349; 'military and civilian' discussed, 14–17; lack of knowledge of, 91; intelligence about, 92–93; choice of, 93–94, 458, 468, 471–472; significance when isolated, 150; significance when dispersed, 150; proportion of crews finding, 156, 157, 163, 178–180, 216, 230–231, 383–384, 395, 423, 434, 448; search for larger, 168–169, 230, 235; identification and location of, 205–210, 211, 218, 219–220, 224, 227, 228–229, 448; methods of illuminating (*see also* Flares), 386–387

Technical Training Command: 84

Tedder, Air Commodore A. W.: 109, 110

Ten Year Rule: 57

Thomas, General Georg: 272, 273

Thomson, Air Commodore A. A. B.: 112fn

Thousand Bomber Raids: effect of single pilot policy on, 309; two go astray, 311, 418; on Cologne, 339–340, 402–410, 465, 485–486; on Essen, 340, 410–412, 486–487; on Bremen, 340, 413–417, 486–487; Harris' views on, 341; object of, 400; referred to, 401; commented on, 417

Thunderbolts P-47s: 450

Tirpitz: 303

Tissandier Brothers: 6

Tizard, Sir Henry: mentioned, 75; and work for Fighter Command, 108; and work for Bomber Command, 114, 121fn; comments on Cherwell's calculations, 333–336; expansion estimates of referred to, 344; suggested to undertake new analysis, 371

Todt, Fritz: 477

Torch: 355, 356, 360

Town Centres: 109

Training: *for a detailed description see Annex III*; state of inter-war, 60–61, 107–120; and operations of night 7th Nov. 1941, 255–256, 257

Training Command: 83, 110

Transport: *see* Communications

INDEX

Transport Command: 84
Trenchard, Marshal of the Royal Air Force Lord: as Major-General, C.-in-C., R.F.C., 35, 39; releases fighters, 36; on air power, 36, 37, 46; opposes separate air service, 38; commands independent bombing force, 39, 40, 43; mentioned, 43, 377; tactics of, 49; becomes C.A.S., 42, 52; plans air force, 52, 54 ff.; on length of pilot's service, 53fn; on tenure of office, 62; on moral effect of bombing, 63-64, 86, 150, 169-171, 298

U-Boats: *see also* Submarines: estimated number destroyed, 303fn; attacks of increase, 325, 328
Udet, Ernst: 480
United States Air Staff: favour air force in U.K., 354; doubt effectiveness of area bombing, 354; favour daylight plan, 354; strategic views of, 364; and 'self-defending' bomber formations, 451; had no intelligence directorate, 471
United States Army Air Forces: mentioned, 10, 31; capabilities of, 126, 320; and M.E.W., 264, 471; and the attack on the German air force, 352; intervention of, 353; British hopes of, 354; build up of, 356; position of, 450; role of, 471
United States Chiefs of Staff: 298, 367
United States Eighth Air Force: and air superiority, 21; and command organisation, 83; destroys alumina plant, 293fn; expansion of, 356; day bombing left to, 435; attack Lille, 441; formation flying of, 445; aim of, 450; no long range fighter for, 450; and attack on ball-bearings, 466; in mind of M.E.W., 469; designed for precision bombing, 471; target intelligence section of, 471; policy machinery for, 472; attacks F.W. factory, 487n
United States Eighth Bomber Command: attack Rouen, 355; expansion of, 360, 450; disaster overtakes, 450; formation flying of, 450; attack fringe targets, 451; disaster to forecast, 454; designed for precision bombing, 466, 471
United States Eighth Fighter Command: 450
United States Naval Staff: 354
United States of America: enters war, 319, 353
United States Special Observer Group: 298, 300
United States Strategic Bombing Survey: *for a detailed description see Annex V*: short description of, 271; criticises M.E.W. estimate, 489fn

V-Weapons: 284
Vansittart, Sir Robert: 169
Venturas: 439, 440, 441
Versailles, Treaty of: 58
Vice-Chief of the Air Staff: *see* Peirse (from April 1940), Freeman (from Nov. 1940)
Vice-Chiefs of Staff: 330fn
Vickers, C. G.: position of, 262; memorandum of, 264fn; and M.E.W.'s role in results of

Vickers, C. G.—*Cont*
bombing, 301fn; advises on direction of air offensive, 465
Victoria Cross: 305fn, 443
Villacoublay aircraft works: 462fn
Vuillemin, General: 136, 137

W.I.F.O.: 287
Wagenfuehr, Dr. Rolf: 276fn
War Cabinet: *for inter-war years see* Cabinet:
    In First World War: and air defence, 35, 36, 37; accepts Smuts report, 38; mentioned, 46
    In Second World War: eager for retaliation, 130; and bombing policy, 136-137, 142, 144, 186, 226, 247; want Berlin bombed, 157; and attack on oil, 159, 160, 161, 289fn, 291; and the war at sea, 164, 346fn; Secretariat helps relations between M.E.W. and services, 262; reconstructed, 328; and expansion of Bomber Command, 343; and attack on French factories and occupied territory, 387, 462
War Office: *see* General Staff
Washington Conference: 59
Washington War Conference: mentioned, 256; decisions of, 320, 329, 353-354, 365
Watson Watt, R. A.: 75, 114
Weather: affects operations, 164, 192, 202-204, 207, 214, 231, 384-385, 397, 399, 470; forecasts of, 204; affects reconnaissance, 231; on night 7th Nov. 1941, 254-255; forecasts for Thousand bomber raids, 405-406, 414-415
Wehrmacht: against Poland, 134; against France, 145; mentioned, 272; members of expected later war, 273; interested in oil, 287
Weir, Lord: 39, 70, 78
Wellesleys: 71
Wellingtons: not available, 71; beginnings of, 72; role of, 75, 125; number in Bomber Command, 81, 129; daylight actions of, 138-139, 192-201, 448; robustness of, 176; armament of, 195; defences of, 197; night operations of, 200, 208, 213, 215 ff., 231, 245 ff.; take night photographs, 222; not suitable for day operations, 235, 454; in attack on German warships, 240; for Coastal Command, 325, 328fn, 333; production of, 333; in attack on French targets, 388; in attack on Lübeck, 392; and Thousand bomber raids, 403-404, 406fn, 410, 413, 414, 416
    Mk. Ia: 235fn
    Mk. Ic: 235fn, 416, 430fn
    Mk. III: 430
    Mk. IV: 430fn
Welsh, Air Marshal Sir William: 403
West Wall: 274, 276
Western Air Plans: described, 94-99; assumptions of, 116; mentioned, 134, 168, 171, 205; in directive of 13th April 1940, 142; one agreed with French, 143; casualties affect, 197; information for, 260; target systems in, 284; and attack on aircraft industry, 294

INDEX

Western Plan: 92
Whitehead, Wing Commander: 426fn
Whitleys: not available, 71; beginnings of, 72; role of, 75; numbers of, 79, 81, 129; leaflet operations of, 140–141, 201–205; night reconnaissance of, 207, 208; night raids of, 210–211, 213, 215, 217 ff.; taken out of service, 309; early *H2S* in, 248fn; for Coastal Command, 328fn; and Thousand bomber raids, 403, 414, 416
Wild Automatic Plotting Machine: 268
Wilhelmshaven: daylight attacks against, 192, 195–201; results of attacks against, 303; in directive of 14th Feb. 1942, 323

Window: 400–401
Wings: 41st: 39
Wimperis, Dr. H. E.: 75, 114fn
Wood, Rt. Hon. Sir Kingsley: 78, 432fn
Wright Brothers: 6
Würzburg apparatus: 400

Zeppelin, Count: 6
Zeppelins: attacks of, 6, 34–36, 38, 44–45; defence against, 48
Zone maps: 475fn